An Historic
of the

An Historical Geography of the Balkans

Edited by

FRANCIS W. CARTER

*Department of Geography, University College
and School of Slavonic and East
European Studies, London, England*

1977

ACADEMIC PRESS
London · New York · San Francisco
A Subsidiary of Harcourt Brace Jovanovich, Publishers

ACADEMIC PRESS INC. (LONDON) LTD.
24/28 Oval Road
London NW1

U.S. Edition published by
ACADEMIC PRESS INC.
111 Fifth Avenue
New York, New York 10003

Library of Congress Catalog Card Number: 77–77367
ISBN: 0–12–161750–5

491 STT
E

Printed litho in Great Britain
by W & J Mackay Ltd, Chatham

Contributors

JOHN B. ALLCOCK — *School of Yugoslav Studies, University of Bradford, Bradford, England*

JOHN L. BINTLIFF — *Corpus Christi College, Cambridge, England*

FRANCIS W. CARTER — *Department of Geography, University College London and School of Slavonic and East European Studies, London, England*

GEORGE W. HOFFMAN — *Department of Geography, University of Texas at Austin, Austin, Texas 78712, USA*

PETER KOLEDAROV — *Bulgarian Academy of Science, Institute of History, 15 Shipka St., Sofia 4, Bulgaria*

RICHARD I. LAWLESS — *Centre of Middle Eastern and Islamic Studies, Department of Geography, South Road, Durham City, England*

JOHN G. NANDRIS — *Institute of Archaeology, 31–34 Gordon Square, London WC1H 0PY, England*

†CENGIZ ORHONLU — *Istanbul Universitesi, Edebiyat fakültesi, Yeniçağ Tarihi Kürsüsu, Istanbul, Turkey*

VELJKO ROGIĆ — *Geografski Zavod PMF-A, 41000 Zagreb, Marulićev Trg, 19/II, Yugoslavia*

MICHEL SIVIGNON — *Faculté des Lettres et Sciences Humaines, Université Paris Nord, Avenue J. B. Clement, 93430 Villetaneuse, France*

GAVRO A. ŠKRIVANIĆ — *Istorijski Institut, Knez Mihailova III, Belgrade 11000, Yugoslavia*

DAVID TURNOCK — *Department of Geography, The University, Leicester, England*

J. MALCOLM WAGSTAFF — *Department of Geography, The University, Southampton SO9 5NH, England*

v

Biographical Notes

JOHN B. ALLCOCK, BA, MA is a graduate of Leicester University and holds a Master's Degree from Carleton University, Ottawa. He is a lecturer in sociology at the University of Bradford and has been teaching there since 1966. His principal teaching interests have been in the field of comparative sociology; while his research concerns have ranged over a variety of problems probing the inter-relations between sociology and its sister social sciences. He has been actively involved in the School of Yugoslav Studies at Bradford, since its foundation; he has held a number of study scholarships in connection with his studies of that country, which is currently the primary focus of his research work.

JOHN L. BINTLIFF studied Archaeology and Anthropology at Cambridge BA, MA and then undertook research for the Ph.D also at Cambridge—title 'Natural Environment and Human Settlement in Prehistoric Greece', which has been completed.

FRANCIS W. CARTER, BA, MA, D.Nat.Sc, Dip.Ed., studied at the Universities of Sheffield, Cambridge, London, Zagreb and Prague. He is currently Joint Hayter Lecturer in the Geography of Eastern Europe at University College and School of Slavonic Studies, London. Whilst at Zagreb he studied under Professor J. Roglić and obtained his doctorate at Charles University, Prague under Professor V. Haüfler. At present he is involved in post-doctoral research at Jagellonian University in Cracow. Publications indicate interests in urban historical geography and modern economic and population problems in Eastern Europe. A book, *Dubrovnik (Ragusa)—A Classic City-state*, published by Academic Press in 1972, reflects his interest in Balkan historical geography.

GEORGE W. HOFFMAN, Ph.D, University of Michigan,

Professor of Geography, The University of Texas since 1949. Visiting Fulbright Professor University of Munich, 1961, 1972, and Heidelberg, 1972. Chairman, Committee on Eastern Europe Association of American Geographers and Committee on Research and Development, AAASS; member, Academic Advisory Board, Institute for Advanced Russian Studies, Woodrow Wilson International Center for Scholars. Research interests in political and historical geography, regional planning South-east Europe, comparative East and West European planning policies, Comecon resource policies and planning. Author of *Balkans in Transition* (Van Nostrand, 1963), *Regional Development Strategy in S.E. Europe* (Praeger, 1972); co-author *Yugoslavia and the New Communism* (Twentieth Century Fund, 1962); editor and contributor, *A Geography of Europe*, 3rd edition (Ronald Press, 1969) with 4th edition in preparation; *Eastern Europe: Essays in Geographical Problems* (Methuen, 1971).

PETER KOLEDAROV is a graduate of the American Grade School in Sofia and of the Law and History Departments, St Kliment Ohridski University, Sofia. He was a senior research officer in the Institute of History at the Bulgarian Academy of Sciences serving there for 25 years. He is also a lecturer in Historical Geography at the University of Veliko Turnovo. His research interests are mainly in historical geography of the Mediaeval Bulgarian State and South-east Europe, together with palaeocartography of the Balkans. His works cover a wide range of topics in Bulgarian and foreign journals and atlases.

RICHARD I. LAWLESS, BA, PH.D, studied at the universities of Durham, London and Paris, and is now Research Officer at the Centre for Middle Eastern and Islamic Studies, University of Durham. His research interests are in the historical geography of the Middle East and North Africa, particularly the evolution of settlement systems. His main publications are on the Maghreb, and he is the joint author of a book *Tlemcen, Continuity and Change in an Algerian Islamic Town* to be published later this year.

JOHN G. NANDRIS, MA, PH.D, FSA, graduated from Trinity College, Cambridge where he completed doctoral work on the prehistoric archaeology of South-east Europe. Has travelled extensively in Europe since the 1950s working in the field and in museums, and spending eighteen months in Greece at the British School of Archaeology at Athens. Has lectured in European archaeology at the Institute of Archaeology, London University, since 1965. Current research centres on the palaeoeconomy and palaeoenvironment of the area from *c.* 10,000 B.C. onwards, with an interest in many of the non-industrial forms taken by human settlement in the region down to the historic present.

†CENGIZ ORHONLU, BA, PH.D, graduated from the Faculty of Letters at Istanbul University and undertook doctoral research on 'Settlement of the Turkish tribes by the Ottoman state between 1691–1696' at the same institution. He spent one year as a research scholar at McGill University, in Montreal. He was Professor of Modern History in the Faculty of Letters, Istanbul University. Unfortunately, during the production of this book Professor Orhonlu died, in June 1976, proving a great Academic loss within the field of Turkish history. Grateful thanks are recorded to Dr Salih Özbaran of the same department for kindly checking the proofs of Ch. 8.

VELJKO ROGIĆ, PH.D is Professor of Geography at the University of Zagreb, Yugoslavia. His research interests focus upon regional development problems, cultural and historical geography. These are reflected in more than forty publications and several textbooks on the regional and economic geography of Yugoslavia.

MICHEL SIVIGNON is a graduate of Lyon University. He was geography assistant at Lyon University and between 1967 and 1970 was Research Director at the National Centre of Social Research, in Athens. He is now lecturer (maître de conference) at the University of Paris-Nord. He has published a book on the Balkans, P. Y. Pechoux et M. Sivignon—*Les Balkans*, Presses Universitaires de France, Collection Magellan no. 16, Paris (108 Bd St Germain) 1971, 284pp. His doctoral research has appeared as *La Thessalie analyse d'une province Grecque* (Lyon, 1975, 576pp).

GAVRO A. ŠKRIVANIĆ, PH.D, graduated from the University

of Belgrade, Yugoslavia and completed research work for his doctoral degree at the Serbian Academy of Sciences and Arts. At present his research interests are concentrated on the historical geography of Mediaeval Serbia. His recent publications are: *The Roads in Mediaeval Serbia* (1974), and *Monumenta Cartographica Jugoslaviae* (1975).

DAVID TURNOCK, BA, MA, Ph.D, a graduate of Cambridge University, developed an interest in Eastern Europe in the late 1960s. This takes the form of a teaching commitment at Leicester University covering the socialist countries and a research interest in Romania, dealing with the country's economic development. This is reflected in a range of publications including a book entitled *An Economic Geography of Romania* (Bell, 1974).

J. MALCOLM WAGSTAFF, BA, Ph.D, graduated from the University of Liverpool and gained his doctorate from the University of Southampton, where he is lecturer in geography, after spending several years in the Centre of Middle Eastern and Islamic Studies at Durham. His research interests lie in Greece and Turkey. They include studies of settlement pattern change and aspects of the geography of the Morea (Pelopónnisos) between c. 1685 and 1830.

Preface

This book is about historical geography, and about the Balkans. Until recently historical geography has been seen as something that involves history and maps, and in more derogatory ways as an illegitimate form of history and as 'hysterical' geography. Likewise the term Balkan has drawn scathing remarks and definitions evoking such phrases as 'inharmonious conditions', 'small antagonistic states', 'hostile nationalities', the 'Balkan problem, question' and other uncomplimentary words. I am sure this book will not completely dispel, or confirm, such beliefs, but it is hoped that at least some myths will be put to rest.

One is fortunate to be the editor of an international team of scholars who have willingly put pen to paper, to place before the reader the results of their recently completed, or continuing, research projects. As editor, early in the preparation of this collective work, certain basic questions had to be decided. One concerned the actual geographical extent of the area to be covered and what was to be its northern limit. The arbitrary decision taken was, of necessity, to exclude Hungary, but include Romania. Another question to be resolved was whether studies should be on a large all-embracing scale, or only local in extent. At the risk of failing on both sides, an attempt has been made to combine themes on a broad canvas covering the whole of the peninsula, with those based purely on a local level. For example, chapters range from an appreciation of the whole peninsula in Neolithic times in Chapter 1, to a close analysis of one small Adriatic island in Chapter 7.

This interdisciplinary study makes use not only of geographers, but also historians, archaeologists and a sociologist. They have each been given a free hand in presenting their views and ideas, but I must stress that throughout the book each author is responsible alone for the various judgements and opinions he makes. I have been particularly fortunate in getting together a number of leading authorities in the field of 'Balkanology'. As an editor I could not have hoped for a better team of contributors who have read each others chapters, made constructive comments, promptly answered my various queries, and have patiently waited for the final outcome. If we can in some way encourage others to foster an interest in this part of Europe, then the whole exercise has been worthwhile.

Finally, I would like to record my gratitude to those people behind the scenes, who have made the final product possible. Members of the Cartographic Unit at University College should be warmly thanked, especially Mr Alick Newman, for his many ideas on layout and presentation. I also acknowledge the help of the secretarial staff of the Geography Department at University College, especially Miss Rosamund Bushell, for the skilful interpretation of my editorial hieroglyphics and for coping with the many strange, often unpronounceable Balkan place-names. To all concerned, my sincerest thanks.

January 1977   *F. W. Carter*

Contents

6
Settlements in the South-Central Pelopónnisos, c. 1618
J. M. WAGSTAFF

197

7
Brač Island, Dalmatia: A Case for Sequent Occupance?
F. W. CARTER

239

List of Illustrations

List of Tables

'Svaki naučni radnik polazi od metode i rezultata koje su drugi stvarali. Svi se mi penjemo, jedni na ramenima drugih.'

(Every scientific worker begins with methods and results which others have made. All of us climb, one on the shoulders of another.)

JOVAN CVIJIĆ (1865–1927)

1

Introduction to the Balkan Scene

F. W. CARTER

The name Balkan, a Turkish word meaning a thickly wooded mountain range or high ridge,[1] has been applied to the eastern-most of the three great southern peninsulas of Europe, since the early nineteenth century. Over the years it has proved very difficult to delimit its exact geographical boundaries, largely due to the peninsula's gradual emergence into the mainland of Europe. Nevertheless, for the purposes of this book the Balkans are defined as that territory covering the modern states of Albania, Bulgaria, Greece, Romania and Yugoslavia, along with the area known as European Turkey (Fig. 1).

The Historical Background

These modern Balkan states share a geographical unity and historical heritage dating back to inhabitation during Lower Palaeolithic times, 200,000–100,000 B.C. The glories of Bronze Age civilization in the Aegean, classical Greece, Illyrian and Thracian culture, Roman conquest, and barbarian colonization all enter the chronology of this south-eastern part of Europe. The early sixth century A.D. saw groups of Slavs, with their developed agricultural tradition, animal husbandry, hunting and fishing, moving into the northern part where the Balkan Peninsula was broadest, and lay open across the lower Danube and Drava rivers to the large plains of Dacia and Pannonia. Here the great longitudinal corridors, the

FIG. 1.

Morava–Vardar, and Morava–Maritsa valleys overran the peninsula, together with the east Adriatic coast, routeways which the
Byzantine emperors were powerless to defend. It was at the expense of this empire, that two Slav states were founded during the
Middle Ages, namely Croatia, with its core area in the middle Sava
and Drava valleys, and Serbia to the south which developed from a
nucleus of river sources and upland basins. In the east the Bulgars,
a Turkish tribe, began crossing the Danube in the seventh century
A.D. and quickly subjugated the Slavic inhabitants. The Romanians or Vlachs, migrated from the Danubian plains into the
mountainous region of Transylvania to live the life of nomadic
shepherds, whilst, similarly in the west the Albanians, descendants
of the old Illyrian population, took refuge in the karstic wastes of
the mountains along the east Adriatic coast. The southern Balkans
saw a slow but perceptible integration of its people under the Byzantine administrative and cultural system, characterized by sporadic
Slavic insurgencies into the more mountainous areas, and vulnera-
bility to attack from the mediaeval states to the north and east.[2]

A common political heritage shared by all the Balkan states was
nearly five centuries of Ottoman rule. The successes of a small
Turkish emirate established during the second half of the thirteenth
century, in north-west Anatolia, lay in the acquisition of a superior
military power based on excellent leadership, organization and a
mobile horse cavalry. At the beginning of the fourteenth century
internal problems slightly delayed the victorious movement into
south-east Europe, but the Ottoman Empire reached the height
of its prestige and power in 1529, when the armies of Süleyman I
(1520–1566) made an unsuccessful attempt to lay siege to the
imperial city of Vienna.[3] Westward expansion had been halted,
and although some territorial changes took place in the Balkans
during the next 150 years, there were no significant indications of
decline until 1683. More important in the Balkan context, it was
able to maintain at least titular control over this area up to 1878.
An important point to remember in this context is that derogatory
ideas on Ottoman civilization are often based on judgements made
from the latter part of its rule, namely in the eighteenth and nineteenth centuries during the period of greatest decline. It is possible, however, that in the earlier centuries the various Ottoman
institutions offered the Balkan population a situation which was

an improvement on the one previously tolerated under native feudal governments. The Ottoman rulers regarded the division of their inhabitants not on the basis of ethnic differences but on religious practice. Thus any individual, by converting to Islam, could become a member of the ruling class.

The success of the Ottoman Empire was dependent on men of ability, combined with strong control by its leaders. Süleyman's reign appears as a watershed in this context for he succeeded a line of remarkable rulers. Of his seventeen successors few were of this calibre and the whole system was riddled with corruption. Among the worst consequences of this collapse of Ottoman government was an increase in lawlessness, throughout the peninsula. Local Muslim rulers increased their importance as central authority weakened, gaining influence through suppressing local skirmishes, bribery, or combating attacks by Christian bands of robbers. Unfortunately such conditions made parts of the peninsula uninhabitable, a situation heightened by the Ottoman wars of the eighteenth century. It was from this background that the seeds of discontent were sown directly leading to the Serbian and Greek revolts during the first two decades of the nineteenth century. Also a contemporary development was the increasing interest in this area by the European powers.

Wars waged in the Balkans not only affected its inhabitants adversely, but also the various political agreements concluded by the larger powers, left them influenced by new ideas on revolution and independence. It was the French Revolution and Napoleonic Wars which clearly signposted the shift from Ottoman domination towards a new era of national revolutions in the nineteenth century. This resulted during much of this century in political and social development, and formation of independent Balkan states. Even more significant was the gradual absorption of the Balkan Peninsula into the cultural and economic orbit of the rest of Europe. The last quarter of the nineteenth century was thus to see the Balkans becoming a part of the European political and economic system, closely connected with the age of imperialism. The Balkans became one of Europe's major crossroads, thanks to the decline of Ottoman rule, increased traffic on the Danube, growth of railways, the building of the Suez Canal, and extension of imperialistic European trends in the eastern Mediterranean.

It is not insignificant that the First World War was begun as a result of Balkan revolutionary nationalism. The break up of old traditional styles of peasant life, the subdivision of peasant holdings resulting from population pressure, and movement of young people towards the towns, all provided a stimulus to revolutionary action. The upheavals of the First World War did little to alleviate the underlying causes of discontent in Balkan society. The frustration of the Bulgarians, Hungarians, Croats and Macedonians, were in some ways counterbalanced by the successes of the Serbs and Romanians after the war, but again some parts of the peninsula were still plagued by old jealousies, agitation and nationalist dreams. These were expressed in the form of two new revolutionary movements namely peasantism and communism. The former movement failed due to weakly prepared programmes of intent, but the latter was much better equipped both ideologically and organizationally. By 1921 each Balkan state had its own Communist party which hoped to benefit from the frustration of peasant discontent and nationalist revolutionary movements. Balkan federation was seen as the best solution for the political and economic misgivings in the peninsula. Such ideas were met with official resistance mainly in the form of land reform, and industrialization in an effort to cope with the ills of Balkan society. Land reform was an unqualified success, such that by the outbreak of the Second World War large landed estates had disappeared from the Balkan scene, except for isolated examples in Romania. Unfortunately the redistribution of land was no answer to rising population pressure and pitiful underdevelopment. Industrialization was seen as the answer to this problem by each Balkan state. This was severely hampered by a shortage of capital so that foreign investors were encouraged to place their assets in various industrial enterprises like the Romanian oil industry.

Economic depression, hardship, and a sense of failure pervaded the Balkan scene in the period prior to the Second World War. In 1945 the Balkan states emerged from German occupation in various degrees of economic and political change. The ideal of a Balkan confederation loomed large in these early post-war years, including an ambitious plan for a united Macedonia based on territory owned by Greece, Bulgaria and Yugoslavia. Such heady plans were never to materialize, and only further reinforced the

consolidation of communist regimes, in Bulgaria, Romania, Yugoslavia and Albania all having varying affinity with the Soviet
Union. Meanwhile Greece and Turkey remained economically and
militarily linked with the western European powers. This led
to an effective split in the Balkan make-up with Greece and Turkey
still encouraging the import of foreign capital and linking their
prices to world markets, whilst the Communist regimes were
developing their economies on a command price system.

This historical background to the Balkan scene may well be
concluded by a recent comment on the present Balkan situation.

'Balkanization may have to be dropped from our dictionaries[4]
one of these days. Europe's bottom right-hand corner and
traditional powder keg is still as divided politically as it ever
was; its two western allies, Greece and Turkey, barely speak to
each other; its two hard line communist regimes, Albania and
Bulgaria, ignore each other; and its two would be neutrals,
Jugoslavia and Rumania, speak to everybody who will listen.
But recently for all these differences, all the Balkan countries
except Albania have been inching toward some kind of regional
union.'[5]

This contemporary comment may have its weaknesses, but it does
kindle a desire for a closer analysis of the Balkans, in an attempt
to explain some of the idiosyncrasies and misnomers that have
arisen about this part of Europe.

An Historical Geography of the Balkans

Historical geography is the study of geographies of the past, and
despite the antipathy of some of the younger generation to
historicism, there is still a widespread and deep-seated desire to
know about the past.[6] This is no more so than in areas of historical
complexity, where historical studies can help to provide a better
understanding of how cultural and economic activities develop,
flourish and decay. Historical geographers have a responsibility
to try and meet this need by writing clear geographical syntheses
of the changing character of regions, places and landscapes. With
reference to the Balkans many tantalizing questions still remain
unanswered. Was the physical impact of the Ottoman controlled

area much different to that of the western Mediterranean, a question that fascinated Braudel?[7] Was the historical geography of the Balkans very different in character from the rest of Europe, or just a mere extension of its influence? Was Serbia very different in historical character, as a Balkan state, compared with, say Bohemia, which was not? Was the definition of the Balkans a term which changed over time, and how do various nationalities perceive the Balkans as a geographical expression? These are all intriguing ideas, though difficult to answer. Perhaps it is therefore opportune at this point to inquire what contributions have been made by earlier historical geographers in their writings on the Balkan Peninsula.

A Question of Definition

This involves some consideration of the term that has become known as 'the Balkans' or 'Balkan Peninsula'. The first person to use the term 'Balkan Peninsula' was the German geographer, A. Zeune in 1889 when he replaced the former name of 'European Turkey' with 'Balkanhalbinsel' or Haemushalbinsel'.[8] Over a hundred years later the Yugoslav geographer Cvijić supported this view stating that he thought there was 'une répugnance évidente' at the description of the Balkans as 'Turkey in Europe';[9] it had however also been called the Byzantine and the Greek Peninsula. In fact this may have been uppermost in Zeune's mind in choosing a term analogous with the Appenine and Pyrennean Peninsulas. His perception of what this constituted, seems to have been much narrower than the present-day term. Zeune saw the northern boundary following the central ridge which enclosed Greece and Macedonia from the north: this was the 'Haemus' ('Catena mundi' or 'Catena del Mondo' of the Renaissance) range popularized in Ptolemy's maps of ancient Rome (Fig. 2). Unfortunately, the imprecision of Zeune's term has meant that only slowly did it gain popular use for reference to this area, even in German scholarly literature. The German geographer, Fischer in 1893 attacked Zeune's definition, stating that a more correct term would be 'the south-east European peninsula',[10] whilst in 1929, Maull renewed this attack on Zeune's imprecision.[11]

The next definite reference concerning the use of 'Balkan' comes from the writings of the French traveller, Boué, in 1847. He had heard of its use from Turkish sources, which referred specifically to the mountain range in northern Bulgaria and was synonymous with the Haemus range of antiquity. Boué understood that 'Balkan' meant 'mountain' but the Turkish translation was the national name for the present day 'Stara Planina' mountains. Regularly, in Bulgarian literature, and also increasingly so in world literature, use is made of national names for local features, and Roglić believes that it is incorrect to preserve Boué's term when referring to the peninsula.[12] Unfortunately, constant use tends to confirm such placenames, so that by 1922, Cvijić had already realized that it was too late to change this term 'Balkan' despite the fact that it was neither a correct regional term, nor had anything to do with the most important mountain in the region.[13] At present, scholars from many countries use the term 'South-eastern Peninsula' or 'South-east Europe', while the term 'Balkan Peninsula' or 'Balkans' is given to a geographically more restricted area.

Where is the northern boundary of the Balkan Peninsula in Europe? Cvijić defined it as a line following the Danube and Sava rivers to the Ljubljana Basin and hence to the source of the River Soča in the west.[14] A Croatian version of 1941 places it from the River Sava through the Postojna Gate, the Vipava Valley to the Bay of Trieste, thus excluding much of Slovenia.[15] Roglić argues that acceptance of this part of the Adriatic Sea as a western limit implies an admission that the eastern limit should stretch as far as Odessa and the northern part of the Western Black Sea Coast.[16] Further analysis may question the use of purely physical characteristics for defining the boundary. Newbigin in 1915 and Melik in 1928 thought this unlikely,[17] but there are few analogous situations where a river like the Danube, besides being a physical boundary, may also have an ethnic and cultural influence. The German physical geographer, Penck, believed that the northern boundary of the Balkans stretched from Medovo (near Plovdiv) to the Bay of Burgas.[18] Chataigueau suggested that part of Romania should be included in the Balkans, namely Dobrugea,[19] whilst a political pact between the 'Balkan countries' in 1934 included Romania amongst the member states.[20] More modern works still reflect this disagreement over the actual area covered by the Balkans. Mately states that 'Romania is often described as a

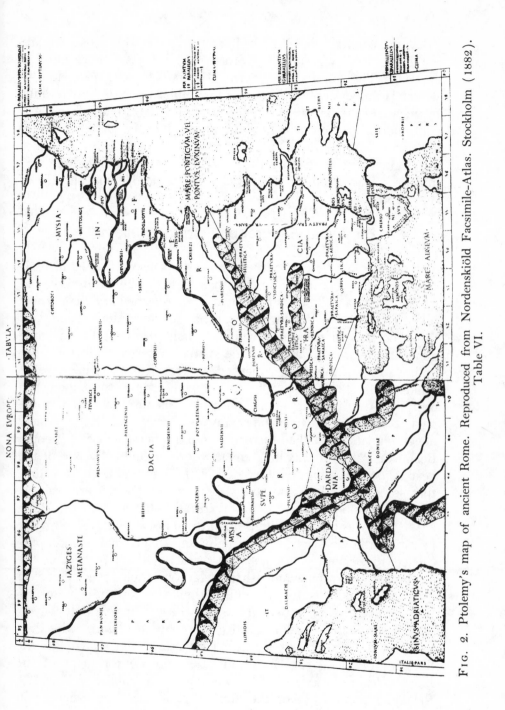

Fig. 2. Ptolemy's map of ancient Rome. Reproduced from Nordenskiöld Facsimile-Atlas. Stockholm (1882). Table VI.

"Balkan" country', but, 'if we characterize it in this sense, we are
not being strictly accurate'.[21] Stoianovich adopts a more flexible
approach but admits 'the term "Balkans" lacks precision!'[22]
whilst Hoffman applies, in one of his publications, the term 'only
to the arc of the Balkan Peninsula running eastward and forming a
continuation of the Carpathian Range south of the Danube'.[23] The
discussion may continue for years to come, and probably the most
important thing is to warn the reader of one's own definition and
interpret it accordingly. This was done in the opening phrases of
the chapter.

Historical Geographies on the Balkans

The number of works produced on the Balkans by trained historical geographers is small, far less than by historians. But historical
geographers are historians second and geographers first; their
major concern is with geographical changes through time and with
the processes of change which may help throw light on some
general principles that determine spatial patterns. Unfortunately,
unlike some of the more advanced western European nations, no
Balkan school of geography developed during the nineteenth
century. Any aspiring geographers at this time left their home
land to study in Austria, Germany or France, so that any early
developments by Balkan historical geographers came via Vienna,
Berlin or Paris. It was in Vienna, where undoubtedly one of the
best schools of geography existed in the late nineteenth century,
that some of the most notable Balkan geographers were trained.
Foremost amongst them one may place Peter Matković (1830–
1898). He was born in Senj, a small town in Dalmatia. As a young
priest Matković studied geography in Vienna and thence proceeded to Berlin, where he soon attracted the attention of the
celebrated geographer Karl Ritter. Matković took a special interest
in statistics and was instrumental in the formation and administration of the Croation Statistical Bureau. His principal work however,
was in the domain of historical geography. He became the Professor of Geography at Zagreb University, and visited all the
libraries of the great European cities looking for maps of the
Balkan Peninsula. Many of his writings were published in *RAD*,
the chief publication of the Academy of Arts and Sciences in

Zagreb. They included articles on mediaeval travellers in the Balkans, and subsequently in the same journal he wrote a long series of well documented articles on Balkan travellers in the sixteenth century. He also contributed to a better understanding of early developments along the Balkan trade routes. In his writings Matković set out important geographical and ethnographical data which still constitute one of the most reliable sources for the study of the Balkan lands in the Middle Ages under Ottoman rule.[24] A contemporary of Matković was Vladimir Karić (1848–1895), a self-taught geographer who in his short life nevertheless succeeded in developing an important academic reputation. He became the first Serbian Professor of Geography at Belgrade University and is best known for his book *Srbija: Opis Zemlje, Naroda i Države* (Serbia: A Description of its Land, People and State) published in Belgrade in 1887. Amongst its 935 pages a very comprehensive and well-illustrated work emerges which carefully describes the life of the people, their physical environment and historical heritage. He received wide praise for this work not only in the Balkans but other European countries and some of his ethnographic maps are of interest if only for the influence they had on other geographers,[25] particularly one of his later pupils, Jovan Cvijić.

Of all Balkan geographers, Jovan Cvijić (1868–1927) is by far the most eminent. In 1889 he went to the University of Vienna and spent four years working with such notable teachers as Albrecht Penck, Eduard Siess, and Eduart Brückner.[26] Although by training a physical rather than a historical geographer, mention must be made of Jovan Cvijić. Like de Martonne and Bowman, Cvijić was initially trained as a physical geographer, but in maturity his mind turned to a wide range of human and historical problems and undoubtedly his writings did much to establish the future Yugoslavia as an independent state. More particularly, his most important work, *La Péninsule Balkanique—Géographie Humaine*, published in Paris in 1918, describes all the essential characteristics of the Southern Slavs, explaining them not only in the light of their natural surroundings but also against a background of cultural influences and historical events, thus including within his scope the whole field of ethnology and sociology. He expressed definite views on the foundations of South Slav civilization, maintaining that the gifts of the Yugoslav peoples could contribute many new elements to world culture. During the First World War, Cvijić worked actively in the defence not only of Balkan interests, but of Slav ones in general. He played an important part at the Peace Conference and his wide scientific knowledge was one of the determining factors in solving many problems related to state frontiers. It was Cvijić who provided the scientific background for claims made by the new Yugoslav state. He also founded and edited a project on the Migrations and Origins of Population, by the Serbian Ethnographical Office. He attached great importance to an investigation into village family origins, particularly where national traditions could be studied locally. Migrations had taken place throughout Yugoslavia under the former control of Turkish rule as well as districts under Austrian and Venetian domination, where the local authorities had noted the origin of all immigrants.[27] Cvijić utilized documentary evidence from Dubrovnik and Venetian archives, from Turkish sources, etc. the results appearing in a monumental work entitled *Naselja Srpskih Zemalja* (The Peopling of the Serbian Lands) and published in many parts from 1902 onwards. It was accompanied by an atlas containing not only maps, but many photographs of villages, house-types, costumes, etc. Recognition for all this work was to follow. In 1920 Cvijić was awarded the Patron's Gold Medal of the Royal Geographical Society for 'his many very valuable works upon the geography of the Balkans states and other parts of Europe'. Numerous other recognitions and distinctions were also accorded to him by home and foreign societies for his scientific research.

Like Cvijić, the German geographer Alfred Philippson (1864–1953) was originally trained as a physical geographer. He studied under von Richthofen in Berlin and later with Karl Ritter. Philippson became Professor of Geography at Bonn University and his main interest was in geomorphology and particularly the problems of the Mediterranean Lands, especially Greece.[28] Even so there is evidence of his sympathy with an historical geography approach as seen in *Das byzantinische Reich als geographische Erscheinung*, published in Leiden in 1939. The idea of a regional historical geography is also seen in Philippson's four volume work *Die Griechischen Landschaften* (Frankfurt, 1951–1959), particularly the chapters written by Hermann Kirsten, (born 1911). He is Professor of

Historical Geography at Bonn University, with a special interest in the Mediterranean.[29] His work on the historical regional geography of Greece, uses not only the rather restrictive written records of the classical period, but also sources dating from later times, which give a more comprehensive and closer insight, than for example Schulten's approach for Iberia.[30] Philippson's influence was also felt in mapping. He travelled extensively in central and southern Greece, and made considerable additions and corrections to earlier maps, without making a complete survey. Even so his map of the Pelopónnisos, (1:300,000) published in 1892, stood as the best map on this area until well after the First World War. He was also quick to realize work done by others. Gustaf Weigand's book, *Die Aromunen*, which clarified ideas about the ethnography of south-west Macedonia published in 1895, was welcomed by Philippson, who praised its value as it was based on extensive personal experience in Macedonia, Thessaly and Albania.

In Bulgaria the earliest evidence of work in historical geography is that produced by Anastas Ishirkov (1868–1937). Like Philippson, he was a student of von Richthofen, and later Ratzel who together kindled his interest in anthropogeography and historical–ethnographic problems. Amongst his many publications he is best remembered for his work on the historical geography of Bulgarian towns, which was the first systematic attempt at their classification in Bulgaria. He became the first Professor of Geography at Sofia Higher Institute in 1898, which was later to become the present day 'Kliment Ohridski' University. His efforts in geographical research ensured that even before his death in 1937, geography was an accepted university discipline in Bulgaria.[31] Comparable development in Romania, is reflected in the work of Constantin Daicoviciu (1898–1973) whose books are helpful for a wider understanding of Romania's historical geography, together with George Vâlsan (1885–1935) and Constantin Brătescu (1882–1945) and even Dimitri Cantemir (1644–1723).[32]

More recent contributions to Balkan historical geography have come particularly from the pens of American and west European authors. In Britain one may mention the pioneer work done by W. G. East[34] and L. Myres[35] or the lesser known work of W. R. Kermack on the historical geography of the Dardanelles.[36] Since the Second World War more British studies have been forthcoming including the work of A. E. Moodie,[37] H. R. Wilkinson[38] and others, which have brought renewed interest in the area. In France the work of André Blanc[39] and Réné Rochefort[40] should be noted, whilst in Yugoslavia articles by Svetozar Ilešič,[41] Ivo Rubić,[42] Josip Roglić[43] and Jovan Trifunoski[44] stand out. One should also include the recent book on the historical geography of Greece by G. Kolias,[45] and that on the Ottoman Empire by D. E. Pitcher[46] to this growing list of works in the field.

The Contributors

Having stated that the historical geographer is a historian second and a geographer first, one may be led to expect a series of essays by such specialists. Unfortunately, this is not so, for only two-thirds of the contributions in this volume (ten) are written by people with geographical training along with two archaeologists, two historians and a sociologist. Nevertheless, the present day emphasis on interdisciplinary study may turn this fact to advantage, for all the contributions may be said to have a spatial approach in discussing their individual problems. Furthermore, it would be unfair to look for coherence of argument and conclusion in specialist essays by different individuals. Although a collection such as this cannot be a continuous story, it does present a picture of centuries. Some chapters, of course are narrow in scope and implication. Others, although restricted in topic, are concerned with critically significant material, whilst others range widely in their field of discussion. However, all contributors, partly because they are writing on topics in which they are directly interested, and partly, one might hope, because of their admiration for, or interest in, the Balkan way of life, manage to be pre-eminently themselves, or at least their professional selves.

Stress must be placed on the chronological approach throughout the book and thus ward off the old adage 'a work of many hands, but no coherent theme'. This was found to be the only workable solution where the contributors had such widely differing interests, backgrounds and nationalities, with four coming from Balkan countries, one from France, one from the U.S.A. and the rest from Britain. Moreover, the very complexity of the area itself, makes a chronological theme the most adaptable, as aptly illustrated by American specialists recently writing on the Balkan Peninsula.[47] This is further supported by Alan Baker's remark that,

> 'because the historical geographer is concerned with studying the past he must learn the trade of historical scholarship and become in many ways an historian. His writings thus assume a dual relevance, both as history and as geography'.[48]

One may take this a stage further and argue that it is the responsibility of all professional students of the past, be they archaeologists, historians, geographers, or any other discipline, to help satisfy the ever present thirst for historical knowledge. This may be in the form of knowledge about the past of different individuals, or on a larger scale of different societies wishing to formulate a collective past. It thus becomes, 'a contribution which affects the quality of life, rather than the standard of living.'[49]

Chapters 2 and 3 are based on archaeological research. The impact of human groups on any region expresses itself in various characteristic ways. Intrusion and settlement provide one of the most important modifications to the geographical environment. John Nandris has examined this fact against the background of the Neolithic period emerging in the Balkan Peninsula, particularly in comparison to regions of geographical proximity, where this had already taken place. John Bintliff takes this a stage further and applies newly acquired archaeological knowledge to a better understanding of increased sedentariness and reliance upon domesticated plants and animals in the prehistoric communities of Greece. Chapter 4 by Gavro Škrivanić, sheds new light on the impact of Roman penetration into the peninsula with an analysis of Roman roads and settlements. Emigrants from the barbarian world entered the Roman Empire, resulting in further settlement in south-eastern Europe, and although much remained unchanged in the landscape, some new features of a permanent character were to be impressed on the countryside.

Subsequent to settlement, it is utilization of the land and other economic activities which become related to an area's geographical setting. Thus it was agriculture conducted from rural settlements, which became a prominent feature of the Balkan landscape during the mediaeval period. The conquest of the plough over woodland,

marsh and heath, increase in population, development and refinement of the settlement pattern, all led to urban development in
parts of the Balkan Peninsula. This theme is looked at more
closely in Chapter 5 with special reference to the western Balkans
tracing growth from a geographic standpoint between the beginning of the thirteenth and end of the eighteenth centuries. In
contrast to this broad chronological canvas, Malcolm Wagstaff, in
Chapter 6, has closely examined settlements in the south-central
Pelopónnisos, around the year 1618. Careful detective work, aided
by reliable documentary sources, has made it possible to reconstruct the settlement pattern of this relatively underdeveloped
economic region, whose primary products were exported to
Venetian territory. The impact of Venetian control is also analysed
in Chapter 7 with reference to the East Adriatic island of Brač.
Settlement evidence is traced back to the Bronze Age in an effort
to test the concept of sequent occupance through the vagaries of
time, right up to the outbreak of the Second World War.

Chapters 8 and 9, are written by Balkan historians. The author,
Leon Dominian, once quoted a striking passage from a national
Turkish poem summing up the duties of the individual: 'He
thrusts, he kills, or fighting dies,' and ends with the statement that
'the history of this great race of conquerors is drawing to a dis-
honoured close before the gaze of the whole civilized world.'[50] It is
therefore refreshing to read the essay by Cengiz Orhonlu on the
state of geographical knowledge in the Ottoman Empire during
the eighteenth century and to realize that such scholars as Kâtib
Chelebi and Bartinli Ibrahim Hamdi were far too busy with the
pursuit of geographical knowledge to worry about their individual
'duties'. Peter Koledarov examines the impact of ethnic and political factors on the geographical placenames of the Balkan Peninsula,
at various levels, local, regional and national. He traces the
pattern through those troubled centuries from the seventh, when
migrants from the east first arrived, up to the more settled conditions of the Later Middle Ages.

The last six chapters in the book range widely, both in scope,
and implication. Chapter 10 by David Turnock examines the
impact of industrialization on Romania during the nineteenth and
first half of the twentieth centuries. The country made considerable
progress based on a well-developed oil industry. By the outbreak

of the Second World War it was arguably the most industrialized nation in south-eastern Europe, a fact ably exploited by the advancing Axis forces. A similar time period is covered in Chapter 11, by Michel Sivignon for Thessaly, and Greece. He examines the transition which took place in this province from being one of peripheral importance under the Ottoman Empire, to that of economic centrality within the new Greek Kingdom. Chapter 12 by Veljko Rogić in some ways continues the story developed in Chapter 5 on urban development. Emphasis is placed on the nineteenth and twentieth century growth of urban centres in Yugoslavia in an attempt to explain the present-day pattern of nodal-function complexes in the country. George Hoffman, in Chapter 13 analyses the present Yugoslavian ethnographic pattern based on the country's historical background and geographical environment, whilst Richard Lawless in the following chapter, looks at Ottoman Greece. After some general comments on provincial life in the Ottoman Empire, he takes a closer look at the economy and landscape of Thessaly. In certain aspects this complements the earlier work found in Chapter 11 on Thessaly. Finally, John Allcock applies a sociological approach to an understanding of Yugoslavia's historical development with particular emphasis on the inter-war period.

Conclusion

In a book covering an area totalling 8 per cent of the European land mass, and ranging in habitable time from at least 150,000 B.C.[51] to the present, there are sure to be some gaps. It was an area long dominated by traditional, peasant styles of life, but, once the Turkish yoke had been discarded, it was rapidly transformed into a provincial variant of the so-called Western style of civilization.[52]

As editor of a book of this kind one becomes only too aware of the gaps. For example, little or no reference, except indirectly, is made to Albania. The strength of some themes, such as settlement, clearly emerge, whilst weaknesses of others, like the impact of agricultural methods, are only too painfully apparent. Furthermore there is probably less evidence than one would like, of a change in paradigm, which has taken place in geography over the past decade. But again quoting Alan Baker,

'The "stresses" created by the new geography have not been followed immediately by adaptions within historical geography to reduce the "strain" on its functioning. Historical geography has a long relaxation time'.[53]

Moreover, in the lesser known parts of Europe there is still perhaps a need to increase the reader's awareness and familiarity on certain topics, such as Balkan historical development. Only then can any new model-based paradigm be geographically utilized to any favourable extent.

1. Notes

1. *Redhouse Yeni Türkçe—Ingilizce Sözlük.* Istanbul (1968), p. 128. Professor T. Stoianovich states that the name 'Balkans' is derived from two Persian words meaning 'high house' or 'mountain'. (See T. Stoianovich *A Study in Balkan Civilization* (Borzoi Studies in History) New York (1967), p. 3.) A considerable number of Persian, Arabic and a few Greek and Italian loanwords have found a place in Turkish topography, and these are commonly combined with genuine Turkish elements. Among the more usual topographic words of Persian origin are 'bala', high and 'khane', house, but 'high house' becomes 'khane boland'.

   A 'mountain' in Persian is 'kuh' or 'dagh'. In Arabic the only word with a similar sound to 'Balkan' is 'balkun', 'balakon' derived from French, for a balcony. In Italian 'balcone'—'balco' is of Germanic origin. In Old English the word 'balca' meant a ridge coming from the Old High German 'balche', (German 'balken') meaning a beam or rafter. It is also possible that 'Balkan' may be derived from one of the Central Asian languages. For example 'Balkash' is the Mongolian name of an inland sea in Central Asia meaning 'Great Lake' whilst the Turkic 'balik' or 'balikh' (Mongolian 'baluk') is a 'city'.

2. F. W. Carter, 'An Analysis of the mediaeval Serbian oecumene: a theoretical approach'. *Geografiska Annaler*, 51, B, Stockholm (1969), 39–56.

3. D. E. Pitcher, *An Historical Geography of the Ottoman Empire,* (from earliest times to the end of the sixteenth century). Lieden (1972, released 1973), 171 pp.

4. To balkanise—reduce to the condition of the Balkan countries, where hostile nationalities are, or were, mixed together. *Chambers Twentieth Century Dictionary.* (New Edition) ed. A. M. Macdonald, Edinburgh (1974), p. 98.

5. Anon; 'The Balkans: safety in numbers' *The Economist* (International Report) (Sept. 27th 1975), 55.

6. A. R. H. Baker, 'Today's studies of yesterday's geographies'. *The Geographical Magazine*, XLIII (6) (March 1971), 452–453.

7. F. Braudel, *The Mediterranean and the Mediterranean World in the Age of Philip II* London (1972), 2 vols, 1, 375pp.

8. A. Zeune, *Goea. Versuch einer wissenschaftlichen Erdbeschreibung*. Berlin (1808). The name was copied from the *Grand Atlas de Robert de Vaugondy* (dates 1757).

9. J. Cvijić, *La Péninsule Balkanique*. Paris (1918), p. 2 and reiterated again in the Serbo-Croat version published four years later 'Sa očevidnom zabunom', *Balkansko Polostrvo*. Zagreb (1922), p. 2.

10. T. Fischer, 'Die südosteuropäische (Balkan) Halbinsel' in A. Kirchhoff, *Landerkunde von Europa*. Vol. II/2, Vienna-Prague-Leipzig (1893), p. 66; also in 'Südosteuropäische Halbinsel oder Südosthalbinsel' in A. Scobel, *Geographisches Handbuch*, Vol. I, Bielefeld-Leipzig (1909), p. 713.

11. O. Maull, 'Länderkunde von Südeuropa'. *Enzyklopedie der Erdkunde*. Leipzig–Vienna (1929), p. 299.

12. A. Boué, 'Some observations on the geography and geology of northern and central Turkey'. *The Edinburgh Philosophical Journal* (1837); also in *La Turquie d'Europe*. Vol. 1, Paris (1840), p. 91.
Further discussion may be found in J. G. von Hahn, 'Reise von Belgrad nach Salonik'. *Bericht der Denkschrift. phil.—hist.* XI, Vienna (1861), 53;
J. Cvijić, 'Struktura i podela planina Balkanskog Poluostrva'. *Glasnik Srpski Kralj. Akademija*, LXIII, Belgrade (1902), 1–71;
J. Roglić, 'O Geografskom Položaju i Ekonomskom Razvoju Jugoslavije'. *Geografski Glasnik*, Nos. 11–12, Zagreb (1949–1950), 11–16;
A Viquesnel, *Voyage dans la Turquie d'Europe. Déscription physique et géologique de la Thrace.* Paris (1868).

13. J. Cvijić, *Balkansko Poluostrva*, op. cit. p. 5.

14. Ibid. p. 5.

15. *Hrvatska enciklopedija*, Vol. II, Zagreb (1941), pp. 144–145.

16. J. Roglić, op. cit. p. 13.

17. M. I. Newbigin, 'The problem of the South Slavs (Jugoslavs)'. *The Scottish Geographical Magazine*, 35 (I), Edinburgh (1919), 1–15;
A. Melik, 'Meja med Balkanskim Polotokom in evropskim trupom' *Glasnik Geografskog društva*, 14, Belgrade (1928), 107–121.

18. A. Penck, 'Die Nordgrenze der Balkanhalbinsel'. *Izvestia na blgarsko geografsko družestvo*, Sofia (1933), pp. 75–86.

19. Y. Chataigneau, 'Les Pays Balkaniques', *Géographie Universelle*, VII, Paris (1934), 396, footnote 2.

20. 'Pacte d'Entente Balkanique', signed in Athens 9th February 1934 between

Greece, Romania, Turkey and Yugoslavia for the maintenance of peace in the Balkans and waiting for the participation of Bulgaria and Albania.

21. I. M. Mately, *Romania: A Profile.* London (1970), p. 9.

22. T. Stoianovich, op. cit. p. 3.

23. G. W. Hoffman, *The Balkans in Transition* (Van Nostrand Searchlight Book) London (1963), p. 12.

24. P. Matković, 'Trgovinski odnošaji izmedju Dubrovnika i Srednje Italije' *R.A.D.* (Jugoslovenske Akademije Znanosti i Umjetnosti). Vol. 15, Zagreb (1871);
Idem. 'Dva talijanska putopisa po Balkanskom poluotoku iz XVI vieka', *Starine,* Vol. 10, Zagreb (1878);
Idem. 'Putovanja po Balkanskom poluotoku XVI vieka' *R.A.D.* 49, 103–164; 56, 141–232; 62, 45–133; 105, 142–201; 112, 154–243; 116 1–122; 124. 1–102; 129, 1–89; 130, 86–188, published between 1879–1898;
Idem. 'Descriptio peregrinationis Georgii Huszthii', *Starine,* 13, Zagreb (1881), 1–38.

25. H. R. Wilkinson. *Maps and Politics* (A review of the ethnographic cartography of Macedonia), Liverpool Studies in Geography. Liverpool (1951), p. 97;
J. Cvijić, 'Vladimir Karić: njegov geografski i nacionalni rad. *Posebna izdanja Geografskog društva,* Vol. 5, Belgrade (1929), 41 pp.;
M. Clement, 'The contribution of the Yugoslavs to geography and ethnography'. *Scottish Geographical Magazine,* 58 (3) 1942, 113–114.

26. J. Roglić, 'Jovan Cvijić i njegovo djelo'. *Geografski Glasnik,* XXVII, Zagreb (1965), 7–18.

27. J. Cvijić, 'Remarques sur l'ethnographie de la Macédoine.' *Annales de Géographie,* 15, Paris (1906), 115–132; 249–266;
Idem. 'The geographical distribution of the Balkan peoples'. *Geographical Review,* 5 (1918), 345–361;
Idem. The zones of civilization in the Balkan Peninsula'. *Geographical Review,* 5 (1918), 470–482;
Idem. 'Les migrations dans les pays yugoslaves: l'adaption au milieu'. *Revue des Études Slaves* III (1923), 5–25; 254–267;
S. Ćulibrk, 'Cvijić's sociological research into society in the Balkans'. *The British Journal of Sociology,* XXII (4) London (December 1971), 423–440.

28. A. Philippson, 'Bericht über eine Reise durch Nord und Mittelgriechenland'. *Zeitschrift der Gesellschaft für Erdkunde zu Berlin,* XXV (1890), 332–406; XXX (1895), 135–162;
Idem. 'Der Isthmos von Korinth', XXV (1890), 1–98;
Idem. Der Kopaïs—See under siene Umgebung, XXIX (1894), 1–79;
Idem. Der Peloponnes, Berlin (1892);
Idem. 'Zur Vegetations—karte des Peloponnes'. *Pertermanns Mitteilungen,* XLI (1895), 273–279;

Idem. 'Die greichischen Inseln des ägäischen Meeres'. *Verhandlungen der Gesellschaft für Erdkunde zu Berlin,* XXIV (1897), 264–280;
Idem. *Thessalien und Epirus,* Berlin (1897);
Idem. 'Beiträge zur Kenntnis der greichischen Inselwelt'. *Petermanns Mitteilungen,* (Ergänzungsheft, 134) (1901) and XLVIII (1902), 106–110;
Idem. *Das Mittelmeergebiet: Seine Geographische und Kulturelle Eingenart,* Leipzig (1904; 1907; 1914; 1922), 256pp.

29. A. Philippson, *Die Griechischen Landschaften,* (eds H. Lehmann, and H. E. Kirsten), 4 Vols Frankfurt (1951–1959);
H. E. Kirsten, *Die griechische Polis als historische-geographisches Problem des Mittelmeerraumes* (Colloquium geographicum; Vorträge des Bonner Geographischen Kolloquiums zum Gedächtnis an Ferdinand von Richthofen; Geographischen Institut der Universität Bonn,) No. 5 (1956), p. 27–154;
Idem. Beiträge zur historisichen Landeskunde von Griechenland, in A. Philippson, *Die Griechischen Landschaften* Vol. I, pp. 259–301, 645–729, 971–1048; Vol II p. 202–266, 558–643;
Idem. *Strabonis Geographica* (with W. Aly and F. Lapp) Bonn (1968).

30. A. Schulten, *Iberische Landeskunde,* 2 vols. Strasbourg/Kehl (1955), p. 57.

31. A. Ishirkov, 'Hidrografija na B'lgriaja' *Godishnik Sofiski universitet 'Kl. Ohridski',* (istoriski-filozofski fakultet) V, 1908–1909;
Idem. '*Grad Sofija' Yubileina kniga na grad Sofija* (1878–1928) Sofia (1928), 1–14;
Idem. 'Sofija po vreme na Osvobozhdenieto' op. cit. 56–64;
Idem. 'Naselenie na Sofija' op. cit. 65–78;
Idem. 'Naukite v B'lgarija dnes–geografija' *B'lgarska kniga,* No. 4/5 (1930);

Idem. 'Isroriko–etnografski pregled na naselenieto na tsarstvo B'lgarija' *Narodna etnografski muzei-Sofija,* X–XI, Sofia (1932). 5–38;
Idem. 'Harakterni cherti na gradovete v tsarstvo B'lgarija' *Godishnik Sofiski universitet,* (istoriski-filozofski fakultet) XXI (7) (1935).

32. Dimitri Cantemir was undoubtedly an historical scholar. His history of the Turkish Empire written 1714–16 foretold its decay. More relevant than this (or his many other works) is the geographical element discernible in his historiography. In the course of an expedition against Persia in 1722 he wrote geographical, archaeological and historical notes on the Caucasus. But the principal work to note must be the *Descrierea Moldovei* written *c.* 1716. Even the title, *Description of Moldavia,* denotes something other than straight history (indeed, it could additionally be described as early ethnography in parts) and at the same time makes frequent reference to historical facts, and contains a map of Moldavia. The first part outlines the physical geography, climate, drainage, boundaries, mountains and minerals,

vegetation, and wild and domestic animals. This for example gives us an account of living *Bos primigenius* in the region where it survived longest in the wild in Europe, although it was then extant only in parks in Poland and was soon to become entirely extinct. This is therefore partly an historical account. There are descriptions of methods of hunting wild horses by driving them into mud flats along the Prut, which may well have relevance even for the Upper Palaeolithic; bearing in mind the explanatory framework of eighteenth century scientific thought as a whole, Cantemir seems to present an undoubted combination of historian and geographer; C. Daicoviciu, *Dacia liberă si Romană*, Bucharest (1964);

Idem. Istoria Rominiei, 4 vols, Bucharest (1960) (editor);

Idem, with E. Petrovici and G. Ştefan, *La Formation du peuple roumain et de sa langue*, Bucharest (1963) Bibliotheca historica Romainiae;

see also A. D. Xenopol, *Istoria Romanilor din Dacia traiana*, 12 vols, Iasi, 1888–1894, and 'One hundred Years of Geosciences in Romania' *Geoforum* 6 (1) (Sept. 1975) especially pp. 76–79.

33. G. W. Hoffman 'Thessaloniki: The Impact of a changing hinterland' *East European Review* 2 (1) (March, 1968), 1–27

34. W. G. East, *An Historical Geography of Europe*, London (1956) Ch. VIII, The Byzantine Empire, Ch. XVIII The Danube Routeway.

35. A. E. Moodie, 'The Italo–Yugoslav Boundary' *Geographical Journal*, 101, (1943), 49–65;
Idem. The Italo–Yugoslav Boundary; A Study in Political Geography, London (1945), 241 pp;
Idem. 'Some New Boundary Problems in the Julian March' *Transactions I.B.G.*, No. 16 (1950), 81–94.

36. W. R. Kermack, 'Notes on the Historical Geography of the Dardanelles', *Scottish Geographical Magazine*, 35 (VII) (1919), 241–249.

37. J. L. Myres, *Geographical History in Greek Lands*, Clarendon Press, Oxford (1953), 381 pp.

38. H. R. Wilkinson, op. cit.

39. A. Blanc, 'Odnos Geografije i Historije: Prikazan na Primjeru Zapadne Hrvatske' *Geografski Glasnik*, No. 14–15, Zagreb (1953), 35–45;
Idem. La Croatie Occidentale: Étude de Géographie Humaine. (Travaux publies par l'Institut d'Études slaves No. XXV) Paris (1957), 498 pp. especially Chs I–III.

40. R. Rochefort, 'Une Cité- État en Meditérranée: Dubrovnik-Raguse' *Revue de Géographie de Lyon* XXXVI (3) (1961), 231–242.

41. S. Ilešič, 'Prvotna kmetska naselja v območju Velike Ljubljane' *Geografski Vestnik*, 5–6, Ljubljana (1929–1930), 154–160;
Idem. Les Systèmes parcellaires des champs en Solvénié International Geographical Congress, Washington, 1952, Proceedings (1957) p. 629–633;

Idem. '*Die Flurformen Sloweniens im Lichte der europäischen Flurforschung* Kallmünz/Regensburg, Verlag M. Lassleben (1959), 132 p. (Münchner geographische Hefte. Hefte 16, Materialien zur Agrargeographie, No. 5);

Idem. 'New contributions to the study of the geography and history of agrarian regions' *Geografski Vestnik,* Ljubljana, 31 (1959), 158;

Idem. Die jüngeren Gewannfluren in Nordwestjugoslawien '*Geografiska annaler,* 43 (1–2) (1961), 130–137;

Idem. 'Preostanki preteklosti pokrajini kot element resničnega geografskega okolja' *Geografski Vestnik* 36, Ljubljana (1964), 3–12.

42. I. Rubić, 'Utjecaj pomorskih i kopenih faktora na razvoj grada Dubrovnika' *Dubrovačko Pomorstvo,* Dubrovnik (1952), pp. 309–322;

Idem. 'O imena otoka Šolta' *Glasnik Geografskog Društva,* 13, Belgrade (1927), 221–223;

Idem. 'Zadar–Split–Dubrovnik' *Geografski Horizont,* VII (1–2), Zagreb (1961) 3–30.

43. J. Roglić, 'Prilog poznavanju Humljačkog stočarstva', *Geografski Glasnik,* No. 18, Zagreb (1956), 1–12;

Idem. 'The Geographical Setting of Medieval Dubrovnik' in *Geographical Essays on Eastern Europe,* (ed. N. J. G. Pounds), The Hague (1961), pp. 141–159.

44. J. Trifunovski, 'The medieval župa of Inogošt *Annuaire,* (Philosophy Faculty; historical-philosophical section, Skoplje University) (1954), 7 (3), 31–40;

Idem. Imenik Geografskih Naziva Srednjovekovne Zete (Istorijski Institut u Titogradu) Cetinje (1959), 104 pp.;

Idem. 'Geografske karakteristike srednjovekovnih vlashkih katuna' *Proceedings of the Scientific Society of Bosnia/Hercegovina,* Sarajevo, (1963), 19–43.

45. *ΚΟΛΙΑΣ, ΓΕΩΡΓΙΟΣ Τ. ΙΣΤΟΡΙΚΗ ΓΕΩΡΓΡΑΦΙΑ ΤΟΥ ΕΛΛΗΝΙΚΟΥ ΧΩΡΟΥ* (2nd Edition) Athens (1969), 338 pp.

46. D. E. Pitcher, op. cit.

47. W. H. McNeil *et al.,* 'History of the Balkans', *The New Encyclopaedia Britannica,* 30 vols, (Macropaedia Vol. 2) 15th edition, London (1974), pp. 611–640.

48. A. R. H. Baker, op. cit. p. 452.

49. Ibid.

50. L. Dominian, 'The Turk, casualty of geography', *Journal of Geography,* 18 (1) (Jan. 1919), 3–13;

see also G. V. Holmes, 'The Turkish Character as shown by History' *Scottish Geographical Magazine,* 58 (1) (1942), 38–31;

Anon, 'The Turk in History and Geography, *Scottish Geographical Magazine,* 35 (IV) (1919), 142–143.

51. Extrapolation from Hungarian dates for pebble tools from Vértesszöllös of *c.* 360,000 has been recorded which is getting to the limit of Potassium Argon. Even bifacial handaxes in Roumania are certainly in the range of 200,000 years.

52. J. Roglić, 'The Geographical Setting and the Internal Relationships of South-Eastern Europe' *Geographical Papers* No. 2, Zagreb (1974), 7–23.

53. A. R. H. Baker, 'Rethinking Historical Geography', Ch. 1, p. 11 in A. R. H. Baker, (ed.) *Progress in Historical Geography* (Studies in Historical Geography) David and Charles, Newton Abbot (1972), 311pp;

J. Langton, 'Potentialities and Problems of Adopting a Systems Approach to the Study of Change in Human Geography' *Progress in Geography* Vol. 4, Edward Arnold, London (1972), pp. 127–179.

2

The Perspective of Long-term Change in South-east Europe

JOHN NANDRIS

This chapter considers some aspects of the perspective of long-term change in south-east Europe over what is relatively speaking a short period, namely the Neothermal. This term is for several reasons more apt and more universal than 'Post-Glacial' for a region which was never subjected to glaciation under the ice-sheets which covered much of northern Europe in the last Glacial. In northern Europe too the climatic amelioration of the Neothermal began later than in mediterranean regions; in south-east Europe we may be justified in taking it back effectively to about the tenth millennium B.C., rather than the eighty-third century as in the Baltic. Short though this period was in relation to man's antecedent development it is long enough to contrast with the perspectives of most historical geography, and to allow for the examination of what have, for modern man, been crucial behavioural innovations.

In this context south-east Europe comprises the eastern parts of modern Yugoslavia (Serbia, Macedonia and the Voivodina); Romania, Hungary and Bulgaria; and Greece as an important adjunct. Central Europe may be defined as parts of north and north-west Hungary, Austria, Czechoslovakia and southern Germany. The south-east reflects very well the variety of resources, regionalism, connectivity, peninsular coastline and other features which have given Europe itself its importance in global civilization.

It is first necessary to define briefly some of our terms, and to give some notion of what processes are envisaged in speaking of 'long-term change'. This must be done if the outline of some environmental and archaeological developments which follows is not to seem altogether unaware of the complexity of the factors involved. The following section is therefore an attempt to allude as briefly as possible to some of these issues before embarking on a more chronologically ordered account in the next section. Every section of this chapter must be understood as a selection of examples, not as a total description.

A Brief Consideration of the Processes Involved

During the period in question one of the most important changes to affect the pattern of human settlement was the emergence of the Neolithic. This term is used here to cover the polythetically defined combination of behavioural changes which emerged in the Neothermal period and resulted ultimately in village settlement. An important part of the basis of subsistence was contributed by agriculture and certain domestic animals, in locally adapted economic combinations, which continued to include hunting, and in all probability an element of seasonality. It must be recognized that there were probably pre-adaptations for this during a very long part of the Pleistocene, in the sense of the utilization by Palaeolithic hunters of plant foods, and of relationships to animals which at least to some extent presaged the wide variety of relationships which we call 'domestic'. The fact remains that there is as yet no specific evidence earlier than the Neothermal period for any mode of behaviour which resulted in the full complement of economic, technological and bio-social traits which define the Neolithic. The definition is best seen as polythetic, implying that a large number of the traits should be present, but that different combinations are possible.

These relationships do not allow for single-factor explanations or definitions of 'the Neolithic'. Environment and chronology are part of the definition, as is implied by the existence of this phenomenon only during the Neothermal. The environmental and chronological definitions on their own do not however distinguish the Neolithic from the Mesolithic hunter-fishers of the Neothermal. These had not indeed adopted such behavioural innovations as regular village settlement, substantial houses, weaving, carpentry, ceramics, harvesting (as opposed to gathering) of plants, or the control of reproduction in certain animal species; but at the same time they shared an environment and climate with, and were the coevals of, people who had done so. Cases of this can be demonstrated in south-east Europe, notably in the Danube gorges.

This complex phenomenon, while it laid a foundation for a much later growth of urbanism, and even of mediaeval settlement, arguably remained quite closely related to the hunter-gatherer mode of behaviour in an economic sense in that it continued to draw its most important resources from an immediately surrounding catchment, whether seasonally or not. This might help towards a definition of urbanism, which constitutes a more fundamental break in patterns of settlement and subsistence. In the Near East the Neolithic in fact evolved by processes of gradualism out of hunter-gatherer modes. One of the problems we face is how far this was true of Europe, especially in the south-east. In the history of the emergence of the Neolithic in temperate Europe, and of the temperate zone as a whole, south-east Europe occupies a particular place. It is in many ways one of the most complex regions of Europe, and the Neolithic itself soon showed an emphasis on regional identity achieved through processes of differentiation. No attempt will be made here to describe these differentiated groups, although mention may be made of some at the end of the chapter, to outline some of the developments which ensued.

The most conspicuous thing about the Neolithic has been its evolutionary success, so far. In other words, this mode of behaviour allowed the utmost flexibility of adaptation, for example to conditions outside the geographical regions in which it evolved, and the greatest possibility of future development. This possibility was seized particularly firmly in south-east Europe, which became and remained until relatively recently the stronghold of an elaborately developed peasant society. The basis for its emergence lay in its relevance not to one but to numerous contemporary parameters, and in a number of pre-adaptations which may themselves have long antecedent histories. There is for example an important functional relationship to population growth, in that agricultural production and cereal consumption admits of higher population densities than those based on meat. In the pyramid of consumers the carnivores at the apex can exist only in much smaller numbers than the herbivores at the base. But Boserup[1] has demonstrated the fallacy of assuming that population increase is causally related to, and somehow necessarily consequent on, agricultural production. In fact she has said that in pre-take-off societies 'population growth elicited an additional effort which would not have been forthcoming in the subsistence sector of the economy in its absence'.[2]

Emerging out of the long-term perspective of population trends throughout human evolution, we might propose one reason why the Neolithic mode failed to crystallize fully out of pre-adaptations which must surely have been present in some of the earlier Interglacials, in south-east Europe as elsewhere. There were not enough people. The answer to the densities of human population which had evolved by the Early Neothermal period was a take-off into sustained growth, with agriculture as its leading sector; and as Rostow points out 'an increase in agricultural production and productivity plays a multiple role in economic development which can hardly be overestimated'.[3] One effect of the new behavioural mode was a gain in female longevity (and not in that of males) of c. 1½ years in the Early Neolithic as against the Upper Palaeolithic,[4] attributable to the impact on child bearing and rearing of the relative security of sedentary existence. This, as Angel has pointed out, means a population surge. The density of known Neolithic sites in south-east Europe certainly seems much greater than that of known Mesolithic sites, although archaeologists are much more aware than formerly of the difficulties inherent in the sampling and preservation of their data. Nevertheless this model of bio-social changes leading to an economic response, which had the reciprocal effect of aggravating the demographic factor, would be a reasonable example of the way in which processes of change in one medium continually deflect processes in another. An essential contribution to our understanding has been the possibility of assessing rates of change afforded by the external frame of dating reference provided by radiocarbon methods.

When we talk of the processes of change, we have to ask several questions, one of which is 'change in what?' Population studies as such are only one aspect of one of the several media in which change takes place, that is to say in the *environment, economy, technology* and in the *bio-social medium*. The very fact that these sectors are interdependent and interact reciprocally in so many complex ways constitutes the reason why in practice they have to be, and are, dissociated into relatively independent fields of study.

As might be expected it is not at present possible to offer an integrated explanation of all the changes that have taken place over the area of south-east Europe during the Neothermal period. The richness and variety of the south-east European environment is one of the primary characteristics of the region, and this has been reflected in the diversity of its human cultures from a very early period. Despite this disclaimer a brief account of some of the main features can be attempted, picking out especially those which have some functional relationship to geographical factors. It remains to consider first the environmental setting, and secondly some of the developments which took place in the human settlement of the region from about 10,000 B.C.

Environmental and Archaeological Developments in the Neothermal

Some Environmental Factors

A demonstration of the exceptional regional diversity which gives south-east Europe its special character might well go back to the conditions obtaining in the glacial maximum of the Late Würm, the period of the Ostashkov stadial in European Russia, for which some broad equivalents are shown in Table I, (in part after Klein).[5a]

Figure 1 helps to illustrate how complex are the vegetational zones within an 800 km radius, centred on the Danube gorges, by comparison with the regions outside this, even in the full Glacial situation. It is not appropriate to take up a great deal of space here in discussing this vegetational situation, and this map and the following ones are intended, like the tables, to speak for themselves.

Transferring from the full Glacial to the modern situation, partly because any presentation of the Late Glacial/Early Neothermal vegetation of south-east Europe would require so much

Table I

Outline of Late Glacial Terminologies for Selected Areas

B.P. 1000 Years	Britain	Netherlands	Alps	Austria	European Russia	Siberia	South-east Europe
							Fagus.
							Picea + QMF
	Neothermal	Neothermal	Neothermal	Neothermal	Neothermal	Neothermal	Neothermal Pinus/Picea transition
10—							12000 B.P. Pinus
—		Temperate Phase Laugerie/Lascaux					Artemisia steppe
	Late Devensian Glaciation { Weichselian Stadial		Würm III Glaciation { Stadial		Ostashkov (Late Valdai) Stadial	Sartan Stadial	
20—							

25,027 ± 360 B	Ohaba Ponor Interstadial A	30,600	
	Lipovskaya Interstadial		Malaya Kheta Interstadial
	Bryansk (Mologo-Sheksna)	Interstadial	
	Paudorf or Stillfried B	Interstadial	
	Wurm II/III	Interstadial	
	Denekamp Interstadial		Hengelo Interstadial
Paudorf Interstadial		Tame Valley Interstadial	Upton Warren Interstadial
— 30 +		— 40 +	

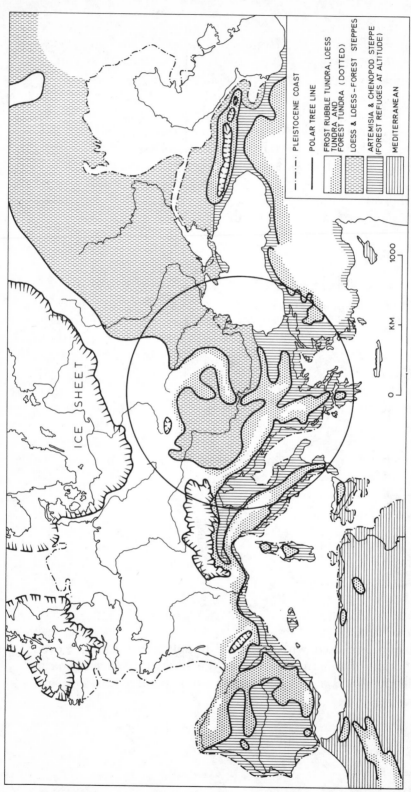

FIG. 1. Vegetation zones during the full glacial (Weichsel) situation, with 500 mile radius from the Danube gorges. (Modified from Büdel's map in Wright, 1961.[32] The most important change to note is the substitution of Artemisia and chenopod steppe around the north Mediterranean, where Büdel claimed deciduous forest.)

Legend:

- – · · – PLEISTOCENE COAST
- ———— POLAR TREE LINE
- FROST RUBBLE TUNDRA, LOESS TUNDRA AND FOREST TUNDRA (DOTTED)
- LOESS & LOESS–FOREST STEPPES
- ARTEMISIA & CHENOPOD STEPPE (FOREST REFUGES AT ALTITUDE)
- MEDITERRANEAN

ICE SHEET

KM   0   1000

qualifying discussion, the picture presented by Fig. 2(a, b, c) (after Hoffman, 1953)[5b] will be seen to give much the same effect. The range of plant species mapped indicates the regional diversity found within the radius of about 500 miles from Lepenski Vir in the Danube gorges. Within this region the cline of Mediterranean influences decreasing northwards can be clearly seen (Fig. 2c). Figures 2a and 2b show the parts played by continental and oceanic influences, reflected in certain plant species. Although this is a rather simple example, there are many indications from areas within this 500 mile radius, such as Romania, that the region is a bioclimatic crossroads of considerable complexity.

In the aftermath of the last glaciation of northern Europe there came vegetational successions which led finally to the establishment of the climax vegetation of the Temperate European Neothermal. This was characteristically a mixed oak forest, in which however it was quite possible for other deciduous tree species, such as lime, to dominate locally, while conifers were important in areas such as Romania. The succession is well known in northern and western Europe, and is usually described in terms of the Blytt and Sernander climatic zones, with the early Neothermal comprising the Pre-Boreal, Boreal and Atlantic periods. Subdivisions of these are beginning to be discussed in the more intensively researched Alpine and north-west European areas.

It should be emphasized that *these periods do not apply directly to south-eastern Europe*, for which the succession is much less well known, although considerable effort is at present being directed to remedy this deficiency. The terms are however, often used, in default of a regional framework, and this opens the possibility of confusion. Not only the vegetational but the chronological successions are different, and unless this is recognized the same disservice is done as when French Palaeolithic terminology is applied in distant parts of the globe, or even in eastern Europe. Markgraf,[6] using dated diagrams from the Alpine region, has demonstrated how zone boundaries do not have an absolute chronological value. This important example should be borne in mind when terms such as 'Atlantic' are used with reference to south-east Europe; even such a locally distinctive feature as the Pinus/Picea transition in Romania cannot be assumed to mark a single point in time throughout various regions.

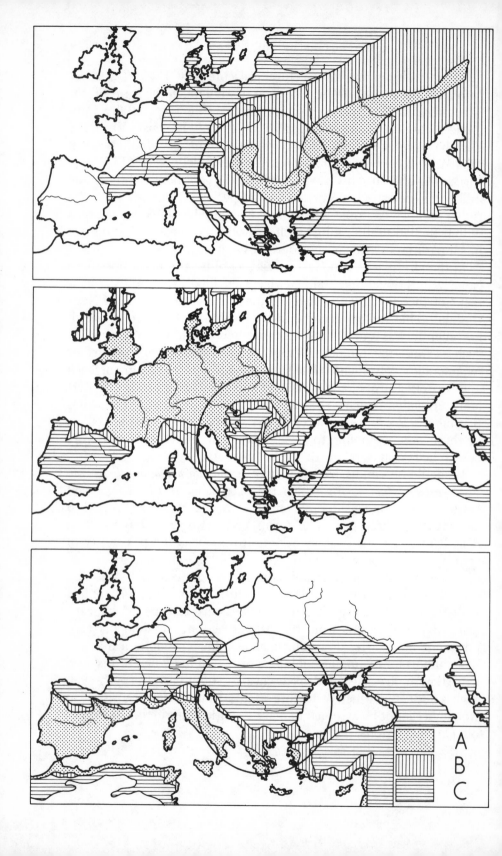

A
B
C

The environmental history of the period is that of the rise of the European forest and then, almost synchronous with its establishment, of its destruction very largely by human agency. It may even be doubted in some areas whether climax vegetation was ever achieved. The forest-clearance activities of Mesolithic man have already been detected in the British Isles, and while neither this nor an impact in pollen diagrams of the agriculturalists, analogous to the northern European Elm Decline and *Landnam* phases, has yet been widely demonstrated in the European south-east there is every reason to believe that in due course their influence will be clearly visible.

The vegetational succession for the Neothermal in Romania worked out by Emil Pop thirty years ago still merits reproduction here with some comments to tie it into the European framework. This pioneer work is being filled out by detailed studies of individual regions, such as that of N. Boșcaiu[7] in south-west Romania. The individual features of the succession belong to south-east Europe, and regional and altitudinal variation have to be taken into account, even when extending it locally.

Pop's[8] annotated succession is as follows, and was drawn up to relate to northern Transylvania.

5. *Fagus* phase   This culminates in the Roman period, and corresponds roughly to the Sub-Atlantic. *Fagus* is a characteristically late addition to the pollen diagrams.

4. *Picea/Carpinus* phase   There is no straight equivalent in central/ south-east Europe for a dry Sub-Boreal phase.

3c. *Picea* maximum   *Quercus* is dominant in the QMF and Corylus falls off significantly.

3b. *Corylus* QMF   *Picea* dominant. This represents a warm maximum which we can now relate to the local Altithermal (equivalent to 'Atlantic' although, like the Neothermal itself, probably beginning earlier in time.)

FIG. 2. (facing page) Variety of climatic influences on vegetation (after Hoffman, 1953), within 500 miles radius from the Danube gorges, as reflected in plant species.
Upper: Continental plants. (A: 7 plants; B: 4–6 plants; C: 1–3 plants.)
Middle: Oceanic plants. (A: 6 plants; B: 4–5 plants; C: 1–3 plants.)
Lower: Mediterranean plants. (A: 6–7 plants; B: 4–5 plants; C: 1–3 plants.)

3a. *Picea* (at higher altitudes) *Tilia, Quercus* and *Corylus* present. (Possibly early local Altithermal.)

Ulmus (at lower altitudes)

2. *Pinus/Picea*   This transition is a very marked feature of the pollen diagrams, readily recognizable over a wide area, and can be attributed to the 'Early Boreal'.

1. *Pinus* phase   This corresponds to the 'Pre-Boreal' and extends back to cover the Late Glacial, characterized in many areas by Artemisia steppe.

This basic succession of Pop's has proved sound, and can be amplified in Table II.[9]

The *Pinus/Picea Transition* of the eighth millennium B.C. is one of the distinctive features of the south-east European succession. This succession is gradually being built up so that it may be compared on its own terms, and in its own terminology, with the better known north-west European succession. An essential refinement lies in obtaining more absolute dates. Even Pop's succession offers a hint that just as the Neothermal itself began earlier in south-east Europe, so the Altithermal which in the north-west corresponds to the Atlantic period, here begins at a time corresponding to the Late Boreal. This realization has an explanatory value. For example the stage of Hunter-fisher Climax in the Danube gorges known as the Schela stage, most notably represented in sites like Lepenski Vir (*c.* 5400–4600 B.C.), has its beginnings in the late seventh millennium. It seems that there may be a functional relationship with the local emergence of Altithermal conditions.[10]

The best general example at present for the Romanian pollen diagrams is that of Tăul Zănoguţi (Fig. 3). This site lies at 1,840 metres above sea level and efforts are at present being directed at obtaining diagrams from lower-lying areas related to archaeological sites. The absence of an effect attributable to the 'Dryas III' cold phase, the decline of the Late Glacial Artemisia vegetation, and the rise of Pinus afforestation at *c.* 10,000 B.C., are features which can be seen in this diagram, together with the very marked Pinus/Picea transition.

The picture in Mediterranean zones, has to be considered, since there much of the southern fringes of the region is included, and views on this have also altered relatively recently. It used to be thought that the forest vegetation belts retreated south into these regions during the last glaciation and that the whole Mediterranean zone constituted the refuges from which southern Europe in particular would have been colonized during the Neothermal. We now know that the characteristic vegetation of almost the whole northern Mediterranean was a cold dry steppe with vegetation dominated by Artemisia and Chenopodiaceae (Fig. 1). Around the northern shores of the Aegean[11] this was supplemented by isolated stands of oak forest, and the main refuge zones would seem to have been localized in montane depressions. The question not merely of succession, but also of altitude, as well as latitude, comes into these developments. South-eastern Europe benefited from its lower latitude in that, as seen at Tăul Zănoguţi, some of the latest cold oscillations, such as the Dryas III, do not find any very marked analogy, and the onset of effectively Neothermal conditions was earlier.

To the first characteristic of south-east Europe, that of natural diversity relative to Europe as a whole, we can add another—a consistent element of primacy in respect of some important developments within the European context. This is seen in relation to the establishment of Neothermal conditions, where the primacy is shared with other Mediterranean environments at comparable latitudes. It is found in the establishment of the Neolithic mode of behaviour, in which the primacy of the south-east is absolute within Europe. It is seen in the emergence of copper metallurgy, which develops early in south-east Europe (from the fourth millennium B.C. at least) and attains a degree of influence which is to be felt even on the establishment of the earliest groups of the central European Bronze Age. In these developments geographical factors, in the sense of variety of environment and richness of resources, were at the least permissive, and probably widely influential. Among these factors the local availability of potential plant and animal domesticates must at least be alluded to, together with some zonations of a climatic, pedological and hydrological nature which are closely relevant to the environment of the earliest farmers.

Table II

Vegetational Succession in the Carpathians: (for contrast with North-west Europe) After Boscaiu, 1971

North-west European terminology	Firbas	Overbeck	Approx. Chronology	South-east Carpathian phases, after Pop, 1929, 1932, 1942, 1943	Phases in Semenic Mts, after Ciobanu, 1948
Sub-Atlantic	X	XII	1000	Fagus phase	Fagus sub-phase ⎫
		XI	± 0		Fagus–Picea–Abies–Carpinus sub-phase ⎬ Fagus phase
	IX	X	–1000		Abies sub-phase ⎭
Sub-Boreal	VIII	IX	–2000	Picea with Carpinus phase	Picea with Carpinus sub-phase
Atlantic	VII / VI	VIII	–3000		Picea phase with Corylus and QMF
			–5000	Picea phase with Corylus and QMF	
		VII	–7000		
Boreal	V	VI		Pinus–Picea transition	Pinus–Picea transition with Corylus maximum

← NEOTHERMAL →

Pre-Boreal	IV	V	—8000		
Dryas III	III	IV		Pinus with low Picea	Pinus with low Picea
Alleröd	II	III	—9000	Pinus with high Picea	Pinus with high Picea
Dryas II	Ic	IIb		Betula episode	Younger dry Pinus phase
Bölling	Ib	IIa	—11000	Pinus and Picea episode	Pinus and Picea episcole
Dryas I	Ia	I	—13000	Older dry Pinus phase	Older dry Pinus phase

⟵ LATE GLACIAL ⟶

Pinus phase (bracket over: Pinus with low Picea, Pinus with high Picea, Betula episode)

Pinus phase (bracket over: Pinus with low Picea, Pinus with high Picea, Younger dry Pinus phase)

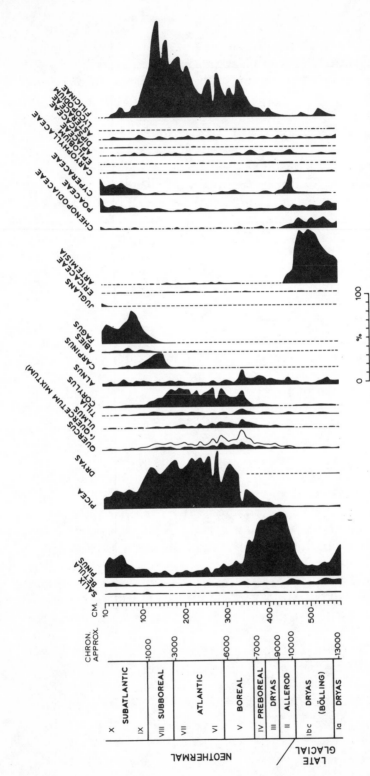

FIG. 3. Pollen diagram from Tăul Zănoguți (Retezat Massif, south-west Romania). (After Pop, Lupșa and Boșcaiu; *in* Pop, 1971.) (Beginning of Neothermal, shown after Nandris.)

It is necessary to view with caution some of the verities regarding the distributions of wild plant and animal species which constituted the economic foundations of the Neolithic mode, especially in south-east Europe. A great deal of work remains to be done on this. Among plants, for example, *Crithodium aegilopoides*, a wild ancestor of einkorn, may have been distributed in the southern parts at least of the Balkan Peninsula[12] Einkorn and emmer, with barley and many other legumes and seeds were staples of Early Neolithic economy. Cattle are an important element of early temperate European husbandry, and their wild progenitor the aurochs, *Bos primigenius*, was widespread in temperate zones[13] as was the wild pig, *Sus scrofa*. The sheep was particularly important in the Greek Early Neolithic. Sheep/goat species, whose intensive exploitation by Early Neothermal hunter-fishers in some Mediterranean regions (e.g. in Greece) almost merits the description which has been applied to it of 'sheep-goat mesolithic', were present in the Carpathians. Although they have sometimes been claimed as components in the fauna of Late Würm sites on the Dniestr[14] they are not attested as local domesticates in south-east Europe during Neothermal times as yet.

A very widely varying spectrum of man-animal relationships in Europe, for example with reindeer in the Late Glacial and red deer in the Post-Glacial, may have laid the foundations for those various relationships which are descriptively oversimplified in the term 'domestication'. These hunter-fisher relationships were especially with herding animals, and Moldavia provides examples of several of the most important species involved, which include *Cervus elaphus*, *Alces alces*, *Rangifer tarandus*, *Equus caballus* (and within the Carpathians *E. asinus hydrantinus*), *Bison priscus*, and *Bos primigenius*. In south Russia the mammoth indeed may just possibly have survived as late as 9000 B.C. according to radiocarbon dating from e.g. Kostienki II (9050± B.C. GIN 93). *Bos primigenius* survived in the wild in Moldavia longer than anywhere in Europe, and the head of the aurochs came to be the main feature of the arms of Moldavia under the Muşat Dynasty, in the fourteenth century, and Stephen the Great in the fifteenth century A.D. These native European cattle were a species particularly important in the economic medium of the early farmers of south-east Europe in Romania and Hungary, and also in the central European primary

Neolithic (the Bandkeramik), in the Copper Age (Bodrogkeresz-túr), the first northern European Neolithic (the Trichterbecher: TRB), and the Early British Neolithic. Like wild pigs (*Sus scrofa*), and the dog, they were abundant in south-east Europe and all three are demonstrably important local domesticates.

Climate and soil, especially on the local scale, are among the factors most crucial for early farmers. The correlation of the central European Bandkeramik farming settlements with loess soils has for long been stressed. We cannot, however, offer a direct correlation between various early farming groups and the soils mapped for south-east Europe in the absence of a conviction that the soil classifications used are appropriate for prehistory. They most usually are not. Nor do they necessarily take account of the continuous history of soil formation, which ensures that very often only a buried soil will bear any relation to the contemporary pedology of a given site. Indeed, all accounts of the catchment or palaeoeconomy of a site must take account of the fact that there is no short cut to palaeoenvironmental reconstruction. It is, however, possible to describe very briefly: 1. a regional zonation of south-east Europe based on climate and 2. a correlation, ultimately climatic, pedological and hydrological, of Early Neolithic sites with the water table in the Tisza region. Both of these relate to the period of the First Temperate Neolithic (FTN), during Altithermal times, and the very existence of a correlation indicates a probably only marginal variation in the broad patterns of climate since that period. Both have been described elsewhere so that only the main features are summarized here.

The regional zonation of south-east Europe shown in Fig. 4 corresponds with some distributions found during the early period of the Neolithic. The known earlier hunter-fisher sites are in general scattered, and the climatic patterns implied were presumably emergent during the Early Neothermal, over the period *c*. 10,000–5,000 B.C., so that this zonation cannot at present legitimately be read further back than Altithermal times. It is however clear that, by the time of the earliest Neolithic, settlement was constrained environmentally by two littoral belts on the west and east of the peninsula. The dry littoral of the coastal Pontic steppe with rainfall below 500 mm, was unsuited to early agriculture. The sites of the earliest Neolithic of Romania (the Criş group of

FIG 4. The First Temperate Neolithic sites of south-east Europe in relation to a regional zonation based on climate. Early Greek Neolithic included. (After Nandris.)

Key:- 1. Macedo–Bulgarian Ecotone
     2. Wet Littoral, >750 mm. p.a. (solid line).
     3. Dry Littoral, < 500 mm. p.a. (dashed line).
     4. Transition to north-central European Bandkeramik.
     5. Forest Steppe : FTN and Southern Bug area.

the larger FTN-complex) stop short at this steppe boundary in
Moldavia and Bessarabia, as well as in Muntenia on the left bank
of the Danube at the edge of the Bărăgan steppe. Further north-
east, on the Southern Bug river, local hunter-fishers adopted
economic and technical traits from the Criş, and these distributions
too are restricted between the steppe boundary to the south-east
(at about Pervomaisk) and the forest to the north (at about
Vinnitsa). The same restriction largely within the important
Moldavian forest-steppe zone is seen in the 'Developed Copper-
using Neolithic' of the fourth millennium, the Cucuteni and Tri-
polje complex.

The south-western littoral on the other hand has a high rainfall,
over 750 mm per annum (it is true that seasonal distributions are
as influential as annual totals of rainfall, but the latter serve quite
well for present purposes). In this wet littoral zone lie the distributions of the Early Neolithic Impressed Ware groups of the
Dalmatian coast, related to the Circum-Mediterranean Impressed
Wares much more closely than to the Temperate European Impressed Wares found within the FTN. It is, however, interesting
to note that the south-western sites of the FTN which break into
this wet zone (e.g. Obre on the Bosna) have archaeological relationships with groups such as Danilo-Kakanj which belong to the
littoral itself. The same transition can be observed further south
in the region of Lake Ohrid or in western Greece. Nearly all the
earliest Greek Neolithic sites (which antedate the Circum-
Mediterranean Impressed Ware sites) lie within about 50 miles of
the Aegean shores of Greece.

Although there are many other regional correlations with this
zonation it remains to comment only on the most important, the
regional transitional between the Greek Neolithic of the Mediterranean zone and the First Temperate European Neolithic. This
region, analogous to an ecotone, is the Macedo-Bulgarian zone
(Fig. 4). Within it are found transitional situations; for example
in Yugoslav Macedonia there are a number of sites important in
the process of extension northwards out of Mediterranean regions
of the Neolithic mode.

Some of the most important of these (Amzabegovo, Rug Bajr,
Vršnik, Džumaljija, Leskovica) lie in the Ovče Polje region and
adjacent Lakavica and Bregalnica drainage. The micro-regional

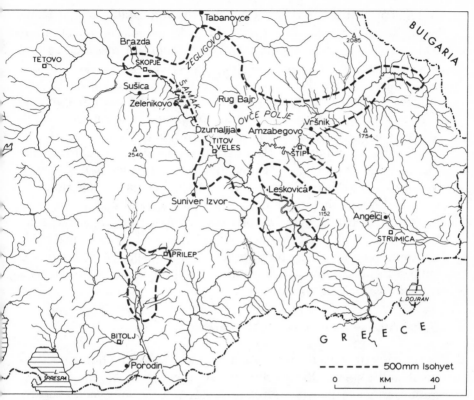

FIG. 5. Yugoslav Macedonia. Early Neolithic sites within the Macedo–
Bulgarian ecotone in relation to the northernmost area locally of 500 mm
annual precipitation. (After Nandris.)

situation is shown in Fig. 5. It is not possible here to argue the full
range of ecological possibilities or the archaeological processes at
work; but the relationship to a localized area of low annual rainfall
(<400–500 mm) very comparable to that obtaining in Greece,
although lying further north locally than any similar region, might
be stressed. There are faunal and other archaeological grounds for
arguing a relationship with Greece at these sites; and at the same
time Amzabegovo is the site furthest south of any at which is
found the V-base bone spoon, prepared from a bovid metacarpal and
exclusively characteristic of the FTN (Fig. 6). The bone in question
was probably derived from *Bos primigenius*[15] but it must be pointed
out that it is precisely the scale of transitional forms between aurochs
and domestic cattle in the FTN region which is of interest.[16]

The correlation of FTN sites with the water table of the Hungarian basin in the Körös region[17] (Fig. 7) is a second distribution which makes some related points. Apart from constituting reasonable evidence for only marginal variations from Altithermal conditions (and indeed the eighteenth and nineteenth century interference with the drainage of the Tisza was more disturbing than any natural processes over the preceding seven millennia) it helps to demonstrate how the well-known, and often only partially valid, correlation between Bandkeramik sites in central Europe and loessic soils is merely a particular case of a more general rule. Where in the Near East and the Mediterranean *water-retentive* soils had been advantageous to the early agriculturalist, in temperate Europe *well drained* soils became essential for the adaptations which took place when the Neolithic mode was transferred, still with its initial repertory at least of wheat species, into a novel environment. South-east Europe is a region whithin which this transition can be observed.

Some Archaeological Developments

It remains to consider briefly some examples of the human settlement and exploitation of this environment, first by the hunters, gatherers and fishermen already present in the area, and then by the farmers in whose economy and technology there is at least an element of diffusion from Mediterranean regions.

An Example of Hunter-Fisher Settlement

In describing some of the environmental factors above, it will already have emerged that hunter-fisher settlement of south-east Europe continued from about the tenth millennium, up to and well past the time, during the sixth millennium, when the Neolithic was established in Greece and the fifth, when it was established in temperate Europe. These Epi-Palaeolithic and Mesolithic sites are scattered in space and time, so that it is not in general possible to give a coherent historical account of hunter-fisher settlement. It may be best to mention just one region, in which something of a sequence is available to form a backbone for the period, and that is the Danube gorges between south-western Romania and northern Serbia.

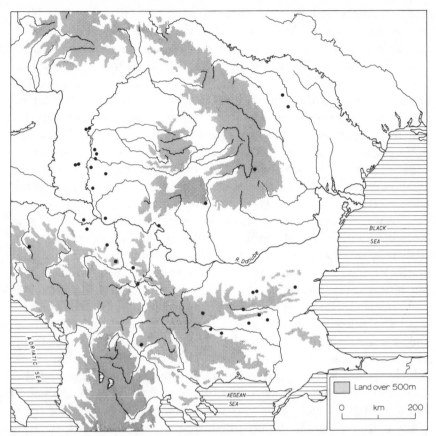

FIG. 6. Distribution of an exclusively First Temperate Neolithic trait: V-based bone spoons made from *Bos primigenius* metacarpals. (After Nandris, 1972.)

The rich biome of the gorges of the Danube above the Iron Gates offered a favourable environment in which hunter-fisher settlement has been radiocarbon dated from the eleventh and ninth millennia onwards. This early settlement, at sites such as Cuina Turcului, contained a lithic industry of small backed bladelets and other components of composite tools. This has been labelled 'Romanellian', although there is no real indication of a connection with the southern Italian site of that name. The forested environment supplied 16 species of mammals at Cuina Turcului in this period[18] among which wild pig, beaver, ibex, goat and bovids predominated, while tortoises, river mussels and snails were exploited, birds were caught, and the river provided fish in abundance. It is to be suspected that an element of seasonality was involved, by inference from the fauna and the climate and hydrology of the river. Certainly some of the sites of the ensuing Hunter-fisher Climax, the 'Schela stage' after Schela Cladovei near Turnu Severin, were flooded for at least half the year, and on a number of grounds one could propose an occupation of these mainly during August, September and October.[19] The Hunter-fisher Climax, which by analogy with a vegetational climax can be seen as the optimum adaptation of a certain set of premisses of exploitation to a given set of environmental circumstances, emerged with the establishment locally of the climatic optimum of the Altithermal, and at Icoana it is radiocarbon dated from the sixty-second century B.C. onwards. The fauna from this site includes 15 species of mammals with pig and red deer dominant, and dog certainly present. It is worth noting that in the tool inventory perforated antler mattocks played a prominent part. Their purpose is not established; but it is certain that the end of this stage of hunter-fisher development overlapped in time, for a period approaching half a millennium, with the presence in the gorges of the earliest agriculturalists, the First Temperate Neolithic people. This is demonstrable at the important site of Lepenski Vir[20] on the Yugoslav shore, which shows also that in favourable conditions a hunter-fisher climax could rise to a settlement type which if not a village was at least a small hamlet. This was succeeded on the same spot by an FTN settlement, which may have been more permanent, whether or not it was entirely perennial. While admitting the novelty of domesticated plants and animals the importance of regional adaptation and the possibility of intimate relationships between Mesolithic and Neolithic modes of behaviour can also be emphasized from the case of Lepenski Vir; for the FTN occupation clearly took up and even extended the range of hunting exploitation of the forest environment, continued to emphasize fishing, and adopted the dog from the hunter-fishers. Indeed the gorges must now seem to be one of the most important European centres of domestication of the dog, which was present in some quantity in the earlier site of Vlasac near Lepenski Vir, and is even claimed from the Romanellian.[21] Even such a modest contribution as the history of the carp in Europe is taken back many millennia by its presence in these sites.

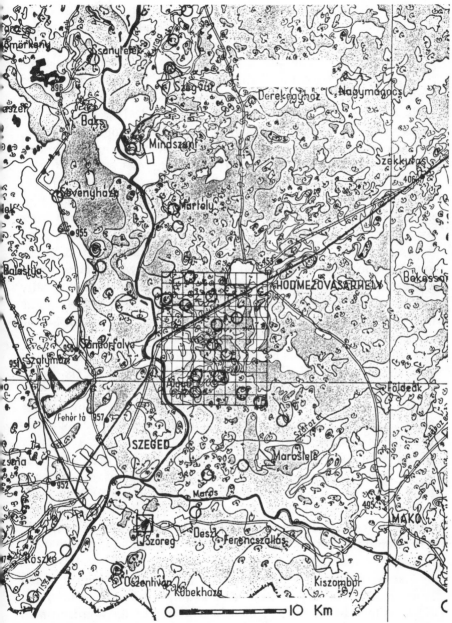

FIG. 7. Relation of First Temperate Neolithic sites of the Early Neolithic along the Tisza (Körös group) to well drained areas of low water table. (After Nandris, 1970a.)

An Example of Neolithic Settlement

It remains to say something about the FTN, the south-east European group which has the distinction of being the first fully formed Neolithic found on temperate European soil, and probably the earliest in any temperate zone of the world. It relates to the earlier Greek Neolithic through the Macedo–Bulgarian region, and something of the way in which diffusion may have operated across this ecotone has been described elsewhere.[22]

The FTN, which extends north from the Macedo–Bulgarian area as far as north-east Hungary and northern Roumania (Fig. 8), is a classic (i.e., quite widely representative of features basic to a polythetically defined) European Early Neolithic village farming culture. As such it cannot represent the process of emergence and formation of this mode of life, about which there is still a great deal to be learned. Its relations with the chronologically earlier Greek Neolithic have been examined elsewhere.[23] The homogeneity of the central European Bandkeramik, which Childe stressed as a classic Early Neolithic, is much more readily apprehended. In the FTN this is to some measure concealed by regionalism already emphasized, for example in Fig. 2b. It is worth noting that such a degree of overt cultural unity was never subsequently displayed over this whole region, to the present day. An outline of the main characteristics of the FTN will give some impression of what is meant by such a Classic Neolithic as a new way of life. While agriculture is attested by carbonized grains or their impressions, sickles, querns and rubbers, there seems often to have been a strong component of hunting or fishing and it may again be stressed that Neolithic economies were regionally adapted, even within such an apparently homogenous group as the Bandkeramik. The Neolithic was distinguished not by economic uniformity but by regional adaptation of its premises of exploitation.

The distribution of the FTN does not stop as abruptly at the River Prut in north-east Roumania as might seem from the map. FTN influences in pottery, in the context of an uninterrupted continuation of local hunting groups can be found as far north as the southern Bug river, and are dated by radiocarbon to the early years of the fifth millennium B.C.

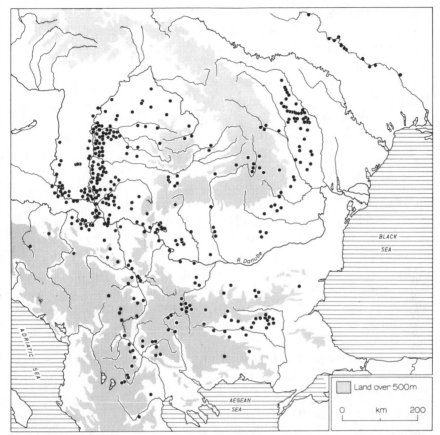

FIG. 8. General distribution of the First Temperate Neolithic, from the Macedo–Bulgarian area to the Hungarian basin and the Southern Bug. (After Nandris.) (Some areas such as the Körös group of the FTN have more sites than can be shown at this scale, and settlement between the Moldavian Criş and the Southern Bug areas is probably continuous.)

The houses of the FTN were usually unitary rooms of daub and timber, several metres square, which, however modest, contrast with the known Mesolithic huts; that from Tiszajenö in the Körös group of the FTN in eastern Hungary measured 8 × 7 metres.[24] They occur in small open settlements, often related to springs or to low river terraces, which lasted long enough to produce one or two metres of deposit. Plans of these villages are rare, but some indications are known from excavations in Bulgaria at Asmaška mogila or Karanovo.[25] At Kazanlik in the northern Maritsa basin corduroy timber flooring is attested from recent excavations, and this feature is also found in broadly contemporary Greek Neolithic sites, such as Servia on the Haliakmon. The Ludvar house model, excavated by Trogmayer from an FTN site beside the Tisza near Szeged, shows a gabled roof with alternately interlocking rafters, and an animal-head terminal on the gable.[26] The gabled roof is also found in contemporary Greek house models. Sometimes the house walls were decorated, and the durable internal remains include domed ovens, clay bins, querns set in clay surround, and clay 'spit-supports'. At Muldava near Plovdiv in Bulgaria[27] fifty vessels were found in a room measuring 7 × 7 metres, and at Divostin in Serbia more than eighty vessels have been found in one room. The number of accessories such as vessels, as well as the bases of some of the vessels, which are ground quite flat, and also perhaps the absence of clay sleeping platforms, must indicate some sort of wooden furniture even at this stage. This is explicitly attested by clay models in the immediately ensuing Neolithic, and like the Neolithic house itself constitutes a fundamental distinction from Mesolithic modes of behaviour.

The attention paid to houses from this time onward marks their importance as a Neolithic trait. The pottery to which archaeologists themselves have paid so much attention is initially merely an adjunct of ways of living, cooking and eating in these houses. It is, however, more than this, since it is as a social signal, bearing in its technology and decoration the imprint of its own society, that it acquired a special importance for its makers and for us. The FTN pottery is vegetable tempered, with a dark reduced core and reddish oxidized surface. There is a wide variety of painted wares bearing black, white or red linear or curvilinear motifs usually on a red ground, with different regional emphasis but closely related. The Temperate European Impressed Wares of the FTN are commoner, especially north of the Macedo–Bulgarian area. These form a unity which may be set against that of the Circum-Mediterranean Impressed Wares. They have finger-pinched or barbotine surface treatment, and sometimes plastic relief figures or faces, or in the Körös area animals recalling Mesolithic art. The incised animals on pottery from Donja Branjevina in the Voivodina also give this impression.[28]

European soil we can see that south-east Europe played a crucial mediating role, by virtue of geographical proximity to regions where the Neolithic had already emerged, and by virtue of a geographical variety favourable to the establishment of what must be viewed as in effect a pattern of behaviour characteristic of the Neothermal period. A better understanding of the course of development of the rich south-east European environment can be seen to be essential. It is as much the way in which the potentialities of a settled way of life were put to use (as for example in the emergence of houses and furniture) which distinguishes the Neolithic from the Mesolithic, as it is the percentage relationships between economic fundamentals. What is conspicuous about this Neolithic is that it was so successful, and allowed of so much future variation on the basic theme and possibilities of future development, which indeed is the only meaning attributable to the term 'progressive'. This is characteristic of evolutionary systems, and the view which sees the Neolithic itself as an episodic revolution was coloured by historical and political modes of thought with which the present evidence and a more modern approach have little in common. It follows from the principles of natural selection that the most complex behavioural patterns of the highest living organisms arise through the selection of pre-existing properties of their functional systems. The possession of such emergent properties is in man complexified and extended socially by the intelligence which is his peculiar attribute. It need not be assumed that the emergence of the Neolithic was inevitable. That it did emerge in the form which it took in Temperate Europe[32] makes it clear both that diffusion took place, and that for a fuller understanding of its emergence we need to know a great deal more about Mesolithic settlement.

2. Notes

1. E. Boserup, *The Conditions for Agricultural Growth*. Allen and Unwin, London (1965).
2. W. W. Rostow (ed.), *The Economics of Take-off into Sustained Growth*. Macmillan, London (1963), p. 405.

3. W. W. Rostow (ed.), op. cit. p. 13.

4. L. Angel, 'Neolithic skeletons from Çatal Hüyük'. *Anatolian Studies*, XXI, 77–98.

5a. R. G. Klein, *Ice-Age Hunters of the Ukraine*. University of Chicago Press (1971).

5b. G. W. Hoffman (ed.), *A Geography of Europe*. Methuen, London (1953).

6. V. Markgraf, 'Waldgeschichte im Alpenraum seit der letzten Eiszeit'. *Umschau* (Frankfurt am Main), 24 (1970), 789–790.

7. N. Boșcaiu, *Flora si Vegetatia Munților Țarcu, Godeanu și Cernei*. Academy, Bucharest (1971), 494pp.

8. E. Pop, 'Contribuții la Istoria Pădurilor diu Nordul Transilvaniei'. *Buletinul Grădinii Botanice și al Muzeului Botanic de la Universitatea din Cluj*, XXII (1942), 101–177;
E. Pop, (ed.), *Progrese in palinologia Românească*. Editura Academiei, Bucharest (1971).

9. N. Boșcaiu, op. cit. pp. 286–287.

10. J. G. Nandris, 'Early Neothermal seasonality and continuity, with special reference to the Danube gorges'. *Fundamenta* (in press).

11. T. A. Wijmstra, 'Palynology of the first 30 metres of a 120-metre deep section in northern Greece'. *Acta Botanica Neerlandica*, 18 (4) (1969), 511–527.

12. J. G. Nandris, 'The development and relationships of the Earlier Greek Neolithic'. *Man*, 5 (2) (June, 1970), 192–213.

13. J. G. Nandris, 'Bos primigenius and the bone spoon'. *Bulletin London University Institute of Archaeology*, 10 (1972) 63–82.

14. R. G. Klein, op. cit. p. 45;
I. P. Gerasimov (ed.), *Ioess-periglatsial-paleolit na territorii Srednej i Vostochnoj Evropy*. Moscow (for VIII INQUA Congress, Paris) (1969).

15. J. G. Nandris, (1972), op. cit.

16. S. Bökönyi *et al.*, 'Vergleichende Untersuchungen am Metacarpus des Urs- und des Hausrindes'. *Zeitschrift für Tierzüchtung u. Tierzüchtungsbiologie*, 81 (1965), 330–347.

17. J. G. Nandris, 'Ground water as a factor in the First Temperate Neolithic settlement of the Körös region'. *Zbornik Narodnog Muzeja* (Belgrade), VI (1970a), 59–71.

18. A. Bolomey, 'The present state of knowledge of mammal exploitation during the Epipalaeolithic and the earliest Neolithic on the territory of Roumania' in *Domestikationsforchung und Geschichte der Haustiere*, ed. Matolcsi, Akad. Kiadó. Budapest (1973).

19. J. G. Nandris, 'Early Neothermal seasonality and continuity with special reference to the Danube gorges'. *Fundamenta* (in press).

20. D. Srejović, *Lepenski Vir*. Thames and Hudson, London (1972).

2 PERSPECTIVE OF LONG-TERM CHANGE 57

1. A. Bolomey, op. cit.
22. J. G. Nandris, (1970), op. cit.
23. Ibid.
24. L. Selmeczi, 'Das Wohnhaus der Körös-Gruppe von Tiszajenö. Neuere Haustypen des Frühneolithikums'. *Evkönyve* (Szeged), II (1969), 17–22.
25. G. I. Georgiev, 'Beiträge zur Erforschung des Neolithikums und der Bronzezeit in Südbulgarien'. *Arch. Austr.* No. 42 (1967), 90–144.
26. O. Trogmayer, 'Ein Neolithithisches Hausmodell fragment von Röszke'. *Acta Anthropologica et Archaeologica* (Szeged).
27. P. Detev, 'Praistoričeskoto Selište pri selo Muldava'. *Godišnik N.A.M.* (Plovdiv), VI (1968), 9–48.
28. S. Karmanski, 'Žrtvenici Statuete i Amuleti sa Lokaliteta Donja Branjevina kod Deronja'. *Arheološka Sekcija, Odžaci* (1968), (typescript).
29. I. Kutzian, 'The Körös Culture'. *Dissertationes Pannonicae 1947*, (Ser. II, No. 23) Text (1947), Plates (1944).
30. J. G. Nandris, (1972), op. cit.
31. J. G. Nandris, (1970), op. cit. Fig. 1.
32. H. E. Wright Jr, 'Late Pleistocene climate of Europe: a review'. *Geological Society of America Bulletin*, 72 (1961), 933–984.

3

New Approaches to Human Geography Prehistoric Greece: A Case-Study

J. L. BINTLIFF

In the prehistory of Greece, there are few studies that pursue the main theme of historical geography—the study of man's interaction with the landscape. Those that exist confine their analysis to general comments on the availability to early settlers of fertile plains, a plentiful water supply and strategic locations.

This chapter is an attempt to demonstrate how the techniques of modern geography and an interdisciplinary approach, applied to the extant remains of human settlement, burial and ceremony over the landscape, as recovered by archaeologists, can yield a significant body of information about the economic and social life of essentially illiterate communities.*

The Region and its Archaeological Sites

A compilation of archaeological sites recorded within a chosen region is the first preliminary to field examination. This sum-

* For clarity and general interest references have been kept to a minimum, and detailed argument omitted. The reader is referred to the writer's Ph.D thesis: *Natural Environment and Human Settlement in Prehistoric Greece*, submitted Cambridge University, 1975, published by British Archaeological Reports, 1976.

marizes the result of surveys of limited areas and with limited objectives, and frequently incorporates numerous chance discoveries. A consideration of the bias in local archaeology e.g. towards larger settlements or sites on prominent defensible hills, sites belonging to periods with easily recognizable pottery, reveals predictable gaps in the maps of sites plotted over time and space. It is reasonable to point out where sites tend to be, but a large sample and persuasive argument are required before one can say where sites tend not to be. Having selected an area, its total surface must be examined for its potential for prehistoric settlement, even if large sectors are devoid of known sites.

Locational Analysis and the Individual Archaeological Site

After excavation and the analysis of stratified floral and faunal remains, the fundamental approach to understanding the function of a particular archaeological site in terms of its immediate natural surroundings is based on the theory of locational analysis, originating from von Thünen and developed by Lösch, Christaller, Haggett and Chisholm. The archaeological application of locational analysis is especially relevant in the work of Higgs and Vita-Finzi and their school.[1]

Not only are fields distant from a particular farming settlement of low 'value' and labour-extensive in their usage, but it is possible that a threshold exists, beyond which economic activity from the home base is barely viable. Further to this point only occasional visits are made with limited use of the resources. With little empirical justification, this threshold has been estimated at about the five kilometre mark in all directions from the agricultural base, ten kilometres with a pastoral or hunting group.

While there is much to criticize in these theoretical guidelines, and application of them requires continual modifications, several years of fieldwork in Greece and the examination of hundreds of site locations have convinced me of the essential truth of these propositions. In almost every case an archaeological site is closely associated with a local concentration of unique resources e.g. good soil, abundant seafood. Often a grading of resource zones conforming to the 'Land Rent' principle can be verified; a soil that is easiest to work and highly fertile forming a first ring around the site, followed by less rewarding but not infertile soil, finally bounded by grazing land (Fig. 1).

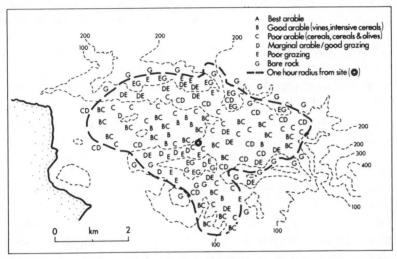

FIG. 1. The modern village of Fournoi (circled asterisk) in the south-west Argolid, is also a key prehistoric site. A grading of land resources available within an hour's walk from the village reveals a characteristic falloff in both land quality and the intensity of agricultural effort. The territory outlined coincides broadly with the fields owned and worked by the village. Further examples of soil zonation around ancient and modern settlements may be found in Figs 2, 3, 4, 5 and 6.

Practical objections to the locational theory involve the criteria of locational values, and the existence of a threshold.

Purely economic considerations seem excessively limiting, and many locations are pre-eminently defensive, or notably well supplied with water resources. The Land Rent principle should surely be distorted by such considerations, especially in Greece where water is scarce, and amongst primitive groups where warfare is supposedly a commonplace activity. A site such as the Argos crag, the Mycenae crag, the Midea–Dendra mountain, the Menelaion plateau, the Malthi hill, the citadel of ancient Melos— these places strike the eye without the need for historical proof, as fortress heights. As for water-supply, Lerna with its mighty

springs, Agios Stephanos and its source, Phylakopi and the great
store of groundwater nearby, the proximity of the main sites in the
Sparta Plain to the perennial Eurotas river—seem equally conclusive. But alternative explanations for these locations point to the
priority of economic considerations, with some concessions made
for example to defence (Figs 2A–C; for Phylakopi see Fig. 4C).

The Threshold Problem

The notion of a threshold to a village or farm territory is a reasonable hypothesis, but quantifying this is problematical. Higgs
and Vita-Finzi made the necessary step in view of changing terrain,
of replacing the 5 and 10 km radius with 1–2 hours walking distance, but the lack of practical proof for the threshold hypothesis
should cause concern to locational practitioners. It seems ad-
visable to seek independent evidence for the spacing of settlements.

Due to exhaustive research in the Late Bronze Age (LBA)
pottery of southern Greece, a given style can be assigned to periods
as brief as a century, often less. It is therefore possible to construct a map of settlements for a given area, where the proof of
contemporaneity is almost certain. Significant patterns and spacings
now become apparent, and intervening distances of 30 min, 15 min
on foot are as frequent as between modern rural communities.
Even the major centres exhibit a territorial radius of only 30 or 45
min, and this space contains lesser satellite communities.

More difficult to separate are the temporal and spatial elements
in a map of sites where dating permits no closer limits than half a
millennium (common in the Neolithic and the earlier part of the
Bronze Age). However even here an examination of all the
archaeological and topographical circumstances can indicate a
strong possibility of contemporaneity, or exclusive territorial
interests (e.g. Early Helladic and Early Minoan rural settlement
discussed later). Again the maximum radius of an hour, is on a quite
inappropriate scale, given the density and small size of the units
of settlement over the landscape.

In all these cases considered, the solution that provides the most
reasonable results is a modification of Locational Territorial
Analysis, which I proposed, on the model of highland British

farm concepts: the In Territory and the Out Territory.

The dictum of E. S. Higgs, that the resources within a ten minute radius of an ancient site are crucial to its locational priorities, underlies the In Territory. Often resources beyond this inner zone are undifferentiated and of lower value; however, power centres in developed cultures such as the Mycenaean may dominate major arable resources from a secure or eye-catching height. Even here, though, the farming community almost invariably occupies a lower town adjacent to the fields.

But clearly a community is normally associated with a body of resources, such as game, seafood, arable and grazing land, which with all but the smallest units of occupation—the farmstead or temporary food-collecting site—requires a larger amount of landscape within its exploited territory. Once the widest reasonable limits of a site's territory are visited and the nearest neighbouring sites are taken into consideration, it is possible to point to a wider potential zone of exploitation—the Out Territory, and this is rarely more extensive in agricultural communities than an hour radius, generally much less. The one hour radius is still an heuristic device to be employed in the field wherever there is no evidence of the contemporary spacing of sites, provided that the site under investigation is of a village or town status. Experience shows that small sites or those of a temporary and seasonal nature exploit far smaller areas of the landscape, and often, with such cases as small fertile shelves, the exact confined zone can be isolated (Fig. 3).

In Fig. 4 we illustrate the 'explanation' of settlement patterns in terms of localized resources. It is clear that a correlation gains strength by repetition. The figures show good correlations of site patterns and particular soils, buried prehistoric coastlines and fishing grounds, (see also Fig. 9).

In the preceding pages, locational preferences exhibited by the individual archaeological site were analysed, using present day features of the landscape and the use made of it by present day rural communities. However, before applying these principles to a given region, we must allow for changes in the economic priorities and technological capacity of human cultures. It is equally necessary to allow for changes in the natural landscape over the time covered by the remains of human occupation.

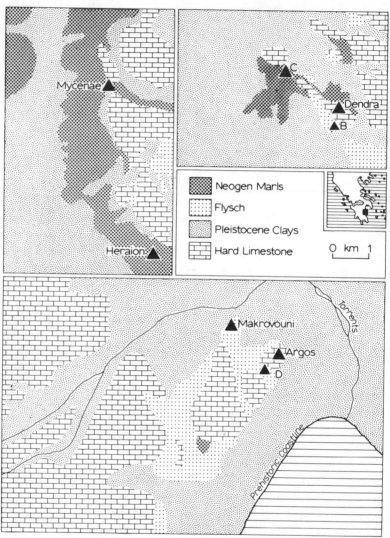

FIG. 2A. The locational preferences exhibited by some famous prehistoric sites. In the Argos Plain, the major early centres of Mycenae, Heraion, Dendra and Argos are in close proximity to the most fertile soils of the region (allowing for the landscape change as indicated)—the Neogen marls and the flysch, while further away the less rewarding Pleistocene clays and rugged uplands are to be found. Even if the citadel occupies an isolated limestone crag, the associated main settlement may be undefended and down amid the best land e.g. site C contemporary to the Dendra citadel, or site D contemporary to the Argos citadel. With the early settlements Makrovouni and Heraion the soil zoning seems to be explanation enough without defensive considerations.

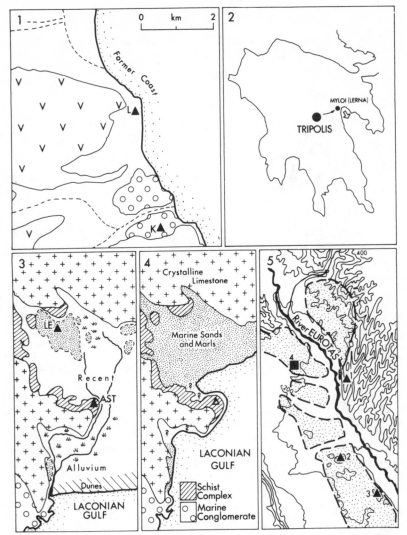

FIG. 2B. The important prehistoric sites of Lerna (L) and Agios Stephanos (AST) are illustrated in 1–4. V infil: hard limestone; circle infill: neogen marls; blank areas: Pleistocene clays; dashed lines: torrents. The present day landscape around Agios Stephanos is compared to that likely in the prehistoric period in 3 and 4. Allowing for that landscape change and that suggested for Lerna in 1 we may say that both sites were originally sites in favourable harbour positions. Notable overseas contacts in the finds of these settlements reinforce this locational evidence, and Myloi, the successor to Lerna (2) was at one time the major port for the Turkish capital of the Peloponnese at Tripolis. Major fishing grounds are likely to be at least as important at Lerna, and perhaps also formerly at Stephanos, while the proximity of significant areas of fine marl soils, in both cases, provides the agricultural basis. Contemporary, and partly contemporary sites amid this arable hinterland (K Kiveri; LE Lekas) are probably complementary locations or even seasonal settlements clearly linked to the main coastal site. In the upper Sparta Plain (5) the three largest settlements in prehistory, and Classical Sparta itself (sites 1, 2, 3 and 4, respectively), despite their proximity to the Evrotas river, and hilltop positions for all but Sparta (4), neatly divide up control over the soil zone of key fertility —the Neogen marl (dotted and enclosed).

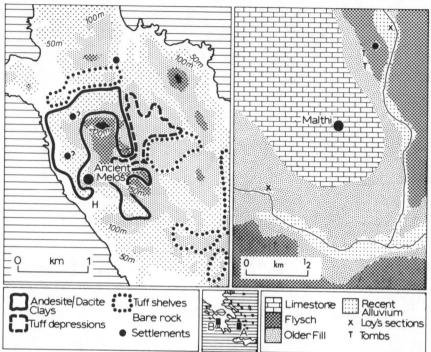

F IG. 2C. The prehistoric centres of Malthi and ancient Melos occupy rugged
hilltop sites like 'acropoleis', but both dominate important expanses of excellent
soils that are rare in their region—the flysch in the Malthi case, in that of Melos
soils developed in tuff depressions, tuff shelves, and from Andesite/Dacite clays.
Bare rock with minimal soil cover occupies the rest of this region of Melos
island. The silted harbour inlet (H) once provided for a small fleet, and is still a
fishing hamlet site. With both Malthi and ancient Melos, additional prehistoric sites associated with the key soils around the main settlement underline
agricultural priorities. In later prehistory the Malthi acropolis may have been
the residence of the elite while the farmers lived at the site indicated amidst the
flysch (Cf. Fig. 2A).

Essentially Human Factors

The overwhelming preference among prehistoric and ancient
farming groups for particular soils (cf. Figs. 4 and 9) is due to
their lightness and high fertility, and to the pre-eminence of
cereals and olives in the agricultural economy. The lack of an
efficient plough and their general nutrient poverty prohibited intensive working of the heavier and stonier soils, particularly the

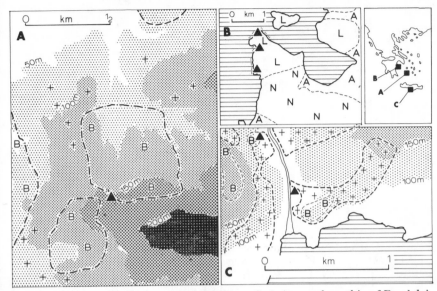

Fig. 3: A. On Melos island, it is common to find sites such as this of Pandelei-
mon, a small cemetery of Bronze Age date, closely associated with two isolated
patches of favourable soil (developed to maturity on shelves and represented
by B), amid exposures of tuff bedrock (crosses) and areas of minimal soil
development (left blank). A family holding?
    B. In the Argolid, three flint sites of Neolithic or Early Bronze Age date
stand apart from other early sites in the region (which normally occupy the
Neogen marls–N), and are located instead on the coast of a bare limestone
peninsula (L). Recent alluvium–A. Their specialist function as shellfish sites
is clear from their association with localized shallow reefs (dense stippling)
and the significance attached to exactly these inshore zones by present day
fishermen.
    C. In the Agiofarango Gorge, Crete, two Minoan collective tombs or 'tholoi'
are sited adjacent to discrete zones of good soil (B–developed on marls and
schist) and connected to rather more extensive zones of poorer but workable
soils (crossed and enclosed). Blank areas are insignificant for agriculture. These
'tholoi' seem to mark family field holdings, and it is traditional Greek practice
to bury the dead by a chapel alongside an ancestral holding.

very widespread Upper Pleistocene colluvium and alluvium,
known as the Older Fill (cf. p. 71 *et seq.*).
    The spread of olive and vine cultivation over Greece during
the Early Bronze Age, as Colin Renfrew has pointed out, may
have stimulated population growth in areas previously sparsely
settled due to limited soil productivity.[2] Surplus production of the
novel cultigens could have been exchanged for imports of local

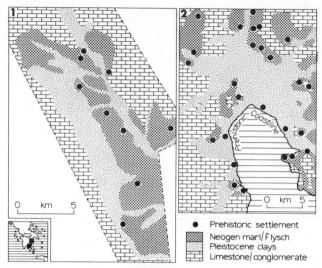

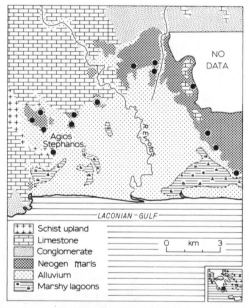

Fig. 4A. Correlation of prehistoric sites and the most fertile soils in the Sparta (1) and Argos (2) Plains. The very fertile but historic recent alluvium is omitted (cf. Fig. 9). In 1, borderlines mark merely the limits of the area I studied.

Fig. 4B. Correlation of prehistoric sites (solid circles) and the most fertile soils available in prehistory in the Helos Plain (South Laconia).

The recent alluvium of the plain proper, with its remnant marshy lagoons was largely formed in later, historic times (cf. Fig. 9). Agios Stephanos is the most south-westerly site (cf. Fig. 2B).

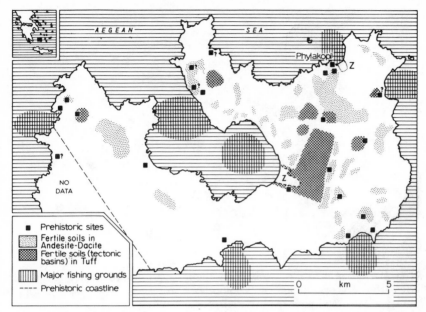

Fɪɢ. 4C. The island of Melos demonstrates a remarkable correlation between its prehistoric sites and highly localized arable and fishing resources. The important Bronze Age 'town' of Phylakopi with a nearby Neolithic fishing station, shows a notable combination of both land and sea resources, though its sheltered harbour is now silted up. The areas in the island marked 'Z' may also once have been harbours.

deficiencies in food, and, increasingly, raw materials such as metals. However, there is no evidence for relocation of settlements in entirely novel micro-environments in response to the new crops, and even possible specialist olive or vine settlements remain closely associated with whatever limited areas are locally available for the staple cereal product (Fig. 5).

An island such as Melos or Thera, with little cereal and olive land, but plentiful vine soil, would have benefited enormously from intensified surplus wine production. Significantly, the vine is a crop which, grown on a large-scale, rapidly outsteps local consumption. Strong fishing interests in the Cycladic isles would have encouraged such exchanges of products. A similar combination can be found in the Hebrides, with low cereal production, strong inter-island fishing movements and the surplus production of woollens.

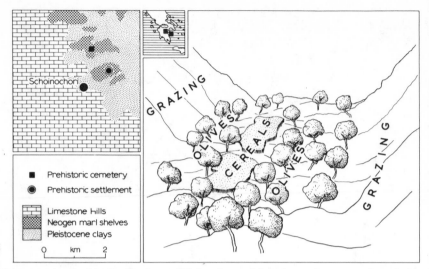

Fig. 5: A. (Left). In the Argos Plain, the prehistoric settlement and cemetery
beside the modern village of Schoinochori, are sited in an area of rugged
limestone hills, and poor quality Pleistocene clays.
   The prehistoric economy is likely to resemble that of the modern village,
extensive olive groves and much sheep/goat herding. A limited but highly
fertile series of Neogen marl shelves, would, however, as today, provide much
of the essential cereal land to enable self-sufficiency to coexist alongside surplus
olive and animal production.
   B. (Right). Many prehistoric sites discovered by the Argolid Survey appear
to represent farmsteads with an extensive associated area of primarily 'olive
land' (uneven terrain, heavier clay soils) where cereals might be grown beneath
the olives in alternate years. But at the core of the site is a central, if small, area
of level land with a very stable and mature soil, ideal for cereal production.
Self-sufficiency may once more be combined in such situations with a surplus
olive-oil production.

Modern dependence on cash-cropping and regional economic
interdependence has led Greek villages to attenuate the locational
links that previously ensured a reasonable self-sufficiency and to
banish the once crucial cereal and olive soils to the periphery of
their exploited territory (Fig. 6).
   Seaworthy boats may open up a new resource—the abundant
mobile fish shoals, but also a whole new way of life with important
consequences for cultural development. Figure 7 illustrates the
results of a study of migratory fishermen in the Aegean and its
relevance to cultural linkage and the movement of ideas and raw
materials between particular regions.

The fishing study reminds us that we must bear in mind the degree of complexity of the community being considered. We would suggest that almost all prehistoric coastal settlements, though often exhibiting evidence for sea-borne exchange in their finds, primarily existed as fishing stations. In early historical times many trading and colonizing cities in Greece correlate closely with major fishing grounds e.g. Aegina, Corinth, Chalcis, Eretria, Thera and Megara. It seems very probable that a similar background of traditional movements in migratory fish and fishermen underlies Phoenician colonization in the western Mediterranean; the continual prehistoric and historic cultural exchange between Brittany, Galicia, Cornwall and Ireland; between peninsula Italy and the Yugoslav Adriatic coast; and between eastern England and the Low Countries.

Essentially Natural Factors

Alluviation Cycles and Climatic Change

A remarkable conclusion drawn from early settlement patterns throughout Greece, up to the Roman period, is the almost complete neglect of the most valuable present day soils, the major expanses of recent alluvial silts. Here are concentrated swarms of modern villages, surrounded by highly profitable irrigated cultures. The dearth of ancient sites on this soil is hard to explain, for those such as W. Loy, who maintain that Bronze Age peoples were as much irrigation farmers as the Greeks today. Others, such as Hope-Simpson and McDonald, hold that these recent alluvial bottomlands were too marshy for early cultivators.

In fact these recent alluvial formations were deposited, in almost their entirety, during and after the Roman period, and up to that time extensive alluvial soils were represented solely by the heavy and generally low fertility Pleistocene formations. Those areas of intensive irrigation cropping today occupy land that was of an entirely different character throughout prehistory— Pleistocene colluvium/alluvium, Pliocene marls, open sea, and to a limited extent—lagoon and delta saltmarshes.

The major breakthrough in this field came with C. Vita-Finzi's studies on the recent geomorphological development of the

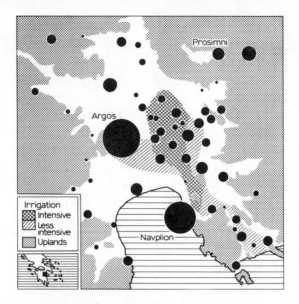

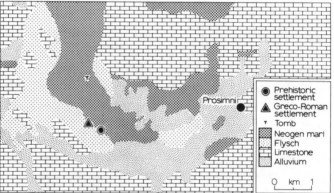

Fɪɢ. 6. An historical change in both environment and crop preference can produce dramatic shifts in settlement patterns.

(Upper) Relative size and distribution of settlements in the Argos Plain in 1928 (size indicated by relative diameter of open circles marking each settlement). Compare this with the prehistoric distribution of Fig. 4A. Argos remains important as the regional centre, and Navplion takes over the several prehistoric ports in its functions. The extreme poverty of settlement in the formerly best soil areas is due to a movement onto recently formed alluvium in the south-east plain, and into the lower irrigable areas of the Pleistocene clays, with irrigated citrus crops the priority in a market economy. The cross-hatched zone was the zone of maximum irrigation in 1928; the hatched zone almost as intensive (contemporary data from Lehmann, H. (1937) *Argolis*). The technical ability to create deep wells for irrigation and the citrus fruits themselves are very recent innovations, while the extensive and moist alluvium is mostly an historic formation (cf. Fig. 9).

Mediterranean valleys.[3] In Figs. 8 and 9 we illustrate schematic valley changes in the Vita-Finzi scheme, the chronology of depositions and correlation with climatic changes, and the reconstructed development of several regional landscapes in Greece (based on my own fieldwork).

Sea Levels and Regional Tectonics

Another important factor that must be evaluated as a dynamic component in the landscape is sea-level fluctuation. Since many famous Classical sites show marine transgressions, attention has frequently been focussed on this phenomenon.[4] Recent discussions highlight two different schools of thought.

The more traditional holds that the sea level is rising absolutely throughout the world, i.e. eustatically, and there is a general rise of *c.* 2m since the Classical period. This rise is a continuing process, and began at the end of the last Glacial period, when there is general agreement on a depressed sea level of at least minus 100m on today's level—due to the water stored in greatly enlarged ice-sheets.

The second school, whose main Mediterranean protagonist is N. C. Flemming,[5] believes that the eustatic rise ceased about 4,000 years ago, and that any major alteration in the relationship of land and sea since that time, is due to local events, such as isostatic rebound in formerly glaciated areas, or long-term tectonic warping of the crust in areas recently active orogenically.

Though Flemming has presented complex mathematical models and calculations in support of his theory, it is difficult to accept that a process of uplift and downwarp over an area as large as Greece and Asia Minor would produce a practically identical relative sea-level rise for numerous ancient sites of *c.* 1m per millennium.

(Lower) Facing page, The village of Prosimni is indicated in Fig. 6A within the general Argos region. T denotes a princely tomb belonging to the ruler of prehistoric settlement—Berbati. It is apparent that prehistoric and ancient communities were, as elsewhere, predominantly interested in the former group of soft and lime-rich soils ideal for cereals and olives. The modern village bases its economy on producing tobacco for export, a crop unusual in its preference for heavy and stony clays (marked here as 'alluvium').

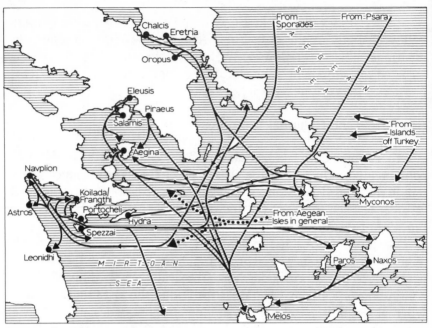

F IG. 7. Seasonal movements of fishermen in the west-central Aegean. Only a limited survey was undertaken, and many more routes remain to be plotted.

These migrations of fishermen, especially in pursuit of the migratory tunny and sardines, can be shown to be highly significant in the explanation of the persistent cultural links within the area of maximum traffic, from the first appearance of tunny, Melian obsidian and alien sheep at Frangthi in the Mesolithic, later with the directional spread of obsidian in the Neolithic and Early Bronze Age and common cultural features throughout the Neolithic and Bronze Age shared within this region. The first sites on the islands can be shown to be settlements of seasonal fishermen (e.g. Saliagos near Paros, Agrilia on Melos, Mavrispilia on Myconos).

An objective examination of his data actually gives far more support to the traditional theory than to his own interpretation. Nor do recent measurements of the trend of crustal movements in Greece provide any evidence of such forces at work.

Before the Classical period, very little is known about the rate at which the ocean rose, and most authors have used a simple extrapolation, into later prehistory, of the rate recorded by submerged historical monuments. Some support for this comes from a recent C14 dated pollen core extracted from Lake Giannitsa in the plain of western Macedonia, and a C14 dated sedimentary core obtained from the Helos Plain in Laconia. Local sea-level heights were obtained for various prehistoric periods, then a comparison was successfully made with a generalized plot of worldwide sea-level rise for the entire Holocene. Between Neolithic and historic times, *c.* 5000 to 500 B.C., the sea rose, on average, by about 1 metre a millenium.

Given the probable height of the sea in prehistory, and the absence at that time of nearly all the recent alluvium, the distance from the shore can be posited for several early settlements, now landlocked amid rich irrigated silts, but then almost certainly fishing and trading stations backed by poor soils (e.g. Tiryns, Agios Stephanos). In many areas of Greece earthquakes and igneous activity have been recorded in very recent times, but the rates of subsidence and faulting appear to be so gradual as not to distort the Aegean eustatic figures from their reasonable fit with other regions, excepting very active parts of Greece, e.g. Melos, Thera, West Crete.

Erosion and Deforestation

It is constantly stated, that the destruction of the primeval wood-lands, by human activity, produced massive erosion, giving rise to the bare slopes and thin soils, the absence of forest, the typical Greek countryside of today. However, the amount of tree cover and the maturity of soils increases as one travels from east to west and from south to north, and from the coast to the mountain ridges. In Fig. 10 we can see this as closely linked to climate and physical geography. Furthermore, we are not to expect vast woods of lofty trees, nor well-developed soils, in the frequently harsh environment of Greece.

Secondly, a woodland is restricted to moderate slopes where soil residues accumulate, and where man is not intensively cultivating. Geographers studying the Minoan palace at Mallia were quick to point out to the deforestation supporters that around the site there have been, for almost uninterrupted millennia, dense arable fields, but for those who bother to ascend into the mountains backing on to the coastal plain they may see, wherever topography permits, fine woodland.

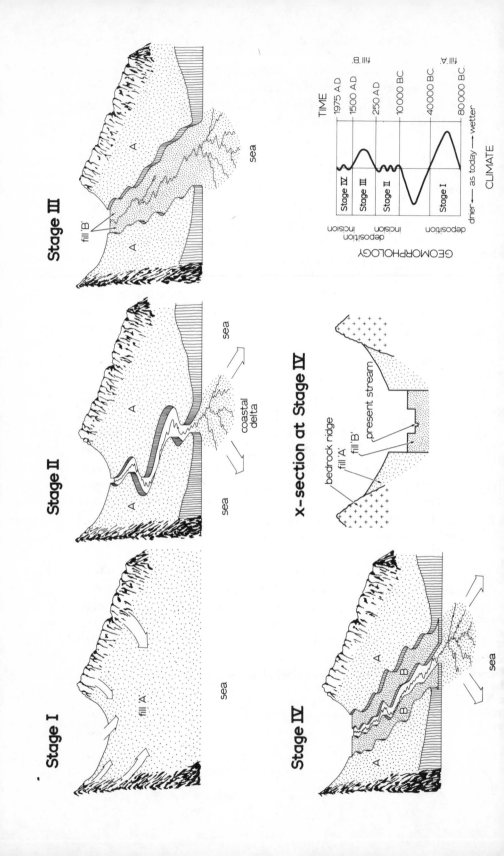

Stage I

fill 'A'

sea

Stage II

A

A

coastal delta

sea

sea

Stage III

fill 'B'

A

A

sea

x-section at Stage IV

bedrock ridge

fill 'A'

fill 'B'

present stream

Stage IV

A

B

B

A

sea

GEOMORPHOLOGY

deposition   incision   deposition   incision

Stage I   Stage II   Stage III   Stage IV

fill 'A'   fill 'B'

80,000 B.C.   40,000 B.C.   10,000 B.C.   250 A.D.   1500 A.D.   1975 A.D.

TIME

drier ←— as today —→ wetter

CLIMATE

Thirdly, a progressive deforestation can be refuted from pollen studies, and the records of travellers to Greece over the last 500 years. Accumulating data suggests that the woodlands of Greece, in favourable conditions, were extensive and able to regenerate up to the last few centuries. At this time massive clearances were effected, for agriculture, industry, fuel and construction, and they are well documented both in contemporary records and dated pollen profiles.[6]

No previous period of human culture left such a scar on the woodlands, although intensive settlement in earlier periods was doubtless associated with temporary incursions in the uplands and rockier areas, more permanent clearances in the arable heartlands. The Roman and Mediaeval moist phase should have encouraged woodland and the return to more typically 'Mediterranean' climate in the last few centuries could have witnessed a natural forest recession in more marginal situations. But the available evidence demonstrates that in characteristic 'Mediterranean' conditions throughout the prehistoric portion of the Holocene, extensive natural woodlands flourished in suitable environments throughout northern and western Greece. Several writers, including at times Vita-Finzi himself, have considered human activity as an important contributory factor to the deposition of the Historical Alluvium by over-grazing, over-cultivation, and deforestation. We have examined the forest cover evidence—significantly, the greatest recorded period of deforestation, the last few centuries, has been

---

FIG. 8. The Late Quaternary development of the Mediterranean valleys, based on the studies of Vita-Finzi. In stages I–IV, we have a schematic reconstruction of the two main phases of valley aggradation (sediment build up by rivers and slope-wash), respectively interrupted and succeeded by two periods of river downcutting and the associated formation of coastal deltas. The 'A' Fill is often referred to as the Older or Pleistocene Fill, the 'B' Fill as the Younger or Historical Alluvium. The chart demonstrates the correlation of these geomorphological features with climatic fluctuations, and the chronology of these events. The evidence of pollen sequences would seem to argue that the moist period of the last Ice Age (Stage I) was confined to Early Würm times, and in contrast to Vita-Finzi, who continued stage I deposition to the end of that Ice Age, the present writer has indicated here a dichotomy of climate and geomorphic process between Early Würm (till c. 40,000 B.C.) and Late Würm (till c. 10,000 B.C.).

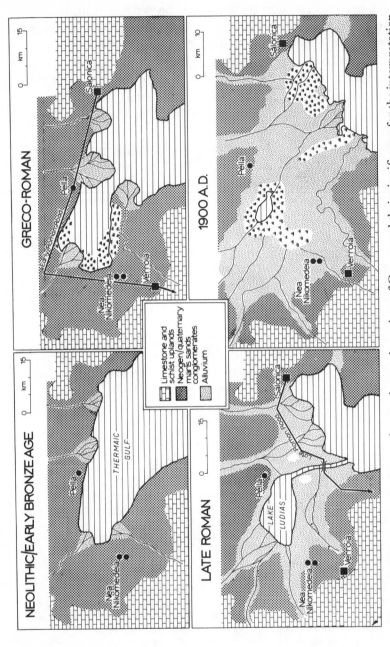

FIGS 9A–D. The recent landscape changes in certain regions of Greece and their significance for the interpretation of associated prehistoric sites.

FIG. 9A. The recent development of the West Macedonian Plain. Prehistoric sites solid circles, ancient cities solid squares. Clearly the changes in soils and accessibility to the sea are very substantial.

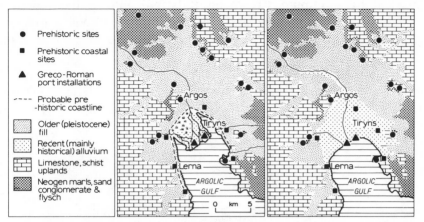

FIG. 9B. The recent development of the Plain of Argos. The left map shows the prehistoric landscapes also the situation by the Greco-Roman period (the additional outgrowth of deltas of recent alluvium); the right gives the present-day landscape. Both soils and accessibility to the sea have altered significantly in this region.

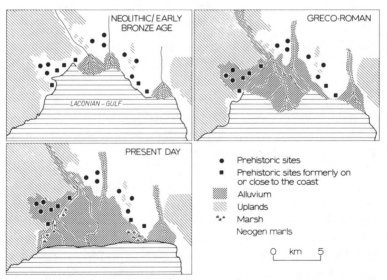

FIG. 9C. The recent development of the Helos Plain. The site of Agios Stephanos is the most southwesterly indicated. Soils and accessibility to the sea have changed dramatically here over the periods illustrated.

marked by minimum stream aggradation, and by incision into previously steeply-graded sediments. This is a strong argument that the sediment load now carried is in fact less than in the high forest phase.

In contrast, some object that it is precisely the abandonment of cultivation, that led to heavy erosion in the Mediaeval period.

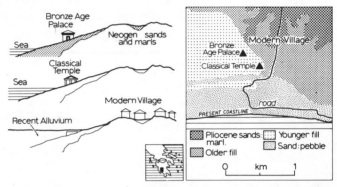

F IG. 9D. The important Early Bronze Age site of Akovitika in south-west Greece lies on the edge of a recent alluvial plain not far from a Classical temple The landscape changes are illustrated schematically in the accompanying diagram.

From field experience, abandonment generally results in the cleared area being overrun by shrub, which acts to preserve the terraced soil. Finally higher growth takes over in the form of woodland. The last phase may be being prevented from regeneration today, but historical and scientific records assure us that in the Late Roman and Mediaeval decline of population, and probably in similar phases recognized in prehistory, the woodland succeeded in reasserting itself. Much the most convincing causation for the Historical Alluviation is the clear evidence for climatic change in Europe during the period A.D. 500–1850, and this is admirably presented in the work of the historical climatologist H. H. Lamb,[7] quite independently of the geomorphological evidence presented by Vita-Finzi.

Finally, some have argued that the goat is a major agent for man in ruining the landscape. Goats thrive on young shoots, but are incapable of making progress in developed woodlands. If man converts the woods into shrub they can prevent reafforestation, but the very recent destruction of forest cover over large areas of Greece argues against progressive attack by the goat—it has been domestic in Greece at least 8,000 years! Far more important is the clearance and maintained openness of landscapes suitable for cultivation. J. F. Kolars, for example, in a study of Turkish villages, related zones of maximum tree loss to predominantly agricultural communities, deforestation 'lows' to goat-rearing villages. Similar evidence is available for the Greek mainland.

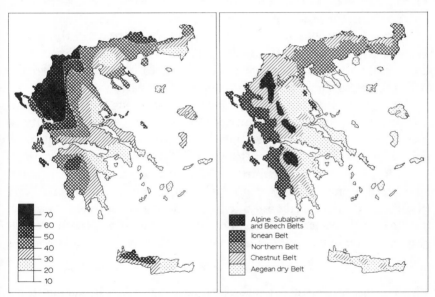

Fɪɢ. 10. Left: Distribution of the rainfall-temperature ratio over Greece (after P. Anastassiades (1949) *Soil Science*). The highest readings demonstrate maximum precipitation and minima of temperature; a definite north-west to south-east cline is clear; as we approach the dry Aegean belt rainfall sinks and evaporation soars.

Right: Generalized Vegetation Zones over Greece (after Anastassiades op. cit.) A similar north-west to south-east cline, upland to lowland cline, is clear; we begin with Alpine flora, passing through continental deciduous growth to typical Mediterranean arid brush. The interaction of depression tracks, mountain features and latitude could be seen as at least, if not more significant than human activity in determining the degree of soil maturity and forestation in e.g. the region of south-east Greece and the Aegean islands.

Social and Political Units of Settlement

We have seen the site-by-site analysis separate out individual priorities as regards arable resources, grazing areas, marine potential. Information about the interaction between the numerous loci of settlement and activity over the landscape, is obtained from a comparative study of the factors of location, the differences observable in extent and probable function of each site, and the possibility of contemporaneity.

Despite the wide bands of time to which we have to assign the possible period of occupation at sites in the earlier phases of prehistory, a good case can often be made for abstracting a settlement pattern from the study of comparative location and function.

A good example arose with the interpretation of the Early Bronze Age (EBA) settlement pattern from the Argolid Survey. In Fig. 11 the EBA pattern is compared to other periods in the area to show a characteristic site density fluctuation.

This general pattern has been seen by previous authors without exception as reflecting the fluctuations in the population density in southern Greece, mirroring the alternating phases of the rise and fall of civilizations. Frequently we read 'historical' reconstructions as follows: after the 'primitive' Neolithic people, living in small groups at some distance from each other, the 'magnificent' EBA civilization witnessed notable agricultural improvements, the first great clearance of all the potential arable areas, the multiplying of settlement numbers and density. A wider use of resources

---

FIG. 11. The changing density of suspected settlement sites within the area of the Argolid Survey is typical for most of southern Greece. To the west can be seen the Argolid Gulf (cf. Fig. 12 for more detail).

FIG. 12. Correlation of prehistoric settlement traces and soil groups in the area of the Argolid Survey. Positive occupation indicated by solid circles, possible by solid circles with question-marks (cf. Fig. 11 for period breakdown). Soil groups: 1. thin and low fertility soils developed on crystalline limestone and conglomerate; 2. moderately deep but high fertility soils developed on serpentine; 3. moderately deep and high fertility soils developed on Neogen marls and sands; 4. recent alluvium and colluvium: a heavy and low fertility clay of Pleistocene date, and a rich alluvial silt known to have been deposited in all essentials in the Late Roman and Early Mediaeval periods. The broken line denotes the probable coastline till historic times.

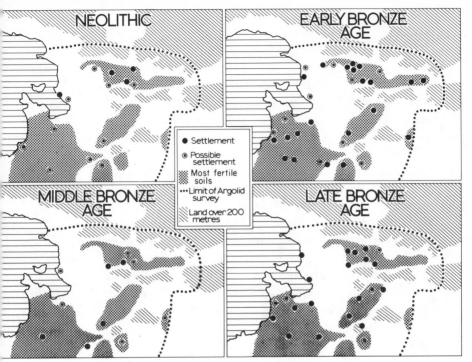

FIG. 11.

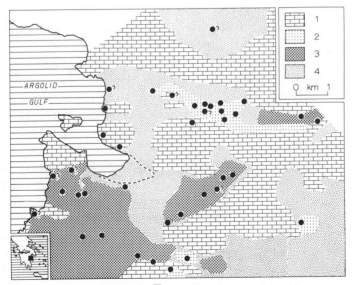

FIG. 12.

is suggested by the frequency of coastal sites. The typical location is a small, low hillock.

But at the end of EBA 2 or 3, (so the traditional 'history' continues), invaders from the north destroyed the centres of these Early Bronze Age folk, and there was a rapid decline in population, deduced from the scarcity of Middle Bronze Age (MBA) sites and large 'empty' areas formerly occupied. The characteristic location is now a steep, defensible hill.

With the rise of Mycenaean civilization, again site numbers shoot up, almost to the EBA figure, and the splendours of the larger centres are matched by the apparent multiplicity of smaller communities, and the obviously extensive use being made of all available resources. The fall of these Late Bronze Age (LBA) folk finds a return, in the following Dark Ages, to a sparseness of sites.

This picture has been elaborated by Renfrew, with mathematical precision, although the basic 'historical' interpretation remains practically the same. But a close study of these settlement changes and their possible significance, from the south-west Argolid data, challenges these orthodox assumptions and their attractive narrative.

Prehistoric Settlement Density and The Argolid Survey

This survey directed by Jameson and Jacobsen is almost unique in Greece for its total coverage of the land surface in the search for traces of past human activity. No *a priori* locations are visited preferentially, every square kilometre is being scrutinized by more than one team of surveyors. The result is an unparalleled picture of absolute settlement numbers and size, from Palaeolithic to present-day.

The final pattern, as can be seen on the maps, conforms closely to the accepted one for each period of prehistory over most of Greece. Correlation with soils and marine resources gave significant results (Fig. 12; see also Fig. 13). A striking feature of the Neolithic and (MBA) pattern is a distinct comparison to the recent village network in the area (Fig. 13A) and to the suggested pattern of Mycenaean (LBA) centres and subcentres (Fig. 13B). The modern trend in Greek rural settlement is to the dispersal of these traditional large nucleated villages into scattered individual farm

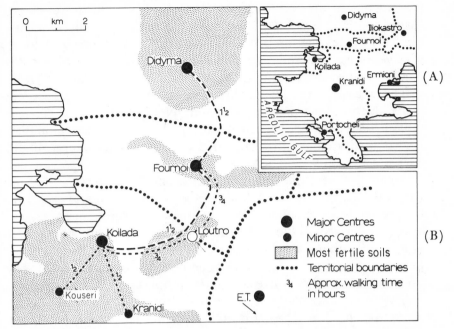

(A)

(B)

Major Centres
Minor Centres
Most fertile soils
Territorial boundaries
¾ Approx. walking time
in hours

F IG. 13. The inset map (A) shows the south-west Argolid Peninsula and its modern settlement territories. The territories of Didyma, Fournoi and Iliokastro villages conform to natural valleys and basins with good soils, surrounded by arid borderland; Koilada and Portocheli villages are primarily ports for the regional town of Kranidi, and major fishing centres, but these villagers also cultivate land within the formal boundaries of the regional capital. Ermioni has a combination of a natural enclosed plain of moderate fertility and a major harbour.

The main map (B) shows a suggested pattern of major centres and subcentres in part of the region during the Late Bronze Age, and the approximate walking-time between them. Possible territories for major centres outlined by lines of dots. The land encompassed in each sphere is comparable in area and location to that supporting the modern villages in Fig. 13A. It can be argued that in Fig. 11, several of the rare Neolithic and Middle Bronze Age settlement sites in key locations may have been hamlet/village sites with a similar size of territories, while the dense 'settlements' of the EBA and LBA very probably represent a combination of villages or 'empty centres' and surrounding dispersed farmsteads. A consideration of the density and scale of findspots in these latter periods, even allowing for shifts in settlement within each period, in comparison to the present village pattern, reveals the necessity for such an explanation. E.T.: Ermioni Tell major centre. The Koilada site may have been the regional centre 'Mases'.

units throughout their territory. The village remains as a centre of trade, worship and social activity. This pattern begins to resemble that of the EBA and LBA. Moreover the *size* of sites alters in the same way: EBA and LBA sites, excluding the exceptional local centres, were generally smaller than MBA and possibly some Neolithic sites.

The conclusive factor is that of distance. The regional landscape is decisive in creating clear spheres of territory for each nucleated village today, each with good arable and harbour resources; all the land is used up in accordance with Land Rent principles (*cf.* Figs. 13A and 12).

An alternative explanation for the changes in settlement density would stress, therefore, the scale of the area being considered. If a handful of modern villages fully exploit a natural territory, so could the few Neolithic and Middle Bronze Age settlements that preceded them in similar or even identical locations; the Early and Late Bronze Age saw a flourishing of farmsteads—overall population numbers need not have changed very much.

In this area conceivably the most important factor being recorded on the period maps is an alternating one, of concentrated and dispersed settlement. The crop changes discussed by Professor Renfrew, could certainly have led to a higher overall population in the EBA, and a greater return from the landscape may have encouraged the dispersed trend of this epoch. Possibly also insecurity in the MBA led to nucleation, relaxed in the 'Pax Mycenaea' that followed. But it does seem likely that the MBA folk exploited the same zones of the landscape as their predecessors. As Lehmann once commented, the location of settlement does change over time, but not the area of settlement.

In the Agiofarango Valley in Crete, a similar result was obtained (*cf.* p. 93) on units of settlement, but other areas of Greece lack the survey cover of the south-west Argolid, and it is not unfair to say that beyond these two surveys, attention has understandably concentrated on—or even been confined to—locating large sites of an obviously dominating nature e.g. the 'fortress towns' of the LBA. Communities smaller than this, unless in strategic positions, receive scant attention, though they certainly existed, and are usually found by accident!

Thus in the Sparta Plain one recorded Neolithic site exists, a typical low mound, found by a Neolithic specialist, while great Mycenaean hill acropoleis run in a line down the plain, studied by acropolis specialists. Nonetheless a study of the admittedly fragmentary settlement evidence here, in the Helos and Argos Plains, and on Melos, suggests that a process of alternate nucleated and dispersed settlement is again at least, if not more, significant than a claimed population fluctuation.

The survey of Messenia province, in the south-west of Greece, by the University of Minnesota (UMME), is a magnificent achievement of interdisciplinary study;[8] but conclusions on population numbers, settlement location and social units, for different periods of prehistory, are highly suspect—simply because the original survey of the province concentrated on the field examination of acropolis-type hills that might have housed towns cited in Homer, the Pylos Palace accounts, and Pausanias' guidebook.

The inadequacy of the sample can be demonstrated from UMME's own statistics (op. cit. pp. 117–147, and Appendix: site register A). Of c. 300 prehistoric sites, only 18 are definitely or possibly Neolithic. The single definite Neolithic open settlement was known before the survey. The five possible open sites, are all high hills. Remaining sites are caves (8) or caches of finds. Only one site could be earlier than Late Neolithic. UMME discovered only one-third of the 35 certain and possible EBA sites. But two-thirds of the certain examples were low natural or artificial knolls. With the Middle Bronze Age UMME is more successful: they found two-thirds of 107 definite and possible sites. But 82 of the MBA sites were new foundations, and c. 77 per cent of the certain sites are now high to medium hills. Of ten cases where the same location was definitely occupied in both EBA and MBA, seven are high sites. In the LBA of c. 195 certain and possible sites, UMME discovered about two-thirds, but about two-thirds of the LBA sites are medium to high locations. Only one definite MBA site was not certainly or possibly reoccupied in the LBA.

In Renfrew's discussion of prehistoric demography, both Messenia and Crete are given steadily increasing population through prehistory while the rest of southern Greece undergoes the familiar cyclical recessions. It seems unwise to use the UMME figures as a real indication of absolute population fluctuations. In fact, in Crete also, the Neolithic and Early Bronze Age periods are very poorly represented in our sample of known sites. An absurdly low number of Neolithic open sites are recorded, hardly any before late Neolithic, while the Early Bronze Age may be characterized by dispersed farmsteads around communal centres—as suggested for the contemporary Mainland (*cf.* below p. 95).

Network Theory

The analysis of a settlement pattern using network theory is increasingly being adapted from geography by archaeologists, to isolate economic and political units over the landscape. Such studies require a sufficient control over the problem of contemporaneity to allow of a balanced settlement picture, and the kind of intensive surveying that is generally lacking in the Mediterranean. Under such circumstances attempts to identify settlement hierarchies, except for the largest units of community, will fall down on inadequate evidence.

However, even within the limits of surveys, such as those of UMME and R. Hope-Simpson, primarily concerned to locate major Mycenaean centres, we can detect significant patterns that provide information on the natural balance of higher and lower order communities, and on the scale of authority and economic organization.

If one considers Hope-Simpson's maps for the settlement picture of any particular region during the Mycenaean age,[9] where we have a very accurate breakdown of pottery groups into 50 or 100 year brackets, a definite regularity in spacing of an approximate kind is visible between those sites held to be key centres. It is generally understood that such a regional power node is characterized by very extensive occupation remains and buildings of a palatial nature. With unexcavated and eroded sites, it is the extent of settlement, and perhaps ancient references, that point to such centres.

Examine, for example, the LBA settlements in the eastern Argos Plain (Fig. 14A). With actual walking distances, regular spacings can be established between the major centres, and a site of uncertain status from excavation—the Heraion, is clearly major.

Another pattern over the landscape fully confirms the settlement analysis, that of the Mycenaean Tholos Tombs. These monumental burial structures were built throughout the LBA. Tholoi are rare and are generally taken outside of Messenia to denote princely

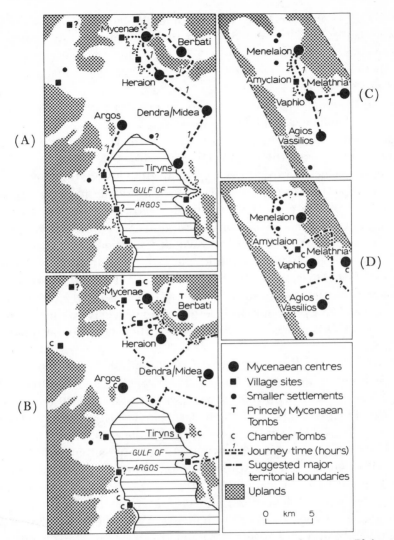

Fig. 14. (A) Regular spacing of Mycenaean centres in the Argos Plain with intervening walking times. The probable line of the prehistoric coastline is here indicated. (B) The location of princely Mycenaean tombs or 'tholoi' within the suspected territory of the major Mycenaean centres. Also of chamber tombs of the 'middle-class' Mycenaeans; their presence accompanies major centres and (without princely tholoi) the next level down in the settlement hierarchy from the major 'palace' centre—the village. Smaller units of settlement are significantly provided with very few, or sometimes no notable tombs.

(C and D) As was seen in Fig. 4 the prehistoric sites in the Sparta Plain relate closely to the distribution of Neogen sands and marls. In these two maps only the Mycenaean sites are shown.

burials, involving control over a skilled labour force and sources of precious wealth (which is found in great quantity in a few un-robbed examples.)

It is no coincidence that a tholos or tholoi can be found not far from Berbati, the Heraion, Dendra and Tiryns, while a group sur-round the citadel of Mycenae. Figure 14B illustrates the location of tholoi in relation to major centres, and the probable boundary of each centre's territory. It is notable that the tholos may be close to or some way from the seat of the living ruler.

Is the prince symbolically expressing the extent of his realm, by placing the family memorial in a striking position in the midst of the fields? The great and splendid tholos north of the Heraion, could never belong to the tiny community it is most adjacent to, at Verseka, nor even the 'border town' at Priphtiani. It is the Heraion tholos, spaced, for effect, amid the rich farming land of Neogen soils. The situation of the Berbati tholos, at the northern end of the fertile enclosed basin of Prosymni, and a good mile from its associated centre, seems to be stating very clearly to those coming down past it from the pass to Mycenae, that 'you are now entering the land of . . .'.

Although smaller communities are doubtless poorly represented in this region, due to survey bias, it is nonetheless clear that traces of a sub-network with regular intervals exists. In Figs 14A and B, villages and hamlets, with their associated burial forms, and hints of regular spacing, are indicated for the same area.

How does even-spacing arise in a primitive situation? A given area is occupied in its most fertile resource sectors, perhaps initially in a fairly random fashion, with an obvious separation of com-munities but no clear minimum or maximum to the intervening distances between pioneer settlements. With the growth of popu-lation and the rise of élite service functionaries (political, religious, technological), several settlement units may crystallize around certain core centres. Competition between these nuclei for land and satellite populations, may result in a 'sorting out' process—regular spacing emerges and territories are adjusted mutually. There are many long-lived prehistoric settlements beginning in the Neo-lithic period in the Argos region, but only certain of these rise to local eminence.

The first clear evidence in this area for a settlement hierarchy comes from the early Mycenaean era, when the centres we have just recognized erect tholoi for their princes, and substantial public buildings begin to be constructed. These princedoms are obviously pretty small territories by our standards, and the petty warfare amongst them may be reflected in later Greek myths. Possibly a counteracting tendency was maintained by regional sanctuaries, perhaps, for example, at the central focus of the Heraion (see below).

Finally a regional supercentre takes a preeminent position, in this case Mycenae. The evidence of the contemporary Linear B documents argues strongly for complete control from each regional palace supercentre over areas as large as north-east Peloponnese (Mycenae), Messenia (Pylos) and Crete (Knossos). This substantially confirms the political situation to be found in Homer.

In locational terms, the rise of Mycenae to greatness far outstripping not only its own region but all other palaces seems paradoxical. It is sited at the northern tail-end of the zone of fertile soils (see Fig. 4A).

Within the Argos Plain, a more obvious choice of regional capital is at Argos itself. Equally advantageous is the Heraion location (Fig. 15A).

But the solution to this paradox lies in the question of scale. In Fig. 15B a much larger area is taken into view, and the preferred soils are emphasized. The place of Mycenae in relation to key soil zones of both the Argos and Corinth regions is equidistant. The importance of Mycenae rests on its central placing between two major resource zones of Greece. The Corinth region lacks a major Mycenaean centre, and significantly, in the Iliad, Agamemnon King of Mycenae is ruler over both Argos and Corinthia.

The settlement network in the Argos Plain should be predictable for other regions. In the Sparta Plain, (Figs 14C and D), we find the same restriction to key soils, the same distances between sites of first and second order. Again it seems likely that the rival 'baronies' became united under a 'supercentre' in the mature Mycenaean age, at the Menelaion. Figure 16 demonstrates the latter's place in the overall region.

In the Argolid Survey area, and in the Soulima Valley in Messenia, we can detect definite regularities in spacing between Mycenaean communities of first or second rank, conforming to the general average (Figs 13 and 17).

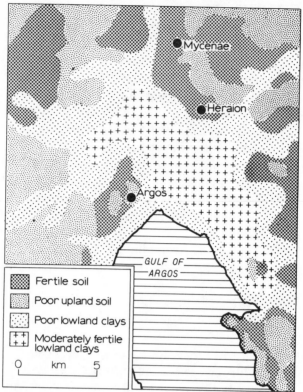

FIG. 15A. The Argos Plain. Coastline as suggested for prehistoric times. The recent alluvium added a new key soil area in later times in the area south of Argos here shown as open sea. A natural centre for this region in prehistoric times, taking account of communications, available soils, the contemporary coastline, might have been expected at Argos or perhaps the Heraion. There is slight evidence for a central ritual function for the latter in the Bronze Age, and such a status is well-attested in ancient historic times. Argos was the regional centre through most of the historic period and is so today, combining its central location in an expanded plain (cf. Fig. 9) with accessibility to both the old priority soil areas and the new irrigated culture zone. With both the prehistoric landscape and inferred soil preferences, and the present-day situation, the pre-eminence in the LBA of the site of Mycenae seems inexplicable in terms of regional geography at this scale.

Ceremonial Sites and the Landscape

In the previous section the value of spatial aspects of burials was demonstrated from the Mycenaean mainland, while the size of a

Minoan periods, and cannot (as some hold) represent, each one, a nearby village, since field calculations prove that each associated arable patch can barely support a few families. As in the Argolid, till recently one nucleated village farmed the whole area.

We suggest that the arable land of the gorge is split up into holdings, associated with a particular kin line. The ancestors of each 'extended family' are buried beside a particular family holding.

Very few of such tombs have been excavated, but where burials have been approximately calculated, a comparison of the number of dead with the duration of use of the tomb, from the pottery and other artefacts, provides us with a reasonable figure of two to four families owning the tomb, and by inference the arable holding, at any one time. The proportions of bones of different age-groups also suggests that all dead community members were interred here.

We find then a parallel pattern to the small EBA farm sites on the mainland, though on Crete there is no noticeable decline of emphasis on the dispersed holding in the MBA.

Where people were actually living in EM and MM times is less clear; there are possible farmstead traces along the valley, and perhaps a village site beside the most extensive of the marl soil patches.

Further confirmation for the family nature of the tombs can be found in their distribution, north of the Agiofarango, in the Messara Plain. Here they are so dense, both in comparison to available land and known settlements, as also to present day village territories, that the hypothesis of one tomb per village can be ruled out. Occasionally, a lone Minoan house near the tomb may represent the family cultivating base of a seasonal or permanent nature.

It seems probable, then, that the Early and Middle Minoan phases on Crete and much of the Early Bronze Age period on the mainland, were times of relative security and a strong emphasis on local kin and cultivation. Similar evidence comes from the Cycladic islands, especially for the Early Cycladic period—when the commonest archaeological site is a small group of burials, that can generally be linked to an 'island' of good soil amid the considerable prevalent expanses of rock and sandy soil (*cf*. Figs 3A and 4C).

Recent parallels abound in traditional island life. On Melos, for

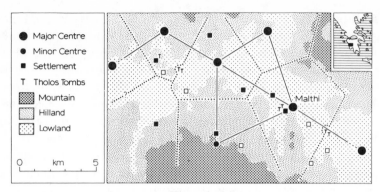

Legend:
- ● Major Centre
- ● Minor Centre
- ■ Settlement
- T Tholos Tombs
- Mountain
- Hilland
- Lowland

0 — km — 5

Malthi

FIG. 17.

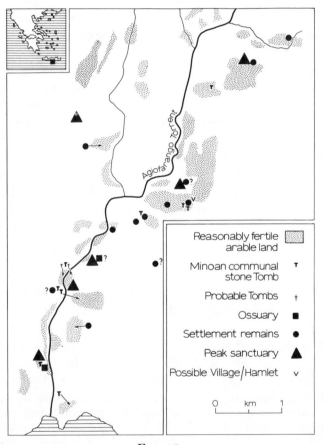

Agiofarango Torrent

Legend:
- Reasonably fertile arable land
- Minoan communal stone Tomb — T
- Probable Tombs — †
- Ossuary — ■
- Settlement remains — ●
- Peak sanctuary — ▲
- Possible Village/Hamlet — v

0 — km — 1

FIG. 18.

example, till very recently, collective village burial was unknown and each family buried its kin by one of the field holdings. Almost all of these discrete areas of good land have an associated chapel, which acted as the centre for burial and ancestor worship for local cultivators. At least 200 of these chapels survive on Melos today.

The same evidence regarding ancient and modern settlements can be demonstrated on Myconos, and could be shown for other islands of the Archipelago.[10]

It is again from ethnography that plausible mechanisms can be extracted to aid the reconstruction of social life in prehistory. A fishing network could introduce a new awareness of wider horizons and different human groups, at the same time providing a way in which material and ideas can circulate in a non-commercial economy. That fishermen are traditionally part-time and spent much of the year as agriculturalists, points up the extent of travel and exchange possible, even within what could well be 'acephalous' self-sufficient economic communities.

Short- and long-distance transhumance with sheep and goats, found throughout Greece, and documented in ancient times, can probably also be assumed for the remotest prehistoric periods as an integrator and medium of cultural and material exchange.

FIG. 17. A pilot study to demonstrate the feasibility of using data from the Minnesota Messenia Survey to establish networks of Mycenaean centres spaced at regular intervals and comparable to Fig. 13 and 14. The best known site in this area (Soulima Valley) is that of Malthi. The major centres are linked by single-lines of apparently regular length; two centres are located just off the mapped area and two close sites both considered major by UMME have been amalgamated. Definite settlements: solid squares, uncertain: open. Suggested territories for major centres are indicated by the broken lines. Only map distances are shown, and walking times are not available; however the lower apparent map distance between major sites in comparison to that seen in Figs 13 and 14 is almost certainly due to the particularly uneven topography of the Soulima Valley, thus increasing the actual walking time for each mapped kilometre separating sites, although one should be very cautious in generalizing from this particular exercise.

FIG. 18. The distribution of the Early and Middle Minoan (Bronze Age) findspots in the Agiofarango Gorge, south Crete. The main torrent and its tributary run approximately north to south across the map to the sea. With the exception of a possible village/hamlet site at 'V', the settlement traces are more of a farmstead or even temporary field hut nature. Substantial finds stem largely from the communal tombs or Minoan 'tholoi', and the significant relationship of these tombs with particular exposures of arable land is indicated by an arrow wherever the tomb does not actually lie within its associated field plot.

However the rise of elaborate architectural complexes in the EBA, and in the later Palace systems, on Crete and the Mainland, associated with evidence for craft specialization and redistribution networks, suggests a definite degree of centralization from the apparently more 'egalitarian' communities that preceded them.

The background to this repeated phenomenon of emergent complexity in a society is discussed below. What is of interest here is the fashion in which a dispersed community, with or without a central focus, is created and maintained as a functioning group that is aware of itself and shares a common culture.

In a key paper in Chang's *Settlement Archaeology*[11] Evon Z. Vogt laid bare the subtle manner in which a region of Mexico achieves renewed integration via religious ceremonial. The modern ceremonial cycle formed a model for the social behaviour of the Pre-Columban Maya (Fig. 19). In Greek anthropology and folklore, parallels are immediately obvious (Fig. 20).

One of the most striking features of Greek history is the continuity and vitality of Greek traditions, despite continued foreign domination. A key role in this strength of tradition lies in these ceremonial cycles, involving all the able-bodied of the community, and every acre of land—whether plain, mountain slope or sea-coast.[12]

The Minoan communal tombs could plausibly be taken to evince the significance of close-kin-relationships, and the deep ties to local ancestral holdings. If religious ceremonial at these centres of integrating tradition nonetheless tended to further social fission and self-sufficiency, or reflected a prevalent contemporary concentration on such aspects of society, it is equally plain that the rise of Minoan civilization saw a conquest of regionalism and kinship fragmentation by some binding influence Minoan civilization maintained itself as a distinct form for millennia, and the visible pattern of the palaces demonstrates control over extensive territories with diverse terrain. Minoan palace texts seem closely comparable to those deciphered from later Mycenaean palaces, and suggest a well-ordered economic and political organization radiating from each palace and tapping all the resources within their respective provinces.

The growing evidence for a widespread system of peak sanctuaries throughout Minoan Crete, is intimately tied up with the rise of that civilization. They begin with the construction of the First Palaces, in early Middle Minoan times, and continue into the Second Palace period and Late Minoan times. In the Agiofarango gorge excellent survey data gave invaluable insight into the spatial significance of these sanctuaries (see Fig. 18). Their distribution and its relation to the tholoi, settlement traces and soil zones, suggests strongly that there are kin group ones, and a possible village (V) one.

In the larger world beyond the gorge, (Fig. 21), we see evidence for more regional peak sanctuaries on major seasonal-pasture mountains. We can expect to isolate similar sanctuaries beside other villages, and we believe that we are seeing key ritual centres in the regional Minoan palaces themselves.

The comparison of the Mexican traditional, the Greek traditional ritual cycles and the Minoan sanctuary system, prompts the suggestion that Minoan ceremonies were also of an ascending order of public significance. The small knoll sanctuaries along the gorge might be important to extended families who were still burying their ancestors in nearby tholoi; but the sanctuary beside the hamlet or village may have been important for the whole valley. The strong likelihood that summer pastoralism took local shepherds to the Asteroussia peaks suggests that there was a much larger catchment area for that peak sanctuary (on the Asteroussia summit—Kophinas), since many other valley populations have traditionally used that upland zone for grazing. Both the Asteroussia summit site and the Mount Ida (Kamares) cave and summit peak sanctuary (the latter a grazing focus for a great area of central Crete as far as Knossos), may have been incorporated into large-scale ritual activity organized from the Phaistos Palace, and almost certainly the ritual cycle in and around the Palace itself, drew in, at one time or another, most of the surrounding and presumably subservient population. The duties or even existence of Minoan 'kings' are controversial problems, though a resident elite living in exceptional luxury, and running the political and economic system, seems assured. Traditions concerning the Knossos Palace ruler suggest a sacred kingship, as does the collective evidence in Evans' studies of the Palace of Minos and its religious significance, and the brilliant analysis of the Minoan palaces by J. W. Graham.[13]

UNITS OF SETTLEMENTS

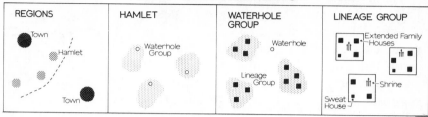

RITUAL MOVEMENTS

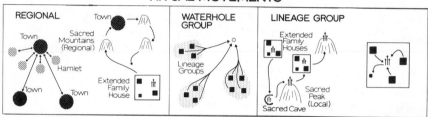

F IG. 19. The relationship of settlement and communal ceremonial cycles in the Zinacantan region of Mexico, based on the study of Vogt.

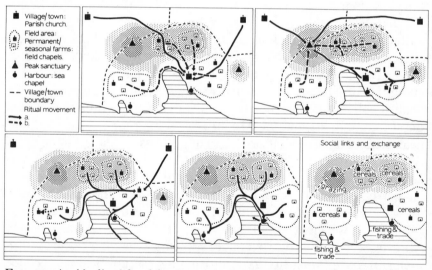

F IG. 20. An idealized local landscape in Greece, illustrating traditional links between communal ceremonial cycles, settlement units and the constituent parts of the traditional economy.

Upper left: Each village has a festival centring upon its parish chapel, attended by occupants of dispersed farms from that village's territory (b routes) and by adjacent villages (a routes).

Upper right: Peak sanctuaries cover most prominent hills and major mountains.

The particular locations of the major shrines, caves and sanctuaries, can be tentatively linked to the nature of the rituals. Sanctuaries of lesser height can be closely linked to associated farming zones, and could involve prayers for crop fertility. Many of the loftier sanctuaries are locations whose only significance is seasonal grazing, and such sites are frequently portrayed in Minoan art with a goddess and goats. Excavations and survey reveal that these summit sites were depositories of figurines of a 'goddess', domestic and wild animals. This sort of coincidence of economic importance and ritual stress is more common than is supposed, and too frequently a 'ritual' explanation for a shrine, just as is the case with 'strategic' locations, is clearly putting the cart before the horse. The whole of the landscape, to the traditional Greek peasant, is alive with religio-economic values—the battle against the devil and destructive forces in general is seen as exemplified in the act of cultivation and renewal of the flocks— harvests of corn and animals are capital won from the forces of evil and based on the original gift of potential fertility to Mankind by God.

The timing of these structures is surely significant, coinciding with the establishment of regional socio-economic centres. The necessary integration was achieved by extending localized cohesive ritual to wider and wider foci of ritual acts.

Within each region one or two have regional significance and attract a widespread congregation at their yearly festivals (routes, left). Lesser sanctuaries act as local shrines (routes, right). It is no coincidence that peak shrines frequently dominate grazing zones occupied seasonally at the time of the peak festival.

Lower left: Field chapels are associated with ancestral field plots, and were the traditional burial place for the family, whether normally resident in a village or amid the fields. Each has its festival, of varying human catchment. Sometimes, as with the example on the left of the map, the congregation represents only those who live or have seasonal holdings in the immediate neighbourhood. But on the right we see a field chapel of some veneration; its festival may involve pilgrimages from the whole region and even adjacent regions.

Lower middle: In various ceremonies throughout the year, pilgrimages are made communally in festivals to bless the fishing fleet, the freshwater sources and the ocean. Each harbour and inlet has its chapel with its own festival.

Lower right: Major values particularly localized in the landscape, whose significance to the peasant community is being celebrated in the various ritual pilgrimages described above. At the same time the different units of settlement within the region are affirming their integration and common socio-cultural background.

The Greek mainland and the islands show the same traditional social mechanisms, and there is abundant evidence that regional religious centres ensured integration within definite provinces during the Archaic and Classical periods. Figure 22A shows major examples, some with possible origins in prehistoric sanctuaries. It is much less clear whether a network of regional ritual foci lay at the cohesive heart of the Mycenaean 'Koine' or cultural sphere.

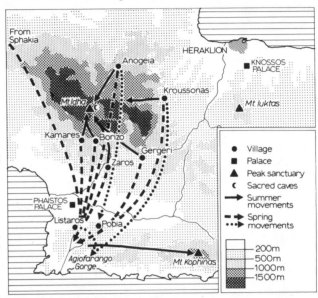

F I G. 21. Central and southern Crete. Above the local level of peak sanctuaries serving individual farmsteads and villages (cf. Fig. 18) regional sanctuaries may be represented by the Minoan sites on the Mt Idha peak, the Mt Iuktas and Kophinas peaks. Significantly the Idha and Kophinas ranges are major summer grazing zones for the surrounding arable lowlands, which in turn once centred upon the major palaces of Phaistos and Knossos. Modern ceremonies at these peaks as Orthodox festivals are naturally during the upland grazing season. Today shepherds from a large number of villages spend the spring in the Agiofarango hills, then summer up in the Idha range; the former villagers of the Agiofarango valley itself, and shepherds from neighbouring valleys, moved with their flocks, in summer, up into the Kophinas range. Source villages for these transhumant moves are indicated on the map, together with the direction of herding movements. We might suggest that similar movements from the lowlands in prehistory were associated with festivals on these major peaks as today; while Mt Iuktas and Mt Kophinas perhaps served only the lowland regions around the Knossos and Phaistos palaces, respectively, it is possible that the Mt Idha peak sanctuary was visited by shepherds and other worshippers from both palace regions as a more 'national' shrine. Pastoral routes from the north-east are not indicated.

Certainly peak sanctuaries and other Minoan shrines appear in Mycenaean art, but this could be simply the contribution of Minoan artistic influences.

However a location discovered on the Argolid Survey has pointed the way to a reappraisal of Mycenaean religion, a Myceaean peak site near Kranidi, with finds and a topography overwhelmingly suggestive of a peak sanctuary.

A growing number of further sites that may represent Mycenaean peak sanctuaries are often in use as such in Classical times, and are generally found to be modern peak sanctuaries, with a wide human catchment and regional importance (Fig. 22B).

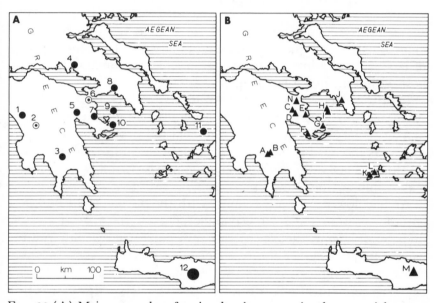

FIG. 22 (A) Major examples of regional and supra-regional ceremonial centres from Archaic and Classical Greece, that served to encourage socio-political and cultural integration within and between the states of the Greek world. Solid circles indicate those with a possible origin in a prehistoric shrine. 1. Olympia; 2. Lynkaion; 3. Amyclaion; 4. Delphi; 5. Heraion; 6. Isthmia; 7. Epidauros; 8. Eleusis; 9. Aegina Oros; 10. Kalauria; 11. Delos; 12. Crete— a notable continuing worship of a communal nature at peak sanctuaries here into historic times.

(B) A. Amyclaion; B. Menelaion; C. Mycenae (Acropolis and Elias peak); D. Heraion; E. Epidauros; F. Kranidi (Argolid Survey); G. Kalauria; H. Aegina Aphaia Temple; I. Aegina Oros; J. Hymettos; K. Melos Agios Spyridon; L. Melos Acropolis; M. Crete-continuity of peak worship into historic times; N. Agia Triadha.

Numerous other possible locations are known on the mainland, and the interpretation of some of them as watchtowers, (recently re-espoused by M. Langdon—in press), needs to be seriously re-examined. Important sanctuaries are recorded in the Linear B tablets of the Pylos Palace, with landed property, slaves and precious wealth.

According to J. Chadwick, (pers. comm.) as our understanding of published Linear B texts deepens, and new tablets appear, the crucial and all-pervading influence of religion to Mycenaean society is becoming very apparent.

Models of Civilizational Growth

In previous sections an analysis has been taken into increasing depth, from the simple requirement of daily bread and the rationale of labour, to the interplay of religion and folk-community awareness within the living landscape.

Finally patterns visible at the regional and national level, will bring us into touch with basic problems in the development of human society. Two aspects of regional political systems are presented as models for the dynamic component in history, the long-term forces activating social and economic growth in Greek lands, and by implication elsewhere.

Archaeologists are preoccupied with the development of differentiation within the socio-economic sphere—the rise of classes, division of labour, the concentration of power and wealth into the hands of a privileged elite. It is clear that this process had already evolved to complex heights by the maturity of the Minoan and Mycenaean civilizations. Professor Renfrew has suggested both a trade model, and a local version of the Coe/Flannery Model for Civilizational Growth. In this scheme, a redistribution from some nodal leader and settlement allows the confederation of landscape zones each with a different resource output, whereby higher culture rests upon the greater economic efficiency of an enlarged community consisting of interdependent smaller communities. Elements of this model are incorporated in the first of our two models.

Evidence is accumulating that both Aegean civilizations arose from stimuli basically internal to southern Greece, and were organizations almost wholly involved in the redistribution of internal, primarily agricultural, resources. Cretan civilization seems to have owed little to external direction, and it seems likely that the Mycenaeans formed a zone of secondary higher culture very much on Minoan lines, if distinguished by singular interest in militaristic activities.

The Sparta Model

This model may be of future value in structuring the various hints of the forces at work to produce the typical settlement—and social —networks and hierarchies to be found in higher cultures. It is based on the actual historical development of the ancient Spartan state, and may parallel the growth of Mycenaean 'civilization in the same region. Figures 23A and B illustrate the model schematically and particular aspects of the Spartan situation.

These factors in operation are bound to be very significant to the rise and maintenance of higher culture, regardless of whether they give birth to a political elite, (the Mycenaean situation?), or reinforce the status of an *a priori* elite, such as a dominant group of external invaders (the Dorians to Sparta, the Spartans to Messenia and Helos).

The Monastery Model

Linked to the previous model, this model isolates another particularly recurrent element, with a possible causative function in the formulation of elite groups and complex stratified societies. An historical study of monastic establishments throughout Greece demonstrates forcibly how a religious minority grew to control most of the land and people of a country, by factors apparently intrinsic to their religious foundations. The following reconstruction is applicable in very general terms to most countries of Europe, and covers the period from later Roman times to the Late Middle Ages.

The original monastic impetus was the desire to dwell alone, or in dispersed groups loosely focussed around a chapel—a life of prayer and simple labour. Frequently a wilderness was chosen, and little effort made to maintain regular contact with the outside

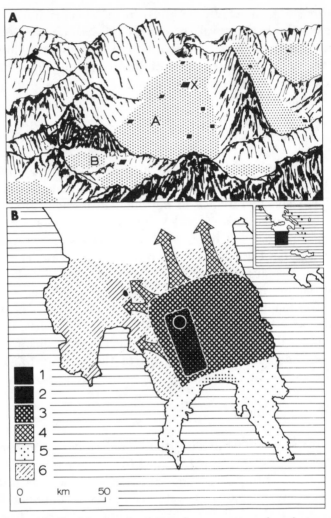

FIG. 23A. An idealized landscape and settlement pattern, based upon the main features of the historic landscape and settlement system of ancient Sparta. The fertile lowland plain is shown as the A zone, with X marking the regional centre; amongst the extensive surrounding mountains and hills (C) are to be seen numerous discrete areas of arable land e.g. patch B; all settlements are shown as in examples, X a lowland town, and Y an upland village.

If we contrast the upland settlements and their available land with the lowland plain communities, certain theoretical conclusions may be drawn for developmental tendencies:

1. The soil is of better quality, and more level, in the lowland thus there is greater return per given area.

2. There is more reasonable soil per sq. km of lowland thus a denser population is supportable.

world. At some point in many areas of Christendom, a subtle change occurred, whereby groups of monks chose a more communal life, and a rudimentary division of labour arose to ensure a continually adequate food and equipment supply. With the more

---

3. Greater per acre returns, thus a smaller holding size is required for self-sufficiency of farmer and this is a further factor increasing population density.

4. Smaller average holding, thus the possibility of surplus of labour arises particularly in lowlands. This extra time for the farmer might be consumed in two main ways: a. further holding may be worked, and this crop exchanged for imported goods, the products of local craftsmen, or the assistance of farmhands; b. with the surplus available via 'a', specialist artisans and administrators/priests may be maintained in the lowlands, ultimately full-time; an intermediate stage might see such roles carried out on a part-time basis with the occupant primarily self-supporting.

5. Denser lowland population, thus there is more purchasing power, and more concentrated demand for created products and imports, as well as more concentrated demand for political and legal 'servicing'. By the law of The Range of a Good the threshold required from local demand to support local centres of artefact production, distribution of imports, and politico-legal servicing, is likely to be first crossed in the dense and mutually accessible lowland community. This establishment in the lowlands provides feedback to the potential for specialization there as in 4b.

6. The lowland is the natural location of regional administration and community activity, being generally the area of easiest communication both within the region and with other regions, and also representing a major proportion (if not the majority) of the regional population total.

FIG. 23B. The development of the ancient Spartan state demonstrates the natural dominance of the 'core-area' of the Sparta Plain, a perhaps predictable conquest or amalgamation of adjacent fertile core-areas, and proof of the concept that to occupy the core-area of a region is sufficient to occupy all of a region. Stage 1: Dorian invaders take over one of the most fertile segments of the Sparta lowlands—the environs of Sparta town itself.

2: All the lowland is conquered from its most fertile sector.

3: The Dorians and indigenous peoples who occupy the poorer uplands around the major lowland area are incorporated with subservient status into an enlarged Spartan state—actual occupation by the Sparta lowlanders not required.

4: The commencement of recurrent conflicts with the forces of adjacent and similarly expansive core-areas for control over intervening zones of lower fertility and lower population, e.g. against Argos over Kynouria, the Arcadian cities over Skirits, Messenia over the Dentheliates.

5: The adjacent core-area of the Helos Plain is annexed by conquest to the Spartan state, providing more high quality land and accessible harbours. Again actual occupation by Spartans is confined to the Helos Plain (indicated by closer area dots), though all the remaining poorer lands of south Laconia come under Spartan control.

6: The adjacent region of Messenia is annexed by conquest to the Spartan state. Only the most fertile areas appear to come under the immediate occupation of Spartans, probably those five indicated by shaded zones.

than average intelligence of the leading monks, their accumulated knowledge of texts on agricultural methods and economics, even the most barren wilderness flowered for the fathers. As noted earlier, the act of cultivation has more often than not been an act of duty and worship.

As the turn to such a life grew in popularity, the power of the secular authorities was declining. The general collapse of many formerly powerful political systems and their economic networks, led to great numbers of people flocking to the secure world of the monasteries, and the secular powers, also, became aware of the relative prosperity of these swiftly multiplying institutions— which acted as balanced, almost self-sufficient centres of production and consumption over the landscape. The monks were given increasingly larger gifts of land to recolonize, as their numbers swelled, and each monastery 'gave birth' to many others; ultimately whole groups of surrounding villages came into a monastery's formal possession. Figure 24 illustrates a schematic plan of the monastery 'system'—dependent villages and sub-monasteries, food and material chains.

The reaction of the peasantry was probably generally favourable. Under the monastery they enjoyed security of subsistence and employment, protection from secular demands and marauders. Furthermore the monasteries set up sophisticated networks for the movement of raw materials and finished goods, at first for necessary utensils, but later to compete with the spiralling demand for the monastery specialist products—woollen cloth, wines. These simple and sophisticated products were distributed to surrounding populations at religious fairs, often held outside the monastery, and the occasion for social and spiritual integration ceremonies as well as the more obviously economic integration. The monastic workshops were the great centres of fine arts, while the literacy of the monks was no less developed in meticulous estate accounts than in the better-known manuscript work. Opportunities for promotion, and responsibility over great areas of land, encouraged a career in the Church for many who in previous centuries would have held high civil posts. For the lesser mortals, the protection against famine and shortage of materials and markets was ensured by the widespread economic links that existed throughout the monastic system; the ritual cycles covering ceremonial activities

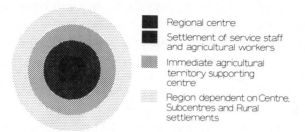

Regional centre

Settlement of service staff
and agricultural workers

Immediate agricultural
territory supporting
centre

Region dependent on Centre.
Subcentres and Rural
settlements

FIG. 24. Notes on the different levels of the Monastery/Palace system: (the scheme applies to both systems, see p. 110 and Fig. 25).

Regional centre: settlement of the elite who deal with the administration of the region,—politically, economically and spiritually. Centre of art and crafts, regional ritual; centre of import and export, and main consumption area of luxury goods (cf. Figs 2C, 4C, 13B, 16, 21).

Settlement of service staff and agricultural workers: associated with the centre, residence of those that maintain the elite settlement and its occupants, as servants, lower craftsmen and cultivators of the immediate surrounding lands (cf. Figs 2A and C).

Immediate territory of the centre: a significant body of fertile arable and/or grazing land, accessible to those servicing the centre and providing its main source of nourishment (cf. Figs 13B, 14B, 16 and 17).

Region of centre: dependent and associated settlements and subcentres: larger region dependent on the centre. Villages, hamlets and dispersed farms, varied agricultural and raw material resources sufficient to maintain regional population and elite (rulers and specialists), as well as providing a surplus for outside exchange. Administered by local 'branches' of the central organization: in the Monastery system for example by dependent smaller monastic foundations; in Minoan Crete probably by both the staff of the country villas and village officials maintained by the palaces; in Mycenaean Greece probably by mayors of dependent villages and hamlets, and district aristocrats dependent on the palaces. Integration furthered on the ritual level by: in the Monastery and Minoan systems—frequent communal ceremonies at the centres and at lesser religious foundations, and at other sacred sites (peak sanctuaries, sacred caves, field chapels), and possibly at the Minoan villas; in Mycenaean Greece perhaps by communal ritual at major and minor centres, shrines in lesser settlements, sacred sites (peak sanctuaries, cave shrines, 'temple communities'—as suggested by the Linear Tablets) (cf. Figs 4C, 13B, 14B, 15B, 16, 17, 21, 23A, B).

Other regions and their centres, dependent settlements: close links between the elites of each regional centre enable exchange of products between regions, cooperation for outside activities (trade, defence). Communal worship at shrines sacred to more than one region may reinforce intra- and inter-regional uniformity of belief and social structure. Ultimately amalgamation may be completed e.g. by elite intermarriage, interchange or conquest (as with the Mycenaean dynasts, the mobility of the higher Monastic priesthood, the conquest policy of the Spartans).

on every corner of the monastery lands created a parallel security on the social and spiritual plane.

It was really only as a result of the local recovery and even prosperity of major agricultural provinces, and the wide commercial links, that in many areas had been largely created by the Monastery system, that the secular powers were able to achieve ultimate integration of large regions into self-sufficient kingdoms and towns began to form significant foci again, and once these two secular forces were re-established, rather naturally, they began to struggle to lessen the Church's hold on the land and the trade, as also the Church's rights over the laws as they applied to Church dependents. This development should be seen as a predictable one, and is closely comparable to the sequence proposed by Adams for civilizational growth in early Mesopotamia and Mesoamerica— Sacred Economy State (which really puts higher civilization 'on its feet' and gives its early stages a characteristic stamp), ultimately overtaken by more secular forms of the State (with a dominant characteristic of expansive militarism).[14]

The key importance of the Monastery or Sacred Economy Stage, is to forge strong links on many levels, between large numbers of people living in different areas, and between different natural regions. The stage occurs either at a very primitive period, or after a cataclysm—when entropy is in danger of disintegrating all but the most local and familial ties, and higher culture of craft or art is all but lost. The cement of this integration process, working outwards from nuclear cells of concentrated elitist organization, is religion; for it is the creation of the Holy City on earth that fundamentally inspired the sophisticated web of the Monastery system, both in its monastic leadership and its co-operating subservient populations. If this ideal became blatantly perverted in the course of time it is really the inevitable consequence of the remarkable efficiency of the organization, and its unconscious take-off from consistent self-sufficiency to commercial profiteering on an international scale.

When we consider the archaeological evidence for the organization of the Minoan and Mycenaean civilizations, we realize we are not prepared—if we had only read Homer. The major novelty is the existence of an all-embracing bureaucracy of great uniformity, radiating authority and complex economic instructions from a series of very similar nuclei—the Palaces. Cultural uniformity, and linguistic, probably also religious, is well-attested within each civilization. The Palaces are engaged in very large scale economic projects, for the regional production and redistribution of food supplies, clothing and metals. Organization for a particular crop or finished product involves numerous stages, taking place in diverse areas of the large provinces associated with each palace, but each stage carefully monitored and recorded by the central bureaucracy. A tremendous harmony of purpose, methodology and belief is manifest by the maturity of each civilization.

We have earlier examined the evidence for a fundamentally religious grounding for these higher cultures, and the case in Crete, at least, if not also on the mainland, for a shift in emphasis from local religious integration to regional ceremonial cycles coincident with the appearance of major local centres of an elitist nature. In Fig. 25 we compare at a detailed level examples of regional centres for definite and suspected 'sacred economies' drawn from diverse backgrounds in areas and time (and cf. also the comparison in Fig. 24).

It is my hypothesis, that future research will demonstrate how the development of sacred economies preceded and paved the way for the mature civilizations in the Aegean. Some centralization of ritual powers may already have occurred with the 'proto-palaces' in Crete and on the mainland, during the EBA, and it is possible that the influence of these foci had already begun to integrate diverse areas within local socio-economic confederacies, cemented by supra-village religious ceremonial. Perhaps these early foci, (as the mature Palaces), were the equivalent of the Mesoamerican Ceremonial Centres, with a staff drawn from the ritual leaders of surrounding communities.[15] On the mainland there was no natural development into the Mycenaean civilization, but in Crete the 'proto-palaces' seem to have developed into the more elaborate and probably more politically powerful First Palaces. When the Mainland did, tardily, achieve its mature civilization, the Mycenaean, it certainly seems modelled on Minoan lines, but there is a difference. The Minoan expanded outside of Crete, in apparently peaceful fashion, but the Mycenaean expansion—amongst other places—onto Crete itself, is typified by an emphasis on militarism.

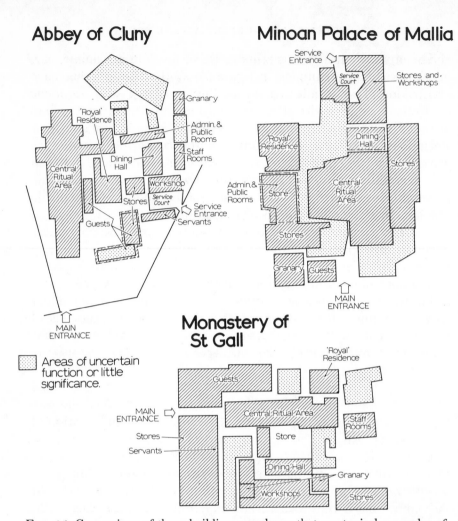

Abbey of Cluny

Minoan Palace of Mallia

Monastery of St Gall

Fig. 25. Comparison of three building complexes that are typical examples of regional centres in Europe during periods when urbanism was either non-existent or of only local significance. In many regions we can point to such centres as the summit of a hierarchy comprising, in addition, numerous dependent villages and farmsteads. In their main functional parts close similarities may be observed. Dotted areas are either of uncertain function or of little significance to the comparison. Even details of access routes and the relative importance of individual shared component parts correspond well. All centres have in common a major ritual area (serving the whole region serviced and ruled by the centre); an elaborate residence for the head of the ruling elite; guests quarters; very extensive storage facilities in which are kept contributions from the harvests of dependent villages, both for the maintenance of the centre and for redistribution to its local agents; important workshops, where we would find both the regional centre for fine arts and a concentrated production of practical artefacts for supplying the surrounding rural population.

These architectural complexes then combine the features of a 'prototown' with those of a 'ceremonial centre' within their region; the example top left is the Abbey of Cluny, bottom centre the Monastery of St Gall (both early Mediaeval from central Europe); the example on the right is the Minoan palace of Mallia on Crete (following the functional analysis of J. W. Graham (1969). *The Palaces of Crete*).

This militaristic aspect is reminiscent of the Adams scheme, and just as with the examples in his study, Mycenaean militaristic expansion did not result in a similar degree of success in regional integration, compared to the careful integration of sympathy and feeling that one is inclined to attribute to the Sacred Economy. The attempt to make Knossos a centre for the occupying Mycenaean warriors was given up after a relatively brief time, and it is likely that the Mycenaeans withdrew from the island. If the Trojan Expedition is as real as Professor Blegen has always maintained, this also seems to have been a brutal attempt at expansion into adjacent and rival spheres of influence, that brought no lasting wider Empire; the Mycenaeans withdrew and very shortly afterwards their higher culture disintegrated in its own homeland.

In many parts of the world, archaeologists are beginning to tackle the crucial transition from simple farming communities to major state units. It is conceivable that the factors isolated in these two growth models will prove to describe essential and decisive elements in the Civilizational Process for areas widely separated in time and space.

3. Notes

1. See particularly C. Vita-Finzi and E. S. Higgs, *Proceedings of the Prehistoric Society*, 36 (1970), 1–37.
2. C. Renfrew, *The Emergence of Civilisation*. London (1972).
3. C. Vita-Finzi, *The Mediterranean Valleys*. Cambridge (1969).
4. For example, cf. D. Hafemann, *Die Umschau*, 60 (1960), 193–196.
5. N. C. Flemming *et al.*, 'Eustatic and tectonic components of relative sea level change' in *Marine Archaeology*, ed. D. Blackman, Bristol (1973), p. 1.
6. Pollen evidence and historical records are consistent on this point from northern Greece (mainly the work of Bottema), and from Messenia (discussed in the Minnesota survey volume). Historical data, particularly the descriptions of recent travellers, corroborate this picture for most other regions of Greece. However, the newly published interpretation of a core from Lake Copais, in central Greece, may indicate a local occurrence of early and progressive deforestation, but we lack reliable dating for events in this core, and the reconstruction as published takes no account of fluctuating lake levels or the exact origin zone of the pollen. It is not impossible

that the draining of the Copais plain for agriculture, perhaps by the Mycenaeans, and a later infill of moist treeless alluvium, is represented in this core, rather than deforestation of surrounding hills. (J. Turner and J. Greig (*Journal of Archaeological Science*, 1 (2) (1974), 177.)

7. H. H. Lamb, *The Changing Climate*. London (1966).

8. G. R. Rapp and W. M. McDonald (eds), *The Minnesota Messenia Expedition*. Minneapolis (1972).

9. R. Hope-Simpson, *A Gazetteer and Atlas of Mycenaean Sites*. London (1965).

10. Since this study was composed Professor Renfrew has isolated communal tomb/family holding groups amongst the megalithic tombs of the Scottish isles, at a similar scale to our Greek examples: C. Renfrew, *Before Civilisation*. New York (1973).

11. K. C. Chang, *Settlement Archaeology*. Palo Alto, California (1968).

12. Nonetheless one must stress the likelihood of recurrent independent 'invention' of such integrative practices. It is not essential, indeed unlikely, that communal ritual e.g. at sacred peaks has continued unbroken from prehistory to the present-day at particular locations. It is surely the appropriateness of certain locations for ritual, given relatively unchanging human involvement with success of upland grazing, field holdings, fishing inter- and intra-village social links, that provides the essential basis for the recurrence of these 'landscape ceremonies'. This is not to deny that memory may survive, even though there are hiatuses in the deposition of ritual offerings. But it is the continuing relevance of the location to new cultures in their everyday life, rather than tradition *per se*, that seems the crucial factor to the present writer.

13. J. W. Graham, *The Palaces of Crete*. Princeton (1969).

14. R. M. Adams, *The Evolution of Urban Society*. Chicago (1966).

15. Here again, since the completion of this paper, Professor Renfrew (1973 op. cit.) has pointed to regular spacings of the prehistoric Maltese temples, each relating to a major zone of arable land—were these also the scene of local integration ceremonies for the surrounding population?

4

Roman Roads and Settlements in the Balkans

G. ŠKRIVANIĆ

The territory of the Balkan Peninsula[1] was exposed to Roman expansion from the third century B.C. until the end of the first century A.D. During their penetration into the Balkan Peninsula, the Romans fought against numerous native tribes—Illyrian, Thrace and Celtic. Their attack on the Illyrians was primarily directed against Ardieans in the area along the River Neretva (229–228 B.C.), then against the Greek towns of Appolonia (today a village called Polina, or Pojani, to the north of Valone) and Dyrrachium (today Durrazo, or Durres-Drach in Albania), which were subdued to Roman rule in 219 B.C. After their victory over Gencie in 168 B.C. the independence of the Illyrians and Macedonians ceased to exist. Following the victory over the rebellious Dalmats in 156 B.C. and Ardieans in 135 B.C. the Dalmatian Coast finally became a Roman Province with its seat in Salona (today Solin, near Split, in Yugoslavia). Definite subjugation of the western territory of the Balkan Peninsula was carried out during the rule of Octavian, in the Illyrian war between 35 and 33 B.C.

Simultaneously, the Romans fought, in the eastern parts of the Balkans, against Celtic tribes, whom they overpowered near Delphe between 280–279 B.C. In 29 B.C. M. Kras penetrated through Serdika (modern Sofia in Bulgaria) into the area along the River Danube, and subjugated the Mezi tribe, who, after the fall of Tribals, had become the principal tribe; their land stretched between the

Danube and the territory of the Hem tribe. This was made into a
Roman Province called Mezia (today part of East Serbia and
Bulgaria) in 6 B.C.

As a result of the subjugation of the Illyrian rising (9 B.C.) in
Pannonia, two new provinces were formed in its eastern part—
Pannonia and Dalmatia.

Thrace, to which Serdika belonged, maintained its nominal
freedom for about two centuries. However, because of internal
disputes and quarrels it became a Roman Province in 46 B.C. In
spite of the more independent rule given to them by the Emperor
Trajan this province was divided into numerous 'strategic'
counties.[2]

Roman conquest in the Balkans is illustrated by three monuments, Tropeion in Adamklisi, Trajan's column and Gema
Augustea. Adamklisi is a place in Dobrudža. Very near the monument of Tropeion is an enormous altar for making sacrifices.
Here are mentioned the names of soldiers killed in this region
(about 2,000 of them). It is thought that this monument was
built in the second half of the fourth century B.C. Trajan's column,
in the Roman Forum, illustrates Trajan's battles in Dacia, namely
it is an idealized representation of Trajan's fighting. Gema
Augustea, dating from the first century A.D. is a cameo from
Kusadak. On the monument is portrayed the coronation of
Augustus with a wreath. Also depicted are Tiberie and Germanik,
the victors in battles with the Barbarians.

The building of roads along the main directions of Roman
penetration is exemplified by work done in the newly subdued
territories. These were main roads called 'via militaris'. For the
safety and the comfort of travellers two types of stations were
built 'mansiones'—inns with sleeping accommodation, a day's
walk distance from each other, then 'mutationes'—for changing
horses. Besides these there were also inns—'tabernae', and in
some places wells were dug—'Ad putea'.

Numerous four-cornered forts with round towers were used to
control these roads 'castella' praesidio and individual towers—
'turres'. 'Castrum' was a fortified military camp, and 'castellum',
a fortified city. Unlike Illyrian forts which were built on hill tops,
the Roman fortifications were made on mountain sides and in
valleys, never in places with difficult access. On the 'limes' there

Serdica itself was another communication centre. Present-day Sofia (Sertica) lies about 500 m above sea level in one of the most beautiful basins in the Balkans, surrounded by high mountains. Diocletian made Serdica a capital of Dacia. A Roman settlement was situated on the site of the present town, and its remains were discovered by Kanitz in the northern part of Sofia near Kursumli Kapu (Lead Gate). There are foundations four m thick and 335 m of preserved walls with four round towers, having a diameter of 6–16 m. Money coined in Serdica had Greek lettering; two important roads intersected here. The first which we are discussing ran from Singidunum to Byzantium (Konstantinopolis), the second from Dyrrachium to Serdica and further along the River Oescus, (present-day Isker), to the Danube, and then along the River Aluta to the Carpathians.[16]

From Serdica the road passed through stations at Sarto (Sparata), Egirica (Egircu), Zyrmis, (Bessapara) and Philippopolis. In the Ihtiman gorge there was once a station at Mansio Egirica, in place of the present-day small town of Ihtiman, where Dorschwan, the best observer of ruins and the remains of old roads, saw a wide road paved with large stones; this was in use in 1553 but has not been repaired. The well-known gorge (Succorum claustra) and village of Klisura contained, even in 1530 and 1553, square Roman forts nearby to the east and west, which were connected by a straight line with a gate which has been well preserved. Half way between Singidunum and Perinthus (Heraclea) there was the well known Trajan's gate, 24 steps high and 15 steps wide. The lower part was made of large square stones, the height of a human being, with Greek lettering, whilst the upper part was vaulted. The Turks destroyed it in 1835, and the place where Trajan's door stood, (in Turkish, 'Kapula Derbend').[17]

After passing through the *Zyrmis* station the road reached *Mansio Lissae*, or Bona Mansio, where a milestone with Greek lettering has been found.[18]

Ancient *Philippopolis* (Philippopuli) was an hour's journey to the north of the present-day town of Plovdiv, where there are the remains of the antique settlement, called Trajan's city. Here the road crossed to the right bank of the River Hebros, present-day Marica, because of extensive marshland on the left bank where rice fields have now been cultivated.[19] The *Burdipta* station was a fortress, protected by a bridge on the River Hebros. Part of the road, between Burdipta and Hadrianopolis was, according to Dorschwan, a paved Roman road in 1553. The name *Hadrianopolis* (today Edirne, Odrin or Jedrene) was derived from Adrian after the Roman Emperor; previously the town had the Thracian name of Uscudana. Hadrianopolis lies at the confluence of three rivers, the Hebros from the west, the Artikos from the south-west (now the River Arda), and the Tunzus from the north, (now the Tundza). Three important roads also met in the town, coming from the Aegean, Propontide and Ponta seas.

From Hadrianopolis the road proceeded towards the south-east to *Perinthus* (Heraclea). It formed a stone bridge with seven arches which crossed the River Ergine at Tzurullum, and then went to Beodizum, after passing through the station; finally it went to the Perinthus station, where the roads from Singidunum and Dyrrachium met. From Perinthus (Heraclea) the road continued through stations at Braunna Callum and Athyra; the old paved road ran through the latter station in an almost straight line, unlike the new road which had many bends. This 'seaway' passed across an estuary with two salt mines, into which a number of streams flowed. These mines were close to the straight main road which lead to Byzantium (Konstantinopolis). There was an alternative road as well, the so-called 'mountain road', which lead through the interior of the country and by-passed the mines at Perinthus on the two stations of Cenofrurio and Melantiady and continued to Byzantium (Konstantinopolis), which was either reached via the Porta Regii, Melandezia, or through the Selivrie gate.

Konstantinopolis emerged from the old Greek town of Byzantium and was built under Constantine the Great in A.D. 330 and proclaimed as the capital of the Roman Empire. It had an exceptionally strategic position, and became one of the largest mercantile and communication centres of the world.[20]

The Via Egnatia

Dyrrachium, and also Roman *Apollonia*, in the south, (present-day village of Pojani, north of Aulona) were starting points for the Roman Via Egnatia, depending on whether the route was from

Bari in Italy to Dyrrachium, or from Brindisi via Aulona to Apollonia and further on to Lychnido (present-day Ohrid in Yugoslavia). Also, the starting point depended on whether one went to Macedonia, or to Greek Epirus. In the first instance Dyrrachium was more convenient for Macedonia, but Aulona was better for Epirus. The Via Egnatia was a continuation of the Roman Via Apiae which led from Rome towards the south of Italy, between the towns of Bari and Brindisi to a place called Egnatia. From there one went by sea to Dyrrachium, or Aulona, and continued overland to the interior of Macedonia. The Via Egnatia went via Thessalonica, which was the mid-point of the road, and to Ipsala (Cypsala). Finally it continued from there under a new name, the Via Militaris, to Byzantium (Konstantinopolis). According to Pouquelle, this was the only real road between Illyricum and Macedonia until the beginning of the nineteenth century. From Dyrrachium to Konstantinopolis the road is 754 Roman miles long, or 1.117 km running via Macedonia and Thracia.

Besides the 'main' track of the Via Egnatia, there were also deviations from it, which eventually met, or rejoined the main route depending on the starting point and choice of destination.

On the road from Dyrrachium to Lychnido there were many stations[22] although the most important are Dyrrachium and Lichnido.

Dyrrachium was founded by colonists of Doric origin from Corfu in the seventh and sixth centuries B.C. under the name of Epidamnos, and later Dyrrachion. The Romans entered Dyrrachium in 146 B.C. when they occupied Macedonia, which then included Dyrrachium together with central Albania. Dyrrachium was a fortified town with a large port. It became a Roman colony in 30 B.C. when it was populated by Italic peasants. It was also an important connection between Rome and the Far East and as such was included in the system of military roads as well as providing one of the two exit points with Thessalonica. During Byzantine rule, Dyrrachium and its territory was of special interest, for it was one of the shortest roads from Byzantium (Konstantinopolis) to Southern Italy.[23]

Lichnido (Lichnidus) was established as an autonomous city Communepolis. Itineraries noted the station was a 'civitas cledo', meaning that the Via Egnatia passed through the town itself, or beside it. During the time of the Empire it was an episcopial seat. The milestones found in Ohrid and Struga have Greek lettering.[24]

From Lychnido the road continued to Thessolonica. In this section the road went through many stations,[25] the most important of which were Heraclea, Edessa, Pella, and Thessolonica.

Heraclea, not to be confused with Perinthus (Heraclea) is situated at Bukovo, two kilometres south of Bitolj in Macedonia. During the Roman rule it was a civitas, which according to archaeological finds had all the elements typical of Greco-Macedonian towns. Heraclea is included on the Tabula Peutingeriana as an important station and start of the road to Stopis (Stobi), with a connection through the Vardar Valley with the main Macedonian roads. In A.D. 347 it became an episcopal seat.[26]

Edessa was traditionally the first Macedonian capital and, like Heraclea during Roman times, had a typical Greco-Macedonian plan. During the early Empire, money was coined in Edessa and later it became a 'civitas'. Furthermore the town was an important stopping place. A milestone was found to the east of the town near the village of Rizari.[27]

Pella was the main centre for Macedonian rulers up to the Macedonian conquest in 168 B.C. The town was situated on Via Egnatia, south-east of Jenidze, near Alkaisi, on the bank of Lake Jenidze. During Roman times it was the centre of the third Macedonian County, but it was constantly under attack. In 30 B.C. it became a colony like others populated by Italic Peasants. Pella enjoyed Italic rights—'ius Italicum'. During the first three centuries of Roman rule money was minted in Pella.[28] In the Itinerarium Antonini (330) Pella was known as Dioclecianopolis, but this name has not survived.

Thessolonica is situated on the same site as it was originally. Before the Roman conquest Thessolonica was strongly fortified, but in spite of this the Romans had the existing fortress walls repaired and reinforced. It was in the central part of the Via Egnatia, and an important communication centre possessing branch roads in all directions. The old road, which was constructed by Macedonian rulers, was called Via Regia, the Romans later called it Via Egnatia and the Byzantines re-named it Leopharos. The Via Egnatia entered the city by the western Vardar gate,

shown that during the Roman times there existed at least three 'castela'.

Transiderna, although it stands beside the main road should be mentioned because of its connections with forts and a bridge across the Danube. The station was near present-day Tekija, and there was a settlement, opposite the Dacian town of Dierna; moreover between Taliata and Transdierna there were numerous castelets and forts, for example between Dierna and the fort of Pontes, near to a bridge-head at present-day Kostol. Prokopie mentions three castles. Also, between Tekija and Kostol, foundations of three castles have been discovered. Castel Pontes lay near Kostol, and was erected at the same time as the bridge, that is during the Troyan–Dacian wars. The bridge was built between Kostol and Turn Severin in Rumania. The castle on the Dacian side was called Theodora, and the town Drobeta, on the right Mesian side was called Transdrobeta. The bridge did not last long. Prokopie states that it fell under the impact of rising river water. Remains of the bridge have been seen during very low water levels (1858). Furthermore the buttresses on both river banks are preserved to the present day. East of the bridge there are remains of a fort. In Kostol, archaeological material indicates the possible existence of a civil settlement.

Egeta Clevora was a seat of a larger garrison and otherwise a larger settlement, but not many traces have been found. In Egeta two roads joined: a short one coming from Taliata over the Miroch mountain, and a longer one going along the Danube.[39]

Ratiaris lay on the site of present-day Archar in Bulgaria. Numerous writings indicate that Ratiaris was a colony. A road from Dyrrachium, via Naissus led to Danubian lands, via Ratiaris.

Oescus (Escus) present-day Gigen, was situated to the west of Nikopolj, and east of the estuary of the River Oescus, (Isker). Near Gigen a Greek milestone was found. Oescus was a colony, and an important road junction, linking the 'Danube road' with a road leading towards the south—thus linking the Danubian lands to the Marica river valley. (This road passed through the stations of Putea, Storgosia, Dorionibus and Melta—today the town of Lovech on crossroads leading to Marcianopolis. Further towards the south it passed through the stations of Sostra and Ad Radices, whilst near Philippopolis, it joined the Via Militaris. According to

K. Jireček, it went from Dyrrachium to Troyan's Dacia through Stopis (Stobi), Pautalia and Aelea. Further along the River Isker (Iskra) the first mentioned road crossed the Danube leading on to Aluta and Carpath.

Ad Novas (Novae) present-day Staklen in Bulgaria, was the site for a central camp of the first Italian legion.

Durostero (Durostorum), is now present-day Silistria. It was a civitas and a municipium dating from the time of Marco Aurelio (A.D. 169–176). Durostero was also the central camp of the eleventh Claudius Legion. It was an important station on the 'Danube road' and was situated on a crossroads. From here the road continued the shortest way from the Danubian lands to Anchialis and further on to Byzantium, passing through the stations of Palmatis, Marcianopolis (today the village of Reka Devna to the west of Varna where the remains of this town are found), Panisso (Panissos), Scatras, Cazalet, Ancialis and to Durostero which Jovan Cimisk named Theodoropolis after St Theodora.

At *Sucidava* (present-day Satunovo) a milestone has been found north-east of the village of Rasovo.

Axiopolis (Axiupoli) was situated near Hinog, in the vicinity of Černa Voda (Romania) where again a milestone has been found and also remains of three castles on the right bank of the Danube near Hinog Island, with old city walls, necropoles, etc. In Černa Voda (Cherne Vode) a milestone has been found.

Noviodunum (Novioduno), today Isacea (Isancha), was on the right bank near the Danube delta, and probably was a civitas. Besides evidence from the old city walls, lettering and ceramics, there are also remains of a Roman-Byzantine citadella and a Christian basilica.

Aegyssus (Egiso), today Tulcea (Tulchea), has remains of an old Roman citadella, while in the city's vicinity there are remains of old city walls, trenches and ceramics etc.

The location of *Ad Stoma* has not been determined, but it is supposed to have been the station near Sulina where two milestones have been found.[40]

From Ad Stoma to Byzantium, along the west coast of the Black Sea (Pontida) the following stations should be mentioned.

Tomis (Tomos) present-day Konstanca on the Black Sea coast was the capital of Scythia (Dobruzda) otherwise polis-civitas. It is a large mercantile centre with numerous archaeological finds indicating that it was a large settlement.

Stratonis lay to the north of Tuzla, and to the south of Konstanca where a milestone has been found.

Odessos (Odisso, Odessus), a Milezian colony, civitas and present-day town of Varna, on the estuary of the River Provadia (Panysus) contains Byzantine ruins. From Odessos the road left for Marcianopolis, Nicopolis ad Istrum, Melta, and from there to Oescus, or Philippopolis.

Ancialis (Anchialus) during Roman times was the best known settlement along the whole of the western Black Sea coast (civitas magna). From Ancialis a number of roads began, running in various directions. One ran to Marcianopolis through a gorge in the Balkan mountains—and further on to Melta; another for Cabyla, and Hadrianopolis, or Philippopolis, via Ranilum. From Hadrianopolis the road went through Plotinopolis and Dymae to Aenos, a port on the estuary of the River Marica. A third road lead to Pudizo, Utsurgas, Caenofrurio, Perinthus, Apris, Aphrodisias, Calipolis and Sestus. A fourth road went via Apollonia, Therae, Buaticum, Scyllam, Philias, Thimea and Sycas to Byzantium.[41] The length of the road from Viminatium to Byzantium (Konstantinopolis) was about 1,045 Roman miles, or 1,547 km.

The Ancient Roads through Greece

The largest portion of the Roman, and generally, the ancient roads went along the seacoast, while those connecting the interior of the country linked to the coastal roads formed a major part of the system. Although affected by the configuration of the Greek coast, the main road system connected Italy on one side with the coast of Asia Minor and Africa on the other. In its western part, starting from Appolonia towards Actia Nicopoli, (Preveza), the coastal road went through the following places.

Apollonia (today the village of Pojani), north of Valona in Albania, was the centre of Greek science during the Roman occupation. It was a civitas, and at the time of the Empire a strongly fortified and lively mercantile emporium.

Aulona, (Valona) was a Roman colony, and port and the main embarking point for the Otrant crossing.

Rutharoto (Ruthrotum), (Butrinto), was also a Roman colony and a lively port.

Actia Nicopoli (Actium Nicopolis) was situated at the entrance to Amraecia Bay near Preveza. (On the opposite side, near Actium, Octavius had defeated Anthony and Cleopatra.) Paleoprevyza lay a little to the north, it was a free Roman city and a Roman colony.

From Apollonia another road went towards Actia Nicopolis, passing through the following stations: Amatria, Hadrianopoli, Ilio, Dodona and Actia Nicopolis. From Actia Nicopolis a road went to Larissa, passing through Trikkala (Tricca), while another road continued in a south-easterly direction between Naupactus and Megara. Naupactos (Naupactus) now Naupuktos was a fortified Corinthian town, a main seat of the Athens sea forces in the Bay of Corinth.

Megara was a capital of the Megara region and today contains the ruins of two acropolei, a water supply system and many public buildings. A milestone has also been found.

From Megara the road continued through the Isthmus of Corinthus, Corinthus itself and the following stations: Cleonas, Mycenae, Argus, Tegaes, Megalopili, Lacedemone, Gythium (Cutmon), Boas (Boeae) and by a ferryboat to Cythera (Cerigo).

Corinthus (Corintho) was a city-civitas, a Roman colony and during the Empire one of the largest towns besides Athens.

Argus (Argos) has many ruins and has retained its original name. From Argus roads went towards the east, to Epitaurus (Epitauro), northwards to Nemea and Sicione and south-west, to Megalopili, and from there to Mesene (Messaenea). On the road from Argus to Megalopili there is a station *Tegeas* (Tegea) which today contains the ruins of a theatre and a marble temple of Goddess Athenae.

Megalopili (Megalopilis), has the same name today. During the Roman period it was a civitas, with ruins of the old town near *Lacedemone.* Nearby lies modern day Sparta on the right bank of the River Eurotas, east of Mistra in the country of Lakonia. Modern Sparta was founded in 1834.

Gythium (*Cytmon, Cutmon*) was the port of Sparta in the vicinity of Marathonisi, near to which there are ruins of a theatre and other buildings.

Boas (Boeas) was the last station in this portion of the road. A few ruins are found near Nauplia (Neapolis).[42]

The portion of the road from Corinthus through Pathras, Olympia and Gythium via Lacedemone varied from the previous one because it followed the west coast of Peoponnese (Peleponnsos). The starting point was the port of Corinthus on the east coast. On this road the following stations have been noted: Corinthus, Lech, Sicione, Aegira, Aegium, Pathras, Dyme, Cyllene, Netide, Olympia, Samoco, Cyparissa, Pylios, Methone, Messene and Lacedemone.

Lech (Lechi) a fortified Corinthian port, on the north of the town to which it was connected by a wall, today it is the tower Baloga.

Sicione, today Vasilika, has ruins of a theatre, water-supply system, arena, etc.

Pathras, which also keeps the same name today, is in the north-west part of Peloponnese. For the Romans it was an important port and a mercantile place, and the only colony in Achaia. The ruins of the Odeon and the water-supply system are of some significance. A milestone has also been found there.

Dyme (Dimis) was an important place during the Roman period, and from the time of Augustus it became a Roman colony. A few ruins are found near Katoachai.

Cyllene (Cilene) was a port and today is called Kyllini; ruins of the town were discovered near Manolada.

Netide (Etide) was the capital of the region of Elis, and today is called Palaepoli; it has the ruins of a temple, rooms with pillars, schools, theatres, etc.

Olympia (Olimpida and Olimpiada) was situated on the right bank of the River Alpheus; it is not a town, but a complex of temples and buildings designed for Olympic games and of great artistic value.

Samoco (Samaco, Samachon) was a fortified town, not far from the sea, and today is called Arene; its ruins lie near a hill, Kaiffa.

Messene, the capital erected by Epaminondas, lies on the south-west slope of a Holy hill, Ithome with Acropolis on the right bank of the Balyra. Today the ruins are seen on the hill of Vurkano, near a village Mavromati.

Olympia was connected with Epitaurus through Melaeneae,

Megalopoli, Tegeas and Argos and Nauplia. Melaeneae is today marked by ruins near Anaziri. Megalopolis has the same name today and lies south-west of Tripolis. Tegeas (Tegea) consists of ruins near Piali. Argos has the same name today and is a town in the region of Argolis. Nauplia, south-east of Argos also keeps its name today. Epitaurus (Epitauro, Epidauro) was in ancient times a well-known spa with the remains of the Temple of Goddess Athene and a fort. Argus and Messene were connected with Sicione, through Nemea. The station Nemea was not a town, but a sacred precinct in a valley; there was a temple dedicated to Zeus here.[43]

The road from Thessalonica to Piraeus passed through the following stations.

Beroe (Borea) is today called Veroia.

Dium (Diume); this station was situated near Malathria, where today there are ancient remains. Dium is a Roman colony.

Sabatium (Sabatum and Sabation), was situated north of modern Platomona, near Pola. A milestone has been found in Vurlama.

Stenas (Senas) is a mountain gorge, through which the River Peneus, (today Salamyria), flows. The station was probably situated at the entrance to the gorge. A milestone has been found near Baba.

Olympu(s) (Olimpius and Olimpium) was situated between Baba and Bakrina, in whose vicinity there are the remains of an ancient marble bridge.

Larissa (Larisa) was a crossroads from which two roads led to Athens. One combined sea and land routes while the other went by land. The first road went towards Demetriade (Demetrias), Opus (Opunto) Chalcide (Calcide), Thebae (Thebis), Oropo (Oropus) and Athenas.

Demetriade lay near Gorica, south-east of Volos. *Opus* consists of ruins lying east of Atalanti. *Chalcide* (today Khalkis) lies on Euboea. These stations were reached by sea. *Thebae* (Thebis) was the oldest and the most important town of the Beotia. *Oropo* has the same name today and lies not far from the estuary of the River Asopus. From there one went by land and by sea to Athenas.

The other road went from Larissa through the following stations, Pharsalus (Grannona, Crannon), Phalara, Thermopylas,

Elatea, Chaeronea, Coronea, Plataeae, Eleusina, Megara, to Athenas and Piraeus.

Pharsalus has the same name today and consists of numerous ancient ruins.

Thermopylas (Thermopilae) derives its name from the warm springs and narrow passes between the Bay of Lamiacus and Mount Ete (Öta). The ancient remains of an aqueduct and fortifications are found here.

Plataeae (Platea) station was situated near the spring of the River Asopus, and has ancient ruins.

Eleusina (Eleusis) lies on the bay opposite the island of Salamine. Here a milestone has been found, and another in Dafne.

Athenas (Athenae) was the largest political, cultural, mercantile and communication centre in ancient Greece and numerous monuments have been preserved.

Piraeus (Pyreon) is the youngest and the largest port of Athens lying to the west of Athens on the Piraeius Peninsula.[44]

The main road of the peninsula into the interior from Thessalonica led through the Vardar Valley to Stobi (Gradsko and Stopis). From there is branched. One road ran to Sofia, through the stations of Astibo, Tranupara, Pautalia, Aelea, Serdica, and further to Esco and the Danubian lands. The second road went from Stobi to Heraclea, through the stations of Euristo, Ceranus, Heraclea and so on to the Via Egnatia.

From Stobi, the road also continued in the other direction, north to *Scopis* (Scupi), today it is called Skoplje, and then ran on to Viciano, Vindenis, Ad Fines, Hammeo, Ad Herculem and then Naissus, and further into other parts.

The Ancient Roads Through Roman Dalmatia

From Aquileia the road led to Dalmatia along the sea coast and through the interior, all the way to Dyrrachium where it joined the Via Egnatia. The road passed through Salona, the capital of the Roman Dalmatia region. The road served as a 'spring board' for the Roman penetration into the interior of the Balkans owing to its well developed sea traffic between the west and east coast and served also as a base for those roads connecting the Adriatic coast with Pannonia. It was one of the main Roman roads, connecting

not only the two capitals of the Empire—Rome and Konstantinopolis, but also the centres of Roman trade along the Adriatic with
that in the central parts of the country.

In order to present a better survey, it has been possible to
divide the road in the following sections.

Aquileia to Senia

This section of the road went from the Aquileia to Ponte Timavi,
Tergeste, Parentium, Pola, Nesactium, Arsia St Alvona, Flanona,
Tarsatica and Senia.

Tergeste, (Trieste or Trst) during the Roman period was an
important coastal and trading city. A milestone has been found in
the direction of *Parentium*.

Pola (Pula, Pola) contains numerous Roman finds and a mag-
nificently preserved arena, remains of aquaducts, temples, etc.
It was a large seaport under Collonia Pietas Iulia (42–41 B.C.).

Nesactium (Vizače-Valtura today) was a municipium with remains of Roman city walls, gates, forts, etc.

Senia, (Senj) during the Roman period was a well known
trading port with good connections with the interior, using the
Salona road. Another road went from Senia to Romula, as part of
the principal road between Romula and Siscia. There was also a
third road going directly from Tergeste to Tarsatica (Trsat-
Rijeka). Furthermore, according to Tabula Peutingeriana there
existed two roads leading from Tarsatica to Senia, one following
the sea coast to the station of Ad Turres, and the other directly
leading through to the interior.

Senia to Salona

This main road passed through the following stations: Avendone,
Arupium, Epidotium, Ancus, Ausancalio, Clambetis, Sidrona,
Hadre, Burnum, Promona, Magnum, Andetrium and Salona.

Of special intest is Burnum (Burno), (Šuplja Stena) near the
village of Ivoševac, which has the remains of the walls, doors,
vaults, amphitheatre and water-supply of a Roman fort. Asseria,
(Podgradje near Benkovac) was a municipium, with evidence of a
Roman triumphal gate.[46]

There was also a road from Iader to Salona, going through

these stations: Iadera, Sardona (Scardona), Ad Pretorium, Magnum, Tragurium, Siclis and Salona.

Tragurium (Tragurio, Tragurion, Trogir) was an old Issean factory; its citizens enjoyed the rights of the motherland (Isse). During the Roman period it was famous for the exploitation of marble from the island of Bauo, today known as (Čiovo, or Buas).

Siclis (Siculi) (Kastel Stafilić) lies to the east of Tragurium. Nearby at Bihać a milestone has been found.

Salona (Solin near Split) has numerous excavations (theatre, amphitheatre, forums, water supply system, and numerous spas, etc.). It was the capital of the Roman county of Dalmatia. From Salona, roads led to all parts of this region, connectiong the city with the whole Empire. Salona became 'oppidum civium Romanorum' (59 B.C.) and in 31 B.C. it became a colony.[47]

Salona to Ad Zizio

This section of the road followed the coastal hinterland and passed through Tiluri, Billubio, Ad Novas, Ad Fusciana, Bigeste, Narona, Ad Turres, Dilunto, Pardua and Ad Zizio.

Tiluri (Tilurium), (the village of Trilj) is situated on the Cetina River, north-east of Split. During Roman times at Tiluri, there was a stone bridge, restored by Commodi (A.D. 184). East of Tiluri near the village of Veliće a milestone has been found.

Narona, (the village of Vid) lies to the north of Metković. In this village numerous finds have been discovered.

Ad Turres was situated near Čapljina, according to the latest research by I. Bojanovski. Even today remains of old roads exist, four metres wide, near the Neretva River, by the village of Tasovčić, and the fort of Turres has been located near the village of Mogorjelo, to the south of Čapljina, where the ruins of two towers can be seen.

Dilunto (Diluntum) is most probably the present day town of Stolac in Hercegovina, where a milestone has been found near the village of Rulići.

Pardua station was situated to the south-east of Ljubinja in Hercegovina, where three milestones mark the Roman road.

Ad Zizio station was probably situated near the modern village of Mosko, to the north-east of Trebinje where three milestones have been found in the vicinity.[48]

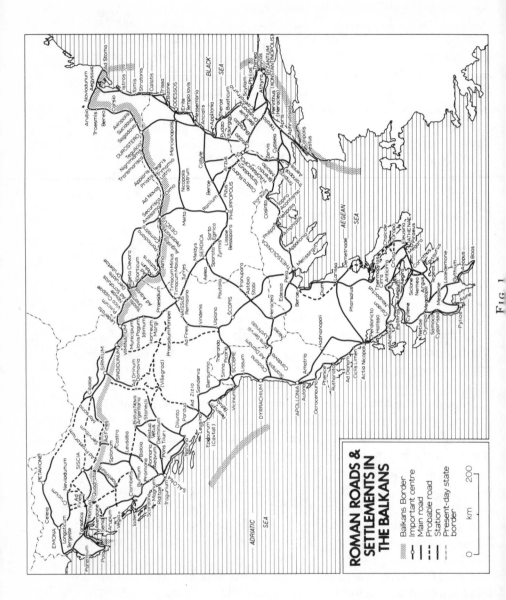

ROMAN ROADS &
SETTLEMENTS IN
THE BALKANS

Balkans Border
Important centre
Main road
Probable road
Station
Present-day state border

0   km   200

FIG. 1

Here this section of the road divided, running in one case to Spalato (Split) from Salona and from there to the headland of the Marjan Peninsula, where there was a temple Ad Diana. The second road went along the coast from Salona to Epetio (Stobreč), Oneo (Omiš), Inaronia (Makarska) and to an unmarked station in the south-east, probably the village of Gradac, south-east from Makarska.[49] Another road also existed running from the station of Ad Zizio to Asamo, Epidaurum and Resinum.

Ad Zizio to Dyrrachium

This road passed through the following stations: Leusino, Sallunto, Sanderva, Varis, Nalata, Sallunto, Bersumno, Sinna, Scobre, Lissum, Pistum and Dyrrachium.

According to the latest research of D. Sergejevski, *Leusino* was most probably situated at the village of Panik, north-east of Trebinje. It then went to the village of Riječani, towards Nikšić. Sergejevski has noted eight milestones here.

In the Šuntulja locality, near Rijecani lay the station of *Sallunto*. Eight more milestones have been noted towards Niksic.

Sanderva (Anderva, Anderba) (is today the city of Niksic). Remains of a Roman settlement are situated in Orgradice at Štedin, to the west of the town.

Bersumno (Bersuminum) station was near present-day Tito-grad (Podgorica), where there are the ruins of Ribnica, at the confluence of the Rivers Ribnica and Morača.

Sinna (Cinna) was probably located at Gradac, north of the village of Kopliku, which is to the north of Skadar in Albania. South-east of Titograd, near the village of Tuzi two milestones have been found. Also traces of a Roman road have been found near the River Cijevna.[50]

Scobre, (Skadar and Scutari) a town in Albania, was a Roman colony containing a highly defensible fort,

Lissum or Lissus (Lješ–Alesio) at the estuary of the River Drin was a well fortified town, at present in ruins and formally a colony. For Dyrrachium (see p. 122. Via Egnatia).[51]

Lissum via Naissus to Ratiaris

One of the roads leading into the interior of the Balkan Peninsula went from Lissum via Naissus to Ratiaris on the Danube in Bulgaria. The road passed through Lissum, Picaria, Creveni, Gabuleo, Theranda, Viciano, Vindenis, Ad Fines, Hammeo, Ad Herculem, Naissus, Timacum Maius, Timacum Minus, Combustira and Ratiaris. The length of the road was 302 Roman miles, or 447.4 km.

Ad Picaria the modern village of Puka, lies to the east of Scutari, on the road to Prizren.

The *Creveni* station was situated in the village of Va-Spasi, the medieval St Spas.

Theranda, was probably situated near Suva Reka.

The *Vindenis* station was situated to the south-west of Podujevo.

Ad Fines (today Kuršumlija); a milestone has been found here.

Hammeo (Hammeum) was situated at Prokuplje.

From there the road went to *Naisso* (Naissus) (today: Niš) and then to Timaco Maiori.

Timacum Maius was probably north-east of Niš, near the village of Niševac, where the remains of an ancient road have been found.

Timacum Minus was where the present day village of Ravna is found, to the north of Knjaževac.

Combustira (Combustica) was situated near the village of Kladorupe, south-west of Vidin in Bulgaria.

Ratiaris, as it was known, was on the right bank of the Danube in Bulgaria.[52]

Remains of ancient settlements are connected with traces of old mining activity in the Kopaonik mountains and in the region of Rogozna. Furthermore ancient writings support evidence that a road existed from Kosovo through the Ibar Valley, going via west Morava into the mining region of Mount Rudnik. From there it went to Singidunum, where traces of Roman mining have been found in the region of the Kosmaj and Avala mountains.

The Senia to Leusinium Road

From the main Senia to Leusinium road which stretched along the hinterland of the Adriatic coast, a maze of roads led into the mining regions of Bosnia and western Serbia, and hence on to the Sana Valley.

The Road from Leusino to the Confluence with the River Drina

This road began at Epidaurum where the remains of an old cobbled road and milestones to Leusino have been identified. It probably then continued via present day's Fatnica to Gacko, and on through the Drina Valley via Višegrad into the Argentaria–Domavia, to the east of Bosnia and west of the Serbia region of Krupanj-Zajača. The road then separated either to the Drina confluence, or to Sirmium. Parallel to this road was the one from Narona, via the Neretva Valley, near the modern towns of Mostar and Konjic, which ran over the Ivan mountains to Ilidža (Aquas) then via the Romanian mountains. It went on to Sokolac and from there to Argentaria, to the stations of Ad Drinum and Sirmium. According to finds from the old cobbled road, traces of Roman mining support the idea that this road was connected with the mining region of present-day Kreševo, Dusina and Dezeva, to the south-west of Kiseljak (Staneclis) lying west of Sarajevo.[53]

From Salona two roads led into the central mining region of Bistua Nova and the region Majdan-Šipovo, west of Jajce, where traces of Roman mining may still be seen today. The first road was from Salona to Delminium, Ad Matricem and Bistua Nova. Delminium was situated in the modern village of Mokronoge, five kilometres north of Duvno in Bosnia, and Bistua Nova which is the present day village of Vitez, south-east of Travnik. The second road went from Salona to Aequum, Ionnaria, Baloia, Leusaba, Ad Fines and Servitium. The station at Ionnaria was near a village called Vaganj, in the northern part of Glamoč Polje in Bosnia. Numerous milestones have been found on the road from Aequum to Ionnaria, as well as towards the station known as Indenea. Castra was situated at Banja Luka in Bosnia. Servitium is the present town of Bosanska Gradiška.

Parallel developments are found with the road from Burnum into the Sana Valley which passed through the stations of Sarnacla (Pecka), Splonum (Stari Majdan), and then crossed the River Sana. It continued along the river's right bank to its confluence with the Una river. A large number of milestones have been found on this road, starting south of Drvar, going north of the Sarnacla station. It is supposed that the road continued from Splonum to Ad Praetorium. Topographical names 'Majdanska mountain' and 'Old Mine', like many others show traces of Roman mining activity indicating the amount of mining done, not only here, but over a large part of central Bosnia. All the above mentioned roads were mutually connected by crossroads, according to remains from Roman settlements, fortress walls, parts of cobbled roads and temples, etc. Also, there existed a main road from the Bihać region and Bosanska Kupa region to the confluence of the River Sana with the River Una. Many finds of Roman remains have been found here. From the confluence of the Sana and Sava rivers it is thought the main road continued through the Una Valley, via Bosanska Kostajnica, and on to the villages of Bačina and Slabinja where two milestones have been found.

At this point the road most probably joined the road leading from Siscia to Servitium, coming from Marsonia to Sirmium. Roman finds in Karlobag, along the coast at Vegia, a Roman station and the milestones at Gospič, all suggest that the main Retinium Road near Bihać was connected with a secondary road near the sea at Karlobag. From Retinium a secondary road ran north-west to the Senia–Romula road and then rejoined the Emona–Crucium road (Mačkovec kod Novog Mesta). Parallel with this was another secondary road which went from Romula to Crucium.[54]

Conclusion

The Romans found an existing road pattern in a large part of the territories which they conquered. Unfortunately Pre-Roman roads are still insufficiently studied; it is thought that some originated from the Neolithic period, whilst certain others could be attributed to the Illyrians, Thracians and Celts. One may conclude that the Romans partly adopted the existing communications network and partly adapted this to their own military-political, needs, and cultural movements. This led to the formation of a specific Roman road-network in the Balkans. Its completion resulted for the first time in a planned projection of roads in the Balkans. Their construction represented a high level of building techniques.

It may be concluded that firstly, the road between Singidunum
and Byzantium (Konstantinopolis) was the most important land
communication which intersected the Balkan interior Peninsula as
far as the Hungarian–Danube Basin. The Romans, possessing this
artery, secured rule over much of the peninsula. The origins of this
road date from prehistoric times, of which there is still little knowledge as yet. Secondly, the so-called 'Danube road' was of importance, coming into existence at a time when the Roman border
coincided with the course of the Danube. In order to protect themselves from the Barbarians living north of the Danube, the Romans
built themselves a complete system of fortifications and roads
parallel with the border known as the Limes. Thirdly, the Via
Egnatia is also included in the group of main roads, for it was the
shortest route between Rome, Konstantinopolis and the Far East.
The two Balkan starting points Dyrrachium and Thessalonica
included this road in a communication network known as the Via
Militaris. Finally, all coastal roads were considered to be main
roads and were the basis for Roman penetration into the Balkan
interior.

From this main network secondary roads branched off to various
parts of the Balkan interior for the purpose of suppressing the
various tribes and for making better access to mineral ores and
other treasures; finally they were used in the colonization of
regions already conquered.

Numerous roads in the interior of the Balkan Peninsula reveal
not only large numbers of populated settlements, but also that
their directions were, in most cases, governed by economic, and
not purely strategic reasons.

For a more correct identification of route directions, apart from
stations, places where milestones have been found should be noted.

The degree of urbanization in different regions varies with the
Roman settlements on the Balkan Peninsula. This is mainly because of the fact that the Romans in the course of their conquests
met with unequal Pre-Roman development, different economic
and political conditions, and lastly different geophysical characteristics of individual regions in the peninsula. These facts also
influenced the governmental organization. Similarly, the urban
complexes were based on Roman principles (e.g. water supply
systems etc.) emphasized by those towns which had mints.

142 G. ŠKRIVANIĆ

In the Balkan and Danubian territories at the beginning of the second century A.D., there were settlements of all sizes originating as native communities (civitates) and ending as regional towns (territorial or provincial towns) holding Latin civic rights. Generally speaking, the Roman urbanization along the Danube, and as a whole on the periphery of the Empire, was based on military–political and not economic reasons.

4. Notes

1. The Northern boundary of the Balkan Peninsula follows a line from Kastav near Rijeka, across the mountains of Rišnjak (Rišhniak), then along the Rivers Kupa and Sava to their confluences, and from there follows the Danube to its southern most tributary at the delta entering the Black Sea.
2. N. A. Maskin, *Istorija starog Rima* (translated by M. Marković), Belgrade (1961), pp. 124, 136, 141, 142;
   K. Jireček, *Istorija Srba*, Vol. 1, (translated by Jov. Radonić), Belgrade (1952), pp. 6–23;
   K. Jireček, 'Vojna cesta od Beograda za Carigrad', (translated by Dj. Pejanović), *Zbornik K. Jirečeka*, Vol. 1, Belgrade (1959), pp. 75–81;
   J. Klemenc, F. Gestrin, 'Naše zemlje u rimsko doba, *Istorija naroda Jugoslavije*, Vol. 1, Belgrade (1953), pp. 30–56.
3. K. Jireček, 'Vojna cesta . . .', op. cit. p. 79.
4. M. Mirković, *Rimski gradovi na Dunavu i Gornjoj Meziji*, Belgrade (1968), pp. 31–32.
5. K. Jireček, 'Vojna cesta . . .', op. cit. p. 78.
6. P. Petrović, 'Rimski natpisi na Djerdapskim stenama', *Stare Kulture u Djerdapu*, Belgrade (1969), pp. 152–157.
7. K. Jireček, 'Trgovački putevi i rudnici Srbije i Bosne u srednjem vijeku' (translated by Dj. Pejanović), *Zbornik K. Jirečeka*, Vol. 1, Belgrade (1959), pp. 254–255;
8. F. Papazoglu, *Makedonski gradovi u Rimsko doba*, Skoplje (1957), pp. 314–315;
   M. Mirković, op. cit. p. 1.
9. N. J. G. Pounds, *The Urbanisation of East Central and South-east Europe*, ed. G. Hoffman, London (1971), pp. 47–50;
   M. Mirković, op. cit. p. 1.
10. F. Papazoglu, op. cit. pp. 312–316.
11. M. Mirković, op. cit. pp. 43–44.

12. K. Jireček, 'Vojna cesta . . .', op. cit. p. 80. The distance is given as 670
    Roman miles, and in K., Miller, *Intineraria Romana*, Stuttgart (1916), pp.
    528–540, it is 631 Roman miles. The same distance is given in *Fontes
    Historicae Bulgaricae*, Vol. II, Sofia (1958), pp. 20–21.

13. K. Jireček, 'Vojna cesta . . .', op. cit. pp. 83–85. Tricornium, at present the
    village of Ritopek lies south-east from Beograd; Monte Aureo, today the
    village of Seona lies south-east of Grocka; Margum Fl., is the modern
    River Morava;
    M. Mirković, op. cit. pp. 56–69, Viminatium is Kostolac.

14. Between Viminatium and Naissus the road passed through the following
    stations: Municipium, Iovis pagum, Idimum, Horreum Margi, where a
    milestone has been found, Presidium Dasmini, Presidium Pompei Gram-
    piana and Naissus, (further details in K. Jireček, 'Vojna Cesta . . .', op. cit.
    p. 85–89.

15. Ibid. pp. 89–92.

16. Ibid. pp. 92–93.

17. Ibid. pp. 95–97;
    Fontes Historicae Bulgaricae, Vol. I, Sofia (1958), p. 20, footnote 14.

18. Ibid. pp. 98–99;
    Fontes Historicae Bulgaricae, Vol. I, Sofia (1958), pp. 20–21.

19. Ibid. pp. 101–106;
    Fontes Historicae Bulgaricae, loc. cit. Between Philippopolis and Hadriano
    polis were the following stations: Ranilum, Pizus, Arzus, Castra Rubra,
    Burdipta (Burdenis) and Hadrianopolis.

20. K. Jireček, 'Vojna cesta . . .', op. cit. pp. 106–112.

21. Th. L. F. Tafel, *Via Militaris Romanorum Egnatia*, Tubingae (1842),
    p. XCIX.

22. From Dyrrachium to Lychnido the road passed through the following
    stations: Clodiana, (modern day Pekini), Scampis, (Elbasan), Ad Dianam,
    Candavia, (Kukes) Pons Servili, (Oraka-Uraka), Lychnido (Ohrid).

23. Tafel, op. cit.;
    Prolegomena, Vols II–IV, pp. XCIX–XCXI;
    Paul Lemerle, *Philippes et la Macedonie orientale*, Paris (1943), p. 74, foot-
    note 3; pp. 3, 170, footnotes 2 to 6; p. 131, footnotes 1–4; pp. 176 and 177;
    B. Nedkov, *Bulgaria i susednite i zemi prez XII vek*, Sofia (1960), pp. 37–
    39;
    O. Cuntz, *Itineraria Romana*, Vol. 1 Lipsiae (1929), p. 48.

24. F. Papazoglu, op. cit. pp. 225–230.

25. From Lychnido the road continued to Thessalonica going through the
    stations of Nicea, near the village of Djavato, west of Bitolj, Heraclea, in
    Bukovo, south of Bitolj, Cellis (Cellae), Edessa, Pella, Dioclitianopolis
    (Deoklecionopol) and Thessalonica.

26. F. Papazoglu, op. cit. pp. 190–192.

27. Ibid. pp. 110–112.

28. Ibid. pp. 111–113.

29. Ibid. pp. 137–158.

30. From Thessalonica to Konstantinopolis the following stations are noted: Melissirgin, Appollonia, Philippis, Neapolis, Acontisma, Topiro, Cosinto, Porsulus, Brendici, Milolito, Timpiro, Trainopoli, Ostidizo, Burdidizo, Bergule, Drusiparo, Thirallo, Perintho, Caenofrurio, Melantrada and Bizantium (Konstantinopolis).

31. F. Papazoglu, op. cit. pp. 158–162.

32. *Fontes Historicae Bulgaricae*, Vol. I, Sofia (1958), p. 18.

33. F. Papazoglu, op. cit. pp. 297–299.

34. Ibid. pp. 296–297.

35. *Fontes Historicae Bulgaricae*, Vol. 1, Sofia (1958), pp. 1, 19, 35, 37, etc.

36. K. Miller, *Itineraria Romana*, pp. 524–525;
O. Cuntz, *Itineraria Romana*, Vol. 1, Lipsiae (1929), pp. 48, 49–50.

37. K. Miller, op. cit. p. 525, fig. on p. 164;
O. Cuntz, op. cit. pp. 48, 49–50.

38. Along the 'Danube road' the following stations have been noted: Viminatium, Pincum (Punicum), Vico Cuppae, Novae, Ad Scrofulas, Faliatis, Gerulatis, Unam, Egeta Clevora, Ad Aquas, Dorticum, Ad Malum (Bononia), Ratiaris, Remetodia, Almo, Pomodiana, Camistro, Augustis, Pedonianis, Oescus, Vio, Anasamo, Securisca, Dimo, Ad Novas, Latro, Trimamio, Pristis, Tegris, Appiaris, Transmarisca, Nigrimiais, Tegulicio, Durostero, Sagadava, Sucidava, Axiopolis, Calidava, Carsio, Bereo, Troesmis, Arubio, Noviodunum, Salsovia and Ad Stoma. Further details: in M. Mirkovic op. cit. pp. 103–104, 105–109; K. Miller, op. cit. pp. 495–516; *Fontes Historicae Bulgaricae*, Vol. I, Sofia (1958), pp. 14–17.

39. M. Mirković, op. cit. pp. 103–107; pp. 114–116.

40. K. Miller, op. cit. pp. 502–507;
Fontes Historicae Bulgaricae, Vol. I, Sofia (1958), pp. 15–17, 26–27.

41. K. Miller, op. cit. pp. 507–514, figs on pp. 157, 158, 159, 164, 165.

42. Ibid. pp. 565–568, figs. on pp. 180, 181, 183.

43. Ibid. pp. 581–584, figs. on pp. 180, 181.

44. Ibid. pp. 573–578, figs. on pp. 180, 181, 183, 184.

45. Ibid. pp. 312–313, 462–471, figs on pp. 96, 97, 135, 136;
G. Novak, *Topografija i Etnologija rimske pokrajine Dalmacije*, Zagreb (1918), p. 8;
A. J. Šašel, *Inscripciones Latinae*, *Situla* Vol. V. Ljubljana (1965), pp. 92, 93, sections 266, 267, 268.

46. K. Miller, op. cit. pp. 463–464, figs on pp. 137, 138, 139, 140;
G. Novak, op. cit. p. 11.

47. K. Miller, op. cit. pp. 474–476;

G. Novak, op. cit. pp. 10, 12, 14;

M. Abramić, O novim miljokazima i rimskim cestama u Dalmaciji, *Vjesnik za Archeologiju i Historiju Dalmatinsku*, Vol. XLIX (1926/27) map enclosed.

48. K. Miller, op. cit. pp. 467–468;

G. Novak, op. cit. pp. 15, 19, 21;

M. Abramić, op. cit. p. 154, and map;

E. Pasalić, *Antička naselja i komunikacije u Bosni i Hercegovini*, Sarajevo (1960), p. 58;

A. Evans, *Antiquarian Researches in Illyricum*, Part 1, 11, London (1883), pp. 92, 93;

I. Bojanovski, Mogorjelo-Rimski Turres, *Glasnik zemaljskog muzeja Bosne i Hercegovine* (1969), pp. 140, 146, 163;

D. Sergejevski, Rimska cesta Narona-Leusinium, *Glasnik zemaljskog muzeja, Bosne i Hercegovine* XXVII (1962), pp. 111–112, with maps;

D. Sergejevski, Rimska cesta od Epidauruma do Anderbe, *Glasnik zemaljskog muzeja Bosne i Hercegovine* XXVII (1962), pp. 78–86.

49. K. Miller, op. cit. p. 482;

G. Novak, op. cit. pp. 17, 18.

50. D. Sergejevski, Epidaurum-Anderba, op. cit. maps II, III, IV;

P. Mijović, Alata-Ribnica-Podgorica, *Starinar* (n.s.) Vols XV–XVI (1964/65), pp. 69–93.

51. K. Miller, op. cit. p. 470;

G. Novak, op. cit. p. 23.

52. K. Miller, op. cit. pp. 556–557;

Font. Hist. Bulgaricae, Vol. 1, pp. 15, 23;

E. Cerskov, *Rimljani na Kosovu*, Belgrade (1969), pp. 44–46;

D. M. Garašanin, *Arheološka nalazišta u Srbiji*, Belgrade (1951), p. 202;

M. Mirković, op. cit. pp. 90–92, 95.

53. E. Pašalić, op. cit. pp. 60–78, and map.

54. Ibid. pp. 12, 35–54, and map.

5

Urban Development in the Western Balkans 1200-1800

F. W. CARTER

A humorist once observed that Yugoslavia's trouble was too much history. Nevertheless it is the aim of this chapter to describe the urban evolution of settlements in the western Balkans (territory of present day Yugoslavia) over six centuries. Furthermore the main historical periods will help to provide a basis for the urban analysis and the Ottoman conquest (*c.* 1500) is a convenient watershed for studying the relations between the spatial urban organization of settlements in the Later Middle Ages and the Early Modern period. Some work has already been published in English on demographic problems and economic development in the Balkans under the Byzantine Empire,[1] which could well form an introduction to the periods under review, whilst J. C. Russell's paper on Late Mediaeval population is also of interest.[2] However, none of these papers have examined urban development *per se*, nor looked at the settlement pattern from a spatial point of view. They have been more concerned with various estimates of total population. Even so

'Scholars are notably hesitant to accept estimates on the ground that they are not accurate. Many who refuse to believe in figures of city population feel free to fill their studies with statements which are quite as questionable as population estimates and feel no qualms about them. In fact all value judgements with a quantitative base about the Middle Ages are about as uncertain as population estimates'.[3]

It has long been realized that cities and villages were, in the past, distributed over the landscape in something like a pattern: villages every few kilometres, small cities a day or so journey away, and large urban nodes at less frequent intervals. In general, the cities would have been distributed more evenly in mediaeval times than at present, since there were fewer concentrations of basic industries to disturb a fairly regular pattern. For example, in the western Balkans castles and monasteries in remote places produced local centres but they were not usually of a large size. Thus, the determining factor in respect of settlement locations from the smallest to the largest appears to have been distance, and friction of the terrain. Both within the slavonic kingdoms and the Ottoman Empire, like all other settlement systems, an hierarchy existed in terms of a capital, regional centres, large market towns, small commercial centres, villages and nomadic stopping points. There was also geographical specialization within these hierarchies, which could have been influenced by patterns of migration. One possibility is that a specialist craftsman or tradesman in a region's largest city sent a member of his family or group to start the same craft in a smaller city, or an agent selling a particular speciality in a series of places, would finally settle in the largest centre where he could spend more time. Various reasons for the hierarchical organization of a settlement system have been studied in central place theories, but here it is hoped to discover from historical sources the basic patterns of urban settlement in the western Balkans over a six-century period.

The territory comprising what is now the Socialist Federal Republic of Yugoslavia straddles the complex system of mountains and river valleys, which through the centuries have served both as a bastion and gateway to south-east Europe. The narrow coastal strip and the offshore islands of Dalmatia link the country to the Mediterranean world; the fertile provinces to the north-east, traversed by the Danube and Sava rivers, connect her to Central Europe, whilst in between there rise the intricate and rugged mountain ranges which cover two-thirds of the state's area and today contain more than half its population. Within or around these highlands lie the valleys through which the migrating peoples and invading armies have passed from the earliest times. The central event of Yugoslav history has been the Turkish invasion, resulting in the destruction of the mediaeval slavonic states, the conversion to Islam of most of Bosnia/Hercegovina, and the dependence of Croatia and Dalmatia on the Roman Catholic powers of Hungary, Austria and Venice for survival. Other historic factors have added their influence on the countryside, including the movement of population from one area to another resulting from a variety of causes. Christian reayas[4] fled from the oppression and reprisals of the Turkish overlords, colonists were brought in to repopulate areas devastated by war or to defend important frontiers, whilst highlanders often migrated to the more sheltered valleys or urban centres.[5] It is within this background that a closer study may be made of the urban development of the country.

The Late Mediaeval Period 1200–1500

Figure 1 shows the distribution of mediaeval settlements constructed on the basis of various historical sources. A total of 1382 settlements have been traced and located (1344 within present boundary), with the heaviest density in the north and west, less evident in the higher Dinaric areas and few in the north-east corner. This latter phenomenon is difficult to explain, but may be related to either the paucity of extant documents or the physical controls of flooding and waterlogged areas. This information was then broken down into various settlement types, (Figs 2 a, b, c, d) where certain regional variations appear. The burgh town with roofed or partially roofed castle (229 examples) predominates in the north-west, whilst the ruined fortified walled town (857 examples) has a much wider distribution. There are fifty-six cases of town colonies mainly in the Sava Valley, whilst this same routeway is predominant in the fortified towns with unroofed castles (240 examples). This picture may be far from complete, for recent finds of charters to different churches during this period suggest that there were more settlements in southern Serbia and Macedonia, including villages and hamlets. The problem therefore arises as to the definition of a 'town' in this context. It has been suggested that the Mongol-Tatar invasion of the thirteenth century may have stimulated town growth by demonstrating the security of living in a community protected by a defensive wall.

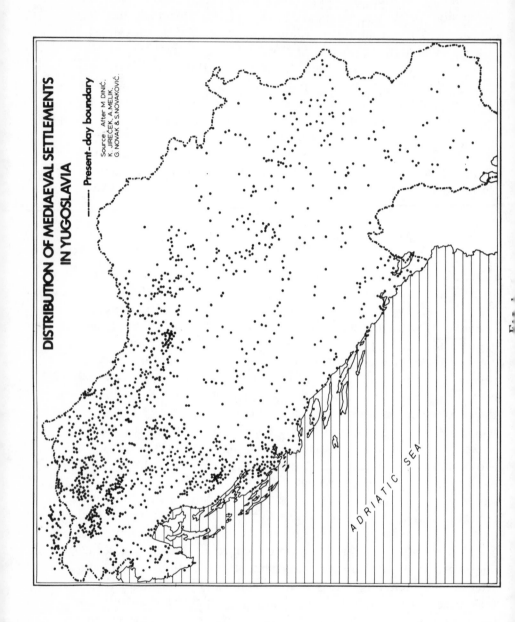

DISTRIBUTION OF MEDIAEVAL SETTLEMENTS IN YUGOSLAVIA

------ Present-day boundary

Source: After M. DINIĆ,
K. JIREČEK, A.MELIK,
G. NOVAK & S.NOVAKOVIĆ.

ADRIATIC SEA

Nevertheless settlements of even 5,000 people were extremely rare in south-eastern Europe (compared with 10–12,000 in Bohemia) at this time, and places with more than 1,000 inhabitants could be classified as 'grad' (town)[3]. Therefore despite its inadequacies Fig. 1 can, at least serve as a basis on which to build up a picture of mediaeval urban development in the various regions of the country.

Serbia[6]

The Serbs arrived in the Balkan Peninsula during the early part of the seventh century A.D. and by the mediaeval period already had a well-developed urban life. Most of the towns were either enlargements of the earlier Pre-Roman sites usually having advantageous geographical conditions, or of later origin and founded for some military, economic or other purpose. Many towns lay on the main artery of the Balkan Peninsula from Belgrade to Constantinople (Singidunum, Viminacium, Horreum Margi, Naissus, Remesiana, etc.) or to a lesser extent on the route from Niš to Thessaloniki.

The first written evidence of urban centres after the Slavic settlement comes from Constantine Porphyrogenitus in the tenth century (reigned A.D. 912–959) [Destinikon (Dostiniku), Megiretos (surely Međurečje), Cernavuskei, Dresneik, Lesneik and Salines (Soli-Tuzla)], but, although most of them cannot be found today, it is thought they were mainly located in the Lim and Drina valleys. Porphyrogenitus calls them 'settled castle, fortified town' (κάστρα ὀικούμενα kastra oikumena) of which the most important appeared to be Destinikon. He also refers to smaller towns in the neighbouring states of Serbia (Zahumlja: 5 settled towns; Trebinje: 5; Zeta: 3). A larger list of town names are found for the beginning of the eleventh in a charter issued by the Byzantine Emperor Basil II, on the organization of the Ohrid bishopric, but curiously does not include those referred to by Porphyrogenitus. The list obviously included the episcopal seats (Belgrade, Braničevo, Niš, Raš, Lipljan and Prizren), but mention was also made of smaller settlements (Niš area: Mokro, Komplos, Toplica, Svrljig; Braničevo area: Moravsk, Smederevo, Groncos, Divisk, Istanglanga, Brodarisk; Belgrade area: Gradac, Omcos, Glaventin and Bela Crkva; Prizren area: Hvosno, Leskovac, Vretos). From

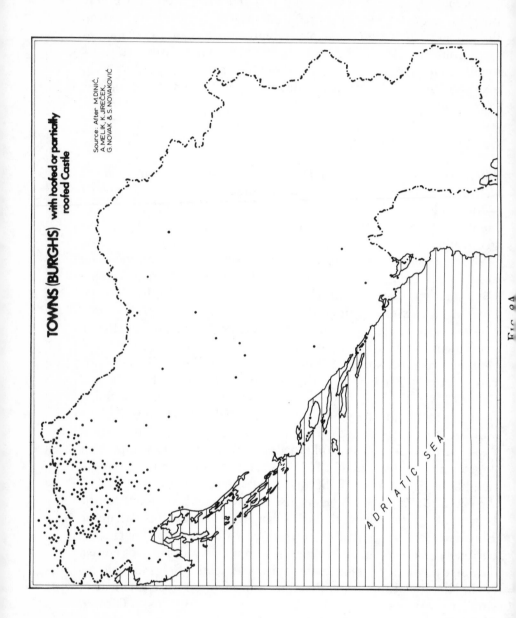

TOWNS (BURGHS) with roofed or partially roofed Castle

Source: After M.DINIĆ,
A.MELIK, K.JIREČEK,
G.NOVAK & S.NOVAKOVIĆ

ADRIATIC SEA

Fig. 9A

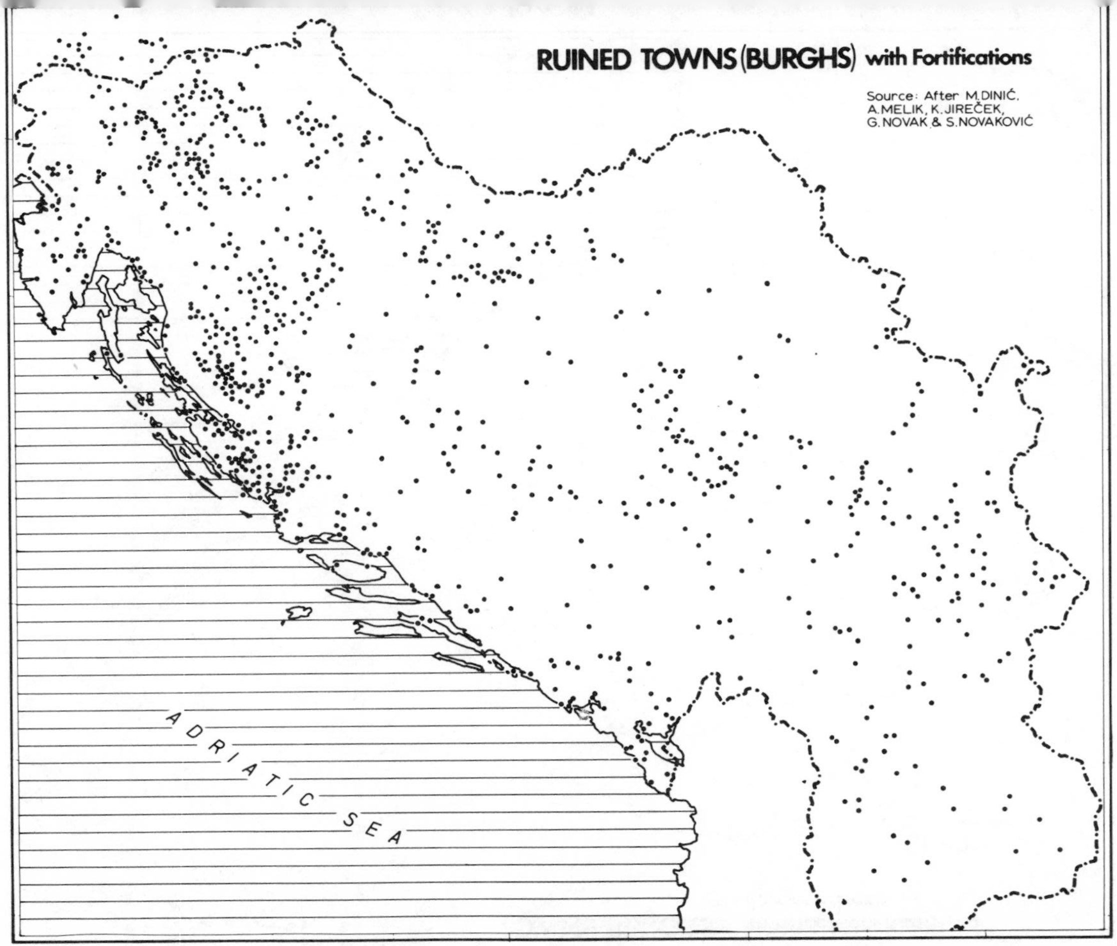

RUINED TOWNS (BURGHS) with Fortifications

Source: After M.DINIĆ,
A.MELIK, K.JIREČEK,
G.NOVAK & S.NOVAKOVIĆ

ADRIATIC SEA

FIG. 2B.

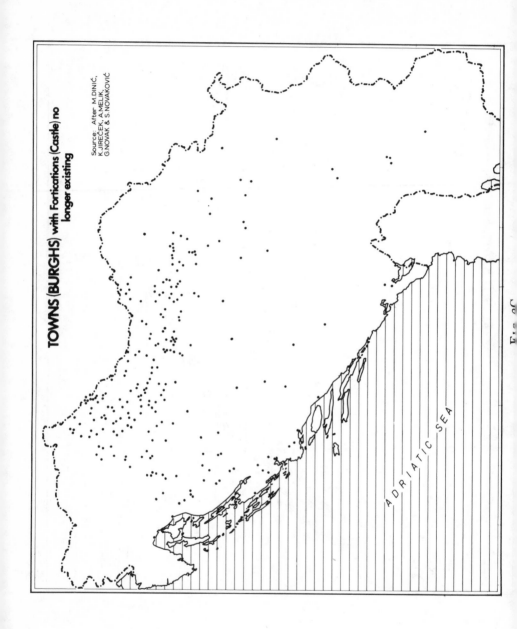

TOWNS (BURGHS) with Fortications (Castle) no longer existing

Source: After M.DINIĆ, K.JIREČEK, A.MELIK, G.NOVAK & S.NOVAKOVIĆ

A D R I A T I C   S E A

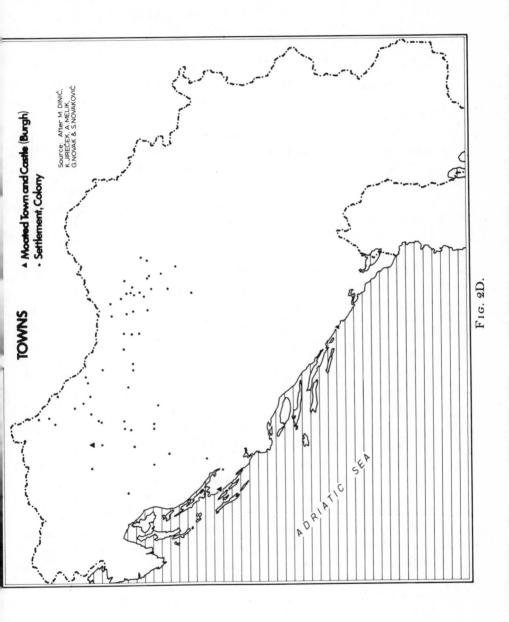

TOWNS

▲ Moated Town and Castle (Burgh)
• Settlement, Colony

Source: After M. DINIĆ,
K. JIREČEK, A. MELIK,
G. NOVAK & S. NOVAKOVIĆ

ADRIATIC SEA

Fig. 2D.

this list it is possible to surmise where some of these places are today: Komplos was near Prokuplje or Gradista near Kurvingrad, Groncos may have been Gruža and Divisisk is Divostin near Kragujevac; Istanglanga is Stalać, Brodarisk is near Paraćin or Jagodina, Omcos is Užice, etc. Some of these names took on a regional application as for example Toplica and Hvosno, but already new settlements were appearing which were later to develop into towns. If some comparison is made between these Serbian areas and those of Macedonia farther to the south, it is seen that the latter not only had important episcopal centres, but also other large settlements (or župa) which were under them. Even at this early date they seem to have been stabilized named settlements with independent status. This basic north–south division, indicates that the southern settlements were more developed due to their longer influence under Byzantium, than these in the 'real' Serbian territory to the north.

Within the mediaeval Serbian state one can distinguish three basic zones of urban settlement, coastal, southern and central. Coastal settlements under mediaeval Serbian rule included Kotor, Budva, Bar, Ulcinj and Skadar and some smaller places such as Drivast, Svač, Danj, Baleco, Sarda and Sapa. The original population nuclei were of Roman descent, with an Albanian element in towns around Lake Skadar, and Slavic inhabitants in some of the centres (e.g. Budva, Kotor). Roman families (Romanorum colonos se appellantes) were still evident as important citizens in Drivast as late as the fifteenth century, but their social status differed greatly in some towns, e.g. Bar, Ulcinj. The extension of the Serbian state to the south in the fourteenth century meant that it now included many towns which had already flourished under Byzantium, and included Albania and Macedonia. New towns were also established and received special mention in Stefan Dušan's code; in Law 124 'Greek towns' obtained 'hrisovulje i prostagme' (χρυσοβουλλα, προστάγμάτα) charters and decrees, whilst Law 176 states that towns 'remained controlled by laws operative under the first czar'.[7] The most thriving urban life appears to have been in the central or 'real' Serbian region, where most of the Roman towns had disappeared, and Byzantine administrative influence had not been strong.

The advent of mining in the mid-thirteenth century formed the basis of urban life in this region. New settlements were established, but in many cases the best developed were in places difficult of access and a long way from the main communication arteries (e.g. Brskovo, Rudnik, Novo Brdo). Many of them were located in the ore rich Kopaonik mountains (Trepča, Janjevo, Plana, Koporič, Livada); in the Podrina (Krupanj, Zaječa, Bohorina, Crnča) and Kučeva areas (Železnik). Even so the urban development of these centres was quite slow as evidenced by an anonymous writer in 1308 who noticed the difference between the coastal (Primorja) and inland (Zagorja) regions. He stated that whereas the coastal region had six towns (civitates), the remaining regions had only 'multa castra, fortalicia et magne ville de tricentis et quadringentis domibus de lignis et asseribus edificatis sine aliqua clausura'. Similar comments were forthcoming from one G. Adam in 1332 who noticed that 'civitates' were only found on the coast, whilst the rest of the state was 'pauca et quasi nulla loca habet forcia vel munita, sed totum est ville et casalia sine fossatis et penitus sine muris'. Both writers agreed that mining was already well developed, but many towns later disappeared from the map when their basis for existence, ore mining, went into irreparable decline.

The population was of varied origin. Saxon miners settled here and were found in many towns, except those of oldest origin; some inhabitants were locals who had ventured into mining, whilst others were merchants and traders who settled here from the coastal region (e.g. from Dubrovnik and Kotor) to help organize the export trade. Many of these commercial agents were Roman Catholics as verified in a papal document from the first half of the fourteenth century which mentions Catholics in Brskovo, Rogozno, Rudnik, Trepča, Prizren, Brvenik, Trgovište, Novo Brdo, Janjevo, Koporič, Plana, Ostatija, Lipnik and other less important places. Gradually the local inhabitants appear to have asserted themselves in the mining industry and also in other branches, such as handicraft production. In Novo Brdo during the first half of the fifteenth century there were a large number of goldsmiths with local names, but they were also found in other professions including butchers, tanners, bakers, carpenters, milliners, tailors, saddle makers and shoemakers. Similarly, Saxon names were found in town lists (e.g. 'snaider', tailor; 'suster', shoemaker) besides mining, and in Novo Brdo there was a 'porta dei susteri'. Some

Saxons are mentioned specifically and their organizational influence was felt in the towns. The first Saxon settlement in Serbia, Brskovo, had one Prince Freiberger, of German origin, as its leader about 1280—'comes Freibergerius et totus populus eiusdem civitatis';[8] in Rudnik a 'notarius Teutonicorum . . . baculus iudicis regis' is mentioned in 1312, whilst during the fifteenth century charters include 'inomici' or nomici' (from Nijemac—Serbo-Croat for 'German') on several occasions. Other important foreigners included merchants from Dubrovnik,[9] who played a leading role in the economic development of these inland towns.

Finally, mention should be made of a group of towns in Serbia which were not dependent on mining for their growth, and were either under Byzantine or Serbian administration. One such town was Prizren, known to have already been in existence in the eleventh century, but under Serbian rule. It had important coastal trade connections via the Bojana river, and inland into central Serbia, but quickly declined when these routes were made unsafe by Turkish incursions. Priština was a well-developed urban centre between 1350 and 1450 on a route which crossed Kosovo polje and near to the mining towns of Trepča, Novo Brdo and Janjevo. At Peć the embryonic form of a town settlement was already apparent, due to the religious importance of several monasteries, whilst other trading centres like Novi Pazar, Trgovište, Kruševac, Prijepolje, Smederevo, etc. were rapidly gaining prominence. Lastly, Belgrade experienced a somewhat different development, first coming under Serbian rule in 1284, when King Dragutin received it from the Hungarian king, and lasting till 1319.[10] The Serbian Despot, Stefan Lazarević, (1389–1427), recaptured Belgrade and gave the town a charter granting special commercial privileges, exemption from customs duties and free access for their merchants to his kingdom. During Hungarian rule, Belgrade was referred to as 'totus populus', but there is little information on town administration or other aspects of urban life.

Bosnia/Hercegovina and Zeta

The early history of this region is completely obscure, the name for Bosnia coming from the River 'Bosante' or 'Bosanius' of classical times and later applied to those Slavic tribes in the area during the seventh century. Zeta was the name given to an area north of Lake Skadar (Scutari), around the present-day Montenegrin/Albanian frontier, and once formed part of Stefan Dušan's realm. The whole area consisted of autonomous tribal units (župe), separated by tracts of difficult country, and possessed no well-defined natural frontier. Information on urban settlement and citizenship throughout most of the area is based on Late Mediaeval sources. Nevertheless, Constantine Porphyrogenitus compiled documents on Bosnia (χωριου Βόσωνα horion Bosona) in the first half of the tenth century and his work records a number of inhabited towns, e.g. Katera (Kotorac) and Desnek. Unfortunately, apart from their names, nothing else is mentioned. There distribution is also of interest, because many of these towns were not located within the main core area of the Bosnian state, but in Zahumlja (later to become Hercegovina). These included the župe of Trebinje, Zahumlija and Paganija (Neretva region), the Pljevska župa (Πλέβα-Pleba), Imotski župa (Εμοτα-Emota) and Livanska župa (Χλεβίανά-Hlebiana). Porphyrogenitus also mentions that already at this time part of the area was under the influence of Dubrovnik's merchants, whilst the first written commercial treaties date from 1186 (with Nemanjin) and 1189 (with Kulin). This lively commercial situation led to the development of towns which were recorded in the other main early source on this area, the chronicle of the priest Dukljanin in the twelfth century.

Attempt has been made to trace and map settlements throughout the area for the Later Mediaeval period (Fig. 3), together these total 1,000 places. Their distribution in turn closely reflects the caravan route network (Fig. 4). Further analysis leads to a breakdown into settlement types. Places recorded in documents as towns (Fig. 5a) reach a total of 258, whilst more than double this number (582) were referred to as villages (Fig. 5b). Further down the settlement hierarchy one finds hamlets (25) and monasteries (54) (Fig. 5c), together with 81 forts (Fig. 3). The century following the death of Kulin in 1204 was a confused period, but by 1330 mining began to play an important role in the commercial life of this area, particularly in the trade and handicraft branches of mediaeval Bosnia, so that more information on urban settlement is forthcoming after this date.

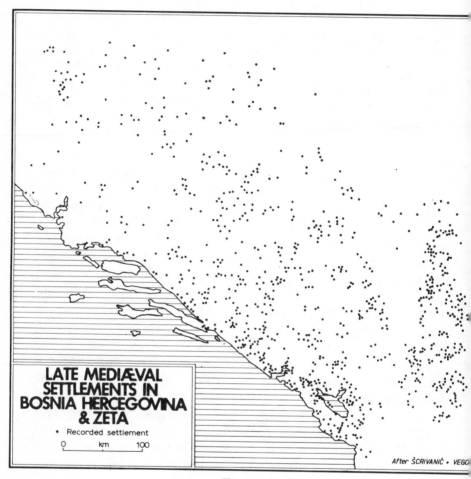

LATE MEDIÆVAL
SETTLEMENTS IN
BOSNIA HERCEGOVINA
& ZETA

• Recorded settlement

0   km   100

After ŠCRIVANIĆ + VEGO

FIG. 3.

FORTS &
CARAVAN ROUTES

● Recorded Fort
— Caravan Route

0   km   100

After ŠCRIVANIĆ · VEGO

Fɪɢ. 4.

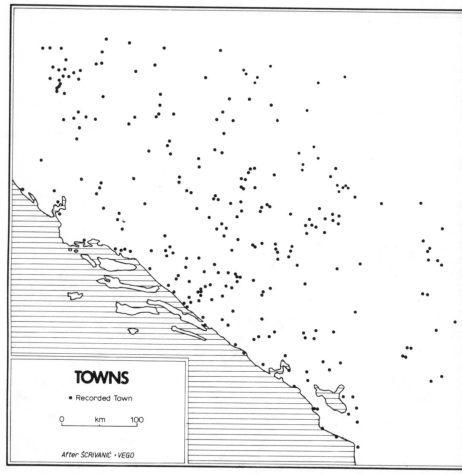

TOWNS

• Recorded Town

0   km   100

After ŚCRIVANIĆ · VEGO

Fɪɢ. 5A.

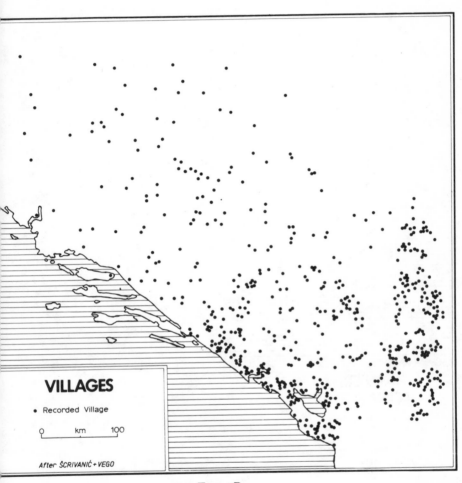

VILLAGES

- Recorded Village

0   km   100

After ŠCRIVANIĆ + VEGO

FIG. 5B.

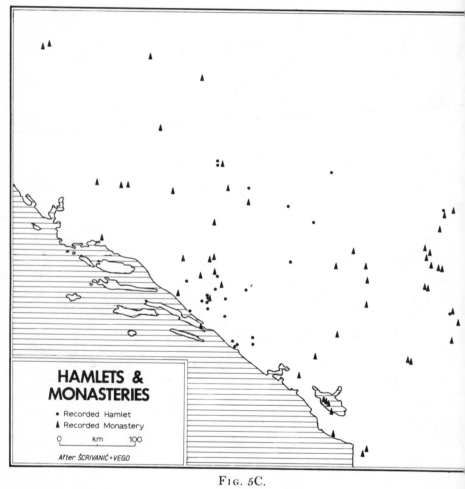

HAMLETS &
MONASTERIES

• Recorded Hamlet
▲ Recorded Monastery

0   km   100

After ŠCRIVANIĆ + VEGO

Fig. 5C.

With this increase in commercial activity, the whole region, and particularly Bosnia, became more stabilized and it was possible to organize important transit trade through the region from the coast to Serbia and Slavonia. The urban settlements tended to develop at points of commercial interest, especially the mining centres (gold, silver, lead for Dubrovnik traders), at nodal points in the caravan network and the royal or ruling towns. For example, Visoki (today Visoko) developed during the second half of the fourteenth century as a trade centre, not only because it was one of the royal capitals with a fort, but also because the main caravan route from Drijeva and the Neretva Valley via Konjica and Ivan-sedla went through the town en route to the mining centres of Olovo, Srebrnica and further to Rudnik in Serbia. Within the mining area of central Bosnia (Lepenica župa), the fifteenth century saw the growth of such towns as Fojnica, Kreševo, Dusina and Deževnica. Olovo, situated in the Krivaja Valley, was first mentioned in 1382, whilst another important mining town, Srebrnica, is included in documents after 1376. This place, according to Jireček, was by the end of the Middle Ages, 'the largest mining and trading town in the whole region between the Sava and Adriatic'. To the north, along the banks of the Drina, lay the towns of Kučlat, and Zvorik (Zvornik), a fortified mining town and market centre. In the upper Podrina region lay the well-known market centres of Hoča (Foča) and Goražde, which from the second half of the fourteenth century developed as caravan route centres on the road from Dubrovnik to Serbia. Other caravan centres included Borač, Prača (royal court of Pavlović), and Blagaj in central and Konjić in northern Hercegovina. Western Bosnia contained several less well-known towns, including Hlebene (Hlivno, Livno) which later played a significant role in the commerce between Bosnia and the mid-Dalmatian towns. During the last ten years of the Bosnian state (1453–63) the town of Jajce, below the fort of Jrvoje Vukčić (an important Bosnian magnate), became the capital of the last Bosnian king, Stephen Tomašević. Travnik was first mentioned in documents in 1480, but it is probable that it existed during the entire life of the Bosnian state. The main coastal town of Bosnia, Novi (Herceg Novi), in the Bay of Kotor, was founded by King Tvrtko in 1382, mainly as an alternative entrepot port to Dubrovnik, during a period of political discontent. Farther south, the Zeta coastal area had the important towns of Kotor, Budva, Bar and Ulcinj. Of these Kotor was by far the most significant commercially, followed by Bar, but, unfortunately, both Budva and Ulcinj had restricted hinterlands which curtailed their independent growth. After Dušan's untimely death in 1355, the Balšić family controlled Zeta and extended their rule as far inland as Prizren, but it was a shortlived episode. The territory was disputed by the Montenegrins, Turks and Venetians, the latter being permitted to fortify the region and gain control of Skadar and Drivast in 1396. Ensuing troubles finally ended with peace in 1423, when the Venetians received Kotor and the Grbalj area, Skadar, the Paštrovići region and Ulcinj.

The urban population throughout Bosnia/Hercegovina and Zeta was very mixed. In many towns foreigners lived for various periods, usually as traders, customs officials or lease holders. The most numerous appear to have been from Dubrovnik and other Dalmatian towns, together with a large Saxon minority working in the mines. It is impossible to say what percentage of the population were of local origin, but it is known that from the end of the fourteenth century a large number of indigenous inhabitants were involved in business, handicrafts, labouring in the mines, transport, etc. Even so there appears to have been a gradual assimilation of foreign elements, especially Saxons, into the urban life of this area. Nevertheless, from documentary evidence there appears to have been a greater variety of minority groups in this area than previously imagined in what Cvijić called 'the ethnical nucleus of our people'. Documentary evidence has revealed the existence of at least thirteen minority groups in the area during the Late Mediaeval period (Figs V—6a and b). The most numerous appear to have been people of Greek Orthodox faith (229 individual documentary references), followed by Jews (50), Latins (49), Španje (45), Bukumiri (27), Giaour (Ottoman Turkish for 'infidel') and Mataguzi (24 each), Magyar (23), Lužani (19), Mataruge (18), Kriči (14), Macure (10), and finally Lutheran (3), giving a total of 536 references. Whereas the Greeks were spread throughout the region, some of the other groups did not show such a wide geographical distribution. This particularly relates to the Kriči and Bukumiri with their highly localized concentration north of Lake Skadar. Some of these groups are thought to be of pre-Slavic origin like the Španje in Zeta who were probably descended from the ancient Illyrians, whilst others were taken from their faiths, e.g. Lutherans, Latins (Roman Catholic) and Jews. The Greeks were probably the most urban conscious, with 26 examples of them residing in towns, but there were also 7 Magyar towns including Tomina and Bjelaj. Clearly more research is needed into this topic, but it is sufficient to say that a complex ethnic situation in the region contributed in some way to its urban development.[12]

The other theme of interest here concerns caravan trade and its influence on urban development. Suburbs (varoš) developed near many of the larger settlements, accompanied by the growth in commerce during the fifteenth century. Numerous traders in the mining settlements, although primarily concerned with various metals, also had secondary interests (e.g. silk production), which attracted the interests of the caravan trade. Village handicraft production had formerly satisfied local needs and those of the feudal lords, but the caravan trade led to a wider basis for their markets. In 1450, Duke Stjepan encouraged his people to produce cloth, arms and other manufactured goods, and established a new harbour (Novi) as an outlet for these products. This was a direct attempt to discourage foreign traders and manufacturers 'from Dubrovnik, Kotor and other places who settle in our towns, and in a short time form large centres (gran citade) for their own purposes'. Nevertheless, despite these efforts and the importance of caravans, towns in mediaeval Bosnia/Hercegovina and even more so in Zeta, were not mature enough by the Late Middle Ages to have developed to a degree where they had their own legal and administrative autonomy. Town laws were under the jurisdiction of local feudal lords or part of the royal domain, which in itself discouraged independent growth. Some signs of greater urban freedom began to appear (e.g. at Novi) but this was curtailed by the Turkish occupation.[13]

Slovenia

The real history of urbanization in the Slovenian region, with its associated coastal towns, began with the establishment of markets, (Latin—forum; German—Markt; Slovenian—trg), and new

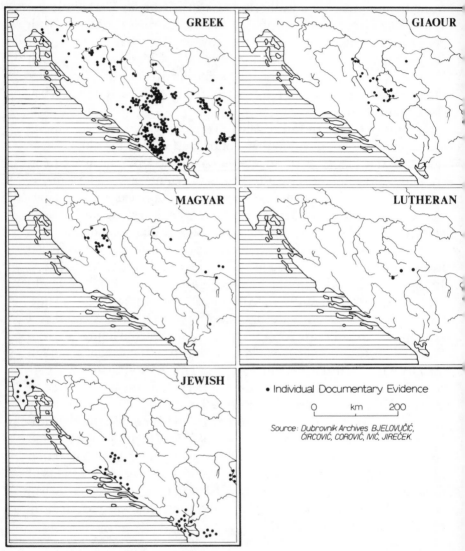

F IG. 6A. Some Late Mediaeval minority groups in the Dinaric regions.

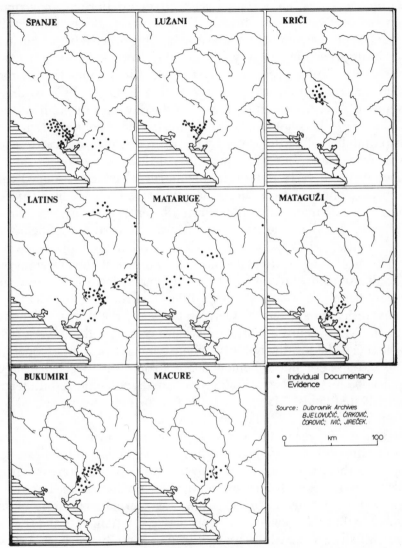

FIG. 6B. Some Late Mediaeval minority groups in the Dinaric regions.

market towns (Latin—civitas; German—Stadt; Slovenian—mesto). These settlements possessed a new social class of people (Latin—forenses, cives, burgenses; German—Bürger; Slovenian —tržani meščani) who mainly lived from trade in handicraft products, or exchange of various goods. This process began during the twelfth century, especially in the Koroska area (around present-day Villach [Beljak]) and reached its culmination in the thirteenth century. Evidence suggests that H. C. Darby's assumption that 'There is not much record of the Slovenes throughout the Middle Ages'[14] is not true, because documentary sources refer to a large number of settlements, each with its own feudal castle and agricultural land, but with apparently little fusion amongst them. Plans of these early town settlements reveal houses grouped together in ones or twos along narrow streets all leading to the market place, many after the thirteenth century were surrounded by fortified walls. The choice of site was often strategic, below a feudal castle, on islands, river bends or between a mountain and river.

The first town settlers in Slovenia were probably foreigners. The Slavic ruling group had been eliminated from early Slovene society before the tenth century, so the chief representatives of the feudal order came from the German lords and the Roman Catholic church.[15] Between the tenth and twelfth centuries there were two basic social classes, the nobility (plemstvo) and peasants (kmeti). The latter were not a homogeneous group[16] in which half-free (polsvobodni) serfs were the best situated and colonized hitherto uncultivated lands. Many also settled in the new towns, helped by the principle that a feudal lord could only seek the return of his serfs up to one year after they had resided in a town. Furthermore, during the period from the twelfth to the beginning of the fifteenth century, the majority of the Slovene rural population obtained their own homesteads and formed their own villages. In the towns the written documentary language was German but it is quite probably that the spoken word was Slavic. Craftsmen in the towns were usually Slavic, whilst traders dealing in credit work and usury were mainly Jews, although they were gradually driven out of the Štajerska, Koroska and Krajnska regions at the end of the Middle Ages.

Most urban dwellers had their own fields, vineyards, etc. together with a share in the parish pasture and forest. Although agriculture was of secondary interest for these citizens, it did take on increased importance during times of economic decline. During prosperous times most activity was centred on the fairs. Many settlements had one or two Sunday fairs a year worked out on a reciprocal basis with other towns in the area. Annual fairs were usually most successful in towns on the main roads through the territory, each town's citizens trying to monopolize handicraft production in their sphere of influence. Unfortunately, they often met opposition from feudal lords and peasants from the surrounding district. Theoretically, handicraft production was legally forbidden for the non-citizen element of a particular region, but this never appears to have been strictly enforced. Village commerce was rarely represented in the Sunday fairs, and only town dwellers dealt exclusively in foreign goods. There were also strict rules on possession within the towns. Citizens could own houses, and be independent traders and craftsmen, but this did not apply to day-labourers, journeymen, nobles or the clergy, despite their residence within the walls. Although many urban centres had their own town council and leading land owners, none of them had political independence. Thus, it is interesting that in the struggle for political rule in the Slovenia region at the end of the Middle Ages most of the strongest developed centres belonged to absent Habsburg owners.

The Slovenian coastal towns saw a blossoming of trade and handicraft production during the twelfth century, each forming a type of autonomous commune within the general political framework. The administrative and legal territory of these towns usually encompassed the surrounding Slovenian villages, but the larger part of the urban population were of Roman origin, with a much smaller Slavic element. Employment possibilities were also on a wider basis, because besides the traditional handicraft and trade activities, some of the citizens were engaged in fishing, salt production and various maritime activities. The drive for independence is best illustrated by the individual administrative laws (written in Latin) promulgated by the autonomous town communes in their statutes. Many Istrian towns did not come under Venetian rule until the thirteenth century (Koper and Izola—1279, Piran—1283, Milje—1420). Trieste was under the independent rule of its bishop until 1369 when it had to recognize Venetian suzereinity, and after 1382 came under the Hapsburgs. Even so these coastal towns continued to foster trading relations with the Slavic hinterland,[17] mainly due to Venetian opposition to the development of their maritime commerce.

Croatia and Slavonia[18]

The extent of mediaeval Croatia is difficult to estimate. In the north it does not always appear to have included Slavonia (between the Sava and Drava rivers), for this strip of territory seems at times to have been more closely attached to Hungary. To the south Croatia was restricted in the Late Middle Ages by the expanding Bosnian state, whilst to the south-west a greater part of Dalmatia was under Venetian rule. Nevertheless, the first growth of urban development dates from the thirteenth and fourteenth centuries when the Arpadović and Angevin rulers granted political privileges to individual new towns. Within the political system there were many individual rulers who formed their own local markets, which even in the earliest written documents were based on monetary exchange rather than barter.

Many of these privileged settlements and suburbs (varoš— Hungarian for suburb) had their own legal form whose origin was closely associated with the colonization process prevalent throughout much of Central Europe at this time. Colonists settled in villages or 'varoš' urban centres, whilst non-agricultural inhabitants were subject to distinct tax burdens, e.g. market dues; one thirtieth of their income to the local ruler, etc. The main characteristic of these settlements, particularly in the Pannonian Basin, was of comparative nearness to each other (Ackerburgerstädte) and lack of cultivated land, often leading to inadequate food supply. Therefore many of the urban dwellers were employed in commerce and manual work, the goods being sold to purchase agricultural produce.

The real key to the development of these towns was the number of privileges accorded them by the local rulers. The largest number of varoš settlements were within the king's territory, some of them being given the title of 'free town' (liberae villae), and possessing their own council (communitas), given them directly by the House of Arpadović during the first half of the thirteenth century. Below the free towns in importance came the market towns, like Samobor and Jastrebarsko, and finally places founded as towns which degenerated into villages, such as Perna (S. of Zagreb). Many of these urban centres had few local craftsmen, so the Croatian–Hungarian rulers encouraged foreigners, especially from Italy, Germany and Hungary, to populate their towns. As patrimonial owners of these lands, they welcomed the arrival of these foreign specialists, seeing them as capable of improving the economic conditions of their territory. These traders and craftsmen, referred to in the Latin documents as 'hospites' (guests foreigners; in Russian Гост—traders) settled in many of the more important centres and found few obstacles to the furtherance of trade and business. The 'hospites' particularly favoured the fortified towns (castra), where they felt secure under the direct protection of the local ruler (župan), often helping him and the king's deputies to organize the local area. Nevertheless, the privileges of freedom given to citizens whether they were local or foreign, varied from place to place and over time. The citizens of Varaždin received their freedom in 1209, Perna—1225, Vukova—1231, Virovitica—1234, Petrinja—1240, Samobor—1242, Zagreb's Gradec—1242, Križevci—1252, and Jastrebarsko—1257. Similarly, the amount of freedom given to craftsmen and traders and their tax liabilities, depended on a town's administration and judiciary (iudex, defensor villae, maior vallae), who decided the type of goods to be exhibited at fairs, taxes at fairs, etc.

Towns not included within royal patronage belonged either to the nobility or the church. The essential difference between these and the royal free towns was their lack of a real independent judiciary, which affected their independent development. Thus, the free towns show evidence of continued growth right up to the Turkish incursions, whilst those urban settlements under the nobility and particularly those in church territory stagnated. This is well illustrated in the case of Zagreb's Gradec. A bishopric here dates back to 1094, and in 1198 the bishop obtained the right whereby the local population were subject to his judicature. Gradec quickly declined until 1242 when full citizens' rights were given to the inhabitants. From then on it developed into one of the best market centres in Croatia at the crossroads of routes from the Adriatic to the Pannonian Basin, and north to the Alps. In 1372 it obtained the right to hold annual fairs, which in turn encouraged its growth as a handicraft centre with its own guild organization (kalendinum Latinorum, confraternitas sclavonicalis). Many foreigners settled in the town and special skills were developed, especially in small handicraft production (needle makers, padlocks, spurs, bows and arrows, etc.).

Adriatic Coast[19]

In spite of migrations into and within the eastern Adriatic coast region over the centuries, the scale and distribution of urban populations varied little from the Early Middle Ages until the beginning of the nineteenth century. After the fall of Rome, the Slavic tribes occupied the agricultural lands outside the Roman towns, e.g. Split, and after several centuries gradually became urban dwellers in these established centres. Two forces appear to have given social continuity to the evolution of the urban system along the east Adriatic coast, one physical the other an established urban network. The rugged mountains, offshore islands and sea all helped create places of refuge for self-selective populations whose main concern was for personal and group independence. The network of towns and villages was already sufficiently firmly established by the Middle Ages to receive these newcomers and easily integrate them into the existing population.

In the North, Venetian Istria had its own urban history. Political opportunities in Istria led to the internal development of urban centres. Towns were formed as independent communes with their own administrative and legal rule (consul and potesta), with their own territory and serfs. After 1209 the patriarchy of Aquila had its own towns and castles with legal and administrative internal rule. Individual towns had their own autonomy and leader, a count (generalis gastaldio) who also had a seat in Kopar, the patriarchal capital. Continual political struggles between Aquila and Venice gradually led to Venetian control of the Istrian towns (Poreč— 1267, Umag—1269, Novigrad—1271, Kopar—1279, Piran and Rovinj—1283, Pula—1331), and by 1420 the whole area was under the Lion of St Mark. Under Venice the economic and political life of the Istrian communes declined. Now town buildings were in the Venetian style, town officials were controlled by Venice and independent economic development was stifled by various Venetian measures to deter free trade. Population also suffered a decline through epidemics (Pula, one of the most important Istrian centres still had only 300 inhabitants in 1638) and emigration.

Urban development in Venetian Dalmatia, along the central portion of the east Adriatic coast, has recently been discussed by Violich.[20] He maintains that during the Early Middle Ages

'virtually all of the urban system was taken over by a predominantly Slavic population',

but that a

'certain continuity of social institutions was maintained through the use of Latin as the official language. Nevertheless, the class structure (in Dalmatia) did place in the hands of a committee group the responsibility for the management of the towns and related villages and seeing that maximum advantage was derived from the social and economic activities'.

The larger centres like Zadar, Split and Dubrovnik, dominated the hierarchy of economic levels during the Middle Ages, since they commanded the strategic positions linking the inland routes with the sea, and prospered through trade and export. Smaller towns along the coast played less important economic roles fixed at certain levels due to their function in serving hinterlands of limited size and fewer local resources, whilst inland urban centres with little contact from the outside world were even more dependent on themselves for development. The latter were more applicable to the idea of the isolated town model previously discussed. Some villages occupying protected inlets gradually grew to importance as small ports serving the interior and, in some cases, became as 'urban' as the larger towns. With the rise of these maritime urban centres, the inland towns and villages on the islands and along the coast, e.g. on Brač Island that had previously flourished as places of safe refuge, remained as agricultural centres within the urban hierarchy.

Finally, mention should be made of the towns in the Zeta Coastal area (Venetian Albania) which today are part of Montenegro. In the eleventh century it was part of the Kingdom of Duklja, but Stephen Nemanja (1169–1196) secured Zeta for the

Serbian Nemanjid dynasty including the important towns of Kotor, Budva, Bar and Ulcinj, and previously discussed under Bosnia/ Hercegorina and Zeta.

The Early Modern Period 1500–1800

Areas under the Turks

One of the biggest problems in the history of the western Balkans under Turkish rule is the question of the role played by towns and the urban economy. Information exists, but there are divergent views as to its interpretation.[21] The source material can be basically divided into two types; there are contemporary travellers' accounts and geographical descriptions; and there is a massive amount of Turkish archival material, much of it not yet investigated,[22] and often found in fragmentary form. Furthermore, many of the towns that experienced Turkish rule have yet to be subject to thorough research although some have detailed written records, which may help in understanding their urban development (number of minarets, schools, public baths, traders, shops, churches, etc.). Some towns also have information on the development of handicrafts, number of soldiers, janissaries, uprisings, fires, epidemics, etc., all useful for creating a general picture of Ottoman urban life at this time.

With these limitations in mind, some attempt will be made to try and highlight the major influences that Ottoman rule had on urban development during their occupation. This occupation within the present area of the Yugoslav lands came in three distinct waves. The first enveloped Macedonia from 1380 onwards, the second was effective in Bosnia and Serbia after 1450, whilst the lands beyond the Sava and Drava rivers escaped the onslaught until 1525. Ottoman urbanization policy was energetically applied to Constantinople, and extended simultaneously to the Balkan interior. Under Turkish rule many smaller towns decayed through economic stagnation, but sites selected as main seats of Turkish administration certainly grew in importance. New towns were founded like Novi Pazar, Sarajevo, Travnik, Köprülü (Veles) and Pirot, whilst for some towns, like Novo Brdo, Ochrida (Ohrid), Srebrenica, the first two centuries of Turkish rule proved unfavourable to their development. In some cases existing towns were expanded, like Plevlje, Prokuplje, Üsküb (Skoplje), Monastir (Bitolj), Belgrade, Valjevo, Užice, Fethislam (Kladovo), Castelnuovo (Hercegnovi), Mostar, Foča, Banja Luka, Zvornik, Jajce and Livno.[23] Some of these towns proved to be important footholds in the Ottoman policy of conquest and in the setting up of the machinery for expansion. In the western Balkans the first centre of significance was Skoplje from 1392 onwards, Smederevo (after 1459), Belgrade (1521) and Banja Luka (1527/28). The Turks actually founded Sarajevo as a governor's residence in 1462, just before the fall of Bosnia in 1463.

Population growth also accompanied urban expansion. Barkan estimates that the population of some cities, including Sarajevo, Monastir and Skoplje, saw nearly a 70% increase between 1525 and 1575. Whatever the exact percentage of urban growth, the town population of the western Balkans unquestionably expanded during the sixteenth century, following the much depleted situation during the previous century, a phenomenon which also characterized the western Mediterranean as a whole.[24] This growth of Balkan towns in turn promoted the spread of trade, Jewish merchants[25] being not least amongst the beneficiaries. The Jewish element in the western Balkan towns rose rapidly between 1500 and 1650 partly as a result of expulsions from Spain. Monastir had about 34 Jewish families in 1525 and 200 by 1591; Skoplje numbered 12 families in 1525, 32 in 1546 and 3,000 Jews by 1688.[26] There appears to have been a decline of the Jewish population after 1660 which continued up to 1800. This may have been related to a stagnation in trade, for many left the ports of Split, Dubrovnik,[27] and some other towns in the Ottoman empire during the eighteenth century for the more expanding economic centres like Trieste and certain west European cities.[28] The Jewish population of Semlin (Zemun) declined from 1,000 in 1680 to less than 100 by 1750.[29] In Belgrade, Skoplje and possibly Sarajevo, some decline in numbers took place at the end of the seventeenth century, although partial recovery to their former demographic and economic strength is noticed during the second half of the eighteenth century.[30] Slowly many towns in the western Balkans became less Jewish, Armenian or even Turkish, and increased their numbers of Greeks, Slavs and Albanians.[31] In Serbia and

Macedonia, many of the original inhabitants fled to Hungary in 1690, so that towns often became more Greek or Albanian in areas previously only inhabited by Slavs. During the Austro–Turkish war of 1683–1690, many cities like Belgrade, Sarajevo, Skoplje, Štip, Veles and Tetovo[32] had large parts of their urban area destroyed. Before 1683 Skoplje had a population of between 40–60,000 and Belgrade more than 50,000, many of the inhabitants being Turks, Jews, Armenians, as well as some Slavs and Greeks. Some fled north, others died of disease or war wounds. Similarly, the Serbs and Christian Albanians in towns like Priština and Prizren, together with other rebellious urban dwellers, migrated northward with the Austrian armies. Repopulation measures both by the Turks and Austrians were only partially successful so that even on the eve of the Napoleonic Wars, Skoplje still only had 6,000 inhabitants and Belgrade 25,000.[33]

The urbanization policies of the Ottoman Empire during its period of ascendence led to the development of trade and handicraft industries in many towns. This gave rise to the founding of foreign merchant colonies in the most successful commercial centres, whilst outside the towns the Turks changed the previous basic production structure of rural life. Mining activity was allowed to stagnate and decline, particularly in precious minerals, whilst livestock rearing was encouraged, often to satisfy war needs. Many products were based on livestock production including skins, capes (aba), covers and blankets. Village production was often based on wax, many shops manufacturing various wax products, e.g. candles; metal handicraft workshops concentrated on manufacturing military equipment. Some of the leading cities had an important textile industry whose products were sold at local fairs and sent for export. However, village economies were mainly based on local markets and the exchange of rural and town manufactures as envisaged in the isolated town model. There seemed little interest in international trade due to the imposition of export duties (gümrük), whilst bazaar traders had to pay further market dues (badz). Yet the expansion of towns, population and industry in western and central Europe[34] during the eighteenth century created a rising demand for rural Balkan products: grains, hides, cattle, meat, oil, wax, silk, wool, cotton, tobacco, and timber. This led to rapid rises in the price of rural commodities, which often aroused jealousy from Ottoman officials, urban and semi-urban proprietors against the landowning classes. This in turn led to the development of protection rackets so that, in many areas, especially near the coasts, in the lowlands and river valleys, the peasant soon found himself paying legal rent to his landlord and protection money, usually in the form of produce, to some urban proprietor.

The urban property owning classes thus acquired a primary interest in the accumulation of wealth through the expropriation of the peasant and exportation of confiscated rural commodities. This wealth was then in many cases used for town buildings, and in turn gave them an Eastern appearance. Provincial administrators and other Turkish aristocrats had their own particular shops, mills, and land within a town, whilst frontier boundary commanders and local sanjak begs erected forts and other monumental buildings within their seat of power; such names as Ishaković (Skoplje), Isabeg Ishaković (Sarajevo), Jahjapasić (Belgrade), Ferhad Sokolović (Banja Luka) and the border commander, Husref-beg in the sixteenth century were connected with the construction of minarets, theological schools (medrese), caravanserai, public baths (hamame), fountains (çeşme), the establishment of cloth markets (bezistan), etc. The various pious foundations (vakf) were also responsible for the erection of schools, minarets and mosques in many urban centres.

Between 1450 and 1550 the basis was laid for many typical Islamic towns in the Yugoslav Balkan lands. The larger towns (şehir) developed at important strategic centres and on commercial cross roads, whilst the smaller urban centres (kasaba) were scattered throughout the country. The recovery of Balkan towns in the sixteenth century was also accompanied by the growth of suburbs or 'varoš',[35] usually reserved for Christian inhabitants, who were forbidden to live in the urban centres. With the decline of the urban nuclei during the War of Candia and the Austro–Turkish wars (1645–1669) there was a modification of this principle in order to allow Christian recruits to perform economic tasks previously done by Turkish moslems, Bosnian Moslems, Jews or Armenians. Sarajevo, for example, had no Christian families in 1520, but by 1655, they totalled one per cent of the population; Banja Luka's Christians formed 6% of her inhabitants in 1655. Varoš's were also used for guarding important route

centres (e.g. Priboj), but those situated in Moslem town settlements (e.g. mining market towns) soon became unstable and
declined because the Islamic population was too authoritarian.

The more stable atmosphere of the sixteenth century and the
settled Islamisized urban population laid the basis for the
distinctive character of West Balkan towns under Turkish rule.
Several quarters were built around the mosque, including a collection of shops and workshops centred on the market place (çarşu)
and bazaar. Houses for the urban dwellers were built in terraces
(as was the Eastern custom) providing the terrain was suitable.
The minaret gave a view over the whole town, within sight of all
the main access routes, many orchards and gardens of the surrounding district. Near the mosque the buildings and courtyards
of the local aristocracy were located, whilst the more unsavoury
parts of the town, around the local well and stables, contained
much squalidness and often produced epidemics and fires. Many
towns had forts. For example there was a very large fort at
Smederevo on the Danube up to 1521 and later at Belgrade (the
Kalemegdan or Town Field). These town forts contained large
garrisons of Turkish and Serbian soldiers who were stationed here
during the sixteenth century, ('martoloz'—Christian sailor from
the Danube in the pay of Turks in their forts; topçu—artillery-
man), together with specialists in fort maintenance. In Belgrade
there was also a large granary for military needs and workshops
for producing gunpowder because of links westward to the
frontier.

Urban settlement in the present-day territory of Vojvodina and
Slavonia was a little different from that experienced in other areas
under Turkish rule. Many towns had already developed from varoš
origins prior to the Turkish occupation, when a product/money
economy meant strong ties with the surrounding villages, and
facilitated the introduction of the Turkish çiftlik system.[36] The
area of Vojvodina today roughly covers the land settled by
Serbians in the sixteenth century, where many urban centres became Turkish administrative and commercial/handicraft towns.
They often had a large Muslim population and possessed a typical
Eastern planning form. Some varoš settlements in the Banat and
Srem areas had exlusively Christian inhabitants (mainly Serbian),
as at Sremski Karlovci. Serbians were also found amongst the

Muslim urban population in Slankamen, Bečkerek, Vršac and Pančevo where they were mainly engaged in commerce and handicrafts, but outside the towns the Serbs were cultivators employed under the çiftlik system.

The period between 1590 and 1650 saw a rapid development of commercial and communication centres in the Turkish-held Western Balkan lands, for the sixteenth-century balance between commerce and industry was now weighted in favour of commerce. This meant the merchant class, like the Ottoman official and land-owning classes, enjoyed an unprecedented period of prosperity. The main urban centres were Belgrade, Sarajevo and Skoplje, and, to a lesser extent Bitolj, Novi Pazar, Užice and Banja Luka where there was a growth in commercial and usurer capital, besides the old established craft industries. As previously, some of the profits were used for the construction of town buildings by feudal lords, army commanders and the richer citizens, but on a smaller scale than previously, for the age of monumental edifices was over. This growth in the urban economy also attracted an inflow of new inhabitants from surrounding villages, especially Muslim peasants; this, in turn, led to complications within the urban social order, for many craft guilds were closed to these second class citizens and a gulf appeared between the ruling richer inhabitants and the poor urban dwellers, especially in Bosnia. Even in Belgrade the situation was very complicated. Ewilyā Chelebi in 1660 described this city as a harbour on the Sava/Danube and important town in East-West trade with 38 Muslim districts (mahalle), 3 Gypsy districts, 3 Greek, 3 Serbian, 1 Armenian and 1 Jewish district. His comment on the urban social order in Belgrade reveals that the

'population is formed into six groups: one group consists of the military personnel, another from overland and maritime merchants, a third from people in service, a small group with vine-yards and gardens, a fifth in shipbuilding and lastly a handicraft group'.[37]

Further urban development at the end of the seventeenth and during the eighteenth centuries was checked by wars and territorial losses. The economic stagnation and decline of the Ottoman economy was closely connected with Hapsburg expansion at the expense of the Turks (most of Slavonia, much of Vojvodina (Srem,

Bačka, and Baranja), part of Šumadija, and northern Bosnia, south of the Sava river). War losses and epidemics of plague led to heavy urban population losses, with many towns having fewer inhabitants in the eighteenth than in the previous century. Surprisingly, the meagre data available suggests that fairs were more animated, and commercially viable in the eighteenth century than ever before. Thus, in the very period in which many Balkan towns were in the throes of prolonged economic crisis, the Balkan fairs bloomed and prospered.[38] What at first appears contradictory is not really so, for the growth of the pre-industrial fair was in fact generally contingent upon the inadequate performance by urban centres of certain manufacturing and exchange functions. This was further stimulated by the increased purchasing power of the Ottoman landlords, officials and merchants which allowed an increase in the importation of 'luxury' products from abroad. Thus, while the commercial sector of the Balkan economy expanded, the overall economy declined. This was accompanied by a breakdown of the Ottoman order which in turn led to anarchy. Individual army commanders and feudal aristocrats, especially in Bosnia and Macedonia, created their own local economies centred on the town with its despotic seat. These individual urban centres in parts of the western Balkans were ruled by independent begs and their agents.[39]

Within Bosnia/Hercegovina and Zeta most of the present day towns retain a markedly oriental appearance. Turkish influence was much stronger here than in the countryside, as the Moslem population contained a high percentage of urban-dwelling landlords and administrators. Places such as Sarajevo and Mostar became famous for their bazaars, where often each street was devoted to a particular commodity or group of commodities. Minarets and poplar trees rose majestically above the fine Turkish houses,[40] whilst streets were narrow and winding. The towns often covered a considerable area in comparison with their population size, since each house usually had its own walled garden. Unfortunately, many towns failed to serve as cultural centres, owing to the stagnation of Turkish life in the later period and to the frequent clash of interests between the Moslem townspeople and the mainly Christian rural population.[41]

Areas Outside Turkish Rule

Outside the Turkish sphere of influence the dependence of Croatia, Dalmatia and Slovenia was on the Catholic powers of Hungary, Austria and Venice. Thus, urban and economic development was often restricted by political considerations. In Dalmatia, Venice subordinated the cities to her own commercial advantage. Though Slovenia was permitted by Austria to make some industrial progress, that of Croatia was subordinated to the interests of Hungary.

In Slovenia the basic urban pattern laid down in the Middle Ages remained unaltered. However, the Turkish occupation of two thirds of the western Balkans had its effect on Slovenian urban life. Firstly, the constant threat of Turkish attack gave many towns greater strategic importance, so that already by the fifteenth century many small market centres were being converted into fortified places and right up to the seventeenth century citizens were armed in readiness to defend their town. Secondly, Turkish expansion meant that all the former commerce with the Hungarian lands ceased, causing a particular loss of wheat, livestock, furs, honey and wax imports.[42] This external unrest was also complicated by internal troubles. Basically, this concerned the struggle between the village-based peasant economy and the urban guild system, for commercial dominance. Some towns remained neutral, whilst some feudal lords protected peasants in the hope that they might themselves monopolize production with serf labour. These problems then faded into the distance with the coming of the Reformation which effected the whole urban population with the exception of Gorica and the coastal towns. The counter Reformation about 1600 led to some emigration from urban centres and the appearance of new monasteries and Jesuit Colleges in many large centres. Guild regulations were the next issue to split urban life, a conflict which reached its culmination in the seventeenth century with the 'numerus clausus' rule for masters and journeymen, and the important part played by guilds in the religious life of the Baroque period.

Little improvement had been made in communications with porters, donkeys and small carts still the main form of transport.

Even so, commerce was lively with the import of sea salt and export of wine (coast and Štajerska region in the north), iron and linen (from Gorenska and Koroška regions) to Italy. Urban dwellers found competition now not only from the villages, but from foreign merchants who obtained monopolistic privileges from local rulers in certain branches of the import/export business. This in turn led to economic decadence in many small towns, where the population of several centres in the seventeenth century was probably no more than it had been in the middle ages. Ljubljana had about 7,000 inhabitants (4,000 within walls); Trieste with 3–6,000 had already surpassed Koper, whilst Gorica and Celovec had between 4–5,000 inhabitants and the remaining towns no more than 2,000 population. Again the social order was noticeably causing a social and cultural split in the urban population. The richer citizens spoke German, the merchant immigrants mainly Italian, particularly after the counter Reformation (except in Gorica), whilst documents were now more commonly written in German than Latin. Also during the Baroque period there was a gradual change in the external appearance of many towns, though the old mediaeval plan remained intact.

The eighteenth century saw imperceptible changes in Slovenian urban life. A new commercial class emerged which lived from large wholesale trading and credit handling, and, although small in number, was concentrated in a few towns (e.g. Zois) and controlled larger amounts of money than the ordinary town merchant. Furthermore, the defeat of the Turks led to the colonization of Slavonia and Vojvodina, which, together with the regulation of the Sava River, once more opened up trade to the east. The declaration of free navigation in the Adriatic and confirmation of Trieste as a free port in 1717, together with Rijeka two years later, was accompanied by the construction of a new road to the interior capable of taking larger carriages than previously. Towns on these new inland routes rapidly grew in importance, whilst former routes like the one via Beljak and the Kanalska valley to Venice declined; similarly, the rise of Trieste meant the contemporary significance of many Istrian Venetian towns was lost.

Finally, after many disappointments, the basis was laid in Slovenia for manufacturing to take place in the larger towns. After 1770 it was decided to abolish the guild system. State bureaucracy increased, accompanied by a growth of the urban population. At the end of the eighteenth century Trieste had about 21,000 inhabitants (25,000 with suburbs), Ljubljana and Gorica about 10,000 each, Celovec over 9,000 and Maribor (with suburbs) 4,500. A large part of these urban dwellers were labourers and other manual workers, whilst town officials and the lay intelligentsia formed an influential minority. By 1800, the larger Slovenian towns were once more changing their appearance with the introduction of street lighting, the demolition of city walls, the building of theatres, improved sanitary facilities and other public services.

The Turkish advance led to modifications in the urban life of Croatia and Slavonia as it had farther north.[43] The history of this area between the twelfth and sixteenth century is closely compounded with the general history of Hungary with its domestic crises, the rivalry of Croatian feudal lords, resistance to the constant Turkish menace and peasant unrest. The latter came to a head in 1573 in a general peasant rebellion (also in Anatolia), linked as already mentioned with a similar movement in Slovenia. Further complications arose between Croatia, Hungary and Austria. After 1527, Croatia had increasing relations with Austria as well as Hungary, which led to a division of loyalty within the country; some of the population looked to Austria rather than to Hungary, particularly those new settlers in the 'Military Frontier' (Militär-grenze, Turkish—Serhat). This was a special marchland against the Turk along the southern frontier and created by the emperor in 1578 and under direct Austrian control. It was a land of forts, watch towers and beacons, and its inhabitants (graničari— frontiersmen), held land by special tenure in return for military service. Depopulation, resulting from earlier Turkish raids, led to weakened defences in the area and its repopulation (mainly Orthodox Serbs, some Germans) was important in this critical area. This repopulation was accompanied by the founding of new towns, of which the strongest in the sixteenth century was probably Karlovac. It received the privilege of being a royal free town in 1587, part of the grant allowed soldiers some rights in the organization of urban life. This led to a mutual understanding with the local citizens and helped in easing the problems of urban growth. In towns where the privileges were limited only to local citizens (e.g. Koprivnica), there was much rivalry and jealousy, particularly in relations between the courts and local ruler, which all in turn contributed to their slower development. In Karlovac, soldiers were exempted from paying local taxes, yet contributed to the general development of the town; in contrast, Koprivnica did not have its first guild until the beginning of the seventeenth century, due to the wrangling between local groups of citizens, and they only managed to agree on the establishment of an annual fair in 1635.

In Slavonia, similar problems arose in the growth of towns mainly due to the various struggles arising from relations between the commoners and the aristocracy. Already by the fifteenth century local counts (grof) set up their own captains to control individual towns, abused local taxes and closed judiciaries. Towns which fared the best were usually under the king's direct rule but some, which had been under local rule since the thirteenth century (e.g. Samobor), saw little progress in urban growth. Later development in the eighteenth century often revolved around local issues, especially the relative strengths of various town guilds. Some guilds were independent, others based on capitalist production methods and yet others concentrated on village production. The abolition of these old guilds by Joseph II in 1783 allowed each specialist his craft and improved the situation in many towns. Unfortunately many guilds were allowed to reform and were only finally abolished in 1859. This led to freer growth of crafts and consequent urban growth.

Along the Adriatic coast economic life was essentially limited to those activities and occupations based on the intrinsic character of the land and sea. The land had little to offer but the sea and its maritime resources governed the location and growth of those towns and cities that provided the link between sea and land. The physical environment of a large part of the east Adriatic coast helped create a system of compact urban settlements at key points and the sea provided a ready-made and vital communication system for the whole region. Even so, many of the villages and hamlets found along this coast today are distinctly urban in character, yet they are only quasi towns since they lack the full range of urban facilities. Many grew by their link function between the sea and inland agricultural areas, such as Slano, Ston, Podobice, Viganj, Sučuraj, Sutivan, Pučišče or Primošten. Others may be found at higher altitudes like Blato on Korčula island which possesses a rich urban history.

Conclusion

This, therefore, concludes a general appreciation of urban development in the western Balkans, in which various parts of present-day Yugoslavia have been examined in the light of their historical development both before and after the Turkish occupation. This chapter has attempted to paint the urban development of the western Balkans on a wide canvas. Care has been taken not to be too concerned with the time dimension but to give due prominence to the principle of geographical inertia. This refers to the fact that spatial patterns often remain relatively unchanged long after the causative forces have disappeared. It has been demonstrated how the flow of goods created by the geographical specialization of the regional centres within the hierarchical structure, the East–West trade routes across the western Balkans, the military demands of the Slavic or Turkish rulers, and the general need for control and integration of the individual states necessitated a well-developed communication and transport network. More regionally, the hierarchical urban structure had a pattern that was organized around routes connecting the regional centres and over this road network the caravans were elements of the spatial organization.

The areas subject to Turkish domination found a spatial organization in which the hierarchical settlement pattern coincided with the administrative structure. The Turkish empire was a large governmental machine which had been developed over time to enable an autocrat to rule a vast empire which lacked racial, geographical, or religious coherence. It was held together only by the overpowering force of a political system and an administration which was also the army. Within it, the economic standing of the peasantry showed wide regional variations, and the towns too often proved alien enclaves in their midst. In such a vast system the land tenure system was used as the key element that would ensure the survival of the central structure, whilst a market economy at a certain level of development proved a prerequisite for the formation of a pre-industrial urban hierarchy. Areas outside the Turkish domain often found the local ruling prince granting such legal and other privileges to win the support of new immigrants, who settled in his towns or villages, against his obstreperous nobility or the majority nationality. Whereas these often pacified their recipients, they also antagonized the more numerous native population. The greater centralization of the state in later years and the gradual passing of power to majority groups eased this problem resulting in freer urban growth.

The six hundred years from 1200 to 1800 brought tremendous changes, in urban development to the western Balkans, where modernization was to be built on the ruins of historical tradition; wars, social change, industrial growth, and finally education gradually prepared the urban pattern of this area to become what it is today.

5. Notes

1. P. Charanis, 'Observations on the Demography of the Byzantine Empire', *Thirteenth International Congress of Byzantine Studies*, Oxford 1966, pp. 1–19;
   M. F. Hendy, 'Byzantium, 1081–1204; an economic appraisal', *Transactions of the Royal Historical Society* (Feb. 1969), 32–52.
2. J. C. Russell, 'Late Medieval Balkan and Asia Minor Population', *Journal of Economic and Social History of the Orient* III (1960), 265–274;
   V. Hrochová, *Byzantska Města ve 13–15 století*, Univ. Karlova, Prague (1967), p. 118.
3. J. C. Russell, *Medieval Regions and Their Cities*, David and Charles, Newton Abbot, pp. 20–21.
4. A reaya was a tax-paying subject of the Ottoman Empire, muslim or non-muslim.
5. R. E. H. Mellor, 'Eastern Europe', *A Geography of the Comecon Countries*, Macmillan Press, London, (1975), pp. 48–52.
6. S. Novaković, *Grad. trg. varoš*, Belgrade (1892);
   Idem. 'Villes et cités du moyen-âge dans l'Europe Occidentale et dans la Péninsule Balcanique', *Archiv für slavische Philologie* (1903), 25, 321–41;
   M. Sufflay, 'Städte und Burgen Albaniens hauptsächlich während des Mittelalters', *Denkschriften der Akademie der Wissenschaften in Wien* (1924), p. 63;
   T. Taranovski, *Istorija srpskog prava u Nemanjićkoj državi* (1931), pp. 83–87; 110–117;
   I. Sindik, *Komunalno uredjenje Kotora od druge polovine XII do početka XV stoleća*, Belgrade (1950);

K. Jireček and J. Radonić, *Istorija Srba*, Belgrade (1952), pp. 83–95; 406–408;

M. Dinić, 'Za istoriju rudarstva u srednjevekovnoj Srbiji, I deo, Posebna izdanja' *S.A.N.* CCXL (1955);

N. Radojčić, *Zakonik o rudarstvu despota Stefana Lazarevića*, Belgrade (1962);

S. Riza, *Rudarstvo Kosova i susednih oblasti*, Priština (1966).

7. M. Burr, 'The Code of Stefan Dušan', *Slavonic and East European Review* 28, (71), 521, 534.

8. Written Прѣбгарь in a charter of King Dragutin, 1276–1316.

9. F. W. Carter, *Dubrovnik (Ragusa)—A Classic City State*, Seminar Press, London and New York (1972), Ch. 6, pp. 223–239.

10. K. Jireček and J. Radonić, op. cit. pp. 189, 201.

11. J. Cvijić, 'Antropogeografski problemi Balkanskog Poluostrva', *Srpski Etnografski Zbornik*, IV, Belgrade (1902), 26.

12. V. Palavestra, 'Folk Traditions of the Ancient Populations of the Dinaric Region', *Wissenschaftliche Mitteilungen des Bosnich-Herzegowinischen Landesmuseums*, I (B), Volkskunde, Sarajevo (1971), pp. 13–98.

13. E. Lilek. 'Riznica porodice Hranića', *Glasnik Zemaljskog muzeja u Bosni i Hercegovini*, I (1889);

C. Truhelka, *Naši gradovi*, Sarajevo (1904);

Idem. Kraljevski grad Jajce, Sarajevo (1904);

Idem. 'Nalaz bosanskih novaca obreten kod Ribiča', *Glasnik Zemaljskog muzeja u Bosni i Hercegovini*, XVII (1905);

H. Kreševljaković, *Esnafi i obrti u Bosni i Hercegovini*, Zagreb (1935);

V. Skarić, *Sarajevo i njegova okolina*, Sarajevo (1937);

M. Dinić, 'Dubrovačka srednjevekovna karavanska trgovina', *Jugoslovenski istoriski časopis*, III (1937);

Idem. 'Trg Drijeva i okolina u Srednjem veku', *Godišnjica Nikole Čupića*, 47 (1938);

Đ. Mazalić, 'Starine po okolini Sarajeva', *Glasnik Zemaljskog muzeja u Bosni i Hercegovini*, LI (1939);

M. Dinić, 'Zemlje hercega sv. Save', *Glas S.A.N.* 1940;

H. Kapidžić, 'Prilozi istoriji grada Klobuka', *Gajret* (1941);

Đ. Mazalić, 'Borač, bosanski dvor Srednjeg vijeka', *Glasnik Zemaljskog muzeja u Bosni i Hercegovini*, LIII (1941);

Idem. 'Starine u Dobrunu'; 'Gradac kod Hadžića, op. cit. LIV (1942);

H. Kreševljaković, 'Vareš kao glavno središte gvozdenog obrta u Bosni i Hercegovini do 1891', op. cit.;

Đ. Mazalić, 'Travnik i Torićan, op. cit. Nova serija III, 1948;

H. Kreševljaković, 'Gradska privreda i esnafi u Bosni i Hercegovini', *Godišnjak Istoriskog društva Bosne i Hercegovine*, I (1949);

Ð. Mazalić, 'Biograd-Prusac, stari bosanski grad', *Glasnik zemaljskog muzeja u Sarajevu*, Nova serija VI (1951);

T. Vukanović, 'Srebrenica u Srednjem veku', op. cit.;

K. Jireček, *Trgovački drumovi i rudnici u Srbiji i Bosni* (trans. D. Pejanović), Sarajevo (1951);

K. Jireček and J. Radonić, *Istorija Srba*, I–II, Belgrade (1952), op. cit.

14. H. C. Darby, 'Slovenia', in S. Clissold (ed.), *A Short History of Yugoslavia*, Cambridge University Press, Cambridge (1966), Ch. 2, p. 13.

15. J. Tomasevich, *Peasants, Politics and Economic Change in Yugoslavia*, University Press, Stanford (1955), pp. 130–131.

16. I. Winner, *A Slovenian Village*: Zerovnica, Brown University Press, Providence (1971), p. 35.

17. F. Gestrin, *Trgovina slovenskega zaledja s primorskimi mesti od 13 do konca 16 stoletja*, Ljubljana (1965).

18. F. Hrnčić, 'Borba između Kaptola i Gradske općine u Zagrebu za ubiranja sajamskih i tržnih pristojbi u srednjem vijeku', *Vjesnik hrvatskog državnog arhiva* (1941);

A. Timon, *Ungarische Verfassungs- und Rechtsgeschichte*, Berlin (1904);

I. Tkalčić, 'O staroj zagrebačkoj trgovini'; *Rad JA* (1909), 176, 178;

N. Klaić, 'Prilog pitanju klasne borbe u zagrebačkoj općini na početku XVII stoljeća', *Historijski zbornik*, III (1950;

Idem. 'O nekim pitanjima feudalne formacije u srednjovjekovnoj Slavoniji', op. cit. IV (1951);

Idem. 'Prilog pitanju postanka slavonskih varoši', *Zbornik filozofskog fakulteta*, Zagreb (1955).

19. G. Cattalinich, *Storia della Dalmazia*, Zadar (1834–5);

C. de Franceschi, *L'Istria*, Poreč (1879);

P. Pisani, 'Mletački posjedi Dalmacije od XVI do XVIII vieka', *Vjesnik za arheologiju i historiju dalmatinsku* (1891);

T. Erber, *Storia della Dalmazia*, Zadar (1892);

B. Benussi, *Nel medio evo. Pagine di storia istriana*, Poreč (1897);

S. Antoljak, *Dalmatinsko pitanje kroz vjekove*, Zagreb, (1944);

G. Novak, *Prošlost Dalmacije*, I–II, Zagreb (1944);

I. Sindik, *Komunalno uredjenje Kotora od druge polovine XII do početka XV stoleća*, Belgrade (1950);

G. Novak, 'Dalmacija i Hvar u Pribojevićevo doba', in V. Pribojević, *O podrijetlu i zgodama Slavena*, Zagreb (1951);

Idem. 'Nobiles, populus i cives-komuna i universitas u Splitu 1525–1797', *Rad JA* (1952), 286;

F. Madirazza, *Storia e costituzione dei comuni dalmati*, Split (1911);

V. Klaić, *Statut grada Zagreba od god. 1609 i njegova reforma god. 1618*, Zagreb (1912);

Idem. Smrt Gregorija Tepečića i njegovih drugova', *Vjesnik hrvatsko-slavonsko-dalmatinskog zemaljskog arhiva*, XIV (1912);

Ibid. Zagreb (1901–1910), Zagreb (1913);

I. Strohal, *Pravna povijest dalmatinskih gradova*, I, Zagreb (1913);

D. Gruber, *Povijest Istre*, Zagreb (1924);

B. Benussi, *L'Istria nei suoi due millenii di storia*, Trieste (1924);

F. Šišić, 'Borba za Jadran do početka XIX stoljeća', *Jadranska straža* (1925);

K. Schünemann, *Die Entstehung des Städtewesens in Süodst-europa*, Berlin (1929);

J. Ravlić, *Makarska i njeno primorje*, Split (1934);

B. Homan, *Geschichte des ungarischen Mittelalters*, Vols I and II, Berlin (1940 and 1943).

20. F. Violich, 'An urban development policy for Dalmatia: Part I: the urban heritage to the time of Napoleon', *Town Planning Review*, 43 (2) (April, 1972), 151–165.

21. N. Todorov, *Balkanskiyat Grad XV–XIX Vek: Socijalno-ikonomichesko i Demografsko Razvitie*, Sofia (1972), 504pp.

22. Such information relates to land known as 'vakf'. Vakf land was designated for the support of religious, educational, and charitable enterprises, such as schools, libraries, public baths, mosques, and convents for priests. Since no vakf property could be confiscated it increased steadily in extent. Other documents include cadastral surveys, reports of the Cadi (judges of Islamic canon law) etc.

23. F. Bajraktarević, 'Usküb', *Encyclopédie de l'Islam*, Vol. IV, Istanbul (1934), p. 1110;

T. R. Djordjević, '*Srbija pre sto godina*', (Prosveta), Belgrade (1946), pp. 21, 153–57, 168;

V. Radovanović, 'Prizren', *Narodna enciklopedija srpsko-hrvatsko-slovenacka*, St. Stojanović (ed.), Vol. III (1928), p. 698;

L. Vojnović, *Dubrovnik i osmansko carstvo*, Belgrade (1898), Vol. I, p. 89;

G. Elezović, 'Iz putopisa Evlije Ćelebije; njegov put iz Beograda u Hercegnovini; opis Užica 1664 godina', *Istoriski Časopis*, I, (1–2) (1948), 113.

24. Ö. L. Barkan, 'Quelques observations sur l'organisation économique et sociale des villes ottomanes des XVIe et XVII siècles', *Recueils de la Société Jean Bodin*, Brussels (1955), 292–293.

25. T. Stoianovich, 'The conquering Balkan orthodox merchant', *Journal of Economic History*, 20, New York (June 1960), 234–313.

26. An anonymous author described Skoplje (1689/90) as a 'vast market town not much smaller than Prague, or perhaps just as large, with a total population of 60,000 (3,000 Jews)'. Compare with Kriegsarchiv, *Feldakten, Türkenkrieg 1689, fasc. 167(13/1)*, Vols 33–35, Vienna.

27. J. Tadić, *Jevreji u Dubrovniku do polovine XVII stoljeća*, Dubrovnik (1937).

28. M. Franco, *Essai sur l'histoire des Israelites de l'Empire ottoman depuis les origines jusqu'à nos jours*, Paris (1897), (Librairie Durlacher).

29. D. J. Popović, *O Cincarima; prilozi pitanju postanka našeg gradjanskog društva*, Belgrade (1937), p. 128.

30. V. Vinaver, 'Tursko stanovništvo u Srbiji za vreme Prvog srpskog ustanka', *Istoriski Glasnik*, Belgrade, No. 2 (1955), pp. 43–44.

31. N. Todorov has analysed the number of towns in the Balkans in the fifteenth and sixteenth centuries, based on the number of households. Towns with over 1,600 householders increased from 2% in the fifteenth century to 22·2% in the second half of the sixteenth century. N. Todorov, *Balkanskiyat Grad . . .* op. cit. p. 30.

    See also M. T. Gökbilgin, 'Kanunî Sultan Süleyman Devri başlarinda Rumeli eyaleti livalari, şehir ve kasabalari' *Belleten*, XX, Istanbul (1956), 252–266.

32. Lj. Lape, 'Prilog kon izučavanjeto na društveno-ekonomskite i politički priliki na Makedonija vo XVIII vek', *Glasnik na Institutot za nacionalna istorija*, II (1), Skoplje (1958), 102;

    M. A. Silahda, *Tarikh*, Vol. II, Istanbul (1928), pp. 490–491 refers to urban areas destroyed in the Balkans during the Austro-Turkish Wars of 1683–1690.

33. Kriegsarchiv, *Feldakten, Türkenkrieg 1689*, fasc. 167, Vienna.

34. Earlier evidence of this trade comes from Turkish account books in Hungary. See L. Fekete and G. Káldy Nagy *Budai török számádaskönyvek 1550–1580*, Budapest (1962), pp. 577, 578.

35. In 1555, Belgrade was described by Busbecq, Imperial Ambassador to the Porte as 'In front of the city are very large suburbs, built without any regard to order. These are inhabited by people of different nations—Turks, Greeks, Jews, Hungarians, Dalmatians and many more. In fact the suburbs, as a rule, are larger than the towns, and together give the idea of a very considerable place';

    E. Wolfgramm, 'Die osmanische Reichskrise im Spiegel der bulgarischen Haidukendichtung', *Leipziger Vierteljahrsschrift für Südosteuropa*, VI (1942), 36.

36. T. Stoianovich, 'Land tenure and related sectors of the Balkan economy, 1600–1800', *Journal of Economic History*, 13, New York (1953), 389–411.

37. *Enciklopedija Jugoslavije* Vol. 3, Zagreb (1958), p. 546.

38. H. Mehlan, 'Mittel- und Westeuropa', *Südostdeutsche Forschungen*, Vol. III, No. 1, Munich (1938), pp. 69–120 (especially pp. 99–100).

39. Edhem pacha, *L'architecture ottomane*, Constantinople (1873);

    E. Stix, *Bauwesen in Bosnien und Herzegovina*, Vienna (1887);

Ć. Truhelka, 'Gazi Husrev-beg', *GZM* (1912);

A. Haberlandt, *Volkskunst der Balkanländer*, Vienna, (1919);

J. Cvijić, *Balkansko poluostrvo i južnoslovenske zemlje*, Belgrade (1922);

H. Minetti, *Osmanische provinziale Baukunst auf dem Balkan*, Hannover (1923);

M. Karanović, 'O tipovima kuča u Bosni i Hercegovini', *GZM* (1927);

G. Elezović, 'Turski spomenici u Skoplju, *Glasnik SND* (1925 and 1929);

G. Szabo 'Spomenici turskog doba u Slavoniji', *Novosti* (1929), p. 89;

V. Tkalčić, *Seljačko ćilimarstvo u Jugoslaviji*, Zagreb (1929);

V. Skarić, *Sarajevo i njegova okolina*, Sarajevo (1937);

H. Kreševljaković, *Vodovodi i gradnje na vodi u starom Sarajevu*, Sarajevo (1939);

B. Kojić, *Stara gradska i seoska arhitektura u Srbiji*, Belgrade (1940);

K. Peez, *Putopis kroz Bosnu, Srbiju, Bugarsku i Rumeliju*, Sarajevo (1950);

A. Deroko, 'Srednjovjekovni utvrđeni karavan-saraj u Ramu', *Starinar* (1951);

J. Krunić, 'Oblici narodnih kučá Ohrida, Kućenice, Galičnika i Kruševa', *Zbornik radova Arhitektonskog fakulteta*, Belgrade (1951);

Lj. Karaman, *Pregled umjetnosti u Dalmaciji*, Zagreb (1952);

H. Kreševljaković, *Banje u Bosni i Hercegovini*, Sarajevo (1952);

A. Bejtić, 'Banjaluka pod turskom vlašću', *Naše starine* (1953);

Dž. Čelić, 'Musafirhana blagajske tekije', op. cit. (1953);

A. Bejtić, 'Spomenici osmanlijske arhitekture u BiH', *Prilozi Orijentalnog instituta*, Sarajevo (1953);

H. Kreševljaković, 'Naši bezistani', *Naše starine* (1954);

Ć. Truhelka, 'Umjetnost dekoriranja u bosanskoj metalnoj industriji', op. cit. (1954);

J. Krunić, 'Šiptarska kula Plava kao tip stana', *Zbornik radova Arhitektonskog fakulteta*, Belgrade, (1954–56);

Dž. Čelić, 'Kuršumlija medresa u Sarajevu', *Zbornik zaštite spomenika kulture*. Belgrade (1956);

I. Zdravković, 'Džamija i česma na Klisu', *Naše starine* (1956);

Idem. 'Spomenici arhitekture turskog doba', *Jugoslavija* (1956);

K. Tomovski, 'Džamija vo Bitola', *Zbornik na Tehničkiot fakultet vo Skopje* (1956–57);

E. H. Ayverdi, *Yougoslaviya da Türk Abidelari ve vakiflari*, Ankara (1957);

A. Bejtić, 'Povjest i umjetnost Foče na Drini', *Naše starine*, (1957);

D. Bošković, *Arhitektura srednjeg veka*, Belgrade (1957);

M. S. Filipović, 'Ćilimi i ćilimarstvo u našim zemljama do sredine XIX veka', *GZM* (1957);

Đ. Grabrijan and J. Neidhardt, *Arhitektura Bosne i put u savremeno*, Ljubljana (1957);

A. Hadžić, 'Barjakli džamija u Beogradu', *Godišnjak Muzeja grada Beograda* (1957) ;

H. Kreševljaković, *Hanovi i karavan-saraji u BiH*, Sarajevo (1957) ;

Idem. 'Sahatkule u Bosni i Hercegovini', *Naše starine* (1957) ;

K. Tomovski, *Pregled na poznaćajnite turbinja vo Makedonija*, Skopje (1957–58) ;

Lj. Nikić, 'Džamije u Beogradu', *Godišnjak grada Beograda* (1958) ;

H. Dekker, *Dakovo i njegova okolica*, Đakova (1959) ;

Dž. Čelić, 'Počitelj na Neretvi', *Naše starine* (1960) ;

H. Kreševljaković and D. Korkut, *Travnik 1464–1878*, Travnik (1960) ;

H. Šabanovic, 'Postanak i razvoj Sarajeva', *Radovi Naučnog društva*, Sarajevo (1960) ; *Istorija naroda Jugoslavije*, II, Belgrade, 1960, pp. 565–570 ;

M. Gojković and N. Katamić, *Grada za proučavanje starih mostova i akvadukata u Srbiji, Makedoniji i Crnoj Gori*, Belgrade (1961) ;

Meric Refik Melul, *Mimar Sinanin hayati, eseri*, Ankara (1965) ;

M. Samić, *Francuski putnici u Bosni i Hercegovini na pragu XIX st. i njihovi utisci*, Sarajevo (1966) ;

Evlija Ćelebija, *Putopis*, Sarajevo (1967) ;

M. Kadić, *Starinska seoska kuća u Bosni i Hercegovini*, Sarajevo (1967) ;

Dž. Čelić and M. Mujezinović, *Stari mostovi u Bosni i Hercegovini*, Sarajevo (1969).

40. In 1655, Sarajevo had 20,000 Muslim houses and 100 Christian houses.

M. V. Butinić, *Djelovanje Franjevača u Bosni i Hercegovini za prvih vjekova njihova boravka* Vol. II, Zagreb (1883), p. 154 ;

Y. Chataigneau, 'Le Bassin de Sarajevo', *Annales de Géographie*, XXXVII, Paris (1928), 306–327.

41. S. Basagić, *Kratka uputa u prošlost Bosne i Hercegovine*, Sarajevo (1900) ;

Ć. Truhelka, 'Tursko-slovjenski spomenici dubrovačke arhive', *Glasnik Zemaljskog muzeja u Bosni i Hercegovini* (1911), 1–162, 303–350, 437–484 ;

Idem. 'Gazi Husrevbeg, njegov život i njegovo doba', op. cit. (1912), 91–234 ;

M. Prelog, *Povijest Bosne u doba osmanlijske vlade*, I–II, Sarajevo (1912) ;

M. Pavlović, *Pokret u Bosni i Albaniji protiv reforama Mahmuda II*, Belgrade, (1913) ;

Ć. Truhelka, 'Bosnjaci i prvi srpski ustanak', *Glasnik Zemaljskog muzeja u Bosni i Hercegovini* (1917), 245–296 ;

V. Ćorović, *Luka Vukalović*, Belgrade (1923) ;

Idem. Bosna i Hercegovina, Belgrade (1925) ;

V. Čubrilović, *Bosanski ustanak 1857–1878*, Belgrade (1930) ;

V. Skarić, *Sarajevo u doba okupacije*, Sarajevo (1937) ;

V. Popović, *Agrarno pitanje u BiH i turski neredi za vreme reformnog režima Abdal-Medžida (1839–1861)*, Belgrade (1949) ;

B. Đurđev, 'Prilog pitanju razvitka i karaktera tursko-osmanskog feudalizma', *Godišnjak Istoriskog društva BiH* (1949), 101–167;

V. Skarić, 'Iz prošlosti Bosne i Hercegovine XIX vijeka', op. cit. (1949), 7–41;

B. Đurđev, 'O uticaju turske vladavine na razvitak naših naroda', op. cit. (1950), 19–82;

V. Bogičević, 'Kako je u Bosni ukinuta rabota i uvedena trećina 1848', *Istoricko-pravni zbornik*, II (3–4), Sarajevo (1950), 181–199;

N. Filipović, 'Pogled na osmanski feudalizam', *Godišnjak Istoriskog društva BiH* (1952), 5–146.

42. Z. P. Pach, The role of east-central Europe in international trade (16th and 17th centuries) *Etudes Historiques* 1 Budapest (1970), 217–264.

43. M. H. Eichel, 'Ottoman Urbanism in the Balkans: A Tentative View'. *The East Lakes Geographer* Vol. 10 (1975), Bawling Green State University, Ohio, pp. 45–54.

6

Settlements in the South-Central Pelopónnisos, c. 1618

J. M. WAGSTAFF

Introduction

The approach of the Maniats to Charles de Gonzague, duc de Nevers, in 1608–09 sparked a chain of events which produced a remarkable document for the reconstruction of settlement patterns in the south-central Pelopónnisos about a decade later. Charles was not only a pretender to the strategically important Duchy of Mantua, but he was also a claimant to the defunct Greek Empire through his Palaeologian grandmother.[1] Although the last vestiges of Greek independence had vanished from the mainland with the fall of Mistrá to the Turks in 1460, rebellion smouldered amongst the people of southern Greece and occasionally burst into flame, especially amongst the Maniats. They were the fierce inhabitants of the bare and windswept peninsula which carries the ridges of the Taíyetos mountains down from the centre of the Pelopónnisos towards Crete and ends in cliffs and deep inlets around Cape Matapan (Taínaron). Limestones and marbles form much of the Maniat countryside. Soils are thin and stony; other resources are minimal. Surface water is scarce. In consequence, malnutrition was probably almost as commonplace to much of the Máni in the early seventeenth century as it was some two hundred years later. Periodic famines occurred as the results of too little rain or devastating winds.[2] But, for all the hardship of life in the region, the Máni offered its people relative security. It was difficult, though not impossible, to penetrate, particularly by land, but by the early seventeenth century it had lost its long tradition of semi-independence.

In 1608–09, the Maniats wanted assistance to free themselves from the Turkish yoke and to restore their ancient liberties. They were already in touch with Spain and the Papacy, but it was probably through their contacts with the Grand Dukes of Tuscany that they were handed on to Charles de Gonzague through Henry IV of France. Nevers agreed to support them in a joint enterprise which would secure their liberties and foster his imperial ambitions. Agents were sent to the Morea, a formal agreement was drawn up and plans laid. Nothing very substantial had been achieved by 1614, when the scheme seems to have collapsed. The Turks appear to have discovered that something was afoot and took harsh measures against local leaders in Lakonía, whilst the assistance on which the whole enterprise had been made to turn was not forthcoming from France and Spain. But the embers of revolt stayed alive.

A new round of negotiations began about 1616. During them the Maniats tried to pressure the duc de Nevers to honour his earlier promises. The immediate results were a flurry of diplomatic activity at various European courts, in which the famous Father Joseph played an important part,[3] and the foundation of *la Melice chrétienne* as the nucleus for a crusading army. In 1618, Philippe de Chateaurenault was sent on a new mission to the Máni. He was accompanied by a Maniat, Petros Medikos (Pierre de Medici), who had already been closely involved in the unsuccessful negotiations with Spain. Detailed instructions were drawn up for the two agents.[4] They were to collect information about the size of Turkish forces in the Morea (Pelopónnisos) and about the terrain and fertility of the Máni, as well as the availability of supplies. Data were also required about the approaches to, and the defensibility of, two of the region's most southerly harbours, Porto de Caille (Porto Kaío) and Porto Vecchio (Porto Yerolimín), which seem to have been envisaged as possible landing places for Nevers' invading forces. Finally, the agents were instructed to pay particular attention to discovering the number of armed men which the Maniats could supply in the event of a revolt and the quantity and quality of the arms they could produce.

Chateaurenault and Medikos made their reports in 1619, but Nevers' 'badly founded and insubstantial plans'[5] were overtaken by events, in particular the preliminary moves of the Thirty Years War (1618–48). The European war not only absorbed the energies of both Bourbon and Habsburg, but also led to the evaporation of the forces raised by the duc. In 1625 he lost his naval squadron. Nevers' succession to the Duchy of Mantua two years later meant the final end of his Greek plans. Various reports and memoranda were left as 'the most valuable result of the agitation'.[6]

The Document

The most detailed document produced through the duc de Nevers involvement with the Maniats was what appears to be a report on the region's manpower resources. It was found in the Naples Archives by the eminent French scholar, J. A. Buchon, and published as part of his corpus of miscellaneous materials relating to Frankish involvement in the Morea following the Fourth Crusade (1204).[7] Although Buchon's transcriptions have been shown to be inaccurate in places,[8] publication was most fortunate in this case since the document is no longer available for study and was most probably destroyed during the Second World War, along with others in the Archives.[9]

As published by Buchon, the document has two parts. The first is headed, in Italian

'The number of hearths in the villages of the territory from Calamata to the Cape of Mayna and back through Colochitia as far as Passava'.[10]

This is followed by a list of villages and the number of 'hearths' estimated to be found in each. At the end the numbers of villages and 'hearths' were totalled (125 and 4,913 respectively) and the number of 'cambattenti' calculated at 10–12,000, 4,000 armed and 6,000 unarmed. The second section of the document begins immediately under another heading, again in Italian

'38 villages under Turkish rule from the mountains neighbouring on Braccio di Mayna, from Passava and Bardugna castles to Londari called Christianopoli'.

There follows a simple list of village names. The whole document ends with a general statement that there were many villages in the mountains which had not been named but which were prepared to take up arms with the districts of Braccio di Mayna.

Buchon made the plausible suggestion that Petros Medikos was the author of this remarkable document.[11] He was a Maniat and, according to a note against the name Prastio in the document, he stayed in this settlement on his mission to his homeland, though the brief note might also indicate that he was born in the village.[12] The original source of the document's information is more obscure. Medikos might have supplied it from his own local knowledge or through his network of local contacts. A meeting between the Maniats and Nevers' agents may have been the occasion for collecting the data, but the apparent predominance of men from the northern Máni at the only meeting mentioned in the available documents[13] suggests that this could not have been the way in which information was collected about the south of the peninsula. Similarly, feuds and local wars make it extremely doubtful that any network of contacts and relatives available to Medikos in a personal capacity would have stretched the length of the region. A much more plausible explanation than either of these is that, directly or indirectly, Medikos gained access to Turkish statistical sources.

The possibility is suggested in several ways. Practically all the names in the first and fullest list can be shown to have come from within the traditional boundaries of the Máni (Fig. 1). This is a distribution which suggests that a recognized territorial unit provided the basic framework for the data. The Máni was treated as a single administrative unit, subdivided into two or three districts, during the brief period of Venetian rule between 1685 and 1715,[14] and it seems probable that the Republic's administrators simply adopted Turkish practice. The names from the second list have a much more scattered distribution suggesting that they may have been added from defective personal knowledge. It was for settlements in the first list, of course, that the numbers of 'hearths' (fuochi) were noted, and these are data recorded periodically in the 'tahrir daftar-i' (statistical registers) by Turkish officials.[15] We are fortunate in possessing a description of the circuits through northern Maniat villages made by Ewliyā Chelebi in 1670 when

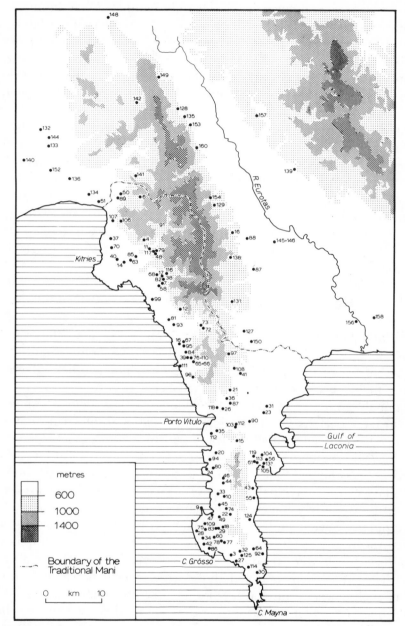

FIG. 1. Settlements in the south-central Pelopónnisos, *c.* 1618—identifications.

engaged in such a survey. He not only estimated the number of houses in each settlement, but also noted the number of musketeers which it could provide.[16] This latter type of information is precisely the sort required by the duc de Nevers and calculated, apparently on the basis of the number of hearths, at the end of the first list in the source under review. Possible survey circuits may be detected by plotting the names from the first list following the order in which they are found in the document. Breaks occur where settlement names cannot be identified, but the sudden shifts from a group of names in one part of the region to another in a different district indicate that a number of genuine circuits lay behind the document as possibly compiled by Medikos (Fig. 2). This is another pointer to Turkish statistical registers as the ultimate source of the document. At the same time, the existence of spatial groups of names within the document proved of some assistance in the identification exercise.

Settlement Identification

The first part of the settlement list contains 125 names. The second has 36 names, though two other places are noted simply as 'another large village of unknown name' and 'another village', presumably because their names had been forgotten or were unobtainable. Identification of the 162 names with settlements known from later periods was guided by the locational information contained in the document's two headings which pointed clearly to the Máni and its vicinity as the area of reference. At a local level the process was helped by following the circuits apparent in the order of names in the original source. Otherwise, the methods used to identify the early seventeenth century names were essentially pragmatic. Seventeenth century maps proved virtually useless in identification, despite their obvious attractions as geographical sources. They were produced on scales which were too small to mark many settlements, and those which were shown often display such a wonderful and intriguing mixture of ancient, modern and imaginary names that they cannot be used successfully in the type of identification exercise being described here. Instead, comparisons were made with names appearing in the lists published by Pacifico and identified by Sauerwein.[17] This was followed by a

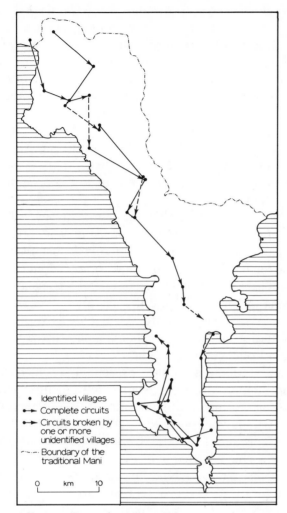

FIG. 2. Examples of possible survey circuits.

similar comparison with names given in a population enumeration and marked on a map of the Morea published by the Commission Scientifique de Morée.[18] An attempt also was made to find modern equivalents in recent sources of settlement information.[19] Where these sources failed to provide clear identifications, recourse was had to the accounts left by travellers who visited the Máni or gathered information about it in neighbouring provinces, though seldom with much success.

Two general and several specific problems were encountered in the identification exercise. The general problems were raised by transliteration and the change of names over time. Italian was used in the headings to the two sections of the document and was employed for the transliteration of settlement names from the original Greek. Direct transliteration was attempted in most cases by the author and it is interesting to observe that the Italian *Ch* was used to render the Greek letters *X* and *K*, perhaps indicating that these had a soft pronunciation in the Maniat dialect of the early seventeenth century, as they do today. The transliteration, however, was neither rigorous nor consistent throughout the document. Italian descriptive or possessive terms were placed before or after a settlement name in several cases, for example, *Paglia* Gianizza and Gliaci-*nova grande*. Sometimes the Greek was partially translated, as in *San* Constantino, but one also finds the forms *Agio* (*"Αγιος*) and *Agia* (*"Αγία*). In one case, the Greek appears to have been completely translated as 'Villa della Madonna di Chelmont' and it was only by very close inspection of the early nineteenth century Carte de la Morée, prepared by the Commission Scientifique, that the suggested identification of Khalasmena Vouni could be made.

Changes in settlement names presented a much more considerable problem. Although some settlements preserved a recognizable form of name down to the early nineteenth century, for example Ardouvista appeared as Androuvista in the enumeration and map produced by the Commission Scientifique, other settlement names have lapsed over the last 140 years (for example, Cutifariagni, Nericista and Nixovo) and, accordingly were difficult to plot accurately. The problem was made even more difficult by a settlement pattern characterized by small dispersed clusters. British Staff Maps,[20] still some of the most detailed which Greek official secrecy makes available to the researcher, gave a general name to several distinct clusters, each of which probably possesses a separate name. Such local names cannot always be discovered from either the available sources or wide-ranging field work for, as W. M. Leake discovered in the Máni as long ago as 1805, 'whenever I inquire of a native of any particular district, he gives me a greater number of names' than the researcher possesses in the lists of place names available to him.[21]

A number of more specific problems were also encountered in seeking to identify the settlements listed in the document. Although Gianizza could be identified with a settlement called Gianitsa *c.* 1830,[22] the suggested identifications of Paglia Gianizza and Panagia di Gianizza which are contained in the appendix were not so obvious. Both settlements appear to have been located in the same general area as Gianizza itself. 'Paglia' is the Italian word for straw and it seemed reasonable to identify Paglia Gianizza with a 'kalyvia' (καλύβια, huts) settlement, consisting of a number of cane and straw huts occupied seasonally from a parent settlement as cultivation or herding requirements necessitated. Such a 'kalyvia' settlement was clearly a dependency and this is often indicated in place names by the attachment of the possessive suffix -'eïka' or -'itika' to the parent settlement's name.[23] It seemed reasonable, therefore, to identify Paglia Gianizza with early nineteenth century Gianitzanika. By a process of elimination Panagia di Gianizza was identified with Kato Gianitsa, a settlement, like Gianitsanika, which was marked on the French map of the Morea but not listed in the early nineteenth century enumeration. There does not appear to have been a settlement called Panagia in the vicinity, either *c.* 1700 or *c.* 1830, which could have been a rival candidate.

A more elaborate but similar process of reasoning was necessary to locate most of the settlements whose names were followed by the phrase 'di Cholochitia'. Two of these settlements, Gognia and Vatas, could be securely identified with early nineteenth century settlements (Gonea and Vata) found in the 'Tmíma' (τμῆμα, section—an administrative unit) of Kolokythia[24] and which have continued in occupation down to the present. The settlements of the early nineteenth century 'tmíma' were arranged largely around the edge of a tract of dissected schist country opening out upon the Bay of Kolokythia. It seemed fair to believe, therefore, that the other 'di Cholochitia' settlements must have been located in the same general area, though Driali di Cholochitia, which could be identified with Driuli (*c.* 1700) and Driali (*c.* 1830), lay a little distance farther to the south. Identification of the basin as Cholochitia seems to be confirmed by the apparent use of the name for a district in the heading to the second part of the document, as well as by Ewliyā Chelebi's reference of 1670 to the six large villages of Kalokituhia. On this basis suggestions have been made for the locations of Castro di Cholochitia, Haitofoglia, Scurta and Voucholia.

Scurta may be Skopá, a tiny island lying off the modern settlement of Kótronas[25] which contains a number of ruins, possibly of mediaeval date.[26] 'Foglia' means leaf in Italian and the name Haitofoglia may have been a partial translation of the name of one of the two settlements which derive their names from plants in the garrigue assemblage—Phlomokhóri (mullein—village) and Riganókhora (marjoram—town/village). Phlomokhóri is preferred here. The settlement contains a mediaeval church at its centre and was probably, therefore, in existence c. 1618. The identification of Vucholia is less certain and was made simply on the basis of similarity in sound between Vucholia and Loukádika, a settlement which appeared in the enumeration and on the map prepared by the Commission Scientifique, though Loudádika can be identified with the settlement called Lusadicu in the first edition of Pacifico's *Breve Descrizzione Corografica del Peloponneso o' Morea*.[27] Castro di Cholochitia appeared to be the most important settlement in the district from its name and estimated population size. With 80 'fuochi' (hearths), it was the largest of the di Cholochitia settlements, whilst its name, Castro ($\kappa\acute{a}\sigma\tau\rho o$), normally meant 'town'.[28] The settlement was probably the same place as Colochina/Colokina/Colocythia mentioned by such late seventeenth century writers as Guillet de Saint-George and Pacifico himself[29] and marked on a number of seventeenth and early eighteenth century maps.[30] Mercator and Kaerius, whose maps were published nearest in time to the document under discussion, both marked it with a symbol indicating its local importance. However, the identification of Castro di Cholochitia with a known later settlement is problematical. Guillet de Saint-George stated unequivocally that Colokina was ancient Gythium[31] and described its location as 'three leagues east-north-east of the island Spatara . . . near to the mouth of the famous river Eurotas'.[32] The position seemed to agree with the identification, for Spatara island was shown on several maps in the correct position for Kranae, the island off the modern town of Yíthion which is partly built over the site of ancient Gythium.[33] Guillet de Saint-George has been shown to be an uncertain guide to topographical identification[34] and no serious assistance could be gained from early maps. The maps did not agree on the location of Colochina/Colocythia, except that it was somewhere on the eastern side of the Máni Peninsular. Some of them showed Colochina and Gythium as widely separated settlements, whilst others marked Colochina and Palaeopoli ('old town'—the actual site of ancient Gythium) as distinct places. In the circumstances, it appeared best to search for Castro di Cholochitia in the early nineteenth century 'Tmíma' of Kolokythia. Local people in the district today refer to the peaked hill which dominates Loukadika as 'the kástro'. Not only has Loukádika already been identified with early seventeenth century Vucholia, but field work also failed to confirm any tentative identification of Loukádika with Castro di Cholochitia. Examination of 'the kástro' hill revealed no traces of fortification such as might have indicated the former existence of a castle there, and thus justified an alternative use of the Greek word 'kástro' (castle) for the settlement. About 30 houses, both occupied or ruined, and many of uncertain date, were found in the village, a number probably insufficient to warrant calling Louká-dika a town. Moreover, available population data suggested that Loukádika had never been the largest settlement in the district.[35] An alternative and more plausible candidate was early nine-teenth century Kotronaes, modern Kótronas. Kótronas has been the largest settlement in the area since at least the early nine-teenth century. It is also located near to the only reasonable anchorage in Kolokythia Bay, a little to the east of Skopá island,[36] so that the settlement could be referred to as a port by late seven-teenth century writers with some credibility.[37] The village is now a fairly compact nucleation containing about 180 houses, with a core of old property near a church at a short distance from the shore, and lies on or near the site of an ancient settlement, Teuth-rone.[38] Its regular street system, together with possession of a number of shops and coffee houses, give Kótronas an almost urban appearance somewhat similar to that of many of the semi-urban communities recognized by the modern Greek census.[39]

The two remaining di Cholochitia settlements, Afungia and Giorgicio-poulo, have not been identified, even tentatively. The fairly large modern settlement of Riganókhora was an obvious candidate for identification with one of them, but there was no means of telling what it should be. There are also a number of

small settlements in the district, such as Loútsa near Loukádika
and Alepoú and Khálika near Kótronas, which could be candidates
for identification with early seventeenth century settlements.
Again, though, there appeared to be no clues to help the investigator, either in the modern place names or in available seventeenth
century sources.

The few examples discussed above should make clear both the
nature and the complexity of the identification exercise. Its full
results are published as an appendix but are summarized in Table I.
Continuity in name seemed to be indicated in 136 cases (78·4 per
cent). Eighty-seven of the 125 settlements named in the first list
have been fairly confidently identified at one or more later dates

Table I

Identification of Early Seventeenth Century Names

Success of identification at different dates	List 1	List 2	Total
No identification	20	5	25
Identification only at c. 1700	2	0	2
Identification only at c. 1830	3	1	4
Identification only with twentieth century names	3	0	3
Identification at c. 1700 and c. 1830	1	2	3
Identification at c. 1700 and with twentieth century names	2	4	6
Identification at c. 1830 and with twentieth century names	56	5	61
Identification at c. 1700, c. 1830 and with twentieth century names	38	19	57
Totals	125	36	161

and suggestions advanced for a further 18, a total of 105. In the
second list, 24 of the 36 names have been identified with reasonable certainty and 7 rather tentatively. In all, 111 names (68·9
per cent) have been fairly securely identified and suggestions advanced for another 25 (15·5 per cent). This measure of success
compares with Sauerwein's proportion of 81·2 per cent for the
whole of the Morea and 76·1 per cent and 79·8 per cent respectively for the Venetian provinces of Messenía and Lakonía, the

units which between them covered the area referred to in the Nevers' document. It must be remembered, however, that there is no way of knowing whether the document aimed at providing a full list of settlements for a particular, but not clearly specified area of the Morea. The first list may be reasonably comprehensive but the second was almost certainly not, as the vagueness over two settlements appears to indicate. In any case, both lists provide a fuller catalogue of seventeenth century settlement names than that which can be assembled from the travel diary of Ewliyā Chelebi who worked in the region in 1670. He mentioned 28 villages by name within the Máni and 8 more from its northern borders towards Londari.

Failure to identify names and thereby to demonstrate continuity between the early seventeenth century and the present is not easy to explain. Abandonment of settlements is one distinct possibility, and it may be significant that a Venetian document of c. 1702 mentioned 14 deserted villages in the Máni,[38] though too much reliance cannot be put on Venetian sources for this region and period since the total of names listed by Pacifico, taking his first and second editions together, is about 78 compared with 125 in the Nevers' source. Any desertion which might have taken place could have resulted either from local wars of the type which were endemic in the region or from the suppression of rebellion by the Turks, as after the Orlov rebellion of 1770 which began in the Máni and was violently suppressed.[39] Neither the Venetian seizure of the Máni in 1685–87 nor the Turkish reoccupation of 1715 seems to have been attended with much violence since the inhabitants assisted at both events.[40] They were also largely successful in keeping the Turkish armies out of the Máni during the Greek War of Independence (1821–29).[41] Emigration, particularly at the end of the nineteenth century, may have been another factor in desertion and hence of the loss of place names. However, three other explanations can be offered for the failure to identify all the names in the Nevers' source. First, the later sources themselves are almost certainly deficient and do not record every contemporary settlement name. There is no way of knowing what has been omitted. Second, some settlement names were probably so disfigured in transliterating the Maniat Greek forms into Italianized spelling that they are no longer recognizable. A final possibility is that settlement names were changed subsequent to 1618 and the earlier forms have not been preserved in the available documentation. A few cases of this are known, for example Tsimova came to be known as 'Areópolis soon after the Greek War of Independence, and there may have been others. Fortunately, a comparatively small number of places remain unidentified and it is possible to reconstruct something of the patterns of settlement in the Máni for the early seventeenth century.

Settlement Distribution

Continuity in name cannot be taken to indicate *a priori* that settlements have occupied precisely the same sites for over three hundred years. Indeed, the frequent destruction of houses and towers in local war and feud, together with the organic process of house rebuilding, should make shifts in settlement site, as well as settlement form, a distinct possibility. However, continuity in name probably means that a settlement has been situated in broadly the same locality since at least *c.* 1618. It is on this assumption that the distribution maps (Figs 1 and 3) have been constructed, using sheets in the *Atlas of Greece* as a base.[42] Figure 3 shows that the settlements in the two early seventeenth century lists were distributed, as the document itself would lead on to expect, mainly along either side of the Taïyetos chain of mountains, which runs for about 115 kilometres from near the centre of the Pelopónnisos to Cape Matapan. A small group was found in the Plain of Messenía, near Calamata, and two rather isolated settlements (Scala and Vlaçhozzotira) were situated on the northern edge of the Helos Plain, which lies at the head of the Gulf of Lakonía. The great majority of settlements, which appear in the first list, lay within the traditional boundaries of the Máni. The concentration of listed settlements in this district is hardly surprising. The first heading in the document provided the clue by referring to Capo di Mayna and the mediaeval fortress of Passava, located in the northeastern corner of the region, whilst the Maniats themselves were ultimately responsible for the production of the document by involving the duc de Nevers in their affairs.

Closer inspection of settlement distribution in the Máni reveals an interesting pattern. Only three settlements were located on the

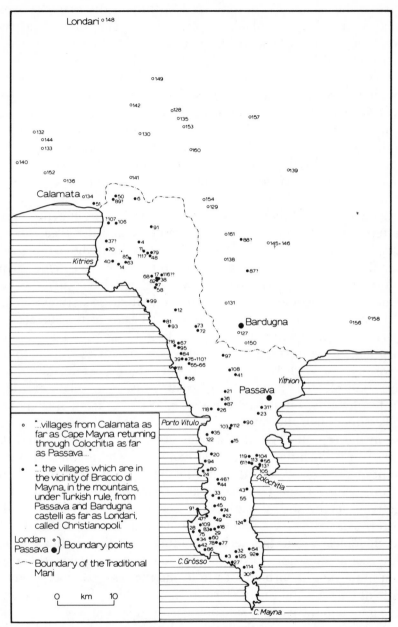

F I G. 3. Settlements in the south-central Pelopónnisos, *c.* 1618—distribution.

coast of the peninsula, despite its length, and the majority were found some distance inland. A possible explanation is the real threat of corsair attack in an area of the Mediterranean where Christian and Muslim disputed control of the seas throughout the sixteenth and early seventeenth centuries. A more likely explanation, however, is that the minute scale of Maniat trade before 1618 rendered coastal settlement largely unnecessary. Such trade as existed could easily have been handled from temporarily inhabited 'skáles', consisting of little more than a few huts and stores near a shore where local craft (caíques) could be beached. Ewliyā Chelebi seems to have been referring to such places when he mentioned the 'harbours' of Zarnata and Milea,[43] since the parent settlements are situated well inland. Most settlements were scattered over moderately sloping terrain behind the great coastal cliffs. They lay rather to the east of, and somewhat above the 'great coastal terrace' which runs along much of the western side of the peninsula.[44] Whilst such a pattern may suggest that security was an element in its development, a peripheral situation may also point to the need to conserve the relatively flat land of the terrace for agricultural production in a region largely classified as 'mixed marginal, agricultural, grazing and waste land',[45] as well as to the importance of slightly deeper soils near the mountain foot. Concentration of settlement was apparent in areas of relatively deep and fertile soils, often where water is available from springs and wells rather than the rainwater cisterns in use almost everywhere else in the region. The area around Ardouvista (No. 7) and the district of Colochitia are the best examples where soil and water conditions are good, but the area in the south-west corner of the region, behind Cape Grósso, is also characterized by patches of relatively fertile soil, though water seems scarce. Away from the western coastal strip, a line of settlements (Nos 23, 90, 112, 103 and 35) picked out the series of interconnecting valleys which allow communication through the mountains between the west coast in the neighbourhood of Vitolo and the east coast between the castle of Passava and the modern town of Yíthion. Few settlements were found on the eastern side of the peninsula, south of Colochitia. The reason was perhaps the lack of cultivable land and good settlement sites in an area marked by steep slopes falling almost directly into the sea, though it seems clear from Ewilyā Chelebi's comments that this was the least visited part of the Máni.

Settlements were totally absent from certain areas. As might be expected, the higher parts of the Taíyetos Mountains in the north of the Máni was one such negative zone. The Kitries Peninsula, where the coastal terrace is widest, and the immediate hinterland of Cape Mayna (Matapan or Taínaron) were also empty. Absence of settlement from these two areas cannot be explained in terms of physical environment. Both areas are characterized by gentle slopes covered with relatively good, cultivable soil and both now contain several settlements. Proximity to the major sea route through the Kíthira Channel (between Cape Matapan and Crete) and its branch towards Calamata, together with the shelter offered by local coves and long narrow bays, may have exposed these two areas to greater corsair attention than that experienced elsewhere.

The largest and most puzzling negative area lay between the north-east coast and a line running through the settlements of Poliazagni, Dombra and Chosea (Nos 97, 41 and 31). Malevri is a district of low, rounded hills and comparatively wide valleys containing perennial streams and it offers the most fertile agricultural land in the region today. It looks ripe for settling. The absence of occupation in the early seventeenth century looks all the more curious, especially when research reveals that the district contained at least 12 settlements by 1830 and contains about 47 now. Failure to collect settlement data is one possible explanation for the observed situation around 1618, but, in that case, it seems odd that the Venetian sources used by Pacifico c. 1700 recorded only one settlement in the district, Lombardo. Several alternative explanations may be offered for future testing. The district provided the easiest route into the Máni and may have been ravaged during the numerous Turkish punitive expeditions launched against the region over the centuries following the fall of Mistrá in 1460. Settlement may also have been discouraged by the presence of Albanian Muslim communities in the Vardhounókhoria which bordered the Máni on the north-east.[46] A more fundamental deterrent to permanent settlement may have been the marshy and malarial condition of the valleys in Malevri. Vita-Finzi has observed a phase of aggradation in valleys throughout the Mediterranean region which may have lasted from perhaps the fifth to the sixteenth century A.D.[47] The valleys in the north-eastern part of the Máni should have shared the experience. Silting, together with a sea level rise of 2 or 3 metres along this section of the coast,[48] may have encouraged marsh formation and led to the spread of malaria which was endemic there, as in the neighbouring Helos Plain, during the nineteenth century.[49] Renewed incision during the seventeenth and eighteenth centuries would have assisted reclamation by improving natural drainage. The stimulus to occupation, however, may have come from population pressure in the rest of the Máni and the Vardhounókhoria and from the need to supply the port of Marathonisi (Yíthion) founded to service the silk industry of Lakonía perhaps during the 1780s.[50] The abundance of state property in the vicinity of Marathonisi shortly after the War of Independence[51] would certainly seem to point to new land becoming available comparatively recently. Late occupation also seems to be supported by foundation stories collected in some of the villages.

Population and Settlement Size

As indicated already, the first list of settlements in the document included a note of the number of 'fuochi' to be found in each community. This was the basis for a calculation of the number of irregular troops which the Máni could supply in the event of a revolt—'at the outside as many as 10–12,000 . . . that is to say, 4,000 armed and 6,000 unarmed'. The figures given for each community are rounded similarly—in units of 10 for 'fuochi' between 60 and 400 and roughly in units of 5 between 20 and 60 —and are clearly estimates. 'Fuochi' themselves appear to be hearths. It is reasonable to assume that the number of hearths corresponded with the number of separate households and that each household was constituted by a single family. If these assumptions are correct, then the total population of the Máni c. 1618 can be estimated. A Venetian document prepared about 1702 gave the total population of the Maniat 'territori' of Chielefa and Zarnata as 3,284 families and 13,462 souls.[52] From these figures, the average size of family at the end of the seventeenth century may be calculated at 4·1 persons. There is no reason to assume that there had been very much change over the century, though the plague of 1687–88 must have had some effect. Accordingly, 4.1 may be used as a multiplier to convert the numbers of 'fuochi' into actual population. The total population of the Máni c. 1618 thus emerges as about 20,704 and that of the average settlement as about 170. The considerable decline during the seventeenth century (36 per cent) may be more apparent than real. The Maniats probably sustained casualties during the Venetian conquest of the Morea (1685–87), in which they played a decisive role, and there must have been some deaths from the plague. However, the possible inaccuracies in Venetian settlement data referred to earlier suggest that the population estimates may also have been suspect.

Population appears to have increased during the eighteenth century to reach a total estimated at about 30,000 in 1805[53] and calculated at 29,037 c. 1830.[54] Natural increase during two hundred years of comparative peace might explain the apparent rise between 1702 and 1830, though there may also have been a certain amount of Venetian-sponsored immigration in the early eighteenth century, possibly from Crete.[55] The early nineteenth century figures, however, suggest that the estimate for 1618 may not be far short of the actual population.

In Figure 4, the estimated number of 'fuochi' in each community have been ranked. It is immediately apparent that the rank size rule, calculated on the formula $Pn = \dfrac{Pl}{n}$ where Pn is the population of the nth settlement in the list and Pl the population of the region's largest settlement, did not apply throughout the series, which was dominated by Vitolo (400 fuochi) and Chelefa (300 fuochi). It almost applied, however, for values below 80 fuochi. Certainly, the rank size rule provided a better fit to the data than its reversal, unlike the situation discovered in rural settlement patterns for modern Ceylon and for at least part of mid-nineteenth century France.[56]

A size distribution completely dominated by two settlements has been described as primate. Such a situation in a pattern of cities has been somewhat tentatively explained by *either* the superimposition of a colonial economy on an underdeveloped country *or* the exercise of political and administrative control from orthogenetic centres.[57] It is perhaps inappropriate to transfer ideas derived from one scale of settlement analysis to another, but in

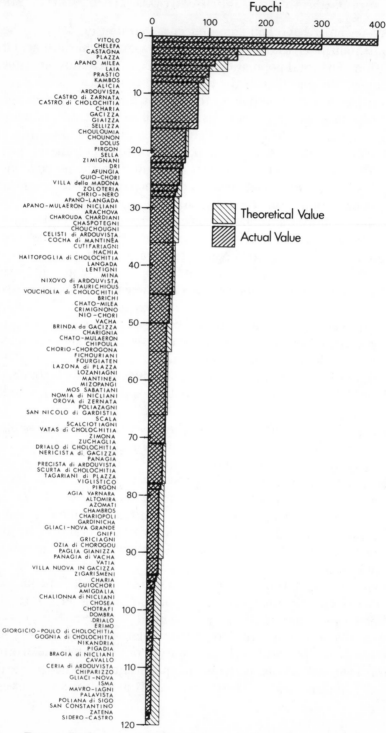

Fuochi

FIG. 4. Rank size order of settlements in the Máni, c. 1618.

this case some interesting results may be obtained. Available economic data for the late sixteenth century and early seventeenth century indicate that the deep bay of Porto Vitulo, near which Vitolo and Chelefa were situated (Figs 1 and 5), was the major port of the region and that the whole of the Máni was not only relatively underdeveloped economically, but was also exporting primary products largely to the territories of Venice, which had itself ruled the region for a brief period at the end of the fifteenth century.[58] Land communication at the time was probably very difficult but Porto Vitulo, situated roughly in the centre of the Máni, would have been accessible by sea from all parts, especially the comparatively densely settled western side of the peninsula. Porto Vitulo may have acted as a collecting centre for local products destined for export and as an entrepot for imports. Vitolo, at least, probably provided the merchants, seamen, drivers and labourers required to handle cargoes at a 'skála' probably situated on the site of modern Karavostási (literally, 'ship stop') on the northern side of the bay. It was the decline of these functions and the curtailment of Vitolo's former commercial privileges which prompted the settlements' leaders to protest to the Venetian governor of the Morea in 1690 about the declined status of their town and which may have led Bellin to comment upon its former commercial importance.[59] At the same time as acting as a commercial centre, Vitolo may have been the centre of an administrative district. The two versions of the original agreement concluded between the duc de Nevers and the Maniats mention the people of Brasso or Bras de Vitulo,[60] along with the people of what appear to have been other administrative units. Chelefa, however, was undoubtedly associated with the administrative centre provided by its neighbouring fortress during the period of Venetian hegemony at the end of the seventeenth century. There is even some evidence to suggest that the fortress was in effect the Venetian capital of the entire Máni at that date.[61] The Venetian 'rettori' at the end of the fifteenth century may also have had their base in the fortress and the Turks may have continued the arrangement during the two hundred years intervening between the two periods of Venetian rule. The date of the foundation of the fortress is crucial here, for its very existence and continuous use, to say nothing of its administrative functions, may go far to explain the relative

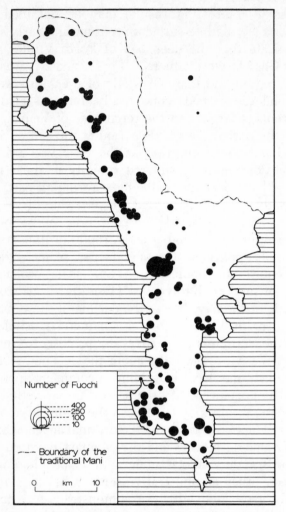

FIG. 5. Size of settlements in the Máni, c. 1618.

importance of the civil settlement, which was first named in the
historical record during 1495.[62] Unfortunately, the origin of the
fortress at Chelefa is a subject of continuing debate. Some scholars
have argued that it must be the same place as 'Grand Magne', a
castle founded in 1249 to contain the Slavs settled on the slopes
of Taïyetos, whilst others have suggested that it may have been a
completely Turkish structure built c. 1669–70, after the fall of
Candia (Iráklion in Crete, 1669) to keep the Maniats in check.[63]

The merits of the various arguments cannot be fully discussed here. Suffice it to say that it is difficult to find an alternative to Chelefa as the site of Grand Magne and that the two may well have been identical, whilst Ewliyā Chelebi referred to the rebuilding of the fortifications in 1670.[64] The existence of the fortress over several hundred years, and its continuous importance as an administrative centre, perhaps go far to explain the size of its neighbouring civil settlement in the early seventeenth century. The administrators, with their clerks and assistants, would probably be accommodated in the village along with their families, whilst the permanent inhabitants of the village no doubt played an important part in the servicing and provisioning of the garrison.

The coexistence of the region's two dominant settlements so close together, but separated by a deep ravine, appears explicable in terms of function. Vitolo was the port and commercial centre and Chelefa the administrative capital of the region.

Most of the second and third ranking settlements were found to the north of Porto Vitulo, though Laia di Chourchougliani lay well south (Fig. 5). The pattern was perhaps the early result of realising the economic potential of the northern Máni, so apparent at the end of the eighteenth century.[65] Administrative arrangements at sub-provincial level may also have been important, though the pattern is almost impossible to recover for the early seventeenth century, despite hints in the agreement between Nevers and the Maniats alluded to above. It was noticeable, too, that the clusters of settlements found in physically favoured areas were dominated by one settlement considerably larger than the rest (Fig. 5 and Table II).

The previous discussion of the location of Castro di Cholochitia has indicated something of the socio-economic, and possible administrative, patterns lying behind this situation. Settlements with 30 or fewer 'fuochi' were concentrated to the south of Porto Vitulo (Fig. 5), in the district traditionally called Mésa ('Inner') Máni. The explanation is probably related to the area's marginal character for agriculture and its limited commerce. Not only are soils thin and stoney, but Mésa Máni is subject to periodic drought and destructive gales. The south always seems to have been the most underdeveloped part of the Máni, sometimes called by non-residents 'Kakavounía' (Evil Mountains) or 'Kakavoulía'

Table II

Ranking of Settlements in Two Specimen Clusters

Ref. No.	Name of Settlement	No. of *Fuochi*
Ardouvista Group		
7	Ardouvista, megali-chora	80
58	Guio-chori	50
68	Lentigni	
82	Nixovo di Ardouvista	40
38	Crimignmo di Ardouvista	35
17	Ceria di Ardouvista	10
Colochitia Group		
13	Castro di Cholochitia	80
1	Afungia di Cholochitia	50
61	Haitofoglia di Cholochitia	40
119	Voucholia di Cholochitia	40
113	Vatas di Cholochitia	30
104	Scalciotiagni	30
43	Driali di Cholochitia	25
105	Scurta di Cholochitia	25
52	Giorgicio-Poulo di Cholochitia	15
56	Gognia di Cholochitia	12

(Evil Counsel) because it enjoyed a terrifying reputation for periodic famines and evil deeds (including piracy and wrecking), whilst possessing a tradition of emigration which can be traced back possibly before the eighteenth century when it is first documented.

Other Information

A number of entries in the document contained notes giving additional information about the settlements. Some of these are straightforward and tell us directly that Prastio was the residence, or possibly the birthplace, of Petros Medikos; Londari was a Turkish town despite its alternative name of Christianopoli; Zatena controlled a pass ('doce e il passo stello'); and that Chariopoli was the seat of a bishop, as it was in later times.[67] Bastan and

Bisbardi were followed by the note 'Albanesi' and Zotira by the phrase 'di Albanesi', which indicate the presence of Albanians in areas from which the Albanian language had vanished by the end of the nineteenth century.[68] This early evidence also disproves Leake's opinion that the Albanian population of the Vardhounó-khoria dated only from the eighteenth century and confirms Philippson's view that it originated with the major Albanian settling of the fifteenth century.[69]

Forty settlements (32·5 per cent) in the first list had a note apparently indicative of possession or association, for example, Precista di Ardouvista and Chounon di Condestauli. The set of such settlements may be divided into 19 subsets (Table III). Eleven subsets contain just one settlement and 3 subsets no more than two places, whilst the rest have 3, 5 and 8 components respectively. Seven settlements carried terms which seem to indicate dependency upon another, larger settlement. The best examples are the Ardouvista group (Table II), in which 5 settlements appear to have been dependencies of Ardouvista itself, and the Plazza grande subset, consisting of 3 settlements. The other 5 subsets consisted of only the 'possessed' or 'associated' settlement (di Chelmont, di Gianizza, di Mantinea, di Vacha and di Zarnata), though in all but one case the 'parent' settlement can also be discovered in the settlement lists (Gianizza, Mantinea, Vacha and Castro di Zarnata). The case of Villa della Madona di Chelmont appears unique and no 'parent' could be discovered. The significance of 'possession' or 'association' cannot readily be discovered. Suggestions which may be tested by further research include the accident of mere proximity resulting from the patchy distribution of relatively good soil, some form of administrative linkage, or possibly a socio-economic relationship, perhaps arising from the foundation of the apparently dependent settlement or settlements by the 'parent' of the group or pair. Three other subsets (di Cholochitia, di Gacizza and di Gardistia) have terms with a form which implies association with a particular district rather than a settlement. The di Cholochitia group is the clearest example. Its territorial associations have been examined already and similar patterns might well be discovered for the other two cases.

A further 7 groups or individual settlements bear phrases which suggest possession or dominance by particular groups of people

Table III

Settlements with Names Indicative of Possession or Association

Name of Settlement Subset		No. of Members
di Chelmont		1
Charouda Chardiani		1
di Chosma		1
di Chorogou		1
di Chourchougliani		1
di Gardistia		1
di Gianizza		1
di Mantinea		1
di Ragusci		1
di Sigo		1
di Vacha		1
No. of Subsets	11	11
di Condestauli		2
di Plazza		2
Sabatiani		(?) 2
No. of Subsets	3	6
da Gacizza		3
di Zarnata		3
No. of Subsets	2	6
di Ardouvista		5
di Nicliani		5
No. of Subsets	2	10
di Cholochitia		9
No. of Subsets	1	9
Totals	Subsets 19	Settlements 41

(Charouda Chardiani, Ozia di Chorogou, Laia di Chourchougliani, 2 settlements di Condestauli, Porastia di Ragusci, Mos and Stio Sabatiani and 5 settlements di Nicliani). All but two of these (di Ragusci and Sabatiani) were found south of Porto Vitulo, that is in Mésa Máni, where clan power appears to have been most well developed and to have lasted longest.[70] Porastia di Ragusci has not been identified, even tentatively. Its name, however, may possibly suggest some connection with the mercantile city-state of Ragusa on the Adriatic but the possibility requires careful examination, despite the known existence of Ragusan colonies in different parts of the Balkans.[71] The other settlements have been located, at least provisionally, and examination of Figs. 1 and 3 shows that, where the subsets have more than a single settlement, all the members are located fairly close together. Spatial proximity may indicate some socio-economic relationship between the settlements. In the case of the di Nicliani group, it is probably significant that the settlements are situated in an area of southern Máni still known as Nikliániko, 'the place of the Nikliáni', and where all the clans acknowledged to be of patrician status are called the 'Nikliáni'.[72] 'Nicliani', the form in the document, is a plural personal name and two explanations of its association with Maniat settlements have been advanced. One, apparently based upon local tradition,[73] is that the name was derived from that of a group of people of mixed Frankish and Greek descent (gasmûli) who fled from Níkli (the mediaeval town on the site of ancient Tegea, near Trípolis in the centre of the Pelopónnisos),[74] at the time of its destruction in 1295 by a Greek army. The theory suggests that this group established itself in Chita, a di Nicliani settlement c. 1618, whose name 'may have some kinship with the Frankish words cité or città'.[75] Although the possibility of such a movement is to some extent confirmed by the early seventeenth century tradition of refugees finding sanctuary in the Máni after the Turkish conquest of the Morea c.1460–1500,[76] it is most unlikely that even 'gasmûli' would have sought safety in one of the core areas of the expanding Byzantine province in the Morea, which had been established in 1262 with the Frankish surrender of the castles of Geraki, Maini, Mistra and Monemvasia together with the territory of Kisterna.[77] Sathas offered an alternative and more convincing explanation of the term Nicliani a long time ago.[78] He thought it was a Neolatin word derived from 'incoliani' (incolae), a term signifying the indigenous possessors of fiefs or possibly of the towers characteristic of the Máni. Some Greek 'arkhóntes' certainly retained their fiefs under Frankish rule[79] and it is possible that the phrase di Nicliani indicates one or more of these. By contrast, the neighbouring settlements bearing the name di Condestauli may have belonged to a Frankish fief, for the name is a direct transliteration of the Greek κοντόσαυλι, itself probably derived from the Old French, 'conestable', signifying the holder of a military office. The existence of fiefs in the Máni is known for the fourteenth century by a grant of 1336 to Nicolas Acciaiuoli and the allocation of 40 fues to Le Meyne in a list of 1391.[90] It seems possible, then, that the settlements bearing a phrase indicative of possession or dominance by a group of people were the components of feudal fiefs and that a mediaeval pattern of socio-economic organization has been fossilized in the early seventeenth century place names. Parallel situations are revealed by some modern English place names. For example, Hurstbourne Priors in Hampshire belonged to the prior and monks of Winchester from before the Domesday Survey of 1086 until the dissolution of the monasteries in the 1530s, whilst Hurstbourne Tarrant, also in Hampshire, was granted to Tarrant Priory, Dorset, in 1266 and retained until the dissolution.[81]

Finally, two names will be found in Table III for which no explanation can be offered at this time (Guio-chori di Chosma and Poliana di Sigo). Failure here reveals the very unsatisfactory nature of much of the foregoing discussion. Much more research clearly remains to be done, but perhaps enough has been said to indicate the importance of the document under discussion as a basis for analysing social conditions in the south-central Pelopónnisos during the early modern period, as well as for the study of settlement patterns in the region. Further research must draw upon documents surviving in local Maniat collections[82] and in Turkey, as well as in the archives of the states (chiefly France, Spain, Tuscany and Venice) whose help the Maniats sought to enlist for their projected rebellion at the beginning of the seventeenth century. Then, indeed, the Maniats agitation will not have been in vain.

Identifications of Settlement Names in South–Central Pelopónnisos,
c. 1618

(names arranged in the order of the Roman alphabet)

Index No.	Settlement name c. 1618	Pacifico c. 1700 (from Sauerwein)	Commission Scientifique c. 1830	Modern
First List (1)				
1	Afungia di Cholochitia			
2	Agia Varnara			
3	Alica	Alica	Alika	Ἄλικα
4	Altomira		Altomira	Ἄλτομιρά
5	Amigdalia			
6	Arachova		Arakhova	Ἀράχοβα
7	Ardouvista		Androuvista	? Χώρα
8	Azomati			
9	Bragia di Nicliani		??Tigani	
10	Brichi	Brichi	Briki	Μπρίκιον
11	Brinda da Gacizza		Brianda	
12	Castagna		Kastania	Καστανέα
13	Castro di Cholochitia		? Kotronaes	? Κότρωνας
14	Castro di Zarnate	Zarnata Fortezza	Fort de Zarnate	
15	Cavallo nel Purcho	Cauallo	Kavalos	(Κάβαλον) Πύρριχος
16	Celisti di Ardouvista		Sélistia	Σελίτσης
17	Ceria di Ardouvista		Tséria	Τσέρια
18	Chaliouna di Nicliani		Kaloni	Καλονοί
19	Chambros	? Colgni		

Continued overleaf

Table IV (*continued*)

Index No.	Settlement name c. 1618	Pacifico c. 1700 (from Sauerwein)	Commission Scientifique c. 1830	Modern
20	Charea	Carea	Karya	Καρέα
21	Charia	Caries	Kéria	Χαριά
22	Charignia	Carignù	Karinia	Καρύνια
23	Chariopoli	Cariopoli	Karioupolis	Καρυούπολις
24	Charouda Chardiani		Karouda	Χαρούδα
25	Chaspotegni	? Chospontinus		
26	Chelefa	Chielefa Fortezza	Kélépha	Κελεφά
27	Chiparizzo		M. Kyparissi	Κυπάρισσος
28	Chipoula	Cipoula	Kipoula	Κηπούλα
29	Chita di Nicliani	Giata	Kita	Κίττα/Κοίτα
30	Chorio–Chorogona		? Korogonianika	? Κορογονιάνικα
31	Chosea		? Khosiari	? Χωσιάριον
32	Chotrafi			Κοτράφιον
33	Chouloumia	Calumia	Kouloumi	Καλούμι/Κουλούμμον
34	Chounon di Condestauli	Cumo	Kouno	Κοῦνος
35	Chouschougni		Kouskouni	(Κουσκούνιον) Σωτήρας
36	Chrio-nero	Crionerò	Kryo-Néro	Κρυονέριον
37	Cocha di Mantinea		? Mandinia	? Μικρά Μαντίνεια
38	Crimignmo di Ardouvista			
39	Cutifariagni		Koutiphari	Θαλάμαι
40	Dolus, detto Chorio	Dolus da basso	Dolous	Δολοί
41	Dombra		Tumbra	(Τόμπρα) Προφήτης Ἠλίας
42	Dri di Condestauli	Dri	Dry	Δρύ
43	Driali di Cholochitia	Driuli	Driali	Δρυαλί
44	Drialo	Drialo	Dryalos	Δρύαλον
45	Erimo		Erimo	Ἔρημος
46	Fichouriani		?? Phrankoulia	? Φραγκούλιας

47	Fourgniaten			? Φουκάλωτο
48	Gacizza–Megali		Mégali-Gaïtsa	Χώρα Γαϊτσῶν
49	Gardinichia		Vardanitsa	Γαρδεδενίτσα
50	Gianizza	Gianizza grande	Gianitsa	(Γιάντσα) Ἐλαιοχώριον
51	Gianizza, Paglia		? Gianitzanika	(Γιαντσάινκα) Φαραί
52	Giorgicio–Poulo di Cholochitia			
53	Gliaci-nova		Gliata	Γλιάτα
54	Gliaci-nova grande			
55	Gnifi	Niffi	Nymphi	Ἔξω Νύμφη
56	Gognia di Cholochitia		Gonéa	Γωνέα
57	Griciagni			
58	Guio-chori		? Xerokhori	Ἔξω Χώριον
59	Guio-chori di Chosma	? Cosma		
60	Hachia		Arkhia	
61	Haitofoglia di Cholochitia		? Phlomokhori	? Φλομοχώριον
62	Ismia			
63	Kambos di Zernata		Kambos	Κάμπος
64	Laia di Chourchougliani	Laià	Lagia	Λάγια
65	Langada		Langada	Λαγκάδα
66	Langada, Apano		Langada	Λαγκάδα
67	Lazona di Plazza		Loutsana	(Λοσνά) Πηγή
68	Lentigni	Leftigni		Λεπτίνι
69	Lozariagni			
70	Mantinea		Mandinia	Μεγάλη Μαντίνεια
71	Mavro-Iagni			

Continued overleaf

Table IV (*continued*)

Index No.	Settlement name c. 1618	Pacifico c. 1700 (from Sauerwein)	Commission Scientifique c. 1830	Modern
72	Milea, Apano ⎫	Milizza	Milia	⎧ Μηλέα
73	Milea, Chato ⎭			⎩ Κάτω Χώρα
74	Mina	Mina	Mina	Μίνα
75	Mizopangi		Pangia	Πάγκια
76	Mos Sabatiani		Somatiani	Σωματιανά
77	Mulaeron Nicliani, Apano	Bularù alto	Apano Boularious	῎Ανω Μπουλαροί
78	Mulaeron, Chato	Bularù basso	Kato Boularious	Κάτω Μπουλαροί
79	Nericista di Gacizza		Nerinda	? Ἀνατολικόν
80	Nikandria		Nikandro	Νικάνδρειον
81	Nio-chori		Néokhori	Νεοχώριον
82	Nixovo di Ardouvista		Nikovos	? Ζαχάρια
83	Nomia di Nicliano	Nomia	Nomia	Νόμια
84	Nomiciagni		Nomitsa	Νομιτσῆς
85	Orova di Zernata	Aroua	Horova	᾽Οροβα
86	Ozia di Chorogou		Okhia	᾽Οχια
87	Palavista		Polovista	Πολοβίτσα
88	Panagia		?? Palaeo-Panagia	Παλαιοπαναγία
89	Panayia di Gianizza		? Kato Gianitsa	
90	Panayia di Vacha			
91	Pigadia		Pigadia	? P. Ρανογιας
92	Piondea	Biondes	Piondès	Πηγάδια
93	Pirgon		Pyrgos	(Πιόντες) ᾽Ακρογιάλιον
94	Pirgon	Pirgo	Pyrgos	Πύργος
95	Plazza grande		Platsa	Πύργος Διροῦ
96	Poliana di Sigo		Polyana	Πλάτσα
97	Poliazagni			Πολιανή
98	Porastia di Rugusci		Polyzaravo	Πολύαραβος

	Prastio		Prastion	Προάστιον
99	Prastio		Prastion	Προάστιον
100	Precista di Ardouvista			
101	San Constantino			
102	San Nicolo di Gardistia			
103	Scala	Scala	Skala	Σκάλα
104	Scalciotiagni		Skaltsotianika	Σκαλσοτιάνικα
105	Scurta di Cholochitia		? Skopa I.	
106	Selizza	Selisma	Sélitsa	(Σέλιτσα) Ἄνω Βέργα
107	Sella		? Selitsanika	? (Σέλιτσα) Κάτω Βέργα
108	Sidero-castro	Sidero Castro	Sidérokastro	Σιδηρόκαστρον
109	Staurichious	Stabri	Stavri	Σταυρίον
110	Stio Subatiani		? Somatiani	? Σωματιανά
111	Tagariani di Plaza		Trakhéla	Τραχήλα
112	Vacha		Vakho	Βαχός
113	Vatas di Cholochitia	Vata	Vata	Βάτα
114	Vatia	Vatica	Vathia	Βάθεια
115	Viglistico			
116	Villa della Madona di Chelmont		? Khalasmena Vonni	Καλομπετσέϊκα
117	Villa nuova in Gacizza		? Biliova–Gaïtsa	? Κέντρον
118	Vitolo	Vitulo	Vytilo	Οἴτυλον
119	Voucholia di Cholochitia		? Loukadikha	? Λουκάδικα
120	Zatena			
121	Zigarismeni			
122	Zimova		Tsimova	Ἀρεόπολις
123	Zinignani			

Continued overleaf

Table IV (continued)

Index No.	Settlement name c. 1618	Pacifico c. 1700 (from Sauerwein)	Commission Scientifique c. 1830	Modern
124	Zoloteria		Soloteri	Σολοτερίον
125	Zuchaglia	Zacaglia		Τσικκαλά

Second List (2)

126	Agia Paraschevi			
127	Agio Nicolo	San Nicola	H. Nikolaos	Ἅγιος Νικόλαος
128	Alevron		Alévrou	Ἀλεύρου
129	Anavreti		Anavryti	Ἀναβρυτή
130	Anustazova	Anastasoua	Anastasova	Νέδουσα
131	Arna	Arua	Arna	Ἄρνα
132	Bastan	Basta	Basta	(Μπάστα) Πλατύ
133	Bisbardi	Bisbardi	Bisbardi	(Μπισμπάρδιον) Ἀσπροπουλία
134	Calamata	Calamata Terra	Kalamata	Καλαμάτα
135	Castagnia	Castagna	Kastania	(Καστανία) Καστόρειον
136	Chazziochono		Katsikova	Κατσίκοβον
137	Chichalo-cori			
138	Chornousta	? Cumusa	Kourtchaouchi	? (Κουμουστά) Πενταλοί
139	Chrizzafa	Crisafà		Χρίσαφα
140	Chuzuna	?? Curzaussi		
141	Chuzzava	Cuzzaua-Caruli	Koutsava Karveli	Καρβέλιον
142	Dorachi	Durachi	Dirakhi	Δυρράχιον
143	Eulogiani			
144	Gaiduro-Chori	Gaidurocori	Gaidourokhori	Ἀριοχώριον
145	Gliandina, Apano }			
146	Gliandina, Chato }	? Clidognia	? Kydonia	? (Κυδωνιά) Κυδωνέα
147	Lapon			

	Londari detto Christianopoli	Leondari Fortezza	Leondari	
148	Longamicho	Longanigo	Longamicho	Λεοντάριον
149				Λογκανίκος
150	Malcina	Malina		(Μαλιτσίνα) Μέλισσα
151	Manezzi			
152	Michrimani	Cuzzucumani	Mikromani	Μικρομάνη
153	Panagia	? Banagia-Loxa	? Panaïti	Φαναΐτη
154	Prasinigo		Barsinikos	? Περγανταίικα
155	Prizza	Brizza		(Πρίτσα) Παλαιόβρυση
156	Scala	Scala	Skála	Σκάλα
157	Stenna		Sitenna	
158	Vlachozzotira	Villachiotti	Vlakhioti	Βλαχιώτης
159	Vriea	? Frizzala	? Fourtsala	
160	Zizzona		Sitsova	Σουστιάνοι
161	Zotira	Sotira	Sotira	Σωτήρα

1. Villagi da Calamata fin al Capo di Mayna et ritorno di Colochitia fin a Passava nel spradetto territorio . . . (. . . villages from Calamata as far as the Cape of Mayna, returning through Colochitia as far as Passava).

2. Villagi 38 chi sono vicini al Braccio di Mayna nelle montagne, sudditi al Turco, da Passava et Bardugna castelli, fin a Londari detto Christianopoli (38 villages which are in the vicinity of Braccio di Mayna, in the mountains, under Turkish rule, from Passava and Bardugna castles as far as Londari, called Christianopoli).

3. H = Hagios, a transliteration of 'αγιος ("saint")

   M = monastery

   P = pyrgos, a transliteration of πύργος ("tower").

Acknowledgement

I wish to thank Professor V. L. Ménage for his kindness in reading the Maniat passages of Ewliyā Chelebi to me. My gratitude is also due to the Cartographic Unit of Southampton University for preparing the maps and to Mrs R. Flint for typing the manuscript.

6. Notes

1. The following account of the duc de Nevers involvement with the Maniats is based on:
Σ. Ι. ΠΑΠΑΔΟΠΟΥΛΟΥ, 'Η κίνηση τοῦ Δούκα τοῦ Νεβὲρ Καρόλον Γονζάγα γιὰ τῆν 'απελευθέρωση τῶν Βαλκανικῶν Λαῶν (1603–1625). Institute for Balkan Studies, Thessaloniki (1966), pp. 26–91, 118–33.

2. W. M. Leake, *Travels in the Morea*, Vol. 1, London (1830), pp. 272, 283, 309; F. C. H. L. Pouqueville, *Travels in the Morea, etc.*, translated from the French by Anne Plumpetre, London (1813), p. 103.

3. A. L. Huxley, *Grey Eminence. A Study in Religion and Politics*, First Collected Edition of Aldous Huxley's Works, London (1956), pp. 125–37.

4. J. A. Buchon, *Nouvelles recherches historiques sur la Principauté française de Morée et ses hautes baronies*, Vol. 1, Paris (1843), pp. 277–79.

5. Cardinal Richelieu's words quoted by M. P. Vreto, 'Tentative d'insurrection dans la Magne au XVIIe siècle', in *Mélanges Néohelléniques*, Athens (1856), pp. 11–20.

6. W. Miller, 'Turkish Greece, 1460–1684', in *Essays on the Latin Levant*, Cambridge (1921), pp. 355–401. The documents concerned are:
    1. Agreement between the Maniats and Nevers. This has to be reconstructed from an undated document (Buchon, op. cit., pp. 262–8) and a memorandum from Nevers to Philip III of Spain dated 1615 (J. A. Buchon, op. cit., pp. 253–61).
    2. Letters from the Maniats to Nevers:
        I. 2 October, 1612 (O.S.). J. A. Buchon, op. cit., pp. 269–70;
        II. 8 October, 1612 (O.S.). J. A. Buchon, op. cit., pp. 270–71.
        III. 8 October, 1612 (O.S.). J. A. Buchon, op. cit., pp. 286–87;

IV. 1618. J. A. Buchon, op. cit., pp. 272–74.

3. Two sets of Instructions, J. A. Buchon, op. cit., pp. 277–79.

4. Reports:
   A. 'On Turkish Forces in the Morea', J. A. Buchon, op. cit., pp. 280–91;
   B. 'Incomplete List of Towns in the Morea', J. A. Buchon, op. cit., pp. 281–82.
   C. 'Two Lists of Villages', J. A. Buchon, op. cit., pp. 283–86.

5. 'Memorandum on the Máni and the Maniats' Design for a Revolt, July, 1619'. M. P. Vrĕto, op. cit., pp. 14–19.

6. 'Speech on the Maniats given by Nevers at Tours on 25 July, 1619'. J. A. Buchon, op. cit., pp. 280–81. See Σ. I. Παπαδοπούλου, op. cit., p. 133.

7. J. A. Buchon, op. cit., pp. 283–86.

8. J. Longnon, and P. Topping, Documents sur le régime des terres dans la Principauté de Morée au XIVe siècle, Paris and The Hague (1969), pp. 20, 32; Σ. I. Παπαδοπούλου, op. cit., p. 133.

9. D. H. Thomas and L. M. Case, (eds.), Guide to the Diplomatic Archives of Western Europe, Philadelphia (1959), p. 145; confirmed by a personal communication from Professor J. Mazzoleni, Director of the Diplomatic and Political Section of the Archivio de Stato di Napoli, dated 2 January, 1970.

10. The Italian of both headings is given at the end of Table IV.

11. J. A. Buchon, op. cit., p. 283.

12. The note reads, Prastio, dove sta il signor Pietro.

13. Letter IV, J. A. Buchon, op. cit., pp. 272–74.

14. A. Pacifico, Breve Descrizzione Corografica del Peloponneso o' Morea, (1st ed.) Venice (1700), pp. 64–69; (2nd ed.) Venice (1704), p. 135.

15. O. L. Barkan, Daftar-i Khākāni, in The Encyclopaedia of Islam, ed. B. Lewis, C. Pellhart and J. Schacht, new edition, Vol. 2, London and Leiden (1965), pp. 81–83;
   Idem. 'Research on the Ottoman Fiscal Surveys', in Studies in the Economic History of the Middle East from the Rise of Islam to the Present Day, ed. M. A. Cook, London (1970), pp. 163–71.

16. Ewliyā Chelebi, Seyāhātnāme, ed. K. R. Bilge, Istanbul (1928) Book VIII, pp. 585–610.

17. A. Pacifico, op. cit., (1st ed.) Venice (1700), p. 69 lists the settlements in Alta Maina and Basso Maina; (2nd ed.) Venice (1704), p. 135 gives settlement names for Territorio di Zarnata and Territorio Maina Bassa.

18. Commission Scientifique de Morée, Relations du Voyage de la Commission Scientifique de Morée, Vol. 2, Pt. 1, Géographie, Paris and Strasbourg (1834), pp. 60–94;
   Idem. Carte de la Morée, 1:200,000, Atlas, Paris and Strasbourg (1835).

19. The most important are:
British General Staff, *1:100,000, Greece*, London (1943), Sheets L6, L7, M6, M7 and N7;
Office National de Statistique, *Population de la Grèce au recensement du 19 mars, 1961*, Athens (1962);
National Statistical Service of Greece, *Atlas of Greece*, 1:200,000, Athens (1965);
Π. OIKONOMAKOY, Χάρτης της Μάνης, 1:100,000, Athens (1925).

20. British General Staff, *1:100,000, Greece*, London (1943), Sheets L6, L7, M6, M7, and N7.

21. W. M. Leake, op. cit., p. 263. He was using the names contained in a poetical description of the Máni written by Nikitas Nyphakos (1748–1818).

22. Commission Scientifique de Morée, *Relations . . .*, op. cit., p. 90;
Idem, Carte de la Morée, op. cit.

23. A. Beuermann, 'Kalyvien-Dörfer im Peloponnes', in *Ergebnisse und Probleme moderner geographischer Forschung. Hans Mortensen zu seinem 60. Geburtstag*, Bremen (1954), pp. 229–38;
A. Philippson, *Der Peloponnes*, Berlin (1892), pp. 583–84.

24. Commission Scientifique de Morée, *Relations . . .*, op. cit., p. 91.

25. British General Staff, op. cit., Sheet M7;
British Admiralty, *Chart 3372, Gulf of Lakonia*.

26. A. Bon, *La Morée franque. Recherches historiques, topographiques et archéologiques sur la Principauté d'Archaïe (1205–1430)*, Paris (1969), p. 508.

27. A. Pacifico, op. cit., Venice (1700), p. 69.

28. Carlo du Fresne, Domino du Cange, *Glossarium ad Sciptores Mediae et Infimae Graecitatis*, Paris (1688), répression du Collège de France (1943).

29. Le Sieur de la Guilletière, (Guillet, A. G.), *Athènes ancienne et moderne*, Paris (1675), p. 56;
Idem. Lacédémone ancienne et nouvelle, Vol. 1, Paris (1676), p. 63;
A. Pacifico, op. cit., Venice (1700), p. 63.

30. G. Mercator, *Morea olim Peloponnesus*, Duisberg (?1595);
P. Kaerius, *Morea olim Peloponnesus* (sic), Amsterdam (?1628);
De Fer, *La Morée et les Isles de Zante, Cefalonie, Ste. Maure, Cerigo . . .* Paris (1686);
D. Randolph, *Morea, olim Peloponnesus*, London (?1686);
N. Visscher, *Peloponnesus, hodie Morea . . .*, Amsterdam (1690);
G. and L. Valk, *Regnum Morae accuratissime divisum in provincias . . . unà cum insulis Cephalonia, Zacynthe, Cythera, Aegina et Sidera*, Amsterdam (?1690);
Sanson, *La Morée et les Isles de Zante, Céfalonie, Ste. Maure, Cerigo . . .*, Paris (1692);
J. B. Homanno, *Peloponnesus hodie Morae Regnum . . .*, Paris (1707).

31. Le Sieur de la Guilletière, (Guillet, A. G.), *Lacédémone ancienne et nouvelle*, Vol. 1, Paris (1676), p. 63.

32. Le Sieur 'de la Guilletière, (Guillet, A. G.), *Athènes ancienne et moderne*, Paris (1675), p. 56.

33. *Π. Ε. ΓΙΑΝΝΑΚΟΠΟΥΛΟΥ, Τὸ Γύθειον*, Athens (1966);
J. M. Wagstaff, 'A small coastal town in southern Greece: its evolution and present condition', *Town Planning Review*, 37 (1967), 255–70.

34. *Biographie Universelle, Ancienne et Moderne*, Vol. 18, Paris (1857),pp. 189–90;
J. M. Osborn, 'Travel literature and the rise of Neo-Hellenism in England', *Bulletin of the New York Public Library*, 67 (1963), pp. 279–300;
J. M. Paton, *Chapters on Medieval and Renaissance Visitors to Greek Lands*, Gennadion Monographs III, American School of Classical Studies at Athens, Princeton, New Jersey (1951), p. 10, note 11.

35. Commission Scientifique de Morée, *Relations . . .*, op. cit., p. 91;
Ι. Ε. Νουχακη, Ἑλληνίκη Χωρογράφα, Athens (1901);
National Statistical Service of Greece, Abstracts from the official censuses, 1920–1951, made for the author;
Office National de Statistique, *Population de la Grèce au recensement du 19 mars, 1961*, Athens (1962), p. 121.

36. The Admiralty Hydrographic Department, *Mediterranean Pilot*, Vol. 4, (8th ed.), London (1955), p. 78.

37. Carlo du Fresne, Domino du Cange, *Glossarium ad Scriptores Mediae et Infimae Graecitatis*, Paris (1688); répression du Collège de France, Paris (1943).

38. Published as an appendix by L. Von Ranke, 'Die Venezianer in Morea, 1685–1715', *Historisch-politische Zeitschrift (Berlin)*, 2 (1833–36), 502.
The revised date was suggested by P. Topping, in *The Minnesota Messenia Expedition: Reconstructing a Bronze Age Environment*, ed. W. A. McDonald, G. R. Rapp. Minneapolis (1972), p. 78.

39. *Τ. Α. ΓΡΙΤΣΟΠΟΥΛΟΥ, Τά Ὀρλωφίκα. Ἡ ἐν Πελοπόννησου ἐπαναστάσις τοῦ 1770 καὶ τά ἐπακολουθα ἀύτης*, Athens (1967).

40. *Κ. Α. ΜΕΡΤΖΙΟΥ, Ποτέ καὶ πώς ἐπεσεν ἡ Μάνη εἰς χεῖρας τῶν τούρκων το 1715', Πελοποννησίακα*, 3–4 (1958–59), 276–87.

41. *Δ. Β. ΒΑΓΙΑΚΑΚΟΥ, Μανιάτικα Α'. Ὁ Ἰμβραὴμ ἐναντίον τῆς Μάνης*, Athens (1961).

42. National Statistical Service of Greece, *Atlas of Greece*, 1:200,000, Athens (1965), Sheets, 3, 29 and 35.

43. Ewliyā Chelebi, op. cit., Book VIII, pp. 589, 595.

44. Naval Intelligence Division, *Geographical Handbook Series, Greece*, Vol. 3, London (1945), p. 200.

45. American Embassy (in Athens), *A General Economic Map of Greece*, 1:200,000, Athens (1947).

46. W. M. Leake, op. cit., pp. 264–65;
Γ. ΚΑΨΑΛΗ, Ἡ Βαρδούνια καὶ οἱ τουρκοβαρδουνιῶτες', Πελοποννησίακα, 2 (1957), 91–140.

47. C. Vita-Finzi, *The Mediterranean Valleys: Geological Changes in Historical Times*, Cambridge (1969).

48. N. C. Fleming, 'Holocene earthmovements and eustatic sea level changes in the Peloponnese', *Nature*, 217 (1968), 1031–32.

49. A. Philippson, op. cit., pp. 216, 487;

M. C. Balfour, 'Malaria studies in Greece. Measurements of Malaria, 1930–1933', *American Journal of Tropical Medicine*, 15 (1935), 301–30.

50. J. B. S. Morritt, 'Account of a journey through the district of Maina, in the Morea', in *Memoirs Relating to European and Asiatic Turkey*, ed. R. Walpole (2nd ed.) London (1818), p. 57;

D. and N. Stephanopoli, *Voyage de Dimo et Nicolo Stephanopoli en Grèce pendant les années V et VI (1797 et 1798)*, Vol. 1, Paris (1800), p. 226.

51. Earl of Carnarvon, *Reminiscences of Athens and the Morea*, London (1869), p. 180. The narrative refers to 1839.

52. L. von Ranke, op. cit.

53. W. M. Leake, op. cit., p. 243.

54. Commission Scientifique de Morée, op. cit., pp. 89–92, using the multiplier of 4.75 suggested by the Commission scientifique on p. 61.

55. Δ. Β. ΔΗΜΗΤΡΑΚΟΥ-ΜΕΣΙΣΚΛΗ, Οἱ Νυκλιάνοι, Athens (1949), pp. 8, 151–58;

La supplica dei Mainotti, in Κ. Δ. ΜΕΡΤΖΙΟΥ, 'Η 'ἐκκλησις τῶν Μανιατῶν πρὸς τοὺς 'ἐνετοὺς κὰτα τῆς Τουρκο- 'Ενετικου Πολέμον,' πελοποννησίακα, 3–4 (1960), 401–4;

Θ. Δ. ΚΡΙΜΠΑ, 'Η 'Ενετοκρατουμένη Πελοπόννησος, 1685-1715,' Πελοποννησίακα, 1 (1956), 315–46; 2 (1957), 247–55;

Σ. Π. ΛΑΜΠΡΟΥ, Δελτίον τῆς 'Ιστορικῆς καὶ 'Εθνολογικῆς 'Εταιρειας τῆς 'Ελλαδος, 2 (1885–89), 228–51, 425–823; 5 (1886–1900), 715–25.

56. A. R. H. Baker, 'Reversal of the rank-size rule: some nineteenth century rural settlement sizes in France', *Professional Geographer*, 21 (1969), 386–92.

57. B. J. L. Berry, 'City size distributions and economic development', *Economic Development and Cultural Change*, 9 (1961), 263–82.

58. The characteristics of Maniat trade were derived from an analysis of cargoes carried by ships sailing to and from the Máni summarized by A. Tenenti, *Naufrages, corsaires et assurances maritimes à Venise, 1592–1609*, Paris (1959), Nos. 18, 83, (?)129, 559, 734, 822, 850, and 946.

Venetian *Rettori del Brazzo di Maina* (1467–76) listed in C. Hopf, *Chroniques Grèco-Romanes*, Berlin (1873), p. 385.

59. Σ. Β. ΚΟΥΓΕΑ, 'Αναφορα τῶν Βοιτυλιωτῶν πρὸς τὴν 'Ενετικὴν Δημοκρατίαν (7 'Απριλίου 1690)', Πελοποννησίακα, 2 (1957), 426–30;

Le Sieur Bellin, *Description Géographiques du Golfe de Venise et de la Morée*, Paris (1771), p. 203.

60. J. A. Buchon, op. cit., pp. 253–61, 262–8.

61. A list of *provveditori* stationed at Chielefa, 1689–1718, is given in Andrea da Mosto, *L'Archivio di Stato di Venezia, indice generale, storico, descrittivo ed anditio, Bibliotheque des 'Annales Institutorum'*, Vol. 5, Part 2, Rome (1940), p. 20.

62. *Δ. Β. ΒΑΓΙΑΚΑΚΟΥ, 'Αρχαια καὶ Μεσαιωνικά τοπωνύμια 'εκ Μάνης*, II,' *Πελοποννησιάκα*, 2 (1957), 302–334.

63. The most recent contributions to the debate are:
   K. Andrews, *Castles of the Morea*, Gennadion Monographs IV, American School of Classical Studies at Athens, Princeton, New Jersey (1953), pp. 25–39;
   A. Bon, op. cit., pp. 502–04;
   K. Kriesis, 'On the castles of Zarnata and Kelefa', *Byzantinische Zeitschrift*, 56 (1963), 308–16.

64. Ewliyá Chelebi, op. cit., Book VIII, pp. 608–10.

65. W. M. Leake, op. cit., p. 310;
   J. B. S. Morritt, op. cit., pp. 109–110.

66. Le Baron L. A. Felix de Beaujour, *Voyage militaire dans l'Empire Othoman ou description de ses frontières et de ses principles défenses, soit naturelles, soit artificilles*, Vol. 1, Paris (1829), p. 39;
   F. C. H. L. Pouqueville, op. cit., p. 197;
   D. and N. Stephanopoli, op. cit., Vol. 2, p. 39.

67. W. M. Leake, op. cit., p. 264.

68. A. Philippson, 'Zur Ethnographie der Peloponnes', *Petermanns Geographische Mitteilungen*, 36 (1890), 1–11, 33–46.

69. W. M. Leake, op. cit., p. 264.

70. J. M. Andromedas, *The Inner Maniat Community Type: A Study of the Local Community's Changing Articulation with Society*, Ph.D. Thesis, Columbia University, 1962; University Microfilms, Ann Arbor, Michigan (1967), especially pp. 71–77.

71. F. W. Carter, 'The trading organisation of the Dubrovnik Republic', *Historickā Geografie*, 3 (1969), 33–50;
   Ragusa's trade with the Morea described in B. Krekic, *Dubrovnik (Raguse) et le Levant au Moyen Age*, Paris and The Hague (1961).

72. J. M. Andromedas, op. cit., pp. 28, 82.

73. *Δ. Β. ΒΑΚΙΑΚΑΚΟΥ, 'Συμβολὴ εἰς τὰ περὶ Νίκλων-Νικλιάνων τῆς Μάνης,' 'Αθήνα*, 53 (1947), 147–94.

74. On the identification of Níkli, O. Markl, *Ortsnamen Griechenlands in 'frankisher' zeit*, Byzantina Vindobenensia, Herausgegeben vom Kunsthistorischen Institut und dem Institut für Byzantinistik der Universität Wien, Bd. I Graz-Köln (1966), p. 48.

75. P. L. Fermor, *Mani: Travels in the Southern Peloponnes*, London (1958), pp. 86–87.

76. J. A. Buchon, op. cit., p. 280;
   M. P. Vréto, op. cit.

77. D. A. Zakythinos, *La Despotate Grèc de Morée*, Vol. 1, Paris (1932), pp. 15–25.

78. C. N. Sathas, *Documents inédits relatifs à l'histoire de la Grèce au Moyen Age*, Vol. 4, Paris (1882), XL–XLI.

79. P. W. Topping, *Feudal Institutions as Revealed in the Assises of Romania*, Philadelphia (1949), pp. 113 and 120.

80. J. Longnon, and P. Topping, op. cit., pp. 20–29; A. Bon, op. cit., Appendix A.

81. W. Page, (ed.), *The Victoria County History of Hampshire and the Isle of Wight*, Vol. 4, London (1911), pp. 288, 319–20.

82. For example, Documents published by:

Σ. Χ. ΣΚΟΠΟΤΕΑ, "Ἔγγραφα ἰδιωτικὰ 'εκ Δ. Μάνης τῶν'ετῶν *1547-1821*,' 'Ἐπετηρὶς τὸν 'Αρχεῖον τῆς 'Ιστορίας τοῦ 'Ελληνικοῦ Δικαίου, *3 (1950)*. 60–117;

Σ. Β. ΚΟΥΓΕΑ, "Ιστορίαι πηγαὶ διά τῆν 'ηγεμονιᾶν της Μάνης (1774–1821)', Πελοποννησιάκα 5 (1962), 60–136.

The last group of documents came from the papers of a branch of the important Grigoraki clan, but the main mass of the Grigoraki archives mentioned by J. M. Andromedas, op. cit., p. 5, are still unpublished.

7

Brač Island, Dalmatia: A Case for Sequent Occupance?

F. W. CARTER

In 1929 Derwent Whittlesey[1] wrote 'Human occupance of area, like other biotic phenomena, carries within itself the seed of its own transformation'. He introduced the term 'sequent occupance' to describe a chronological series of successive cultural geographies of an area and compared it to plant succession in botany. Further he noted that, 'Not only does the recognition of sequent occupance place the current stage in its proper relation to antecedents and to successors; it throws it into true perspective'. The analogy between sequent occupance and plant succession in botany appears obvious, but the former is more difficult to explain. The latter is concerned with only one subject, plant associations, but sequent occupance involves the human occupance of areas, and must take account of changes in any of the complex elements of the natural environment, and equally in the complex cultural forms. Such changes as occur from the inherent character of a particular mode of occupance follow a normal pattern and at length give way to a new consequent mode of occupance. Unfortunately, normal sequences are rare because extraneous forces often interfere with the normal course of events, which in turn alter either its direction or rate, or both. Sometimes they are of a natural physical origin, such as severe earthquakes, landslides, floods, pestilence, etc. but there may also be interruptions of the cultural order. These changes occur more commonly and involve the shifting of political boundaries, revolutions, and enactment of different laws. Other factors are also capable of disturbing the thread of sequent occupance such as movements of population, which carry with them certain attitudes completely novel to the new environment, or create social friction; moreover the introduction of new technology, or changes in the mode of communication affect the method of contact with outside regions. Whittlesey admits that,

'the student of sequent occupance of area is beset with an intricate problem',

but,

'the concept of sequent occupance, when a sufficient number of studies have been made, should point the way to simplification, based on exact statement and detailed observation, whereas all indications suggest the probability that in nature relatively few sequence patterns have ever existed.'

Brač Island

Whittlesey based his conclusion on experience gained in New England, but here it is proposed to examine a small island in the Adriatic off the coast of Yugoslavia. Brač, off the Central Dalmatian mainland, occupies an area of 394·57 km² (Fig. 1). It has been chosen for study because of its wealth in documentary information concerning settlement and urban development. This small island may be described today as a chalk limestone massif, which was formerly part of the mainland, but with the post-glacial rise in sea level has been cut off from the main mountain section. Much of the island consists of bare rock exposures, but there are pockets of fertile flysch and marls, clay and löess deposits scattered throughout the area. The northern coast is precipitous in places and possesses several dry valleys, whilst the southern coast has less steep slopes, and some fertile flysch valleys, particularly around Bol. The highest part of the island reaches 778 metres (Vidova Gora). The climate is Mediterranean, with an average annual temperature on the coast of 16·5°C and 13·8°C inland. The island is exposed to various winds throughout the year, the Bora along the northern coasts, and Burin in the south during the winter, whilst in summer the Mistral and Sirocco are regular visitors. Parts of the island are covered with a tangle of pioneer, deciduous and coniferous, second

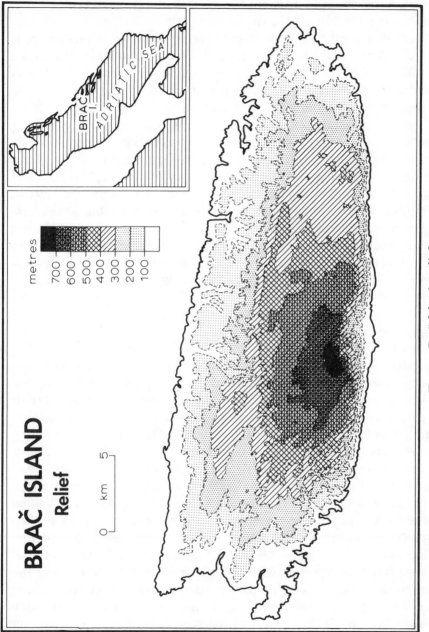

Fɪɢ. 1. Brač Island: relief.

growth forest, whilst inland the gentler slopes have been cleared of forest for cattle and sheep pasture.

On this small Dalmatian island each generation of human occupance has been linked to its forebear and to its offspring, and each exhibits an individuality expressed in some elements of its natural and cultural characteristics. Moreover the life history of each discloses the inevitability of the transformation from stage to stage. The present stage of human occupance was preceded by a long period of farming, mainly in the form of livestock rearing, in which cattle and sheep were allowed to graze over much of the island interior. Preceding this farming stage of occupance, the area had been virgin mixed forest and its human inhabitants had lived a migrant life, depending chiefly on collecting from the forest berries, fuel and game. On the evidence of the present day occupance, and increasing rural depopulation,[2] the future can be forecast with some certainty as an occupance once more by forests, and scrub vegetation, that will be periodically cut by the remaining population for timber etc.

Earliest Evidence

Evidence of settlement on Brač, dates from the Early Stone Age with finds in several parts of the island. Occupance during the Bronze Age gradually gave way to the formation of an Illyrian culture during the Iron Age as witnessed by a number of village settlements and the existence of dry walls found at Bobovišca (Ložišca) etc. The Greek colonization of the Adriatic[3] in the fourth century B.C. appears to have left Brač (xpateiaí-Brateia) unaffected except for two settlements one near Bobovišca and the other which was later to become the village of Škrip. This is the oldest known settlement on present-day Brač, and Rubić believes it came from the Greek word 'skirros' (limestone) and concludes that it was an important quarry for the Greeks.[4] This was an ideal settlement because it had an adequate water supply and use could be made of the stone there.[5] It is possible that another Greek settlement existed on the south-west side of the island near a cave which even today bears the name 'Grka' (Greek) but the proximity to the coast and piratical attacks led to its decline.

Throughout this Graeco-Illyrian period human occupance appears to have been based on hunting. Support for this idea comes from Mayer[6] who believes the island's name originally came from the Illyrian word 'brentos' (deer) and it was later given the Greek equivalent 'Ελαφος hence Elaphusa. With the advent of the Roman occupation cattle and goat breeding became an important branch of the island's economy, together with the exploitation of limestone quarries. Pliny the Elder (A.D. 23–79) mentions Brač's goats in his great work *Natural History* ('Contra Tragurium Baro et capris laudata Brattia'), whilst material for Diocletian's palace in Split came from Škrip (Scripea, 'civitas'; oppidum). Nevertheless the predominant population of Brač at this time was still Illyrian, for both the Greek and Roman elements still remained insignificant minorities throughout the island. The cultural impact of the Romans however, must have been felt for there are still many historical monuments of their work at Donji Humac, Nerežišća, Škrip, Novo Selo and Bol and Roman sarcophagi have been found at Škrip, Dračevica and Bol. The Roman settlements were sited either well inland and dependent on cattle breeding, or on the northern coast of the island within easy reach of quality limestone quarries (e.g. they fortified Scripea in 79 B.C.). Donji Humac and Nerežišća were of the former type, whilst Dol and Podgradišća characterized the latter (Fig. 2). One Roman settlement was located on the southern coast at Bol; it was an important water source, had fertile terrain and harbour facilities for fishing. Even so only three of today's settlements remain from the Roman period, Škrip, Bol and Bunja (at Novo Selo).

Roman Period

Romanization of the island was intensified early in the seventh century. In A.D. 614 the Roman city of Salona, near Split was razed to the ground by the invading Slavic tribes and many of its inhabitants escaped to Brač. Some families later returned to the mainland, but others stayed. According to Ciccarelli over 200 families remained on the island obtaining various privileges and helping to renovate the ransacked town of Scripea, whose inhabitants had moved to the southern coast around Bol, as a result of incessant piratical attacks. With the fall of the Roman Empire, Brač became a neglected backwater off the Dalmatian mainland, which in A.D.

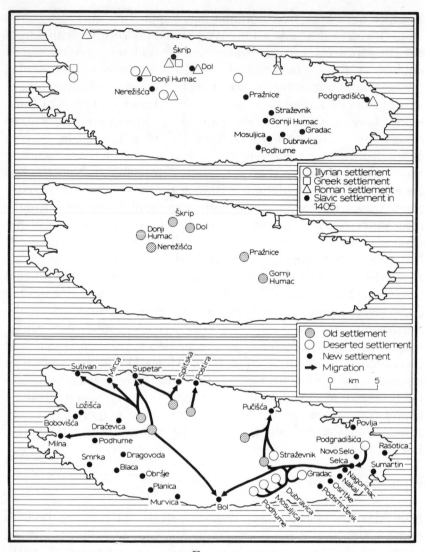

Fig. 2.

670 only had one main settlement, Scripea. Formally it was now under the protection of Byzantium, and a Byzantine fleet was stationed near Gradac. Most of the Romanized population lived in the southern part of the island and in A.D. 872 suffered from a Saracen raid on Bol. Sometime during the first half of the ninth century Slavic colonization of the island began. Immigrants came from the

Neretva region of the Dalmatian mainland and were known as 'Neretljani'. They gradually Slavicized the Brač population, but did not readily assume the former practice of cattle breeding and did not rapidly adopt Christianity. Their main centre, Gradac (gradac uzvišenje—the exalted, elevated place) was inland at the south eastern corner of the island. The Neretljani were still there when, in A.D. 1000, the Venetians occupied Brač. Venetian rule was centred first at Bol and later inland at Nerežišća. The main economy of the Brač population at this time was still cattle breeding and some farming, but the Venetians must have encouraged the development of shipping and commerce; already by the eleventh century the island's trade was subject to attack by piratical groups from the Neretva region.

Early Mediaeval Period

Throughout its early mediaeval history, Brač's inhabitants seemed less worried by foreign domination than by the continued piratical attacks which constantly affected the island's trade and settlement pattern. The Saracen raid of A.D. 872 had forced many of the island's inhabitants to retreat into the interior and in 1175 pirates attacked the monastery at Povlja. Evidence, though meagre, does mention inland settlements dating from the eleventh century. In A.D. 1111 Straževnik is mentioned for the first time, and in A.D. 1184 a monastery document refers to the towns of Gradac, Pražnice and Gorni Humac. Pražnice is the oldest Slavonic settlement on the island, its name derived from 'prag' and 'nica' (—pražiti) which refers to the special primitive process of burning scrub to create new agricultural land; it was noted for cattle breeding. This settlement therefore helps in the recognition of sequent occupance on the island. The period of collecting maintained itself as long as exploitation did not become destructive, but when aboriginal resources failed, the destruction of the forest and scrub itself ushered in the period of farming. Thus the era of idle land and renascent forest, with some incidental grazing prior to more permanent settlement, is seen to represent not a distinct mode of human occupance, but a transition period, in which vestiges of the former casual migratory grazing of marginal areas, gave way to a more permanent settlement pattern.

Other small permanent settlements now appear, such as Mirca, two kilometres from the northern coast, on excellent pasture land and first mentioned at the beginning of the thirteenth century; Murvica, first mentioned in a document dated 1286 as a colony settlement near Bol, was a hamlet noted for its mulberry trees, ('murva'—mulberry). One further piece of documentary evidence from this early mediaeval period is the 'Povaljskoj listini' (an inventory) of 1250, which records names of all the families and settlements on Brač.[7] This old Christian document mentions 150 families on the island, most of them engaged in cattle breeding, but also growing wheat and tending vineyards. The document, written in the cyrillic script, seems to suggest that Brač was already Slavicized by the middle of the thirteenth century.[8] Already during the second half of the eleventh century, Brač had come under the rule of Croatia, and remained until 1279 subject to the Croatian-Hungarian king's authority. Many families had settled on Brač having come from the eastern Neretva region to continue their struggle against the Venetians. Constant fear of attack from either the Venetian galleys or the marauding mainland pirates, meant that no stable settlements were developed along the coast. Some coastal settlements existed, as at Stipanska Luka and Pučiški Dolac near Pučišca, but when attacked the inhabitants fled to the stable inland centres of Pražnice and Straženik.

Between 1278 and 1358 Brač was once more under Venetian rule, and relied on its protection from the pirates of Omiš and the Neretva. After 1358 the island had many owners, including the Croatian-Hungarian king of Bosnia and Dubrovnik.[9] Rule by these various states led to an increase in population growth by immigration. This in turn induced the establishment of new settlements like Dubravica (from 'dubrava'—grove, wood, woodland) first mentioned in 1388, and Podgradišća (from 'pod'—'Gradac'—under the exalted place) a deserted Roman settlement that was recolonized.[10] Thus between the tenth and fourteenth centuries Brač provided a domicile for many people from the Balkan mainland, of which two main migratory streams appear to predominate. The first resulted from the expulsion of Bogomils[11] from Bosnia to avoid religious persecution, and the second was related to people fleeing from Tartar raids (c. 1242) on Split and its immediate hinterland.

According to the Brač poet Dujam Hranković, the population of the island in 1405 was no more than 6,000 inhabitants. He mentioned the names of twelve villages, all inland, eight of which exist today,[12] and two hamlets Gomilje (founded in 1064) and Zajezerčane (1397) which have long disappeared. Population numbers, however, fluctuated greatly as a result of the plague.[13]

Venetian Period

In 1420, Brač once more returned to Venetian rule (until 1797), but, more importnat, in 1444 the Venetians finally conquered the mainland town of Omiš, the main pirate centre, and freed the whole area of further piratical incursions. Prior to this date, all settlements were located inland, away from attack and were dependent on cattle-breeding and goat rearing for their existence. After 1444 many inland settlements were abandoned and coastal centres were established (Fig. 2). This provided a much better situation for the local populace. Previously the inland villages had occupied convenient sites in the karst landscape and the population was largely self-sufficing, procuring from outside only luxuries and some utensils and implements, purchased with the small available surplus of wool, hides and meat. Now the fear of marauding attacks by Turkish and other pirates was passed, and the coastal areas provided improved conditions for the raising of vines, the cattle could be brought nearer to the sea, fishing could be developed and it was also possible to encourage sea communications and trade. Some of the inland villages remained, but the new coastal settlements were to form the embryo of the present day pattern along the northern coast, and around Bol in the south. After the fall of Omiš, many cattle raising villages were abandoned and the people moved towards the sea. The inhabitants of Donji Humac went to Sutivan, Mirca and Supetar. The last place became the harbour for the inland village of Nerežišća and its name was derived from the local St Peter's (Sv. Petar) church. People from Škrip moved to Splitska (the main exporting harbour for stone to Split)[14] and Supetar, from Nerežišća to Supetar, Bol and Milna (from 'milo prud pličina'—a pleasing shallow sand bank), from Dol to Postira (probably from Latin 'pastura'—pasture), and from Straževnik, Gornji Humac and Pražnice to Pučišća. Other inland settlements in the eastern part of the island became depopulated leading in some cases to deserted villages (e.g. Gradac, Podgradišća, Dubravica, Podhume and Straževnik), their inhabitants resettling in Selca, (from 'selo'—village; pluralia tantum—selca), Bol and probably Gornji Humac.

The inauguration of an occupance stage can be set in motion when certain intermediary factors begin to alter, either subtly or grossly, the previous situation. A political instance of the principle appears in the unification of a large and diverse area under a single system of government; despite advantages derived from solidarity, the inhabitants of marginal areas feel the application of many of the laws as hardships. Such was the case with Brač, when the island became part of the Venetian empire, after 1420. Their occupation affected the island's economy in three main ways, in agriculture, boatbuilding and immigration. The first two topics were developed to help support the empire's population and wars of conquest, the latter to provide an outlet for the people from the mainland who wished to escape from Turkish domination, and those from Venetian territory under constant threat from Ottoman attack.

The Venetian officials on Brač wished to improve the island's agricultural economy, but this was immediately fraught with problems. In the days before Venetian rule the division of pasture and cultivated land was made on a communal basis. It was a rule, even in Roman times, that cattle belonged to the owner on whose pasture they grazed, and the inhabitants associated together as a community when discussing the problem of land ownership, a tradition carried over to the first centuries of Slavic colonization. The church also owned land during the mediaeval period; for example the Croatian bishopric had possessions around Bol, as did the Benedictine monastery at Povlja. With the advent of Venetian rule, and its emphasis on agricultural development, the first struggles over landownership took place. The centre of the dispute arose over individual farmers wishing to feed their cattle on reduced pasturage because much had now been converted to arable. Only three years after the Venetian takeover the question of pasture ownership led to the Brač Statute of 1423. The document refers to a consultation between ten of the island's noblemen (5 from the higher villages, 5 from the lower) from whom the Venetian officials required decisions on pasture rights. The nobles found that there were 119 pastures under private ownership (called 'stani')[15] on Brač. In future the landowner could now keep one thirteenth of his pasture, the remainder to be utilized for cultivation; in addition he was asked to cultivate the arable land and failure to do so after three years meant automatic loss of the land. Use of the church's land for cultivation by a farmer carried a rent equal to one sixth of his annual income to be paid to a church official. This situation led to many quarrels and involved much cheating and deception on the part of the farmers and landowners over the next two centuries; in 1603 an order was given that all arable land must be ploughed and not used for any other purpose. Generali Providur Marossini in 1623 stated that 'If anyone in future takes even the smallest area of arable land and change back its real purpose e.g. to that of grazing, the owner must immediately change its alternative use to one of cultivation.' Further, Marossini prohibited the use of common land by individual owners as it was there for the benefit of all inhabitants. In spite of these various laws the Venetian officials had to intervene over pasture disputes on many occasions, and illustrates how the Venetian Republic, whether intentionally or not, was involved in settling the agrarian problems of Brač.

Greater safety at sea, the establishment of new coastal settlements and the emphasis on diversified agricultural production all led to changes in the human occupance of Brač which entered upon a new stage of development. Cattle breeding from now on was far less important in the island's economy, though still significant inland, and greater emphasis was placed by the Venetian officials on the cultivation of vines, olives, figs, mulberry trees and various Mediterranean fruits. Vine growing had been known on Brač since Roman times, but inland sites had never favoured their development. Olives were also grown but usually in poor soils on steep hill slopes. Better coastal sites for both these crops increased production; some of the best wine in Dalmatia was made on Brač, especially from the vineyards of the Hvar bishopric on the southern facing slopes around Bol. The island was self-sufficient in wine, the surplus being exported to Venice or sold to the Venetian army, according to a report by two Venetian officials (A. Dieda and B. Giustiniano) in 1552,[16] but a disastrous frost in 1550 had harmed the fig trees and the Venetian government forbad low quality figs

from being exported for several years. Many fig trees were uprooted and the land put to arable but again this led to Venetian
intervention; their officials had to prohibit the export of oxen for
they were now in great need for ploughing. The new arable land
was given over to cereal production (the island's supplies increasing from two months to nine/ten months of annual demand and
planting olive groves; even so supplies were still inadequate and
had to be supplemented by imports of oil from Apulia and cereals
from the Dalmatian mainland. Fishing also became important,
particularly for sardines and mackerel.

Evidence for industrial activity on Brač during Venetian rule
mainly refers to boatbuilding and quarrying. Many of the islands
and towns of Dalmatia were well known for their boatbuilding
activity, e.g. Dubrovnik,[17] Hvar, Korčula, etc.,[18] but there is very
little information concerning Brač. Admittedly, the long period of
confinement to inland settlements had not encouraged the growth
of any tradition in the boatbuilder's art, but the raw material base
for the trade, namely the Brač jasmine and black pine forests, was
in plentiful supply on the island during the Venetian occupation.
In 1511 a Brač prince lent the town of Split 22 boats and 400
people, and the Venetians used parts of the southern coast for their
galleys' winter quarters near to the arsenal at Bol. Other galleys
used the harbour at Pučišća on the northern coast (from Latin
Puteus = brook, stream), established in 1467 in one of the most
wooded parts of the island.[19] Thirteen fortresses surrounded the
settlement from possible Turkish attack (hence its alternative
name of 'Luka-kula' = harbour fortress) and it is possible that
boatbuilding was pursued here but there are no extant documents
to prove it. Unfortunately neither Bol nor Pučišća provided safe
shelter from the Bora and Sirocco winds. One document does confirm that boatbuilding did take place at Bol during the sixteenth
century. Dated 1576, it refers to a Venetian syndicate (D. and A.
Gustiniano) that had gained concessions to build houses near the
boatyard, on land close to the flood-gate (li detti moli),[20] and
mentions an earlier letter of 1574 concerning house building near
the yard by a local person Marco Veniero. On the basis of this
document it appears certain that boatbuilding activity did exist in
Bol during the latter decades of the sixteenth century. One reason
why boatbuilding during this period may have been veiled in

secrecy, results from the presence of Uskok pirates from Senj (Zengg, N. Dalmatia), who may have utilized boats made on the island. In 1586 there was an Uskok settlement at Pučišća, whilst in 1596 one Juraj Lenković asked the Pope for protection against the pirates from Brač. In some cases Brač inhabitants solicited the help of the Uskoks in their struggle against the Venetians, and one Christopher Valieri noted in 1596 that the island was becoming another Senj (quasi nuova Segna). A year later a document records (24/VI/1597) that Giovanni Bembo besieged Brač for the Vatican and found 300 Uskok pirates.[21] It is interesting that in previous centuries the inhabitants of Brač had lived in fear of piracy and welcomed the occasional help of the Venetian warships, but once the Venetians gained control of the island its people looked to their former enemies for help in resisting the Lion of St Mark. Little evidence of boatbuilding is found for the later years of Venetian rule, but in one petition written at the end of the eighteenth century it states that boats built on Brač were used to carry products throughout the Adriatic, Mediterranean and Black Seas. The same document contains a plea by Brač citizens for free trade in wheat from mainland areas, and asks to be allowed the free export of goods without the taxes or dues.[22]

Brač stone has been famous since antiquity as a building material. By the second century A.D. the Romans were using stone from the Brač quarries for constructing the town theatre in Salona (Split), as evidenced by a stone tablet found near Škrip ('centurio Quintus Silvius curagens theat/ri/'). The Brač chronicler Vicenzo Prodi (1628–1663) in a document dated 1662[23] mentions the use of Brač stone for building Diocletian's Palace at Split ('taglio de sassi nella Brazza per la construczione de Palazzo, at latre Fabriche di Diocleziano'). At the beginning of the nineteenth century Ciccarelli states that in A.D. 286 best quality Brač stone was chosen for building the Emperor's palace at Split and that even today (1802), the stone quarries can still be seen below Škrip and above Splitska.[24] The Emperor even had special boats built (naves lapidariae) to convey the stone from Brač to Split. On completion of the palace in A.D. 305 the quarries seem to have been abandoned, but again reappear in documents of the fifteenth century. Brač stone was used in the construction of Šibenik cathedral as mentioned in a treaty of 1451 ('quod ipse se proximo trafferet ad insulam Brazae et ibi sibito laborabit'). Another document dated 1455 states that Andri Alesi, a stone mason on Šibenik cathedral, made an order for the purchase of Brač stone[25] and later used the same material on work in Italy (Tremiti). In 1493, Nicola Firentinac, a stone mason, wrote about the qualities of Brač stone and in 1502 used it to build a church in Valvedere (Italy) choosing 'dove ando a taiair le piere e pagar le maestranze'. Although most of the quarries were located around Škrip, another important place at this time was at Straževnik.

The Venetian occupation of Brač also affected the island's economy through immigration. As Whittlesey maintains

> 'Interruptions of the cultural order engendered by man occur even more commonly: shifts in political boundaries, . . . movements of population which carry with them mores and attitudes novel to their new habitat . . . are capable of breaking or knotting the thread of sequent occupance.'[26]

The situation on Brač was fundamentally altered by the Turkish occupation of the Balkan interior and subsequent 'open-door' policy of the Venetian government towards refugees fleeing from the Ottoman incursions. Increasingly during the second half of the fifteenth century there was a flow of immigrants to the Venetian held Dalmatian coastland from those areas subject to the dangers of Turkish attack. Many people came to the Central Dalmatian islands; for example between 1463–1469 immigrants from Hercegovina (as witnessed by their surnames, Kukretić, Cikarelović, Ostojić) came via Poljica on the coast to Brač, whose numbers by 1500 totalled 150 emigres.[27] A Venetian official recorded the island's total population as 5,000 inhabitants in 1503, which indicates that the emigres still only formed a small part (3 per cent) of Brač residents. Further estimates of population size are difficult, but in 1525 two Venetian officials recorded that 900 men on Brač were fit for military service.[28] Jutronić has estimated that for every 100 inhabitants, 20 were fit for military service (i.e. 1:5), and on this basis the island's population in 1525 would have been 4,500 people.[29] In 1537, the Venetian Republic captured part of the mainland opposite Brač from the Turks (Poljica). Despite further immigration from here and other areas, the Venetian officials stated in 1553 that the island had a total population of only 2,700 inhabitants (of which 600 were suitable for conscription).[30] Brač had twelve important villages and seven good harbours. Therefore comparison between Brač's population in 1405 (Hranković: 6,000 inhab.), and 1553 shows a decline of 3,300 people in spite of immigration from other areas, a great loss over the 145-year period. This deficit is best explained by successive plagues in 1425–1427 (two-thirds population died),[31] again in 1434–1436,[32] and 1526, and the wreck of the island's galleys in 1489 with large loss of life. In 1490 there were only 231 houses on the island and the people were extremely poor.[33]

In contrast to this dismal picture on Brač, the general situation in Dalmatia, according to the English traveller T. G. Jackson, was very different. He states that despite

'the terror of Turkish invasion which from this time forward hung like a cloud over the country till the Turkish power itself began to decline, Dalmatia under the settled government of a great commercial power advanced rapidly in wealth and prosperity. The arts flourished, noble buildings sprang up, the treasuries were enriched with beautiful work of the goldsmith or silversmith'.[34]

It is perhaps true that the Venetians did not feel the full onslaught of the Turk until after the defeat of Hungary at Mohacz in 1526, and despite their differences and their periodic warfare, Christian and Turk settled down to live side by side. The coming of the Turk had, however, further increased the Slav character of the coastal cities, for refugees from the interior entered Christian territory (e.g. Brač). These new immigrants founded several settlements on the island. Bobovišća, in the western part, was 3 km from the sea on fertile pasture. The name is derived from 'Bobovac' a village in Bosnia, and the original home of many immigrants who came here after the Turkish invasion. The first recorded family in Bobovišća was Krstulović, a surname still found in Bobovac today. Another new settlement near here was Dračevića, at the western end of Nerežišća polje. Records again reveal the first occupants to be the Simunović family from Poljica, and along with other early names indicate that the inhabitants came here from the Dalmatian mainland; emphasis was probably on horticulture and viticulture, the name Dračevića coming from the slavic word (draza) referring to the enclosure of vineyards and gardens with wooden fencing. People from the Makarska region of the Dalmatian coast also settled at Selca during the Turkish invasion, whilst others founded the small hamlet of Dragovoda ('precious water') near Nerežišća, for cattle breeding purposes. Similarly, Blaca hamlet nearby was also established by families from Poljica in 1550.

The pirate community of Uskoks from Senj, themselves in origin a band of refugees, through their piracies in the Adriatic, directly led to a renewal of war between Venetian and Turk during 1571–1573. The reports and diaries of Venetian agents provide an extremely interesting picture of the relations between Christian and Moslem along the Dalmatian frontier itself at this time, the various raids, challenges to single combat, rough courtesy and chivalry, to be met with amongst the antagonists of the two faiths, for as one Venetian wrote, 'no nation are all evil alike'.[35] The peace of 1573 left the Dalmatian frontier more or less as it had been, each party regaining what had been lost, but for Brač it meant a share in the 350 families from Poljica who were allowed to settle on Venetian territory. According to Dukla Moceniga[36] there were forty refugee families living in the eastern part of the island on 31/XII/ 1574; at this time a village was established here by Poljica families ('Nove Selo = New village') as a result of the Venetian re-population policy.[37] In 1579, August Valiera, Bishop of Verona, visited Brač and gave information on the names and population of individual settlements. He notes that on the coast Sutivan had 150 inhabitants, Mirca 12, Supetar about 60, Postira about 100, Pučišća 250, Bol 400 and Splitska had 5 houses; inland he found that Dol had 140 people, Škrip 200, Donji Humac 70, Nerežišća 500, Gornji Humac 120 and Pražnice 230.[38] If one assumes that each house in Splitska had five people then the new coastal settlements totalled 997 inhabitants and the older inland centres 1,260; thus of the overall total population (2,257), 56 per cent still lived inland. Ten years later a Venetian official, Mateja Zane, recorded that Brač had a population of 3,544 inhabitants, of which 873 (25 per cent) were fit for military service.[39] This large increase between 1579 and 1588 was not due to natural increase only but to continued immigration from Poljica, to be further incremented at the end of the century by people from the mainland. In 1596 the Turks captured Poljica and 300 families came onto Venetian soil.

Church records on Brač from the early part of the seventeenth century refer to this new wave of immigration, for example in 1612 there were 37 'pastures' amongst the eastern villages of the island and specifically refers to one 'Stjepan Ostojić and the other new population' who possess pasture at Goranjice;[40] families from Poljica were recorded at Postira in 1616, and Sutivan in 1626.[41]

War between Venice and Turkey did not break out for over seventy years after 1573. In 1645, the pasha of Bosnia entered Dalmatia at the head of a large army and after intermittent warfare in Dalmatia and elsewhere, peace was declared in 1669. The Candian War, as it was known, led to further immigration to Brač. In 1645 the Venetian Republic issued an edict whereby women and children from the Makarska region could go to live on Brač, and resulted in 500 new immigrants; by 1669 there was a total of 230 new immigrant families on the island,[42] supplemented by a further 180 families in 1672.[43] One settlement in particular dates from the Candian War (Fig. 3). Sumartin, one of the eastern villages was founded in 1645 by people from Bosnia and Hercegovina, especially from the Imotski region. It is one of the most recent settlements on the island and was formally called Vrh Brača ('Bračian Heights'), but changed to its present name in 1890, after the church of St Martin. Hostilities again broke out between Venetian and Turk in 1684. The Lion of St Mark captured the Morea and its armies were able to drive the Turks back from the seaboard of Dalmatia into the interior, leading to the Treaty of Carlowitz in 1699, one of the most disastrous treaties suffered by the Turks.

During the War of Morea another 25 families arrived on Brač in 1684 from Makarska, many of them originally having come from Bosnia/Hercegovina as a result of the Turkish occupation,[44] whilst two years previously a Venetian official, Cornaro, recorded Brač as having 5,224 inhabitants (2,579: male; 2,645: female).[45] Thus despite Brač being the largest island in Central Dalmatia and successive waves of immigration, it still did not have the population of nearby Hvar (7,243); however it did have more than the major mainland town of Split and its suburbs (4,567).

One piece of information referring specifically to settlement was recorded by the Brač poet, Prodi, for the mid-seventeenth century. He gave a list of places which included two towns, three villages

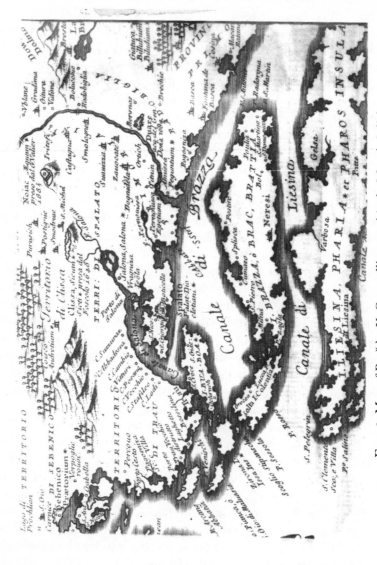

FIG. 3. Map of Brač by V. Coronelli 1678. (Arch. Muzej, Split).

Table I
Population of Brač Island: 1682
(from Cornaro's Census of Venetian Dalmatia 1682)

	Men	Women	Boys	Girls	Total
Brač Island	1,688	2,040	891	605	5,224
Whole of Venetian Dalmatia	23,530	25,686	14,649	14,432	78,285
Brač's per cent	7·17%	7·94%	6·08%	4·19%	6·67%

on the coast, four villages inland, four castles and several hamlets in the island's interior.[46] Although probably not a complete list, it does support the other evidence in the establishment of new settlements on the coast. Actual and estimated population for Brač between 1579 and 1763 (Fig. 4) shows a growth for most of the coastal settlements, whilst some of the inland centres like Gornji Humac, and Pražnice declined in numbers.[47] Many of the new settlements were located along the northern coast due to favourable harbour sites, whereas the southern coast consisted mainly of uninhabitable karst and steep cliffs. During the eighteenth century changes also took place in its economy when cattle-breeding was superseded by olive and vine growing. This led to the further decline of many inland centres dependent on cattle for their livelihood. Two accounts by Fortis[48] in 1774 and 1778 state that Brač had nineteen settlements and 13,000 inhabitants (av. 684 inhab/ each), which according to Garagnin[49] only reached 10,988 people at the fall of the Venetian Republic in 1792.

Emphasis throughout the period of Venetian occupation of Brač has been on immigration, but there is also evidence to suggest that some emigration from the island to the Dalmatian mainland took place. Documents in Split archives record the movement of people from Brač to Split between 1570 to 1830 and these have been recently analysed by Jutronić.[50] He found that people from Brač came to Split (which is only 14 km from Sutivan) for various periods, some permanently. From the various birth, marriage and death certificates he found 624 cases of Brač inhabitants moving to the mainland; many people were born in the northern coastal settlements, particularly Sutivan, Supetar, Pučišća and Postira.

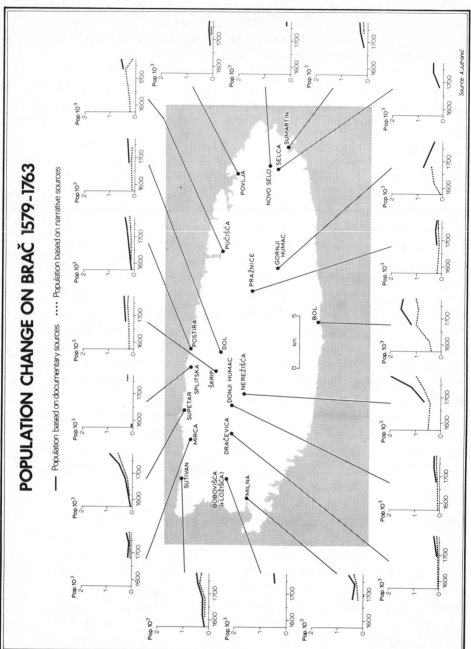

FIG. 4. Population changes on Brač: 1579–1763.

The era of Venetian rule came to an end on Brač in 1797. Perhaps the greatest impact it had was in agriculture. The gradual colonization of Brač from the fifteenth to the nineteenth century led to strong agricultural development. Albert Fortis during his second journey to Dalmatia (1787) stated that Brač had more vineyards than previously (1774) but trade in wood and livestock had decreased. Pasture on the Brač hills was excellent and both the sheep and goat meat was of good quality. Emphasis was placed on sheep rearing because they were less dangerous to the young forests than goat herds. Cheese from Brač was not well known and the island's wool was of bad quality. Honey production was important, the beehives being constructed using local slate. Brač wine was the best in Dalmatia and there had been an increase in the number of olive, almond and fig trees planted; cereal production satisfied local demand and saffron had been successfully grown, but fishing was declining in face of competition from other islands like Vis.[51] The decline of livestock production formerly so important for the island's economy when it was centred inland, resulted from the Venetian insistence on agricultural diversification, leading to the desertion of some inland villages for the more amenable, coastal sites. By the fall of the Venetian Republic in 1797, Brač's livestock compared unfavourably with other parts of Central Dalmatia:[52]

Table II
Livestock in Central Dalmatia, 1797

	Oxen	Sheep and goats	Pigs	Horses, mules, asses
Split	2,210	20,000	600	1,000
Poljica	1,000	7,000	700	200
Korčula	200	4,000	250	500
Hvar and Vis	60	3,000	100	600
Brač	73	3,000	94	700
Total for Dalmatia	80,292	1,032,970	18,280	22,730
Brač as percentage of Central Dalmatia	2·06%	8·10%	5·38%	23·33%
Brač as percentage of Dalmatia	0·09%	0·29%	0·51%	3·07%

One other aspect of Whittlesey's notion of sequent occupance follows on from his assertion that

'A political instance of the principle appears in the unification of a large and diverse area under a single system of government; . . . ultimately the political unit breaks up or becomes a federation of loosely connected entities with a large degree of local autonomy'.[53]

The case of Brač before, during and after Venetian rule regarding local autonomy is relevant in this respect. By the Late Middle Ages many Dalmatian towns operated their own municipal charters, even under Venetian control. The island character of Brač stimulated the evolution of an independent administrative system which began in the fourteenth century and continued to function, though less effectively, in the seventeenth and eighteenth centuries, until the end of Venetian occupation. The statute of Brač (1305) based on Roman antecedents, is considered to be one of the oldest in Dalmatia, and served as a model for other islands,[54] covering urban as well as rural residents. The statute dealt especially with the relationships among people whose main occupature, oleoculture, cattle and sheep rearing, fishing, cereal production and other forms of limited agriculture. The regulations dealt specifically with the relations between peasants and landowners, arable and grazing land held by a municipality, restrictions on grain exports and wine imports to protect the local producers. While Brač remained a separate entity within the Venetian Republic, often in competition with other Dalmatian islands, all under differing degrees of autonomy, the similarity of the basic system provided an ideal framework for regional cohesion. This led to a certain degree of population interchange, e.g. from Poljica, and valuable experience in the evolution of a legal system; both significant factors for consistency and homogeneity in urban development. Violich, for example, has recently asserted the importance of administrative institutions in the urban development of Dalmatia.[55] Autonomy reached its peak on Brač at the end of the seventeenth century, coupled with vigorous settlement growth. Unfortunately, stricter Venetian control during the eighteenth century weakened local autonomy on the island, and with the fall of Venice in 1797 a struggle began between the Brač noblemen and landowners for control of the island. Any vestiges of autonomy that remained were virtually extinguished at the beginning of the following century by Napoleonic forces.

Contemporary Scene

The present stage of human occupance on this small Adriatic island was immediately preceded by a thoroughgoing subjection of the land to viticulture. All the gentler slopes were used and some of the scrubland cleared to accommodate for the increased wine demand in the nineteenth century. The prosperity from the vineyards increased during the second half of that century when places like Sumartin had important links in the wine trade with the northern Adriatic ports of Trieste and Fiume (Rijeka—Susak). This in turn stimulated other branches of the economy, such as boatbuilding concentrated around Bol, and the island's population rose from 10,683 inhabitants in 1813[56] to 24,408 by 1900 (Fig. 5). Unfortunately, this prosperous period was not to last for as Whittlesey points out

> 'Strictly speaking, normal sequences are rare, perhaps only ideal, because extraneous forces are likely to interfere with the normal course . . . so called acts of God, whereby one or another element of the natural complex becomes abruptly and profoundly modified. Such are . . . insect or other biological pests'.[57]

On Brač, as in other parts of Dalmatia, the first decade of this century witnessed the arrival of phylloxera, a genus of plant-lice related to the aphids, which attacks the grape vine, and systematically destroyed many vineyards not only here but in other parts of Europe. As attested by numerous walls and foundations of boulders and by written record, the vineyards fell into disuse many never to be revived; the people, disillusioned, began again but many decided to emigrate to the New World. The close of this stage of occupance might have been postponed by the construction of improved transportation (roads) and consequent modification from subsistence to more interdependent agriculture, had not the shipping companies at the same time opened to settlement and to competition the far more favoured lands of North America and Australia. Left to itself, land on Brač promptly began to recreate

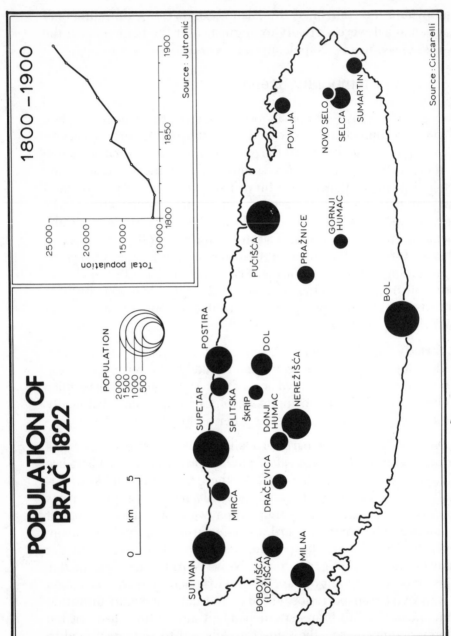

Fig. 5. Population of Brač: 1822.

forest and scrub, which has ironically again become one of the keys
to the island's future. This time it is to be utilized in conformity
with the present day patterns of human occupance in Yugoslavia—
as an export potential for scenic tourism, and timber for constructing summer cottages and second homes. Thus not only does the
recognition of sequent occupance place the current stage in its
proper relation to antecedents and to successors; it throws it into
true perspective. In the Brač Island example the present era of idle
land and renascent forest, with some grazing, represents not a distinct mode of human occupance but a transition period in which
vestiges of the farming epoch linger on in the more fertile parts of
the island. Similarly, many of Brač's present inhabitants reflect
former immigration to the island for recently Jutronić has analysed
the surnames of 844 families living on Brač prior to the Second
World War. Surname origin revealed that 54 per cent of the families had initially come from the Dalmatian mainland and islands,
whilst a further 22 per cent were very old Brač names; the rest
(24 per cent) had arrived from other parts of Yugoslavia and
abroad (Fig. 6), indicating the areas of strongest in-migration
during the preceding four centuries.[58]

Conclusion

This study of Brač Island has been based on a genetic approach, in
order to find out how things came to be where they are, or were,
and the agents behind them that generated change. Use of Whittlesey's concept of sequent occupance has provided a useful framework for guidance, and certain influences give strength to his
arguments. Two main forces appear to have prevailed in lending
sequent occupance to the evolution of the settlement on Brač
Island. One was the physical character of the area, its ruggedness
and isolated valleys affording places of refuge for self-selective
populations whose concern for personal and group independence
was paramount. The other was the existence since early times of a
network of towns and villages already sufficiently firmly established to receive these newcomers and integrate them into the local
population. Further, among the smaller inland settlements there
was less contact with the outside world and even more dependence
on themselves for development. Conversely, the small ports,

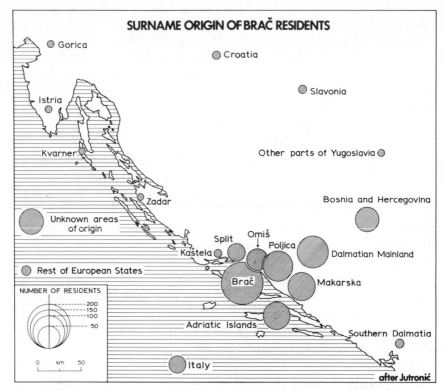

F IG. 6. Surname origin of Brač residents (after Jutronić 1940).

established during the Adriatic peace secured by Venice, became as 'urban' as the larger mainland towns, whilst the inland centres remained as agricultural settlements with a lower level of cultural development. Some of the coastal towns, however, succeeded in forming links with inland agricultural areas (e.g. Sutivan and Pučišća) and led to their growth in the seventeenth and eighteenth centuries, despite Venetian restrictions on commercial development.

Further exploration and recognition of sequent occupance on this Yugoslav island appears an attractive path to follow, which hopefully would lead to an understanding of the complexity which springs from the infinite interplay of many elements of the natural and the cultural landscape common to many other studies. In fact as Whittlesey maintains

'the concept of sequent occupance, when a sufficient number of studies have been made, should point the way to simplification impossible under the purely descriptive discipline. . . . Instead, the continuous but varicolored woof of human life is woven with the firm but not uniform warp of areas into a strong yet supple texture, pleasingly varied but always orderly in pattern'.[59]

The question therefore arises as to whether Brač Island fitted the pattern of sequent occupance first envisaged by Whittlesey? Certain negative factors suggest that this is not the case. Firstly, the application of any theoretical model to test and explain sequent occupance on Brač would have its difficulties. The two basic factors of production at the pre-industrial level, land and man-power, had to increase to achieve growth in the surplus product. Manpower on Brač was constantly being ravaged by plague, shipping disasters or compulsory military service, whilst certain areas of coastal land were uncultivatable up to the mid-fifteenth century due to constant piratical attacks. Transport facilities were limited on the island, whilst other factors, such as social organiza-tion, autonomy and the legal system, would be difficult to quantify in such a model. Admittedly, inland Brač must have come close to an idealized closed system together with its agricultural hinter-land, but little is known of local control groups and their influence over surplus production to calculate such facts as maximum settle-ment size. Secondly, there are obvious weaknesses in Whittlesey's assumption that development progresses in orderly preordained sequence of steps as in the biological analogy. In the history of the occupance of an area there is no predictable sequence of events, and therefore no inevitable progression from stage to stage as in genetic geomorphology or vegetational succession. This criticism has been adequately stated by Prince that

'Human landscapes neither grow in an organic sense nor do they die. They are made and are worn out and the human groups that occupy them may abandon their work for a variety of reasons, at their own volition or under pressure from outside forces'.[60]

This has been aptly illustrated on Brač Island with the movement from the inland to coastal settlements after the supression of pira-tical incursions. Furthermore,

'Occupants may if they so decide move. Areas may be colonized and invaded from elsewhere and the cultures of resident populations may be transformed by contacts with alien cultures. Unlike landform or plants people can learn to change their habits, their behaviour and their activities . . . Human landscapes are not evolved in isolation, they are shaped by complex processes of cultural transference, acculturation, absorption and replacement'.[61]

Therefore, suffice it to say that Brač Island has illustrated the life history of each generation of human occupance, but not independent development in situ, as this is very much the exception rather than normal in human history.[62]

7. Notes

1. D. Whittlesey 'Sequent occupance' *Annals of the American Association of Geographers*, 19 (Sept. 1929), Cambridge, Mass., 162–165. Amongst the literature on this subject one may also include:

Stanley D. Dodge, 'Sequent occupance of an Illinois prairie', *Bulletin Geographical Society Philadelphia* 29 (1931), 205–9;

L. F. Thomas, 'The sequence of an areal occupance in a section of St. Louis Missouri', *Annals of the American Association of Geographers*, 21 (1931), 75–90;

J. O. M. Broek, *The Santa Clara Valley, California: A Study in Landscape Change* Utrecht (1932);

S. D. Dodge, 'Bureau and Princeton community', *Annals of the American Association of Geographers*, 22 (1932), 159–209;

R. B. Hall, 'The Great Lakes' 167–8;

Derwent Whittlesey, 'New England', 168–70, contributions to 'Round Table on Problems in Cultural Geography', *Annals of the American Association of Geographers*, 27 (1937);

Richard E. Dodge, 'The interpretation of sequent occupance' *Annals of the American Association of Geographers*, 28 (1938), 233–7;

E. A. Ackerman, 'Sequent occupance of a Boston suburban community', *Economic Geography* 17 (1941), 61–74;

Alfred H. Meyer, 'Toponomy in Sequence Occupance Geography: Calumet Region, Indiana-Illinois', *Proceedings of the Indiana Academy of Science* 54 (1945), 142–59;

J. S. Matthews, *Expressions of Urbanism in the Sequence Occupance of North-eastern Ohio*, Chicago (1949);

Shannon McCune, 'Sequence of plantation agriculture in Ceylon', *Economic Geography* 25 (1949), 226–35;

Norman L. Nicholson, 'The establishment of settlement patterns in Ausable watershed, Ontario', *Geographical Bulletin*, 1 (1952), 1–13;

Preston E. James, 'Towards a further understanding of the regional concept', *Annals of the American Association of Geographers* 42 (1952), 195–222;

E. C. Highoe, 'The Three Earths of New England', *Geographical Review* 42 (1952), 425–38;

R. S. Thomas, *The Changing Occupance Pattern of the Tri-State Area, Missouri, Kansas and Oklahoma* (Chicago, 1953);

Alfred H. Meyer, 'Circulation and settlement patterns of the Calumet region of north west Indiana and northeast Illinois', *Annals of the American Association of Geographers*, 44 (1954), 245–74; 312–56;

M. W. Mikesell, 'Comparative studies in frontier history', *Annals of the American Association of Geographers*, 50 (1960), 85–97;

P. L. Wagner and M. W. Mikesell (eds), *Readings in Cultural Geography*, University of Chicago Press (1962), Chicago, pp. 218–47;

M. Mikesell, 'Landscape' Enc. of Soc. Science, University of Chicago Press (1970).

2. M. Friganović, 'Suvremeni Geografski Problemi Naših Otoka' *Geografski Horizont*, VIII (1–2), Zagreb (1962), 10–24.

3. F. W. Carter *Dubrovnik (Ragusa) A Classic City State*, Seminar Press, London and New York (1972), 710 pp., Fig. 9;

A. Jutronić 'Kako je Brač dobio ime' *Večernji Vjesnik*, No. 95 Zagreb (5/IX/1957), p. 9;

D. Rendić, 'Da li je i na Braču bilo grčkih kolonija?', *Brački Zbornik*, No. 2, Split (1954), 10–21.

4. I. Rubić, *Naši otoci na Jadranu*, Split (1952), p. 120.

5. A. Ciccarelli, *Osservazioni sull' isola della Brazza e sopra quella nobilità*, Venice (1802), p. 207.

6. A. Mayer, 'Studije iz toponomastike rim. provincije Dalmacije', *Vjesnik za arheologiju i historiju dalmatinsku*, Zagreb (1932).

In old documents the island is referred to as Braxia, Bractia, Brettia, Brachia, Britanide, Brattia, Bracia, Elaphusa and in Italian Brazza.

See A. Jutronić, 'Bračka naselja i proijeklo njegovog stanovništvo', *Brački Zbornik*, Split (1940), 8;

I. Ostojić, *Benediktinska opatija u Povljima na Braću*, Split (1934), pp. 176.

7. J. Vrana, 'Kulturnohistorijsko značenje povaljske ćirilske listine iz godine 1250', *Filogija*, 3 Zagreb (1962) 201–218.

8. This is the first time the Slavonic name 'Brač' appears in a document, which Fisković believes is a later development of the Italian 'Brazza'. C. Fisković, 'Javni spomenici starijeg doba u Dalmaciji', *Nova Doba* (25/XII/1939), Zagreb, p. 3.

9. F. W. Carter, op. cit., p. 193–194; from 1358 to 1390 Brač was under the Bosnian king; by 1394 again under a Croatian-Hungarian king; 1403–1413 under Duke Hrvoj Vukčić, 1413–1416 it belonged to the Dubrovnik Republic; 1416–1420 under Sigismund of Luxembourg, and in 1320 returned to Venice until 1797.

10. A. Jutronić, *Naselja i porijeklo stanovništva na otoku Braču?* Zbornik za narodni život i običaje J.A., Zagreb (1950), p. 8.

11. A. Solovjev 'Bogumulentum und Bogomilengräber in den Südslavischen Ländern', *Völkern und Kulturen Südosteuropas*, München (1958), p. 173–199; M. Spinka, *A History of Christianity in the Balkans*, Chicago (1933).

12. A. Jutronić, 'Dujam Hranković i njegov opis Brača iz g. 1405', *Brački Zbornik*, XLV, Split (1951), 37–51; A. Ciccarelli, *Osservazioni sull' isola della Brazza e sopra quella nobilità*, Venice (1802), pp. 91–94.

13. *Diverzi pubblici decreti terminazioni privilegi et indulti a favor della magnif. Communita della Brazza*, Udine (1656), pp. 19–20, and 80.

14. P. Didolić, 'Historijski Brački Kamenolmi', *Brački Zbornik*, No. 3, Split (1957), 98–106.

15. A. Jutronić, 'Agrarni odnosi na Braču u doba Mlečana, *Nova Doba*, Vol. 7, No. IV, Split (1928), pp. 23–34. The pastures were divided between Nerežišća (54), Donji Humac (9), Škrip (7), Dol (11) and Pučišća-Bol (38).

16. S. Ožanić, *Poljoprivreda Dalmacije u prošlosti*, Split (1955), pp. 11–36.

17. F. W. Carter, op. cit., pp. 308–313.

18. B. Kojić, 'Brodogradnja na istočnom Jadranu kroz vijekove', *Pomorski Zbornik*, Vol. I, Zagreb.

19. A. Ciccarelli, *Narazione istorica di Castel Pucischie nell' Isola Brazza*, Venice (1823), Archaeological Museum, Split (Document No. 48 H. 22).

20. A. Jutronić, 'Brodogradalište u Bolu na Braču u 16 stoljeću', *Pomorstvo*, No. 1–2, Split (1955) p. 31.

21. *Pomorska Enciklopedija*, Vol. I, Zagreb (1959), p. 557, (Nak. Lek. Zav. F.N.R.J.).

22. ibid., p. 558.

23. V. Prodi, *Cronaca dell' isola della Brazza* (1662), pp. 2. (Document in City Museum, Split); A. Jutronić, 'Vicko Prodić i njegova "Cronaca dell" isola della Brazza' *Starine J.A.* 45, Zagreb (1955), 331–388.

24. A. Ciccarelli, op. cit., p. 208.

25. Zadar State Archives (2/V/1455), *Fond:stari splitski*; archiv svez XXV, Civil V, fol 1676.

26. D. Whittlesey, op. cit., p. 165.

27. M. Sanudo, *Diarii*, Luglio (1496) (Split Archives), p. 92; A. Pivčević, *Povijest Poljica*, Split (1921), p. 61.

28. Relatio nobilium Leonardi Vinerio et Hieronymi Contareno sydicorum ad partes Dalmatiae. Presentat 27 octob. 1527, pp. 18–19, *Monumenta spectantia historiam Slavorum meridionalium. Commissiones et relationes Veneta*, Vol. VIII, Tome I (S.L. Ljubić) Zagreb (1887).

29. A. Jutronić, 'O stanovništvu i naseljima srednjedalmatinskih ostrova od početka XV do sredine XIX vijeka', *Glasnik Srpskog Geografskog Društva*, XXXII (2), Belgrade (1952), pp. 129–137;
A. Jutronić, 'Bosansko-hercegovačko porijeklo nekih Bračana', *Zbornik radova Srpska Adakemija. Nauka*, Belgrade (1951), pp. 203.

30. Itinerario di Giovanni Batista Giustiniano, Monumenta . . . op. cit., pp. 217–223.

31. Diversa pubblici decreti op. cit., pp. 19–20.

32. A. Ciccarelli, op. cit., p. 56.

33. Diverza pubblici decreti, op. cit., p. 80.

34. T. G. Jackson, *Dalmatia, The Quarnero and Istria*, Vol. I, Oxford (1887) p. 143.

35. J. Gardner Wilkinson, *Dalmatia and Montenegro* Vol. II, London (1848), pp. 297–350, which gives long extracts from these reports and diaries for the period 1571–1574.

36. Diverzi pubblici decretia, op. cit., pp. 105–106.

37. M. Vrsalović, 'Otoka Brača' *Obzor*, No. 8, Zagreb (11/I/1935).

38. A. Jutronić, 'Apostolska vizitacija otoka Brača g. 1579', *Croatia sacra*, No. 5, Zagreb (1933), pp. 62–88.

39. Ibid., p. 71.

40. G. Vitnico, *Privilegi della mag. Comunità della Brazza. Terminazioni de Sindici, molte Parti, Decreti e Atti Pubblici, Commissioni de Rettori et diversi casi segnati per ordine de tempi copiati nel presente Libro*, Venice (1765), p. 181.

41. G. Novak, *Hvar*, Belgrade (1924), pp. 115–117.

42. G. Mladineo, *Libro primo di Diverze ducali e Terminazioni intorno l'armamento della Gallea, della Brazza*, Archaeological Museum, Split (1670), pp. 91–94.

43. F. Madirazza, Storia e costituzione dei comuni dalmati, Split (1911), p. 64

44. G. Novak, 'Naseljavanje otoka srednje Dalmacije u novum vijeku', *Jadranska straža*, No. 3, Split (1938), p. 99.

45. Venetian State Archives, *Descrition dell'anime della Provintia di Dalmatia et Isole de Quarner, fatta l'anno 1682 per ordine del Ill.mo et Ecc.mo Sign. Gir.mo Cornaro. Proved. Gen. in Dalm. et Alb.*, Relazioni, Coll. V. Secreta Fasc. 72.

46. V. Prodi, *Cronaca dell' Isola della Brazza de Dalmatia,* Split Archives, (1660), p. 2.

47. A. Jutronić, 'O Stanovništvu i naseljima . . .' op. cit. pp. 129–137.

48. A. Fortis, *Viaggio in Dalmazia,* Vol. II. Venice (1774), p. 279; *Idem., Topografia Veneta,* Venice (1787), p. 377.

49. G. L. Garagnin, *Reflessioni economico-politiche sulla Dalmazia,* Vol. I, Zadar (1896); V. Lago, *Memorie sulla Dalmazia,* Vol. I, Zadar (1896), pp. xxvi–xxvii.

50. A. Jutronić, 'Prilog poznavanju veza Splita s Bračanima' *Brački Zbornik,* 3 Split (1957) 10–16.

51. A. Fortis, op. cit., (1787), p. 258.

52. S. Ožanić, op. cit., p. 36.

53. D. Whittlesey, op. cit., p. 162.

54. *Statuta municipalia ac Reformationes Magnif. Communitatis Brachiae,* Vtini MDCLVI apud Nicolaum Schirattum. (Written in 1305, published in 1656); K. Kadlec, 'Statut i reformacije otoka Brača '*Monumenta historico-juridica Slavorum meridionalium* Vol. XI, Zagreb (1926), p. 11; A. Cvitanić, 'Srednjovjekovni Statut Bračke Komune iz god. 1305', *Brački Zbornik,* 7, Supetar (1968), 18–32.

55. F. Violich, 'An urban development policy for Dalmatia. Pt. 1: The urban heritage to the time of Napoleon.' *Town Planning Review,* 43 (2), Liverpool (April 1972), 162–163.

56. Copia del prospetto officiale al No. 6595 dell' anno 1815 dal governo di Zara . . . con la chiusa dell' anno 1813, ossia del dominio franceze' in V. Lago, *Memoria sulla Dalmazia,* Vol. I Zadar (1869), pp. XXVI–XXVII; A. Ciccarelli, Narazione istorica . . . 'op. cit., statistical supplement at end of work; *Almanaco della Dalmazia per l'anno 1831,* Zara (1831), pp. 226–227; *Manuale provinciale della Dalmazia,* Zara (1845), pp. 29–48.

57. D. Whittlesey, op. cit., pp. 164–165.

58. A. Jutronić, 'Historički i Umjetnički Spomenici na Braču', *Brački Zbornik,* Vol. 1, Split (1940); *Idem.,* 'Naselja na Otoku Braču', *Brački Zbornik,* Vol. 4, Zagreb (1960).

59. D. Whittlesey, op. cit., p. 165.

60. H. C. Prince, 'Real, imagined and abstract worlds of the past', *Progress in Geography,* Vol. 3, E. Arnold, London (1971), pp. 12–13.

61. Ibid., p. 13.

62. M. W. Mikesell, 'The rise and decline of "sequent occupance": a chapter in the history of American geography' in *Geographies of the Mind,* ed.D. Lowenthal and M. J. Bowden, Oxford University Press, New York (1976) Ch. 6, pp. 149–170; P. Šimanović, *Brač,* Zagreb (Grafički Zavod Hrvatske) 1976.

8

Geographical Knowledge Amongst the Ottomans and the Balkans in the Eighteenth Century According to Bartinli Ibrahim Hamdi's Atlas

Cengiz Orhonlu†

In Islamic civilization, works written on the various aspects of geography have titles such as *Sūrat al-ard, al-Masālik wa'l-mamālik, Ilm al-Turuk,* and *Kitāb al-Buldan* ('The Navel of the Earth', 'Roads and Countries', 'Science of Roads' and 'Books of Countries'). Al-Biruni considered his *al-Masālik* as a science which dealt with fixing the geographical position of places. Al-Mukaddisi in a work called *Ahsan al-takāsīm fi ma' rifat al-akālīm* ('The Best Classification for Acquiring a Knowledge of the Provinces') comes to the conclusion that geography has a specific number of special aspects. Various Ottoman geographical works can be added to these, though the absence of the word 'geography' from their titles shows that it had not yet attained widespread usage as the term for the science of geography, although it did start to come into use from the twelfth century onwards,[1] and was used by the Ottoman Turks.

At the same time, use was made for a while of the term 'atlas'. This word came into prominence in the seventeenth century with Kâtib Chelebi, and was used in the eighteenth century as a

† Deceased.

synonym for the word 'geography'. The use of 'atlas' was greatly
assisted by Mercator's work of the same name; this did much to
found a new approach to geography, and as it was translated into
Turkish the word 'atlas' later acquired comparatively widespread
usage as a description of geography and related subjects.[2] In the
same way, towards the end of the seventeenth century (in 1685),
the work Ebu Bekir bin Behram Dimishki was translated into
Turkish with the name 'Atlas Major'.[3] The meaning of the word
'atlas' is basically clear; it is the name given to a collection of
geographical maps brought together to give compact and coherent information about the economic situation, the physical
geography of a region, a country, or the world.

The beginnings of Ottoman geographical knowledge go back
to the fourteenth century. The first works in this field are bound
up with cosmography and, the best work of the genre is Yazící-
zade Ahmed Bican's (?–1456) *Durr-i Mekun* ('Well-preserved
Pearl'). The same author translated into Turkish from Arabic
a cosmography called *Adjāib al-makhlūkāt* ('Wonders of Creation') by Kazvini (?–1283). Other translations of this work
exist, and one by a certain Ruknettin Ahmed was presented to
Mehmed I.

This work first described the world as oval and from here the
idea passed into other geographical works. In the Islamic world,
Ptolemy's (*c.* A.D. 90–168) 'Geography' held sway for a long time.
At Mehmed II's command it was translated from Greek into
Arabic.[4] Islamic geographers were familiar with the Ptolemy
(called Batlamyos) system; it dominated the world of the Middle
Ages for a long time.[5] After Nicolaos Copernicus (1473–1543)
had hypothesized that the sun was the centre of the universe and
that all the other heavenly bodies, including the earth rotated
round it, Ptolemy's theory gradually lost ground in the scientific
circles of Europe. However, Ottoman geographers continued to
uphold the old system for some time to come.[6] The reasons why
Europe made such progress in the spheres of science and knowledge from the eleventh century onwards, while the Islamic world
lagged behind, lie outside the scope of this chapter. Yet, despite
this stagnation in the field of science and an obvious lack of the
spirit of research in the Islamic world, the scientific progress of
Europe in the seventeenth century was in some ways indebted to it.[7]

The Introduction of the New Geographical Knowledge into the Ottoman State

In the seventeenth century Kâtib Chelebi's (1609–1657) cautious efforts introduced European geographical knowledge to the Turkish Empire and this, being added to Ottoman geographical theory, began to alter the traditional approach. Works by Mercator (1512–1594)[8] and Abraham Ortelius (1527–1598)[9] were translated into Turkish with the help of Sheik Mehmed Ikhlāsī (a convert to Islam who had originally come from France) in an abbreviated form with the title *Atlas Minor*. Kâtib Chelebi also revised this translation of this work under the title *Levamiün-nūr fi zulumât-i Atlās Mīnōr* ('Light in the Darkness Atlas Minor').[10] Kâtib Chelebi made use of Western sources in the writing of the last part of his work *Djihānnumā* ('View of the World').[11] Unlike his predecessors in the field of geography, Kâtib Chelebi attached great importance to the map, whilst his method of presentation was to examine the surface of the earth by dividing it up into continents. He established a close relationship between the subjects of mathematical geography and the geography of a country.[12] At the same time, it must be noted that he speaks of astronomy in accordance with Ptolemy's system and, makes no mention of the new theory current in Europe. It is possible that Kâtib Chelebi made no reference to this system because it had not won acceptance, in religious circles, rather than because of the backwardness to the Muslim world.

Copernicus's system was first openly mentioned in the Turkish Empire in the second half of the seventeenth century. Ebu Bekir bin Behram Dimishki translated into Turkish the joint work of the Dutch father and son, Wilhelm and Joan Blaeu, during the years 1675–1685 under the title *Djughrāfyā-yi-Kebir* and *Atlas Major*.[13]

Basically the work gives a brief exposition of Copernicus's system; thanks to this translation, Copernicus's system became known to the Ottoman world 145 years after it had first been propagated, that is to say, in 1685. At the same time, Ptolemy's system was not rejected. Ebu Bekir bin Dimishki's work is not so much a translation but in places almost gives the impression of a compilation.[14]

Ottoman Geographical Knowledge in the Eighteenth Century

Along with Kâtib Chelebi's (1609–1657) work there was a continual current of interest in the science of geography which must
not be underestimated. The net result of this interest was the
appearance in the eighteenth century of several translations and
compilations and in this way it can be seen that, from the point of
view of the content of geographical knowledge, the new ideas and
component subjects had won acceptance. The man who printed
Kâtib Chelebi's work *Djihānnumā* and was the founder of the
Turkish printing press, Ibrahim Müteferrika (1674–1745), was
also a geographer. While *Djihānnumā* was being printed, the
missing sections on Arabia and Anatolia were completed from the
work translated by Ebu Bekir bin Behram Dimishki. After adding
to the beginning of *Djihānnumā* information concerning elementary
geometry, he mentioned such scholars as Copernicus and Tycho
Brahe (1546–1601) and their views on the system of the Universe
and proceeded to discuss them; he referred to them as 'First
doctrine' (Ptolemy's system), 'Second doctrine' (Copernicus's
system) and 'Third doctrine' (Tycho Brahe's system) respectively. He spent proportionately less time on Tycho Brahe's
system than on Copernicus's.[15] At the same time, he showed a
certain circumspection in pointing out that Muslim scholars did
not accept these new theories. He mentioned in passing magnetism
and magnetic deviation. By adding such items of information as
these he managed to bring *Djihānnumā* up to date in comparison
with the European learning of his time.[16]

His work *Füyūzât-i miknātisiye* belongs to the field of geography
and is basically a compilation; it was printed in 1732. In this work
he discussed the invention of the compass and magnetic peculiarities. However, this work is essentially a foreign work.[17] It is noteworthy that several of the works on geography written during the
eighteenth century show the influence of Kâtib Chelebi and indeed
seem almost to have taken his work as a direct model. Basically,
Kâtib Chelebi believed that geography was the natural ancillary
of history and this is clearly demonstrated in his work; not surprisingly, the works of those who followed in his footsteps belong

to the field of historical geography. One such writer was Shehri-zāde Mehmed Sa'id (?–1764). One can follow Shehri-zāde's ideas on this subject. According to him, geography and history were mutually necessary subjects; from the historical point of view, when discussing the conquest of a place, it is essential to give a geographical description of it. It is essential, too, for those in charge of the nation's affairs to know the two disciplines of history and geography; a statesman who does not know both cannot be effective in matters of state.[18] Shehri-zāde Mehmed Sa'id Efendi made use of both Kâtib Chelebi's work, *Djihānnumā*, and Ebu Bekir bin Behram Dimishki's translation.[19] Shehri-zāde Mehmed Sa'id Efendi, being a man bound mentally to the traditional theory of geography, does not mention Copernicus's system.[20]

Another fact which shows that a new theory had become established in the Ottoman concept of geography was that cartography achieved a place for itself, and plans, maps and sketches are found wherever appropriate in writings on this subject. Several people became famous for their skill in cartography and the number of maps drawn increased significantly.[21] For example, Ibrahim Müteferrika himself drew several of the maps and diagrams in *Djihānnumā*; others were transferred from the original. In addition to this, a map of Asia Minor drawn in 1726 is a model of painstaking industry in the field of cartography.[22]

Sources

Almost all the works written in the eighteenth century were derived from the West. Works written in European languages are translated directly into Turkish. The eventual result of this activity[23] was that the new theory of geography became firmly rooted in Ottoman scientific circles. After the opening of technical colleges such as the Imperial Ottoman School of Engineering (founded in 1769) in which scientific subjects were taught on western lines, geography began to be taught as part of the curriculum, along with other scientific and technical courses. In fact, from the time of its inclusion into the curriculum, geography began to be taught in a systematic way, incorporating the very latest geographical information.[24] But the efforts of those concerned with geography before it reached this stage and the contributions they made to Ottoman geographical knowledge must not be forgotten.

When one examines the existing works one sees that some of them continued to follow the traditional system of Ptolemy, while others followed the new method of geography, which was current in Europe from the time of Copernicus. Those who wrote in what could be called Kâtib Chelebi's field of historical geography, a field that was comparatively bound to a geographical system, formed what could be considered a separate group, for example such writers as Shehri-zāde Mehmed Sa'id and Bartinli Ibrahim Hamdi.

When one considers the contents of these works though, another classification suggests itself. As a result of such an examination one could classify them as 'general geography' and 'geography of a country'. The majority of works written in this century are concerned with the individual geography of countries, particularly with the geographies of several countries belonging to one continent, generally Europe. In the works written in this field of the geography of a country, the emphasis is given to contemporary history. On the other hand, it must be pointed out that in these works concerning the geography of a country, one has much difficulty in finding statistics concerning the population of the region. One does find records giving the distance between one town and another, and details of their latitude and longitude. The explanation lies in the degree of interest of the writer and his level of erudition; in some works one frequently encounters statistics.

While Sheikh Hasan Esīrī (?–1727), commander of the munitions officers corps was busy with Kâtib Chelebi's Arabic work *Fezleke*, he journeyed much in the Ottoman lands. The information which he collected on these journeys he added to Kâtib Chelebi's work and, with the further addition of contemporary maps, a new work was born. He gave the title *Miyāru'd düvel ve misbārü'l-milel*[25] to his work, which was probably written in 1729.

The work of the German, Bernhard Varenius printed in 1664,[26] was translated from German into Turkish be the deputy interpreter at Belgrade Castle, Osman bin Abdulmennan, in 1750.[27] Above we touched on the additions made to *Djihānnumā* when it was printed, and spoke of Ibrahim Müteferrika's work *Füyūzât-i*

Miknātisiye (Istanbul, 1732). At Ahmen III's command, Ibrahim Müteferrika translated the work of the Dutch geographer, Andreas Cellarius,[28] under the title *Mecmu'a-i hey'et-i kadime ve cedîde* ('Collection of the Old and the New Life') adding several notes of his own. He took from amongst the additions made to *Djihānnumā* those relating to astronomy and cosmography and placed them at the beginning of this work and then discussed the significance of the added diagrams. It was necessary, to use this work, to complete the additions on cosmography and astronomy made by I. Müteferrika in *Djihānnumā*.[29]

As was explained above, several works were written and translated on the subject of Europe's position and its human geography. The movement towards the westernizing of existing institutions together with the desire to become acquainted with the West, that is to say Europe, must have played a large role in these endeavours. In this way, it is possible to classify the observations made in travel accounts (Sefāretname)[30] written by ambassadors sent to the various European centres as geographical works of a sort. If one were to classify travel literature (Sefāretname) as a separate genre, it would probably be more favourable to travel literature. However, no analysis has been made of the information contained in these travellers' accounts. There is an anonymous work, directly concerned with Europe and written between 1725–1726 (h. II38), called *Idjmāl-i ahvāl-i Avrupa*.[31] It begins by saying that the world is divided into the four regions of Europe, Asia, Africa and America, and goes on to discuss Austria, Venice, Spain, Portugal, England, Holland, Denmark, Sweden, Poland and Russia (Muscovy) and ends with a brief account of the Ottoman lands.[32] The second part of this work is directly concerned with geography and is a translation. After explaining that the science of geography concerns the actual contitions of the various tribes and nations on the face of the earth (folio 23b), it goes on to say that this science needs illustrations, diagrams and maps in order to be able to do this and to disseminate knowledge. This treatise was written with the intention of proving the usefulness and, indeed, the necessity, of geography.

Ahmed Resmī Efendi, the well-known statesman and writer, felt a keen interest in geography and wrote works in this field. He wrote *Eflâk djoğhrafyāsi* ('A Geography of Wallachia'),[33] in

1760; this is a regional geography. He also wrote *Djoğhrafyā-yi Djedīd*; a general work of geography prepared on the basis of what he had seen and read during his time as Ambassador in Prussia.[35] A certain Petros Baronian, who was interpreter to the embassy of Holland, translated Jaques Robbs' work[36] into Turkish with the title *Risāle-i djoğhrafyā* or *Cemnūmā fi fenn-i djoğhrafyā*. This consists of an introduction, followed by four chapters and a conclusion. While he was translating the maps, diagrams and tables of this work (1733) he was the chief interpreter in the embassy to the Kingdom of Sicily.[37]

One of the compilations written during this century was that composed by Ibrahim Hamdi. This work, completed in 1750, was called *Atlas*; today only the second part survives; the first part has been missing for a long time.[38]

Ibrahim Hamdi was born in the village of Enduz, which belonged to the district of Ulus in the province of Bolu. During his youth he spent some time with his father in the castle of Temešvar in Transylvania during Mustafa II's (1695–1703) campaign against Austria. Ibrahim Hamdi stayed in this city until 1716 to complete his education. Later he was stationed in Tirnova castle in Bulgaria and from there was transferred to Chotin (Hotin) castle. At first, he worked as clerk to the Munitions Store (djebekhāne), but later, as he was both literate and capable, he was made accountant of the secretariate. Chotin castle is situated close to the Polish border, and while living there he was able to learn a great deal about conditions both in Poland and in the neighbouring countries. His tour of duty in Chotin must have continued until about 1727–1728. In 1727 he visited his native town of Amasra, situated on the north-west coast of Anatolia. In 1733–1734, he was in Istanbul. During 1736–1737, he was at the front, on the border, in the war with Russia. In this way, a significant part of his life was spent in the Balkans. It is reasonable to conjecture that between the years 1738–1748 he was carrying out researches and gathering material for his work, and was most preoccupied with it in 1749. By his own account, 1st March 1750 is the date on which he put the final touches to his work. The information concerning himself which he gives in this work, stops here.

Having nominally finished writing his work on 1st March 1750, the author continued to make additions in the margins at various dates.[39] The dates and events noted in these additions show that Ibrahim Hamdi must have been still alive in the 1760s. The loss of the first part of this work prevents one from knowing more about the author. The first part must have dealt with Arabia, Anatolia and other countries in Asia.[40] The only extant version of the Atlas, preserved in the Es'ad Efendi section[41] of the Süleymaniye General Library, is the second part. When one examines it, one is struck by the fact that Ibrahim Hamdi was an intelligent man, comparatively well-read in the field of scientific literature. It is also noteworthy that the author is extremely honest and open in acknowledging the sources he has used. This meticulous procedure is illustrated in many of the geographical observations. His principal sources are: Ebu Bekir bin Behram Dimishki's *Atlas-i kebir* or *Djughrāfyā-yi kebīr* (folios 14a, 85a, 176b, 214a, 221b, 243b), Kâtib Chelebi's *Djihānnumā* (folios 121a, 124b); Pîrî Reis's *Kitāb-i Bahriye* (folios 220b, 401a); he made use of Pîrî Reis's work in the section on the Aegean Sea. *Atlas-i Djedīd-i Felemenk* (folio 217b) and *Djoğrafyā-yi Djedīd* (folios 218b, 219b, 273b) are mentioned, but it is not clear whether the *Cemnūmā fi fenn-i djoğrafyā* or *Djoğrafyā-yi Djedīd*, attributed to A. Resmî, is intended. Other works used for reference are: Sipahi-zāde Mehmed's work called *Takvim*;[42] Sherīf Muhammed Idrīsī's work (folios 82a and b);[43] Abu al-Fida's (not mentioned by name) *Takvim al-buldān* (folios 120a, 219b) and Yakut al-Hamavī's *Mu'cem al-buldān*. These are some of the Islamic geographers whose work is used. Amongst the historical sources used are Abu al-Ferec's *Muhtasar al-duvel* ('Summary of the States') (folio 120b) and Ibn Šihna's *Ravzāt al-manāzīrīn* (folio 480b). For Ottoman history, the work he used most abundantly was Mustafa Cenābī's work (folios 121b, 206a, 221b, 130a).[44] In some places, for stories about the walls of Istanbul (folio 121a); he made use of *Künhu'l-akhbār* by the great sixteenth century historian, Mustafa Alî he made use of the seventeenth century historian Abdurrahman Hibrî's work *Enīsü'l-müsāmīrīn* for information on Edirne and its surroundings (folio 188b). Finally, he used an anonymous work called *Beč* (*Viyana*) *vekāyiï* (folio 360a) for information about Vienna and the siege of Vienna (1683). For information on the events and geographical details of the Crimea, Kuban, Özü (Oczakow) and the surrounding region, he also made use of a work called *Kefere tārihi* (folio 290b), (the exact nature of which it has not been possible to establish). Although no sources are given for the information on the protocol and legal procedure of the Ottoman State, there can be no doubt that such information was taken from the protocal books and law codes. In the sections on the Maritime Arsenal and the navy (folios 164b–169b) one cannot but mention Hezarfen Huseyin Čelebi and his work.[45]

Ibrahim Hamdi wrote about the geography, or rather the historical geography of the places he had not visited himself with the help of the works we have noted, intermingles with his original work. In writing of the places which the author had personally seen and lived in, he achieves an exceptional level of vivacity, particularly when speaking of Rumelia, Istanbul and the places he had visited in Anatolia. One can take the information given in such observations as the result of first-hand experience. Another important point is that the writer was able to sift the works he used with a critical and analytical understanding based on his own experience.

The Historical Geography of Rumelia According to Ibrahim Hamdi's Atlas

It could be said that Ottoman geographers first became acquainted with Europe and the Balkans by way of the sea. It could be said, too, that Ottoman knowledge of maritime geography made a great leap forward in the sixteenth century. Pîrî Reis's *Kitāb-ı Bahriye* ('Book of the Navy') is an example of this. The word 'Balkans' meant for the Ottoman Turks the chain of mountains on that peninsula. Basically, the word 'Balkan' was used in Turkish with the sense of 'steep, forested place', 'forested mountain'; the word could be used either alone or in combination with other words, as for example, Emine Balkanî, Koca Balkan.[46] Ami Boué[47] gave the name Balkan Chain to these mountains (Emine Balkanî, Koca Balkan) in the first half of the nineteenth century. Although the name 'Balkans' had appeared earlier in an atlas of 1757,[48] it was essentially the name used for the mountain chain from the early nineteenth century onwards, later becoming generalized to refer to the whole peninsula.

The Ottoman Turks used the term 'Rumelia' for the Balkan

addition of those founded later, eleven provinces; the existence of such vassal states as Wallachia, Moldavia, Transylvania and the Crimean Khanate has also been pointed out. In the first half of the eighteenth century, that is to say in the period of Ibrahim Hamdi's *Atlas*, there were in Rumelia the following provinces: Belgrade,[52] Morea,[53] Bosnia, Özü (Oczakow), Temešvar. In the *Atlas* the Ottoman administrative units in the Balkans are referred to by the name of the country or district, this means, however, the administrative units which came after the provinces ('eyalet') are intended. The majority of the places mentioned by the name of the country, or district were in fact 'sancaks' (provinces) of the same name. Bearing this in mind, amongst the places referred to by the name of the country or district are the following: Vize, Silistre, Nikopol, Vidin, Edirne, Čirmen, Sofia, Alacahisar (Kruševac), Semendre (Semendria), Gelibolu, Selânik (Thessalonika), Köstendil (Kjustendil), Üsküp (Skopje), Tırhala (Trikala), Egriboz (Euboea,) Morea, Inebahtı (Navpaktos), Karlıili, Yanya (Ioannina), Elbasan, Ohri (Ohrid), Prizren, Vulčitrin (Vučitrn), Dukakin, Bosnia, Hersek, Klis, Izvornik (Zvornik), Hirvat, Seksar (Szekszard), Istoni Belgrad (Stuhlweissenburg), Budin, Usturgon (Esztergom), Yanik (Raab, Győr), Pecuy (Pecs), Sigetvar (Szigetvar), Simontorna (Simontornya), Kanije (Kanisza), Temešvar, Segedin (Szegedin), Egri (Eger) (folios 175 onwards).

The sancaks of Egri, Budin, Kanije, Szigetvar, Istoni Belgrad and Szegedin which are mentioned here actually passed into Austrian hands in 1685; and constituted the territory ceded to Austria under the Treaty of Karlowitz in 1699. However, the author was aware of this fact: he writes about the loss of former Ottoman possessions, explaining that they used to be in Ottoman hands and that later they passed into Austrian hands (folio 200a). In talking about the former Ottoman province of Kamanice, he recounts how it was conquered and made into a province, then how it was lost and restored to Poland (folios 343b, 344a–b). On the subject of Wallachia, he first of all discusses it from a historical point of view, then recounts that it became a 'beylik' (district governed by a Bey) and gives various details about the capital, Bucarest (folio 272a). However, in describing Wallachia's borders, he makes an error when he says that Poland lies to the north. While describing Moldavia, he mentions that its name (in Turkish

'Bugdan') comes from a certain sort of wheat (Turkish 'bugday') that is grown there. The interesting thing about the information given here is the fact that our author was stationed on the northeast frontier of Rumelia and, while going to Istanbul, he passed through places in the right wing of Rumelia which he describes so well, and stayed in those parts. It is highly probable that while he was stationed on duty in castles, such as Temešvar and Chotin, he often went to Wallachia and Moldavia to obtain provisions, etc. A point which strengthens this supposition is his short but extremely valuable description of the organization of the principality ('voyvodalık') of Wallachia.

It is necessary at this point to repeat a few of the ideas set forward in the introduction to this article. When speaking of Ibrahim Hamdi's sources, it was stated that the *Atlas* is a general work of geography and that he used Pîrî Reis's *Kitāb-ı Bahriye* ('Book of the Navy'), Kâtib Chelebi's *Djihānnumā*, and, most abundantly of all, Ebu Bekir bin Behram Dimishki's translation *Djughrāfyā-yi kebīr*. Amongst the geographical works which we conjectured belonged to the eighteenth century are *Atlas-i Djedīd-i Felemenk* and *Djoğrafyā-yi Djedīd*. Bearing this in mind, there is nothing at all, from the point of view of geography, that is new. Basically, the writer was not a harbinger of the new geographical theories of his age; he did not pretend not to know of the existence of Copernicus's system, and remained bound to the traditional Ptolemaic system. What is original in his work is the information he gives about the Balkan lands which he saw with his own eyes and about other countries of which he knew. From this point of view, one must consider his work to be a form of historical geography. Below, the parts of his work which are original in this respect will be indicated.

Ibrahim Hamdi spent his youth in Temešvar and remained in this city until 1716. As a result the information which he gave about Temešvar is of great value; for example, he gives a very colourful description of the siege of Temešvar castle in 1716 and its passing, with much destruction, into Austrian hands (folios 255b, 256a), his coming to Temešvar during the years 1695–1696, the many events he witnessed there during his childhood and youth, and the rich intellectual life of the city (folios 254a–b, 255a–b, 253b). However, the information about Buda, no longer in Ottoman hands, he learnt from Pîrî Ahmed Efendi, who came to seek refuge in Temešvar; and so he also relates that in Pec there were 27 medreses (Moslem theological schools) and that there was such an abundance of water in the city and that in every house there was the murmuring of running water, plus other such details (folio 359b).

Amongst the items of information given about Transylvania, which was in Austrian hands while Ibrahim Hamdi was in Temešvar, details concerning trade are of particular interest. According to the information given here, the extraction of various minerals in Transylvania was attributed to Nišovalı Ibrahim Zaîm (Ibrahim Zaîm of Nišova). Ibrahim Hamdi lived in Chotin until 1727–1728, and worked as Accountant to the Secretariat and collected much material, which is an important addition to what is known about that period (folios 275b, 276a–b, 277a). He tells in great detail about the extensive, new repairs made to Chotin castle. Apart from this, he gives detailed information about the town itself and about cities such as Ak Mescid (Simferopol), (folio 275b), Babadagı (folio 173a), Tırnova (folio 183a), Lofca (folio 183b), Arcar (folio 185b). Thus, the town of Cebire, which lies between Rahova and Nigbolu (Nikopol), received its name from the refugees who founded it in the course of their flight, which was occasioned by the fall of Temešvar and Belgrade to the Austrians in 1717 (folio 185a); the information which he gives about some of the Christian communities on the peninsula of Morea is of this sort. For information on the places which the author was unable to visit himself, he has recourse to the accounts of those who had been there, and in this way overcomes his handicap. For example, he writes about Moscow and St Petersburg and their surroundings with the help of what he had learnt from the commanders of Özü (Oczakow) and Chotin, the pashas Yahya and Kolcak, who had spent some time in Russia as prisoners of war. Isakca (Isaecea) (folio 179b), Šumnu (Shumen) (folio 181b), Kamanice (Kamnets Podolski) (folio 344b), Akkirman (Belgorod Dnestrovski) (folio 281b) and Kefe (folio 284b) are some of the other towns and cities that he describes.

Much of the information noted down about the vassal states of the Ottoman Empire, Wallachia (folios 271b–273b), Moldavia (folios 273b–274a) and the Crimean Khanate (folios 284b–293a),

concerns their crops. While speaking of Wallachia, the observations made concerning the capital Bucarest are based on writings
belonging to the first half of the eighteenth century; he mentions
the rich salt deposits in Wallachia and Transylvania (folio 262a)
and comments on their fame (folio 272b). After giving a general
survey of Moldavia, he gives a short but extremely valuable
account of the history and human geography of the towns of Yaş
(Iaši) (folio 273b), Galati (folio 273b), Sucuva (Suceava) (folio
274a). While he is talking about saltpetre deposits here and its
manner of extraction, he mentions that in his time there was a
forest here and describes how the Moldavians had cultivated this
forest themselves.

Ibrahim Hamdi says that formerly the Crimea contained about
forty towns. He explains, that in spite of the fact that this is what
the history books say, when he was travelling in those parts he
saw only a fraction of this number, and he mentions Bahcesaray
and the town of Karasu, which certainly could not be called a city.
(folio 293a). As has already been mentioned, he also gives information about various communities as he did in Morea. In the
same way, one of the communities about which he writes is that of
the Lipkas, a Tartar group who live in Poland; the information he
gives about them is considerably richer than that to be found in any
other source. While he was stationed in Chotin castle, he was fully
cognizant of several of the problems of the region. He was in continuous contact with these Lipkas, who, for a number of reasons,
had left Poland and settled in Chotin and the surrounding area; at
the same time, he was also obliged to be in contact with their relatives in Poland. The eventual result of this was that he learnt their
dialects. Ibrahim Hamdi's knowledge came in useful in the question
of the existing border between the Ottoman Empire and Poland
and also on the question of the Lipkas, a matter which concerned
both countries.[54] Thus, it was through these Lipkas, a community
divided, because some of them lived in Ottoman lands while others
lived in Poland, that Ibrahim Hamdi came to collect information
about the Polish State; he noted down in his work the information
that he thus obtained. (folio 342a–b).

If one considers the actual nature of the work, then it must be
admitted that the author spends too much time on the city of
Istanbul and the organization of the Ottoman State. After giving

an account of the founding of Istanbul, he speaks of its mosques (folio 124b) and the Galata (folio 151), Eyup (folio 130b) and Scutari (folio 131b) quarters of the city, then goes on to relate the laws of the city and the formation of the trade-guilds (folios 133a onwards) and finally passes on to the military organization of the army. He also dwells on the laws and regulations in force in the various parts of the state (folios 161b, 162a etc.). It may be conjectured that the author made use of Hezarfen Hüseyin Čelebi's work called *Telkhīsu'l-beyān fī kavānīn-i āl-i Osmān* ('Clarifying the Laws of the Ottoman Empire') and Kâtib Chelebi's *Tuḥfetu'l-Kibār fī esfāri'l-bihār* (Istanbul, 1329) ('Elderly in Voyaging the Seas') for information connected with the organization of the State. It is noteworthy that in this instance the author does not mention his source. In the discussion on the organization of the army, he does in places give statistics on its fighting strength at that time (folios 161a, 166a).

As has already been explained, the bulk of geographical information in Ibrahim Hamdi's work was gathered from works belonging to the seventeenth century. Use was also made of one or two translated works belonging to the eighteenth century. He is not a harbinger of the new geographical works appearing at that time in Europe.[55] At the same time, he made use of many sources in the writing of his work and it is therefore of great worth in the field of historical geographical research. This is the most valuable aspect of this work. The addition of his own first hand experience in the information which he gives on the Balkans, which we have already discussed, gives particular value to these sections. At the same time it must be pointed out that the most original material concerns the east Balkan lands; that is to say, the eastern Bulgaria, Wallachia, Moldavia, the Crimea, Özü (Oczakow), Chotin Transylvania and its environs. These are the lands in which the writer frequently travelled, either on duty or on some other errand.

8. Notes

1. For further information on the knowledge of geography in Islamic civilization see S. Maqbul Ahmad, 'Djughrafya', *Encyclopaedia of Islam* II (1960–1965) pp. 575–587.

2. *Atlas minor, Gerardi Mercatoris A. S. Hondio Plurimis aenis atque illustratus*, Arnheim (1621).

3. The original name was *Atlas major seu cosmographia blaei ana qua solum, salem, coelum accuratissime describuntur* and belonged to the Dutch father and son Wilhelm Janszoon and Joan Blaeu. First printed Amsterdam (1662).

4. Adnan Adıvar, *Osmanlı Türklerinde ilim* ('Science amongst the Ottoman Turks'), Istanbul (1970), pp. 23, 29.

5. At the same time, from the twelfth century onwards there had been a growing awareness that Ptolemy's system for the explanation of the movement of the heavenly bodies was inadequate. See Besim Darkot, 'Sema hareketleri ve Doğu âlemi' ('Movements of the sky and the Eastern World'), *Coğrafya Enstitüsü Dergisı*, 9, İstanbul (1958), 1–10.

6. For the science of geography amongst the Ottomans, see F. Taeschner, 'Die Geographische Literatur des Osmanen', *Zeitschrift der Deutschen Morgenlandischen Gesellschaft*, LXXVII (1923), 31–80.

7. See Aydın Sayılı, 'Islam and the rise of the Seventeenth Century Science', *Belleten*, 87 Ankara (1958), 353–368.

8. The work is called *Atlas, sive Cosmographiae meditationes di fabrica mundi*. Hondius completed the work in 1606 and printed it.

9. *Theatrum Orbis terrarum*. Antwerp (1570).

10. The work was completed on 29th July 1655 (25 Ramażan 1065) and there is very fine copy in the Istanbul University Library (T.Y., 2350). This work starts with a general information about each of the continents of Asia, Europe, America and Africa in turn, and then continues with a descriptive geography of the countries of Europe, starting from the north; the section on Europe is very detailed, but information on the other continents is given in a much shorter form. The translation omits various places.

11. Apart from Abraham Ortelius's work, his sources include Ph. Cluverius's *Introductio geographica tam vetera quam nova* and Lorenzo of Calabria's *Fabrica Mundi*.

12. According to Hamid Sadi Selen, Kâtib Chelebi wrote two different versions of *Djihānnumā*. In the first, he only made use of Islamic writers; this has not come down to us. The second text is the one he wrote with the help of Western sources; the printed text, which İbrahim Müteferrika completed, is not Kâtib Chelebi's original text 'Cihannuma, Kâtib Çelebi, Hayati ve eserleri hakkinda incelemeler' ('Djihānnumā and the studies on the life and works of Kâtib Çelebi'), *Türk Tarih Kurumu*, Ankara (1957), pp. 122, 123–130).

13. The original name of the translation is *Nuşretu'l-islâm ve's-surûr fī terceme-i Atlas Mayor*. There is a copy of this translation in nine volumes in the Baghdad Kiosk Library, in Topkapı Palace Museum (No. 325–333). There

is also an abridged version of two volumes in Köprülü Library in Istanbul (No. 173–174).

14. Adnan Adıvar, op. cit. pp. 135, 136.

15. *Djihānnumā*, İstanbul (1145/1732), pp. 23, 46, 47.

16. See Besim Darkot, 'Kâtib Çelebi-İbrahim Müteferrika ve sema hareketleri' ('Kâtib Çelebi-İbrahim Müteferrika and the movements of the heavens'), *Coğrafya Araştırmaları*, II, İstanbul (1958), 4–19.

17. Adnan Adıvar, op. cit., pp. 149, 150. The original of the translation, which was published in Leipzig in 1721, is possibly the work of William Whiston.

18. *Ta'rikh-i Nev-Peydā*, Istanbul University Library, T.Y.3291, folio 9 a.

19. *Ta'rikh-i Nev-peydā*, folio 80 a and other places. This is essentially a historical work; it was completed on 29th July, 1756.

20. Shehri-zāde Mehmed Sa'id Efendi wrote an appendix to Kâtib Chelebi's *Djihānnumā* in 1740 called *Ravḍatü'l-enfus*. According to F. Babinger there is a copy in Berlin (*Die Geschichtschreiber der Osmanen und ihre Werke*, Leipzig (1927), p. 297). A part of the work called *Ta'rikh-i Nev-Peydâ* (folios 79a–95a) is a geography of the Ottoman lands.

21. No serious work has been done on this subject. For the time being see Abdurrahman Aygün, 'Türkiye'de ilk harita basımı ve ilk asrî matbaa' ('The first map printing and the first modern printing press in Turkey'), *Haritacılar Mecmuası*, IV (İstanbul), 83–88.

22. Fâik Reşid Unat, 'Ahmed III devrinde yapılmış bir Ön Asya haritası' ('A map of Asia Minor made in the reign of Ahmed III'), *Tarih Vesikaları Dergisi*, 2, İstanbul (1941), 160.

23. It is noteworthy that many of the translators worked in the state service as interpreters.

24. İbrahim Hakkı Akyol, 'Tanzimat devrinde bizde coğrafya ve jeoloji' ('Geography and Geology in our country during the Tanzimat period'), *Tanzimat* I, İstanbul (1940), 15.

25. There are two copies of this work in Turkish Libraries. The first is in the Es'ad Efendi Library (No. 2109, 2110), the second is in the Hekimoğlu Ali Pasha Library (No. 803). The Es'ad Efendi copy is in two volumes and is complete; the Hekimoğlu Ali Pasha one consists of the first volume only.

26. *Geographie generalis in qua affectionnes generales tellaris explicantur.*

27. He compiled it with a translated work, including an introduction, six chapters and a conclusion. Osman bin Abdülmennan began his translation with the encouragement of the commander of Belgrade, Köprülü-zâde Ahmed Pasha. There are two extant copies, one in the Es'ad Efendi Library (No. 2041), the other in the Köprülü Library (No. II/175).

28. The original name is *Atlas Coelestis* or *Harmonia Macrocosmica* and was printed for the first time in 1665.

29. Adnan Adıvar, op. cit., p. 154.

30. For travel literature (Sefāretnāme) see Fâit Reşit Unat, *Osmanlı sefirleri ve sefaretnāmeleri* (*Ottoman Ambassadors and their travel Accounts*), Ankara (1968).

31. There are two extant copies of this treatise, one in the Atıf Efendi Library (in İstanbul, No. 1885), the other in the Topkapı Palace Museum, Revan Kiosk Library (No. 1648). See V. Ménage *Three Ottoman Treatises on Europe, Iran and Islam*, in honour of W. Minorsky, Edinburgh (1971), pp. 421–433).

32. In the Ravan copy, the section on the necessity of geography comes after the second folio. At the end of it, there is 'Idjmāl-i Aḥvāl-i djezire-i Malta' (folio 38 a, b) and a part of the heading 'Zikr-i ahvāl-i djezire-i Aḳritoş (Crete)' taken from Hezarfen Hüseyin Efendi's work *Tenḳıhu't-tevārikh* (folios 39a–40 b).

33. There is only one copy in Turkey (Hazine Library, Topkapı Palace Museum, No. 445). Two more copies of this work have recently been found. M. Guboğlu has made known the existence of the copies found in the collection of V. A. Urechia in Galati, Rumania, and has published a summary of their contents. See *Doua Manuscrise Turcesti de Ahmed Resmi Efendi in Biblioteca 'V. A. Urechia' din Galati privind Tarile Romane*, Galati (1974), pp. 133–155.

34. C. Orhonlu, 'Ahmed Resmi Efendi's Geography of Walachia'. Paper read at the III International Congress of South-east European Studies, The Turkish text is being published in *Güney-Doğu Avrupa Araştırmaları Dergisi*, Istanbul (No. 4).

35. There is a fine copy of this work in the Husrev Paşa Library in İstanbul (No. 296). However, in the same Library, there is another copy (No. 268) written at the beginning of the translation, called *Risāle-i Djughrafya*.

36. The original name of the work is *La methode pour apprendre facilement la géographie*. There is a translation of the work in the Reval Kiosk Library (No. 828); a second copy may be found in the Hazine Library (No. 444), at the Topkapı Palace Museum.

37. In this translated work, there is information on new theories in mathematics and physics. The work has 29 folios; 'some geographers divide the Globe into four continents: the first is the Region of Asia, Africa and Europe; the second, America, that is to say the Region of the New World; the third is the North Polar Lands, about which nothing is known; the fourth is the South Polar lands, again, territory unknown' (folio 25).

38. For detailed information on the work and the author, see Cengiz Orhonlu, 'XVIII. yüz yılda Osmanlılarda coğrafya ve Bartınlı İbrahim Hamdi'nin Atlas'ı' ('Geography of the Ottomans and Bartınlı İbrahim Hamdi's Atlas'), *Edebiyat Fakültesi Tarih Dergisi*, 19, İstanbul (1964), 115–140.

39. Ibid., pp. 118, 119, 120ff.

40. Information on the first volume is based on the extracts which Talat Müm-
    taz Bey edited and annotated. This author from time to time published parts
    of the section which is in his possession; he has published the following
    parts: '200 sene evvel Konya, Uluslu İbrahim Hamdi Efendi 'ye göre'
    ('Konya and its surroundings two hundred years ago according to İbrahim
    Hamdi'), *Konya Halkevi Dergisi*, II/22–23, Konya (1938), 1208–1219;
    Idem., 'Cihānnumā'nın ilâveli bir nushası' (An enlarged copy of Dji-
    hānnumā), *Ülkü Halkevleri Dergisi*, XV, Ankara (1940), 41–49, 147–154,
    248–257. However, he wrongly considers the *Atlas* to be an enlarged copy
    of *Djihānnumā*.

41. The first volume had earlier been purchased by Ahmet Tevhit from some-
    one's estate; Talat Mümtaz gave notice of this in his work of 1934; later
    this first volume passed into Talat Mümtaz's possession; he wrote the
    articles mentioned in Note 40 with the help of this work. However, it has
    been learnt that this manuscript perished in a fire that broke out in his house
    in Kastamanu, a city in Northern Turkey. The first writer who wrote about
    the *Atlas* and who made use of it was Ahmet Tevhit Bey; Ahmet Tevhit in
    an appendix to Karaçon İmre's article ('İbrahim Müteferrika', *Ta'rikh-i
    Osmānī Encümeni Medjmu'āsı*, I, İstanbul (1328), p. 188 relates from İbra-
    him Hamdi's work *Atlas*, a description of the paper factory in Yālāḳābād
    (Yalova) and how the paper was manufactured in it.

42. It is not stated which of the two works are intended, *Esāmi-i djibâl ve buldān*
    or *Evzāhu'l-mesālik fī ma'rifeti'l-buldāh ve'l-memālik*.

43. *Nuzhat al-mushtāḳ fī ikhtirāḳ al-āfāḳ.*

44. Cenabi's work is called *Al-'Aylam al-zāhir fī aḥvāl al-avāil ve'l-avākhir.*

45. Hezarfen Hüseyin Efendi's work is called *Telkhisü'l-beyān fī kavānin-i āl-i
    Othman*. See R. Anhegger, 'Hezarfen Hüseyin Efendi'nin Osmanli devlet
    teşkilâtına dâir mülâhazalar'ı ('Hezarfen Hüseyin Efendi's observations on
    the organization of the Ottoman state'), *Türkiyat Mecmuası*, X, İstanbul
    (1953), 365–393.

46. Today in the north-west of Turkey the word 'Balkan' is used to mean a
    stony place. See, *Türkiye'de halk ağzından Söz derleme Dergisi*, İstanbul
    (1939) Vol. I, p. 159.

47. *Turquie d'Europe*, Paris (1840).

48. Robert de Vaugondy, 'Grand Atlas'; in Besim Darkot, *Balkan*, *Islâm Ansik-
    lopedisi*, İstanbul (1949) Vol. II, pp. 280–283.

49. Demetrius J. Georgacas, *The Names for the Asia Minor Peninsula*, Heidel-
    berg (1971), pp. 122, 123, 124.

50. Not only the Danube's south shore, the opposite shore to Kilia and Akker-
    man, were subject to the province of Rumelia.

51. Şerafettin Turan, 'XVII. Yüzyılda Osmanlı İmparatorluğu'nun idarî
    taksimatı' ('Administrative divisions of the Ottoman Empire in XVIIth

CENGIZ ORHONLU

Century'), *Atatürk Üniversitesi Yıllığı*, 1961, Erzurum (1963) 210, 211 etc.

52. Belgrade and its surroundings were in Austrian hands between the years 1718–1738.

53. Morea was in the hands of the Venetian Republic between 1699–1715.

54. See Cengiz Orhonlu, 'Lipkalar', *Türkiyat Mecmuası*, XVI, İstanbul (1971), 57–87.

55. A. Wolf, *A History of Science, Technology and Philosophy in the Eighteenth Century*, London (1951), pp. 410–425.

9

Ethnical and Political Preconditions for Regional Names in the Central and Eastern Parts of the Balkan Peninsula

PETER S. KOLEDAROV

Ethnical processes and political events have always left an imprint on geographical nomenclature. This is most vividly seen in southeastern Europe, and in the Balkans in particular because compared with the other regions of the Old World the former have been subjected to frequent and profound changes.

A study of the emergence and the evolution of local names in this area shows that not only have they been replaced by other names or had their image or sound modified, but in certain cases the old toponyms were preserved, though with a new content, or cropped up in entirely new localities. The study and elucidation of these phenomena and the causes for their emergence reveal certain patterns and also help to eliminate the numerous errors and delusions about the past and present of the Balkans.

It is impossible, within the framework of a single chapter, to examine comprehensively the complicated question of geographical nomenclature in all of this part of Europe. It is for this reason that we shall deal only with the more important regional names in the eastern and central parts of the Balkans. The differentiation of that area also justifies the restriction of the subject in relation to its geographical scope. In Antiquity the eastern part of the peninsula was inhabited by Thracians and Dacians, and the western part by Illyrians. Whereas the former fell under the influence of Hellenism and largely retained its traditions, the latter maintained closer ties with Rome. This ethnical differentiation in the period preceding the division of the Old World, as well as the proximity of Constantinople in cultural and geographical aspects, determined that the area under review remained in the Empire's eastern part. After settlement in the area by the Slavs and Proto-Bulgarians, that differentiation was aggravated and could be traced in the ethnical and political development of the following centuries.

Byzantium, being the heir to Rome, took over its administrative division and its nomenclature. The names of the provinces Thrace, Illyria, Macedonia, Scythia, Dacia,[1] etc. were established and adopted by the old inhabitants of the Balkans, since in general terms they corresponded to the countries settled in by the various groups (ethnicons). These names of provinces were not only administrative units but became geographical concepts. During their continuous usage in the course of the first six centuries A.D. the Roman nomenclature of the provinces and dioceses in the Balkans gained a wide popularity and a definite significance in all parts of the Old World including its western domains. It should be stressed that a precondition for this was a combination of political and ethnical factors.

Radical changes occurred in the territorial scope and the ethnical composition of the Byzantine Empire in the sixth and seventh centuries (Fig. 1). The Emperor in Constantinople was able to keep under his sceptre barely a third of the territory, he had ruled in earlier centuries. The Arabs and the Persians conquered considerable parts of his domains in Africa and Asia, whilst at the same time his rule over Italy and the Balkan Peninsula was already very much restricted. The waves of 'barbarian' invasions were followed by prolonged and even more devastating raids by the Slavs (Sclavinians)[2] during the last decades of the sixth century. The Sclavinians, a south-eastern Slavic group were also called 'Dacians' or 'Bulgarians', and eventually provided the basic component of the Bulgarian nationality.[3]

Benefitting from the unprotected northern Byzantine frontiers

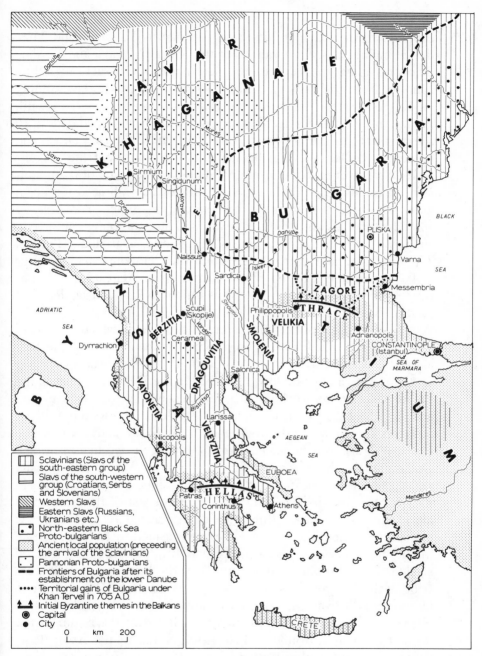

FIG. 1. Ethnic and political changes in the Balkans towards the end of the seventh century A.D.

(a result of warfare waged by the Empire in Asia) the Sclavinians
came down from their initial base in modern Wallachia and Moldavia, mainly along the valleys of the Rivers Morava and Vardar.
They occupied the land to the south and south-east, to a line
running from the estuary of the River Koloubara at the Danube,
passing across the ridges of the Roudoka, Stolova and Kopaonik
mountains and the north Albanian Mountain Range, and ending to
the north of the town of Dyrrachion (the Old-Bulgarian Drach and
present-day Durresi in Albania) and the Shkodra Lake.[4] Their
settlements were most densely populated in the heart of the peninsula, in the diocese of Macedonia (which also embraced Greece).
The new settlers used it as their second base, and from it they
spread eastwards and south-eastwards. Thus, the Slavs cam permanently to the former provinces of Moesia, Dardania, Thrace,
Thessaly, Epirus, Central Greece and the Peloponnesus, reaching
as far as the coasts of the Black, Adriatic and Aegean seas. Separate groups crossed in their vessels (monoxyles) and landed also
on the islands of the Archipelago as well as in Asia Minor.[5]

A second important ethnical and political factor which decisively
influenced the outlook and geographical nomenclature of the Balkans at this time, was the arrival of the Proto-Bulgarians, who set
up their state along the lower reaches of the Danube, as far as the
Balkan Mountains to the south, and received recognition *de jure*
and *de facto* by Byzantium in A.D. 681. After continuous raids—
both on their own and in alliance with Slavs and Avars—the
Proto-Bulgarians established their domiciles in two main regions.
One embraced the former provinces of Scythia Minor and Moesia,
and the other was located in central Macedonia. Led by Asparouch,
they arrived in Moesia from the northern coast of the Black Sea,
after Koubrat's 'Great Bulgaria' disintegrated *c*. A.D. 650. At
almost the same time, the second group, headed by Kouber, settled
in the area between Thessalonica and Bitolja, with their central
settlement in Ceramea, in the midst of the land of the Sclavinain
tribe of the Dragouvites. This group arrived from Pannonia, or to
be more exact from the area of Sirmium (modern Sremska Mitro-
vitsa, Yugoslavia), which then was included in the realm of the
Avar Khaganate. Kouber's Proto-Bulgarians being Avar dissi-
dents, Constantinople counted on breaking up the mass of Slavs
and their alliance with the Avars, so Byzantium welcomed them

and asked its allies, the Dragouvites, to provide food supplies.[6]

A part of the local population of the plains withdrew to the mountains, while another, the Hellenized and Romanized elements, went to the towns and to the territories where the Empire was still in a position to protect them. Along with the Aegean islands, Thrace was the most significant bulwark inland, as the latter was of vital importance for the defence of the capital city. In the rest of the peninsula, the Empire had under its control only Thessalonica* and some of the stronger fortresses with the adjacent strips of land along the sea coasts and the more important highways. The power of the Emperor was only nominal in the territories occupied by the Slavs as Sclavinian chiefs (princes) were in control there. The territory of each tribe acquired the name 'Sclavinia' ($\Sigma\kappa\lambda\alpha\nu\iota\nu\acute{\iota}\alpha$), obviously in accordance with the proper name of the Slavs from the south-eastern group. The term was in common use most often by Byzantine writers in the plural—$\alpha\acute{\iota}$ $\Sigma\kappa\lambda\alpha\nu\iota\nu\acute{\iota}\alpha\iota$ or in the vulgarized version $\Sigma\kappa\lambda\alpha\beta\iota\nu\acute{\iota}\alpha\iota$, the Latin form being 'Sclaviniae'.

The Czech historian, Lubor Niedelie, first drew attention to the fact that since the middle of the seventh century that name meant Macedonia.[7] Most of the writers interpreted the term as a designation of independent[8] Slav principalities, which were found outside Bulgarian territory[9] or more generally, as 'Slav land'.[10] The oldest references (at the turn of the sixth century)[11] to 'Sclaviniae' relate to the land, inhabited by Slavs and located along the left bank of the Danube, i.e. their first base in present-day Wallachian lowland.

In the chronicles of Theophanes the Confessor,[12] dealing with events between 658 and 809–810, the 'Sclaviniae' already implied the principalities west of the River Mesta, while in *Narratio anonyma e Codice Vaticano* and in *Scriptor Incertus de Leone Armenio* (the excerpts about the Byzantine–Bulgarian Wars of 811 and 814)[13] the term has a different meaning. The first mention of 'the surrounding Sclaviniae' ($\kappa\alpha\grave{\iota}$ $\tau\grave{\alpha}s$ $\pi\acute{\epsilon}\rho\iota\xi$ $\Sigma\kappa\lambda\alpha\beta\eta\nu\acute{\iota}\alpha s$) probably refers to the principalities near Pliska, along the western and northern frontiers of Bulgaria (the Timokites, Moravites and principalities to the north of the Danube) and the second mention namely, 'all Sclaviniae' ($\kappa\alpha\grave{\iota}$ $\pi\acute{\alpha}\sigma\alpha s$ $\tau\grave{\alpha}s$ $\Sigma\kappa\lambda\alpha\beta\eta\nu\acute{\iota}\alpha s$), also refers to those in modern Macedonia. The lack of data makes it impossible

* (Salonica).

to discern the basis of the relationship between the Bulgarian
Khan Kroum and the Slav principalities. One may assume that the
relationship was based on an alliance with the Bulgarian state, and
that the Sclavinian principalities were buffer areas between it and
the Avar Khaganate. The Slavs obviously sided with Khan Kroum
in his struggle against Byzantium, but it seems that they preserved
their independence. It is in this sense that the term Кнѧжєннє
should be interpreted in the name given (in the 'List of Names of
the Bulgarian Khans') to the territory along the left bank of the
Danube, Кнѧжєннє оүбою страноү Доүнаю. Thus, it should be the
Slav-Bulgarian synonym of the Byzantine 'Sclaviniae', and reveals
the political status of independence of the Sclavinian tribes. The
latter, as we shall see later, gave their names to the regions they
occupied.

The latest mention of the 'Sclaviniae', as a collective concept,
appears in Anastasius the Librarian's *Chronographia tripertita*
(compiled in the second half of the ninth century). The reference
in the passage concerning events in 785, when Constantine VI
conquered the Sclaviniae of Macedonia ('Sclavenias penes Mace-
doniam'). We may draw the conclusion that in this case, Macedonia implied the proper province of Antiquity. It is mentioned for
the sake of clarity, because of the very wide territorial scope of the
concept of 'Sclaviniae' at that time.

Although this term (as a collective concept, in the plural), used
to denote 'the land of the Sclavinians' disappeared from the sources
towards the end of the ninth century, certain names of the separate
Sclaviniae, named after the tribes that inhabited them, proved to be
more stable. They were retained as regional toponyms for centuries. Among the few that have been preserved in written documents and in oral tradition even to the present day, the following
may be listed: Berzitia (Βερζιτία) after the Bursyatsi in Central
Macedonia (the areas of Bitolja, Ochrida, Prespa and Veles);
Dragouvitia (Δραγουβιτία) after the Dragouvites to the west and
south-east of Thessalonica, along the lower reaches of the Vardar
as far as Mount Olympus; Veleyezitia (Βελζητία, Belegezitia)
after the Veleyezites in Thessaly and as far as Thebes; Vayonetia
(Βαγενετία, Vayonetia) after the Vayonites in the Epirus, between
Arta and Gjirokastra; Smolenia after the Smoleni in south-eastern
Macedonia, between the lower reaches of the rivers Strouma and

Mesta; Velikiya in the Western Rhodope; Rupchos after the Ruptsi in the central Rhodope as far as Mount Strandja, etc.

These radical ethnical and political changes in the seventh century brought down Byzantine rule and the ancient administrative organization in the eastern and central parts of the Balkans. They marked the end of an epoch—Late Antiquity. The following eighth and ninth centuries constitute the transition towards the Middle Ages in that part of the Old World. The ancient names of the regions reflected natural conditions as did the rule of the Empire. The new conditions already imposed the use of another geographical nomenclature in practice, in conformity with the existing state of affairs.

Lower Moesia (Moesia Inferior) and Scythia Minor, devastated and void of its old population, received the name of their new lords, Bulgaria. Having no longer any relation with their ancient ethnical content, these provinces rapidly lost their names. Only the Byzantine writers, who were bent on archaization, called the Bulgarians 'Moesians' and 'Scythians', and for them 'Moesia' was the synonym of Bulgaria.[14] The central part of ancient Macedonia, inhabited by Kouber's Proto-Bulgarians was also called 'Land of the Bulgarians' (τῶν Βουλγάρων χώρα) and was the second Bulgaria in the heart of the Balkans.[15] The other tracts of land, occupied by the Slavs outside the new Bulgarian Empire on both sides of the Danube, were marked by the collective concepts of 'Sclaviniae' or called after the name of the corresponding tribe.

The very use in Byzantine literature and in other documents of the new names, Bulgaria and Sclaviniae, shows that people in the Empire fully understood the magnitude of the radical changes that had occurred in the Balkans. Their rulers, however, did not want to comply with these changes. That is obvious, firstly from the numerous assaults against the Bulgarian Empire and the Sclavinian principalities, and secondly from the basic transformations in Byzantine military and administrative organization in the eighth and ninth centuries. These aimed at the merger of civic and military power for greater efficiency. The marked thinning out of the old local population similarly led to the formation of bigger territorial units. These were named after the army unit, known as the 'theme' and could be called up if necessary as a militia, composed of local inhabitants and military settlers who were established in the 'theme'. The first themes were set up in Asia Minor to facilitate waging the wars against the Persians and the Arabs, and later, also in the Balkans, for the campaigns against the Proto-Bulgarians and the Sclavinians. With the appearance of the Bulgarian Khanate, the theme of Thrace was established[16] and between 687 and 695 the theme of Hellas (in Central Greece) for action against the Slavs.[17]

Yet, the threat to Byzantium and to its capital city in particular, was not contained. In the struggle for the return of its rule in the Balkan Peninsula, the Empire incessantly formed new themes, segments of the chain, which should have encircled the Bulgarians and the Slavs. Towards the year 800, to protect Constantinople, the theme Macedonia, with its centre in Adrianople, was set up, and for offensives against the Slavs, c. 805 or 807, the theme of Peloponnesus. Some time later, there appeared also the themes of Cephalonia (composed of the Ionian Islands), Dyrrachion and Thessalonica.[18]

The theme Macedonia included the basin of the River Maritsa and the Rhodope area, thus restricting the territory of the initial theme Thrace only within the scope of its south-eastern confines, i.e. the neighbouring hinterland of Europe on the Sea of Marmara and the southern strip of the Black Sea coast.[19] The newly-formed military and administrative unit took its name from the population of the former Roman and Early Byzantine provinces and diocese of Macedonia. The refugees, who were driven away by the Sclavinians and who were hostile to the new settlers in the Balkans, constituted the most reliable and belligerent element in the warfare waged by the Empire against the newcomers. The militia were reinforced by Armenians, Syrians and other resettled peoples from the Byzantine domains in the Near East. The settlements were grouped mainly in the plains of the Maritsa Valley and in the long run, thanks to its numbers, the Slavonic population that had penetrated into ancient Thrace also, took the upper hand. It assimilated the poorer strata of the indigenous population and of the emigrants from the East. In this respect, an important part was also played by the dualist concept brought over from Asia, which gave rise to the Bogomil heresy in the area of Philippople. From there it became widespread in Bulgarian lands and in Byzantium.[20]

In all probability, it was the heresies in Thrace which formed the link and led to a united front against Constantinopolitan rule and its Church by discontented military settlers and the Slav population, hostile to the Empire. Only those who were directly linked to and associated with the Byzantine rule and culture remained loyal to the Emperor and to Hellenism.

The themes of Macedonia and Thrace were of signal military and political significance in subsequent events in the Balkans and in the coming duel between Bulgaria and Byzantium for the affiliation of the Slav popular masses. For this reason, and also to a certain extent because of ethnical and ancient traditions, these themes imposed their names as regional ones on the territories where they were situated. The correctness of the ethnical explanation for the use of the mediaeval name of Macedonia for ancient Thrace, and in general for the practice, handed down from Antiquity, of imposing on the country the name of part of its population, is confirmed by another example. In the ninth century, when Khan Kroum deported the inhabitants of the theme Macedonia to his domains across the Danube, the region where they settled was given the name Macedonia during their brief stay there.[21]

However, the structure of the Byzantine theme did not always have the effect of forming a new geographical nomenclature for regions (as was the case with the setting up of the military and administrative unit of Macedonia; there was the additional factor in this instance of migration). This is distinctly seen in other, previously mentioned themes, as well as in those created later (Voleron, Philippopolis, Strymon, etc.). Their names were linked with towns or diverse geographical landmarks, but not with the ethnicon. An exception is the theme of Thessalonica, whose name relates to refugees from Thessaly—Hellenized elements who took shelter in Thessalonica and its vicinity after their homeland was taken over by Slavs. The part of ancient Macedonia along the Aegean sea coast, held by Byzantium, acquired the name of Thessaly.[22]

For a century and a half after its establishment along the Lower Danube, the Bulgarian Empire succeeded in winning to its side, and incorporating a large portion of the Sclaviniae. A major contribution was made to this end by Byzantium itself, and in particular its reprisals against the Slavs who rose to arms: c. 805–807 in central Greece, c. 837 against the Smoleni and other tribes in the northern hilly areas of Thessalonica, c. 847 in Peloponnesus (Morea), etc. In spite of the fact that the uprisings were crushed, the Empire was unable to restore its old rule over the peninsula. It consolidated only its hold on the coasts and created strongholds against the Slavs with the newly-established themes. Between 837 and 842, during the reigns of Khan Presiam (836–852) and his son Boris I, a considerable number of the Sclavinians in ancient Macedonia acceeded voluntarily and by peaceful means to the Bulgarian state. Byzantine chroniclers have left no information on the military activities of the Bulgarian khans against the Slavs; if there were such activities, they would not have been overlooked.

The formation of regional nomenclature in the eastern and central parts of the Balkans followed the general pattern of ancient traditions throughout the Middle Ages. The name for a piece of territory in a given country or province was closely related to ethnographical origins. A typical example is Macedonia. The political factor was also important in establishing a given name, in cases in which the name of the people was given to the military-administrative region or land (e.g. Bulgaria, Wallachia, Thrace, Dalmatia, etc.). These names gave meaning and touched lightly on the surrounding nationalities, and came to have more general geographical meaning.

Names designated for administrative units, which did not follow ethnographic traditions, were short lived, for example Paristrion, Strimon, Voleron and others. This was noticeable throughout the period of Ottoman rule when districts and areas were created which bore no resemblance to ethnographic composition and urban tradition. Later, more lasting names for the particular people of a region were based on how the land was divided up (for example Dolna and Gorna Zemia, Zagora etc.), or on ethnical and political considerations.

As a result of the almost complete isolation of the Balkan interior from the rest of the Christian world for centuries and because of the despotic rule of the sultan, traditional names for towns and regions remained unknown. This isolation from the West existed for a long period. Under the strong influence of the humanists and in the Renaissance, there were *a priori* reasons for the eastern and central parts of the Balkan Peninsula retaining the known Roman provincial nomenclature. This was without reference to the actual situation and ethnic attitudes and also did not take into account practical application and usage in urban settlements, which had retained the traditions of successive centuries.

It is at that time that the term 'Sclaviniae', which was of relatively short duration, disappeared from the literature and from everyday life. It was replaced by the name of the state, of which these principalities became an inseparable part. The establishment of the rule of Bulgarian khans in ancient Macedonia was only a minor reason for it receiving the name Bulgaria. There were also the following decisive preconditions for the change of name and its establishment.

1. Similar ethnical components in the population of the ancient provinces of Moesia and Macedonia, namely, Slavs of the same tribal group (Sclavinians), Proto-Bulgarians and some remnants of the old indigenous population, who did not take refuge in Byzantium.

2. A single process, occurring simultaneously, of the formation and consolidation of the Bulgarian nationality in the Balkans in the ninth and tenth centuries.

3. The fact that the central part of ancient Macedonia had gained popularity as the Land of the Bulgarians as early as the beginning of the eighth century, after the arrival of Kouber's Proto-Bulgarians there.

It is for this reason that in his Lexicon (compiled in the twelfth century), John Zonaras without any hesitation explains that Sclavinia is a synonym for Bulgaria. This is so because it was obviously the homonym of the country, in whose realm the Sclavinian tribes were included in the first half of the ninth century.

After the new mediaeval name for Macedonia was permanently established in ancient Thrace, Byzantine writers at the end of the ninth century, almost without exception, applied the name Bulgaria to the ancient provinces of Macedonia and Dardania. The ancient names of these two areas were forgotten both by the local population and by the neighbouring peoples. The presence of a theme of the same name in another part of the peninsula and the removal of its ancient ethnicon to the new location played an important part in this.[23]

The names of the individual Sclaviniae (Dragouvitia, Smolenia, Velikiya, etc.) were similarly lost, or mentioned only in the titles of bishops, although those of the Sclaviniae which remained for longer outside of the domains of the Bulgarian Empire (Vayonetiya, Veleyezitia, etc.) were preserved longer. They were eventually replaced however by the ancient names Epirus and Thessaly, which were reintroduced. This was after the fourteenth century, with the return of ancient traditions under the impact of Renaissance ideas, and in particular after the later re-identification of the local Slavs as Greeks.

In connection with the frontiers of the Bulgarian Empire, there appeared regional names, such as Zagore or Zagoria, having an initial meaning of 'land, situated across a mountain'. These are common names for numerous localities in the territories, inhabited by Bulgarian Slavs, where a mountain massif separated their state from another, or served as a frontier.[24] Examples of this are the plains beyond the Balkan Mountains, the Rhodope, Mount Zagrazhden and Mount Pirin. Plains in the periphery of the main areas inhabited by the Slavs were also named Zagore, if located across large mountain massifs, such as Pindus (in Epirus), Shar (in Kossovo Polje), the Carpathians (in Transilvania), etc., as were small plains between a mountain and the sea-coast, for example to the east of Pelion in Magnesin, the Helicon Mountain in Boiotia, etc.[25]

The Bulgarians called their vast state territory, bordering on the three seas, 'Bulgarian land' or 'Bulgaria'. With the administrative structure of the new arrivals, the land was divided into three main parts. In accordance with tradition, and hypsometric relationships, the land situated closer to the seas were called 'lower', and conversely the land farthest from the sea, 'upper' (Fig. 2). For instance, the Roman province of Moesia Inferior opened towards the Black Sea, while the upper province (Superior), opened towards the interior of the peninsula. To the Bulgarians 'lower' was the land facing the warm Aegean Sea, toward which they descended. In addition to these general definitions in accordance with hydrographic and orographic features of the sites, a decisive part was played by another custom, brought by the Proto-Bulgarians.

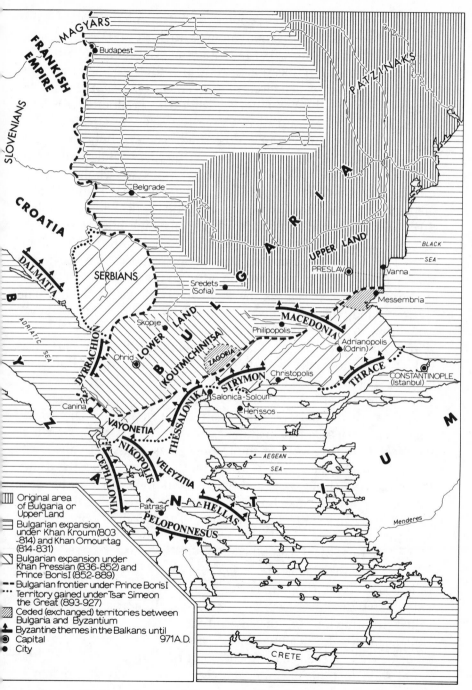

FIG. 2. Ethnic and political changes in the Balkans from A.D. 800–972.

To this day among certain peoples in central Asia, the definitions 'upper' and 'lower' are synonymous with East and West, respectively.[26] It is only, thus, that mountainous Macedonia (both in its ancient and modern location), contrary to hypsometrical relationships, could be called, according to an ancient tradition, 'Lower Bulgaria' or the 'Lower Land',[27] while the predominantly level Moesia and Thrace, was called 'Upper Bulgaria' or 'Upper Land.'

In addition one may confirm the subdivision of Bulgarian lands into three parts in the Middle Ages by the List of Bulgarian Archbishops of the twelfth century (also known to scholars as the *Catalogue of Du Cange*). In it there is a report that Prince Boris I dispatched Clement of Ochrida as a bishop of Tiberiople (modern Stroumitsa, Yugoslavia) and Velikia,[28] charging him 'to supervise also the third part of the Bulgarian Kingdom, i.e. from Thessalonica to Herissos and Canina or Tassipiyat.[29] Herissos is located in the Chalkidike Peninsula, and the latter, on the coast of the Adriatic Sea. If this report uses the popular division into 'Upper' and 'Lower' land, then obviously the third part is the 'Lower land', called thus in other script monuments.

It is feasible to assume that the shaping of the three parts was linked chronologically with the great expansion of the Bulgarian empire. The first was 'Upper Bulgaria', the initial territory of the state with the capital at Pliska, and later Preslav. It incorporated Moesia with the part of Thrace already conquered. The second part was 'Trans-Danubian Bulgaria', a large portion of which, as far as the middle reaches of the Danube, was annexed by the khans Kroum and Omourtag early in the ninth century, after the downfall of the Avar Khaganate and the division of its territory between Bulgaria and the Frankish Empire. The third, greater enlargement of Bulgaria came with the unification of the kindred population of ancient Macedonia and the greater part of modern Albania. This took place towards the middle of the ninth century.

It is known from *Legenda Bulgarica* by Theophylakt of Ochrida Bulgaria's Archbishop, that during the reign of Prince Boris I (852–889) the south-eastern part of the Bulgarian Empire was called Koutmichinitsa, the Byzantine transcription of a Proto-Bulgarian word, meaning 'newly-acquired' or 'newly-annexed' land. In view of the rapid expansion of the Bulgarian Empire, that name soon lost its meaning and was replaced by the names of the main towns of the new arrivals, i.e. Devol, Stroumitsa, etc.[30]

The traditional and popular division of Bulgarian lands was retained even after mediaeval Bulgaria ceased to exist. The tradition was preserved also in the coat of arms in its last dynasty, that of the Shishmans: three lions, placed one above the other, as symbols of every part of Bulgaria's domains. Subsequently, in designing the coats of arms of the three main Bulgarian regions: Moesia or Bulgaria, Thrace and Macedonia, the three lions were separated, each forming a basic element, in accordance with the common practices of heraldry. Again three similar symbols— greyhounds—also appeared in the coat of arms of Bulgaria in a heraldic inventory of Hungary in 1766.[31]

In A.D. 1018 Bulgaria fell under Byzantine domination. With the downfall of the First Bulgarian Empire, the barrier which checked the raids by the Turkic peoples, such as the Patzinaks, Uses, etc. at Europe's eastern gate, also disappeared. The military and administrative structure of Bulgaria's territories, conquered by Byzantium, was evolved in view of the new tasks: to make secure the north-eastern realm of the Empire. The themes of the Danubian towns Paristrion and Sirmium were created from the two ancient Moesias in the Upper Land. The Western part of Trans-Danubian Bulgaria fell under the rule of the Magyars, while Byzantium held a part of the eastern territory for a short while. Thus, in present-day Bessarabia, between the rivers Proutul and Dnjestre, the theme Mesopotamia of the West, was set up. It disintegrated, however, in the first decades of the eleventh century under the blows of the invaders from the East.[32] The Lower Land, where towards the end of its existence after the capture of the capital city Preslav in A.D. 972, the centre of the Bulgarian state was transferred to Ochrida, a new Byzantine theme was established with Skopije as its centre (Fig. 3). It alone retained the name of the conquered state—Bulgaria. The seat of the Bulgarian Patriarchate, transformed by the conqueror Basil II Bulgaroktonus into an autocephalous Bulgarian Archbishopric, remained in Ochrid.

For the third time, by virtue of administrative decisions and for terminological and political reasons, ancient Macedonia re-established its name—Bulgaria. At that time it took a regional sense, without, however, replacing the general name of Bulgaria,

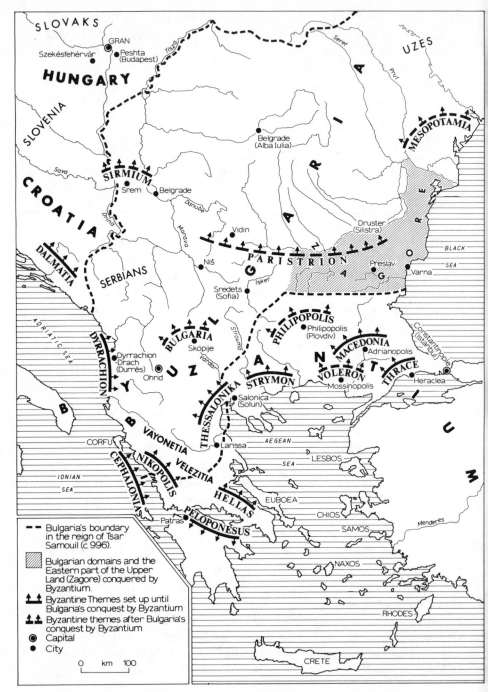

FIG. 3. Political changes in the Balkans, A.D. 972–1185.

existing simultaneously with it, or the archaized Byzantine term of Moesia, in the sense of the lands, inhabited by a Bulgarian population. The Bulgarians, however, stuck to the division of their homeland into the customary three parts.

There was a change with the restoration of the Bulgarian Empire in 1185. Its centre again returned to the Upper Land, and Turnovo became the capital city. From the viewpoint of the population of the Lower Land (i.e. ancient Macedonia), as well as that of the Byzantine themes Macedonia and Thrace the Upper Land was called Zagoré. (Note that the regional name Zagoré was given to land which was inhabited by a homogenous population, which, however, was separated by a mountain, serving as a frontier.) This was possible, after its fall under Byzantine rule in 972. At that time, mountain massifs, serving as frontier areas with the Byzantine Empire, separated it from Bulgarian lands, with a state centre in Ochrida, which remained free and independent until A.D. 1018. Being a shorter term, Zagoré was the preferred form and a synonym of the Upper Land or Upper Bulgaria for the inhabitants of the Lower Land.

After Turnovo was proclaimed capital and the seat of its Archbishop (and later Patriarch), the rulers and the head of the Bulgarian Church acquired the name Zagorski or Zagorian. This name would have been widely used in the spoken language, by the people and for this reason it was adopted by the authorities as well.[33] The name Zagoré, given to the heart and centre of the Second Bulgarian Empire by the inhabitants of the Lower Land, was taken up also by the neighbouring peoples. As early as the thirteenth and fourteenth centuries it was adopted by Serbians, Italians, Byzantines, and later also by the Ottoman Turks during their invasion of the Balkans. Thus Zagoré became the synonym of Bulgaria in general and acquired a secondary meaning.[34] In the Late Middle Ages, the term passed into Italian cartographic images of the Balkans and then was used in some German and other maps.[35]

The Ottoman conquest of the Balkans found regional names, well established among the local population, which had formed as a result of ethnic changes and the political state of affairs in the Middle Ages (Fig. 4). The name Bulgaria was retained along with that of Lower Land, Lower Bulgaria or Lower Moesia, respectively, chiefly for the western territories,[36] ancient Macedonia,

FIG. 4. Names of regions and countries, established during the Second Bulgarian Empire.

populated by Bulgarians. The north-eastern parts were called Zagoré or Upper Land (Upper Bulgaria),[37] while the basin of the River Maritsa in ancient Thrace, in accordance with the Byzantine theme structure, was called Macedonia. Owing to the long duration of Bulgarian rule over its northern and western parts, it was known as Bulgarian Macedonia.[38] South-eastern Thrace (which was the only one to retain the name of the ancient province, Thrace, thanks to the Byzantine theme of the same name), as well as the Adrianople area were also called Romania, because of their prolonged affiliation to the Empire. In fact, the Ottoman Turks, on reaching the Balkans, clashed with the Byzantines and for this reason they called the territories conquered by them, Rum-ili or Roman Land; later this was a general name for their other European domains. It is from this term that the later west European one, 'Rumelia', was derived. By a religious criterion that name was given to all lands inhabited by Eastern Orthodox Christians in the central and eastern parts of the Balkans belonging to the sultan's realm. The Ottoman Sultan placed them under the Greek Patriarchate of Constantinople, which had abolished the Turnovo Bulgarian Patriarchate towards the end of the fourteenth century.

Some of the small independent states, set up after the decline of the central power in Byzantium and in Bulgaria introduced new names to countries, such as Wallachia, Albania, etc. The former came into being as a state in the fourteenth century in a part of Bulgaria's territories across the Danube, when its Second Empire was in the period of feudal dismemberment.

The rule of the sultan could not impose new names on regions and areas by its imperial organization, and to a large degree, the latter conformed with the territories of the separate feudal possessions, and not with the nations inhabiting the Balkans. Fortresses, near which decisive battles were fought during the conquest of the peninsula, were selected for centres of the sanjaks. The fortresses lent names to the administrative unit, e.g. Nicopolis Sanjak, in which the territories of the Turnovo Tsardome to the north of the Balkan Mountains at its subjugation were incorporated; the land of the Dobroudja Principality was included in the Silistra Sanjak; the domains of Tsar John Sratsimir–in the Vidin Sanjak; those of the Dragash despots—in the Kyustendil Sanjak, etc.[39] As in the Middle Ages administrative units that were named after their town-capitals, without taking into account the ethnical composition of the population, could not form durable toponyms. It is for this reason, that, even after both Bulgarian and Byzantine administrative organizations were destroyed, the traditions of mediaeval regional, geographical nomenclature were not impaired in the concepts and consciousness of the indigenous population.

Both monuments in local script and a number of foreign observer-travellers in the fifteenth to eighteenth centuries bear testimony to the preservation of the names of regions and areas, established during the Middle Ages. The majority of travellers passed along the old military highway from Vienna via Belgrade and Sofia to Constantinople. Those that had closer contact with the population report that after crossing the Rivers Morava and Nish, they entered 'Bulgaria', and after the mountain pass 'Trajan's Gates', into 'Macedonia' with its main towns Philippople and Adrianople.[40]

These local traditions of the Middle Ages, however, clashed with the concepts in the West concerning the names of countries and of the population in south-eastern Europe. These concepts were formed under the influence of Renaissance ideas, and as a result of the respect held by cartographers for the traditions of the Roman provincial structure. Also, the names of the Roman administrative nomenclature were not fully effaced from mediaeval maps of the world, where the Roman provinces continued to be marked, along with certain new facts and changes that had taken place after the downfall of the World Empire.[41]

Christians in Western Europe had incomplete and sparse information on the Balkan Peninsula, and on its interior regions in particular, owing to its almost entire isolation. They believed that the descendants of Greeks, Thracians, Dacians, Macedonians and Illyrians still lived there, but that their religion was 'Greek', i.e. Eastern Orthodox. Thus, they continued to call by their ancient names those inhabitants of the Balkans who were oppressed and stereotyped under the Ottoman yoke. For people who were imbued by humanistic ideas, these countries were veiled in mystery and were adorned in the imagination with the beauty of Antiquity and the attractiveness of Eastern exotics. In Western Europe, the classical geographers enjoyed an irrefutable prestige. Thus, in more modern times, the traditional Roman geographical nomenclature was not only retained, but found fresh arguments in Claudius Ptolemy's *Cosmography*. For a long time, it remained the main source of information on the state of affairs in that part of the old World. As a consequence, the names Thrace and Macedonia covered areas, both in the literature and the cartography of western Europe, they had in Antiquity. In the Balkans, there had been little progress since the second century A.D., when they were described by the Alexandrian cartographer.[42]

'Moesia', which was not related to an ancient ethicon, was replaced by 'Bulgaria' in the mediaeval tradition, as there was information about the existence of such a country and people. However, only the space between the Balkan Mountains and the Danube was left and allotted to them, after the map had been divided into the countries of the glory-covered Macedonians of Alexander the Great and of the Thracians of Orpheus. Thus, in the maps of more modern times, three provinces, actually non-existent in the Ottoman administrative structure, are formed in the central and eastern parts of the Peninsula. In fact the inhabitants of these regions held totally different concepts of the locations and scope covered by these names.[43]

Towards the middle of the nineteenth contury, modern geographical science undertook a systematic study of the unknown hinterland of the Balkans. These investigations helped in the gradual dissipation of stratified delusions that they formed a 'Hellenic world' and a 'Greek Peninsula', both ethnically and culturally. The 'discoveries', however had no effect on the widespread use of an ancient regional nomenclature in free Europe.[44] In spite of everything, it remained valid and unaltered. Moreover, step by step, after relations with Western Europe and the penetration of its civilization became brisker, the peoples, subjugated to the Sultan, began to hear of this nomenclature and it was adopted by the indigenous population although the mediaeval names and meanings were lost.

9. Notes

1. Since the reign of Emperor Aurelianus (A.D. 270–275) Dacia has been situated to the south of the Danube, where a considerable part of the

population of Trajan's Dacia fled after the invasion of the Carps in A.D. 245.
A similar instance of shifts of names of countries is the case of Moesia in
Asia Minor, where a part of the Thracian tribe of the Moesians resettled
from the Balkan Peninsula. As a rule, countries' names are in a definitive
relationship with those of their inhabitants and follow their settling in new
domiciles.

2. The barbarian invasions and the settlement of the Slavs is abundantly
elucidated in the general course of Byzantine and Balkan history.

   For greater detail on the penetration of the southern Slavs into modern
Greece and Albania see:

   А. М. Селищев, *Славянское население в Албании.* София (1931);

   L. Niederle, *Manuel de l'antiquité slave.* Paris (1939);

   M. Vasmer, *Die Slaven in Griechenland.* Berlin. APAW, Philos.-hist. Klass.
No. 12 (1941);

   P. Lemerle, 'Invasions et migrations dans les Balkans depuis la fin de
l'époque romaine jusqu'au VIIIe siècle'. *Revue Historique* CCLI (April–
June, 1954), 270 *et seq.*;

   Д. Ангелов, *Образуване на българската народност.* София (1971),
pp. 141 *et seq.*

3. See Д. Ангелов, op. cit. (1971), pp. 103 *et seq.*

4. For the areas of settlement of the two South-Slavonic groups (the Serbo-
Croatian and the Bulgarian) see L. Niederle, *La Race Slave. Statistique,
antropologie, demographie,* Paris (1916), and especially the map supplied by
him, giving the state of settlements in the seventh to eighth centuries. The
distribution of the ethnical groups on the Balkan Peninsula is given at the
time of their establishment and the formation of Slav nationalities and the
boundaries of the spread of South-Slavonic languages are indicated there.

5. In addition to references in note 2, see also:

   Ив. Д. Шишманов, 'Славянски селища в Крит и другите острови',
Български преглед, 4 (1897), 97 *et seq.*;

   P. Charanis, 'The chronicle of Monemvasia and the question of the Slavonic
settlements in Greece. *Dumbarton Oaks Papers* 5 (1950), 39–166;

   A. Bon, *Le Peloponèse byzantin jusqu'en 1204.* Paris (1951).

6. *Miracula Sancti Demetrii,* II, V, 197.

7. L. Niederle Manuel, op. cit. I, 104–105.

8. One can judge the status of Slavonic territories, after they were reconquered
by Byzantium from the report of Emperor Constantine VII Porphyrogenitus
in *De administrando imperio* ed. by Gy. Moravcsik and R. J. H. Jenkins,
Budapest (1949), 50, 1–180, p. 232. The Morean Sclavinians were
described as 'independent' and 'autonomous and self-ruling'.

9. В. Н. Златарски, *История на българската държава през средните
векове,* Vol. I (1), София (1918), pp. 17 *et seq.,* 136, 160 etc.;

П. Мутафчиев, *История на българския народ*, Vol. I, София (1943), pp. 82, 144, 160 etc.;

F. Dvornik, *Les Slaves, Byzance et Rome au IXe siècle*. Paris (1926), pp. 12 *et seq.*;

Idem. *Le légende de Constantin et de Méthode vue de Byzance.* Prague (1933), pp. 15 *et seq.*

10. Ив. Дуйчев, 'Славяни и първобългари'. *Известия на Института за българска история*, Vols 1, 2 (1951), pp. 197 *et seq.*

11. See Fr. Dölger, Ein Fall slavischer Einsiedlung im Hinterland von Thessalonike im 10. Jahrhundert, *Sitzungsberichte der Bayerische Akademie der Wissenschaften, Philosoph.-historiche Abteilung* I (1952), 25 *et seq.*

12. Theophani Chronographia, rec. *C. de Boor*, vol. I, Leipzig (1883), pp. 364, 430, 486 etc.

13. Ив. Дуйчев, 'Нови житейни данни за похода на Никифор I в България през 811 г.' *Списание на БАН*, LIV (1936), 149–150;
Scriptor Incertus de Leone Armenio, Leonis Grammatici Chronographia, rec. *J. Bekkeri*. Bonn (1842), p. 347.

14. For the use of the names 'Moesians' and 'Moesia', meaning 'Bulgarians' and 'Bulgaria' see Gy. Moravcsik, *Byzantinoturcica*, II, Berlin (1958), 207–208.

15. *Nicephori i archiepiscopi Constantinopolitani Opuscula Historica*, ed. by C. de Boor, pp. 55, 56;
Theophani Chronographia, p. 430 etc.
The first to attract attention on that report was G. Cankova-Petkova, 'Bulgaria and Byzantium during the First Decades after the Foundation of the Bulgarian State', *Byzantinoslavica*, XXIV (1), Prague (1963), 41–53.

16. In accordance with the explicit mention of Constantine Porhyrogenitus in his work *De thematibus* ed. by A. Pertusi, *Studii e testi*, No. 160. Città del Vaticano, No. 86 (1952).
D. Obolensky, *The Byzantine Commonwealth, Eastern Europe, 500–1453.* London (1971), pp. 76 *et seq.*;
N. Oikonomidès, *Les listes de préséance byzantine de IXe et Xe siècles.* Paris (1972), pp. 76 *et seq.*

17. Г. Острогорский, 'Постанак тема Хелада и Пелопонес', *Зборник радова САН*, I, (1952), 64–76.

18. П. Коледаров, 'Образуване на тема Македония в Тракия', *Известия на Института за история*, 21 (1970), 222*et seq.*

19. Ibid. 236 *et seq.*

20. P. Koledarov, 'On the initial hearth of Bogomilism', in *Materiaux du symposium international 'Tirnovo et l'Etat bulgare moyenageux—centre de mouvements heretiques' (XII–XIV s.)*, V. Tirnovo (1973).

21. Georgii Hamartoli Chronicon (ed. by E. de Muralt, Petropoli (1859), pp. 724–725.

22. In the Old-Bulgarian translation of *Legenda Ochridica* by Demetrius Chomatianus, Archbishop of Ochrida, written early in the thirteenth century, 'Thessaly' is translated as the 'Thessalonica area'. Obviously, in the minds of mediaeval Bulgarians Thessalonica was the centre of Thessaly, and not of Macedonia. The theme 'Macedonia' of that time had its centre in Adrianople.

23. The ancient meaning of the name 'Macedonia' was preserved only in parchment manuscripts and maps in the Middle Ages, to reappear again from time to time as a parachronism. Only the more conservative-minded ecclesiastic circles, and occasionally single members of the Byzantine literary circle used it for a couple of centuries after the setting up of the theme 'Macedonia' in Thrace. These are mostly cases when they were forced to use the term at times of ultimate danger for their homeland, Byzantium, in order to produce arguments in support of their claims on ancient Macedonia and to draw on its grandeur and might. They took the ancient Kingdom from oblivion with the aim of stimulating the patriotic feelings of the population of the Empire, but even in such cases, the name 'Macedonia' had only a regional and geographic content, and not an ethnic one. Many of these writers, when they archaize, deem it necessary to explain what they have in mind, namely the ancient Macedonia, and not the contemporary one. This is the case for instance with Anastasius the Librarian (in *Vita Hadriani* II, 636), and Theophylact of Ochrid, Archbishop of Bulgaria (in the *Vita of the Tiberiople martyrs*—J. P. Migne, PGr, Vol. 126, col. 151). The theme 'Macedonia' imposed its name to such a degree on Byzantine everyday life that, in certain cases, it became the cause for retrospective actualization: in its mediaeval scope and location the name 'Macedonia' was transposed to events that took place prior to the formation of the theme, and in fact in the confines of Thrace in Antiquity.

24. P. Koledarov, 'More about the Name "Zagoré".' *Bulgarian Historical Review*, 4, (1973), 100, 106.

25. Ibid. pp. 93, 99.

26. Thus, for instance, in the Turkmenian language the word 'okari' denotes 'East', i.e. the point where the sun rises, and 'oshag' denotes 'West', i.e., where the sun sets. See Э. М. Мурзаев, 'Основные направления топономастических исследований' in *Принципы топонимики*, Москва (1964), p. 31.

Even today in Bulgarian dialects the East Wind is called 'Gornyak' i.e. coming from the Upper Land (Gorna zemya), while the West Wind is the opposite, 'Dolnyak', coming from the Lower Land (Dolna zemya).

27. It is found, for instance, in the deed of King Constantine Asen (1251–1277),

granted to the monastery of Virginsko Burdo near Skopije, in the Old-Bulgarian translation of *Manasses' Chronicle* and other Bulgarian documents of the Middle Ages.

28. According to reports by Theophylact of Ochrida in Legenda Bulgarica, as 'First Bishop in the Bulgarian language of the Dragouvites and of Velikia'. See quotations in П. Коледаров, 'Климент Охридски, "Първи епископ на български език" на драгувитите в Солунско и на Великия в Западните Родопи' in *Константин-Кирил Философ*, София (1969), pp. 160–161.

29. Ibid. pp. 157 *et seq.*

30. Ibid. pp. 158–159.

31. Francisco Carolo Palma, *Heraldicae regni Hungariae spesimen*, Vienna (1766). The Proto-Bulgarians held the lion and the dog as sacred animals.

32. For the Byzantine theme across the Danube see Ив. Вожилов, 'Към въпроса за византийското господство на Долни Дунав в края на X в.', *Studia Balcanica*, 2 Sofia (1970), 81–95; Oikonomidès, op. cit., pp. 263, 269, 363.

33. P. Koledarov, op. cit. (1973a), pp. 100–102.

34. Ibid. pp. 102–104.

35. Ibid. pp. 104–105. Idem. 'The Bulgarian State in Medieval Cartography' in *Etudes historiques*, Vol. IV (à l'occasion du VIIe Congrès international des études slaves—Varsovie), Sofia (1973), p. 48.

36. For the use of the terms by Bulgarian men-of-letters in Macedonia in the nineteenth century see P. Koledarov, op. cit. (1969), pp. 161–162.

37. P. Koledarov op. cit. (1973a), pp. 100 *et seq.*

38. See, for instance, the Dechani Synodikon of the twelfth century in В. А. Мошин, 'Сербская редакция Синодика в Неделю православия, *Византийский Временник* XVII (1960), 347–348.

39. See П. Коледаров, 'Към въпроса за развитието на селищната мрежа и на нейните елементи в средищната и източната част на Балканите от VII до XVIII век', *Известия на Института за история*, 18 (1967), 108.

40. Certain instances for such testimony and findings are given in P. Koledarov op. cit. (1970), p. 239, footnote No. 18.

41. See P. Koledarov, op. cit. (1973a), pp. 37–51.

42. For greater detail see P. Koledarov (1973). 'Traditions of antiquity and the Middle Ages in the regional nomenclature in the modern map of the Balkans', *Byzantinobulgarica*, IV, 171–174.

43. Ibid. pp. 156 *et seq.*, pp. 173–174.

44. Ibid. pp. 173–174.

10

The Industrial Development of Romania from the Unification of the Principalities to the Second World War

D. TURNOCK

Introduction

In common with her neighbours in south-east Europe, Romania has achieved remarkably high rates of economic development in the post-war period. Although considerable emphasis is now being placed on the intensification of agriculture and the modernization of transport the main concern remains with the manufacturing sector, a priority repeatedly underlined by political statements.[1] Strategic consideration within the communist bloc have lost some of the impetus gained during Stalin's life, but the national forces which have to some extent replaced them have led to only a limited shift in investment priorities. Moreover, Romanian communications media also convey the impression that this forceful progress since the Second World War followed a long period of relatively limited achievement. Thus, a major geographical work concludes a brief examination of statistical data with the opinion that distribution patterns were irrational and even chaotic in the days of 'România burghezo-moşierească,' the polemical label frequently applied to both the old Kingdom ('Regat')[4] and Greater

Romania ('România Mare'), the enlarged state which emerged from the First World War.[2]

This historical perspective strengthens the impression of recent revolutionary progress. The author has argued that the communist model applied since the late 1940s is merely one of a series of radical solutions applied to solve the country's economic problems.[3] Some significant progress was recorded in the late eighteenth century and early nineteenth century, especially after a constitution was provided for Principalities in 1832 in the form of the Organic Statutes. Still greater efforts followed in the period after the unification of Moldava and Walachia in 1959, (and the achievement of independence in 1878), and again, during the short interlude between the two World Wars. It is with these two periods that this essay is concerned, periods which offer strong contrasts in development patterns arising from technological change and from major differences in the international climate and in the political make-up of the country (Fig. 1). Considerable statistical information is available and there are several valuable contemporary accounts.[5]

The Socio-Political Context

The country's agricultural endowment includes a large area suitable for arable farming with a range of climatic conditions from the temperate towards the sub-tropical[6] but the best land in the Bărăgan and Dobrogea suffers from the rigour of a steppe environment and irrigation is needed to overcome the risks of severe drought. Sugar beet, sunflowers and soya beans are suitable industrial crops but among the textile plants the traditional crops of flax and hemp tend to be most prominent. Cotton was tried during, and more especially after, the Second World War but results were unsatisfactory. The mountainous areas are an obvious base for lumbering. They also favour pastorialism in view of the fodder available from hayfields (fînete) and rougher grazings (pașuni) unsuitable for arable farming. The development of stockraising on the plains has been inhibited in modern times by the priority given to cereals, a most convenient export crop, but intensification is gradually allowing more land to be switched to fodder production. The mineral endowment of the 'Regat' consisted mainly of oil

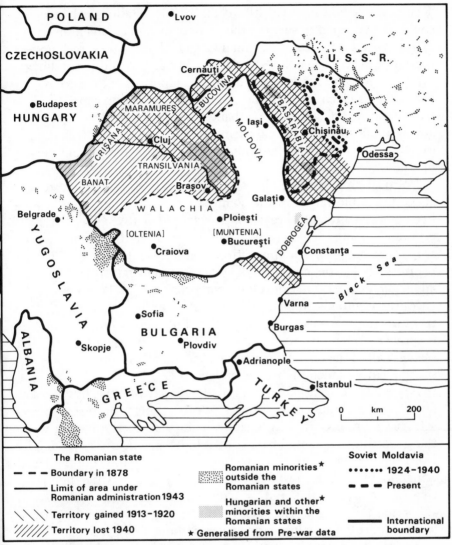

FIG. 1. Location map.

reserves that furnished a secondary export staple (after 1900) and provided power for the food processing, sawmilling, textile and cement industries established before the First World War. Engineering industries, of great strategic importance to the country, were compromised by a lack of iron ore or coking coal within the old Kingdom. Metalliferous ores were comparatively plentiful in

Transilvania however and the established metallurgical industry
could be expanded to support the growth of Romanian engineering
in the 1920s and 1930s. Unfortunately, despite new techniques,
mostly perfected since the Second World War, to allow metallurgical use of low grade resources domestic supply of both ore and coal
has failed to catch up with the growth of production capacity. The
vast deposits of salt and methane gas have however created a
strong domestic base for the chemical industry, though technological constraints again limited the possibilities for the present period
of study.

Political circumstances have not always been favourable to the
sustained exploitation of the country's resources but a new stability emerged after the Treaty of Adrianople of 1828. The Ottoman
economic monopoly was broken and progressive Russian influences
helped to build an administration restored to the care of native
princes. Modest development of agriculture and industry[7] prompted
advocacy of a national development programme: bounties might
encourage suitable industries, especially textiles, and afford protection against excessive competition. But there were few sources
of power and political weakness was not overcome until the
second half of the century when the Principalities were unified[8] and
subsequently gained their independence.

Beyond the Carpathians, in Transilvania, there were, by contrast,
fewer political upheavals and a greater range of resources to
attract capital in spite of the centralizing tendencies instinctive to
the great imperialisms of the time. Independence freed Romania
from the stranglehold of a suzerain power, but the country faced
a formidable defence problem, with a very long frontier line relative to the area of the state. Furthermore, with limited industrial
skills and unstable world prices for primary export commodities,
it was difficult to maintain progress without foreign financial and
technical assistance. Growth on an autarkic basis has been invariably regarded as politically desirable. Thus, in the years after
independence, there were strong voices urging protection,[9] voices
that have been favourably reviewed in recent times.[10]

Generous concessions were made available to indigenous
industrialists supported by a growth of financial institutions and
vigorous programmes of education and railway construction, but
the heady years of economic confrontation gave way to a more

accommodating attitude to foreign capital crucial in the development of the oilfields and the sale of oil abroad. Heavy protection was also injurious to agricultural exports a special economic concern because of the strong political position of the boiars, the native landowning aristocracy. The class structure may well have inhibited investment in social overhead capital for the benefit of all sections of the population and help to explain why a period of unprecedented expansion was marked, in 1907, by a full-scale peasant revolt.[11]

Romania emerged from the First World War with a far greater area, population and industrial capacity. There was a substantial growth potential emerging from the union of both sides of the Carpathian arc and a new social structure, forced by the war experience and the enhanced political awareness of the peasantry, promised land reform in 1917;[12] land reform destroyed the *latifundia* and the political strength of the Conservative party[13] transferring ascendancy to the Liberals with their strong urban-industrial power base. Vested interests in industrial growth and hostility to foreign capital were strong underpinnings to an intensely nationalistic programme inspired by the dictum 'prin noi înşine' (by ourselves alone). But Romania was faced with serious problems after the war in creating a stable economic foundation and integrating the new provinces.[14] These tasks were not eased by unstable world market prices that prevented the accumulation of trade surpluses large enough to service foreign debts and thereby necessitated relatively stringent methods to mobilize funds internally. Despite import tariffs among the highest in Europe by 1927, and export taxes that depressed the agricultural sector, the Brătianu regime was unable to generate investment capital and consumers were caught in a price scissors where low agricultural prices were set against rising costs for manufacture.[15]

Romania was brought back more fully into the world economic system in 1928 by the National-Peasant government. Tariffs were moderated and foreign loans contracted. The new economic policy gained considerable publicity through the writing of Virgil Madgearu, who argued that industrial development required an adequate home market which in turn depended upon progress in the agricultural sector, where the productive power of small and medium farmers needed stimulation. Stronger credit institutions would support the land improvement recommended by the researches of Gr. Antipa and G. Ionescu-Şişeşti, but this popular policy was undermined by the depression, since falling prices for primary exports reduced the resources that could be ploughed into agricultural development. The monarchy came more directly into the political arena for Carol II spent the 1930s perfecting 'monarchofascism', with an economic philosophy veering to the Liberal view of unbalanced development to favour key industries.[16] Closer economic links with Germany provided some welcome stability in the exports of primary commodities and permitted increased imports of industrial plants.[17] The German link was strengthened in 1939 under growing political pressure as mixed companies were envisaged in such fields as mining and mineral processing. Industries of strategic importance were emphasized, notably armaments and chemicals, and this encouraged expansion of steel output which doubled from 145,000 tons in 1933 to 277,000 in 1938. This orientation reached a climax during the Second World War when Romanian raw materials and manufactures were invaluable to the Axis cause, seen by many as the only vehicle for some restoration of frontiers that collapsed so dramatically in 1940.

Policies may seem sharply contrasting in retrospect. Certainly the National-Peasant government attempted to place democracy and the smallholder at the centre of the stage. Yet all parties were agreed on the basic need for industry, especially where this involved the valorisation of domestic raw materials. All parties likewise sympathized with arguments for protection[18] and even post-war literature has made some positive comment over support for the idea of a national plan for industry canvassed by such eminent economists as M. Constantinescu and V. Madgearu.[19] It might even be argued[20] that all parties accepted the need for foreign assistance, with the reservation that national interests should not be subordinated, for even Liberal policy in the 1920s envisaged a degree of cooperation with foreign interests and regarded self-sufficiency only as a temporary measure to increase the share of Romanian capital in major enterprises. Governments may have sought new relationships with foreign capital through changing international conditions but the element of continuity in policy imposed by the objective conditions of the country should not be obscured.

The Fuel and Power Question

The well documented geography of fuel and power resources is important in providing an essential context for the study of industrial location problems. Romania's oil resources are associated with Tertiary rocks folded during the Carpathian mountain building. The most important oil bearing structures comprised a series of structural alignments between the Buzău and Dîmboviţa valleys roughly parallel to the grain of the Carpathians. West of the Dîmboviţa, exploration effort, beginning in the 1930s, was not rewarded until about 1950. There are also oil deposits in the eastern Carpathians in the Bacău area, where there are eighteenth-century references to the use of oil as cart axle grease and for lighting the homes of the aristocracy.[21] The Treaty of Adrianople created conditions for international trade in oil and small companies were operating in the Moineşti area, by 1835, working shallow wells lined with impermeable clay and supported by some timber or wickerwork. A burst of drilling activity in the early 1860s, coinciding with the American Civil War, was not sustained and it was not until after 1890 that output was substantially increased. Meanwhile more remarkable developments were taking place in the Prahova Valley. Hand-dug wells, with ventilation and winding provided by horse power,[22] persisted until the turn of the century by which time depths of 250 metres (attained after three to four years digging in hazardous conditions) were not unknown, but from 1885 when mechanical drilling at Drăgăneasa on the Cantacuzino estates produced a flow of some 10,000 tons per annum, large scale operation produced the bulk of the output. Generally the small scale of activity had made it difficult to finance mechanical drilling programmes which would keep the industry fully competitive with the growing American counterpart. However, the industry received a major fillip in 1890 through government acceptance of foreign oil companies. The legal position was tidied up by the Mining Law of 1895 and almost immediately the largely German financed 'Steaua Română' went into operation.[23]

By 1898 their deep boring in the Cîmpina-Buştenari area had doubled production from that field and in 1904 came still greater success with the discovery of oil in the second structural alignment at Moreni. Moreni, with neighbouring structures of Boldești, Gura Ocniței and Ochiuru, produced 67 million tons of oil up to 1937, nearly 63 per cent of all recorded Romanian production up to that time. From only 10·3 thousand tons in 1890 Prahova production soared to a pre-war peak of 1·68 million tons in 1913, its contribution to national output rising from 19·3 to 89·0 per cent. Despite a clear concentration of effort, encouraged by a few particularly successful discoveries and the high cost of operation in rough country away from main lines of communication, it should not be overlooked that both production and exploration areas were considerable.[24] Many sites in Prahova county (and in adjacent counties of Buzău and Dîmbovița) had been studied and some interest was shown in the counties of Gorj and Vîlcea as early as the 1880s (Fig. 2a).

After the First World War the oil companies faced the task of restoring the damaged oilfields in an economic climate of low prices and a political climate in which Romanian national interests were strongly pressed. After narrowly escaping complete surrender of the oil industry to the Berlin controlled Öelpacht, under the Treaty of București of 1918 a national exploration company was formed in 1919, Creditul Minier and 1920, Industria Română de Petrol' (I.R.D.P.).[25] A new Mining Law in 1924 placed the state in a strong directing role throughout the industry and revised terms of working in favour of Romanian nationals. The national companies[26] had only limited resources but only the

---

FIG. 2. Oil resources: a. progress to 1918; b. progress to 1944; c. oil refining. Sources: M. Pizanty (1938, 1947) *op. cit.*; *Enciclopedia romăniei, 3, 650 op. cit.* *Key* *Oilfields in Buzău, Prahova and Dîmbovița Counties:* 1. Drăgăneasa; 2. Cîmpina; 3. Telega; 4. Buștenari; 5. Vărbilău; 6. Popești; 7. Tega; 8. Doicești; 9. Glodeni; 10. Colibași/Valea Reșca; 11. Runcu/Scorțeni; 12. Vîlcanești; 13. Scăiosi; 14. Copăceni; 15. Matita/Păcureți; 16. Aninoasa/Teiș; 17. Viforîta; 18. Gorgota; 19. Ochiuri; 20. Mislea/Bordeni; 21. Măgurele; 22. Podenii Noi; 23. Udrești; 24. Apostolache; 25. Dragomirești; 26. Razvad; 27. Gura Ocniței; 28. Moreni; 29. Filipești; 30. Băicoi; 31. Liliești; 32. Țintea; 33. Boldești; 34. Cornet-Cricov; 35. Călugăreni; 36. Berca; 37. Arbanași; 38. Comișani; 39. Bucșcani; 40, Mărgineni; 41. Aricești; 42. Valea Călugărească/Chițorani; 43. Ceptura; 44. Srăata Monteoru; 45. Mănești/Vlădeni; 46. Brazi; *Oilfields in Bacău and Neamț Counties:* 1. Zemeș/Tazlău Sărat; 2. Lucăcești/Moinești; 3. Comănești; 4. Darmanești/Plopu; 5. Cucuieți; 6. Dofteana; 7. Grozești-Hîrja; 8. Călcîi; 9. Schitu Frumoasa; 10. Stanești/Solonț; 11. Cîmpeni/Parjol; 12. Tețcani/Scorțeni; 13. Berzunți.

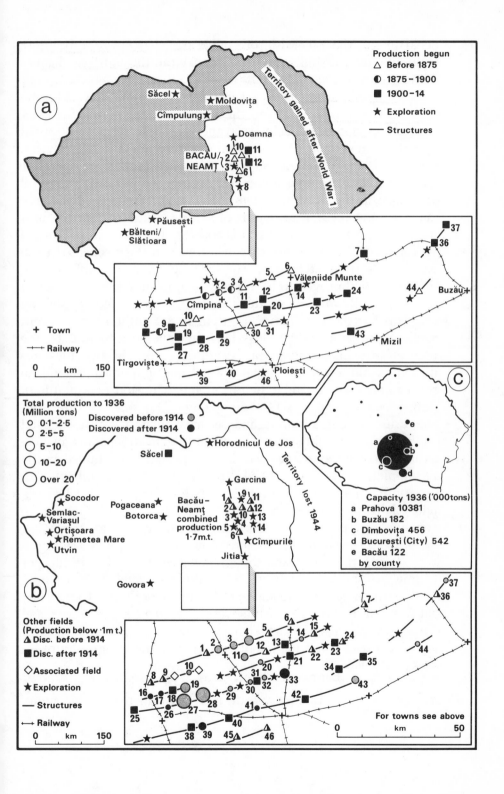

a

Production begun
△ Before 1875
◑ 1875–1900
■ 1900–14
★ Exploration
— Structures

Săcel ★ ★ Moldoviṭa
Cîmpulung ★

Territory gained after World War 1

★ Doamna
1 10 ■ 11
BACĂU 2 △ △ ■ 12
NEAMṬ 3 ★ 6
7 ★ 8

★ Păuseṣti
★ Bălteni/
Slătioara

■ 37
■ 36
7 ★

★ ★ 2 3 4 5 △ 6 + Văleniide Munte
1 ◑ △ ■ 12 14 ■ 24
Cîmpina 11 ■ 20 23
44 △
10 △ ★ Buzău +
+ Town 8 ◑ 9 30 31
★ 19 ■ 43
— Railway 27 28 29 + Mizil

0 — km — 150
Tîrgoviṣte + 39 40 46 + Ploieṣti

c

b

Total production to 1936
(Million tons)
○ 0·1–2·5
○ 2·5–5
○ 5–10
○ 10–20
○ Over 20

Discovered before 1914 ●(grey)
Discovered after 1914 ●(black)

★ Horodnicul de Jos
Săcel ■

Territory lost 1944

★ Garcina
Bacău– 1 △ 9 ★ 11
Neamṭ 2 △ 10 ★ 12
combined 3 ★ ★ 13
production 5 △ 4 ★ 14
1·7 m.t. 6 ★ Cîmpurile
Jitia ★

Capacity 1936 ('000tons)
a Prahova 10381
b Buzău 182
c Dîmboviṭa 456
d Bucureṣti (City) 542
e Bacău 122
by county

Socodor ★
Semlac– ★ Pogaceana ★
Variaṣul ★ Botorca ★
★ Ortiṣoara
★ Remetea Mare
★ Utvin

Govora ★

Other fields
(Production below ·1m t.)
△ Disc. before 1914
■ Disc. after 1914
◇ Associated field
★ Exploration
— Structures
↔ Railway

0 — km — 150

◑ 37
△ 36
7 △

6 △ ★
1 △ 2 ★ 3 ●5 4 ★ 14 15 ★
△ + 11 12 13 21 22 ■ 24
23
8 10 ◇ 20 35
★ 9 ◇ 31 33 ● 34
16 19 32
17 18 29 30 42
25 ■ 26 28 27 41 ●
38 39 40 45 △ 46 43

For towns see above

0 — km — 50

departure of the Liberals from office paved the way for a more equitable partnership with foreign capital through the further Mining Law of 1930.[27]

In view of the intensive activity between 1895 and 1914 and some further progress during the war years, the number of completely new oilfields developed in the inter-war period was small. The main developments were immediately north of Tîrgovişte, where Răzvad, Aninoasa and Teiş continued the Moreni anticline and at Bucşani some ten kilometers south of the town, where oil was found in the third alignment (Fig. 2b). Previous efforts here had been unsuccessful at depths of some 600 metres but the productive structures, at depths of 1,500–2,000 metres were reached by 1934. Within two years, in what was an unprecedented flush even by Moreni standards, output reached 2·18 million tons. However 1936 proved to be a watershed, for not only did Bucşani production, obtained from thin Meotic layers, tailed off sharply after this but the total national output of 8·7 million tons was not regained until the early 1950s. This time the need to increase the area of proven reserves was generally accepted but the case argued by the companies, that special encouragement should be given to prospecting and exploration in new regions, was not fully acknowledged by the 1937 Mining Law. This gave private companies insufficient initiative and security though it made special provisions for remote areas: a major exploration effort in new areas came only after the 1942 act. Exploration continued in the old mining areas but moved just west of the Dîmboviţa to Dragomireşti and Şuţa Seacă.[28] Under the stimulus of accelerating industrialization in the late 1930s, continued until 1943 owing to Romania's support for the German war effort, a major parcelling out of concessions in new regions was envisaged and exploration work during the war years, though concerned mainly with deeper drilling in established regions, nevertheless included probes near Arad on the western plain and in the counties of Putna (Cîmpurile) and Rm. Sărat (Jitia).[29] Results were disappointing, however, and it took several years of further work after the war to uncover new deposits in the Getic Piedmont and modify the geography of oil production.[30]

The oil refineries[31] were located close to the individual sources of crude but usually sited beside railways and the largest units, owned by the foreign companies, tended to cluster in and around the principal towns, convenient for services and for contact with the oilfields as a whole. It was some time before these tendencies became clear in the geography. In the Bacău area, Moineşti was the principal centre with Steaua Română refinery (first built in 1926) having a capacity of 60,000 tons per annum. But, before the railway link from Comăneşti to Moineşti was completed, refining units were more scattered—most were in Lucăceşti and Valea Arinilor but others at Luncani. Some 'pull' was exerted by the Bistriţa and Trotuş valley railways and refineries were located at Mărgineni, Buhuşi and Rosnov in the former case and at Oneşti in the latter. In the Buzău area Buzău itself and the immediate environs attracted small refineries. Tîrgovişte in Dîmboviţa county became important with the discovery of oil at Gura Ocniţei but the principal units, however, were in Prahova county—in Cîmpina, Ploieşti (including the 'suburbs' of Brazi/Tătărani, Teleajen etc.) and at smaller railway station locations such as Băicoi, Mizil and Măgurele/Plopeni. Small units in relatively remote areas remained a feature of the geography up to the Second World War, notably to the east of the Ploieşti-Vălenii de Munte railway: Păcureţi, Podeni and Matiţa. Changing locational emphasis is considered in Table I. The combined capacity of the nine refineries in the Moineşti-Lucăceşti area in 1936 is given as 104,000 tons (and 90,000 tons of this relates to two units, Steaua Română at Moineşti and Moldonaphta at Lucăceşti). By contrast, the fourteen refineries in Ploieşti had a combined capacity of almost 7·0 million tons, varying in size individually from Luciana's 5,000 ton unit to Astra Română's huge installation, the largest in the country, approaching 2·0 million tons. There was a relative absence of units on the coast. However, a seaboard refinery in the early twentieth century would presumably have required co-operation between companies as well as confidence in the world trading position. Furthermore, the export flow of oil upstream from Giurgiu as well as seawards from Constanţa, served to emphasize the value of Ploieşti, at the centre of the pipeline network, and as a suitable location for an export refinery.[32]

Very pure methane gas was discovered at Sărmăşel in Transilvania in 1908 in the course of prospecting by the Hungarian Geological Institute. It appears that the discovery was quite accidental

Table I

Oil Refining 1840–1936

Period	Refineries established in the county of:					Total	Average Capacity ('000 tons per annum)
	Bacău	Buzău	Prahova	Dîm-boviţa	Others		
1840–1869	2	—	1	—	—	3	1.3
1860–1879	7	—	3	1	—	11	5·8
1880–1899	5	4	12	6	4	31	36·9
1900–1919	4	1	9	3	1	18	*
1920–1936	1	1	6	1	5	12	170.5

*Not available

Note: Capacity figures must be treated with caution since they are based on data referring to the situation in the census year and not when the refineries were first built.

Sources: M. Pizanty (1939) 3, op. cit.

Enciclopedia româniei 3, op. cit.

and it was three years before the flow came under control. Successful searches were made by the Hungarian state before the First World War: the Şincai field was found, immediately south-west of Sărmăsel, and other fields were proved at Bazna, Copşa Mică, Saroş and Zău de Cîmpie in central Transilvania.[33] Further exploration gathered pace after 1930, but success was limited to Nadeş, north of Sighişoara, first tapped in 1936, and Noul Săsesc where a very large field was opened in 1939. During the war, another important field was found at Cetatea de Baltă. Short pipelines were built to neighbouring towns: by 1918 gas was supplied to Dicio San Martin (now Tîrnaveni), Mediaş and Turda and, after 1930, further pipelines were laid to Tg. Mureş (1930) Sighişoara (1936) and Sibiu (1937). Expansion of armaments and chemical industries in Transilvania required the connection of Noul Săsesc with Făgăraş and Braşov, achieved by 1944. Both Noul Săsesc and Cetatea de Baltă were expected to supply Bucureşti, but work was still in progress at the end of the war. Casing-head gas, however, was available in the Prahova oilfields and the particularly rich reserves at Măneşti justified a pipeline to Bucureşti, which was ready in 1943.[34]

Like the natural gas,[35] Romania's principal coal reserves lay in the new provinces developed with the introduction of coke smelting at Reşiţa metallurgical works in 1846. Additional supplies were subsequently found in the Danube defile. The most extensive hard coal reserves are in Jiu valley near Petroşani. The best coking coal is found in the west where tectonic pressure was greatest but even this material was not found suitable for metallurgical uses until after the Second World War and the Hunedoara furnaces had to import. Mining began in 1840, on the northern flank close to Petroşani itself (Dîlja, Lonea and Petrila), but extended to Aninoasa later and by 1868 the southern flank was worked at Uricani, followed by Lupeni 1881 and Vulcan 1895.[36] Production rose from less than a thousand tons in 1868 to 2·2 million tons in 1913 and 2·7 in 1943. Deposits of brown coal are found in the Mesozoic and Neozoic formations, but are frequently small and difficult to work.[37] Thus, the Bahna coal near Drobeta-Turnu Severin was worked at the turn of the century but abandoned in 1910 because the seams were badly eroded and large-scale working was impossible. But brown coal at Cŏmaneşti, first worked to supply the railways of Moldova and a local power station, has had more long-term importance. The smaller fields of Ţebea near Brad, and Aghireş, near Cluj have, also maintained a local importance, supplying power stations adequate for the needs of the Apuseni mining region, based on Gura Barza and the city of Cluj respectively. Finally, there are substantial deposits of lignite related to continental lacustrine facies of the Pliocene, which are found especially on the outer arc of the Carpathians. The large deposits in Gorj, around Motru and Rovinari, have only been worked for a few years since their exploitation awaited large scale equipment for opencast working and suitable techniques for power station consumption of this very low grade fuel. Smaller deposits which were easily tapped did however prove commercially attractive from the late nineteenth century both as a local fuel and for use in locomotives and boilers mixed with fuel oil residue. The first use of lignite in power stations came in 1930, when the Schitu Goleşti station was completed near Cîmpulung (Muscel) and connected with Bucureşti and Ploieşti by a 60 kv transmission system.

Romania possesses considerable water power resources, but

these have not proved easy to exploit due to highly variable river discharges and a lack of large natural reservoirs. The most attractive sites for large scale development to be located far from the principal markets; while the Bistriţa in Moldova and the Danube at the Iron Gates offered prospects for the modernization of backward regions, the scale was out of proportion with immediate demands, which could be met most economically by oil-fired generators.[38] Only sites of modest capacity lying close to demand were really viable. Thus Sinaia supplied the oilfields from 1900 (though part of the load was supported by Steaua Română's Cîmpina thermal plant after 1907). Sadu supplied Sibiu, and through a 60 kv grid, the Mediaş area as well, while Văliug supplied Reşiţa (Fig. 3). Larger works were considered, but the only concrete results were obtained close to Bucureşti, with the completion of the Dobreşti station; the 20 MW generators were linked to the capital through a 110 kv line, which formed the nucleus of the national grid.[39] Clearly Romania had ample resources for power generation particularly after the First World War.[40] Although a comprehensive grid systems, based on hydro and lignite burning stations, could cover the bulk of the country and allow railway electrification.[11] Unfortunately, the abundance of fuel oil destroyed the simple logic of those who wanted oil revenues to finance the relatively costly installation of water powered generators. And the ideal of regional supply systems was only being realized in the Bucureşti and Sibiu areas by the Second World War.[42] Implicitly, therefore, large power consumers would have limited locational choice. The lack of pronounced industrial growth in Brăila, Constanţa and Galaţi, despite the obvious advantages of port location, must be seen in part in the context of a limited electricity system. The advantages of location close to the oilfields, and more especially the gas fields, remained clear.[43]

Small-scale Industry

Although emphasis over the last century has been given to large-scale activity ('industria mare'), the small scale peasant industry ('industria casnică tărănească') is an essential component of the whole industrial pattern. As in other parts of central Europe, there is a distinction to be drawn between the artisan working full-time

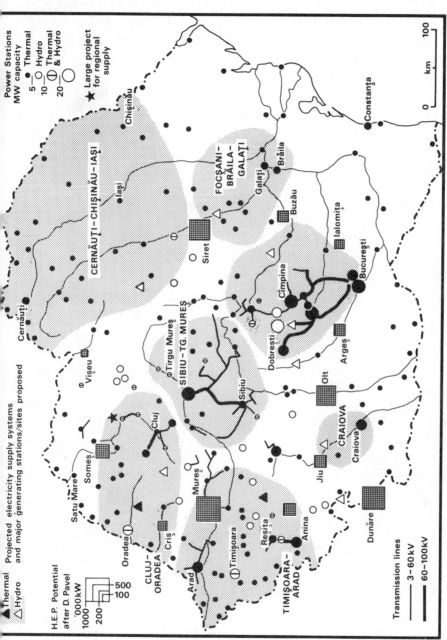

FIG. 3. Electricity. Sources: *Encyclopedia românieì*, 3, 108, *op. cit.*; D. Pavel quoted by S. Fischer Galaţi, ed. *Romania*, Praegar, New York (1957) p. 280; I. Veverca in N. Lupu-Kostaky et al. (1939), pp. 172–173 *op. cit.*

at a particular trade, usually in the town, and the villager who may follow various part-time activities, especially in the winter months.[44] But in contrast to the upland country of Saxony and Bohemia, the rural craft industries of Romania generally failed to achieve high levels of quality and sophistication, though they developed in the first place as a result of similar stimuli—limited agricultural endowment and suitable industrial raw materials and power supplies. It was predominantly amongst the hill and mountain dwellers that craft industries developed with vigour.[11] The plains' peasants were engaged more fully in the rhythm of agricultural work. Thus the wanderings of the woodworkers and meal chest makers of the Apuseni, the Petroşani Basin and Prahova Valley (especially Proviţa de Jos) among the villages and fairs of the Bărăgan reflect limited agricultural opportunities at home and valuable local timber resources, at a time when these materials were not being processed extensively by factory industry. Expansion of small-scale activity in certain sectors continued in the late nineteenth century as the state favoured unbalanced growth of large industry in key sectors of the economy.[46]

Private co-operative and trading organization however could play a useful role. In the late nineteenth century the Furnica organization won big military orders, giving work to numerous individual weavers in the towns and villages of Argeş, Dîmboviţa, Ilfov and Prahova, counties closest to the capital, and the Munca clothing enterprise offered employment to poor families in the Bucureşti suburbs. Promotional work through international exhibitions helped stimulate a demand for quality textile products embodying high standard of peasant art in home weaving combined with larger-scale organization for combing, carding and finishing.[47] Interestingly, however, the effort was most marked in the relatively advanced upland regions close to Bucureşti and the Prahova Valley resorts: Breaza de Sus (Prahova), Cetăţenii din Vale (Muscel) and Pietrosiţa (Dîmboviţa) were outstanding as were Caşin (Bacău) and Tazlău (Neamţ) in Moldova. It is very unfortunate that little detailed material is available on these essentially part-time occupations.

The full-time artisans were most numerous in Bucureşti. By the early seventeenth century there was considerable specialization: coat and blanket makers, leather workers, shoe makers, furriers and brandy distillers are mentioned in such waterside districts as Cotroceni, Mihai Vodă and Vacăreşti on the Dîmboviţa and Fundeni on the Colentina. The selection of Bucureşti as the capital Walachia in 1659 led to further growth and the north-eastern sector, with each street tending to house members of a particular craft, was becoming a significant industrial suburb by the end of the seventeenth century, when the riverside sites had begun to suffer from congestion.[48] The English traveller, J. Bentham, mentions the glass and leather industries in his diaries of the 1780s, while I. Ghica reports favourably in the nineteenth century on the fine silks and furs, as well as on the fine cotton goods, 'testemeluri' much sought after abroad.[49] Regrettably, these crafts were destroyed in the late nineteenth century by competition at home and abroad from cheaper factory products, a situation which added further weight to the case for protection and development of national industry which progressives had been urging since the 1830s. The importance of small scale industry, omitting part-time peasant crafts, emerges from the census of industrial establishments carried out by D. P. Marţian in 1860. The census records a total of some 13,000 establishments employing 83,000 people. Rather more than half these installations (6,800) were flour mills, mostly located in the villages and using wind or water power. Other important groups were brandy (ţuica) distillers (1700), potters (600), sawmillers (600), limeburners (500) and cloth makers (400). The latter group, in particular, was decimated by exposure to foreign competition.[50]

The 'anceta industrială of 1901–2 allows some further quantitative assessments of small scale activity[51] which indicate rapid growth over previous decades.[52] V. Madgearu[53] states that 410 units of 'large' industry employed 35,466 workers, 87 in each enterprise on average, whereas 61,778 other industrial units employed 132,732, or approximately two to each enterprise. From further studies by G. Zane[54] it appears that 279 of these 'other' units were large artisan concerns which did not have any source of mechanical power but employed more than 10 workers. Rather more than half these enterprises were concerned with food processing and shoe making and a further quarter dealt with textiles, leather, wood and building materials. Such enterprises illustrate a tendency for small workshops to combine into larger co-operative

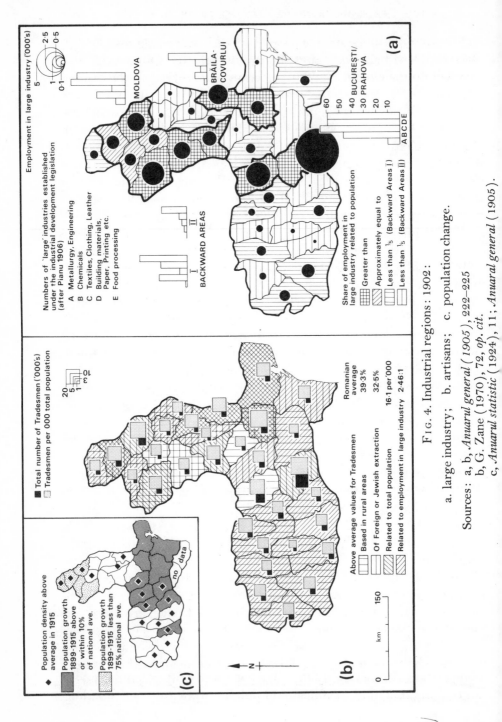

FIG. 4. Industrial regions: 1902:

a. large industry; b. artisans; c. population change.

Sources: a, b, *Anuarul general* (1905), 222–225
b, G. Zane (1970), 72, *op. cit.*
c, *Anuarul statistic* (1924), 11; *Anuarul general* (1905).

legacy of Ottoman guilds   1830's - Romania had more autonomy than other parts of the empire.

10   THE INDUSTRIAL DEVELOPMENT OF ROMANIA   337

ventures. One example of these craft workshops (atelierele meşteşugareşti) is the furniture business in Focşani where four workshops combined, each one then specializing in one part of the process. A similar arrangement emerged at Tg. Neamţ where a coat-making concern was established with the formerly separate units now specializing in carding, spinning, weaving and finishing. Other significant examples include the tannery and shoemaking enterprises of Gr. Alecsandrescu and I. Bradea in Ploieşti and Brăila respectively and the brewery of S. Pedrone in Brăila. Usually it was in the towns where these large artisan activities were most prominent, many employing more than 20 people; the woodworking and furniture business of M. Ganca in Bucureşti, with only five workers in 1884, had become a 'large' industry employing some 300 people by 1911. But there were exceptions, notably the crown properties at Bicaz in Moldova, where a complex of activities was fostered, including cloth, rope making, leather working, wood processing and basket weaving. Furthermore, weavers in the country districts might be employed casually by textile mills in the towns such as those of T. Conescu in Cîmpulung (Muscel) and T. Danovici in Ploieşti, enterprises which tended to attract workers from the nearest villages. Hence, villagers where such casual work was most prominent tended to be clustered around the principal towns: Bucureşti, Cîmpulung, Giurgiu, Ploieşti and Tîrgovişte. This established lines of specialization which persisted into modern times.[55]

There was considerable regional specialization: the majority of the country's musical instrument makers, sieve manufacturers, brass workers and wood tile and shingle makers came from the Bacău, Teleorman, Fălticeni and Gorj/Prahova districts respectively. At the local level, too, specialization was evident. In the case of the pottery industry in Oltenia, Glogova concentrated on plates, while Hurez produced luxury items and Şişeşti de Jos has a reputation for preserving jars. In general, because of the growing competition from larger scale producers, there was a decline in the number of small industries in the towns (with a concentration in sectors least exposed to competition) and a growing bias towards the rural areas. Not that the villages were immune from outside competition, for village dying shops survived only when there was a good organization to collect and deliver work over surrounding areas, but their relative strength increased especially in the pottery and ceramics sector, where 98 per cent of the small operators were based in rural areas in 1901 compared with 69 per cent in 1860. There were substantial regional variations. The emphasis on the rural areas was greatest in the more backward regions, where towns were small and had not yet collected a wide range of central place functions. Whereas only 17·4 per cent of tradesmen in Ilfov (which includes Bucureşti) were based in the villages and 17·2 in Iaşi, the figures for Gorj and Romanaţi were 87·3 and 91·8 per cent respectively. Furthermore, in the small towns in backward regions, such as Calafat and Tg. Jiu, small scale industries were still on the increase. These observations point to a considerable element of dualism in the Romanian economy, not only between large and small industries but equally between advanced and backward regions.

Regional variation was also evident in the inter-war period. If the whole of Banat, Crişana, Maramureş and Transilvania is considered then the proportion of all industrial workers employed in small enterprises (employing 1–5 persons) falls from 64·4 per cent in 1900 to 56·5 in 1910 and 35·4 per cent in 1930. In absolute terms the numbers of small enterprises increased from 92,060 in 1900 to 105,737 in 1910 and then fell to 54,974 in 1930, while units employing 6 or more increased steadily from 2,072 in 1900 to 4,066 in 1930 (of which 461 in 1900 and 1,040 in 1930 comprised units employing more than 20). But while trends in other regions were similar, the stage reached varied very considerably. In 1930, Muntenia and Transilvania had only 28·9 and 36·8 per cent respectively of their industrial workers in units employing 1–5 persons (and roughly 75 per cent of the remainder in plants employing more than 20). But Oltenia and Dobrogea had 60 per cent of their workers in small units and only about half the

due to switch to heavy manufactory or was efforts or !

FIG. 5. (facing page)
a. large industry 1935;   b. large industry 1938 (by ţinoturi);
c. industrial centres 1940.

Sources: *Enciclopedia romaniei 2/3, op. cit.*
Anuarul statistic (1939), 380
b, V. Madgearu (1940), 142, *op. cit.*
c, *Anuarul statistic* (1939), 478
d, L. Georgescu, *Localizarea şi structura industriei româneşti*,
Cartea Românească, Bucureşti (1941).

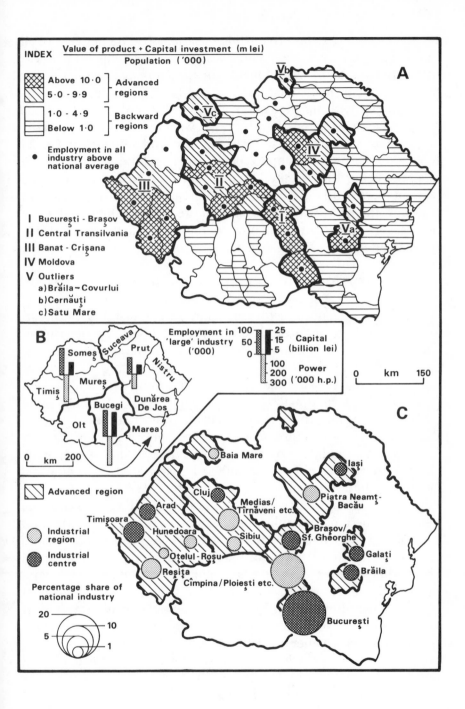

INDEX $\dfrac{\text{Value of product} + \text{Capital investment (m lei)}}{\text{Population ('000)}}$

Above 10·0 ⎤ Advanced
5·0 - 9·9 ⎦ regions

1·0 - 4·9 ⎤ Backward
Below 1·0 ⎦ regions

● Employment in all industry above national average

I Bucureşti - Braşov
II Central Transilvania
III Banat - Crişana
IV Moldova
V Outliers
 a) Brăila – Covurlui
 b) Cernăuţi
 c) Satu Mare

A

Vb
Vc
IV
III
II
I
Va

B

Someş
Suceava
Prut
Nistru
Timiş
Mureş
Dunărea De Jos
Bucegi
Olt
Marea

Employment in 'large' industry ('000)
100
50
0
Capital (billion lei)
25
15
5
Power ('000 h.p.)
100
200
300

0   km   150

0   km   200

C

◨ Advanced region

⬤ Industrial region

⬤ Industrial centre

Percentage share of national industry
20
10
5
1

Baia Mare
Iaşi
Cluj
Medias/Tîrnăveni etc.
Piatra Neamt-Bacău
Arad
Timişoara
Hunedoara
Sibiu
Braşov/Sf. Gheorghe
Galaţi
Oţelul - Roşu
Reşiţa
Cîmpina/Ploieşti etc.
Brăila
Bucureşti

remainder in large concerns, while Basarabia had 68 per cent of all industrial workers in small enterprises and only some 40 per cent of the remainder in large units.[56] In the more backward regions peasant industrial installations reached new levels of sophistication, notably with the perfection of water-powered sawmilling, the 'joagăr' being occasionally integrated with the corn mill (moară) and perhaps a further unit for washing wool and fulling cloth (piuă) to form a veritable 'complex de industrie ţărănească', a notable example being that on the Olteţ at Polovragi (Gorj), but, while peasant corn mills still survive in areas remote from modern bakeries, the post-war expansion of large scale clothing and wood processing industries has now eliminated virtually all these peasant enterprises.[57]

Development of Large-scale Industry to 1918

Attempts to introduce factory industry to the Iaşi and Bucureşti areas in the late eighteenth century were upset by the Russo-Turkish Wars and a sustained effort was delayed until the 1830s. Considerable attention was given to road building to link the northern districts with the Danube, emerging as an important highway of international commerce and graced by a number of planned towns of which Brăila, Turnu Măgurele and Drobeta-Turnu Severin are impressive examples. The princes were prepared to foster industry by awarding privileges such as monopoly rights and tied labour. Food industries appeared at Brăila and Galaţi, though Bucureşti saw the greatest development.[58] The Gh. Assan milling, oil-pressing and brandy distilling enterprise of 1853 was the most notable single example, being one of the first factories in the country to use steam power. Production of cloth and domestic utensils was also well established in the Bucureşti area, while further afield the shipbuilding of Giurgiu and Zimnicea, glass making of Namaeşti, near Cîmpulung, porcelain at Tg. Jiu, sawmilling at Rm Vîlcea and tanning at Dumbraveni near Craiova may be mentioned. In Moldova milling, meat packing and glass industries are mentioned in the Bacău, Huşi and Iaşi districts, but other ventures were relatively ephemeral. A sugar beet industry was mooted by Gh. Asache in 1835, but it was felt to be inappropriate in relation to the low level of demand: as in Walachia, this industry did not appear until later in the century. A paper industry at Piatra Neamț in 1841 was a short-lived venture[59] and until a national industry was firmly established in the late nineteenth century the Principalities were dependent on imports from Transilvania where capacity included small water-powered undertakings which were flourishing in the Alba district and Zărnești.[60] Similar dependence on Transilvania is evident for iron. This was produced at Reșița in the Banat and, in smaller quantities, from a number of furnaces in the Poiana Rusca, an upland area lying to the west of Hunedoara which offered iron ore, timber and water power. C. Mihailic de Hodocin considered the possibility of an iron industry in the Bistrița valley of Moldova using local charcoal and the ores but lack of financial backing upset this visionary scheme.[61]

Heavy industry began to make its appearance only after the unification of the Principalities in 1859.[62] In 1859, Marin Mehedinteanu opened his refinery near Ploiești for the production of kerosene, while the 1860s saw significant progress in foundry and engineering industries. The army arsenal was built in București in 1862, while private foundries were opened in București in 1864 and 1867 by Lemâitre and Freud respectively. Substantial expansion was also achieved at the D. Wolff foundry, which had first opened in 1853. These units were sited in the Dîmbovița Valley, for it was the suburbs on the floodplain and lowest river terrace which attracted most activity until the opening of the first railway brought growth to Filaret, on higher ground immediately south of the river. București was the obvious location for large industries in view of its administrative and local market importance, not to mention its proximity both to the Danube and the oil-producing districts of Buzău and Prahova. But there was a danger of generating a centre-periphery situation in which the large capitalist units of the southeast contrasted with an economy based on agriculture and craft industry, in Oltenia and northern Moldova especially. While private capitalists were not unnaturally wary of investing in remote areas where transport and administration would have been particularly suspect, it was open to the state to encourage some convergence by directly sponsoring large concerns in areas where high transport costs could be set against the advantages of skilled labour and security from attack. An interesting case is the military clothing works of M. Kogălniceanu, established between 1858 and 1862 at Tg. Neamţ.[63] The Neamţ monastery had a considerable reputation for woollen textiles which had resulted in a diffusion of skills in the district. Various domestic workers were integrated into the factory system with its carding, spinning, weaving, dying and finishing sections and the monastery equipment was incorporated following the secularization of church lands. But the impact of machinery through Galaţi proved difficult because of the atrocious road conditions.[64] Nevertheless, the industry survived until the 1880s and it may be seen as one of a group of enterprises, including linen at Tg. Ocna, for which the local skills and security offered by the hill country were particularly relevant. The natural resources of the hill and mountain country also attracted investment in large scale saw-milling as the railway system developed in the 1870s.[65]

All industrial development at this time was constrained by virtually free trade conditions for exchanges with Austria–Hungary, Germany and Russia, negotiated in the 1870s. While this new situation was favourable for agricultural exports, it proved ruinous for industry. In 1886, therefore, tariffs were levied in a bid to protect native industries (leading to a tariff war with Austria–Hungary until 1891) and in the following year a law was introduced allowing for positive state encouragement of industry: Măsuri generale pentru a veni în ajutorul industriei naţionale. These measures, offering concessions over land acquisition and taxation, followed the encouragement given to certain specific industries some years earlier, notably paper in 1881 and sugar refining in 1882.[66] They were measures applied only to large industry (industria mare.)[67] Although the planners aimed at little more than the development of industry capable of transforming raw materials (industrie transformatoare) and providing to some extent for the country's defence, the results of the policy were substantial. The measures of 1887 were not an isolated initiative but part of a complex of measures for the modernization of the country, a policy with which Carol I consistently identified himself. Measures were taken to improve education and banking while the railway network developed across the country, forging international connections with Hungary (Orşova, Predeal and Ghimeş), Austria (Suceava-Burdujeni) and Russia (Iaşi-Ungheni and Galaţi).

București remained the principal industrial centre with the engineering, textile, food and leather sectors particularly well represented.[68] It could be regarded as the principal node on an industrial axis extending from the Danube to the Hungarian frontier at Predeal, an axis which enjoyed rail communication with international connections at both ends (though with a ferry crossing needed at Giurgiu) and tapped the principal oil and lignite fields of the country. Giurgiu had a ship repairing business and sugar factory, Ploiești was a centre of leather and textile production but, more significantly, shared with Cîmpina the Prahova oil refining and oilfield engineering business. Further north lay the Comarnic cement works, the Azuga clothing, sugar and brewing enterprises and the woollen cloth, paper and lumbering works of Bușteni. A second obvious focus lay in northern Moldova a combination of two elements. First, the city of Iași and other towns such as Botoșani and Roman, close to the political core of the old principality of Moldova, with a relatively mature urban tradition strengthened by the prominence of Jewish businessmen. Second, the Siret corridor, a principal rail and water axis which enjoyed good railway contacts with Austria, Hungary and Russia as well as the port of Galați. It could exploit not only the skilled labour of the Bacău and Neamț districts but also the rich stands of resinous timber in the eastern Carpathians and the fuels of the Bacău district.[69] There was food processing (sugar at Roman and Sascut near Adjud and flour milling at Botoșani), textiles (at Iași, Buhuși near Bacău and at Bacău itself), paper, cellulose and saw milling (at Bacău and Piatra Neamț), along with oil refining in the Moinești area and railway workshops at Pașcani. Then both Galați and Brăila, forming a third industrial concentration, were important for engineering, saw milling and flour milling, while Brăila also boasted textile and cement industries. Development outside these three areas, with their particular advantages in terms of transport, labour and energy, was much more modest.

Although the changing geography cannot be accurately measured because of a lack of comparable statistics the distribution pattern at the beginning of the twentieth century emerges with some clarity through the ancheta industrială of 1901–2 and the study of firms receiving state encouragement carried out by N. I. Pianu in 1906. This latter study is not as complete as the official census which is therefore preferred as the basis for analysis, but detail in Pianu's study permits certain calculations which would not otherwise be possible. A simple relationship of share of total population to share of total employment in excess of the share of population (including a few highly marginal cases) are grouped into three regions: Ilfov-Prahova (including Bucureşti and Ploieşti), Brăila-Covurlui (the towns of Brăila and Galaţi) and northern Moldova including Botoşani, Iaşi, Roman and Suceava plus the Carpathian districts of Bacău, Neamţ and Putna. The remaining counties, all with shares of industrial employment well below their share of population are grouped into two categories of backward area (Fig. 4a). The details of this basic regional pattern are set out in Table II and their respective employment structures are examined. Ilfov-Prahova shows a remarkable balance in its employment structure, while Brăila-Covurlui shows a bias towards food processing and metallurgy and Moldova is prominent in food processing and wood/paper industries. While the weaknesses of the most backward counties is clear on account of the exaggerated importance of food processing, the less backward, perhaps intermediate areas do not seem to combine their lower intensity of industrial employment with marked structural inferiority. Their share of chemicals is higher than in Brăila-Covurlui and Moldova, their share of metallurgy is greater than that of Moldova and the food share lower than in Brăila-Covurlui.

Two other points should be considered. First, the cushioning effect of small scale industry: the contrasts between advanced and backward regions are considerably reduced when artisans and their apprentices are included in the picture (Fig. 4b). Secondly, the figures listed by Pianu for the opening of large industrial concerns indicate some spread. In 1887, Ilfov had 43·2 per cent of large industrial units, Brăila-Covurlui and Moldova together had 25·0 and all backward areas 31·7. During the first expansion phase to 1895 (when foreign investment in the oil industry began), the figures were modified slightly to 41·6, 36·0 and 22·4 respectively. Over the next decade, the Ilfov-Prahova share showed further marginal contraction, while the backward areas improved their share at the expense of the other two advanced regions. These figures do not offer conclusive evidence, because nothing is known of the size of each firm and the extent to which the labour force

Table II

Industrial Regions of the Regat

A. Industrial Structure 1902

	Industrial regions						Backward areas			
	București–Prahova		Moldova		Brăila–Covurlui		I		II	
	a	b	a	b	a	b	a	b	a	b
Metallurgy and mining	52·1	17·9	16·7	11·8	15·6	21·1	14·6	13·1	1·0	2.9
Chemicals	43·8	16·5	22·9	17·6	9·5	14·1	21·9	24·5	1·9	5·9
Leather, textile and clothing	71·4	23·4	12·1	8·1	5·5	7·0	6·6	5·6	4·4	11·8
Building materials, wood and paper	41·0	21·1	31·2	33·1	6·2	12·7	17·4	23·4	4·2	17·6
Food	30·9	21·1	20·9	29·4	16·8	45·1	20·4	36·4	11·0	61·8
All industries	44·5	100·0	21·7	100·0	11·3	100·0	17·1	100·0	5·4	100·0

a. Share of total national employment in each sector
b. Importance of each sector in the employment structure of the region
Backward Areas have a share of employment in large industry substantially below their population share. Backward Areas II have a share of large industrial employment smaller than one fifth their share of population.

B. Changing Relative Importance 1902–1930

	Percentage share of: Population		Employment in large industries		Employment in industry inc. artisans	
	1902	1930	1902	1930	1902	1930
București–Prahova	14·3	17·6	46·6	54·9	31·6	44·8
Moldova	17·4	17·3	27·4	22·2	21·6	18·4
Brăila–Govurlui	4·9	5·1	8·5	7·7	7·6	6·1
Backward Areas I	32·7	33·0	15·0	11·1	23·5	19·1
II	28·6	27·0	2·6	4·0	15·7	11·6

Note: The improvement of backward areas II in employment in large industries is due entirely to investment in the Argeș textile industry.

Sources: *Anuarul General* (1905), 22 *et seq.*
Anuarul Statistic (1939), 330

was increased subsequently. There are details of installed power in the industrial census but their usefullness is reduced by the calculation in terms of steam engines rather than horse power units. On the face of it all regions except Ilfov-Prahova had higher shares of installed power than they did of employment, a surprising observation as regards both Ilfov-Prahova (49·8 per cent of employment but only 36·2 per cent of steam engines) and the backward regions (17·6 per cent of employment but 21·4 per cent of steam engines). But the population evidence paints a rather different picture for the 1899–1915 period. The fastest growing countries between the 1899 census and 1915 were all in the southeast (Fig. 4c), and although migration was almost certainly a factor in this expansion unfortunately no natural increase data for counties is available. Some of the growth could be explained in terms of agricultural colonization of the steppes but the dynamism of Bucureşti and Ploieşti over this period of rapid oilfield development and the virtual stagnation of Iaşi[70] gives ground for speculation that the years immediately before the war were bringing renewed build-up in the metropolitan region.

Development of Large-scale Industry 1918–1944

After the First World War by the territorial changes that gave rise to a new order of priorities. On top of the relatively local problems of distribution within the historic provinces of Moldova, Muntenia and Oltenia, there was the wider national problem of integrating the new territories under the influence of Bucureşti and constructing a new industrial geography. This aimed at the integration of the Regat with the industrial axis of Transilvania, extending from Braşov through Sibiu to the Banat, with metallurgical, engineering, textile, leather and paper industries represented. There were industrial centres in north Transilvania, notably Baia Mare, Cluj and Satu Mare but Basarabia, administered by Russia from 1812 to 1918, was a relatively backward area with a small industrial complex in the leading town, Chişinău, and a scattered textile industry, silk particularly, in the Cetatea Albă region.[71] State and private interests could hardly lose sight of the obvious energy centres in the Prahova-Dîmboviţa oilfields, the Transilvanian natural gas and the hard coal of Petroşani and Anina. The principal mineral wealth was clearly in the western half of the country, while towns close to the mountains would be easiest to supply with hydro-electricity. Against this the plains had a high potential for food production that could generate a processing industry. There was also the advantage of easy access to the Black Sea ports. But the weight of international trade would require only the modest expansion of port facilities (complicated by the competition between Brăila, Constanţa and Galaţi) with long-term potential as industrial complexes of international proportions requiring solutions of the energy problem and the exhaustion of domestic raw material base. Additionally, the relatively low incomes of the eastern regions, their inferior communication and proximity to the sensitive Russian frontier would tend to inhibit growth.

The scope for development after the First World War was enormous and the comment that Romania was 'standing at the threshold of a great industrial development' is typical of the optimistic assertions of the inter-war period.[72] However, other commentators were more guarded for even with stable international relations the peasant character of the country would only have changed slowly, but despite the inability of the powers to create a stable world order, a short time span of two decades, complicated by the depression[73] and the peculiar short-term problems arising from the First World War,[74] there were impressive structural changes (Table IIIa). The inter-war period saw major expansion of metallurgical and oil refining chemical industries, details of which are given elsewhere. A third growth industry was textiles. The cotton industry was concentrated in the Banat towns of Arad, Lugoj and Timişoara and in Bucureşti, with Iaşi as a secondary centre. Imports of raw cotton rose sharply during the 1930s and the level of demand was high enough for consideration to be given to cotton growing in Romania in the lower Danube valley and in the Banat near Timişoara. To the woollen industries of the Regat, at Bacău, Bucureşti and Buhuşi, were added the substantial capacities in Timişoara and the Braşov and Sibiu areas, where small textile producing regions already could be identified. Rayon and staple fibre were produced in the late 1930s in new plants: Apretura at Popeşti-Leordeni on the southern outskirts of Bucureşti and Viscosa Romanească at Lupeni near Petroşani.

Table III

Industrial Structure

A. National Pattern 1914–1938

	Regat				Greater Romania			
	1914		1921		1930		1938	
	a	b	a	b	a	b	a	b
Metallurgy	16·2	9·8	25·3	17·0	19·0	18·1	18·7	20·8
Textiles and leather	17·4	11·7	11·2	6·2	24·0	11·7	30·1	12·4
Wood, paper and printing	28·4	21·9	30·2	19·5	23·1	20·2	20·3	15·7
Food	16·8	34·9	17·5	28·6	14·5	25·3	13·3	18·3
Chemicals	7·6	12·0	5·9	16·6	6·9	13·2	9·8	24·6
Building materials	13·0	9·7	9·8	11·7	9·4	11·4	7·8	8·1
TOTAL	53·3	n.a.	148·5	481·2	174·2	492·7	289·1	746·8

B. Regional Pattern 1919–1938

Region	1919		1928		1933		1938	
	a	b	a	b	a	b	a	b
Regat	40·2	39·4	44·5	41·5	46·1	42·3	45·6	52·6
Transilvania and Panat	51·8	55·0	46·9	50·9	45·1	50·6	46·5	41·6
Bucovina and Basarabia	8·0	5·6	6·6	7·6	8·8	7·1	7·9	5·8
TOTAL	157·4	481·2	206·5	472·3	184·8	529·9	278·9	722·6

Notes: a. employment ('000 persons)
b. installed power ('000 h.p.)
All figures are percentages except for totals where actual figures are given (discrepancies due to rounding)

Sources 1919 C. C. Rommenheller (1926), 230–235, *op. cit.*
1928 *Anuarul statistic* (1929), 186
1933 *Anuarul statistic* (1934), 236
1938 I. Veverca in N. Lupu-Kostaky *et al.* (1939), 159, *op. cit.*

Even so, there was widespread cultivation of flax and hemp by peasants who were able thereby to produce their own clothing. The leather and shoe industries were prominent in Cluj, Oradea and Timişoara.

The timber industry developed quickly to supply export markets; the main emphasis was placed on both flanks of the eastern Carpathians as well as Bucovina, areas with a wealth of resinous timber which was grossly overcut. But the whole timber industry was over-expanded in relation to normal forest yield and this factor, coupled with growing competition in export markets, led to a slackening in the pace of investment in the 1930s. The saw-milling sector was most significant but there were wood distillation plants in the Banat, furniture industries in Bucovina and Transilvania and major paper and cellulose plants at Bacău, Buşteni and Zărneşti near Braşov. The cement industry saw rapid expansion during the 1920s: the pre-war plants at Brăila, Cernavoda, Drobeta-Turnu Severin (Gura Văii) and the Prahova Valley were supplemented by the Transilvanian plant at Braşov and Turda and a new works in the upper Ialomiţa Valley at Fieni.[75] Glass and ceramics were prominent in Ploieşti but especially on the Transilvanian natural gas field where Vitrometan of Mediaş and Fabrica de Sticlarie of Turda were located. Finally, the food industry was a prominent sector by the time of the First World War both in Bucureşti and the Danube ports. It was also important in the principal towns of Transilvania, Banat and Crişana where brewing and sugar refining were prominent. Further expansion of capacity was recorded but the relative importance of the sector fell.

There are useful case studies for individual cities[76] but broad geographical analysis is frustrated by limited statistical data. Information supplied annually for the historic provinces, show the Regat increasing its share of employment (40·3 per cent in 1919 rising to 45·6 in 1938) at the expense of Transilvania, with a modest advance in Bucovina-Basarabia, largely due to expansion of Bucovina's timber industry and expansion of light industry in Cernăuţi, well-positioned to supply Basarabia. More importantly, the census of 1930 gave population and employment data for each country (judeţ), though without distinction between large and small scale activity.[77] Furthermore, the Enciclopedia României recorded N. P. Arcadian's survey of 1935 on the importance of large industry in each county, in terms of investment, employment, installed power and value of production. Finally, in 1938 there was a detailed statistical compilation in the Anuarul Statistic, unfortunately of limited interest because of the use of a new and short-lived regional system of ten regions (ţinuturi) instead of counties or historic provinces. Using the 1935 data, an index embracing investment and production values was calculated as a basis for identification of the principal concentrations. Employment data were also used as a secondary indicator (Fig. 5a). The Bucureşti-Braşov industrial region is most important but there are three others though with a reduced level of importance: Central Transilvania, Banat-Crişana and Moldava. Hunedoara and Bihor countries were included in the Banat-Crişana region because of their high level of employment and diversified industrial structure. Then four 'outlying' areas appear: Satu Mare (which included the town of Satu Mare and the complex of non-ferrous, metallurgical and chemical industries around Baia Mare), Cernăuţi in Bucovina and Brăila-Covurlui. Finally, the backward counties are grouped into two categories. Employment structures were then calculated to fit this regional pattern and the results are tabulated in Table IVa.

There are striking contrasts in industrial structures. Both classes of backward region are relatively prominent in the food processing and timber/paper sectors and the first group was also important for building materials, glass and ceramics. By contrast, the advanced regions have above average proportions for chemicals, metallurgical industries and textiles: textiles are prominent in all four, while metallurgy is strongest in Banat-Crişana and the outliers, and chemicals are most prominent in Bucureşti-Braşov and Transilvania. If the number of jobs in each sector are related to population (Table IVb), then Bucureşti-Braşov emerges as a class of its own with 40·82 jobs per thousand of the population, followed by the other advanced regions with figures ranging from 19·10 to 22·26 (average 20·73). The two classes of backward area are clearly much weaker, recording values of only 7·03 and 1·21 respectively. A further examination by sectors shows that Bucureşti-Braşov comes out consistently with more than double the national average employment rate, but with a particularly high positive deviation in chemicals (Table IVc). The other advanced regions are always above the average, but only in the case of metallurgy is the average rate doubled. The first backward area group shows rates marginally above the average for wood/paper industries (where the advanced area rate is exceeded) and in food processing, but weakens in the chemical, textile and metallurgical sectors is very clear. The second group of backward areas shows relative strength in wood/paper and food processing but even here values do not reach even a third of the national average. The chemical and metallurgical sectors are particularly weak. On the whole, therefore, there are strong contrasts, but these are structured to a considerable extent. Clearly, the industrial core of the country embraces București-Brașov, Transilvania and Banat-Crișana, regions which are adjacent to one another but each exhibits a degree of specialization, but the industrial weight of Moldova and the four outliers shows that no simple centre-periphery model can be assumed. It may be conceded, however, that Moldova tends to be strongest in the less sophisticated sectors apart from textiles: wood/paper and food processing. Yet its status as an industrial region is difficult to deny, even though it has become somewhat reduced in size on account of the failure of Botoșani, Putna and Suceava (renamed Fălticeni, and later Baia, after 1918) to maintain their earlier rates, of growth.

The position of the backward areas was alleviated to some extent by migration to the principal growth areas and by the relative importance of small scale industry. An indication of the strength of migration currents emerges from study of birth-place statistics accompanying the 1930 census. After balancing in-coming and out-going movements, it appears that 5·4 per cent of the population of Muntenia in 1930 had moved in from other regions. By contrast, there were net losses in all other historic provinces, the excess of out-migrants amounting to 1·0 per cent in Moldova, 1·3 in Basarabia, 1·9 in Transilvania, 2·7 in Bucovina and 4·4 in Oltenia. The low figure for Basarabia is rather surprising. Migration before the First World War would obviously have been difficult, though this could apply equally for Bucovina and Transilvania. Possibly lower cultural standards acted as an insulating factor. It should be emphasized, however, that these calculations do not take account of seasonal migration, which would have also offered

Table IV

Employment Structure of Industrial Regions 1935

A. Total Employment

Sector	București–Brașov		Other advanced regions:								Backward areas				Romania	
			1		2		3		4		1		2			
	a	b	a	b	a	b	a	b	a	b	a	b	a	b	a	b
1	12·9	17·8	4·1	15·9	16·9	35·7	0·4	2·0	6·9	35·0	3·3	8·7	0·2	2·5	44·7	19·5
2	14·4	19·8	5·9	22·9	3·1	6·6	0·4	2·3	2·2	10·9	1·3	3·5	0·2	2·5	27·5	12·0
3	20·7	28·5	8·2	31·6	14·5	30·7	9·1	46·0	5·2	26·5	5·2	13·6	1·2	19·1	64·1	27·9
4	9·0	12·4	1·0	3·9	4·2	8·8	3·4	17·4	3·1	15·6	8·1	21·2	1·8	29·9	30·7	13·4
5	12·4	17·0	3·6	13·9	4·8	10·2	6·2	31·7	2·0	9·9	17·4	45·7	2·5	40·4	48·9	21·3
6	3·2	4·4	3·1	11·9	3·8	8·1	0·2	0·8	0·4	2·0	2·8	7·3	0·3	5·6	13·8	6·0
TOTAL	72·7	100·0	25·9	100·0	47·3	100·0	19·7	100·0	19·7	100·0	38·1	100·0	6·2	100·0	229·7	100·0

a. Total employment 1,000s (large industry only).
b. Percentage (discrepancies due to rounding).

B. Employment Related to Population (per thousand)

Sector	București–Brașov	Other advanced regions				Total	Backward areas		Romania
		1	2	3	4		1	2	
1	7·26	3·14	7·65	0·44	6·69	5·20	0·61	0·03	2·52
2	8·10	4·52	1·41	0·50	2·10	2·14	0·24	0·03	1·55
3	11·63	6·24	6·58	10·23	5·07	6·81	0·96	0·23	3·61
4	5·08	0·77	1·90	3·86	2·98	2·15	1·49	0·36	1·34
5	6·94	2·75	2·18	7·05	1·90	3·06	3·21	0·49	2·76
6	1·80	2·34	1·73	0·17	0·38	1·37	0·52	0·07	0·78
TOTAL	40·82	19·77	21·44	22·26	19·10	20·73	7·03	1·21	12·94

C. Employment Related to National Average Rate
(National Average = 100)

Sector	București-Brașov	Other advanced regions	Backward areas 1	Backward areas 2
1	288·1	206·3	24·2	1·2
2	522·6	138·1	15·5	1·9
3	322·2	188·6	26·6	6·4
4	379·1	160·4	111·2	26·9
5	251·4	110·9	116·3	17·8
6	230·8	175·6	66·7	9·0
All Industry	315·5	160·2	54·3	9·3

Notes

1. Sectors are:
   1. Metallurgy and engineering
   2. Chemicals and glass
   3. Textiles and leather
   4. Food processing
   5. Wood, paper and printing
   6. Building materials

2. Advanced regions are:
   1. Central Transilvania
   2. Banat-Crișana
   3. Moldova
   4. Outliers (Brăila-Covurlui, Cernanți and Satu Mare).

3. Backward areas grouped as in Fig. 5a.

Sources: *Enciclopedia României 4, op. cit.*
Anuaral statistic (1939), 380

some solution to local underemployment.[78] The importance of small scale industry can be measured by relating the 1935 survey data to the results of the 1930 census. Results must be handled with caution because of the time gap separating the collection of the two sets of data, a period which saw a substantial increase in employment in large industry (from 174,227 to 230,797) despite the intervening depression. While large scale industry accounted for 49·0 per cent of all industrial workers in Bucureşti-Braşov and 41·6 per cent in other advanced regions, the proportion falls to 31·2 in the first group of backward areas and 9·4 in the second. However, relating the employment in small-scale industry to total population there is still a clear gradient from Bucureşti-Braşov, with 42·51 jobs per thousand of the population, and the other advanced regions with 29·15, to the backward regions, where the first group records 15·52 and the second 12·86. This range of values, although relatively moderate, suggests that development of large industry could be a positive factor in the development of small enterprises, at least indirectly through higher living standards stimulating the growth of light industry.

A critical question at this stage is obviously the changing degree of polarization over time. Unfortunately, there are few other regional statistics which allow meaningful comparison with earlier or later periods. However, if the counties of the Regat are taken from the 1930 and 1935 surveys, then a limited comparison against the 1902 results, is possible (Table IIb). This shows that Ilfov-Prahova has increased its share of the population from 14·3 to 17·6 per cent, while its share of industrial employment has risen from 31·6 to 44·8 and the share of large-scale industry has grown from 46·6 to 54·9. By contrast, shares of all other regions have fallen, except in the case of the large scale industry share of the second backward area group. Here, however, the advance from 2·6 to 4·0 per cent is due entirely to expansion of the textile industry in Argeş county. These results may give some support to the view that the Ilfov-Prahova area was advancing rapidly immediately before the First World War, or alternatively changes could be related to the inter-war situation with sharper competition as a result of the exposure of the Regat economy to industry in Transilvania. There is some further support for this latter view when changes in the late 1930s are examined. Aggregation of county data for 1935 to fit the administrative regions (ţinuturi) used in 1938 data tabulation allows comparison over a critical three-year period during which remarkably rapid growth was achieved (Table V). The number of industrial enterprises increased by only 4·1 per cent, but investment went up by 16·4 per cent, installed power by 28·1 and employment by 25·3 per cent. The bulk of the investment went to the chemical, metallurgical and textile sectors which took 65·9 per cent of the increased employment and 92·5 per cent of the additional power.

Results by individual region show local variations which cannot be usefully interpreted. But combination of the ten regions into three groups embracing the Bucureşti-Braşov axis (Bucegi region), Transilvania, Banat, Crişana and Maramureş (Mureş, Someş and Timiş regions) and the remainder reveals a more generalized and informative pattern (Fig. 5c). While Bucegi's share of installed power and employment in 1935 was 31·3 and 39·0 respectively, its share of additional power and employment recorded in 1938 was 77·0 and 47·1 per cent. Transilvania's shares in 1935 were 42·6 for power and 44·5 for employment, but share of additional power and employment were 21·7 and 36·4. Other regions absorbed only 1·7 per cent of the power installed between 1935 and 1948 and 16·5 per cent of employment compared with shares of 26·1 and 16·4 respectively in 1935 (Table IV). For installed power, especially, the relative growth of the Bucegi region is very clear. This was an area with advantages in terms of power and infrastructure, not to mention considerations of national security. The Bucegi region was also given priority in the extension of the natural gas pipeline system, although the connections through to Bucureşti were not finished until after the Second World War. In the other regions there were significant advances in terms of employment but modest increases in installed power in Oltenia and the eastern regions emphasize the long-standing imbalance. The overall impression, therefore, is that the vigorous measures taken to modernize the economy during the first four decades of the twentieth century were producing strong industrial regions indicated by the work of L. Georgescu (Fig. 5d). But the backward areas show little sign of advancement, although some individual counties, notably Constanţa, were growing relatively fast. The impression of weakness in the industrial sphere is

Table V

Industrial Development 1935–1938 by Groupings of Ținuturi

A. Overall Change in Employment and Installed Power

Region	Population (millions)		Employment (thousands)		Installed Power (thousand h.p.)			
	a	b	a	b	a		b	
1	3·82	21·2	80·7	39·0	181·1	31·4	130·3	77·0
2	5·06	27·9	85·7	44·5	246·2	42·6	36·8	21·7
3	9·18	50·9	57·4	16·4	149·8	26·0	2·1	1·3
TOTAL	18·08	100·0	223·8	100·0	577·1	100·0	169·2	100·0

B. Growth in Leading Sectors

	Region 1				Region 2				Region 3			
	Employment		Power		Employment		Power		Employment		Power	
	a	b	a	b	a	b	a	b	a	b	a	b
Metallurgy	12·9	9·6	21·9	19·6	23·4	−1·3	76·1	18·8	7·3	2·1	15·0	3·7
Chemicals	13·7	1·7	48·5	83·0	6·5	3·4	46·8	0·5	2·1	0·8	3·4	1·2
Textiles	23·2	10·9	24·4	13·0	24·3	8·4	22·6	13·0	17·1	3·5	18·7	1·3
Total: Growth Industries	49·9	22·2	94·8	115·6	54·1	10·5	145·4	32·3	26·5	6·4	37·1	6·2
Other Sectors	30·8	5·5	86·3	14·7	31·6	10·9	100·6	4·5	30·9	3·3	112·7	−4·1
TOTAL: All Industry	80·7	27·7	181·1	130·3	85·7	21·4	246·2	36·8	57·4	9·7	149·8	2·1

Key: a. 1935   b. Growth 1935–1938   (Percentage figures underlined)

Ținuturi Groupings: 1. Bucegi
2. Mureș, Someș and Timiș
3. Dunarea de Jos, Marea, Nistru, Olt, Prut and Suceava

Source Anuarul statistic [1939] 478 et seq.
Enciklopedia româniei, etc. etc.

strengthened when other socio-economic criteria are considered, (Fig. 6). But only long term programmes could solve the backward area problems[79] and significant improvements in education and transport were a basis for more rapid industrial expansion in the 1950s.

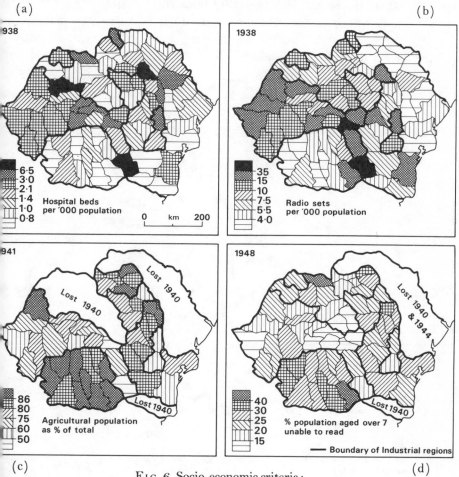

(a)

(b)

(c)

(d)

FIG. 6. Socio-economic criteria:
a. medical facilities 1938;   b. radio licences 1938;
c. agricultural population 1941;   d. illiteracy 1948.

Sources: a. *Anuarul statistic* (1939), 206
b. C. Kormos (1944) 75–76, 81–82 *op. cit.*
c. R. Cresin, *Recensamentul agricole al Românîei din 1941*, Inst. Central de Statistica, Bucureşti (1945), Table 21.
d. A. Golopentia and D. C. Georgescu, *Populaţia R.P.R. la 25 Ianuarie 1948*, Inst. Central de Statistica, Bucureşti (1948), 37–41.

A Case Study: Metallurgy and Engineering

Romania has a very long history of metal working with evidence of activity at Bocşa and Reşiţa dating back to Dacian times (Fig. 7). At Valea Caselor, near Ghelar, in the Poiana Rusca, the principal centre of iron ore mining at present, smelting was apparently going on in Roman times and tools were being manufactured in

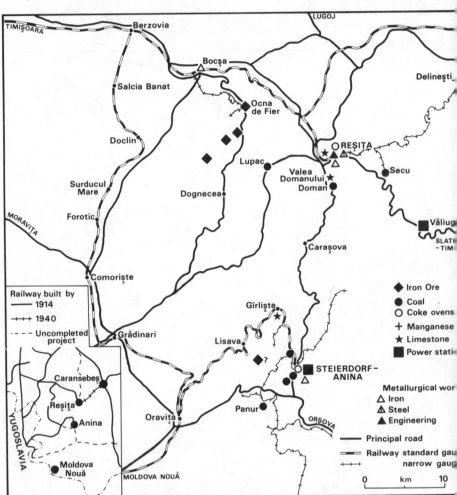

FIG. 7. The metallurgical industry: Reşiţa. Sources: Romenholler (1926), 239–245, *op. cit.*; topographical maps and field work.

small workshops at Cinciş, Ghelar and Teliuc. The gold of the Apuseni was a powerful attraction to the Romans, who brought their best metallurgists from Albania and Dalmatia to expand production at Zlatna (Ampelum). The modern industry however dates from Habsburg interest in the area after the Turkish withdrawal in 1699. Following the discovery of iron and non-ferrous ores small furnaces were built during the 1720s at Bocşa, Dognevea, Oraviţa and Sasca Montană, some skilled labour being drawn from Austria. Reşiţa was then charcoal supplier for Bocşa but due to its large waterfall and ores found in close proximity it became an important centre of production in its own right. When Maria Theresa decided to build a large furnace to replace Bocşa, it closed in 1768. Work started in 1769 and two years later twin furnaces plus a finishing plant and tool works went into production, output rising to 1,000 tons per annum by 1814. A considerable immigration of German workers took place in the 1770s and 1780s. Encouragement during the reign of Maria Theresa was also instrumental in the expansion of the iron industry in the Poiana Rusca. Numerous small furnaces are mentioned in the Hunedoara area in the 1780s, but, by the early nineteenth century, the principal units were Nădrag and Ohaba Bistra (later known as Ferdinand and today as Oţelul Roşu) in the western section and Ghelar, Govăjdia and Limpert to the east. Other units were built in the Orăştie area, notably Cugir (where the puddling process was introduced in 1830) and Sibişel. In Harghita (east Transilvania) the Vlăhiţa furnace was lit in 1856. Capacities were small, although the industry had far more than local importance since metal was carted to the main Transilvanian towns and to Moldava and Walachia. A spirit of emulation in the Principalities provoked some investigation into the possibilities for an iron industry in the Bistriţa Valley in Moldova but, as noted above, there was no sustained interest by capitalists.

The momentum for further development in the Banat and Transilvania arose from the discovery of coking coal near Reşiţa, first at Doman and Secu, later at Anina. Iron ore came from the Ocna de Fier–Dognecea area, south of Bocşa, and manganese from Delineşti. Coking and coal washing plant, together with new rolling mills and machine shops for the production of sheet, rails and wheel rims emerged from a major overhaul carried out between 1840 and 1854. Bessemer converters were introduced in 1868 and 1875, but the open hearth steel process proved more suitable and capacity consisted exclusively of Siemens Martin furnaces (built 1876–1890) by the First World War. Blast furnaces were rebuilt between 1880 and 1893, when there were three units each producing 60–80 tons of iron each day.[80] Owned now by Österreichesche Staatseisenbahngesellachaft, the works were closely tied up with railway expansion in imperial Hungary. Reşiţa was also a significant centre of engineering, while other metal-using industries developed in the vicinity at Bocşa, Anina and Topleţ.

But the strong raw material and fuel orientation in the location pattern made for transport difficulties in marketing. Some 1,500 peasants were impressed to cart ore and finished metal, and in 1872, when the first steam locomotive was built at Reşiţa, its despatch for exhibition in Vienna called for twenty-four pairs of oxen to haul it across rough country to the nearest railhead, Oraviţa, which was linked with the Danube via the Buziaş terminal in 1854. The peasant community at Cîlnic developed mainly to provide transport for the iron works, which remained essential until a direct rail link was provided from Budapest via Timişoara in 1909 (though a narrow gauge line to Bocşa was open in 1873). In addition, there was the problem of local transport for coal and ores supplied to Reşiţa. This called for a considerable narrow gauge rail system around Reşiţa and Anina and standard gauge connections between these two centres, though the latter route was very circuitous, via Oraviţa and Berzovia, compared with the more direct course, via Caraşova, taken by the estate road (Fig. 7). Anina was linked with Reşiţa by electric cable in 1917 since the 8 MW thermal power plant built on the Anina fuel base was the largest in the area. Reşiţa itself had some 6 MW of thermal plant, burning coal and furnace gas and an approximately similar capacity of hydro power arising from the harnessing of the Bîrzava near Văliug at Grebla (1904) and Braşova (1916), the latter associated with the electric steel furnace at Reşiţa started in 1915. By this time, the works was outgrowing its natural resource base: in 1913 32,000 tons of a total ore consumption of 143,000 tons came from Austria-Hungary and Serbia, comparable figures for coke (imported from Austria-Hungary) being 17,000 and 157,000.[81]

Elsewhere, Siemens Martin furnaces were built in the Bistra Valley in 1891 and 1903, replacing the puddling method still in use when the works was enlarged in the 1870s as a producer of agricultural machinery. It seems to have received at least some of its iron from Călan which was in direct rail communication with the Bistra Valley after the opening of the Caransebes–Subcetate rack railway in 1907. This 'import' may have been necessary because of the inadequacy of the local Ascuţita and Bouţari ores, the works being retained on a specialist basis because of the availability of water power locally (500 h.p. capacity installed by 1896) and, conceivably, because dispersal was strategically desirable. The linkage resulted from the formation of Kronstadter Verein A.G. in 1859 with interests in the projected Arad-Petroşani railway, the Ohaba Bistra works and the Petroşani coal mines. The works near Găvojdia, established by Sebastian Meislinger in 1845 on the basis of ore (Tincova) and charcoal at the western end of the Poiana Rusca, were greatly handicapped until a narrow gauge railway was completed in 1894. From then until the First World War brought a halt to activities the Nadrager Eisen Industrie was a significant iron producer. The Călan works had opened in 1869, intermediate between the ores of Teliuc in the western Poiana Rusca (richer deposits but less accessible than outcrops further east) and the charcoal of Petroşani. Since materials were being drawn from a relatively wide area development here had to await rail communication. From 1884 the ores of Ghelar were smelted with local charcoal at Hunedoara, a works which was converted to coke smelting in 1896 (using imported coke) and concentrated on the supply of pig iron for the Diosgyor works in Hungary. Output reached 87,000 tons in 1910, compared with Reşiţa with 114,000 and the Bistra Valley 15,000. In the Regat, meanwhile, there was no comparable industry and the engineering works were dependent on imported metal. In Bucureşti, the Arsenal Armatei opened in 1863, the workshops of Louis Lemaître were built in 1864 and those of E. Wolff in 1877. 1860–1880 was a formative period in which foreign assistance and technical training were more important and when interest was necessarily restricted to a few centres: Bucureşti with Craiova and Iaşi to a lesser degree. At the local level, however, the trade schools turned out Romanian craftsmen who worked under Austrian, German or

Hungarian management in small workshops and forges up and down the country. After 1900, the development of the oilfields stimulated the engineering industry in Bucureşti and Sinaia. At Galaţi, a convenient location for imported metal, five major companies set up there between 1890 and 1911 following the Naval Arsenal in 1879. Railway workshops were opened at Buzău, Drobeta-Tr. Severin, Iaşi and Paşcani[82].

The enlarged state faced a serious problem of repairing war damage. Some works were in need of overhaul, while others had been dismantled. The Călan and Bistra works had fallen into the hands of the Budapest Rimamurany firm in 1896/97 and plant was removed to Ozd when war involved Romania in 1916. Under the postwar reconstruction, Uzinele şi Domeniile Reşiţa remained the leading producer with two blast furnaces (rebuilt in 1923 and 1936) and a total capacity of 146,000 tons, complemented by five Siemens Martin 50 tons steel furnaces and the smaller electric furnace of 30 tons built in 1915. Five finishing lines turned out a range of rolled and laminated products. Coking plant capacity was doubled to 80,000 tons in 1933. Refractory products were made locally. With the failure of the plan to establish a large thermal power station at Rusca Montană for the benefit of the whole southwestern region each centre of demand had to make its own arrangements. Reşiţa may have increased its thermal power capacity by oil burning, but the full development of the hydro potential of the Bîrsava was not achieved until after the Second World War and the piping of gas from Transilvania was also delayed. Production of metal continued to rise, reaching 106,000 tons of iron and 235,000 tons of steel in 1945 (approximately two thirds and three quarters respectively of national output), although this was straining supplies of coke, refractories and scrap to the limit. Finishing sections expanded and the development of engineering took in electric motors (1919), steam locomotives (1923) and machine tools (1936). Finally, with German assistance, armaments workshops were installed between 1942 and 1944. The Reşiţa works was rather isolated for rail transport and goods had to travel via Timişoara. There were grandiose plans to forge new links across the mountains to the main Orşova to Caransebeş line, a plan first considered by the Hungarians in the 1870s. Effort was concentrated on the Reşiţa–Caransebeş line, completed in 1938.

It is interesting to note that, apart from their interest in the Năd-rag ironworks, U.D.R. maintained a small iron furnace and engineering shops at Anina. When this enterprise started is uncertain but it may have been around 1913, when coking capacity was transferred from Reşiţa. The blast furnace could also have emerged from relocation following overhaul of plant at Reşiţa. The new development, although soon to be hit by the depression, is an expression of the resource base with local coal linked with limestone from Gîrlişte and iron ore, presumably, from mines near Lişava in the Oraviţa area which were close to the Oraviţa-Anina railway line.

The second group of works focused on Hunedoara, where the six blast furnaces, with a combined capacity of 142,000 tons were unsupported by steel making plant until 100,000 tons capacity was installed, between 1937 and 1941.[83] Production was gravely affected by difficulties in maintaining ore output from Ghelar and Teliuc, where known reserves were anyway limited. The import bill for the ore, plus the coke which Petroşani could not provide satisfactorily at the time, could not be sustained and severe disruption occurred in 1931/32, when all the metallurgical companies combined to form the Socomet Cartel. In 1938, domestic production of iron ore amounted to 137,000 tons, whereas imports from Yugoslavia and the U.S.S.R. totalled 114,000 tons. The industry revived under the stimulus of rising armaments output in the later 1930s and at the beginning of the Second World War the first steps had been taken to transform the works into the integrated complex which now exists. The remaining small producers were eliminated, apart from Vlăhiţa, the charcoal furnace in the Harghita area, which concentrated on cast iron for domestic utensils, and the three small producers in the west which were integrated into the Societatea Titan-Nădrag-Călan. Through the iron ore mines of Teliuc, the charcoal blast furnace at Călan (rebuilt with an 80,000 tons capacity by 1935) steel works at Ferdinand (formerly Bistra) and rolling mills at Nădrag and Titan (Galaţi)[84] the firm could claim to be an integrated concern.

The problems of increasing domestic output in the Banat and Transilvania ensured that the inherited dualism between the western and southeastern locations would continue. Industria Sîrmei of Cluj was equipped with a wire works in 1920 and an electric furnace, producing special steels for cable making, in 1928, while a similar unit was opened in Brăila in 1929. The former example is interesting in illustrating the importance of the natural gas fuel, obtainable in the new works sited beside the main line railway at Cîmpia Turzii near Turda. By contrast, persistence of the lower Danube units rested in large measures on the lower costs of imported metal compared with that brought overland from Western Romania. Galaţi was also an important shipbuilding town, while Brăila had engineering works to serve. Furthermore the strategic advantage (in the event of a partial invasion of the country) in having major centres of production: Banat-Transilvania and the Lower Danube strengthened the case for blast furnaces and steel works at some tidewater location. But this would have required very heavy investment in plant and infrastructure and would have exacerbated balance of payments problems at a time when the established producers in the west might still be enlarged and supported by domestic resources to be provided through intensified mineral prospecting. Instead the increased concern for state security in the 1930s prompted renewed integration. Such considerations as railway connections with Germany, power supply and security from enemy attack seem to have contributed to the decision to reinforce the Bucureşti-Braşov-Hunedoara–Reşiţa axis. In 1936 a number of engineering works were selected for expansion and conversion to war production, with technical assistance provided largely by the Czech firms Skoda and Zbrojovka. But reference must also be made to several notable new developments.

In Bucureşti mention should be made of precision instrument firms such as Industria de Optica Română and also the Malaxa works, a major producer of locomotives, diesel motors and machine tools; the firm had its own rolling mill and seamless tube works (Stiefel system), as well as electric and Siemens Martin steel furnaces, equipment mostly installed between 1941 and 1943. The steel furnaces may have worked up pig iron from Hunedoara or alternatively imported scrap. The availability of battlefield scrap from Basarabia and Transnistria in 1942 is thought to have enabled national steel output to reach a record 350,000 tons in that year, although this would still have been far below total capacity, estimated at 500,000 tons. Ploieşti was the location of the Concordia armaments and munitions works, while close by was the munitions factory of Mărgineanca near Plopeni. Brașov and its surrounding area provided an ideal location and several works were built. The Malaxa shell factory at Tohanul Veche near Zărnești and the bomb-filling factory at Satulung were outside the town itself. Within the town were the armaments workshops of the Astra group, a com-bination of interests drawn from Arad, Satu Mare and Brașov, all basically concerned with railway rolling stock. Also important was the aircraft works (Industria aeronautică română) opened in 1937, which used engines and other components made largely in Romania at a variety of locations including Azuga, București, Pitești-Colibași and Cîmpulung (Muscel). An aircraft parts fac-tory at Tg. Ocna in Moldova was proposed in 1939. Further west were Avrig and Orăștie shell filling and assembly works and the small arms and artillery works of the Societatea Copșa Mică și Cugir, started in 1929 but not significantly developed until 1936.[85] Non-ferrous metallurgy was drawn into the picture with firms pro-ducing copper, zinc and aluminium laminates for supply to arma-ments factories established in Brașov and București. In addition, the Cîmpia Turzii works was extended to deal with zinc wire (1938), and the electrolysis of copper (1941), while zinc metal was produced for the first time in Romania, at Copșa Mică in 1941. Development of the processing capacity clearly fell to locations close to main line railways and gas supplies.

This brief interview demonstrates that heavy industry has been a long-standing concern of Romanian governments, despite the limited resource base. Equally significant, however, are the loca-tion problems which accompanied the growing dependence on im-ported coke, ore and scrap. The principal producers could receive imported materials by rail and, especially in the case of Reșița after the Caransebeș railway was completed in 1938, river-borne freights could be brought in through Orșova. But raw material and power problems were stimulating consideration of the fea-sibility of new integrated plant at a more convenient assembly point. One such point was a railway node in central Transilvania. More specifically Teiuș was suggested on account of its local water supply, from the Mureș, and the methane gas nearby (easily the cheapest source of power in Romania).[86] In addition, there were good rail links with Hunedoara and Petroșani (for ore and coal respectively), as well as with Galați (for imported materials), especially if a railway was built through the Buzău Valley. Although developments at Cîmpia Turzii and Copşa Mică followed the logic of this argument, no major development was attempted since it was deemed preferable to improve infrastructure at Hunedoara and Reşiţa. A second possibility was the emphasis of a tidewater location, particularly Galaţi. This would require the supply of fuel from the western part of the country for generating electricity, but there would be obvious advantages in terms of reception of imported ore and coke, as well as distribution of finished products. Economists, such as M. Constantinescu, appreciated the convenience of imports of Russian ore from Krivoi Rog but this market was ruled out for political reasons. Galaţi was also exposed to attack from the east and, furthermore, government would probably have been unwilling to make what might have been a premature decision in favour of imported materials.[87] Realization of this project was only to be achieved under conditions of changed political affiliations, national systems of electricity and gas, and a greatly increased metal consumption which even major expansion of the established centres could not meet.[88]

Conclusion

Despite some controversy over degrees of emphasis[89] large-scale industrialization has been a basic objective of all Romanian governments in modern times. Encouragement was sustained in the late nineteenth century through the law of 1887 and the efforts to build up effective systems of transport, education and government. Although there was a considerable spread of large manufacturing units, concentration was maintained by spatial inequalities in power supplies and the special attractions of Bucureşti and the main seaports. While there is not enough data to justify a definite assertion, it is likely that the rapid growth of the oil industry in and around Ploieşti emphasized the advantages of Muntenia, to the detriment of Moldova and Oltenia, in the period after 1895. After the First World War the natural gas of Transilvania attracted a good deal of new industry to the small area served by the distribution system. But the oilfields retained their importance for industrial location supported by the political programme of the new state, to extend the influence of Bucureşti over the new provinces. But the insecurity of frontier regions also spelt a preference for central location, well illustrated by the rapid progress of Brașov. Furthermore, the loss of the northern provinces in 1940 and Romania's subsequent development as part of the Axis war machine, ensured that the final phase of growth in the pre-communist era would endorse the primacy of the advanced regions whose advantages in terms of skills, infrastructure, fuels and raw materials were supplemented by industrial sites in wooded valleys well-serviced yet sheltered from enemy aircraft. Such installations as Avrig and Ucea de Sus (now Victoria) emerged from the war relatively undamaged and proved useful in the first years of socialist development.

So in 1945 as in 1918 the Romanian economy exhibited striking regional contrasts. The major industrial regions show a clear pattern of specialization, partly the result of policies of sectorially unbalanced growth, as exemplified by the priority for heavy industry in the late 1930s. But they are all very sharply differentiated from the backward areas where much of the employment in industry was provided by the small-scale activities of artisans and tradesmen. The progress of the poorer counties was largely dependent on the wealth generated by their more highly industrialized counterparts and the preliminary attempt to achieve maximum growth nationally (commensurate with the international climate). Concentration on the most promising regions has therefore been regarded by some economists as inevitable, irrespective of the social system prevailing.[90] In the Romanian case the integration of formerly separate industrial areas inherited from the old political order, as well as strategic questions, made consolidation in the inter-war period all the more difficult. Unfortunately there is very little research in Romania directed to objective study of documentary evidence dealing with the historical location problems discussed here. And although fieldwork in Romania and contact with Romanian scholars has built up a valuable perspective, this essay has been constrained by the limited amount of published material on the subject held in British Libraries. Hopefully further investigations may throw more light on the perception of locational questions from both the company and government standpoints, perhaps casting a new light on the backward area problem with which the present régime is now heavily preoccupied.

10. Notes

1. N. Ceaușescu, *Romania on the way of building up the multilaterally developed socialist society*, Meridiane, București (1969–70), 4 vols.
2. *Monografia geografica a R.P.R.* Academiei, R.P.R. București (1973), p. 108.
3. D. Turnock, *An economic geography of Romania*, G. Bell and sons, London (1974).
4. The Romanian spelling has been used for the names of the historic provinces.
5. C. D. Cioriceanu, *La Roumanie économique*, M. Giard, Paris (1928);

   D. Șt Emilian, *L'industrie en Roumanie*, Socec, București (1919);

   Gr. Antipa, *Dunărea și problemele ei științifice economice și politice*, Cartea Românească, București (1921);

   N. P. Arcadian, *Industrializarea României: studiu evolutic istoric economic si juridic*, Monitorul Oficial, București (1936);

   G. Bley, *La Roumanie*, Giard and Briere, Paris (1896);

   C. D. Busila, *Industria românească în decurs de 50 de ani (1881–1931)*, Göbl, București (1931);

   D. Z. Furnică, *Industrie și dezvoltarea ei în Țările Românești*, Tiparul Românească, București (1926);

   C. Ianculescu, *Problemele agrare și dezvoltarea industrială a României*, Leopold Geller, București (1934);

   N. Iorga, *Istoria industriilor la Români*, Societatea Națională de Credit Românească București (1927);

   C. Kormos, *Rumania: basic handbook*, British survey handbooks, 3 vols, Cambridge (1944);

   Emm de Martonne, *La Valachie*, A. Colin, Paris (1902);

   P. N. Panaitescu, *Studii asupra industrieid in României*, Göbl, București (1915);

   N. Razmiritza, *Essai d'économie roumaine moderne 1831–1931*, Lib. Générale de Droit, Paris (1932);

   Fr. Schmalz, *Grossrumânien: wirtschaftlich politisch u. kulturell*, Verlag, F. A. Perthes, G. A. Gotha (1921);

   C. Teodorescu and G. Simionescu, *Geografia României*, Steinberg, București (1905);

   A. Tibal, *La Roumanie*, Rieder, Paris (1930).
6. N. A. Rădulescu, *et al. Geografia agriculturii României*, Științifică, București (1968).
7. I. Corfus, *Agricultura Țarii Românești în prima jumătate a secolului al XIX-lea*, Academia R.S.R. București (1969).
8. W. G. East, *The union of Moldavia and Wallachia 1859*, Cambridge University Press, Cambridge (1929).

9. P. S. Aurelian, *Terra nostra*, Academia Române, București (1880).
   Also available in *Opere economice* published by Academia R.S.R. (1967).

10. A. D. Xenopol, *Studii economice*, Lib. Samitca, Craiova (1882).
   Also available in the author's *Opere economice* published by Academia
   R.S.R. (1967).

11. S. Fischer-Galati, 'Romanian nationalism', *Nationalism in eastern Europe*,
   ed. by P. F. Sugar and I. V. Lederer, Univ. Washington Press, Seattle
   (1970).

12. I. L. Evans, *The agrarian revolution in Roumania*, Cambridge University
   Press, Cambridge (1924).

13. G. C. Ionescu-Șișești, and N. Cornatizianu, *La reforme agraire et ses consequences*, Academia Romănă, București (1937).

14. I. Pasvolsky, *Economic nationalism of the Danubian states*, Allen and Unwin,
   London (1928).

15. P. N. Panaitescu, *Politica industrială în o țara agricolă și în special în România*,
   Tip. Libertatea, București (1932).

16. H. Bolitho, *Roumania under King Carol*, Eyre and Spottiswoode, London
   (1939).

17. A. Basch, *The Danube Basin and the German economic sphere*, Kegan Paul,
   London (1944);
   K. Brandt *et al.* (1953) *Management of agriculture and food in the German-
   occupied and other areas of fortress Europe*, Stanford University Press,
   California (1953);
   P. Einzig, *Hitler's 'New Order' in Europe*, Macmillan, London (1941).

18. M. Manoilescu, *The theory of protection and international trade*, P. S. King
   and Sons, London (1931).

19. A. Puiu, *Valorificarea supericară a resurselor naturale*, Academia R.S.R.,
   București (1969).

20. Constantinescu was an advocate of the Liberal policy of development *prin
   noi înșine* and contributed an important three-volumed work on national
   industrialization: *Politica economică aplicată*. Madgearu held basically
   similar views on the need for industrialization but had reservations on the
   wisdom of developing industries for which there was a limited resource base,
   e.g. ferrous metallurgy. He also expressed qualms about the economic
   relationship with Germany since there was a danger of Romania's options
   being restricted (Madgearu 1940). Constatinescu's defence of national
   interests through his work at the National Bank has also been recognized
   by the present leadership (Ceaușescu 1969/70, *op. cit.*, Vol. I, p. 354). Because Romania was exchanging the labour of 600,000 peasants for that of
   60,000 industrial workers in other countries permanent protection should
   be given to industries whose productivity surpassed the average for the
   country irrespective of the availability of cheaper imports and the short-

term sacrifice which the consumer is required to make. The widespread influence of this line of argument is discussed by Montias (1967, p. 196). A thorough and scholarly review of these ideas is provided by Todosia (1967).

M. Montias, *Economic development in communist Rumania*, M.I.T. Press, Cambridge, Mass. (1967);

V. Madgearu, *Evoluția economiei românești după războiul modial*, Independența, București (1940);

M. Todosia, *Teorii burgheze din pericada interbelică cu privire la industrializarea României*, Universitatea 'Al. I. Cuza', Iași (1967).

21. A. A. Demidov, *Travels in southern Russia and the Crimea through Hungary, Wallachia and Moldavia* I. Mitchell, London (1853).

22. The earliest comprehensive picture of the Romanian oil industry emerges from the work of C. Alimănestianu, V. Brătianu and L. Mrazec who formed a commission in 1901 to study the oil regions of the country in the aftermath of the political crisis over the Standard Oil concession (L. Mrazec *et al.* 1904). Other important technical studies were made at this time (L. Edeleanu and I. Tănăsescu, 1903; L. Mrazec, 1907; I. Tănăsescu and V. Tacit, 1907). Useful general descriptions in A. P. Iancoulesco (1928), G. Rommenholler (1926), M. Pizanty (1930, 1939) etc.

L. Edeleanu, and I. Tănăsescu, *Studiul petrolului român*, Asociația română pentru dezvoltarea și înaintarea științei, București (1903);

I. Tănăsescu and V. Tacit, *Exploatarea petrolului în România*, Göbl, București (1907);

L. Mrazec *et. al.*, *Lucrările comisiunii însarcinate în studial regiunilor petrolifere din România*, Ministerul Lucrărilor Publice, București (1904).

L. Mrazec, *Despre formarea zăcămintelor de petrol din România*, Göbl, București (1907).

G. Gane, *Problema petrolului în România*, Göbl, București (1938);

A. P. Iancoulesco, *Les richesses minière de la nouvelle Roumanie*, Lib. Universitaire, Paris (1928);

M. Pizanty, *Le petrole en Roumanie*, Eminescu, București (1930);

M. Pizanty, *L'industrie du raffinage en Roumanie*, Cartea Românească București (1939);

G. Rommenholler, *La Grande Roumanie*, Hijhoff, The Hague (1926).

23. Further foreign investment followed with Dutch capital in 1899 but a Conservative government proposal to sell state oil-bearing lands and allow the construction of a pipeline to Constanța generated a political crisis which brought the Liberals to power and delayed the penetration of American capital until 1904 when Standard Oil's Româno-Americană company was registered (Pearton, 1971, pp. 21–34; Sturdza, 1906).

Polemics against foreign capitalists were again strong in the 1950s (Badrus, 1954).

Gh. Badrus, 'Dominația monopolurilor străine în industria petroliferă a României burghezo-moșierești', *Probleme economice*, 7 (1) (1954), 85–98; M. Pearton, *Oil and the Romanian State*, Clarendon Press, Oxford (1971); D. Sturdza, *Petrolul Romăniei*, Voinita Natională, București (1906).

24. 'Those producers who have wells on their own lands, but far from any railway station, and work them in a primitive fashion, often suffer great losses in bad weather, the conveyance to the nearest collecting railway stations over the bad country roads being very difficult and attended by considerable cost' (G. Benger, 1900, quoted in D. Warriner, ed. 1965, p. 195); D. Warriner, ed. *Contrasts in emerging societies*, Athlone Press, London (1965).

25. C. Pohl, *Die rumänische Petroleumindustrie während des Krieges 1914–1918*, Friedrichs-Wilhelms Univ., Berlin (1926).

26. The interest in nationalization dates from the crisis of 1900, the case being strongly articulated by the work of V. Brătianu and C. Hălăceanu in 1911, *Politică de stat în industria petrolului*, updated after the war (Brătianu, 1919; Hălăceanu, 1919 and 1922). The theme is fully discussed by other authors (Pearton, 1971; Serdaru, 1921).
V. Brătianu, *Petrolul și politica de stat*, Independența, București (1919); M. Pearton, *Oil and the Romanian State*, Clarendon Press, Oxford (1971); C. Hălăceanu, *Pacea de la București și chestiunea petrolului*, Independența, București (1919); Ibid., *Punerea în valoare a zăcăminteler de petrol de pe proprietățile statului*, Poporul, București (1922); V. S. Serdaru, *Le pétrole roumain: aperçu historique économique politique et législatif 1825–1920*, Jouve, Paris (1921).

27. The oil industry, however, remained exposed to political pressure and divergent interests of the state, for higher taxes, and the companies for greater profits, led to serious friction, especially during periods of sluggish demand. The 1937 Mining Law reintroduced the distinction between national and foreign-capital companies. This legislation was overtaken by events even more rapidly than its predecessors for the agreement with Germany in 1939 allowed for a major German stake in the industry.

28. M. Pizanty, *Aria exploatării petrolifere în Romănia*, Univ. Populară Nicolae Iorga, București (1938); Ibid., *Privire retrospectiva asupra industriei petrolifere în perioada 1930–1939*, Cartea Românească, București (1940).

29. C. N. Jordan, *The Romanian oil industry*, N.Y.U., New York (1955).

30. Exploration during the war years was largely in the hands of the German company *Kontinentale Öel A.G.*, since its possession of drilling equipment

made it an appropriate partner for the established companies. Between 1940 and 1943 the effort was concentrated overwhelmingly in Dîmboviţa and to a much lesser extent Prahova and Buzău. Only a modest beginning was made in Putna and Arad. There were concessions in Moldova but no action was taken (Pizanty, 1947).

M. Pizanty, 'Consideraţiuni preliminare asupra sondajelor de explorare efectuate în România', *Monitorul petrolului român* 9 (10) (1947), 1–30.

31. Oil refining started in 1840 and more than 70 small installations were erected by 1900. Refining concentrated on the kerosene fraction and heavier distillates, which yielded lubricating oils when treated with sulphuric acid. The residue was burnt as waste until ways were found to use it as locomotive and boiler fuel (mazout)—through difficulties arose because of high ash content. Large units with a continuous distillation process did not appear until 1897 when Steaua Română's refinery opened at Cîmpina. By this time, benzine, for use in cars and in the chemical industry, was coming into demand. In 1927, in response to increasing demand for benzine (or gasoline), rather than kerosene, and the need for higher quality lubricants, new refining methods were developed for cracking of the residue after the primary distillation to remove paraffins. Cracking was common by 1930.

32. The Wallachian Petroleum Company's project at Brăila in the 1860s is an interesting exceptional case. The company invested heavily in the Băicoi Buştenari areas and built a refinery at Brăila which was to be linked with the oilfields by barrels (hardae) carried on ox carts. The rapid exhaustion of capital, coupled with heavy losses of draught animals and a fire at the refinery, forced the dissolution of the company. Besides a small unit at Galaţi in the early twentieth century, there was the Colombia refinery opened at Cernavoda in 1900: with a capacity of 146,000 it was then the fourth largest unit in the country (after Cîmpina (Steaua Română), Ploieşti (Concordia) and Băicoi (Aurora) and the first to introduce cracking (1927). But it had evidently discontinued operations by 1936. No installations were ever built at Constanţa apart from storages, although refineries had been planned in expectation of the pipeline project of 1900 but when this was dropped the companies concerned switched policy to expand their oilfield plants. In 1927, when the possibility of increasing the capacity of the Constanţa pipeline was under discussion, Liberal politicians saw the prospect of the additional capacity being taken by national companies, who would combine for the purpose of setting up a refinery at Constanţa, a move which would presumably increase the competitive position of Romanian oil abroad. But the increased capacity was not realized before the change of government. Only in 1973, under conditions of rising imports of crude oil, was a seaboard oil refining and petrochemical complex announced for Constanţa.

33. Anon., *Enciclopedia româniei* 4 Vols, Bucureşti, Vol. 3 (1939–43), pp. 652–659.

34. C. N. Jordan, *The Romanian methane gas industry*, Mid-European Studies Center, New York (1956).

35. Natural gas is an excellent fuel, allowing complete and controlled combustion without ash or smoke. Heavy local demand was needed to justify laying pipes and due to the dispersed nature of the market and the heavy competition from fuel oil residues, relatively little use was made of the gas until the Second World War. Methane gas has proved to be a valuable raw material for the chemical industry and was used at Copşa Mică and Tîrnaveni for carbon black and synthetic ammonia. The manufacture of acetylene by dissociation of methane gas with oxygen, offered many possibilities; for not only is acetylene itself valuable in welding and as a raw material for the manufacture of plastics, rubber and pharmaceuticals but also by-product hydrogen may be combined with other products obtained from carbon black manufacture to make ammonia, which, in turn, is basic in further manufacturing processes aiming at fertilizer, plastics and synthetic fibres. These were possibilities however which were out of reach for financial and technical reasons, although German support for the Romanian chemical industry was promoting rapid progress, until supplies were cut off in 1944.

36. Anon. *Enciclopedia româniei*, 4 vols, Bucureşti, Vol. 3 (1938–43), pp. 68–692.

37. N. Sophian, *Schita zăcămintelor de cărbuni din România*, Inst. Geologie al Romaniei, Bucureşti, (1925).

38. D. Leonida, Perspectivele economice legate de Valea Bistriţei Moldovene *Buletinul S.R.R. de Geografie* 42 (1923), 100–152.

39. D. Leonida, and N. Caramfil, *Scurt istoric al inştalatiilor în România*, Tip. Göbl, Bucureşti (1938).

40. L. Fundăteanu, 'The problem of Roumania's energy and economy', *The economical situation and organisation of Roumania in 1926*, Bucureşti, (1926), pp. 75–86.
    D. Pavel, *Capacitatea energetică a României*, Imprimeria Naţională, Bucureşti (1930).

41. S. Pascariu, *Industria uzinelor electrice în România*, Soc. Natională de Credit Industrial; Bucureşti (1929).
    I. G. Rarincescu, *Electrificarea României*, Institutul Român de Energie, Bucureşti (1930).

42. However, after 1939 a further programme for developing hydro-power was drawn up with priority for the Bicaz project on the Bistriţa and serious consideration for the Iron Gates (to be achieved through a Romanian–Bulgarian–German concern). Such developments would enable railway

electrification (especially Bucureşti–Braşov–Sighişoara) and growth of electro-chemical and electro-metallurgical industries (Lupu-Kostaky 1939). But the programme was not implemented until after the war.

N. Lupu-Kostaky et al. '*Aspecte ale economiei româneşti: material documentar pentru conoşterea unor probleme în cadrul planului economic'*, Consiliul Superior Economic Oficiul de Studii, Cercetări şi Indrumari, Bucureşti (1939).

43. St. Chicoş, *Groupement territorial de quelques industries en Roumanie*, Curierul Judiciar, Bucureşti (1926).

M. Manoilescu, 'Isvoarele de energie si asezărea geografică a diferitelor industrii în Romania', *Buletinul S.R.R. de Geografie 40* (1921), 23–61.

44. R. G. Wanklyn, 'The artisan element in the Slav countries', *Geographical Journal 53* (1944), 101–119.

Useful references include V. Diculescu, *Bresle negustori şi meseriaşi în Ţara Româneasca 1830–1842*, Academia R.S.R., Bucureşti (1973);

C. C. Giurescu, *Contribuţii la istoria ştiinţei şi tehnicii romaneşti în secolele XV-începtul secoluliu XIX*, Ştiinţifică, Bucureşti (1973);

I. Lungu, et al. *Meşteşuguri şi meşteşugari din sud-vestul Transilvaniei*, Ştiinţifică, Bucureşti (1970);

T. Morariu, Piuăritul în valea Someşului *Buletinul S.R.R. de Geografie 55* (1936), 118–136;

St. Pascu, *Meşteşugurile din Transilvania pînă în sec. XVI*, Academiei R.P.R., Bucureşti (1954).

45. V. Cărăbiş, 'Mori şi pive pe valea Jaleşului (Gorj) în sec. al XVII–XIX', *Studii*, 15 (1962), 931–952;

I. Simionescu, *Tara noastră: natura oameni muncă*, Fundaţia Regele Carol II, Bucureşti (1938).

46. Postwar Romanian interpretations are less charitable (Zane 1970, p. 37) and emphasize the need for clear separation of agricultural and industrial occupations, while frowning on the alleged tendency to regard the traditional way of life with its low material standards as utopian. However, as postwar experience so clearly shows, capital and skill as well as organization is required and the importance of craft industries was therefore emphasized in the industrial programmes of the late nineteenth century progressives, such as M. Eminescu. See *Enciclopedia Romaniei I*, 282, *op. cit.*;

G. Zane, '*Industria din România în a doua jumătate a secolului al XIX-lea'*, Academia R.S.R., Bucureşti (1970).

47. A. A. C. Sturdza, '*La Terre et la race roumaines'*, J. Rothschild, Paris (1904), p. 128.

48. D. Berindei, *Oraşul Bucureşti: resedinţa şi capitala Ţarii Romîneşti 1459–1862*, Soc. de Ştiinţe Instorice, Bucureşti (1963);

C. C. Giurescu, *Istoria Bucureştilor*, Literatura, Bucureşti (1966);

49. D. Warriner, Ed. *Contrasts in emerging societies*, Athlone Press, London (1965), pp. 164–7.

50. M. G. Obédénare, *La Roumanie économique d'après les données les plus récentes*, Leroux, Paris (1876).

51. Tradesmen who had served their apprenticeship could set up in business anywhere, and with increased emphasis on industrial training after independence together with social changes wrought by the 1864 land reform, many new businesses were formed (Adam and Marcu, 1954; Adaniloaie and Berindei, 1966). After the agrarian reform of 1864 there was a greater emphasis on full-time craft work and hence the industrial surveys of the period became increasingly comprehensive. However there remained many households practicing a variety of seasonal occupations and even where these activities involved sale of goods and services to others, as opposed to cloth making, wood working or food preserving for the family, it is possible that complete statistics were not collected until after the Second World War when such activities would have come under the co-operative system.
I. Adam, and N. Marcu, 'Reforma agrară de la 1864 şi unele aspecte ale dezvoltării capitalismului în agricultura Romîniei', *Problema economice* (1954), 7 (5), 124–141, (7) 75–101, (8) 121–144.
D. Adăniloqie and D. Berindei, *La réforme agraire de 1854 an Roumanie et son application*, Academia R.S.R., Bucureşti (1966).

52. *Anuarul General* (1905), 222.

53. V. Madgearu, *Rumania's new economic policy*, P. S. King and Sons, London (1930).

54. G. Zane, 'Politica economică a principatelor în epoca unirii şi capitalul străin', *Studii*, 12 (1) (1959), 223–261.

55. I. Stefănescu, 'Meşteşguri sateşti în regiunea Ploeşti', *Probleme de geografie*, 6, (1959), 253–260.

56. V. Madgearu, *Evoluţia economiei românesti după războiul moudial*, Independenţa, Bucureşti (1940).

57. Details of water mills and other small industrial installations can be obtained from publications of Muzeul Brukenthal of Sibiu (e.g. C. Irimie 1966). An open-air museum Muzeul tehnice populare with structures collected from different parts of the country is maintained at Dumbrava Park in Sibiu and small scale industry also features in the 'Village Museum' beside Lake Herăstrău in Bucureşti;
C. Irimie, *et al.* (1966). *Moara cu dube din satul Fînaţe*, Muzeul Brukenthal, Sibiu.

58. D. Mihailache, 'Date cu privire la începuturile industriei din oraşul Bucureşti', *Rev. de statistică* 8 (9), (1959), 50–56;
E. Mihaly, and S. Mihaly, 'Dezvoltarea industriei oraşului Galaţi în perioada 1857–1873', *Studii şi articole de istorie* 9 (1967), 123–138.

59. V. Popovici, 'Inceputurile industriei hîrtei în Moldova', *Analele şt. Univ. 'Al. I. Cuza' din Iaşi Şt. Soc.* 1 (1955), 87–110.

60. Al. Bărbat, 'Fabrica de hîrtie de la Zărneşti 1852–1878, *Studii şi articole de istorie* 4 (1962), 197–221.

61. G. Dobre, 'C. Milhalic deHodocin', *Buletinul Inst. Politehnic Iaşi* 9 (1963), 469–474.

62. G. Zane, op. cit. (1959).

D. Berindel, *L'union des principautés roumaines*. Academia R.S.R., Bucureşti (1967).

63. L. Boicu, Despre stadiul manufacturier al industriei în Moldova' *Studii şi cercetări ştiinţifice ale Academiei R.R.P. filiala Iaşi istorie* 11 (1960a), 127–137

G. Chirita, 'Date noi privind fabrica de postav de la Tg. Neamţ' *Studii* 17 (1964), 1391–1407.

64. L. Boicu, 'Mijloacele viteza şi preţul de cost al transporturilor în Moldova la începutul secolului al XIX lea', *Studii şi cercetări ştiinţifica istorie* 14, ale *Academiei R.P.R. filiala Iasi* 14 (1963), 249–257.

65. D. Ivănescu, '*Din istoria silviculturii românesti*', Ceres, Bucureşti (1972).

66. D. Şt. Emilian, (1919), *op. cit.*

67. 'Large' industries were enterprises employing at least 25 workers and requiring capital investment in excess of 50,000 lei and operating for more than five months of the year (*Monografia geografică*, 2, 80). Building sites were given exemption and there was relief from customs duties on imported machinery. Legislation was strengthened in 1912, varying the extent of concessions according to the type of industry and the degree to which home produced raw materials were used. Concessionary railway rates were granted and free use of water power allowed. The definition of large industry was revised to take in enterprises with more than 5 h.p. of installed machinery or a labour force of more than 20 (apart from administrative staff). There was also some encouragement for associations of artisans. In 1920, this legislation was extended to the new provinces (Rommenholler, 1926, pp. 493–502).

C. G. Rommenholler, (1926), *op. cit.*

68. D. Mihailache, 'Industria din oraşul Bucureşti la ancheta industrială din 1901–2', *Rev. de Statistica* 9 (9), (1960), 47–59.

69. I. Şandru, and P. Poghirc, 'Cîteva trăsături geografice ale dezvoltării industriei Moldovei în ultima sută de ani', *Analele şt. Univ. 'Al. I. Cuza din lasi* 2, (1958), 4.

70. Gh. Platon, 'Populaţia oraşului Iaşi de la jumatatea secolului al XVIII–lea pina la 1859', *Populaţie şi societate*, Pascu, Şt. ed. Cluj, Dacia, (1972), pp. 259–343.

71. S. Panaitescu, Privire economic asupra oraşelor Basarabiei, *Buletinul Institutului Economic Românesc* 2, (1923), 355–366.

72. C. U. Clark, *United Roumania*, Dodd Mead, New York, (1932).

73. E. Grunberg, *L'industrie roumain et la crise mondiale*, Paris (1936).

74. Gr. Antipa, *L'occupation ennemie de la Roumanie et ses conséquences économiques et sociales*, Presses Universitaires, Paris (1929).
    D. Mitrany, *The effect of war in southeastern Europe*, Newhaven, Yale University Press, Newhaven (1936).

75. E. Hesselman, and G. Ioanitiu, 'The cement industry in Roumania', *L'Économiste roumain*, 2 (1926), 302.

76. M. C. Herbst, (1971). *Geografia industriei municipiului București*, Universitatea 'Babeș-Bolyai'—Cluj, București (1971);
    C. Petrovici, 'Anchete economice: industria Galaților', *Buletinul Institutului Economic Românesc*, 3 (1924), 178–201.
    Al. Ungureanu, 'Evoluția comparativă a zonării funcționale a orașelor Iași și Galați', *Analele șt. al' Univ. 'A.I. Cuza IIc*, 18 (1972), 75–83.

77. Anuarul Statistic (1939);
    S. Manuila, and D. C. Georgescu, *Populația României*, Națională, București (1937).

78. T. Morariu, 'Maramureșul în organismul etnic și politic al țării Românești', *Buletinul S.R.R. de Geografie*, 60 (1941),23–44.

79. W. E. Moore, *Economic demography of eastern and southeastern Europe*, League of Nations, Geneva (1945).

80. I. Desmireanu *et al. Uzinele Reșița în anii construcțici socialiste*, Academia R.P.R., București (1963).
    C. Mitea, and St. Zidărita, *Hunedoara și Reșița: giganți ai industriei românești*, Politică, București (1964).
    I. Zejiu *et al, Reșița: istorie și contemporaneitate*, Comitetul Municipal Reșița al P.C.R., Reșița (1972).

81. Șt. Burileanu, *Industria metalurgică a Banatului si a Transilvanici Buletinul S.R.R. de Geografie* 39 (1920), 27–80;
    M. Manoilescu, 'Isvoarele de energie și așezărea geografică a diferitelor industrii în România', *Buletinul S.R.R. de Geografie*, 40 (1921), 23–61.

82. M. Iosa, 'Despre dezvoltarea industriei în Romînia la sfîrșitul, secolului al XIX-lea și inceputul secolului al XX-lea (1880–1914)' *Studii și materiale de istorie modernă*, 3 (1963), 353–429.

83. I. S. Gruescu, *Gruparea industrială Hunedoara—Valea Jiului: studiu geografic —economic*, Academia R.S.R., București (1972).

84. In addition to the Titan works at Galați, integrated with other units in Transilvania, there were various other units installed in the southeast: The Goldenberg works at Brăila (later Intreprinderile Metalurgică Dunărene) and the Industria Fierului plant in București. Both were at least partly dependent on imported metal, in the form of pig iron or scrap.

85. C. Orghidan, *Industria metalurgică din România* Imp. Națională, București (1940).

86. M. Manoilescu, op. cit. (1921).

87. M. Constantinescu, (1939–41) *Comerţul exterior al României 1928–1937*, Cartea Românească, Bucureşti, 12 vols.

88. The Galaţi plant was started in the 1960s. However, before the decision was taken an alternative strategy was proposed, building up on the tube works built at Roman and Iaşi. Although convenient for exchanges with the Soviet Union a major expansion in northern Moldova would have required heavy investment in infrastructure and plans were linked with the canalization of the Prut and the diversion of water from the Siret over the watershed into the Bahlui valley in which Iaşi stands.

89. O. Constantinescu, 1973 *Critica teoriei România—ţara eminamente agricolă* Academia R.S.R., Bucureşti (1973).

90. K. Mihailovic, *Regional development; experience and prospects in Eastern Europe* Mouton, The Hague, (197?).

11

The Demographic and Economic Evolution of Thessaly (1881-1940)

M. SIVIGNON

Introduction

The Significance of the Liberation of 1881

During the early centuries of Ottoman domination Thessaly derived many advantages from being part of one of the most advanced
European States in which law and order was well established. By
contrast, after the beginning of the nineteenth century, the country suffered as a result of the progressive decline of the Empire.
The fact that the Greeks in Thessaly rose in revolt a number of
times between 1821 and 1878 showed that attachment to Greece
corresponded to the wishes of the majority.

Thessaly was simply a marginal province of the Ottoman
Empire, functioning as a defensive zone for land to the south,
being situated far from the great cities of the Ottoman state, and
having little economic importance. In Greek hands, however,
Thessaly became an essential component in the Kingdom providing Greece with the greater part of its grain supplies and containing the largest, most fertile stretches of lowland in the
country. By becoming part of Greece, Thessaly associated itself
with what was undoubtedly still a backward country, but one where
centralized power was better obeyed, the people more educated,

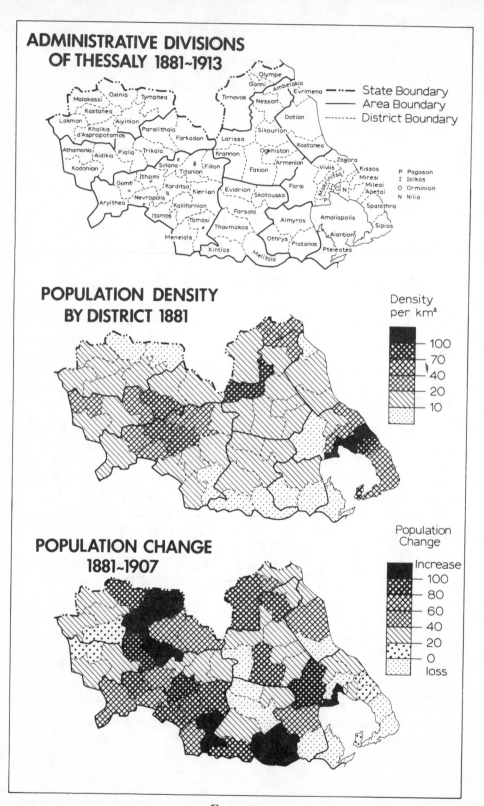

FIGS 1–3

and their economy more developed than in Turkey in 1881 (Fig. 1).

From Liberation to the Balkan Wars (1881-1912)

The Population of Thessaly

Densities

According to the census of 1881, Thessaly had 270,886 inhabitants, but this was undoubtedly less than the real figure, because on one hand the female population was underestimated and on the other some of the Turkish residents were excluded from the census

Densities were low, with an average of 21 persons/km² which contrasted with 32/km² for Greece at the same date. The population of Thessaly was very uneven in its distribution, with the district of Othrys recording on 4.9 persons/km² whilst in the Iolkos district, on the Gulf of Volos, the figure reached 365/km² (Fig. 2.)

Three zones of high population density emerged. First, the Pilion region where more than 100 persons/km² were recorded in six districts, although these were small shoreline districts, with Volos, for example, containing fewer than 5,000 inhabitants. Densities decreased away from this central zones but remained above 40 persons/km² throughout the region. The second zone covered the Plain of Trikkala and the lowest section of the Pindus Chain, in the county of the Agrafa (literally 'the country without a written name'), which was never under direct Turkish control. The high densities recorded in the Trikkala and Larissa districts were explained by the presence of the two most important towns of Thessaly. In addition, there was a third region with above average densities of population. This involved the Lower Olympus and Ossa mountains situated on either side of the lower valley of the Pinios.

The remainder of the province supported very low densities of population, normally less than 20 persons/km², but in some places falling to half that amount. Some areas were almost entirely empty. Those included the country along the Macedonian frontier, the Othrys district and the hills of Revenia. Fakion district, quite close to Larissa, supported only 7 persons/km².

Thus, the highest densities were not found in lowland areas but in semi-mountainous country, such as the Pilion region, the Lower Olympus and the Pindus mountains. Some lowlands were virtually without population, which represented an inversion of the population densities, a characteristic pattern found in Mediterranean countries at this time.

Demographic Characteristics

The population of Thessaly exhibited a very young age structure, with people under 20 years of age representing 48 per cent of the total. By contrast, only 3·7 per cent were more than 65 years old. Local differences were not very great, with the proportion under 20 years ranging only from 49·8 per cent in the eparchy of Farsala and Domokos to 43·3 per cent in Tírnavos eparchy. However, the eastern part of Thessaly displayed a slightly older population structure than further west.

Table I

Population of Thessaly 1881

Eparchy	More than 65 years per cent	Less than 20 years per cent
Tirnavos	3·6	43.3
Ayia	3·1	46·6
Larissa (Eastern Thessaly)	3.0	46·7
Almyros	2·8	47·2
Volos	5·3	44·1
Trikkala	2·7	49·3
Farsala and Domokos	3·2	49·8
Karditsa (Western Thessaly)	3·6	49·0
Kalambaka	3·1	47·9

Changes in Population (Fig. 3)

Because of its age structure, it is not surprising that the population of Thessaly grew rapidly. If one excludes the eparchy of Domokos which was attached to the Phtiotide for administrative purposes, the population of Thessaly grew from 255,000 in 1881 to 380,000 in 1912, and the average density increased from 21 to 30 inhabitants/km².

Very few districts registered population losses during this period. Apparent reductions in the number of residents in the Vlach districts of the Pindus (Athamania and Khalkis) were of little importance since they were linked to the chronology of pastoral movements, as stockmen moved with their transhumant flocks and herds. By contrast, the Platanos district, in the southern Othrys mountains, and the districts in the central Pilion region (Aiantion, Kissos, Mileai, Miresi, Orminion) most probably experienced their peak populations before 1881. The Central Pilion, the little haven of Trikeri and Othrys mountains represented important areas of emigration to Egypt.

The rest of the Aegean part of Thessaly experienced only modest increases and the same was true for the Pindus Mountains in the nomos department of Trikkala the hills of Revenia, and the countryside around Farsala.

By contrast, rapid increases occurred in the Tirnavos region. This seems to have resulted from the replacement of Turks by Greeks, who came from elsewhere in Thessaly or from the Peloponnesus. Population growth was also important in the southern parts of the lowland, which had been almost without inhabitants in 1881, and in the whole of western Thessaly where birth rates were high.

In general, trends of population change produced densities that conformed with the carrying capacity of each part of Thessaly.

Ethnic Composition of the Population of Thessaly (Figs 4 and 5)

According to the census of 1881, 90 per cent of the population of Thessaly was Orthodox, 9·1 per cent was Muslim, and 0·9 per cent was Jewish. Orthodox inhabitants were Greeks and Vlachs and

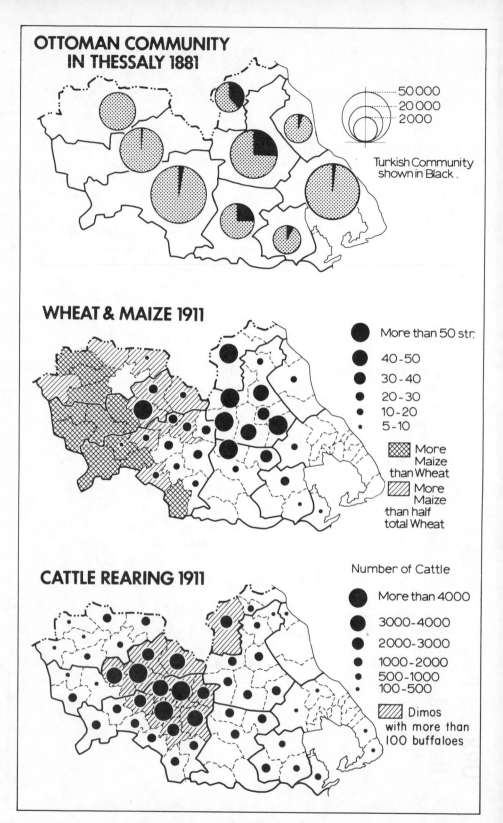

OTTOMAN COMMUNITY
IN THESSALY 1881

50 000
20 000
2000

Turkish Community
shown in Black.

WHEAT & MAIZE 1911

More than 50 str.
40 - 50
30 - 40
20 - 30
10 - 20
5 - 10

More
Maize
than Wheat
More
Maize
than half
total Wheat

CATTLE REARING 1911

Number of Cattle

More than 4000
3000 - 4000
2000 - 3000
1000 - 2000
500 - 1000
100 - 500

Dimos
with more than
100 buffaloes

FIGS 4, 6, 7

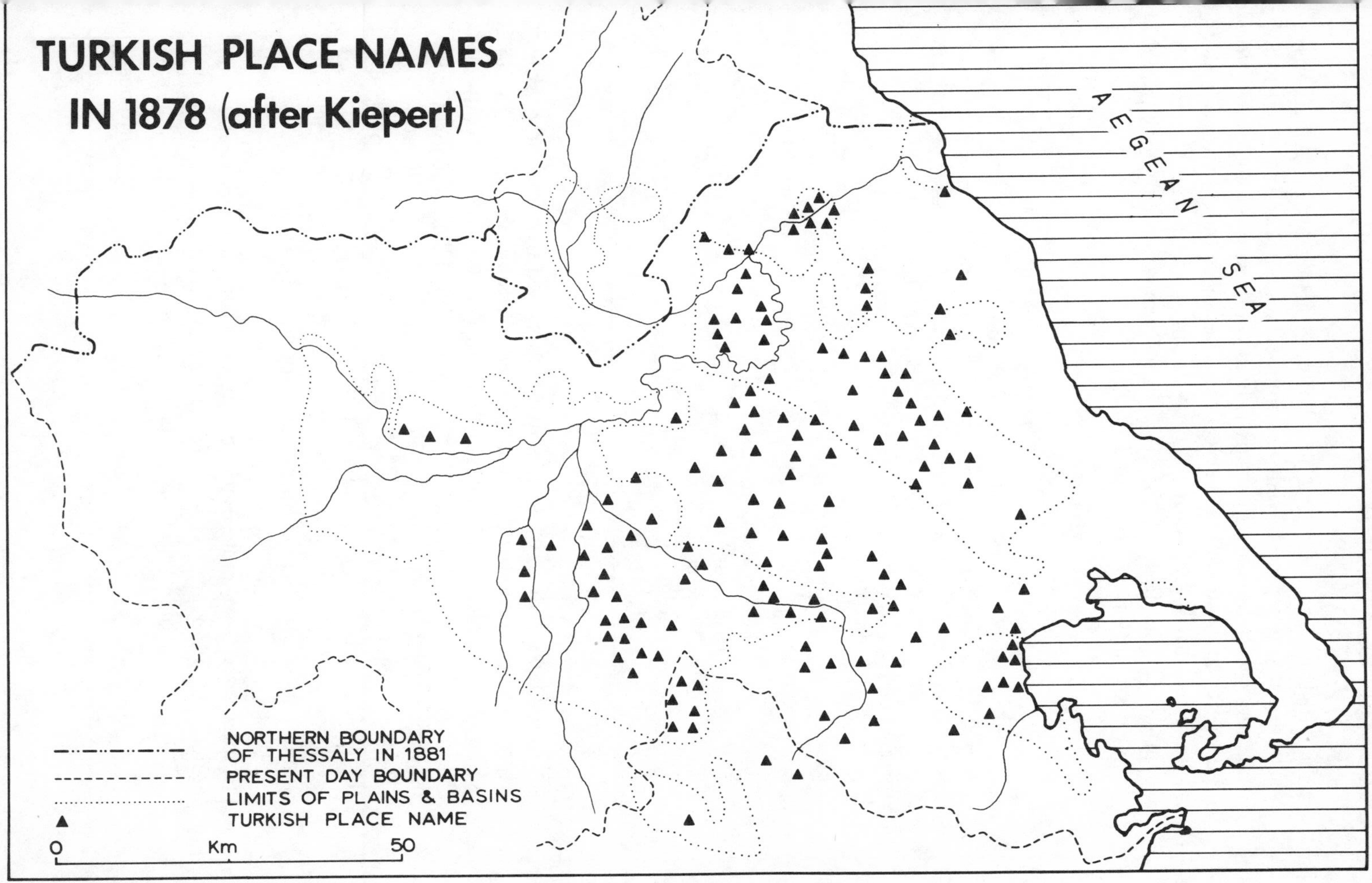

TURKISH PLACE NAMES IN 1878 (after Kiepert)

AEGEAN SEA

NORTHERN BOUNDARY
OF THESSALY IN 1881
PRESENT DAY BOUNDARY
LIMITS OF PLAINS & BASINS
TURKISH PLACE NAME

Km   50

0

FIG. 5

the Muslims were mainly Turks but also included some Albanians. The most important Jewish community was at Larissa, (with 68 per cent of all Jews in Thessaly), being followed by Trikkala (20 per cent) and Volos (12 per cent). The ancestors of these Jews, like those in Salonika, had come from Spain in the fourteenth century. Turks formed the most important minority group and their distribution is shown in Table II.

Table II
Muslims in Thessaly in 1881

Eparchy	Proportion of Muslims per cent
Larissa	24·7
Ayia	4·7
Almyros	11·8
Volos	2·4
Farsala and Domokos	23·8
Tirnavos	30·0
Trikkala	2·4
Karditsa	4.9
Kalambaka	0.0

The Turks called Koniarides were supposed to have come from Konya. They owned small peasant holdings and lived in a score of villages like Dereli (Gonni), Balamut (Itea), Baba (Tempi), Mousalar (Rodia), Karadzoli (Aryiropouli), Utmanda (Makrikhori), Kiserli (Sikourion), Toivasi (Kalokhori), In addition, Turks were found in some large villages between Farsala and Domokos, around Velestino and near to Almyros. They also lived in urban centres, where they were officials, soldiers, craftsmen and landowners. The largest number was ound in Larissa.

Turks had earlier been more numerous. The map drawn by Kiepert[1] gives valuable evidence on Turkish placenames and thus reflects to a certain extent the density of former Turkish settlements. Areas of Turkish influence in eastern Thessaly, stand in contrast with areas to the west where the peopling process remained Greek. The area of Turkish placenames corresponds with that of the chifliks.

Whilst the Turks were enumerated separately, this was not the case either for the Vlachs who were Orthodox and strongly influenced by the Greeks, or for the Sarakatsanes who were Greek-speaking shepherds. The Vlachs were all bilingual. They included the Koutsovlachs, who had long been settled in their summer villages on the Pindus, and the Arvanitovlachs who arrived later from Albania, possibly in the eighteenth century and spoke Albanian, as well as Greek and their own language. Mention must also be made of the Koupatsarei, who spent the summer in the mountain villages of the Grevena region and the winter near to Tirnavos and who were perhaps Vlachs who had been influenced by the Greeks.

Together with Weigand,[2] Wace and Thompson[3] and other authors, one might wonder if the peasants of the lowland of western Thessaly are also Vlachs. They are known as Karagounides, and still possess distinctive costumes, with their womenfolk wearing black and white dresses with red patches. The fact that the Vlach population of Epirus along the Albanian frontier and of Etolia-Arknania are known as 'Karagounis' suggests that this may be so.

The ethnic variety of Thessaly in 1881 soon became simplified, especially because of the rapid reduction of the Ottoman minority group.

The Departure of the Turkish Community

The Turkish departure started before 1881 and it is probable that the migration took on important proportions during the troubled period between 1878 and 1881. The treaty of 1881 gave the Turks the right to continue to live in Greece and retain their property, but still the exodus continued. B. Ornstein[4] visited Larissa in 1882 and he estimated that at that time the population was composed of 4,900 Greeks, 4,600 Turks, 2,200 Jews, 1,000 Vlachs and 500 Gipsies. But the town contained 26 mosques, and the Turks held 10 schools whilst the Christian population had nine and the Jews only three. The Turks left Thessaly only on the occasion of the Graeco-

TurkishWar of 1897. Greek peasants fled before the advancing Turkish armies and the Koniarides Turks joined in the common cause of their compatriots, but such participation was to their disadvantage. When after a year the Greeks took possession of the province again the Turks fled, and this is why the census of 1907 recorded only 2,795 Turks, making up less than one per cent of the total population of Thessaly. The most important Turkish group (638) was at Larissa. A few were still to be found in the towns, but the Koniarides villages had been emptied of their Ottoman population. Turks had represented 30 per cent of the residents of the Tirnavos eparchy in 1881 but by 1907 only 186 remained.

Economic Progress

Communications

Improvement of the communications network was essential before economic advance could be made. The Greeks were primarily concerned with being able to transport cereals from Thessaly through Volos. This matter was immediately taken in hand in 1884 as two narrow-gauge lines (1m) joined Kalambaka to Volos through Trikkala and Karditsa and also linked Larissa to Volos. By contrast the constitution of the normal-sized railway line between Athens and Larissa was much slower, partly because of difficult terrain but also because of strategic concern to avoid following a coastal route. The railway from Athens reached Larissa as late as 1908 and in 1912 came to a halt at Papapouli on the Turkish frontier. Not until after the beginning of the First World War was Greece linked to the European railway network in 1916.

The railway was a particular advantage to Volos and allowed the province to maintain contacts with the outside world. Advances in agricultural production were stimulated as a result.

Agriculture

In the absence of adequate figures, apart from data on tobacco and other supervised crops, the agricultural enquiry of 1919 will be used to depict Greek farming just before the Balkan Wars.

The small area of cultivated land is the most important point. Land recorded as 'usable' also included woodland, marshes, rough grazing land, and pastures, and covered an area of 7,015 km² out of a total surface of 12,191 km². Land that was effectively cultivated, excluding fallow, represented 1,945 km², some 15·8 per cent of the total. Table III indicates land devoted to the main crops. In addition, one must mention the large area of fallow land (71,420 ha) which was about half of the surface under cereals, also the fact that 2,520 ha were used for secondary crops, especially beans which followed the maize crop. The range of products grown had changed little since 1881. Thessaly continued to provide Greece with wheat and this had been a grave problem in 1897 when the province was occupied by the Turkish army.

Table III

Crops grown in Thessaly in 1911

	ha
Cereal crops	149·300
Orchards and gardens	18·120
olive groves	8·630
vineyards	7·600
Industrial crops	13·250
tobacco	6·490
sesame	5·680
cotton	690
Vegetables	9·930
vetches, lentils	5·680
chick peas	1·670
beans	1·010
Vegetables	3·050
cucurbits	1·650
Lucerne	850

Wheat (Fig. 6) was grown on the plain of Larissa and in the central hilly country of Révénia. Maize replaced wheat at higher altitudes, in the Pindus, Lower Olympus and Pilion mountains. Throughout western Thessaly the area under maize represented half that sown with wheat. Barley covered a larger surface than maize in eastern Thessaly. In the west, barley (19,800 ha) occupied less land than maize (27,300 ha). Thus one can contrast western Thessaly, and its typically Balkan production of maize, with the eastern part of the province where wheat and barley were grown as in other typically Mediterranean areas. The continuing importance of traditional leguminous crops indicates the relative stability of the agricultural system. Beans grown as a secondary crop were a speciality of the damper parts of western Thessaly.

Sugar beet was not listed in the agricultural statistics. This crop had, however, been introduced into Thessaly by a large landowner called Zographos, whose main landholding was situated some 20 km from Trikkala. Zographos constructed a sugar refinery, but progress was slow. Since the peasants lacked technical expertise the plants became diseased and, above all, the government was not concerned about rising sugar prices and preferred to import sugar from abroad. Cotton production was of limited importance, and thus contrasted with its considerable development during the Turkish period. This was due to competition from Egypt and America. Olives and vines were, however, important. Olive growing was restricted by climactic factors to areas close to the west and the production of vines was limited to the hillslopes surrounding the two plains.

The value of the main agricultural crops emphasizes the predominance of cereal production in the province.

Information on livestock was incomplete in the 1911 enquiry, since nomadic herding was excluded from these and other agricultural statistics. The contrast between western and eastern Thessaly appeared once again, with western Thessaly containing larger numbers of livestock than in the east where climactic conditions were less favourable for stock raising (Fig. 7).

Cattle raising was a speciality of the West, with almost all districts with more than 2,000 cattle apiece being found there. Sheep were more numerous in the East in 1911, but we do not know where the nomadic flocks were recorded. There were more goats than sheep in the mountainous regions (Pilion, Othrys, Ossa, and

Table IV
Value of Agricultural Production in 1911

Agricultural production	Value (million drachmas)
Wheat	24·0
Maize	6·9
Barley	3·0
Beans	1·0
Tobacco	6·0
Cotton	0·25
Vines	4·2
Oil	6·0
Olives	6·0
Total	57·35

Agrafa). Only in the lowlands and central hilly areas were there twice as many sheep as goats (Fig. 8).

Pigs were almost entirely absent from the Pilion area and few were found throughout eastern Thessaly. By contrast, they were characteristic of the western plain and the Agrafa area. Their distribution corresponded in part with the former distribution of Muslims. (However, Turks had not settled in the Pilion area.)

Few buffaloes were kept in 1911. They were more numerous than cattle in only two villages and these were located on the western plain. Indeed, almost all the districts where buffaloes exceeded 10 per cent of the cattle population were found in this region (Fig. 8). The distribution of buffaloes partially corresponded with marshy areas. But why should they be absent from the shores of Calle Karla and Calle Nessonis in eastern Thessaly? In our opinion this must be explained by cultural rather than physical factors.

The table showing agricultural production and the information on stock raising indicate something of a paradox. Western Thessaly was more populated and possessed a broader range of resources, but this region was backward in technical terms. The

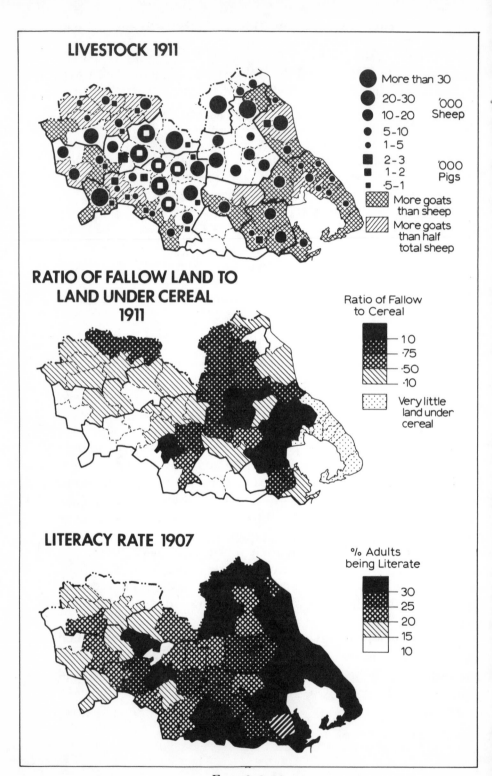

LIVESTOCK 1911

More than 30
20-30
10-20   '000
5-10   Sheep
1-5
2-3
1-2   '000
·5-1   Pigs
·5-1

More goats
than sheep

More goats
than half
total sheep

**RATIO OF FALLOW LAND TO
LAND UNDER CEREAL
1911**

Ratio of Fallow
to Cereal

1·0
·75
·50
·10

Very little
land under
cereal

LITERACY RATE 1907

% Adults
being Literate

30
25
20
15
10

FIGS 8, 9, 10

importance of beans and other legumes and the presence of maize, pigs and buffalo indicate that the western part of the province was part of the central Balkan realm and indeed part of central Europe. By contrast, eastern Thessaly was much more open to innovations and more Mediterranean.

But a study of land use and production does not provide an adequate summary of the agricultural economy. This functioned within the framework of communal practice which will not be summarized. As far as we know, no documents have been written on this subject. Our information is derived from verbal enquiries conducted between 1963 and 1971 which give some idea of what must have been the situation at the beginning of the twentieth century. Thessaly forms part of a much larger zone comprising the eastern section of the Balkan Penninsula where settlements are scattered and agricultural land is divided into a number of fields that are subject to obligatory rotations. Enclosure is forbidden. These fields are known as damka (or domka) in Greece, and this word is very likely of slavic origin. From the information we obtained, obligatory rotations were enforced until 1940–50 in the plains of Karditsa and Trikkala and in the eparchies of Elasson and Fársala, but, by contrast, it is likely that these constraints disappeared at an earlier stage on the plain of Larissa, perhaps even before the First World War.

The system of rotations was closely linked to the practice of fallowing. In general land was left fallow every other year, with cereals being sown and the land being divided into two fields. The biennial system was the most widespread, but there were others. In some cases the soil was too poor for cereals to be grown every other year and thus a kind of shifting cultivation operated. For example, in 1911, 3,090 ha were cropped in the district of Almyros and 4,250 ha left fallow (Fig. 9). More frequently, land was left fallow for three years and then sown with wheat for the other two, as in the Larissa region. Around Karditsa wheat was sown and then legumes (beans, chick peas, lentiles, vetch), with the land being left fallow for the third year, but in very damp areas, where the water-table was close to the surface, fallowing was rare. For example, in Trikkala district, wheat covered 4,730 ha in 1911, maize 2,510 ha and fallow only 270 ha.

The system of fallowing survived longer than that of obligatory rotations. This phenomenon was not special to Thessaly but involved at least half of the low-lying areas of Greece in 1911. Winter floods covered a good part of the lowlands each year. Maize was planted as soon as the water drained away, with marshland being abandoned to wild ducks and buffaloes.

Fallow, rough grazing, periodically-flooded land, and 'meadows' covered a large area, namely 295,000 ha in 1911, by comparison with the cultivated surface of 194,500 ha. Some 6,740 ha of meadowland belonged to the peasants, but with the exception of the 71,420 ha of fallow and the cultivated land, the remainder belonged to the state or to the rural communities. Livestock grazed these areas according to the system of stubble grazing, which was linked to obligatory rotations and partially to communal tending of animals. This latter feature was even more widespread than obligatory rotations, and survives to the present day in the Karagouni country of western Thessaly, even though obligatory rotations have long since disappeared.

In addition, there were many specialist shepherds especially Vlachs and Sarakatsanes. It is difficult to be precise, but there may have been 10,000–20,000 shepherds. The Vlachs occupied the northern Pindus and the present area where their villages are found corresponds with that distinguished by Wace and Thomson[3] at the beginning of the twentieth century.

The Sarakatsanes did not have villages in the mountains, but had groups of huts situated in the Agrafa, to the south of the Vlach Pindus; or else in precarious positions in the middle of the Vlach villages, or else in Macedonia much further to the north in the Vermion or Kaimakchalan areas. All these folk, plus the Koupatsarei of Grevena and a part of the peasant population of the Agrafa came down to winter on the plain of Thessaly with their flocks. The new frontier established in 1881 certainly prejudiced these pastoral movements, since many shepherds had frequented summer pastures that were in Turkish control but winter grazings that had passed into Greek hands. Each period of tension between Greeks and Turks, such as that described by Wace and Thompson, ended with incidents along the frontier which was closed for varying lengths of time. Shepherds from the Samarina region, who habitually moved down into Thessaly in winter, frequently decided to spend the cold months in Epirus or in Albania.[5]

Industrial Progress

Progress in industrial activity was more marked than in farming. These advances did not own much to the ancient craft activities, and little reference was made to the embryonic metallurgical industry, which had been set up at Drakotripa the Pindus where sword blades, cannons and pistol parts were made. The textile industry, which had produced turbans and oriental cloths, suffered serious contraction after the Turkish army adopted western-style uniforms in 1877. The final blow came after 1881 with European dress becoming more and more widespread. Some villages such as Tirnavos, Zarkos, and Ayia continued to dye thread and print cloth using woodblocks, but their sale market was in Albania, which was the most backward region of Europe.

By contrast, industrial activities flourished in Volos between 1881 and 1912. It became a metallurgical centre, and two important firms employed several hundred workers making ploughs, harrows, seed-drills and, at the end of the period, threshing machines driven by steam power. Volos became the leading centre for the production of agricultural machinery, but was overtaken by Pireus for foundry and copper work. At the same time, a modern textile industry was established, with an important spinning-mill for cotton being opened in 1906. From 1890 through to the present, the Matsangos factory made Volos a centre for processing tobacco and manufacturing cigarettes. In addition, many food-processing firms started production of pastry and canned fish. Flour mills had the advantage of processing local wheat, whilst mills in Pireus used Russian wheat.

Much of the capital required for these industrial activities derived from the investments of migrants who settled in Egypt. Capital was also drawn from the profits of the port of Volos which was the only trade outlet of the province. The necessary banking facilities were established in Volos in association with the Epiro-Thessaly bank. The town became the most important in Thessaly, with its population rising from 4,987 in 1881 to 23,563 in 1907. Its distinctiveness derives from the fact that it is an industrial town, a rare situation in Greece, with a working class and an important bourgeoisie with a tradition of investing in manufacturing activities. However, Volos was something of an exception in Thessaly. This point is stressed in Table V which shows industrial activity in Thessaly in 1918. Almost all manufacturing was located in the eastern section of the province and particularly at Volos.

Table V

Industry in Thessaly (After Andréadis, 1918)[6]

	Eastern Thessaly		Western Thessaly	
	No.	Workers	No.	Workers
Potteries	1	22	1	2
Agricultural machinery works	2	216	3	44
Spinning mills	1	75		
Weaving mills	3	242		
Mills	12	247	23	120
Pasta manufacture	1	12		
Preserves	2	30	3	6
Glass works	2	11		
Tanneries	15	93	4	8
			(Electricity works)	
Wood industries	2	21	1	16
	41	969	35	196

Problems

This picture of consistent economic progress should not conceal the fact that Thessaly continued to experience two major problems: the socio-cultural backwardness of its population and the problem of agrarian structures.

Cultural Backwardness

The census of literates undertaken in 1907 showed considerable differences between the departments of Thessaly. The situation was best in the eparchy of Volos, where 43·7 per cent of the population was literate. But in eastern Thessaly only Karditsa eparchy reached the 25 per cent literacy rate. At the district level, a clear contrast existed between urban areas, which were more favoured, and the countryside. Literacy rates in Volos (53·3 per cent) and

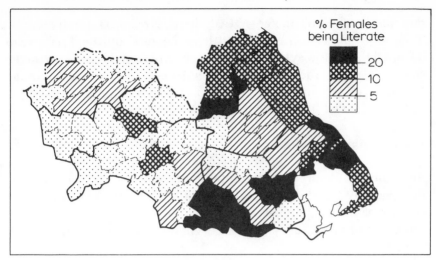

FIG. 11. Female literacy 1907

Larissa (47·8 per cent) were much higher than in the towns of western Thessaly (Trikkala 34·6 per cent and Karditsa 33·0 per cent). Coastal districts also had high rates, such as Nilea and Miresi where more than 40 per cent of the residents were literate. In contrast in Trikkala eparchy almost all districts registered literacy rates of less than 20 per cent. Some contrasts were particularly striking: Ambelakia district (36·6 per cent) in the mountains of Ossa was much more developed than those of the plain. Ferrai district which was the only one in Volos eparchy outside the Pilion region was clearly the least advanced (Fig. 10).

To the West, uncultivated land covered the undeveloped mountain areas of the Khassia where the percentages of literates were the lowest in the province of Thessaly (10·8 per cent in Oxinia district, 12·8 per cent in Tyrmphaia district). Rates were also low in lowland districts, such as Paralithaia (16·1 per cent), Pialia (16·3 per cent), Aiyinion (18·9 per cent), and Sillana (14·0 per cent). By contrast, percentages were much better in the Agrafa area (Nevropolis 29·4 per cent, Ithomi 25·3 per cent). Rates of female literacy varied in a similar fashion and emphasized the contrast between two parts of Thessaly (Fig. 11). The Aegean coastlands and the Pindus were open to innovations by virtue of proximity to the sea, the operation of pastoral movements, and the fact that the Turks had never settled here. By contrast the central, lowland section of Thessaly had been peopled by the Turks who installed the chiflik system. In this second part of Thessaly marshes were extensive and malaria was endemic. The persistent backwardness of the lowlands emphasized that the peasantry in the chifliks achieved little after the Turkish departure.

The Agrarian Problem

According to Andréadis[6] the total number of villages in Thessaly included 192 free villages and 466 chifliks. By 1918, 204 of these chifliks had been purchased by their inhabitants. Other sources[7] confirmed these figures: 270 free villages and 400 chifliks were recorded in 1896.

Chifliks were few in number in the eparchy of Volos and Aghia in 1917, 4 and 5 respectively. But 127 were still in existence in the plain of western Thessaly and 100 in the eastern lowlands of the province. In western Thessaly, each chiflik covered an average of 752 ha. and involved 40 or so families apiece. Large properties still covered 60 per cent of the cultivated surface in lowland regions in the departments of Karditsa and most probably of Trikkala in 1971.

The system of large properties was linked to a very rigid social structure. Large landowners cultivated the land with the help of sharecroppers (Kolligas) and agricultural labourers (parakentedes), whose social status was even poorer than that of the sharecroppers. In addition, very small landowners operated tiny holdings especially in regions of broken relief.

The chiflik system was disastrous in both social and economic terms. Large property owners simply amassed profit from the land and very few encouraged any kind of progress. The system was also prejudiced to public order. Philippson[8] emphasized that Phtiotide and Thessaly were the only provinces where large land-holdings survived and it was in these areas that banditry was rife. The bandits were protected by the large landowners and used by them at election-time to terrorize their opponents.

The system of large landowners influenced many aspects of life in the countryside of Thessaly.

Between 1881 and 1911 legislation was changed only slightly. However the social situation worsened and the agrarian problem was labelled the 'Thessalian problem'. Agricultural labourers organized themselves into groups and in 1911 the army opened fire on demonstrators at Kileler and Larissa, killing several of them. In 1907 piecemeal measures led to the purchase of 51 large holdings throughout Greece and the installation of 4,398 peasant families and 2,628 refugee families from Bulgaria on the land.

In 1909 the liberal party of Venizelos came to power and the constitutional charter was modified to authorize expropriation, by declaring the installation of poor farm labourers on the land they worked to be in the public interest. However the decade of wars between 1912 and 1922 deferred the application of these measures.

From the Balkan Wars to the Second World War (1912–1940)

Solution of the Agrarian Problem

The solution to the agrarian problems of Thessaly was linked to the arrival in Greece of refugees from Asia Minor. Not that they were very numerous in Thessaly. The 1928 census listed only 34,000 out of 493,000, representing 7 per cent of the total population. Refugees made up more than one-tenth of the population of only Volos eparchy, with almost a third of all the refugees (11,000) settling in that town. The highest density of refugee settlements occurred in the eparchy of Elasson, which had recently been attached to Thessaly. Peasant refugees were installed on land that had been abandoned by the Turks who had made up 12 per cent of the total population in 1912. But nowhere were refugees sufficiently numerous to act as a stimulus for agricultural renovation, as was the case in Thrace or Macedonia. However, it was the arrival of these refugees in Greece which brought a solution to the agrarian problems of Thessaly.

A series of laws and decrees, of which the latest dated from 1924 and 1925, led to the breaking up of large landed properties in Greece. All units of land ranging from 8–15 ha according to province that had been worked by tenants or sharecroppers were expropriated. Owner-operators were allowed to retain between 50 and 200 ha, according to province. In Thessaly the maximum was 100 ha.

400 M. SIVIGNON

However, 'plantations, woods, large industrial works located on properties, and pastures that were not suitable for cultivation but were vital to the peasantry' were excluded from expropriation.[9] All landless heads of households who were more than 21 years old had the right to benefit from this reallocation of land. Thessaly was the main beneficiary from these new regulations, as is shown in Table VI which depicts the number of properties subject to expropriation.

Table VI
Distribution of Alienable Properties

Thessaly	571
Macedonia	341
Epirus	308
Thrace	4
'Old Greece'	272
Total	1,496

Each beneficiary received an average of 13·25 ha in eastern Thessaly and 4·85 ha in the west. This was because of the higher density of population in the western part of the province.

Agrarian reform did not produce a perfectly egalitarian rural society. The contrast between west and east has already been noted. In addition, there were no properties qualifying for expropriation in two thirds of the villages and inequalities between rich and poor peasants remained. Finally, leaving in mind the varying number of beneficiaries in each village, the division of the chifliks created a contrast between rich villages, where everyone received an adequate portion of land, and poor villages, where everyone had to be content with much less.

Undoubtedly the consequences of agrarian reform were favourable in social terms. Heavy dependence on large landowners was replaced by less burdensome indebtedness to the State. Agrarian reform managed to weld together a much more egalitarian society.

The results were less clearly positive in an economic sense. J. Sion[10] noted that many drainage activities that had been regularly maintained on large properties became neglected once the land was divided between peasant landowners. Malaria became even more of a problem. The same author noted that '. . . apart from the grazing lands, that were often held communally, half of the agricultural land was sown each year with wheat. Only 10–15 per cent of the other fields received barley and oats. The rest was fallowed for a year.'

In addition, this period saw the creation of the Agricultural Bank, an important public organization affecting all aspects of agricultural life in Greece. The Agricultural Bank made loans available, used its technical advisers to instruct the peasants, helped finance agricultural co-operatives, and intervened in other ways. The creation of the bank had been conceived as an essential adjunct to agrarian reform.

Consolidation of Economic Progress

The period between the two world wars was one of consolidation, when the economy was restarted and society slowly recovered from the shock of the catastrophy of Asia Minor and the arrival of the refugees. Thessaly remained an essentially agricultural province, as the 1928 census showed.

Table VII
Employment (by percentage of Total Workforce) 1928

	Agriculture	Industry, transport	Commerce	Other branches
Eastern Thessaly	58·8	25·7	8·3	7·0
Western Thessaly	83·6	9·6	3·6	3·0
Thessaly	70·8	17·9	6·0	5·1
Greece	61·1	22·4	8·6	7·7

The area of cultivated land increased by 45 per cent from 196,900 ha in 1911 to 315,80 ha. in 1936, whilst the population rose by only 30 per cent over the same period.

This increase in cultivated land resulted from marshland drainage and clearance of rough grazing land, either by peasants from the villages or by the semi-nomadic Vlachs and Sarakatsanes who became sedentary farmers. These marshes and rough pastures had been excluded from agrarian reform, and, as a result, some large landholdings were created anew.

However the enlarged agricultural surface was used in rather different ways than before. The proportion devoted to cereal production declined, but that planted with vegetables, fodders, and industrial crops increased, with advances in the production of potatoes, tomatoes, alfalfa and cotton being particularly significant.

Volos continued to dominate Thessaly's manufaturing activities, since a large number of firms had been established in that town earlier in the century. In 1930 Volos was the fifth town of Greece in terms of industrial employment (5,943 workers), coming after Athens, Pirens, Salonika and Patras. But Thessaly accounted for only 5·8 per cent of Greece's total industrial workforce and consumed only 4·9 per cent of the industrial energy used throughout the country.

According to the industrial census of 1930, two thirds of Thessaly's factories employing more than 100 workers apiece were located at Volos.

Table VIII
Industrial Firms Employing More Than 100 Workers in 1930

Industrial Sectors	Thessaly		Volos	
	Number	Workforce	Number	Workforce
Mineral products	2	334	2	334
Building	6	1,728	2	311
Mechanical engineering	2	310	2	310
Textiles	3	654	2	546
Paper	1	106	1	106
Tobacco	1	536	1	536
Transport	3	895	2	601
	18	4,465	12	2,744

There were no important changes in the major industrial firms in Thessaly. The Glavanis and Stamatopoulos works dominated foundrywork, coppermaking, and mechanical engineering. The most important weaving mills were those operated by Papageorgiou and Leviathian at Volos, Kazantzis at Larissa, and Tegopoulos at Trikkala. The Adamopoulos spinning mill was located at Volos and the same town contained the Matzangos cigarette factory.

The arrival of refugees from Asia Minor provided the industries of Volos with a cheap labour force, but the newly arrived workers, generally lacked adequate capital to start new firms, unlike the refugees who settled in Macedonia and in the suburbs of Athens.

The Position of Thessaly in Greece on the Eve of the Second World War

At first glance, Thessaly appeared to be important in the Greek nation. The province accounted for 17 per cent of the national surface devoted to cereal production, 12 per cent of that under legumes and fodder crops, 8 per cent of the land under industrial crops, and 8 per cent of the orchards, even though Thessaly occupied only 6·5 per cent of the total area of Greece. In addition, the province was in fourth position among all the provinces of Greece in terms of industrial production.

However, an examination of socio–economic indices shows that Thessaly was in a fairly mediocre position. Death rates were quite high, and were raised further in some years because of epidemics. At the same time, the birth rate was above the national average.

Table IX
General Mortality Rates

	1933	1936	1938
		per cent	
Eastern Thessaly	15·9	18·0	13·4
Western Thessaly	19·4	17·4	12·7
Greece	16·9	15·5	13·2

Table X
Birth Rates

	1933	1936	1938
		per cent	
Eastern Thessaly	26·5	28·0	27·0
Western Thessaly	31·3	31·0	33·7
Greece	28·7	28·0	26·1

Tables IX and X shown above indicate a clear difference between eastern Thessaly, where conditions approximated to the national average, and the western part of the province, where demographic conditions remained much more primitive. At the same time, the age structure of the population emphasized the relative youth of the inhabitants of western Thessaly.

Table XI

Age Structure of Thessaly: Census, 1928

	0–14	15–39	40–59	60 + over
		per cent		
Eastern Thessaly	32·3	40·8	18·1	8·6
Western Thessaly	36·9	39·2	16·7	7·0
Thessaly	34·3	40·1	17·5	7·9
Greece	32·1	40·7	18·1	8·9

The same contrast between eastern and western Thessaly emerges again from an examination of illiteracy rates.

Table XII

Proportion of Illiterates

	1920 per cent	Rank position among Greek departments	1928 per cent	Rank position among Greek departments
Eastern Thessaly	45·2	7th	37·5	5th
Western Thessaly	57·7	28th	50·2	33rd

Conditions in western Thessaly became relatively worse during the interwar period and was partly due to the arrival in eastern Thessaly of refugees from Asia Minor who had been better educated than Greeks living in Greece.

A further economic index confirms the mediocrity of conditions in Thessaly (Fig. 12). This shows the total amount deposited, by departement, in Saving's Banks during 1938, which may be considered as an average year. Although containing two of the leading towns of Greece, eastern Thessaly occupied 17th position

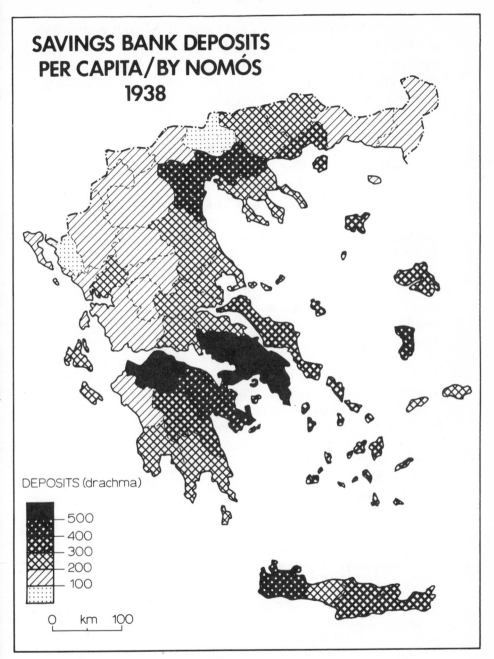

SAVINGS BANK DEPOSITS PER CAPITA/BY NOMÓS 1938

DEPOSITS (drachma)

500
400
300
200
100

0   km   100

Fig. 12

among the 38 Greek departments, with western Thessaly coming in 33rd place. Undoubtedly this index is far from perfect since it tends to emphasize regions of commercial farming, such as Crete, and the northern Peloponnesus, but it gives an idea of the relative economic importance of the various regions of Greece.

Conclusion

One ends up with a kind of paradox. On one hand Thessaly undoubtedly experienced demographic and economic growth between 1881 and 1940. Farming made considerable progress and one industrial town rose to national importance, but on the other hand, Thessaly was still marked by a clear cultural division which most likely originated far in the past Eastern Thessaly was more urbanized, more open to the outside world of the Aegean, more educated and more receptive to progress, so that it contrasted with the predominantly rural western part of the province, where the population had come under Greek influence more recently. The western part was less well educated, more inward-looking, and characterized by very high birth rates and fluctuating death rates. This final feature was due to inadequate medical services. Western Thessaly formed part of the least favoured region of the peninsula that might be called 'The Deep Balkans' like the American 'Deep South'. It had long experienced foreign domination and for several centuries had been the most politically unstable zone of the Balkans. By contrast, the Aegean part of Thessaly had belonged to a more stable political world, had suffered fewer changes, had more often been the master of its own destiny.

11. Notes

1. H. Kiepert, 'Die Neue Griechische-Turkische Grenze', *Zeitschrift für Erdkunde*, Berlin (1882).
2. G. Weigand, *Die Aromunen*. 2 vols. Leipzig (1894/95).
3. A. B. J. Wace and N. S. Thompson, *The nomads of the Balkans*, London (1914).
4. B. Ornstein, *Elf Wochen in Larissa*, Berlin (1882).

5. M. Sivignon, 'Les pasteurs du Pinde septentrional', *Revue de Géographique de Lyon*, 43 (1) (1968), 5–43.

6. V. A. Andreadis, 'Les progrès matériels de la Thessalie depuis sa libération *La Revue de Grèce* (1918), pp. 5–21.

7. A. Wogasli, 'La question agraire et sa solution en Grèce', *La Revue de Grèce* (1919).

8. A. Philippson, *Thessalien und Epirus*, Berlin (1897).

9. Ch. Evelpidis, *La réforme agraire en Grèce*, Athens (1926).

10. J. Sion, 'En Thessalie', *La Géographie*, Vol. LXI (1934), p. 13.

12

The Changing Urban Pattern in Yugoslavia

VELJKO ROGIĆ

The geographical distribution of the hierarchically formed system of centres in a certain territory reflects the complex factors of the socio-economic organization of its space. The contemporary system of Yugoslav urban centres is the outcome of recent social and economic developments, but certain relationships between the highly varied geographical structure of Yugoslav territory and the distribution of its centres can best be emphasized by the historico-geographical differentiation of the individidual stages marking the formation of this system.

Before the Roman conquest of most of Yugoslavia's present territory, and excepting the Greek colonies on the Adriatic,[1] the Pre-Illyrian, Illyrian, Thracian, Celtic and Celtic–Illyrian tribes did not develop any urban settlements. The many topographical localities called 'Gradac', 'Gradišće' or 'Gradina' which can be found on pre-historic archeological sites in Yugoslavia point to the existence of numerous fortified centres. Thus, the term 'gradinska kultura' used in historical and archaeological literature relates chiefly to the period after the Indo–European colonization of Yugoslavia's territory.[2]

While archeological and historical investigations to date have not been sufficient to allow a precise establishment of the functions of pre-historic fortified centres, it is highly probable that most of them were refuges for small, local farming communities. It was only the Roman state organization which brought into being a permanent system of urban settlements on Yugoslav territory in order to meet the military, administrative and economic requirements of the empire.

The geographical distribution of the main known Roman urban centres[3] within the area of modern Yugoslavia is highly characteristic. Most of these centres emerged in a narrow strip of the Mediterranean coastlands, in Macedonia (which before the Roman conquest was under strong cultural influence from the Greeks), in the marginal zone of the great Pannonian Plain, along the 'limes' on the Danube, in the sub-alpine region of what today is Slovenia, through which ran important communication routes from Italy to the Danubian Plain, and finally along the Morava–Vardar corridor which was the most important geographical and trade link between Pannonia and the Aegean Basin.

The mountainous interior of Yugoslavia's territory was in general an area of sparse Roman settlements. Roman urban settlements in this area had a special status and wide local autonomy ('decuriae' under local governors—prepositi) in contrast to the numerous centres on the fringes where administrative organization was based on the system of 'civitates',[4] i.e., a system of towns which acted as centres of Romanization and controlled administrative territorial units, the size of which depended on the importance and functions of the respective urban centres.

Major towns or, according to the hierarchic system, towns of the first category, obtained the status of colony (i.e. Roman civic rights) at a very early stage. (A 'colonia' was a settlement of Roman 'citizens' from the beginning; this is what distinguished it from any other settlement.) At the same time they were centres of Romanization, administrative and political centres and important trading centres. Their geographical distribution confirms the importance of the marginal zones of Yugoslavia's present territory.

The oldest Roman colonies (dependencies) to emerge on the Adriatic were Aquilea and Salona. While the former played a great military role as the main base for the Roman conquest of most of what is present-day Yugoslavian territory, the latter developed as the administrative centre of the largest territorial and political unit—the province of Dalmatia. Similar in importance were Poetovio (Ptuj), the first centre of the province of Pannonia (later Upper Pannonia) and Sirmium (Sremska Mitrovica), the centre of Lower Pannonia. Viminatium (Kostolac), the main centre of the province of Upper Mesia, developed at one end of the Morava–Vardar trade corridor, and Salonika, the main centre of the province of Macedonia, at the other. In the alpine region, the role of main centre was played by Virunum (near Klagenfurt), as the centre of the province of Noric.

With the spread of Romanization, new towns emerged which, as the centres of newly formed provinces, also became towns of prime importance over a period of time. These towns included Siscia (Sisak), the centre of the province of Pannonia Savia, Scodra (Scutari), the centre of the province of Praevalitana, and Scupi (Skopje) the centre of the province of Dardania. Most of the towns with colonial status developed along the Adriatic coast, where Roman influence was at its strongest: Tergeste, Pietas Julia Polensis, Colonia Iulia (Poreč), Jader (Zadar), Aequum (Čitluk near Sinj), and Narona (Vid), while in the mountainous interior there was only the mining centre, Domavia (Srebrenica), which gained the status of colony. (colonia).

Similarly, there were numerous urban centres of secondary importance, i.e. along the Adriatic coast, in the Alps, on the border of the Pannonian Plain, and in the Morava–Vardar corridor, but secondary centres were rare in the interior.

There was a disintegration of the Roman towns in the Middle Ages in the interior. A certain continuity of urban life can be observed only on the Adriatic coast where under the protection of Byzantium, some old towns survived into the Middle Ages, either as continuations of former Roman settlements (Trieste, Koper, Poreč, Pula, Krk, Osor, Rab, Senj, Zadar, Trogir, Kotor, Budva, Bar, Ulcinj and Skadar), or as new urban creations near former Roman towns (Split, Dubrovnik, Biograd and Šibenik). In the interior, however, and with a few exceptions, towns began to re-emerge only much later (in the twelfth and, especially, the thirteenth centuries). Some of the old coastal towns were able to preserve the continuity of urban life and especially of economic functions; when trade activities were resumed towns on the Adriatic coast soon played a leading role.[5] Almost the entire Yugoslav territory looked towards the Adriatic for trading purposes. This mediaeval Adriatic orientation is borne out by many documents connected with trade and transport which point to the dominant importance of the trade routes that ran transverally through the mountain region towards the Adriatic Sea.[6]

The main trade routes of the Yugoslav territory were in fact those of the individual coastal towns, from which they also derived their names: Dubrovački, Senjski, Istarski (for Istrian towns and Rijeka). Towns on the southern Adriatic coast were linked with what was called the Zeta route.

The re-appearance of towns in the interior was chiefly due to the growth of trade along these routes and to the revival of crafts. On the sites of old Roman centres there emerged many new mediaeval towns, either under names derived from their original Roman names (Celje, Kranj, Ptuj, Sisak, Niš) or under new names (Zàgreb, Belgrade, Ljubljana, Novo Brdo, Varaždin).

The political fragmentation of the territory in feudal times, the absence of a strong authoritative state organization, and the low level of crafts and trade in comparison with that of other parts of Europe prevented the development of any major towns in the interior. In the north-western part of what today is Yugoslavia, there emerged numerous, more or less autonomous, urban communes surrounded by walls.[7] These communes differed from other settlements in their outer appearance which was marked by a dense urban pattern and strong walls guaranteed the communes' special status. They were similar in type to west and central European mediaeval towns and possessed small populations, averaging between 1,000 and 2,000, as at Zagreb.

The urban settlements which re-emerged in the country's mountainous interior and eastern regions during the Middle Ages were completely different in character. They usually developed next to royal forts as settlements of traders and craftsmen,[8] most of whom had come from coastal towns, primarily Dubrovnik. These people regarded themselves mainly as citizens of their respective home towns on the coast, and looked upon their settlements below the royal forts only as their trading colonies. These settlements in the interior and the eastern parts of Yugoslavia did not develop into compact settlements, i.e. towns with the same autonomous status as that of towns in north-western Yugoslavia. In contrast to the geographical and socially homogenous towns on the coast and in mediaeval Croatia and Slovenia, which were surrounded by walls and in most cases possessed municipal rights, towns of Mediaeval Serbia, although they were sometimes major settlements, had quite a different character. They were not built as compact urban settlements surrounded by walls, within which similar homogenous urban communities could gradually develop.

The differences between the towns in the north-western parts and those in the south-eastern parts of the Yugoslav territory became especially marked following the Turkish conquest. One of the reasons for the rapid successes of the Turkish advance—apart from a number of historically known reasons, such as organizational supremacy of the centralized Turkish Empire and idealogical unity of political action, as opposed to economic and social crisis, religious division, dispute and political disorganization due to feudal particularism—was the low development level of independent towns in the south-eastern part and the central mountainous region of Yugoslavia.

The whole of modern Yugoslavia, except its extreme north-western part, was under Turkish rule by the second half of the fifteenth century. Turkish administration was based on towns of a completely new type. Most of them were without defence walls and large in area. They consisted of a differentiated trading Turkish-market quarter (čarsija) and residential (mahala—Turkish district) sections and a separate fortification (hisar—Turkish Castle). Towns became not only the basic strongholds of Turkish rule, but also the main centres of an oriental civilization infused with Islam. Thus, for the first time after the Roman period, there emerged a certain hierarchic system of urban centres in a large part of what today is Yugoslav territory.

Large centres (šehirs—first class centres) developed along the main trading routes leading from the Aegean coast to Pannonia, and in the central mountain region. Thus, Skopje, Smederevo and Belgrade developed along the Morava–Vardar corridor on the main communication route from the Aegean coast, and Sarajevo grew up in the central mountain region. Similar to them in size, hierarchic category and central functions were the Turkish Budim (later the administrative centre of the Turkish part of west Hungary and a part of Slavonia) and Temisvar. According to existing studies and published historical sources,[9] these main urban centres considerably exceeded the old mediaeval towns both in number of inhabitants and in the social organization of urban life.

The second hierarchic category of the Turkish urban system consisted of minor trading and administrative centres.[10]

The geographical pattern of the urban system began to undergo considerable changes in the first half of the nineteenth century when, with the retreat of the Turks south of the Sava and the Danube, Yugoslav territory was reorganized under Hapsburg rule and the first independent national political organizations came into being in Serbia and, much later, in Montenegro.

Figures 1, 2 and 3 show the geographical distribution of centres according to size in the early nineteenth century, in mid-nineteenth century, and in 1910. They illustrate well the basic factors in the formation of the urban system in Yugoslav territory.[11]

The situation in the early nineteenth century is highly characteristic of Turkish influence. If we except Novi Sad, Sombor and Subotica (whose size was determined by a high proportion of agrarian population and large agrarian areas incorporated in the towns), the two biggest cities in Yugoslav territory—Sarajevo and Bitola—were within the frontier of Turkey. Sarajevo, with about 20,000 inhabitants[12] was the only major town because it continued to act as the political and economic centre for Bosnia and Herzegovina, the largest socially and economically organized single unit in Yugoslav territory. Bitola and Skopje were of secondary importance because the entire south-eastern part of Yugoslavia was economically orientated towards Salonika. The remaining area of Yugoslavia, which formed part of the Hapsburg Empire, contained no major urban centres, but gravitated towards the foreign cities of Vienna and Budapest, and, to a certain extent, Graz. Trieste, too, developed into an important economic centre, but although lying within Yugoslav ethnic territory, it was dominated by foreign economic and political elements.

In those parts of the present Yugoslav territory which were out-

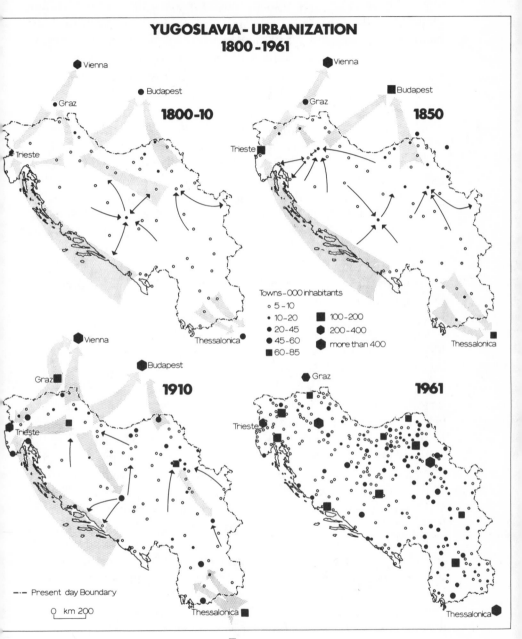

YUGOSLAVIA - URBANIZATION
1800 -1961

1800-10

1850

1910

1961

Towns –000 inhabitants
- ○ 5 – 10
- • 10 – 20
- ● 20 – 45
- ● 45 – 60
- ■ 60 – 85
- ■ 100 – 200
- ⬢ 200 – 400
- ⬢ more than 400

Vienna
Budapest
Graz
Trieste
Thessalonica

—·— Present day Boundary

0   km 200

F I G s 1–4

side Turkish rule, the following towns developed in the early nineteenth century into leading centres or centres of first category:
Ljubljana, Zagreb, Rijeka, Osijek, Karlovac, Subotica, Novi Sad,
Sombor, Zadar, Split, Dubrovnik, Skopje and Bitola. Not one of
the leading centres, except a few towns in Vojvodina,[13] had more
than 10,000 inhabitants. The main trading route of that politically
heterogenous territory was the Danube–Sava–Kupa waterway,
with road links to northern Adriatic ports, especially Trieste.[14]
There was also some orientation towards Graz, Vienna, Budapest
and Salonika, while the Adriatic region was orientated exclusively
towards Trieste.

In liberated Serbia, Belgrade had not yet developed into a major
centre, and, according to the number of inhabitants, corresponded
to the small urban centres of the first category in the Yugoslav
part of the Habsburg Empire.

The map of urban centres in the 1850s (Fig. 2) shows that in
contrast to the continuing lack of a marked differentiation of centres
on Yugoslav territory, there was a rapid growth of the previously
mentioned foreign cities. While the largest Yugoslav towns hardly
reached a population level of 20,000, Vienna, Budapest, Graz,
Trieste and, in a smaller measure, Salonika were developing
rapidly, in comparison with the situation at the beginning of the
nineteenth century. With the development of railways, the Vienna–
Trieste transport route gradually increased in importance and
began to replace the former major transport route along the
Danube, the Sava and the Kupa. Similarly, the Hungarian radial
railway system (Budapest–Rijeka, Budapest–Osijek–Vinkovci–
Slav. Brod, and Budapest Subotica–Zagreb) destroyed the primacy
of the former natural transpiration system along the Sava Valley,
and artificially promoted the gravitational orientation towards
Budapest.[15] It was situated at the intersection of the main transport
and trade routes which ran towards Trieste, Vienna and Budapest,
and playing a mediating role in relation to Bosnia. Furthermore it
was just beginning to take over the role of main administrative
and economic centre for inland Croatia. Other places such as Osijek,
Sombor, Subotica, Vršac and Zrenjanin, were comparatively important centres because of the large proportion of agrarian population rather than because of any highly developed urban functions.

Belgrade was only beginning to develop as the new national capital of liberated Serbia, while Sarajevo retained its role as the main administrative, political and economic centre of Bosnia and Herzegovina, and Bitola was developing into Macedonia's strongest centre. In fact, with the exception of some centres in Vojvodina, only Ljubljana, Zagreb, Sarajevo, Belgrade and Bitola could be classified as centres of the first size category.

A marked differentiation of urban centres could be observed for the first time in the second half of the nineteenth century and in the early twentieth century after the completion of the main railway lines and the beginning of industrialization. However, in 1910 the urban system in Yugoslav territory was still poorly developed and, except for Trieste, large centres, (i.e. big cities in the real sense), developed exclusively outside Yugoslav territory (Fig. 3). However, even at the time of its greatest prosperity and despite its primary links with the Yugoslav hinterland and a high proportion of Yugoslav national elements, Trieste could not establish itself as a national centre of the first category. In contrast to Vienna, Budapest, Graz, Salonika and Trieste, no town in Yugoslav territory reached a population of 100,000. If Subotica[16] is excepted, the largest towns—Zagreb and Belgrade—could not be compared with in size with other foreign cities. Sarajevo, Ljubljana, Subotica, Bitola and Skopje, which as late as the 1850s were in the first category, began to acquire the character of secondary centres. It should be noted that at that time, the second category included for the first time the town of Rijeka, which was rapidly expanding and (together with Sušak) had a larger population than Ljubljana. Pula, which in the first half of the nineteenth century was still a small settlement of the fourth category, was rapidly developing into a secondary centre. In 1910, Skopje and Bitola already belonged to the same category. During the same period Osijek definitely lost its former importance as an urban centre of the first category to become only a centre of the third category thus joining the category of Novi Sad, Sombor, Niš, Mostar and Maribor. The emergence of Split as the largest Dalmatian town marks the beginning of the differentiation of centres on the Adriatic coast. Some centres, which in the early nineteenth century were in the first category (e.g. Karlovac and Varaždin), were reduced to the level of small towns of the fourth category and hardly differed from many local centres.

The period between the two World Wars was marked by a definite polarization of the two leading centres Zagreb and Belgrade[17] and the emergence of a slightly changed group of towns in the second category (60,000–100,000 inhabitants)—Subotica, Ljubljana, Sarajevo, Skopje and Novi Sad.[18] The practical stagnation of Subotica, the rapid development of Novi Sad, the powerful expansion of Ljubljana and Skopje, and the slightly slowed growth of Sarajevo suggest the changed but not stabilized conditions forming a new hierarchic structure of centres in the second category. Apart from the Vojvodina centres which had a high proportion of agrarian population (Senta, Sombor, Zrenjanin), only Maribor, Split, Mostor, Kragujevac and Niš appear as urban centres of the third category with 30,000–50,000 inhabitants.[19] A general characteristic marking the development of urban centres in the 1921–1931 period.[20] is the fact that the bulk of the increased urban population[21] is absorbed by major centres with more than 50,000 inhabitants. This trend continued after the Second World War as was shown by the first post-war census taken in 1948 when 46·31 per cent of the country's total urban population[22] lived in towns with more than 50,000 inhabitants.

It is only in post-war Yugoslavia, especially in the period between the two censuses of 1953 and 1961, that large towns with more than 100,000 inhabitants and towns with 50,000–100,000 inhabitants had smaller rates of increase than those with 20,000–40,000 inhabitants[23] (Fig 4). However, the most important changes in the structure of the urban system have taken place in centres of the second category. What marks the Yugoslav urban system (1961) is a lack of centres of the second category (200,000–400,000 inhabitants). Sarajevo, the largest centre after Zagreb and Belgrade, comes nearest to this medium size, and owes its growth to its situation on the crossroads of transport routes in the central mountain region and to its function as the regional centre for Yugoslavia's main areas of basic industry.

If only the number of inhabitants and the rate of population growth are considered, then Sarajevo, Lubljana and Skopje show much smaller differences in comparison with such dynamic centres as Novi Sad, Rijeka and Split, than they show in comparison with Belgrade and Zagreb (excepting, of course, the laters' functions as national capitals). The rapid growth of Novi Sad (33·4 per cent), Rijeka (33·2 per cent) and Split (31·4 per cent) between 1953 and 1961 shows that they may take over the role of secondary centres in the third category (100,000–200,000 inhabitants). A similar tendency can be noticed in the case of Maribor, which, with a highly urbanized surrounding area closely linked with it in a functional sense and developing at a much faster rate than the town itself, is already entering into the third category. Niš with its high rate of growth (38·2 per cent in 1953–1961) also appears to be emerging as a secondary centre.

Towns belonging to the next two lower categories (the fourth and the fifth) are also marked by an uneven development trend. Characteristically, despite a higher number of inhabitants and a more favourable macro-regional situation, Osijek in the latest inter-census period developed at a lower rate (25·1 per cent) than did Banja Luka (38·6 per cent) and Tuzla (50·9 per cent). Similarly, Subotica (13·2: increase of population from 1953–1961), despite its tradition as an old urban centre, lagged considerably behind such dynamic growth, although still small centres such as Banja Luka, Tuzla, Zenica (33·9 per cent), Mostar (36·6 per cent), Kragujevac (29·2 per cent) and Zrenjanin (26·5 per cent) had important increases. There is an obvious tendency towards the gradual emergence of a specially differentiated group of centres of the third category, such as Subotica, Osijek, Banja Luka, Mostar, Tuzla, Zenica, Bitola, Karlovac, Kragujevac and Zrenjanin, despite the still existing differences between their numbers of population. The extremely rapid and dynamic development of Titograd (a population increase of 87·4 per cent from 1953–1961!) and Priština (61·5 per cent) shows that, although still moderate in size, these two centres may be expected to fill the existing 'gaps' in the system of centres of the third category in the near future.

Pula, which began to develop rapidly in the second half of the nineteenth century, has become absorbed by Rijeka's wider gravitational region just as the old Dalmatian centres Zadar, Šibenik and Dubrovnik have entered into the gravitational zone of Split. In general, centres of the fourth order in the sixth size category

1971

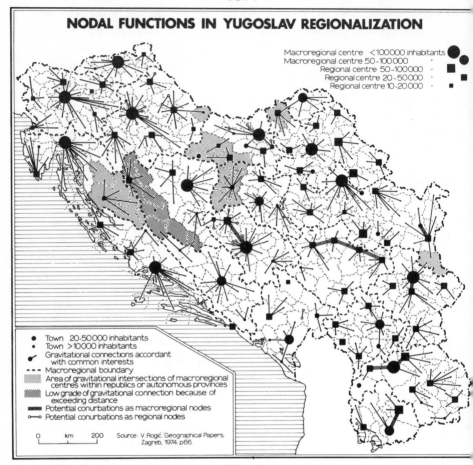

NODAL FUNCTIONS IN YUGOSLAV REGIONALIZATION

Macroregional centre <100000 inhabitants
Macroregional centre 50-100000   ˮ
Regional centre 50-100000   ˮ
Regional centre 20-50000   ˮ
Regional centre 10-20000   ˮ

• Town 20-50000 inhabitants
• Town >10000 inhabitants
🖋 Gravitational connections accordant
   with common interests
--- Macroregional boundary
▨ Area of gravitational intersections of macroregional
   centres within republics or autonomous provinces
▨ Low grade of gravitational connection because of
   exceeding distance
▬ Potential conurbations as macroregional nodes
o—o Potential conurbations as regional nodes

0   km   200   Source: V. Rogić. Geographical Papers.
                                   Zagreb, 1974. p.66.

FIG. 5

are developing chiefly as centres of economic, primarily industrial activity, and with central functions of very limited importance.[24]

Recent dynamic socio-economic development stresses the need for a study of functional connections between geographically different regional complexes. The scheme for a nodal-functional regionalization is most important in this context (Fig. 5). It is evident that the definition of different gravitation levels, i.e. the central zones of urban influence, as in other countries throughout the world, represents a vast field of research. In spite of numerous studies dedicated to these problems much remains to be examined.

The first geographical studies stressed the importance of regionalization, based on gravitation or nodal functions, and provided prototypes for the first such regionalization schemes in Serbia,[25] Slovenia[26] and Croatia.[27] They, in turn, had an influence upon the process of forming definite ideas of approach to this work, so necessary in every day life. The pioneer work of I. Vriser on zones of influence in our cities[28] is the best geographical study within the Yugoslav network of cities. It should be noted that the useful research on gravitation regarding the local polling functions of centres is not the only or main criterion for nodal-function regionalization. Each complex has to be a well-rounded territorial unit with its own centre within which there are formed similar well-rounded units inside and containing a hierarchy level and corresponding centres.

The gradual formation of nodal-function related to the recent development of urban patterns is a dynamic and complex process. Tendencies within them to date have not been completely understood, researched and explained. Spatial planning in Yugoslav communes aims to find the best solutions for development within the framework of specific common interests. These are instigated and made possible by the segregation of territorial groups, which have themselves the character of nodal-functional complexes. The first draft of four basic Croatian macro-regions first published in 1962[29] was accepted and partially modified by the annexation of the West-Shavonian region, this bordered on the Osijek macro-region, the Lika region, and the Rijeka macro-region. Thus four basic Croatian macro-regions were established in 1965.[30] Plans for their development were made for the periods: 1965–1970 and 1970–1975. Today they represent the optimum organizational spatial units in the socialist Republic of Croatia, utilizing an 'intermediate level' between republic and commune. The problems associated with their borders, already existing in 1962, have not yet been settled.[31]

There is a strong tendency among Yugoslav communes for co-operation in order to find rational solutions to socio-economic problems of development. These tendencies have to be considered in order to fully understand the complex components of the nodal-function regionalization process. A basic scheme for nodal-function regionalization for Yugoslav contemporary needs result in the following demands:

1. more clearly defined tendencies regarding communal interests and their ensuing co-operation;

2. the acceptance and application of theoretical conceptions regarding spatial planning practice. This is in order to outline the basic regional complexes both at republic and at commune level;

3. tendencies, connecting communes of similar interests were first perceived in the four Croatia macro-regions. They are also present in the eight intercommunal spatial plans for the Socialist Republic of Serbia.[32] The regionalization of Bosnia/Herzegovina was carried out on the same basis. Till now this is the most complete regional division of Bosnia/Herzegovina with its four macro-regional commune groups around Sarajevo, Banja Luka, Tuzla and Mostar.[33]

Beside the contemporary larger republican centre and Autonomous Regions, the city functions at the highest macro-regional level and is performed by settlements with more than 100,000 inhabitants. Such cities, as Split, Rijeka, Niš, Maribor have almost reached the same category as Osijek, Subotica, or Banja Luka. Also towns like Titograd and Priština have an unquestionable function of primary regional centres, in spite of their inadequate population size. It appears therefore that regions distant from existing primary centres contain centres approximately the size of Titograd and Priština. This applies also to Tuzla, Mostar and Bitolj. It is characteristic that according to Vrišer's town centrality classification[34] not only do Republican and Autonomous Regional centres have the highest hierarchy level, but that only Maribor, Split, Rijeka, Osijek, Subotica, Niš, Banja Luka, Tuzla and Mostar have the central characteristics apparent in the next hierarchy level. Experience has shown that there is a need for new centres outside the 100 km perimeter of a dominant large centre with more than 100,000 inhabitants; or, even a potential partially developed centre with fewer inhabitants. The position of Rijeka, Osijek and Split in the Socialist Republic of Croatia in this respect is very clear. It was not by chance that around them the earliest mutual co-ordination and group planning of communes was found at a macro-regional level. For example, the location and size of the traditional regional communes of Bosanska Krajina and their distance from Sarajevo clearly show that Banja Luka, Tuzla and Mostar fully conform to the third criterion. Niš is the most typical example of a macro-regional centre. The whole of south-eastern Serbia gravitates towards it due to its size, location and its tradition of being a regional centre. It is the only spatial complex which regarding territorial size and position demonstrates the need for strengthening its still undefined focus and relationship to the border zones.

Differences, as to the number of inhabitants between the 18 nodal-function primary centres, are of a relatively minor significance in the definition of their role as first class foci. The 18 basic macro-regional groups, plus a nineteenth that has conditionally been named 'West-Moravian Macro-region', are most important with regard to their location, infrastructure and development and tradition of being centres of numerous communes. Furthermore, the zones are well-established and influential and spatially similar to each other in the number of inhabitants.

1. The Ljubljana or west Slovenian region, covers 15,486 km² and contains 1,209,305 inhabitants. It encompasses groups of Slovenian communes, whose centre is within a 100 km perimeter of Ljubljana. Population concentration is 17·6 per cent of Ljubljana as a town, i.e. 21·3 per cent in the Ljubljana commune. This is extremely important due to the extensive area of the suburban, metropolitan region. It has a good basis for strengthening the process of nodal-function integration at the macro-regional level, because of its secondary centres, which is strongly felt despite the influence of Zagreb and Rijeka on its outlying territories.

2. The Maribor or east Slovenian macro-region, covers 4,765 km² and has 515,783 inhabitants. It is the second most important spatial unit in Slovenia. Maribor's importance is derived from a route convergence and has a beneficial influence on the whole region. Maribor itself has a population concentration of 22 per cent, i.e. 33 per cent for the whole commune. This is a quite realistic figure and helps integration.

3. The Zagreb or central Croatian macro-region covers 19,655 km² and has 2,132,620 inhabitants including communes more or less within the 100 km perimeter from Zagreb. There is only one important exception namely the Podravina sector which includes Virovitica. The 26·5 per cent population concentration

for the city itself and 28·2 per cent for the surrounding agglomⁿ eration clearly illustrates the conditions favourable for regional integration.

4. The Rijeka or west Croatian macro-region including the territory of Lika (poor gravitational integration) covers 14,005 km² of which a considerable part is outside the 100 km perimeter (central and southern Lika). Demographic concentration of the macro-region totals 605,391 inhabitants and is relatively high. This amounts to 26·7 per cent for Rijeka itself and 32·2 per cent for the surrounding metropolitan area within the Rijeka commune boundaries.

5. The Split, Dalmatian or south-Croatian macro-region contains 11,758 km² and has 830,074 inhabitants. The theoretical significance of the influence of the perimeter's 100 km cannot be applied here because of its peculiar shape. However, this does not diminish the macro-regional integrity of Dalmatia and of Split's metropolitan function as a whole. Population concentration in the macro-region totals 18·3 per cent for Split, and 22·2 per cent for its metropolitan area. This reflects a favourable relationship between the macro-region and its focus.

6. The Osijek, Slavonian or east Croatian macro-region covers 11,090 km² and has 858,136 inhabitants. Communal centres stay more or less within the 100 km perimeter from Osijek. The Osijek's impact as a macro-regional focus for central Slavonia is weak. It has a poorly developed transportation network and the lowest population concentration with only 10·9 per cent for the city itself and 16·7 per cent for the surrounding metropolis area within the Osijek commune.

7. The Belgrade (central Serbian) macro-region, within the boundaries of Serbia proper, encompasses an area with a perimeter of more than 100 km due to the size and importance of Belgrade. The territory of eastern Serbia (Timočka Krajina) is a clearly defined and so is that of south-eastern Serbia. In spite of widely differing ideas on the delimitations of the central Moravian–Sumadian and western regions of Serbia[35] it is evident that the Belgrade (central Serbian) macro-region[36] must include it. Even today this regionally controversial area is included in the territory of Belgrade itself. A spatial complex of 50 communes[37] covering 29,907 km² and containing 3,393,712

inhabitants is obtained by eliminating the territory of eight east Serbian communes[38] 29 communes in south-eastern Serbia[39] and 26 communes in south-western Serbia.[40] The east Serbian areas cannot be considered as a macro-regional entity due to its lack of a developed ᵢcentre. It is in a border zone where the influences of Belgrade and Niš meet. Therefore it seems justified to include it into the Belgrade macro-region, if consideration is given to its marked regional integration at a lower level. New motorways, which for the first time in history have 'opened-up' the east Serbian region towards Belgrade justify the growth of the Belgrade macro-region covering 37,273 km² and containing 3,739,110ᐧinhabitants. Demographically the Belgrade (central Serbian) macro-region has a concentration of 20·0 per cent. If Greater Belgrade (15 communes encompassing 3,122 km²) is included this rises to 32·2 per cent.

8. The dominant influence of Niš as the second largest urban metropolis in Serbia 'proper' spreads throughout Upper Pomoravlje or south-eastern Serbia. This is well illustrated by the joint spatial planning of 28 communes covered by the Chambers of Commerce from Niš and Leskovac. The Upper Pomoravlje or Niš spatial complex covers 14,536 and Leskovac. The Upper Pomoravlje or Niš spatial complex covers 14,536 km² and has a total of 1,144, 131 inhabitants. Its shape (spreading southwards) indicates the gravitational influence of Niš. This is diminishing to the north and north-west because of Belgrade's influence but is more strongly felt in the south. Niš evidently fulfills all the requirements for becoming a macro-regional centre, in spite of the considerable size and dense population of the Upper Pomoravlje region. The latter has a population concentration of 11·4 per cent in the Niš agglomeration this rises to 16·9 per cent.

9. After the exclusion of central Serbian/Belgrade macro-region and the Niš/Upper Pomoravlje region within Serbia proper there remains an area which, with regard to its distance from Belgrade and Niš, should theoretically develop a nodal-functional focus of its own. The individuality of the west Moravian area has been stressed in all the regionalization drafts of the Socialist Republic of Serbia.[41] It constitutes together with a part of the Dinaric Mountainous region of Serbia its own entity as defined by

gravitational circulation within the west Moravian centres of Titovo Užice, Čačak, Kraljevo and Kruševac. Joint spatial planning is in progress for 16 communes of the Kraljevo Chamber of Commerce covered by territory and a further 10 communes, the economic life of which is organized by the Titovo Užice Chamber of Commerce.[42] Together the 26 communes cover an area of 14,620 km² and contain 958,838 inhabitants. These figures correspond with the Yugoslav average nodal-function macro-region. Unfortunately, none of the five west Moravian centres comply with all the requirements of a macro-regional centre. Furthermore it is unreasonable to expect a strong development by any one of them, which would automatically suit it for the role of a macro-regional metropolis. It is certain, however, that the interrelationship of west Moravian centres, will become stronger in the future. It is therefore necessary to consider the possibility for the development of one or two con-urban communities which would take over the role of nodal-function foci for that territory. Vojvodina, is treated quite logically as a regional entity of Serbia. However, it is evident with regard to the Novi Sad size and significance that there is a marked disproportion, if Vojvodina is considered as a nodal-function macro-region of Novi Sad. This is best illustrated by the very low extent of its population concentration—only 7·8 per cent.[43] Subotica, has the character of a macro-regional centre based on its size and central place functions and it is therefore only logical to regard Vojvodina as an area consisting of two nodal-function complexes.

10. The Novi Sad macro-region covers 19,119 km², and contains 941,027 inhabitants. The extent of its population concentration is 9·0 per cent (i.e. 12·7 per cent if the metropolitan area is added, within the boundaries of the commune and comes closer to the expected figure).

11. The Subotica macro-region has an area of only 2,387 km² with 253,857 inhabitants. Population concentration totals 35 per cent[44] but on the other hand, it is best suited to the influence of Subotica's nodal-function in a territorial framework.

12. Kosovo, is the fifth macro-regional entity in the Socialist Republic of Serbia. Priština is its indisputable nodal-function metropolis focus geographically due to an extremely important

process of marked polarization within its socio-economic development. The importance of the distance to the perimetre the size of the territory, (10,887 km²) and density of the population (1,244,755 inhabitants) is stressed by the nondal-functional integration of the Kosovo territory. In spite of Priština's rapid population growth (69,524 in 1971) the extent of population concentration has not been significantly affected. It still amounts to only 5·6 per cent for Priština itself,[45] but the metropolitan zone within the boundaries of the commune rises to 12·3 per cent. In the case of Priština this is quite justified.

The question arises as to whether Macedonia, with its 25,713 km³ and 1,611,069 inhabitants, can be called a unique macro-region. Skopje is the third largest city in Yugoslavia, but can it be set apart as an exclusive regional centre? Regionalization-based on the principle of a specific orientation in production, i.e. of economic specialization, demands that such regional integration of the Macedonian Republic should take place in Yugoslavia.[46] Skopje has a strong influence outside the bounds of the 100 km perimeter, due to its size and the strong influence. It is also due to the fact that it is an important communication node. This influence is especially noticeable along the double 'axis' of the Vardar Valley and the ancient modernized communication corridor from Stip-Strumica), but the southwestern part of Macedonia is outside the range of Skopje's direct influence. The historical and geographic functions of Ohrid and Bitola have shown very significant regional interrelationship in the past. They can be clearly defined as the so-called 'Western Region' in the economic regionalization of the Socialist Republic of Macedonia.[47] The relatively slow development of present-day Bitola, (65,851 inhabitants) is because it does not have the character of a completely equipped macro-regional centre. This in turn effects the development of a west Macedonian or Bitola nodal-function macro-region. The proximity opportunities and needs of a well-balanced development dictate a strengthening of the mutual relations between Bitola and Prilep. This would refer to an objective establishment of a specific con-urban community functioning as a nondal-function focus for the west Macedonian area.

13. In this way the Skopje/central Macedonian macro-region,

i.e., a group of 20 communes covering 17,231 km² and containing 1,202,032 inhabitants could be created. Demographically the concentration in Skopje amounts to 26 per cent (i.e. 32 per cent if the Skopje metropolitan zone is considered.

14. The Bitola or west Macedonian macro-region consists of a group of 10 west Macedonian communes. This covers 8,476 km² and has 445,072 inhabitants. Population concentration reaches 14·7 per cent in Bitola, and indicates that such a division would be justified. The conditions are evidently favourable for strengthening and expanding mutual function connections between Bitola and Prilep, which in turn provides yet another argument for such a division.

15. Montenegro covers an area of 13,812 km² and contains 531,213 inhabitants. It offers all the pre-requisites for stronger integrational processes within the framework of an undivided nodal-function entity. This is based on its size population density and the location of Titograd. The rapid development of Titograd clearly illustrates this, based on the declining and final disappearance of incongruities between its function as a primary centre and lack of population concentration. The completion of a modern communication network, now in its final stage, is a further argument in favour of this idea. Demographic concentration in the city vis-a-vis the republic macro-region already totals 10·3 per cent, whereas the metropolitan zone has already reached 19·1 per cent.

In Bosnia and Hercegovina there are five primary urban centres With the exception of Sarajevo only Banja Luke, Tuzla and Mostar can function as gravitational macro-centres due to the towns location.[48]

16. The central Bosnian/Sarajevo-Zenica macro-region includes a group of 32 communes covering 11,798 km² and a population of 996,736. It is functionally best integrated towards Sarajevo regarding its position, function and importance together with the economic significance of the Sarajevo-Zenica Basin as a focus. According to the first draft for the regionalization of Bosnia and Hercegovina eight communes (Doboj, Tešanj, Teslić, Maglaj, Derventa, Bosanki Brod, Odjak, Modricha) grouped around Doboj in the Peripannonian area, have been separated from the Sarajevo-Zenica macro-region and added to

that of the north-west/Tuzla macro-region. It is certain that the focus attraction of Sarajevo-Zenica with its traditional importance as the Bosnian communication route has recently increased. Thus the various economic structures, which complement each other, suggest its incorporation into the Sarajevo-Zenica macro-region. The population concentration of Sarajevo in relation to the central Bosnian macro-region is 24·5 per cent and covers 32 communes, i.e. 29·3 per cent if the metropolitan area is included. If the eight communes around Doboj were added, the concentration for Sarajevo itself would still remain above 15 per cent.

17. The separation of the Hercegovina/Mostar macro-region results more from tradition and a tendency for a stronger communal integration in this area, based on common interests, than from Mostar's actual impact on the macro-region. Mostar, including 18 communes covers 11,504 km², and has 467,660 inhabitants. This forms 10·2 per cent of the population, (i.e. 19·1 per cent of the metropolitan area).

18. Bosanska Krajina is based upon traditional connections between the west Bosnian, Dinaric, mountainous area and Peripannonian region.[49] The impact of Banja Luka as a macro-regional centre in this large area is very weak outside the 80 km perimeter. This follows from its weakly developed communication network, and poor connections with Banja Luka itself. The Bosnian Krajina/Banja Luka macro-region contains 28 communes covering 17,593 km² and consisting of 1,064,185 inhabitants. It is functionally the least integrated large entity in Bosnia and Herzegovina. On the other hand, Bihac in spite of its very dynamic development does not have any opportunities for asserting itself as an independent macro-regional centre. Unfortunately possible advantages gained from its position regarding traffic routes convergence have been almost completely ignored. It is evident that Banja Luka will have to strengthen its gravitation pull in this area. So far this has proved to be too great for Banja Luka's present size and power of attraction. The population concentration of Banja Luka within the Bosanska Krajina only totals 8·4 per cent and there is no significant increase if the suburban area is added amounting to only 14·8 per cent.

19. The north-eastern Peripannonian Bosnian territory of

Bosnia including a small part of the mountainous region has all the prerequisites for becoming a functional macro-region. Since the second half of the sixteenth century Banja Luka has been the largest if not the main centre of Bosanska Krajina. This is in spite of its difficult situation based on great distance from other large centres of mountainous surroundings. Even up to the second half of the nineteenth century there was no leading centre in north-east Bosnia. Tuzla succeeded Zvornik as administrative centre. The development of Tuzla however was primarily determined by its production function, not by its importance as a regional centre. The north-eastern Bosnian macro-region includes 28 communes,[50] covering an area of 10,234 km² and containing 1,188,205 inhabitants. It is functionally a poorly integrated region. The demographic concentration of Tuzla only reaches 4·5 per cent and even with suburban settlements only has 9·0 per cent. This is far below that of any other potential Yugoslav nodal-function macro-region. Tuzla has a very marked production: it is the centre for chemicals and a leading goal and power producing area in Bosnia and Hercegovina. It is acquiring, increasingly, the character of a specific, spatially diffuse agglomeration. This in turn provides a different and geographically more realistic, definition of its urban area. Even so, the fact remains, that the demographic concentration of the north-eastern Bosnian macro-region is still exceptionally low. Nevertheless this macro-region illustrates the most recent attempts at trying to organize space in Yugoslavia.

This chapter has tried to describe Yugoslavia's basic spatial entities during the most recent historico-geographical period, on the basis of certain synthetic variables. Thus regions which are more or less geographically homogeneous fit into the system of nodal-function entities, which are at present being evolved. Furthermore they also help to stress the country's complex regional structure.

12. Notes

1. Greek colonies, the first real urban settlements in a geographical sense, were set up along the adriatic coast: Lumbarda in the island of Korčula: P. Lisičar, *Crna Korkyra i kolonija antičkih Grka na Jadranu*, Skopje (1951); Issa on the island of Vis: G. Novak, *Vis*, Zagreb (1961); Pharos on the island of Hvar: G. Novak, *Hvar Kroz stoljeća*, Zagreb (1960); Tragurion; Epetion; Salona; Aspalathos—Split: G. Novak, *Povijest Splita I*, Split (1957); and Heracleia (exact location still unknown): G. Novak, op. cit.; D. Rendić, 'Da li je bilo na Braču grčkih kolonija', *Brački zbornik II*, Split (1954); P. Lisičar, op. cit. According to pseudo-Skilaks: K. Müller, *Geographya Graeci minores I* (1855) one may assume the existence of a colony near Ulcinj (mentioned by Pliny, *Nat. hist. III*, 26th ed. Teubner, Leipzig (1906), Cavtat, near Dubrovnik and, later on, Narona in the Neretva estuary. There are indications for the existence of a city of colonial status (Asseria) in the Zadar hinterland. *Cf.* G. Novak, 'Stari Grci na Jadranskom moru', *Rad JAZU*, Vol. 322, Zagreb (1961).

2. M. Garašanin, 'Jedan osvrt na prvobitnu istoriju naše zemlje', *Istorijski glasnik*, Belgrade (1948), No. 2.

3. Our knowledge of the geographical distribution of the Roman urban centres mentioned by ancient authors is the result of systematic archaeological investigations which began in the second half of the nineteenth century. In addition to general encyclopaedic works recording the results of these investigations (especially Pauly-Wissova *Real Encyklopedie der Class. Altertumswiss*), many studies have appeared in various Yugoslav publications and certain works of synthesis covering major areas of Yugoslavia, especially E. Pašalić, *Antička naselja i komunikacije u Bosni i Hercegovini*, Sarajevo (1960).

4. M. Rostovtzeff, *La vie économique des Balkans dans l'antiquité*, Belgrade (1936);
   Idem. *Historija naroda Jugoslavije*, Vol. I. Belgrade (1950).

5. According to H. Pirenne *Histoire économique de l'occident Medieval*, Desclee de Brouwer (1951), the period of vanishing trade activities, return to natural economy, and the destruction and disappearance of west European towns following the disintegration of the Roman Empire was followed by a new era which brought a revival of urban life (tenth to eleventh centuries). In the territory of Yugoslavia, apart from the Adriatic coastal belt, this revival started later than it did in Western Europe.

6. This is confirmed by K. Jireček's classical work *Die Handelstrassen und Bergwerke von Serbien und Bosnien während des Mittelalters*, Prague (1879),

which is still the most complete existing study on the directions of trade from Yugoslav territory in the Middle Ages.

7. K. Schuneman, *Die Entstehung des Stadtwesens in Südosteurope*, Berlin (1929);

B. Homan, *Geschichte des Ungarischen Mittelalters I, II*, Berlin (1940);

N. Klaić, 'Prilog poznavanju postanka slavonskih varoši', *Zbornik Filozofskog fakulteta*, Zagreb (1955).

8. K. Jireček, op. cit.;

J. Erdeljanović, *Trgovački centri i putevi po srpskoj zemlji u srednjem vijeku*, Belgrade (1899);

S. Novaković, 'Villes et cites du Moyen Age dans l'Europe Occidentale et dans la peninsule Balcanique', *Archiv für slawische Philologie* (1903), No. 25;

M. Šufflay, 'Städte und Burgen Albaniens hauptsachlich während des Mittelalters', *Denkschrifte der Akademie der Wissenschaften in Wien* (1924), No. 63.

Especially characteristic are descriptions given by an anonymous writer in 1308 and by G. Adam in 1332 which point out that in contrast to Adriatic towns the interior of the country contained only trading settlements without walls (*cf*. S. Novaković, op. cit.).

9. J. Hammer, *Geschichte des Osmanischen Rieches in Europa*, Pest 1827/35; N. Jorga, *Geschichte des Osmanischen Reiches*, Gotha (1908–13);

Afet Inan, *Apercu General sur l'histoire économique de l' Empire Turc-Ottoman*, Istanbul (1941);

Busch-Zantner, 'Zur Kentniss der Osmanischen Stadt', *Geogr. Zeitschrift* (1932);

H. Šabanović, 'Upravna podjela jugoslovenskih zemalja pod turskom vladavinom do Karlovačkog mira', *Godišnjak Ist. društva BiH*, IV, Sarajevo (1952);

P. Matković, 'Putovanja po Balkanskom poluotoku XVI vijeka', *Rad JAZU* 56, 62, 71, 84, 100, 104, 105, 112, 116, 124, 129, 130, 136.

10. Unfortunately, on the basis of the available sources it is impossible to draw a definite distinction between large regional centres ('šehirs') and minor centres ('kasabas'). An interesting attempt at establishing the nature of a 'kasaba' as a minor centre (N. Mastilo, 'Kasaba kao vrsta naselja', *Geografski pregled* Vol. III, Sarajevo (1959) has revealed the difficulties in distinguishing 'kasabas' on Yugoslav territory from one another and, especially, in relation to šehirs'. The relation of small centres ('pazars' and 'palankas') to 'kasabas' still remains an open question.

11. A study of the situation as it existed in 1810 (inherited from the preceding century with slightly new changes), in mid-nineteenth century or in 1869 (period of change before railways began to be developed), and in 1910 (the last census year for that part of Yugoslavia which belonged to the Austro—

Hungarian monarchy, i.e. the period of change before the First World War) will give a good idea of the gradual formation of different centres in Yugoslav territory during the period of capitalist development before the First World War.

12. According to M. Bašeskija (V. Škaric, *Sarajevo i njegova okolina*, Sarajevo (1937), in the second half of the eighteenth century Sarajevo had a population of about 22,500, i.e. about the same number as at the beginning of the nineteenth century.

13. Towns in Vojvodina (Subotica, Novi Sad and Sombor) are exceptions as regards absolute number of inhabitants (e.g. in 1810 Novi Sad had 14,000, Subotica 22,000, Sombor 12,000 inhabitants). However, this is not a measure of their importance, because they have a very high proportion (50–70 per cent) of agrarian population and their territories include the surrounding villages as well.

14. The main route running from Vojvodina along the Sava valley to the North Adriatic developed during the eighteenth century, and up to the period of railway construction continued to serve as the backbone of a loose system of transport routes in the politically and economically heterogenous territory of what now is Yugoslavia. The best geographical evidence on the moderate volume and poor organization of trade on that route concerns the insignificant urban centres at key points (Becej, Novi Sad, Zemun, Slavonski Brod, Sisak and Karlovac).

15. The unsuccessful struggle in the Croatian Parliament for an integrated railway line along the Sava valley linking Zemun with Rijeka, to take over the function of the former combined river-and-road route, reflected conflicting interests within the Austro–Hungarian monarchy. Although different, the Austrian and the Hungarian concepts of a railway system had one thing in common: they 'cut up' the economically most important parts of the Yugoslav Pannonian area by promoting the domination of foreign urban centres at the expense of urban centres in Yugoslav territory (*cf. Denkschrift über die Notwendigkeit und die Bedeutung einer Eisenbahn von Semlin nach Fiume*, Vienna (1864).

16. Although the 1910 census recorded a population of 94,610, without the high proportion of agrarian population and large rural but incorporated areas it actually was a centre with less than 50,000 urban inhabitants.

17. Between the two censuses of 1921 and 1931, Zagreb's population increased by 72 per cent and that of Belgrade by 100·2 per cent. However, between the two towns there were considerable differences as regards the causes of their growth. Belgrade's expansion was chiefly due to the rapid development of its central functions, while in Zagreb economic activities prevailed.

18. The individual rates of increase of population during the period between

the 1921 and 1931 censuses were as follows: Subotica 9·9 per cent, Ljubljana 2·1 per cent (this low rate does not correspond to the actual growth of the urban agglomeration because it was worked out on the basis of the town's central administrative area, the population of which increased from 53,294 to only 59,765 whereas the fastest increase was recorded actually in the outer suburban communes); Sarajevo 17·8 per cent (since the growth of the town's suburban areas was very slow, this rate of increase comes nearest to the new situation which reflects the considerable decrease of Sarajevo's central functional importance in comparison with the Austrian period); Skopje 50·7 per cent (becoming Macedonia's functional centre in contrast to the former division of central functions between Skopje and Bitola); Novi Sad 50·7 per cent (definitely becoming Vojvodina's centre of economic activity and administration, with peripherally situated Subotica declining in importance.

19. The rate of growth of Maribor (13 per cent) does not correspond to the town's real growth, which centres on the suburban areas outside the town's central administrative territory. As regards other secondary centres, figures on their urban populations give an almost exact picture of their growth because their suburban areas were still very poorly developed: Split 74·5 per cent (it was only in pre-war Yugoslavia that Split definitely became the centre of Dalmatia); Kragujevac 74·0 per cent; and Niš 41·6 per cent.

20. What prevents a real, statistical establishment of changes in pre-war Yugoslavia is the lack of data for the 1931–1941 period, when many important changes took place, since because of the war no census was taken in 1941.

21. The figures published by D. Vogelnik 'Urbanizacija kao odraz privrednog razvoja FNRJ', *Ekonomska biblioteka*, Vol. 13, Belgrade (1951), p. 57 suggest that the proportion of the urban population of Yugoslav towns with more than 50,000 inhabitants increased from 31·27 per cent in 1921 to 40·41 per cent in 1931. *Cf.* M. Macura, 'Stanovništvo kao činilac privrednog razvoja Jugoslavije', *Ekonomska biblioteka*, Vol. 7, Belgrade (1958).

22. D. Vogelnik, op. cit., p. 57.

23. During the 1953–1961 period, towns with 20,000–30,000 inhabitants increased by 33·1 per cent; towns with 50,000–100,000 inhabitants by 28·9 per cent; and towns with over 100,000 inhabitants by 29·1 per cent (M. Sentić, D. Breznik, 'Demografska kretanja i projekcije u Jugoslaviji', *Stanovništvo* (April–June 1964), Belgrade).

24. Characteristically, the first systematic presentation of the functional classification of urban centres in Yugoslavia (D. Vogelnik, op. cit., pp. 282–286) which is based on statistics obtained by the 1953 census shows that most of the towns with 'industrial specialization' belong in fact to the group of centres of the sixth size category (Sisak, Zagreb, Varaždin, Kranj,

Slavonski Brod, Vukovar, Valjevo, Titovo Užice, Smederevo and Kosovska Mitrovica).

25. V. Djurić, 'Problematika Geografske Regionalizacije Srbije', *Zbornik Radova V. Kongresa Geografa Jugoslavije, Cetinje* (1959).

26. Sv. Ilešić, 'Problem Geografskog Rejoniranja ob Primeru Slovenije', *Geografski Vestnik*, Ljubljana, Vol. XXIX–III (1958).

27. V. Rogić, 'Fizionomska i Funkcionalna Regionalizacija Hrvatske', *Zbornik Radova VI Kongresa Geografa Jugoslavije*, Ljubljana (1962).

28. I. Vrišer, 'Vplivna Območja Jugoslavenskih Mest', *Filozofska Fakulteta Univerze*, Ljubljana (1972).

29. V. Rogić, *op. cit.* (1962).

30. The regional development of the Socialist Republic of Croatia during the period 1966–1970. The Republic Planning Office Zagreb, March 1966; compare: V. Rogić, 'Les differences qualitatives de la regionalisation a grande et petite échélle—L'example de Croatie', *Bull. de la fac. des letters de Strasbourg* (Avril–Mai 1969).

31. V. Rogić, 'Prostori općeg makroregionalnog centraliteta Zagreba, Rijeke, Splita i Osijeka u odnosu na regionalizaciju ekonomskog programiranja', *Zbornik Radova VIII kongresa geografa SFRJ*, Skopje (1968).

32. B. Piha, 'Medjuopstinski prostorni planovi na području SR Srbije', *Komuna* No. 1, Belgrade (1972).

33. Collective work, 'Regionalizacija i centri drustveno-ekonomskog razvoja u Bosni i Hercegovini', *Ekonomski institut Ekonomskog fakulteta i Rep. zavod za planiranje i ekonomska istrazivanja*, Sarajevo (1969).

34. I. Vrišer, 'Centralna naselja u Jugoslaviji', *Ekonomska revija*, Ljubljana (1968).

35. 'Prostorni plan SR Srbije I, Element valorizacija i ocena prostora SR Srbije', *Zavod za urbanizam stambene i komunalne delatnosti*, Belgrade (1970).

36. Ibid. p. 86.

37. These are the 15 communes belonging to the metropolitan zone of Belgrade; eight communes from the so-called Braničevo community working on a joint intercommunal spatial plan under the supervision of the Belgrade Chamber of Commerce; 12 communes from the territory of the Kragujevac Chamber of Commerce, and 15 communes from the areas of Valjevo and Šabac.

38. 'Društveni dogovor općina Istočne Srbije o formiranju medjuopćinskih ustanova, organa i sluzbi'; *Komuna* No. 11, Belgrade (1972).

39. The territory included in the intercommunal spatial planning for the areas of Niš and Leskovac. B. Piha, op. cit.

40. The territory included in the spatial planning for 10 communes, the economic life of which is organized around a Chamber of Commerce at Titovo Užice and 16 communes belonging to the Kraljevo Chamber of Commerce.

41. Prostorni plan SR Srbije, op. cit.

42. B. Piha, op. cit.

43. Quite understandably, the exceptionally strong influence of Belgrade has not been considered here. It is especially dominant in Eastern Srijem and Banat.

44. In the case of Subotica there is no justification for considering the metropolitan area of the Subotica commune outside the statistical area of Subotica itself when determining demographic concentration because of its markedly rural character.

45. One of the main reasons is the high birth rate in the autonomous Province of Kosovo, each year.

46. 'Ekonomska regionalizacija na SR Makedonija', *Ekonomski institut na Univerzitetot "Kiril i Metodij"*, Skopje (1971).

47. Ibid.

48. Collective work, 'Regionalizacija . . .', *Ekonomski institut*, op. cit. (note 33).

49. Ibid.

50. Ibid.

13

The Evolution of the Ethnographic Map of Yugoslavia A Historical Geographic Interpretation

GEORGE W. HOFFMAN

Anyone studying the complex ethnographic map of Yugoslavia which shows the distribution of the national structure of the Yugoslav peoples must obviously be aware of the close relationship between historical experiences and the geographical environment. Geography and history have interacted in this area bringing about a complex cultural landscape with great regional differences and a 'heterogeneous grouping of cultural variable and a political system that has been in constant flux as a result of external pressures and internal instability.'[1] Historical events have played an important role in this region with its often cited 'crossroad' or 'bridge' position linking Central Europe with the Near East (Levant).[2] This is usually explained by its easy outer accessibility, which made possible movements by many different people and ideas from neighbouring power centres into important peripheral regions and through its corridor valleys into the heart of the region. Of even greater importance was the impact of the rugged and diverse relief of large segments of the area which produced great inner fragmentation, encouraging particularism and isolationism, and thus impeding important historical processes.

The national structure of the Yugoslav population and the distribution of its various nationalities as shown in Fig. 1 has posed a serious social and political problem for the people of Yugoslavia and its complexity has long been a challenging problem for scholars to contemplate. The literature is rich with many outstanding studies of Yugoslavia, the cultural differences among the Yugoslav nationalities, the complex problem of national relations or with studies of the individual nations, nationalities or other national and ethnic groups of the country.[3] However, in spite of the abundance of historical writings in many different languages on various aspects of Yugoslavia's nationality problem, no authoritative history (not to speak of a historical geography) has been published relating the map of the ethnic distribution of all the Yugoslav peoples to the processes and the reasons for the distribution.

This study, therefore, should be considered as an experiment only, or an opportunity to discuss in the space assigned the many complex reasons for the mosaic of conflicting linguistic and religious patterns of today's ethnographic map of Yugoslavia. Perhaps this study could also point the way to opportunities available in this type of scholarly research—either for studies in greater depth concerning Yugoslavia's complex ethnographic settlement pattern, or in countries with similar problems. Its basic aim is to analyse the impact of Yugoslavia's ethnic diversity. The study will be divided into two major parts and a brief introduction. Its major section consists of an analysis of the ethnographic map of Yugoslavia and the various population movements in today's territory of Yugoslavia and the impact of these movements which affected every aspect of the current social and political problems of the country. Finally, the reader should be aware at the outset that the following discussions can do no more than, in the opinion of this author, cite a selected number of the most important of these population movements and their impact in certain key regions of the country.

Introduction

The area of today's Yugoslavia, in spite of its largely mountainous topography has a number of well-defined passages permitting relatively easy access to most parts of the country. The importance

---

FIG. 1. (Facing page) Ethnic distribution by communes, 1971.

The ethnic distribution of the Yugoslav people, as shown in Fig. 1 and the various related tables showing the national structure of the Yugoslav population, permit a number of observations:

1. Most of the people of Yugoslavia (20,522,972 on March 31, 1971) listed their nationality (98·1 per cent) with 86·7 per cent belonging to one of the six nations (called national groups or nationalities in earlier censuses of the post-war period) of the country and 11·4 per cent as one of the nationalities or other national and ethnic groups (in earlier censuses referred to as national minorities); 1·6 per cent of the Yugoslav peoples did not give their nationality—0·2 did not answer this question at all, 1·3 declares themselves as Yugoslavs and 0·1 listed their regional affiliation only.

2. The Yugoslav population increased between 1948 and 1971 by 30·3 per cent, but the ratio among the nations and nationalities remained nearly unchanged. The percentage of the peoples listed under 'nations' changed from 87·4 per cent to 86·7 between 1948 and 1971 (83·1 in 1921).

3. Changes among the nationalities and other national or ethnic groups (national minorities) have been more noticeable (a decrease from 16·9 per cent to 11·4 per cent between 1921 and 1971, but an increase from 12·6 to 13·3 for the period 1948 and 1971). There are a number of reasons for these changes: (i) changes due to the Second World War, especially the emigration by Germans, Hungarians,[11] Italians and Turks (9·4 to 3·0 per cent between 1921 and 1971); (ii) the differences in the rates of growth of individual nations and nationalities with the Albanians, Moslems and Turks having the highest rate of natural increase (and a rapidly declining mortality rate). Most other nationalities having a very low rate of net population increment due to decreasing births and increasing ethnically mixed marriages (with a low birth rate or as a result of children reporting a different nationality from parents), and (iii) a fluctuation in the size of some national groups, specifically due to a different declaration in the early post-war censuses, e.g., Romany-Gypsies (prefer to be called 'Romi'), Wallachians, Germans, Hungarians and Albanians. They listed their nationalities as the same as the nearest ethnic group among whom they lived. A good example are the Albanians in Macedonia and Kosovo. Their dissatisfaction is indicated in the 1953 census

when the number of Turks increased dramatically between the 1948 and 1953 census.[12] Obviously, many Albanians suddenly indicated their nationality as Turkish, perhaps in the hope of benefitting from the permission given to the Turkish population to emigrate to Turkey. The impact of the changes in the classification of the Moslem people is discussed below and presents a special case. Petrović pointed out that 'the influence of the subjective factor in the selection of nationality on the size of a group was stronger the less numerous the group.'[13]

4. The position of the ethnic Moslem Population (Muslimani po etničkoj pripadnosti) deserves a word of special explanation. Whether they can be classified as a nation is a difficult question to answer, especially in view of the census classification before 1945 in terms of language and not as nationality. Their secular status was not recognized between 1878 and 1945. In addition, Turks and Albanians were also ethnic Moslems. David Dyker in a recent article goes into some detail on their background and summarizes the constant changes in the statistical practice.[14] Most of the ethnic Moslem live in Bosnia and Hercegovina, as can be seen in Fig. 1 (89·1 per cent in the 1971 census) and in Serbia proper (Sandžak), Kosovo and north-east Montenegro. The origin of the Moslems in Bosnia and Hercegovina is subject to controversy, but according to most scholars they are descendants of the Bogomils.[15] They have grown in absolute numbers, especially in the period 1931 to 1948 but due to changes in census practices their exact number was not available. Also Bosnia and Hercegovina had disappeared after 1931 as an administrative unit.[16] At the first post-war census in 1948 the ethnic Moslems were encouraged to identify themselves (opredeliti se) as either Serbs or Croats, but only those classified as 'undeclared Moslem' (neopredeljeni Muslimani) were listed separately as ethnic Moslem. In the 1953 cenus the category 'undeclared Moslem' was abolished and a new category was established, Moslem of Yugoslav ethnic origin and they were classified as 'Yugoslav-unspecified or undifferentiated' (Jugosloveni neopredeljeni) unless they opted for a separate group (Serbs, Croats, Turks, Macedonians, etc.). Presumably this group of 'Yugoslav-unspecified' contained also both Serbs and Croats. Their total number was close to the 1948 census figure. The 1961 census recognized a new category, ethnic Moslem (Musliman po etničko

pripadnosti), but the category 'Yugoslav-unspecified' was retained. The total of both categories together remained almost identical with the 1953 figure. The 1971 categories were similar to those of 1961, but

> 'methodological solutions and their modifications together with other circumstances, have created a certain degree of incomparability of data on the exact number not only of Moslem but also of other national groups recorded in the 1948, 1953, 1961 and 1971 censuses.'[17]

5. As can be seen from Table I, the actual number of Moslems, Albanians, Macedonians and Turks increased above the average national rate of Yugoslavia's population, while the number of Serbs, Slovenes, Croats, Montenegrins, Slovaks, and Romany-Gypsies increased less than the national average with the other nationalities actually declining. The census figures of the post-war period permit the conclusion that the proportion of Moslems, Albanians and Macedonians increased, while the proportion of all other nations and nationalities decreased. The proportion of the Turkish population alone remained unchanged. It would go beyond the aim of this paper to analyse in detail the reasons for these changes, but suffice to say that they are due to a number of factors, e.g., differences in the increases of natural population, emigration, both as a result of the Second World War and those since mid-1960 for the purpose of seeking employment outside the country,[18] inter- and intra-regional migrations, largely from rural to urban areas; changes brought about by personal decisions due to various causes such as the earlier discussed criteria applied in individual censuses, inter-marriage, the decision to limit the size of their families and changes in perceptional feelings of the individual nationality.

6. The distribution of the Yugoslav peoples shows that every nationality is represented in every republic and autonomous province. Not a single commune is populated by people from one nationality only.

7. Communes with the largest number of nationalities are obviously the industrial cities and administrative centers (see Table IV in the earlier cited study by Petrović), with the rural areas usually the most homogeneous, except in the Vojvodina.

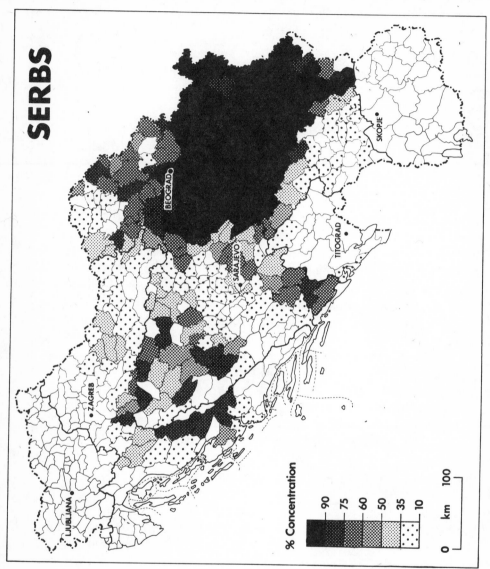

SERBS

% Concentration

90
75
60
50
35
10

0   km   100

Fig. 2(A). Territorial concentration of the Peoples of Yugoslavia: SERBS.

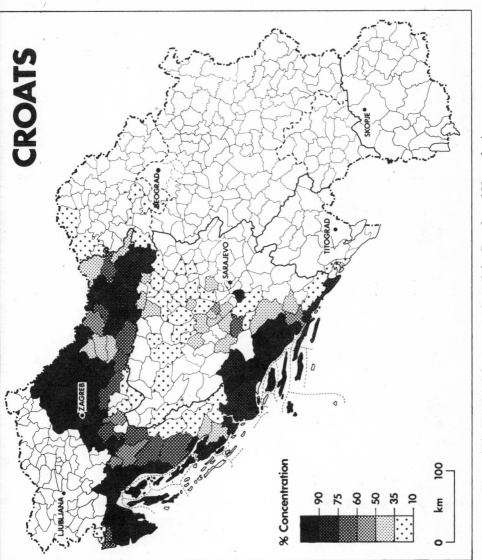

CROATS

% Concentration

90
75
60
50
35
10

0   km   100

Fig. 2(B). Territorial concentration of the Peoples of Yugoslavia: CROATS.

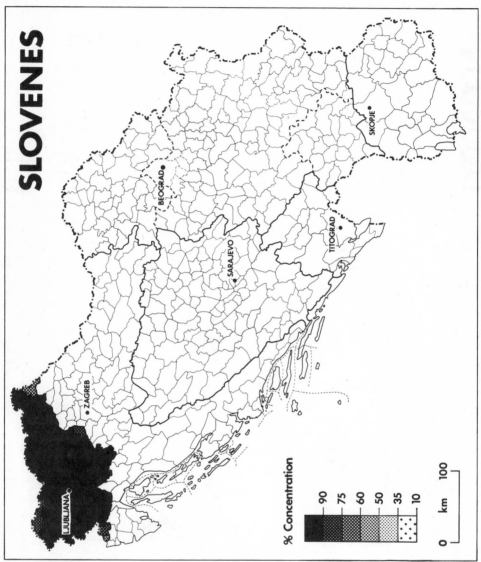

SLOVENES

% Concentration

90
75
60
50
35
10

0   km   100

FIG. 2(C). Territorial concentration of the Peoples of Yugoslavia: SLOVENES

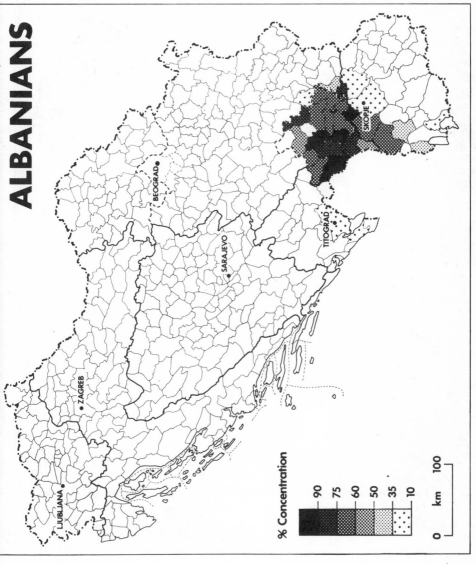

ALBANIANS

% Concentration

90
75
60
50
35
10

km

0   100

FIG. 2(D). Territorial concentration of the Peoples of Yugoslavia: ALBANIANS.

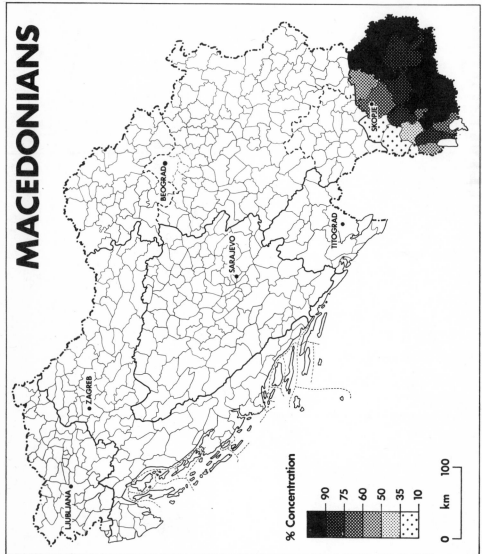

MACEDONIANS

% Concentration

90
75
60
50
35
10

0 km 100

LJUBLJANA

ZAGREB

BEOGRAD

SARAJEVO

TITOGRAD

SKOPJE

Fig. 2(E). Territorial concentration of the Peoples of Yugoslavia: MACEDONIANS.

MONTENEGRINS

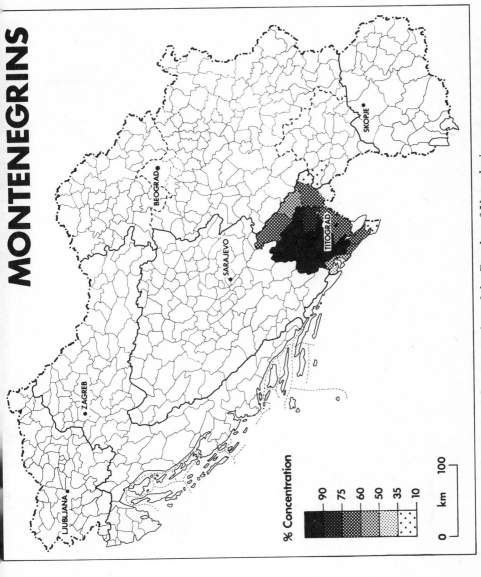

% Concentration

90
75
60
50
35
10

0 km 100

FIG. 2(F). Territorial concentration of the Peoples of Yugoslavia: MONTENEGRINS.

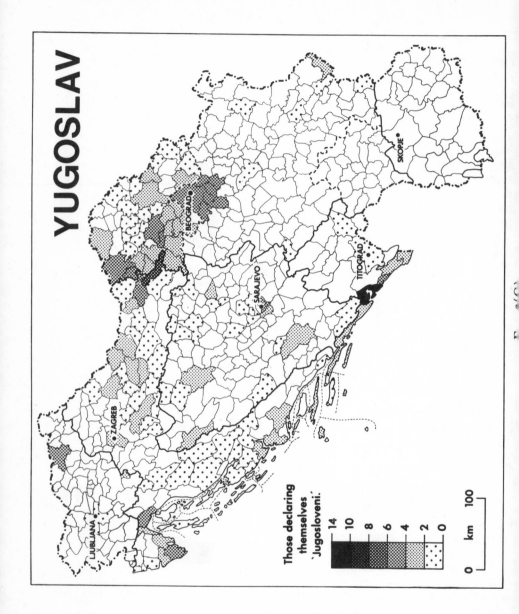

YUGOSLAV

LJUBLJANA

ZAGREB

BEOGRAD

SARAJEVO

TITOGRAD

SKOPJE

Those declaring
themselves
'Jugosloveni:'

14
10
8
6
4
2
0

0   km   100

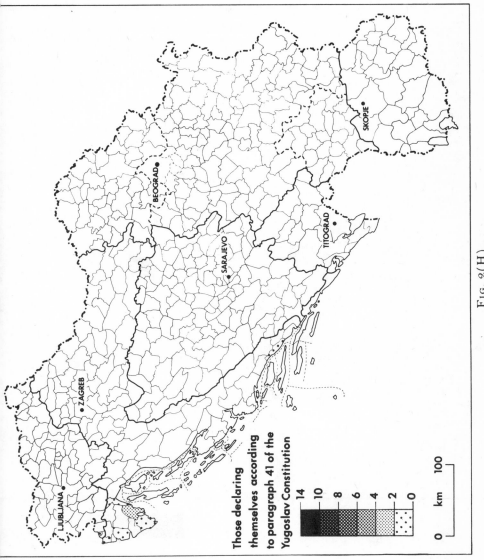

Those declaring
themselves according
to paragraph 41 of the
Yugoslav Constitution

14
10
8
6
4
2
0

0   km   100

FIG. 2(H)

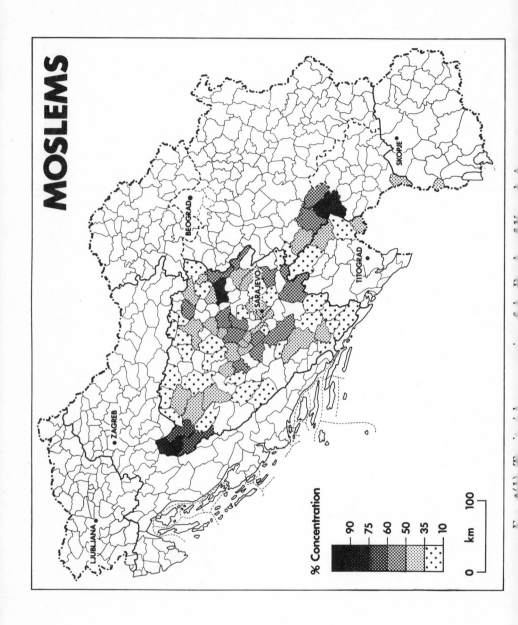

MOSLEMS

% Concentration

90
75
60
50
35
10

0   km   100

TURKS

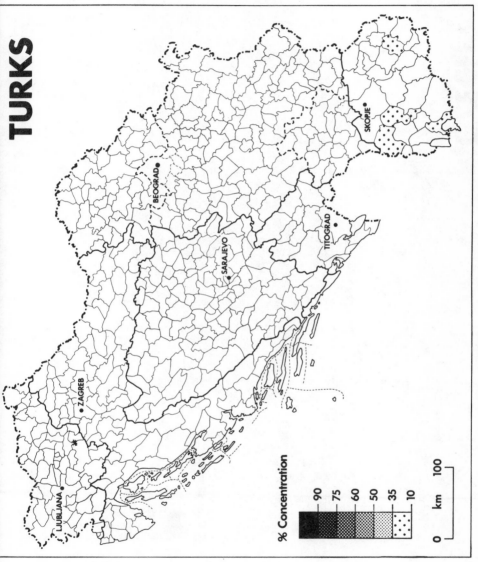

% Concentration

██	90
▓▓	75
▒▒	60
░░	50
░░	35
∴∴	10

0   100
└── km ──┘

FIG. 2(J). Territorial concentration of the Peoples of Yugoslavia: TURKS.

CZECHS

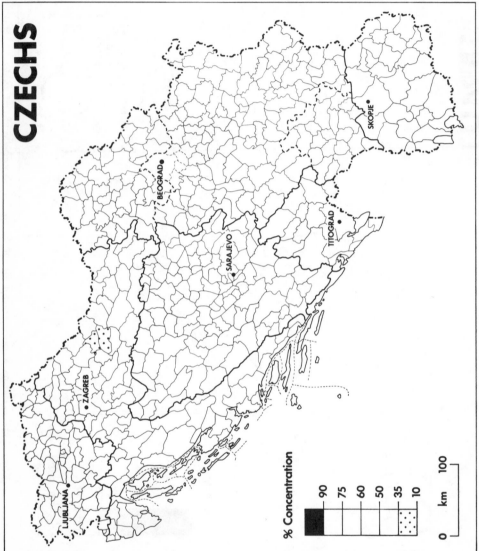

% Concentration

| 90 |
| 75 |
| 60 |
| 50 |
| 35 |
| 10 |

0   km   100

FIG. 2(K). Territorial concentration of the Peoples of Yugoslavia: CZECHS.

SLOVAKS

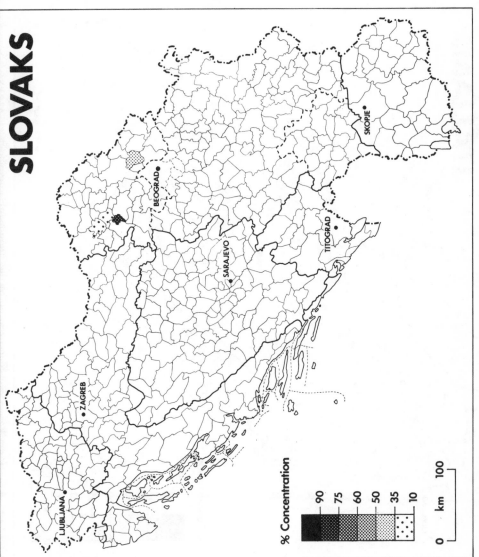

Fig. 2(L). Territorial concentration of the Peoples of Yugoslavia: SLOVAKS.

% Concentration

90
75
60
50
35
10

0   km   100

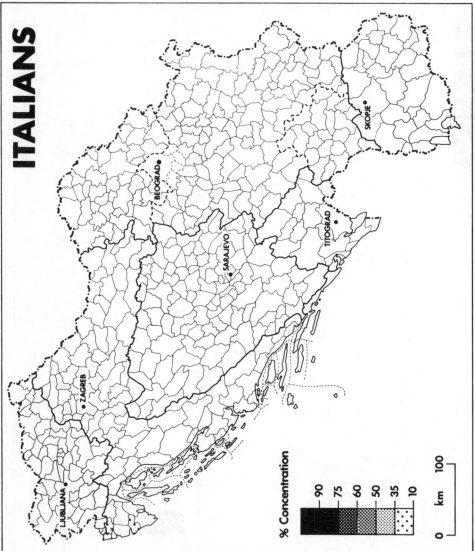

ITALIANS

% Concentration

90
75
60
50
35
10

km

0   100

Fig. 2(M). Territorial concentration of the Peoples of Yugoslavia: ITALIANS.

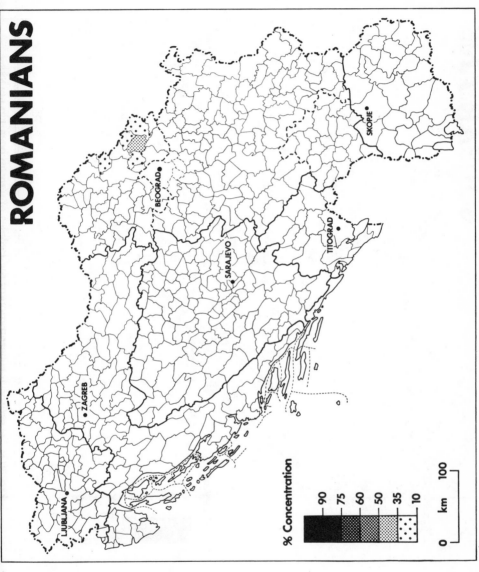

ROMANIANS

% Concentration

90
75
60
50
35
10

0   km   100

Fig. 2(N). Territorial concentration of the Peoples of Yugoslavia: ROMANIANS.

BULGARIANS

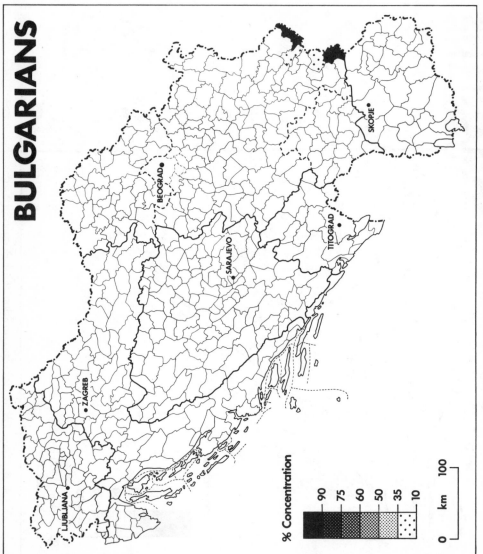

% Concentration

90
75
60
50
35
10

km
0   100

FIG. 2(o). Territorial concentration of the Peoples of Yugoslavia: BULGARIANS.

RUSSIANS

% Concentration

90
75
60
50
35
10

0   km   100

Fig. 2(p). Territorial concentration of the Peoples of Yugoslavia: RUSSIANS.

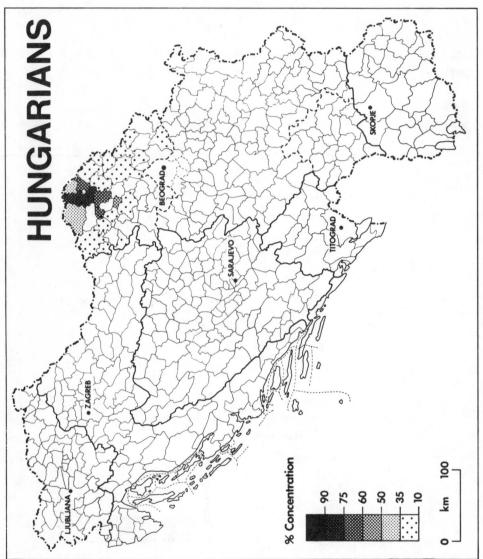

HUNGARIANS

% Concentration

90
75
60
50
35
10

0 km 100

FIG. 2(Q). Territorial concentration of the Peoples of Yugoslavia: HUNGARIANS.

8. It also is evident from studying Fig. 1, which shows the territorial distribution of the peoples of Yugoslavia, that in spite of a great degree of national differentiation the most populous part of each nation and nationality is concentrated in a relatively restricted region, which becomes their core territory (see Table II and Figs 1 and 2 (A) to (Q) which show clearly the proportion of territorial concentration of the peoples of Yugoslavia).

It is obvious from Table II that in spite of the large national differentiation of the Yugoslav population a considerable part of each nation and the major nationalities are confined to a specific territory, referred to as the 'core territory of a national group.' This does not mean the region in which its members make up the majority of the population, but the region in which the majority of this group lives. In some cases these two elements coincide.

The highest degree of territorial concentration can be found in Slovenia with the Slovenian population showing a concentration of 97·1 per cent in 1971. Only six communes show a Slovenian population of less than 90 per cent and they are border communes (Piran, Izola and Koper on the coast, Jesenice with its important iron and steel works in the north, Metzika on the Croatian border and Lendava on the Hungarian border). Slovenia is followed by Macedonia with a territorial concentration of 95 per cent in the republic and a sprinkling of Macedonians distributed in a number of communes in Serbia proper. According to the census of 1971, 85·9 per cent of all Moslems lived in Bosnia and Hercegovina, which is considered a very heterogeneous republic. As a result, their proportions among the individual communes vary greatly, from zero (Gruda) to 96·5 per cent (Cazin) and 89 per cent in the neighbouring commune of Velika Kladuša.[19] Outside Bosnia and Hercegovina, larger concentration of Moslems are found in the Sandžak of Serbia proper and the north-eastern part of Montenegro; 77·6 per cent of all Croatians in Yugoslavia live in Croatia, a highly heterogeneous republic, with the result that the proportion of Croats varies greatly in individual communes, being highest in the Zagorje (north of Zagreb) and lowest along the north-western part of the old Austrian-Turkish Military border.[20] Over 17 per cent of the Croats live in numerous communes distributed in Bosnia and Hercegovina. The largest concentration of Croats is found in the western part of Bosnia and Hercegovina, with no commune having a concentration of Croats

Table II

Territorial Distribution and Degree of Concentration of Nations and Nationalities by Republics and Provinces, March 31, 1971

	Slovenes	Macedonians	Moslems	Croats	Serbs	Montenegrins	Hungarians	Albanians
Yugoslavia—total	100·0	100·0	100·0	100·0	100·0	100·0	100·0	100·0
Bosnia-Hercegovina	0·2	0·1	85·9†	17·4	17·1	2·5	0·2	0·2
Croatia	1·9	0·4	1·0	77·6‡	7·7	1·9	7·4	0·2
Macedonia	0·1†	95·9	0·0	0·0	0·5	0·6	0·0	21·3
Montenegro	0·0	0·0	4·0	0·2	0·4	70·3	0·0	2·7
Serbia	0·8	3·5	8·9	3·9	74·1	24·4	90·4	75·6
Serbia proper	0·6	2·1	7·2	0·8	48·2*	11·2	1·1	5·0
Kosovo	0·0	0·0	1·5	0·1	2·6	6·1	0·0	70·4
Vojvodina	0·2	1·4	0·2	3·0	13·3	7·1	89·3	0·2
Slovenia	97·1	0·1	0·2	1·9	0·2	0·3	2·0	0·0

Source: Ruža Petrović, 'National Structure of the Yugoslav Population,' *Yugoslav Survey*, XIV (February, 1973), 5. The quotation below in the next paragraph is taken from the same source. See also *Statistički Bilten*, No. 727 of December, 1972 published by the Federal Bureau of Statistics.

Note: When using different official publications, statistical data are not always consistent. The figure printed for Serbia (74·1 per cent) is correct, but the figure for Serbia proper* should be 58·2 instead of 48·2 as printed in the Yugoslav Survey to derive the total for Serbia. Some obvious mistakes were corrected †, and others ‡ were left due to different data in the official figures.

of under 90 per cent. In some communes in central Bosnia, Croats have also a majority. About three per cent of the Croats live in the Vojvodina. The territorial concentration of the Serbs is relatively low with 74 per cent of the Serbs living in Serbia though nearly 60 per cent of them living in Serbia proper; 17 per cent in Bosnia and Hercegovina, (a range in individual communes from zero to 90), 13·3 per cent in the Vojvodina largely the southern part of the province where they account in certain communes for over 70 per cent of the population, and 7·7 per cent in Croatia, predominantly in the territory of the former Military Border. The degree of Albanian concentration in Kosovo amounted to 70·4 per cent. Over 21 per cent of the Albanians settled along the western part of Macedonia. Thirty per cent of the Montenegrins live outside Montenegro. Their low territorial concentration is equalled by the Serbs. A quarter of the population live in Serbia, widely distributed in both Serbia proper and the autonomous provinces. The Hungarian territorial concentration is largely in northern Vojvodina (northern Bačka), 89·3 per cent. Others live mainly along the Hungarian border. Bulgarians, Rumanians, and Italians are concentrated largely along the borders with their parent countries; 84·8 per cent of the Turkish population lives in Macedona with their highest concentration in the communes of Debar, (36·6 per cent of the population), Kruševo (21·2 per cent) and Gostivar (16·0 per cent). The western part of Macedonia is, therefore, considered the core territory of Turkish settlers. Slovaks (85·5 per cent of their number) and Ruthenians are concentrated in the Vojvodina, where they were among the earliest settlers brought in by the Austrian authorities in their colonization efforts. Slovaks reach in some communes as much as 77 per cent of the population (Bačka Topola 76·9 per cent of the total population, Kovačica 38·4 per cent, Stara Pazova 17·9 per cent). Ruthenians reach 14 per cent of the population of Kula, 10·9 per cent of Vrbas.

The high degree of territorial concentration is one of the reasons for the close ties and loyalty of the people to their region which according to some was typified by the last census when 15,000 people indicated the regional origin only. It is also clear that a relatively high homogeneity within a republic or province or commune, contributes to greater territorial consciousness. The national composition, their homogeneity or heterogeneity has a strong territorial and historical basis, but the rapid economic development in the post-war period left its impact on the national structure. While the percentage share of the most numerous groups in the total population has remained relatively stable,[21] only the percentage of Montenegrins living in Montenegro has declined in absolute terms (90·7 per cent in 1948 to 67·1 per cent in 1971). This degree and the trends of national differentiation by republics and autonomous provinces can be observed in the Table III below showing the percentage share of the most numerous group of the population and the coefficient of differentiation.

This table clearly shows that Bosnia and Hercegovina was the most heterogenous republic (same coefficient as for Yugoslavia as a whole), followed by the Vojvodina, while Slovenia and Serbia proper are considered the most homogenous parts of the country with the lowest coefficient.

The Burden of History

Population Movements in the Early National States

Yugoslavia's complex ethnic structure resulted from a long succession of human settlements which included Illyrians, Thracians, Greeks, Romans, Goths, Slavs (Slovenes, Croats and Serbs), Byzantine Greeks, Bulgars, Hungarians, Venetians, German-Austrians, Ottoman Turks and Albanians.[22] The discussions here aim to trace the major settlement waves which explain the present ethnographic distribution.

As part of such an explanation it is of importance to point toward the decisive role played by the triangular shaped, mountain ranges stretching for nearly 500 miles from the valleys of the Sava and Kupa in the north to the Ibar Valley and the basins of Kosovo and Metohija in the south. This mountainous heartland coincides with the Dinaric ranges. The varied relief separates the people of one valley from those of another, bringing about local particularism and political fragmentation. Great diversity characterizes these ranges, from the barren dissected and waterless ranges in the west to parallel forested mountain and hill lands and fertile basins connected with sheltered intercommunicating interior valleys in the north and north-east. Each of the major regions of the

Table III

National Differentiation of the Population by Republics and Provinces, 1948 and 1971

Territory and the most numerous national group	Percentage share of the most numerous group in total population		Coefficient of differentiation*	
	1948	1971	1948	1971
Yugoslavia				
Serbs	41·5	39·7	140	152
Bosnia-Herzegovina				
Serbs	44·3	—	125	—
Moslems	—	39·6	—	152
Croatia				
Croats	79·2	79·4	26	26
Macedonia				
Macedonians	68·5	69·3	45	44
Montenegro				
Montenegrins	90·7	67·2	10	48
Serbia				
Serbs	73·9	71·2	35	40
Serbia proper				
Serbs	92·1	89·5	8	11
Kosovo				
Albanians	68·5	73·7	45	35
Vojvodina				
Serbs	50·6	55·8	97	79
Slovenia				
Slovenes	97·0	94·0	3	6

*The coefficient of differentiation shows how many members of all other groups taken together (inclusive of those who did not declare themselves nationally) there are per 100 members of the most numerous national group.

Source: Ruža Petrović, 'National structure of the Yugoslav population,' *Yugoslav Survey*, XIV, 1 (February, 1973), 21.

mountainous heartland played a major role in the historical processes throughout the centuries.

Three areas expecially in the mountainous heartland played an
important role during the early settlement of the South Slavic
tribes. Two additional peripheral regions also played an important
role: The southern valleys of the Eastern Alps were settled by the
Slavic Slovenes, and the valley of the Vardar in the south became a
settlement area of the Macedonian Slavic people, but the exact
area included under the term 'Macedonia' has varied from time to
time and until recently has never been identified with any single
administrative or political unit. The mountainous heartland itself
was settled by three Slavic people: the area from the north-west
to the southern part of the Dalmatian coast (Dubronik) by the
Croatians, the southern region of the heartland by the Serbians
and between these two people stretched the territory of Bosnia
which was first colonized by people with various tribal names.

Several South Slavic tribes found their way into this area in the
sixth and seventh centuries. Those that went south—the modern
Serbs and Macedonians—came under the influence of Byzantium
from which they accepted Christianity and thus became Orthodox
Christian. The tribes that went north-west and westward, primarily the modern Slovenes and Croats early came under Germanic influence, but the most important influence was that of Rome
and Catholicism.[23] Many people of Bosnian origin became Islamized during the early Turkish occupation.

The least accessible region, which is perhaps historically of
greatest interest is the western karst zone (the High Karst)
averaging some 40 to 50 miles in width and located between the
Adriatic and interior of the country. It stretches for some 350
miles parallel to the Adriatic in a north-west to south-east direction and comprises a series of barren, deeply fissured limestone
mountain ranges at an altitude from about 1,000 to 5,000 feet,
with many caverns and underground streams. This region played
an important role from the earliest times until the most recent
history as frontier, as refuge and fortress in time of war, and as a
population reservoir in times of peace. This vital role of the Karst,
especially its forested and important high mountain pastures, once
again became decisive during the Second World War when numerous German divisions were tied down by a numerically weak

Partisan force. The karst region served as a refuge for many people, e.g., the Latin speaking and pastoral nomadists 'Morlaci', (from Greek Μαυρόβδαχφ—literally Black Vlahs), Bosnian people fleeing from Hungarian rule, Serbians escaping from Turkish conquests. The area of the Neretva Valley, where climate is more mild and the elevation is lower, was the region where some 40,000 Bosnians were resettled in 1448. Their ruler, Stjepan Vukčić (Hrvatinić), received the title of the Duke of St Sava and the country was renamed 'Hercegovina,' meaning duchy. The southern karst region was part of the original Serbian settlement area and was known first as 'Dioclia', then as 'Zeta' and finally as 'Crna Gora-Montenegro' (Black Mountains) though it did not cover exactly the same territory. It served as refuge for those Serbians fleeing from 'Old Serbia' before the Turkish advance. It defended itself successfully and remained quasi-independent during the period of Turkish occupation as well as from Venetian conquest.

The significance of the central and southern karst area lay in its extensive stock breeding economy with its summer mountain pastures, but geographical conditions allowed its inhabitants to keep only a small number of livestock.[24] Traces of Pre-Roman and Illyrian settlements are found all through the karst and the Romanized Vlah shepherds speaking a Latin dialect and known under different names (Aromanians, Kutzovlacs, Tsintsars), grazed in these lands, including high Montenegro of present day and Stari Vlah (south east part of the Dinaric mountains, the heart of Raška). This also served as the territory from which in the Middle Ages the merchant republic of Ragusa (Dubrovnik) received its greatest economic strength through its important caravan trade. The imposing Bogomil tombstone monuments (stećci) in the Dubrovnik hinterland in south-west Hercegovina and other nearby regions are a reminder of the one time wealth of the stockbreeding economy.[25] This region, by supporting the vital caravan trade, facilitated the prosperity and rise of Ragusa and at the same time, the caravan routes with their important crossroad and relay stations also contributed to the rapid expansion of the early Serbian state of Raška with its nucleus at Novi Pazar. The Ottoman occupation brought great population changes in this frontier zone and a considerable displacement of the Vlah shepherds and ultimately a discontinuance of numerous caravan roads.

The difficulty of penetrating the mountainous region during the early settlement period contributed to the creation of the first Slavic national states: The Slovenes in the upper Sava Valley and in southern Carinthia were probably the first South Slavic people to arrive in the latter part of the sixth century (Fig. 3). Their independence was shortlived. In 748, they submitted to the Franks and were converted to Christianity by the Western Church at an

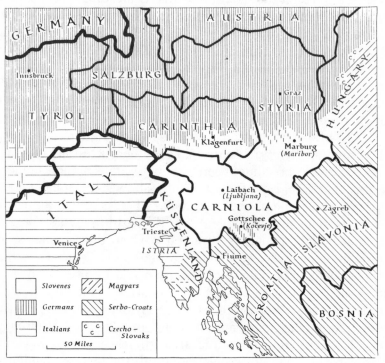

FIG. 3. The Slovene lands (pre-1918 frontiers). Figures 3–10 and 12 are taken from S. Clissold (Ed.) *A Short History of Yugoslavia*. Cambridge University Press (1966).

early period. They formed part of the duchy of Carantania and German (Austrian) influence became predominant. They were part of the Holy Roman Empire and were organized as a March against Magyar raids. In the mid-fourteenth century, a number of Germans were settled in the southern part of Slovenia at Gottschee (Kočevje), where they remained until 1944.

To the south of the Slovenes were the Croatians. Their independence was first reported in the ninth century and Tomislav (crowned in 925) was their first king (Fig. 4). Their core region centred at Nin, north of Zadar, later in Biograd. Though records are very scanty the early Croatian kingdom at certain periods occupied the whole region south of the Drava River (today's Slavonia) to the Drina and Neretva, including the whole Dalmatian coast. The period between the defeat of the Avars and the arrival of the Magyars was a relatively peaceful period for the peoples bordering the Pannonian plains. When succession disputes

FIG. 4. Croatia about A.D. 1070.

arose in 1089 Ladislav I, King of Hungary, who was related to the Croatian royal house, took control of Croatia in 1091 and established a bishopric in Zagreb. In 1102 Croatia and Dalmatia were joined to Hungary, but the hereditary claims to Dalmatia were sold by the Croatian king Ladislav of Naples to Venice in 1409. The Croatian contacts with the flourishing Latin cities of the Dalmatian coast played an important part in the cultural influences and development of its people. The whole country at first was part of the archiepiscopal province of Spalato (Split). Croatians were

Christianized from Rome, but at first their native Glagolite alphabet (similar to the Cyrillic one) and only after the sixteenth century with the increasing influence of western culture was the Latin alphabet introduced in their Slavic language.

The Serbian tribes arrived south of the Danube during the early part of the seventh century, probably after other Slavic tribes had already moved through the valleys of the Morava and Vardar. According to some reports, they were granted territory known as 'Serblia,' a frontier march of the Byzantine Empire against the Avars and later the Magyars. The various loosely connected clans settled in two groups. The western settlements were known as 'Dioclea' or 'Zeta,' in today's Montenegro and Hercegovina. The eastern group was settled between Raška and Novi Pazar, astride the strategically important 'Bosnian Way' overlooking both the Danubian and upper Morava plains and the Kosovo Basins.

After a lengthy period of internal warfare and lack of cohesion the various Serbian clans were united during the Nemanja dynasty and quickly expanded their territory in Zeta to the Adriatic coast, including the cities of Scutari and Kotor, and advanced into the nearby fertile Kosovo and Metohija basins. The Serbian rulers availed themselves of the opportunities offered by the loosening of the control exerted in this region by the Byzantine Empire. During a period of nearly 200 years the mediaeval Serbian state expanded south into the Basins of Kosovo and the Vardar Valley in an area generally referred to as 'Macedonia', and never lost control of this vital area. With Byzantine suzerainty shaken off, the Bulgarian Empire, which for a time extended westward to include Niš, Skopje and Ohrid and allied with Ragusa, was defeated. The Serbian frontier was pushed southward, their capital moved from Novi Pazar, to Prizren and to Skopje indicating their steady southward advance which ultimately led to the Aegean Sea and Thessaly. (Fig. 5). Under Stephen Dušan (1331–1355) the Serbian state reached its greatest extent.

Both foreign expansion and internal economic development went hand in hand. With the help of German miners (colonists from Hungary known as 'Saxons'), the well-known mines from the Roman period in the Kopaonik Mountains, east of the Ibar river, were mined for copper, tin, silver and gold. The silver mines

FIG. 5. Serbia under the Nemanjid dynasty.

of Novo Bródo near Pristina were expanded and so were the
Ragusian trading privileges. Trade on the old East-West Roman
roads flourished with wine, oil, salt, manufactured and even luxury
goods moving from the coast to the interior and metals, timber,
wool, skin, cattle and leather from the interior to the coast. The
Serbian archbishopric of Peć was raised to a partriarchate, in spite
of opposition from Constantinople, and Dušan was crowned in
Skopje Emperor of the Serbs and Greeks (later changed to Emperor and Autocrat of the Serbs and Greeks, the Bulgarians and
Albanians). At a time when the Byzantine emperors enlisted the
support of the Ottoman Turks (1345 and 1349) to stop the advancing armies of Dušan, the Emperor suddenly died. The diverse

units of his empire quickly broke into numerous feuding fragments. Local chieftains assumed power and even tried to enlarge their territory. The Balša family in Zeta established their independence and founded Montenegro. The way was now open for the Ottoman advance into the South Slavic lands, which was completed when the last Serbian city, Smederevo, was captured by the Turks in 1459, i.e. 24 years after Sarajevo. This capture was soon followed by the Turkish advances into southern Hungary, and only Montenegro, whose population was increased by the many Serbian refugees, remained semi-independent.

Without doubt, the most interesting development in the mountain heartland was in Bosnia, which derived its name from the River Bosna. Its nucleus was within western Illyricum and, therefore in the Latin part of the Roman Empire. It was a

'borderland of an unusual type, not a corridor country in the midst of which competing neighbours have established a mutual frontier, but a well-protected fastness which happened to be so situated that during the formative period of the nationality it came under equal and opposite influences from neighbouring civilisations.'[26]

Its semi-independent people entered the region during the seventh century (Fig. 6). The earliest capital was at Sutjeska and the main commercial and administrative capitals moved from the south-west to the north-west and finally was established at Jajce, in an area of advantageous communication near a pass linked with the fortress city of Travnik in the Basin of the Upper Bosna. Trade from the coast was conducted by the merchants from Ragusa, with the main caravan route leading across the mountains via Kalinovik to Sarajevo.[27] The rulers of Bosnia slowly expanded their territory south of Ivan Pass, the territory known as Hercegovina, and thus for the first time had control of part of the coast between Split and the Neretva River. While the physical geography differed greatly between Bosnia and Hercegovina, with the latter part largely consisting of barren karst limestone, the two parts have remained united as one administrative unit to the present time. Other territory incorporated into the expanding mediaeval Bosnian state was the fertile plain of Livno, located between the parallel ranges of the Dinaric Alps, and settled to this date by

Roman Catholic Croats. Bosnia also extended its territory slowly toward the north-west beyond the Una River with a population consisting of Roman Catholic Croats, an area part of the old Croatian kingdom. Its population was forced to flee during the early part of the Ottoman occupation, but its landscape has a decidedly Croatian character and since the Turkish conquest has been called 'Turkish Croatia'.

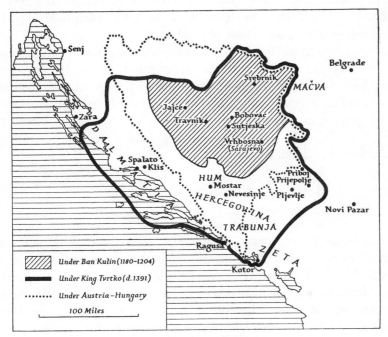

FIG. 6. Mediaeval Bosnia.

Perhaps it should be pointed out briefly that the borderland role of Bosnia referred to earlier concerned her position astride the frontier of the Eastern and Western churches. As a result, the 'state church of the Bosnian kingdom was of an intermediate character.'[28] In spite of this, or perhaps because of this intermediate character, the state persecuted the numerous adherents of the Bogomil sect which lived in the valley of the Upper Bosna.

Due to the great dissatisfaction and persecution of the Bogomil population by the Roman Catholics, the advances of the Turkish armies into Bosnia found little resistance. Some districts with less strong Bogomil ties held out somewhat later, but the conquest was made complete when the last king surrendered in 1463. With the arrival of the Turks, most Bosnian nobles accepted Islam, the nobles thus preserving some of their property and power and the serfs acquiring land, or 'ćiftlük', free of feudal obligation.[29] Thus a sizeable proportion of the Slavic people of Bosnia and Hercegovina became Moslems and tended to identify themselves with Turkey rather than with the Slavic lands. To this date, the people of this region show a curious phenomenon. Thirty-nine (39·6) per cent of the population are Moslem by religion and even nationality, but most of those are Slavic by race. Catholicism became in time restricted to the barren karst area of Hercegovina (esp. Livno Polje) with many fleeing into the Croatian-Slavonian or Vojvodina part of today's Yugoslavia. For the most part, Serbs, Vlahs and other Orthodox people moved to (or were forced to move) northern Bosnia which even today shows a large percentage in its border communes.

The Impact of the Ottoman Period

In the wake of the Turkish advances, the Bulgarian and Serbian states, already torn apart by internal dissension, were defeated and Ottoman administration was imposed. The Serbian defeat (with soldiers from other Slavic people participating) at Kosovo Polje in 1389 opened the way for the Turks to enter the mountainous heartland. The movements of the Turkish armies were made easier by the defection of dissatisfied people, especially in Bosnia. The mediaeval kingdoms of Serbia and Bosnia and Hercegovina with the exception of Montenegro (which at that time consisted largely of an area approximately the size of the present-day commune of Cetinje) became part of the Turkish Empire.

As a result of the Turkish advances, major ethnographic changes occurred in three regions. One was the area of the mediaeval kingdom of Bosnia and Hercegovina in the central mountainous heartland, where the indigenous population rapidly accepted Islam, and where also major population changes occurred, especially along the northern and north-western border of the Ottoman Empire. The second area is located to the south of the original Serbian nuclear settlement, the area of Raška, on the northern fringes of the Kosovo and Metohija Basin. It is the Basin of Kosovo with its striking 'contrast between the *planina*, the high mountain region on its confines, and the *župe* or *pays* which are found at lower altitudes in the plains and on their fringes.'[30] Their economic independence is a key factor in the understanding of the problems of Kosovo. Kosovo was a frontier zone between the Byzantine, Bulgarian and later Serbian Empires, between the Eastern and Western Roman Empires, between Christianity and Islam and between Vlahs, Albanian[31] and Serbian settlers. The importance of controlling the Kosovo and Metohija Basin, with its two major routeways, the Bosnian and Zetan Way, has, as pointed out by Wilkinson in his admirable study, 'each played a great part in the history from the time of the Roman Empire until today.'[32] The strategically located crossroad basins of Kosovo, with its key routeways, was the goal of the mediaeval Serbian Empire, but it remained in Turkish hands after the Serbian defeat at Kosovo Polje in 1389 to the end of the Balkan Wars in 1913. As a result of the northward movements of the Serbs, Albanians slowly encroached on the basins until today they amount to over 70 per cent of its inhabitants.

The third area where major ethnographic changes occurred was located in southern Hungary, a region known as Vojvodina and to a lesser extent in neighbouring Slavonia. The changes here are related to the large scale movements of the Serbian population to the north of the Danube river after 1389. Reports of 1483 already speak of close to 200,000 Serbs settled during the four-year period. By 1538, it was estimated that one half of the population of Hungary consisted of Serbs.[33] Serbian settlers participated in the colonization efforts by the Austrian authorities after the defeat of the Turks in 1699 (Treaty of Sremski Karlovci-Karlowitz), when the empty lands of southern Hungary were resettled with people from every part of the Austrian Empire. So many different nationalities settled in Vojvodina and parts of Slavonia that ever since that time this part is referred to as an 'ethnographical museum'. The peace treaty marked a turning point in the history of south-eastern Europe.

The migrations mentioned were largely the result of indirect Turkish pressures extended over several centuries, though some migrations were fostered by the Turks, largely in connection with the transplanting of people from one region to another for military and political reasons, especially noticeable at the northern border of Bosnia and Hercegovina. Most of the migratory movements were outward movements from early settlement areas or those which were incorporated by the early Slavic states, such as (Kosovo and Metohija) and Macedonia; by withdrawals of the Slavic population from the plains and areas of important communication arteries and centers either north across the Danube or into the protection of the mountainous heartland. This was in many ways a repetitious strategy used by the early Vlah population. The Islamized Albanian people moved from the mountains to the fertile and vacant areas of Kosovo and Metohija and north-western Macedonia, a movement which assumed great importance after the mass emigration of Serbs in 1691 (estimated at 30–40,000 families) following their patriarch of Peć across the Danube to settle in southern Hungary. The constant population pressure exerted by the Albanians[34] and furthered by the Ottoman authorities contributed to the continuous movements of the Serbian people toward the north, its speed influenced by the turn of events, a pressure still going on, as may be seen in the figures of the post-war censuses. These mass movements of the largely Serbian and Albanian population were made possible because of their pastoral economy, the absence of a crop economy, and the decline in the late eighteenth and nineteenth century of animal husbandry.

Finally, a brief summation detailing specific migratory movements induced as a result of the Ottoman occupation of the South Slavic lands showing their long term impact on today's ethnographic map.

1. Outward movements occurred largely by the Serbian population from south to north, across the Danube into southern Hungary, the Vojvodina, and into the protection of the mountainous heartland. These two areas, the Vojvodina and the mountainous heartland, have seen the largest number of refugees from the Turkish occupation and the Vojvodina has seen the greatest ethnographic changes of permanency in all of the territory of today's Yugoslavia. The settlements in southern Hungary started before the expansion of the Turkish occupation north of the Danube, but reached its zenith after the Turkish defeat and the resultant peace treaty in 1699. It was after that time that the planned colonization

of the empty lands of Vojvodina by the Austrian authorities com-
menced and mass settling into planned villages got under way.
While Serbian settlers were in the majority in Vojvodina, settlers
from all parts of the Austrian Empire and beyond were attracted to
these rich agricultural regions with promises of assistance and
special privileges, including religious freedom. Besides Serbs,
there were a number of Croatian settlers mostly in the western
part of Vojvodina and a smaller number in the Backa region
around Subotica in northern Vojvodina.[35]
2. Other Serbian migratory movements from the Kosovo and Vardar region went to Bosnia,[36] Montenegro and Dalmatia and their
place was generally taken by either Turkish settlers transplanted
from Anatolia (largely to Macedonia) or by the earlier mentioned
Islamized Albanians. Due to the earlier described flexibility of the
Serbian settlers, migration was not an especially difficult problem
for most.
3. Not all migrations are due to Turkish pressure. Some are connected with the overpopulation of the mountainous heartland, but
they too went largely north of the Danube into the Vojvodina and
to a lesser extent to Slavonia with small numbers moving into
Slovenia and even south into the Greek lands. It is interesting to
note here that the migrations from the mountainous heartland into
the fertile agricultural lands of Slavonia and especially Vojvodina
continued until the early 1950s.
4. A counter-migration (return migration) occurred at the time
when some Serbian areas were freed from Turkish occupation and,
due to the pressures of the Catholic Austrian overlords, including
efforts to convert the Orthodox Serbians to Catholicism, a number
of Serbs moved back into this free territory south of the Danube.
When Turkish armies counter-attacked, the Serbs did little to help
the Austrians. These 'return migrations' increased as the liberation of Serbian territory expanded all during the nineteenth century.
5. Major migratory movements occurred all along the depopulated
and underpopulated Turkish-Austrian frontier region (Fig. 7).
The earlier mentioned Austrian military frontier offered a refuge
for many Orthodox Serbian fugitives from Turkish pressures and a
sizeable number of people settled along today's southern border of
Croatia, a fact clearly shown on the ethnographic map of 1971. In

addition, Catholic Croatians from so-called 'civilian' Croatia and
Slavonia settled in the military frontier as they were attracted by
promises of special privileges. The origin of the sizeable Serbian
population in today's Croatia, nearly 15 per cent, dates to these
settlements.

6. The Turkish occupation of Bosnia and Hercegovina, in addition
to the earlier mentioned mass conversion to Islam of most Bosnian

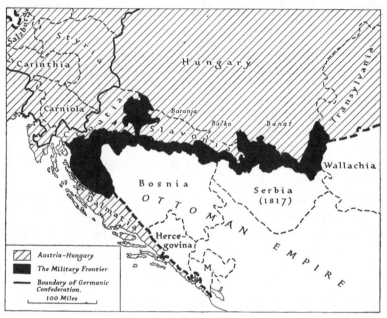

FIG. 7. The 'military frontier' of Austria and Hungary, M. Montenegro.

people, caused a variety of population movements which left their
long term impact on the ethnographic makeup of this region.
Catholic influences generally disappeared. For the most part the
Catholic people were either expelled or left voluntarily, often
with Austrian armies who moved through the northern part of
Bosnia, e.g., nearly 40,000 Bosnian Catholics, presumably Croats,
left in 1697, moving into the military border region and many
fleeing to Hungary. A few Catholic Croatians fled to Dalmatia and
thus increased the Catholic element of the Dalmatian coastal
towns. A few migrated to Slovenia and Hungary. Sizeable numbers
of Serbs and a few Vlahs from interior Bosnia and Hercegovina
were settled at the frontiers of the Turkish Empire in northern

Bosnia. These population movements extending during the period of the lengthy Ottoman occupation explain, to a large part, the heterogeneous settlement of today's map of Bosnia and Hercegovina.

Pan-Slavism and the Yugoslav Idea

The spirit of independence burned fiercest among the Serbs. Starting in 1804 they initiated a series of revolts which finally brought them their full independence in 1878. But under the fiery Serb nationalists, proud of their long suffering as well as their successes, the new state now became attached to the idea of Pan-Serbianism, its leaders dreaming of the mediaeval empire of Dušan, hoping to include in their territory Bosnia and Hercegovina, Macedonia, Kosovo, as well as southern Hungary, and the Vojvodina, with its larger Serbian population (Fig. 8). The Serbs of Vojvodina were greatly disappointed, when after siding with the Austrian emperor and the Croats during the Hungarian revolt in 1848, they received no reward. This became especially clear in the Austrian-Hungarian Ausgleich of 1867, when the hoped for autonomous status for Vojvodina was not realized. From that time on, the Serbs of Hungary worked closer and closer with the growing Serbian state to the south, seeing this as the only way to avoid losing their national identity in the face of strong Magyar pressures. Table IV shows the ethnic composition of Vojvodina and indicates the linguistic mosaic created by the migrations after the region was liberated from the Turkish yoke.

The several wars of liberation fought by the Serbs during all of the nineteenth century against the Ottoman Turks and the slow, but step by step retreat of Turkish power from Europe, culminated in the settlement of the Treaty of Berlin in 1878. This brought major changes to the map of the Balkan countries. Serbia gained territory and complete independence, but north of its original nucleus, in the valley of the Morava and south of the Danube. 'Old Serbia', including Skopje still remained outside their reach and within the Turkish Empire. Bosnia and Hercegovina exchanged Turkish occupation for that of Austria-Hungary, which was more favourable to the Croats, but still a detested foreign power to the Serbs. Austria and Hungary became worried by the growing talk

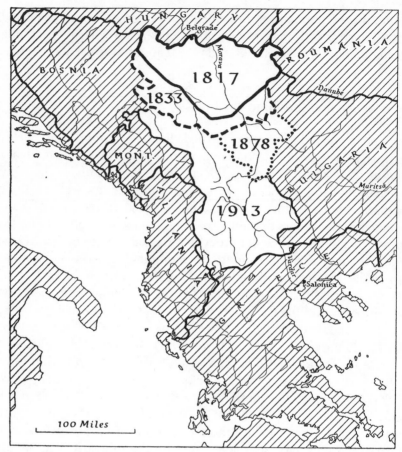

FIG. 8. The growth of Serbia, 1817–1913.

of South Slavic union, 'the possibility of some union among the various Southern Slav groups was never lost sight of during the nineteenth century,'[37] first mentioned under Napoleon's 'Illyrianism' (Fig. 9).

'The twin nationalisms of Serbia and Croatia were blended inextricably with their respective religions. What counted in determining who was a Serb and who was a Croat was more religion than place of residence or ethnic origin. This was particularly true in Bosnia, where it was virtually impossible to untangle the population on a strictly ethnic basis, and in Croatia,

Table IV
Estimated Ethnic Composition of the Vojvodina

	(1)	(2)	(3)	(4)
	1910	1921	1931	1942
Serbs	381,872 ⎫		461,864	404,600
Croats	6,559 ⎬	502,415	16,000	9,000
Bunjevci and Šokci	62,904 ⎭		68,000	61,000
Slovenes	—	7,105	7,700	3,000
Magyars	421,567	376,107	385,500	472,000
Germans	301,035	316,579	317,300	315,500
Roumanians	75,806	69,530	71,950	76,000
Slovaks, Ruthenes and other Slavs	58,003	65,434	71,200	74,400
Others	12,152	9,357	16,292	12,500
	1,319,898	1,346,527	1,415,806	1,428,000

Based on (1) the Hungarian Census of 1910; (2) the Yugoslav Census of 1921 in which Serbs, Croats, Bunjevci and Šokci are collectively classified as Serbo-Croat; (3) an estimate for 1931, based partly on ecclesiastical figures, as no linguistic statistics were given in the Yugoslav Census of 1931; (4) the Hungarian Census of 1942 for Baranja and Baćka together with an English estimate for the Banat.

Source: Stephen Clissold (ed). *A Short History of Yugoslavia.* Cambridge University Press, Cambridge (1966) page 122.

where several hundred thousand persons of Orthodox faith, Serbs or not were considered Serbs.'

Also the Orthodox Church, strongly anti-Roman Catholic, was able to give Pan-Serbianism a special Orthodox flavour which brought it more and more into conflict with the Roman Catholic Croats.[38]

As a result of Austria-Hungarian annexation of Bosnia and Hercegovina in 1908 Serbia's hopes for incorporating this area in its territory received a setback. New interests were more and more directed toward 'Old Serbia' and Macedonia and, by means of various alliances formed between Greece, Bulgaria, Montenegro and Serbia, the Turkish armies quickly were defeated. Serbia occupied Skopje and incorporated northern and central Macedonia,

FIG. 9. The Illyrian provinces, 1809–14.

a subsequent frontier adjustment divided the Sandžak of Novi Pazar between Serbia and Montenegro. Only the much coveted outlet to the Adriatic coast, blocked by a newly founded state of Albania on the initiative of Austria and Italy, eluded Serbian dreams.

Perhaps the richest prize was the Serbian acquisition of ethnically diverse Macedonia. The literature about the ethnic affinity of the Macedonians is enormous and at times it is difficult to distinguish between facts and propaganda (Fig. 10), but the fact remains that in all the years of Turkish occupation the preponderance of the Slav element remained. Macedonia's ethnic complexity has for a long time been extremely controversial with the origin, distribution, and the character of its Slavic population uncertain.[39] In addition, it has a large number of minorities, Vlahs, Albanians, Turks, Greeks and Gypsies. The various population claims by

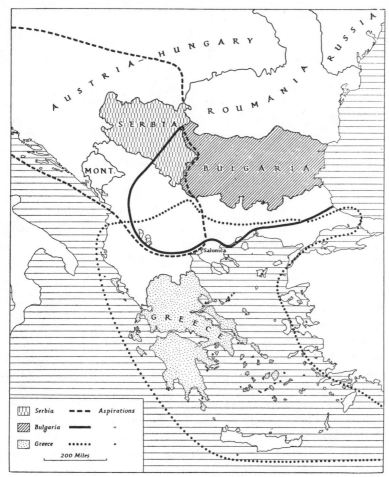

FIG. 13.10. Conflicting claims in Macedonia, 1912.

rival nationalities can be seen in Table V.

With the Serbian occupation of Macedonia in 1912–13 and its incorporation into the Serbian State as 'South Serbia', a large scale planned colonization by the Serbians now began. Due to the lack of a proper explanation in the detailed statistical data in the 1921 and 1931 censuses listing all Serbo-Croatian people under one heading, no detailed population information was available until the first postwar Yugoslav census in 1948.[40] Only 2·6 per cent of the population of Macedonia, or about 30,000, were listed at that time as Serbs with 68·5 per cent or close to 800,000 as Macedonian. The Albanians accounted for 17·1 per cent and the Turks for 8·3

Table V

Macedonia: Nationalities as Viewed in Serbian, Bulgarian, Greek and
German Literature

	(1)	(2)	(3)	(4)	(5)
	Serbian view, 1889	Bulgarian view, 1900	Greek view, 1889	German view, 1905	Turkish view, 1904
Turks	231,400	489,664	576,600	250,000	1,508,507
Bulgars	57,000	1,184,036	—	—	896,497
Serbs	2,048,320	700	—	—	100,717
Macedo-Slavs	—	—	454,700	2,000,000	—
Greeks	201,140	225,152	656,300	200,000	307,000
Albanians	165,620	124,211	—	300,000	—
Vlachs	74,465	77,267	41,200	100,000	—
Other	101,875	147,244	91,700	—	—
Total	2,880,420	2,248,274	1,820,500	2,850,000	2,911,721

1 to 4 from Jovan Cvijić, *Questions Balkaniques*.
(1) Serbian view: S. Gopčević, *Bevölkerungsstatistik von Altersbien und Make-donien*, Vienna (1899).
(2) Bulgarian view: V. Kŭnchov, *Makedoniia, Etnografiia i Statistika*, Sofia (1900).
(3) Greek view: C. Nicolaides, *Makedonien*, Berlin (1899).
(4) German view: K. Oestreich, 'Die Bevölkerung von Makedonien', *Geographische Zeitschrift*, XI (1905), 292; these figures are estimates.
(5) Yusef Hikmet Bayur, *Türk Inkilabi Tarihi*, Istambul (1940), Vol. I, p. 512.
Source: Stephen Clissold, (ed.). *A Short History of Yugoslavia*. Cambridge University Press, Cambridge, (1966) p. 136.

per cent, a percentage reduced to 6·6 per cent in the 1971 census. Being unable to make comparisons with pre-war censuses it is difficult to judge how many Serbian settlers indicated Macedonian and their nationality. The Serbian population migrated from areas of overpopulation, especially the inhospitable southern parts of the mountainous heartland, into the plains and they, in turn, were part of a systematic colonization effort by the Serbian government to move people into Kosovo and Macedonia. It was not until after the changes brought about by the Second World War and the changes in the administrative setup of post-war Yugoslavia with the establishment of a Socialist Republic of Macedonia (encompassing the area of pre-war Macedonia in spite of territorial claims by Bulgaria) and an autonomous region later province of Kosovo (also known for certain periods of Kosovo and Metohija, or Kosmet), that this Serbian migration and colonization came to a halt. This was due largely to the indigenous settlers, the Macedonian Slavs and the Albanians of Kosovo (Fig. 11). With the Turkish defeat in the Balkan Wars, sizeable parts of the Turkish population withdrew with the Turkish armies, an emigration which has continued until the late 1950s. The migrations of the Turkish settlers back to Turkey have been estimated to number more than 100,000.

FIG. 11. The *Balkans* in August 1913. The arrangement between Serbia and Montenegro respecting the partition of the Sanjak of Novi Pazar was not made until 4 November. From G. W. Hoffman *Regional Development Strategy in Southeast Europe*. Praeger Publishers, 2nd printing (1974).

Changes in the Ethnographic Map Resulting from Two World Wars

The First World War resulted in a unified, though as proven only too early not very viable state. Serbian wartime propaganda espoused South Slavic unity though under Serbian leadership. The Yugoslav idea quickly came to the forefront as the likelihood of a collapse of the Austro-Hungarian Empire meant that Slovenia, Croatia and Bosnia and Hercegovina had a real stake in working out a solution of collaboration among the various South Slavic nationalities before peace came. In 1918, shortly before the Armistice, a National Council of Slovenes, Croats and Serbs was organized and the Croatian parliament voted to end its eight hundred year ties with Hungary. The Austrian-Slavs aimed at a federal-type state, with a carefully delineated autonomy for the three major South Slavic ethnic groups. The Serbian government finally agreed to Yugoslav unity under the name of the Kingdom of the Serbs, Croats and Slovenes.

When the new state was established in 1918 it comprised a population of about 12 million with over two million non-South Slavic people. In addition to the independent kingdom of Serbia and the kingdom of Montenegro, it obtained Croatia–Slavonia, hitherto part of Hungary and from Austria, Dalmatia, Carniola, part of Styria, a small section of Carinthia, a small part of Istria, the rest having been assigned to Italy and Bosnia and Hercegovina formerly jointly administered by Austria and Hungary. From Hungary the new state obtained Bačka, part of Baranja, the western part of the Banat (all part of present-day Vojvodina), together with the districts of Prekomurje and Medjimurje. To bring all South Slavic people into the new state a sizeable number of Hungarians, no less than 450,000, were also incorporated.

Much disagreement arose over the Italo-Yugoslav frontier and it was not until October 1920 that the final border was drawn with Italy receiving all of Istria, the city of Zadar (Zara) and the islands of Cres, Lösinj and Lastovo. Fiume (Rijeka) was to become an independent free city, but in November 1919 was seized by Italy. It was only in 1924 as part of a new Italo-Yugoslav Treaty that Yugoslavia officially recognized Fiume as part of Italy. In return she received Fiume's suburb Susak. The problem of drawing a border with Austria was complicated by the German-Slovene linguistic frontier in Austria's southern provinces of Carinthia and Styria. The final border was drawn after an inter-allied supervised plebiscite with the border on the Karawanken crest and following roughly the linguistic line in the province of Styria. Over 10,000 Slovenes evidently voted for inclusion with Austria. In the southern part of the new country the border with the newly organized state of Albania was indeed a thorny issue and was not settled until 1926 when roughly half a million Albanians were assigned to Yugoslavia. A small border rectification at the expense of Bulgaria affected only few people. Other population changes affected the Germans—a relatively small number returned to Austria— and the earlier mentioned Hungarian minorities, a number of whom emigrated from the newly formed Yugoslav state, but their total number was not large.

Of all the political and economic changes Yugoslavia has undergone since its organization in 1918–1919 none had more far-reaching results than those brought about by the Second World War. After having been occupied and divided up by its neighbours during the war (Fig. 12), a new Yugoslavia emerged as a multi-national Communist state.[41] The Federal People's Republic of Yugoslavia (later changed to Socialist Federal Republic) is administratively divided into six socialist (first called people's republics, which roughly coincided with the ethnic divisions of the population. The post Second World War period uprooted a large number of people and it is estimated that as many as half of Yugoslavia's population were affected. This was followed at the end of the war, first, by migrations largely from the traditional population refugee areas, the mountainous heartland, to the agricultural regions between the Drava and Sava (Slavonia), the Danube–Tisa Plains, Vojvodina, and the Vardar river valley of Macedonia. Thousands of German settlers in Vojvodina and Slavonia retreated with the German armies or were forced to leave their ancestral homes (see Table I). Into these empty lands moved settlers from the population surplus regions of the country. This explains, for example, the Macedonian and Montenegrin minorities on the ethnic map of Vojvodina; respectively eight and nine per cent of the communes Pancevo and Plandište are Macedonians. This territorial mobility

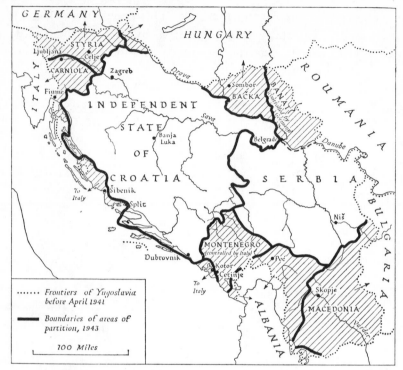

FIG. 12. The dismemberment of Yugoslavia, 1941.

of both the nations and nationalities assumed large proportions
with the result that in 1961 37·1 per cent of the Yugoslav people
live away from their place of birth. Of those, one-third had moved
only a short distance, usually within their commune; one-fifth had
moved outside the commune but relatively short distances and one-
half of the migrants moved greater distances. The largest of the
migrations occurred among the Serbian population, followed by
the Croats with the Albanians and Moslem of Bosnia and Hercegovina showing the least territorial mobility.

Only few population changes occurred as a result of territorial
changes after the War. As a result of the Yugoslav–Italian changes
about 128,000 Italians left the country between the end of the war
and 1971, but the rights of the remaining Italians were spelled out
specifically in the 1954 four-power agreement on Trieste. Of the
roughly 500,000 Germans in Yugoslavia, the largest minority
group lived in Vojvodina and Slavonia. Only about 20,000 re-

mained by the first post-war census, though a few and especially those married to persons of other nationalities, may well have declared the nationality of their spouse. Their numbers have continued to decline (12,000 in 1971). Yugoslavia also lost around 60,000 of its Jewish population during the war and most of the remainder, close to 7,000 emigrated to Israel shortly after the war. Finally, over 100,000 Turks emigrated to Turkey during the 1950s, roughly half of the Turkish population of Yugoslavia (the figures and the appropriate periods reported vary slightly in Turkish reports: 1946 to 1960—102,000; 1950 to 1958—104,372). A small number of Moslems from Bosnia also emigrated to Turkey. The settlement changes of the post-war period again left an important impact on the ethnographic map of the country. It reduced the number of its national minorities—most of all the Germans, followed by the Turks and Italians. Of far greater importance than these changes, were the large scale migrations during all the post-war period, migrations from overpopulated mountainous areas to the fertile lands of the plains, the inter-commune and republican movements, the reverse movements from rural to urban areas and the sizeable emigrations as foreign workers. It must be recognized, however, that certain inter-regional movements in Yugoslavia are complicated because of the difference in the areas involved in language, religion and even alphabet.

The Problem

The centuries long migratory movements with their resultant territorial dislocations of a sizeable number of the Yugoslav people have resulted in a very complex socio-economic history. In addition, as Phyllis Auty stressed, the great 'geographical diversity has thus tended to preserve differences through the history of the country.'[42] The mountainous heartland has thus provided a refuge encouraging the continuation of traditions and their institutions, as well as contributing to tensions among the various cultural-ethnic groups. These repeated population dislocations during much of Yugoslavia's history left their impact not only on he ethnic distribution of the Yugoslav people, but they also explaint the major reasons for the widely differing levels of economic development which resulted for the most part from the constantly recurring political tensions of the post First World War period. It is, therefore, not surprising, as Ivo Lederer pointed out in his penetrating study, that, in 'this society of undying memories and emotions' and strong regional-ethnic loyalities, 'in the sixties symbols of economics have been translated into the terminology of cultural rivalry.'[43] Repeatedly, the tensions between individual republics or intra regional differences have been attributed to the great disparity in regional socio-economic differences. Regions with below average per capita income—Macedonia, Montenegro, Bosnia and Hercegovina and Kosovo—while making considerable progress in the socialist society, are still far behind in their standard of living when compared with the more affluent northern republics. Questions of economic policy repeatedly have been looked upon with suspicion by the closely related nations because historical experiences. Tito's frequent intervention and appeal for unity and restraint have clearly shown the dangers to the viability of the state. It is easy to overstress these national prejudices, as they are related to economic attitudes, but the fact remains, as was pointed out so succinctly in a recent study,

> 'economic demands of today deepen existing national prejudices, making nationalistic interpretations of the rights of the republics, the role of Belgrade in the economic and political system, and so forth, more, not less plausible . . . economic controversies in Yugoslavia have awakened old national emotion, but not given them a radically new content, nor created nationalism where none existed before.'[44]

The developments of the past twenty-five years have not erased the legacy of ethnic identity of the peoples of Yugoslavia. In spite of the basic purpose of the federal-type Constitution of the country (Amendment XX, Art. 2), The Socialist Federal Republic of Yugoslavia, and its explicit statement

> 'voluntarily united and equal peoples and their socialist republics, including the socialist autonomous provinces of Vojvodina and Kosovo which form part of the Socialist Republic of Serbia based on the rule of and self-management of the working class and all working people . . .'

the recent census has again verified that relatively few people in the country consider themselves Yugoslavs first. The ethnic loyalties rooted in history continue to exist and[45] the people have not thus far been able to identify themselves with the larger Yugoslav nationality.

Acknowledgements

This study is the result of many years of study of the political-geographic transformation of the Yugoslav society. Appreciation is expressed to colleagues both in Yugoslavia and the United States for their careful reading of the original draft manuscript. Special mention goes to the anonymous readers of the manuscript selected by the editor. Obviously in a manuscript with numerous statements based on interpretation of various historical developments, the author must assume final responsibility. Secretarial support provided by The University Research Institute of The University of Texas at Austin is acknowledged. The author also wishes to acknowledge with thanks permission received from his various publishers to quote freely from his publications, i.e., The Twentieth Century Fund (together with Fred Warner Neal: *Yugoslavia and the New Communism*, 1962), Van Nostrand Company (*Balkans in Transition*, 1963), Praeger Publishers (*Regional Development Strategy in Southeast Europe*, 1972).

13. Notes

1. Jack C. Fisher, *Yugoslavia-Multinational State*, Chandler House Company, San Francisco (1966), p. 19.
2. The late German historian Fritz Valjevac called it a 'Bindeglied, Kulturbrücke, or Völkerbrücke.' Fritz Valjevac, 'Die Eigenart Südosteuropas in Geschichte und Kultur,' *Südosteuropa Jahrbuch*, I (1956), 54–55.
3. It would simply be an impossible task to list all the important books and articles which served as background for the preparation of this study. Among the most valuable for this study were the books by Paul Diels, Francis Dvornik, Edgar Hösch (translated by Tania Alexander), J. Peisker, George Stadtmüller, L. S. Stavrianos, Robert Lee Wolff. Also the books edited by the following selected number of authors contain a variety of contributions which served as background for this study: Henrik Birnbaum

and Speros Vryonis, Stephen Clissold, Francis H. Eterovich and Christopher Spalatin, Charles and Barbara Jelavich, Robert J. Kerner. A number of scholarly contributions, too numerous to mention, also served as background material. Studies in historical geography on individual regions or nationalities are also numerous. Among the most valuable contributions are those by Dimitrje Djordjević, Jovan Cvijić, Vaughn Cornish, B. Ž. Milojević, M. I. Newbigin, Josip Roglić, Wayne S. Vucinich, H. R. Wilkinson, to mention only a few.

4. H. R. Wilkinson, 'Jugoslav Kosmet: The Evolution of a Frontier Province and its landscape,' *Institute of British Geographers*, 21 (1955), 183, describes clearly its vital position in the Middle Ages not only as frontier between pastoral and feudal society, but also between the Greek Orthodox (Serbs and earlier Byzantine and Bulgars) and Roman Catholicism (Albanians).

5. F. Valjevac, op. cit., pp. 54–55.

6. Joseph Velikonja, 'Territorial identification and functional relations in Yugoslavia', Paper presented at annual meeting of the Association of American Geographers (1966), p. 3.

7. The use of the term 'South-east Europe' is in many ways an arbitrary one, though it is possible to make a strong case for the use of this term in view of the locational aspect within the European triangle. The best explanation and strongest argument in the defence of the term for South-east Europe was made by Josip Roglić, 'Die Gebirge als die Wiege des Geschichtlichen Geschehens in Südosteuropa,' *Colloquim Geographicum*, Band 12, *Argumenta Geographica* (Festzeitschrift Carl Troll) (1970), 225–239.

8. When using the term 'ethnic' the author refers to the various peoples of Yugoslavia. In specific cases the author uses the official Yugoslav terminology, as used in the 1971 or earlier censuses, i.e., nations, nationalities and other national or ethnic population in 1971 and national groups and national minorities in the 1961 census. *Yugoslav Survey*, XIV, 1 (February, 1973), 1–2 explains the 1971 census classification of the Yugoslav population into two major categories: those who stated their nationality and those who did not. The first category was classified into the nations of Yugoslavia: Croatians, Macedonians, Montenegrins, Moslems in the national sense (hereafter called 'Moslem'), Serbs and Slovenes; the nationalities (i.e., national minorities): Albanians, Bulgarians, Czechs, Hungarians, Italians, Rumanians, Ruthenians, Slovaks and Turks and other national and ethnic groups: Austrians, Germans, Greeks, Jews, Poles, Romany-Gypsies, Russians, Ukrainians, Wallachians and the collective group 'others.' Those who did not state their nationality were classified into (a) those who did not give any answer (according to Art. 41 of the Federal Constitution), (ii) those who declared themselves as Yugoslavs (not to be

considered a statement of nationality), and (iii) those who indicated a regional origin.

9. The commune (opština) is the smallest socio-territorial unit in present-day Yugoslavia, but the number of communes and their boundaries have undergone considerable changes (774 in 1961 and 500 in the 1971 census). The republican boundaries have seen only one minor revision in the whole post-war period, between Montenegro and Bosnia and Hercegovina in 1949. See the excellent contribution by Jack C. Fisher, 'The Yugoslav Commune,' *World Politics*, 16, 3 (April, 1964), 418–441 and a summary in George W. Hoffman and Fred Warner Neal, *Yugoslavia and the New Communism*. The Twentieth Century Fund, New York (1962), pp. 224–228.

10. The 1971 distribution of the Yugoslav peoples is taken from *Statistički Bilten* No. 727 of December, 1972 published by the Federal Bureau of Statistics including the Annex. All figures used on the following discussions, if not otherwise stated are based on the official data, especially those summarized in the article by Ruža Petrović, 'National Structure of the Yugoslav Population,' *Yugoslav Survey*, XIV, 1 (February, 1973), pp. 1–22.

The following information explaining the various census data is taken from Paul F. Myers and Arthur A. Campbell, *The Population of Yugoslavia*. International Population Statistics Reports Series P-90, No. 5. United States Government Printing Office (1954), pp. 28–40, 52–55, 150–155.

The 1921 and 1931 censuses compiled the population by size of commune (opština) and not by size of village or inhabited locality. Inasmuch as a commune usually consists of more than one locality, data based on the size of the commune is not very meaningful for showing the distribution of the population by size of inhabited locality. After the Second World War the 'commune as the unit of rural agglomeration' was replaced by the unit called 'territory of the local People's Committee'. At the 1948 census Yugoslavia had 7,975 of these territories plus 877 cities. Also the 1921 and 1931 censuses were based on 'mother tongue'. In addition to language, the 1921 census also used religion and the 1931 census nationality. But the nationality figures of the 1931 census were considered so unreliable that they never were officially published. German sources in Vienna published those data during the Second World War. Attention also is drawn to the fact that Macedonians, Montenegrins and Bulgars are not listed as separate entities on the 1921 and 1931 censuses; they were all entered as Serbians. This obviously reflected the Greater Serbian influence prevalent during the inter-war years. All post-war censuses are based on 'nationality' and this is generally considered the best criterion because it permits the listing of distinct nationality groups. The reader is especially referred to the explanation on pp. 150–155 in evaluating specific data in the first post-war census in 1948.

11. Hungary and Yugoslavia concluded an agreement in September 1946 to exchange an equal number (40,000) of Hungarians from Yugoslavia and Yugoslavs from Hungary.

12. See Tables IX and XIII in R. Petrović, op. cit., pp. 17 and 19.

13. R. Petrović, op. cit., p. 15.

14. David A. Dyker, 'The ethnic Muslims of Bosnia—some basic socio-economic data,' *The Slavonic and East European Review*, L, 119 (April, 1972), 238–256. See also the earlier cited source by Petrović, op. cit., pp. 11–12.

15. The so-called sect of the 'Bogomils', also known as Patarini, Bosnian Christians, or the 'Bosnian church' lived in the mediaeval Bosnian state and was of Gnostic and Neo-Manichaen character. The members of the Bogo-mils sect were considered heretics and were persecuted by both the Roman Catholic and Eastern Orthodox churches. As a result of these persecutions they were quickly Islamized during the Ottoman occupation. There is con-siderable literature on the nature and significance of the Bosnian church;
for a brief summary of the special character of the Bogomils see Vaughn Cornish, 'Bosnia, the Borderland of Serb and Croat,' *Geography* XX (1935), 269.

16. The administrative structure of Yugoslavia was reorganized in 1931 into a series of banovina. Bosnia and Hercegovina comprised four of those: Vrbaska, Primorska, Zetska and Drinska. It also should be pointed out that the Moslems in Bosnia and Hercegovina are not only descendants of the Bogo-mils, but also of other religions, mainly Roman Catholics who were the only religious group in the territory before the appearance of the Bogomils and before the Turkish invasion.

17. R. Petrović, op. cit., p. 12;
see also the discussions by D. A. Dyker, op. cit., pp. 238–41.

18. For a detailed discussion of the impact of migration see George W. Hoff-man, 'Currents in Yugoslavia: Migration and Social Change', *Problems in Communism*, XXII (November–December, 1973), 16–31.

19. There are two reasons for the very high concentration of Moslems in the communes of Cazin and Velika Kladusa. The communes Bihać and Bos. Krupa have also a relatively high concentration of Moslems: (i) when the Turks occupied that part of Croatia it became the most north-western part of the territory. They therefore preferred to have here a Moslem popula-tion. They brought a number of already Islamized population from earlier occupied parts of Bosnia and they forced the domestic population to change its religion and to become Moslems, and (ii) the Turks occupied consider-able Croatian territory on the west, like the regions of Lika and a part of Banija and Kordun. They Islamized a portion of the population there, but when they were forced to retreat from these territories in 1699, the

Islamized population retreated with them to the nearest Turkish region and this was the country around Cazin. Cazin was made a key border fortress. It was also a center for Turkish trade with Croatia. In the eighteenth and nineteenth centuries the Moslems there formed a center of opposition to the Sultan's reforms.

20. The military border (also referred to as 'confine militares', 'Militärgrenze', or 'Vojna Krajina') was located between the borders of the Habsburg Empire and those of the Ottoman Turkish Empire between the first half of the sixteenth century (it became a separate territory in 1578) and until 1881.

   During the eighteenth and nineteenth centuries the border was divided into Croatian–Slavonian and Banat frontiers and was organized into territorial military units, governed by military authorities responsible directly to the Austrian Emperor. Their purpose was to organize a defence against the Turks, both in time of war and peace, including plunder raids and for the purpose of controlling the pest and trade. The people who settled along the frontier were to a large extent refugees of Eastern Orthodox faith and peasants from Turkish territory and some from parts of 'civil' Croatia and Slavonia. Though these settlers received special privileges, e.g., freedom of religion, taxation, serfdom, they had permanent military obligations and were among the most valued soldiers of the Austrian Empire (peasant soldiers). These former refugee settlers with their ethnic and religious diversity are the reason for the mixed Croatian and Serbian communes on the present population map in the former military border region. See also the two excellent books by Gunther F. Rothenberg, *The Military Border in Croatia 1740–1881*. The University of Chicago Press, Chicago and London (1966) and *The Austrian Military Border in Croatia, 1522–1747*. The University of Illinois Press, Urbana, Ill. (1960). The same author also wrote several articles on related topics.

21. See the tables in R. Petrović, op. cit., pp. 16–20.

22. The name Albanians is the official name for the people of Albanian origin living in the Kosovo. Before 1968 when Kosovo was elevated from an autonomous region to an autonomous province these people were called Shiptars in Yugoslavia and the region was called Kosovo and Metohija or 'Kosmet'.

23. The Southern Slavs took to Christianity before the Schism, which meant that during the period of Cyrill and Method, who Christianized them, all of them recognized Rome and all were tied to Rome in spite of the fact that the mentioned apostles came from the East.

24. For an excellent contribution see the article by Ian M. Matley, 'Transhumance in Bosnia and Herzegovina,' *The Geographical Review* LVIII (1968), 231–61.

25. Frank W. Carter, 'Dubrovnik: the early development of the pre-industrial city', *The Slavonic and East European Review*, XLVII (January, 1969), 354–368;

see also *Idem.*, *Dubrovnik (Ragusa): A Classic City-state*. Seminar Press, New York and London (1972);

George W. Hoffman, 'Thessaloniki, the impact of a changing hinterland', *East European Quarterly*, 2 (March, 1968), 1–27;

Josip Roglić, 'The Geographical Setting of Medieval Dubrovnik', in *Geographical Essays on Eastern Europe*, Indiana University Publications, Russian and East European Institute, Vol. 24 (1961), pp. 144–159.

26. V. Cornish, op. cit., pp. 261–2.

27. F. W. Carter, 'Dubrovnik, the early development' . . . op. cit., 361–62.

28. V. Cornish points out here that 'the conversion of all the Serbian communities dated from before the Great Schism of East and West, and Western Illyrium, in which Bosnia is situated, was within the Patriarchate of Rome.' Being located close to the historic division between Latin and Hellenic halves of the Roman Empire opened the country to overlapping cultural influences and gave it a very special character. For example, church services followed the Eastern rite, but in the native language and with the approval of the Pope. They were held as late as the 1930s in the Bosna Valley. V. Cornish, op. cit., pp. 268–9;

see also the discussions in Stephen Clissold, (ed.), *A Short History of Yugoslavia*. Cambridge University Press, Cambridge (1966).

29. Wayne S. Vucinich, 'Yugoslavs of the Moslem faith', in *Yugoslavia*, ed. by Robert J. Kerner. University of California Press, Berkeley and Los Angeles (1949), pp. 262–3 reports based on the work of Vladimir Corović, a Yugoslav historian, 'that just as many Bosnian nobles and rulers had earlier adopted Catholicism to free themselves from Magyar attacks, or to secure Magyar support, so in the fifteenth century, for similar reasons they went over to Islam. The Bogomils were the first to adopt the new faith, but soon after the fall of Bosnia, in 1463, they were followed by the nobility of other faiths. In the seventeenth century, and with the appearance of the janizaries, many peasants also adopted Islam';

see also the discussions in Jozo Tomasevich, *Peasants, Politics, and Economic Change in Yugoslavia*. Stanford University Press, Stanford (1955), pp. 95–96.

30. H. R. Wilkinson, 'Jugoslav Kosmet . . .', op. cit., p. 171.

31. Albanians are generally considered, in common with Vlahs, descendants of Illyrian-Thracian settlers seeking refuge in the western uplands of Southeast Europe, though they do not speak Latin. Some writings even suggest that the basins were the homeland of the Vlahs from which they dispersed into several directions before the advance of the Serbian clans in the twelfth century.

32. H. R. Wilkinson, 'Jugoslav Kosmet . . .', op. cit., p. 175.

33. H. C. Darby, 'Serbia', in Clissold, op. cit., p. 103 reports that 'in 1483 Matthias Corvinus, king of Hungary, wrote to the pope that 200,000 Serbs had settled in the south of his kingdom in four years; and, in 1538 Cardinal Matinuzzi stated that Serbs formed half of the population of Hungary. However doubtful these figures may be, it seems fairly clear that by the sixteenth century there was a very considerable Serb population in the area.'

34. The Albanians accepted Islam in the second half of the fifteenth century and lived in their homeland until the seventeenth century. They expanded north and north-east either into empty Serbian settlement areas or forced the Serbs to accept Islam or migrate northward. Vucinich, op. cit., pp. 261–62.

35. The Croatian settlers of Subotica came under the leadership of Franciscan friars from Dalmatia and Hercegovina and Bosnia. These Croatian settlers in Subotica were the reason for the Serbian demands in 1918–19 for the inclusion of the sizeable Hungarian population which lived around Subotica. Even the 1971 ethnographic map shows 31·6 per cent of all settlers in the Subotica commune were Croatians (49·5 per cent Hungarians and 13 per cent Serbs), while the Hungarian population reached in the surrounding communes anywhere between 72 and 88 per cent of the population of individual communes.

36. Before the Turkish invasion there were no Serbian people in Bosnia at all. They came with the Turks as their soldiers—a special type of soldiers, the so-called 'Martolozi.' They settled together with their families in the border regions of Bosnia. Their percentage is higher in the north-western part of Bosnia because that part was later occupied and the majority of the original Croatian population had enough time to flee from that region, which was not the case in the eastern, central and southern parts of Bosnia. Therefore, the Serbians who were settled in the north-western parts of present day Bosnia (or the earlier mentioned 'Turkish Croatia' at that time), became immediately the majority of the population.

   The Croatian population that had to remain and their descendants are still here either as Croats (if they are still Catholics), or as Moslems if they changed their Catholic religion to Islam. Besides a question of timing, the Croats of Bosnia are on the Dalmatian side for a variety of reasons: the protection of the mountains, Moslem tolerance of the Franciscan monastic centres by treaty right, commercial and other ties with the Venetian-held coast. It should be noted that the whole question of the original settlers of Bosnia is much disputed. The viewpoint presented here is only one of many and considered a highly reliable one by the author.

37. S. Clissold, op. cit., p. 154.

38. George W. Hoffman and Fred Warner Neal, *Yugoslavia and the New Communism.* The Twentieth Century Fund, New York (1962), p. 55.

39. The literature in western languages discussing the Macedonian question is abundant. For geographers the studies by Wilkinson and the Serbian geographer Jovan Cvijić are of special interest: Jovan Cvijić, 'Die ethnographische Abgrenzung der Völker auf der Balkanhalbinsel,' *Petermanns Mitteilungen*, 59.1 Halbband (1913), pp. 113–118, 185–189; 244–246;

La Péninsule Balkanique. Géographie Humaine. (Librairie Armand Colin, Paris (1918);

H. R. Wilkinson, 'Jugoslav Macedonia in translation', *The Geographical Journal*, CXVIII, Part 4 (December, 1952), 389–405;

Maps and Politics. A Review of the Ethnographic Cartography of Macedonia. Liverpool University Press, Liverpool (1951);

two additional valuable studies are:

Milorad Vasović and Jovan Petrović, 'Aspects regionaux du Monténégro', *La Revue Mediterranée*, 4 (July–September, 1963), 3–35;

Dennison I. Rusinow, 'The "Macedonian question" never dies,' *American Universities Field Staff*, XV, 3 (Yugoslavia), DIR-3'68.

40. The large Bulgarian population in the two border communes is the result of the peace settlement after the First World War. By the Treaty of Neuilly of November 27, 1919 (which came into force on August 9, 1920), Bulgaria ceded to the Kingdom of the Serbs, Croats and Slovenes four small but strategic areas, one in the Timok Valley in the north, west of Vidiin; the town of Tsaribrod and surrounding territory; the upper part of the Dragovshtitsa Valley, west of Sofia; and the western half of the Strumitsa Valley which Bulgaria had acquired in 1913.

In the north-eastern part of Serbia, particularly around Bor and on Homoljske Mountain, there live many Vlahs—officially 6·9 per cent of the Bor commune, though it is estimated that as many as 50 per cent of the total population of that commune are Vlahs. They declared themselves as Serbians in spite of the fact that they, especially the women, do not even speak the Serbian language, or they speak it very poorly. Among themselves they speak the so called 'Valachian language' which is in fact a dialect of the Romanian language. There are several explanations possible for this phenomena. Professor Michael Petrovic explained it in a letter to the author as follows: first, Vlahs have always inhabited the mountain regions of Serbia, from mediaeval time; second, the mines at Bor have attracted Vlah workers, and third, these Vlahs may be modern Romanian immigrants who fled from Transylvania in the late eighteenth century as the result of peasant disturbances (the Horia, Closca and Crisan uprising) or who came from the Old Kingdom (Regat) into Serbia to get away from Phanariot taxes.

41. The literature of a multi-national society is sizeable. Three studies by Yugoslavs closely connected with this problem are cited:

Alex Bebler, 'Die Stellung der nationalen Minderheiten in Jugoslawien,' Lecture before the Austrian Society for Foreign Policy and international relations (June 14, 1960) 42p;

Anton Vratusa, 'Seminar on the multi-national society', organized by the United Nations in cooperation with the Government of Yugoslavia, background paper, SO 235/3 (2) EUR (1965), 39p.;

Majda Strobl, 'The problems of nationalities and of national minorities in federal states (Yugoslavia).' Paper presented at the North American–Seminar on Federalism, Indiana University, June 1–7, 1967, 20pp.

42. Phyllis Auty, 'Yugoslavia: Introduction', in *Contrasts in Emerging Societies*, ed. by Doreen Warriner. The Athlone Press, London (1965), p. 285. Jovan Cvijić, the well-known Serbian geographer was much concerned with the origin and migratory movements of the population of particular regions. See his summary presentation in 'The geographical distribution of the Balkan People', *The Geographical Review*, 5 (5) (May, 1918), 356–61. He discussed the whole problem of the relationships between patterns of migrations and the development of national consciousness after the Battle of Kosovo in his outstanding work *La Péninsule Balkanique. Géographie Humaine*. Librairie Armand Colin, Paris (1918);

also his monograph series *Naselja i porelko stanonista* (Settlements and Origin of Population) discusses the movements and origin in certain regions.

43. Ivo J. Lederer, 'Nationalism and the Yugoslavs', in *Nationalism in Eastern Europe*, ed. by Peter F. Sugar and Ivo J. Lederer. University of Washington Press, Seattle (1969), p. 438.

44. Paul Shoup, 'Les dimensions economiques de la question nationale yougoslave', *Revue de l'Est*, 3 (Oct. 72), 75–92;

See also the very excellent study by Fred B. Singleton, 'The economic background to tensions between the nationalities in Yugoslavia', in *Probleme des Industrialismus in Ost und West*. Festschrift für Hans Raupach, ed. by Werner Gumpel and Dietmar Keese. Günter Olzog Verlag, Munich and Vienna (1972), pp. 281–304.

45. A good summary is the report by Dennison I, Rusinow, 'The Other Albanians', *American Universities Field Staff*, XII, 2 (Yugoslavia), DIR-2-'65. It should be mentioned here that declaring oneself 'Yugoslav' was actually discouraged (for the first time and to Tito's distress) in the 1971 census.

14

The Economy and Landscapes of Thessaly During Ottoman Rule

RICHARD I. LAWLESS

Among the many emirates which emerged in Anatolia during the second half of the thirteenth century, that of the Ottomans, situated in the hinterland of Brusa overlooking the Sea of Marmora, was the only Turkish outpost facing unconquered Byzantine territory. Because of its geographical position and the prospect it offered of new conquests and booty in the Balkans, the new state was able to attract numerous Turkish adventurers and refugees to its service. It was this magnetism and expansive impetus which enabled the Ottomans to extend their control over the Balkan Peninsula and later over the whole of Anatolia.[1] As a consequence, the maintenance of Ottoman rule in the Balkans came to be seen as an essential part of the traditional base of loyalty to the Sultan which explains why the Ottomans refused to relinquish their control of these provinces even though, after the seventeenth century, they were of only limited financial and military value to the Empire.[2]

At the height of its power in the fifteenth and sixteenth centuries, the Ottoman Empire embraced the entire Balkan Peninsula with the exception of Slovenia and western Croatia, held by the Habsburgs. After the sixteenth century, the empire entered a period of defeat and contraction but its final disintegration and partition did not take place until after the First World War. Thus,

much of the Balkan Peninsula experienced between four and five
centuries of Ottoman rule.

The evidence available for these centuries is considerable. In
Istanbul, there survives a vast body of archival material on the
economic life of the Ottoman provinces in the fifteenth and sixteenth centuries, but research into this valuable source has only
just begun. For later centuries, the archives are less informative,
and, apart from the visible remains of the Turkish occupation in
the Balkan landscapes (Fig. 1), heavy reliance must be placed on
the numerous accounts of European consuls and travellers which
vary greatly in their detail and accuracy.

Fig. 1. Turkish bridge in Thessaly.

Interpretations of the impact of Ottoman rule have been varied, but for many writers—especially those from the Balkan states—the occupation was a period of unrelieved tyranny and oppression. This, however, appears to be an oversimplified and misleading interpretation of events. The early centuries of Ottoman rule brought relative peace and security to regions which had suffered two centuries of incessant wars and exploitation. The newcomers introduced a less oppressive feudal system and the average Balkan peasant had more favourable rights of tenure than his counterpart in Western Europe. The Balkans were never subjected to systematic and sustained proselytism, and mass conversions to Islam occurred only in a few parts of the peninsula. Christians did not have religious equality but were granted a substantial degree of religious freedom. The Patriarch of Constantinople was invested with full ecclesiastical authority over members of the Orthodox Christian community and with considerable civil powers. In this way, the Orthodox Christian hierarchy became a vital arm of the Ottoman political administration. The officials, both lay and clerical, who held church offices were almost exclusively recruited from the Greek community in Istanbul,[3] and their influence, which was greatly resented by the Serbians and Bulgarians, resulted in a growing Hellenization and centralization of the Orthodox Church in the Balkans during the period of Ottoman rule.[4] Furthermore, the Turkish practice of taking a tribute of male children from poor and remote villages in the Balkans—the devshirme system—gave the subject peoples access to the Ottoman ruling class. As slaves of the royal household, many of these villagers came to hold important positions in the army and administration, and a few rose to the highest offices in the empire.

After the sixteenth century, the Ottoman empire, a state organized for conquest and expansion, failed to adjust imperial institutions to a period of defeat and territorial losses. There was a decline in government efficiency, a breakdown in law and order, and widespread corruption in both the administration and army. At the same time, economic institutions and practices in Western Europe were being transformed, leading to the creation of an expanding and dynamic capitalist economy. The impact of these changes on the Ottoman state was profound and far-reaching. In the Balkans, commercial agriculture expanded rapidly, new crops (e.g. maize) were introduced, the volume of trade with Western Europe grew and there was some industrial expansion—developments which only served to accentuate the economic dependence of the Ottoman Empire on the West. The new economic conditions resulted in the formation of a native class of Balkan merchants and shipowners, who were to play an important role in the development of national consciousness. Unfortunately, these economic changes also led to a deterioration in the condition of life of a large section of the rural population following the introduction of a more oppressive landholding system.[5]

The aim of this essay is to present a study of the impact of the Ottoman occupation on the economy and landscapes of one part of the Balkan Peninsula, Thessaly in Greece; to examine in particular the spatial aspects of the economic and social changes which resulted from Turkish rule; and to attempt to isolate and evaluate the processes which brought about these changes.

Like the plains of Macedonia, Thessaly forms one of a series of deep depressions situated around the edges of the Aegean Sea. The depression, a result of permanent subsidence during the Tertiary period, was subsequently filled with marine and lacustrine deposits and later covered with alluvium, giving rise to level plains which are divided into two parts (the upper and lower plains) by a range of low hills (Fig. 2). The plains are bounded on the west by the first range of the Pindus Mountains, which rises steeply from the plain below to over 2000m, and in the south by the Plateau of Othrys rising in parts to 1000m. In the north, several spurs of the Khasia Mountains and the foothills of Mount Olympus extend southwards into the plains enclosing a series of lowland bays. To the east, Mount Ossa and Pelion, rising to 1978m and 1551m respectively, separate the lower plain from the Aegean Sea.

Cut off from maritime influences by the surrounding mountains, much of the region experiences a continental climate with cold and occasionally harsh winters[6] and high summer temperatures. In part, this explains the sharp contrasts in vegetation between the coastlands, characterized by Mediterranean trees and shrubs, and the bare steppe landscape of the plains. Some depressions from the west do reach the region in spite of the barrier formed by the Pindus mountains, and the upper plain receives an annual rainfall

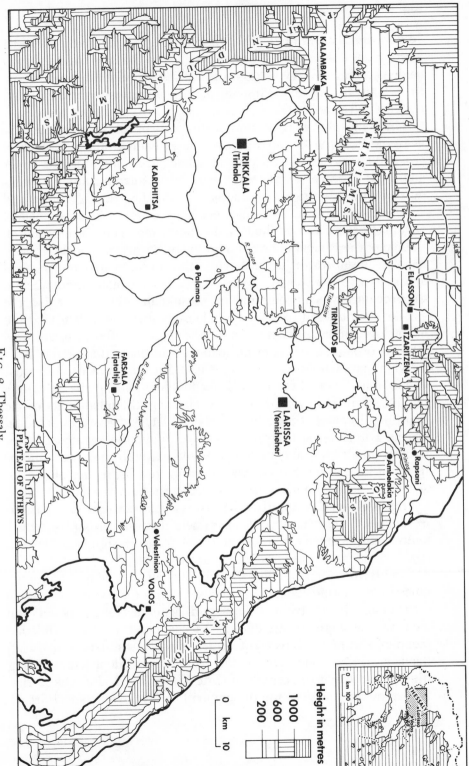

FIG. 2. Thessaly.

of 750 mm. But rainfall, which is characterized by marked irregu-
larity from one year to another, declines to the east and the lower
plain receives only 450–500 mm. Maximum rainfall is in autumn,
with very little rain falling during the summer months of July,
August and September.

Until the new measures of water control carried out after the
Second World War, the region was very badly drained, a result of
instability and continued crustal subsidence. Much of the upper
plain, which receives several rivers and streams from the well-
watered Pindus ranges, was subject to flooding during winter and
spring, and some depressions were permanently filled with water,
forming extensive marshlands. In the lower plain changes in the
course of the River Pinios resulted in large tracts of poorly drained
land to the north of Larissa, while the southern part of the plain
drained to the extensive Lake Karla from which there was no
regular outlet to the sea. In short, a difficult environment, but the
challenge it offered to man was taken up at an early date, and the
stamp of human activities on the landscapes of the region was
already profound when the Turkish occupation began.

Many prehistoric sites are known in Thessaly of which the most
notable are Sesklo and Dimini near Volos. During the Neolithic
period excavated evidence has revealed that the inhabitants of the
region cultivated wheat, barley and millet, and reared goats and
sheep. Later, in classical times traces of numerous settlement sites
indicate that Thessaly was well-populated, with the main concentrations in areas with good natural drainage. The modern towns of
Larissa, Tirnavos and Elasson all occupy sites inhabited continuous-
ly from classical antiquity. Yet is spite of considerable natural
resources, Thessaly, in contrast to neighbouring provinces, never
emerged as a strong political unit, nor played a significant role in
the general history of Greece during this period.[7]

The Romans made Thessaly part of the province of Macedonia
and the Byzantines later incorporated it in the province or Theme
of Hellas.[8] By the twelfth century, a large part of the population
consisted of linguistically distinct Vlachs, descendants of Thracian
peoples who had occupied the central Balkans and trans-Danubian
lands until they were dispersed by invasions of Slavic tribes during
the sixth and seventh centuries. The Vlachs of Thessaly were described by the Jewish rabbi, Benjamin of Tudela, who visited Greece

about the middle of the twelfth century and the name commonly applied to Thessaly by Greek writers of the later Byzantine period was 'Great Valachia'. During the following centuries, many Vlachs were gradually assimilated within the Hellenic community—a process in which the Orthodox Church played an important role— and a large part of the population of Thessaly, though of mixed origin, became Greek in language, religion and culture.

After the conquest of Constantinople by the knights of the Fourth Crusade in 1204, from which the empire never completely recovered, Byzantine rule in Thessaly was challenged by the great landowners, who were able to expand their estates by absorbing holdings belonging to free peasants, by a series of independent local rulers, and by a succession of foreign invaders, Catalans, Venetians, Serbians and finally the Turks. Crippled by territorial losses, financial exhaustion and military weakness, the Byzantine rulers were able to maintain effective control for relatively short periods during the thirteenth and fourteenth centuries which were characterized by civil wars, revolts and invasions. The death of Stephen Dušan in 1355 and the subsequent disintegration of the Serbian Empire removed the only ruler strong enough to check the advance of the Turks into the Balkans, and by 1385 a Turkish army was on the northern borders of Thessaly. At the beginning of 1386, Khairaddin Pasha entered the eastern plain and Larissa appears to have fallen to the Turks by the end of that year. Trikkala, however, was not taken until 1393. A cryptic note on a manuscript reveals that 'in the year 1403–1404 the infidel was in control of Great Valachia'.[9] Thessaly became a 'sandjak' or province of Rumelia, Turkish Europe, and remained under Turkish rule until it was united with the Kingdom of Greece in 1881.

The Early Ottoman Period

The conquest of Thessaly by Ottoman forces set in train important population movements. The mass deportation of the native people from particular areas by the Turkish authorities was common at this time,[10] while some of the wealthier Christian families no doubt chose to migrate to lands beyond Ottoman control. But more significant were the movements which occurred within the province, in particular the migration of the Christian population from villages in the plains and from the main urban centres to seek refuge in the mountains far from the main lines of communication and from Turkish authority. This is a phenomenon recognized throughout the Balkan Peninsula at this time.[11]

The scale of the movement is unknown, but the evidence available suggests that it was considerable. These migrations, which may have begun before the conquest, in response to the insecurity, war and exploitation which characterized the last centuries of Byzantine rule, were also to have far-reaching economic and social consequences. In particular, they resulted in a new phase of forest clearance, the creation of new villages isolated and difficult of access, and the intensive exploitation of limited natural resources in the mountains.

The first centuries of Ottoman rule also brought changes in the composition of the population, though the impact of these changes was not as great as in the frontier areas of the Balkans. At an early date, Turkish settlers were introduced into the region, first during the reign of Bayezid I (1389–1402) with a second colonization during the reign of Murad II (1421–1451). Military considerations no doubt made necessary a policy of colonization and some groups may have been forcibly settled in the newly conquered territories. But the Ottomans certainly encouraged voluntary migration from Anatolia, parts of which appear to have been comparatively over-populated during the fourteenth century.[12] A number of Turkish colonists were settled as farmers in new villages, often on land abandoned by Christians—e.g. the Koniáridhes who occupied the plains between Larissa and Mount Olympus—and they did not usually mix with the native population. Their villages, in which each house was built in the middle of a garden, were quite distinct from the villages of Graeco-Mediterranean type inhabited by Orthodox Christians. The majority of the new colonists, however, were urban dwellers. Many Jews fleeing from racial prejudice and persecution in Christian Europe, particularly Spain, and attracted by the religious tolerance of the Ottoman Empire, also settled in the urban centres of Thessaly during the fifteenth and sixteenth centuries,[13] where they were joined by small numbers of Armenians, Arabs and Negroes. The Turkish historian O. L. Barkan has calculated that at the beginning of the sixteenth century, the Turko-Muslim community in Thessaly contained some

12,347 households (18 per cent of the total number of households in the province) and the Jewish community, 387 households.[14]

From the outset, however, Muslim and non-Muslim communities remained geographically and socially segregated. Orthodox Christians, who formed the majority of the population in Thessaly, Muslims and Jewish subjects were divided on the basis of religion into autonomous communities known as 'millets'. Members of each millet were free to practise their own faith and to retain their institutions, laws and traditions under the direction of their religious leaders who became both the civil and military authorities. By ensuring that persons of different religions were separated from one another as much as possible, the millet system enabled the Ottoman ruler to exploit the wealth produced by his subjects with the least possible resistance and friction. The various regulations which applied to Christians and Jews with regard to residence, clothing and social conduct were essential elements in the basic Ottoman social structure, and similar regulations applied to members of the Muslim community. Their purpose was not to discriminate against non-Muslims but to provide visible signs of each person's position in society so that others could recognize it, thus reducing the possibility of friction.[15] As a consequence, there were few losses to Islam. The different communities did not merge into an organic society but remained intact, apart and distinct.

The early centuries of Ottoman rule brought a definite improvement in the material condition of the majority of the population. During the later Byzantine period, the great landowners had been free to misrule and overtax with little control from Constantinople. But with the Ottoman conquest, Thessaly was incorporated into a strong and highly centralized state with an efficient administrative system able to maintain peace and security —sometimes described by historians as the 'Pax Ottomanica'. Furthermore, many of the local and inherited rights and privileges were actually retained. All subjects and lands belonged to the Sultan who alone had the authority to exploit sources of wealth within the empire. Some land was retained by the ruler and by members of the imperial family. A second category of land was that known as vakf/vakuf, land designated for the support of religious and educational institutions, e.g. mosques, public baths and schools. Other lands, especially in the plains, were granted as fiefs to cavalrymen (spahis), who formed the bulk of the Ottoman army during the early conquest, in return for military and later administrative services. As the spahis were of two ranks, there were two types of fief, large fiefs 'ziamets' held by ziams and small fiefs, 'timars' held by timariots. This new feudal system was first introduced into Thessaly by Bayezid I about 1397 and by the first half of the fifteenth century, there were an estimated 60 ziamets and 344 timars in the province.[16] The majority of these estates were granted to members of the Turkish aristocracy, but a number of timars were also given to the pre-Ottoman military class or aristocracy; in 1455, for example 36 out of 182 timariots in the district of Trikkala were Christians.[17]

Under the new land holding system, customary dues were rendered more often in labour and services than in money and goods. The spahis were only permitted to collect the head-tax—a tax charged to all non-Muslims because they were excluded from military service—which they passed to the government, and a land-tax consisting of a fixed proportion, generally a tenth, of the annual produce, which they retained. The fiefs were not hereditary, and relations between the peasants and the timar holders were strictly controlled by Ottoman officials. As many officials had entered the Ottoman ruling class through the devshirme system, they retained some sympathy for the subject peoples. The villagers therefore held their land under conditions which were much more favourable than their counterparts in the West. In areas not divided into fiefs, especially the mountainous regions, each village retained a substantial measure of self-government under its own elders so long as taxes were paid regularly to the government tax collectors. Thus, in certain areas, and in certain spheres of life, Ottoman rule impinged scarcely at all on the daily lives of the non-Muslim population.

Other economic and social consequences followed the Ottoman conquest. The new state possessed a centralist system of government, and, just as the relations between Muslim and non-Muslim, peasant and fief holder were carefully regulated, so a considerable degree of control was exercised over the economic life of each province.

To this end, the state carried out surveys of population and of all taxable resources of the empire every thirty or forty years during the Early Ottoman period and the results were entered into various kinds of registers. They list the adult male population, a person's legal status, his economic and social position and the amount of land he held. Many of the registers have survived and they contain a wealth of detail not only about the population of the provinces but about land use, customs revenues, markets, fisheries and mines together with the numerous regulations controlling production and distribution.[18] Their study has only just begun, but the first results of research carried out by Turkish historians have already appeared, and in the future this valuable collection of documents should provide us with much more information about the economic and social structure of the Balkan provinces during the fifteenth and sixteenth centuries.

The researches of O. L. Barkan and his team have shown that the first two centuries of Ottoman rule were characterized by the rapid expansion of the urban population in the Balkans. The Ottomans appear to have adopted a systematic policy of creating new towns and of repopulating earlier foundations which had declined as a result of the conquest and earlier wars and civil disorders. This was achieved in many cases by bodily transplanting settlers from other areas. The policy was spectacularly successful in the case of the capital, Istanbul, which grew from less than 100,000 inhabitants in the second half of the fifteenth century to an estimated 700,000 inhabitants at the end of the sixteenth century.[19] In Thessaly, Barkan has calculated that the population of both Larissa and Trikkala increased by 68 per cent between 1525 and 1575.[20] As a result of the policies pursued by the Ottomans, Turkish peoples made up a high proportion of the country's urban population. In Larissa, for example, the Turkish community represented about 90 per cent of the total population and in Trikkala 36 per cent,[21] while almost all the inhabitants of Farsala were Turks. Moreover, contrary to popular belief, not all members of the Turko-Muslim urban community were soldiers and administrators. Of the 355 Muslim heads of household in Larissa in 1454, 217 were craftsmen, and in Trikkala in the same year 121 out of 255 Muslim heads of household were craftsmen.[22] This suggests that the Ottoman government, in the tradition of many Middle Eastern States, believed that artisans were indispensable in reviving and developing an urban centre.

The growth of Istanbul had a profound effect on the economy of the Eastern Balkans. It has been estimated that the inhabitants of the capital consumed each day between 300–500 tons of wheat and every year some 200,000 cattle, 4 million sheep and 3 million lambs. The provisioning of the city, which Braudel[23] has described as 'an urban monster', was therefore a problem of vital importance to successive Ottoman rulers. The problem was solved in two ways. First by authorizing private traders and trade associations to purchase foodstuffs and other commodities at prices fixed by the state or by appointing official government buyers, and second, by forcing provinces such as Thessaly, together with Macedonia, Thrace and Roumanian principalities to reserve a large part of their surplus production—grain primarily, but also sheep, cattle, horses, butter, tallow, honey, wax and timber—for export to the capital.[24]

In contrast, urban centres in Thessaly, like other Ottoman provincial towns, represented concentrations of population on a very small scale, though they were comparable with centres elsewhere in the Mediterranean at this time. Trikkala, for example, had a population of only about 4537 in 1520 and Larissa 4224.[25] Nevertheless, the provisioning of these centres was a matter of constant concern to the Ottoman government, and a series of laws and regulations were enacted to ensure a regular supply of basic foodstuffs and raw materials. The state prohibited the export of a wide range of basic commodities and also controlled domestic trade. Grain, for example, could not be moved from one district or province to another without a special authorization from the state.[26] There were regulations to ensure that the cultivation of certain crops was maintained and some farmers were compelled to supply a part of their annual production at fixed prices. The transport of foodstuffs and raw materials was entrusted to a privileged group of traders, and markets were prohibited outside the urban centre. Retailing was closely supervised, including the fixing of maximum prices, in order to provide a regular and adequate supply of basic commodities for the urban population and to eliminate speculators.[27]

The state exercised a similar control over urban industry which was greatly stimulated by the protectionist and urbanization policies of the Ottomans. This was achieved by strengthening the guild system in the cities. Each guild had a monopoly of one particular branch of industry and a craftsman was not allowed to set up in business without the permission of the guild. In this way, the number of craftsmen engaged in the various branches of industry could be restricted and controlled. In return for certain rights and privileges which the state granted, the guilds, through their officials, had to ensure that regulations concerning the purchase and distribution of raw materials, the quality and price of manufactured goods and the marketing of finished products were strictly enforced. They were expected to settle disputes between members, and they often performed certain social functions. As well as bringing order to the economic life of the cities, the guild system also became a valuable framework for the administrative and fiscal control of the urban population.[28]

The Later Ottoman Period

It seems clear that the key to understanding the impact of Ottoman rule on Thessaly during the early period of the occupation lies in the Ottoman approach to the organization of government and society. The Ottoman system of government, as it emerged during the fourteenth and fifteenth centuries, consisted of a complex series of different but interlocking classes, institutions and organizations, each carefully regulated and strictly controlled by an efficient administration, and held together and made to function as a workable whole by the person of the ruler himself. This highly centralized system worked efficiently when directed by a succession of strong and able rulers, but from the late sixteenth century a series of feeble and incompetent rulers resulted in a gradual weakening of central control. This was accompanied by a fundamental change in the character of the administration. In place of a ruling class composed of specially trained slaves devoted to the Sultan, and promoted on the basis of merit, there developed an administrative system in which each position went to whoever could make the highest bid. The collection of taxes was likewise farmed out to the highest bidder. The result was inefficiency, misrule, a decline in state revenues, disorder and anarchy. Precious metals from the New World combined with the great population increases experienced during the sixteenth century and after, only intensified the chronic inflation and the financial, economic and political chaos that characterized Ottoman society from the beginning of the seventeenth century.[29] There was also a decline in Ottoman military strength as the standing army of infantrymen (the janissaries), who had been permitted to marry and to supplement their incomes by engaging in trade and industry, degenerated into a privileged but ineffective militia of city traders and artisans. At the same time, new unified states in Western Europe were developing formidable armed forces, possessing superior techniques and equipped with more efficient weapons. Ottoman military superiority therefore disappeared, the period of expansion (except for Crete) came to an end, and the state was forced to fight a series of defensive wars. In Western Europe, traditional economic institutions and practices were also being transformed and replaced by an expanding and dynamic capitalist economy. The old merchant guilds gradually gave way to joint-stock companies able to trade on a wider scale, while the craft guilds were slowly replaced by the entrepreneur with capital to purchase the necessary raw materials, engage workmen and to sell the finished products at market prices.[30] The Ottoman Empire did not experience these revolutionary changes, and as trading privileges, 'capitulations', were extended to western merchants, the state became merely an economic dependency of the West, a source of raw materials and a market for the expanding manufacturers of Western Europe. The profound economic and social changes which occurred in Thessaly during the second half of the Turkish occupation resulted from a combination of these factors, from the weakening of central control, the growing economic influence of the West, and the inability of the ruling class, convinced of the superiority of Ottoman ways, to respond and adjust to the new age.

Perhaps the most important effect of the progressive weakening of central government was the gradual collapse of the timar landholding system in the Thessalian plains and the expansion of quasi-private properties known as 'çiftliks'. In the early centuries of Ottoman rule, as we have seen, the state strictly defined and carefully controlled the obligations, rights and privileges of both fief holders and tenants. Fief holders had no title to their estates but enjoyed the revenues in return for military service. The tenants were obliged to pay tithes to the spahis, taxes to the state and to render certain customary dues, but they could not be evicted and had hereditary use of their lands. From the late sixteenth century onwards, however, many spahis began to transform their estates into heritable holdings and to ignore the legal limitations which the state set on the tenants' obligations in order to increase their revenues. On occasion, and in return for a suitable payment, the state itself was willing to legalize the right of heredity to a timar, or to dispossess the spahis and convert their timars into civil holdings. Furthermore, local officials (ayans) from the towns began to acquire properties of peasants unable to pay their taxes, and to convert fiefs into private estates. In the early nineteenth century, for example, the ayans of Larissa possessed most of the farmland in the plains surrounding the city. The janissaries, who had begun to supplement their incomes by industrial and com-mercial activities and were therefore badly hit by the decline in the size of the urban market after 1600, also began to turn their attention to the land. Together with other outsiders, they took ad-vantage of the disorder and brigandage which had become preva-lent in the province by offering 'protection' to the peasants in return for a proportion of their crops. In this way, many tenants were forced to acknowledge two landlords. Sometimes loans were extended to farmers against future harvests and when they were unable to make the necessary repayments their properties were confiscated by their creditors.[31] In these various ways, çiftliks spread through most parts of the plains during the seventeenth and eighteenth centuries, and in the early nineteenth century the area under this type of landholding system was further extended when Ali Pasha of Janina, who ruled much of Thessaly between 1784 and 1822, gained control of many free villages in the northern part of the province and transformed them into çiftliks.[32] It has been estimated that in the second half of the nineteenth century 460 villages out of 658 in Thessaly formed estates (çiftliks) owned by landlords.[33]

As land became concentrated in the hands of landowners who held their estates as personal and hereditary possessions, so the position of the peasants deteriorated. The new landowning class no longer fulfilled military obligations to the state and were more concerned with their own personal enrichment and prosperity. Peasants on the çiftlik estates lost their hereditary right to culti-vate the land and were reduced to the level of sharecroppers who could be evicted if they refused to accept the landowners tenancy terms. In general, though there was considerable variation within the province, these arrangements took two forms. In the lower plain, the landowner provided the seed and paid half the taxes in return for one half of the harvest. In the upper plain the tenants provided their own seed and paid all the taxes giving up only one third of the harvest to the landowner. In addition to increases in rent, the tenants were also expected to perform field, transport and other labour services for the landowner. The demands of the state tax collectors and estate managers merely accentuated the onerous nature of the new landholdings system and many tenants retained only one third of the harvest. They were therefore forced to borrow from the landowner at high rates of interest in order to survive and until the debt was paid in full, the tenants were bound to the estate. Indeed, they were often transferred, together with the land, buildings and implements, when an estate was sold. In order to keep tenants on the land and to protect their estate, bands of armed irregulars (kirjalis) were employed by the new land-lords.[34] Nevertheless, peasants did escape from villages in the plains, and Leake observed[35] at the beginning of the nineteenth century that some landowners near Larissa had been forced to bring Turkish peasants from Anatolia to cultivate their estates.[36]

These changes in the land tenure system were accompanied by the introduction of a new type of rural settlement—the estate or çiftlik village—together with significant changes in the number, size and form of existing villages. The çiftlik village was an architectural and social complex distinguished by a large central square surrounded by lines of small cottages built of mud-brick and roofed with thatch, occupied by Christian sharecroppers. The houses along each side of the square were joined together so that their outer walls offered a measure of protection for the inhabitants against attack. Inside the square was the 'konak' or manor house of the landowner (Fig. 3), a square stone tower some three storeys high with a stone staircase leading to a door in the second floor.[37] The manor house was often surrounded by a stone wall enclosure with a tower and observation post at each corner. It served as an occasional residence for the landowner and his agent, the estate office, and often the garrison for a detachment of kirjalis.

Both Braudel[38] and Barkan are convinced that the çiftlik villages

FIG. 3. Remains of a Konak tower at Anavra.

were new creations, colonization villages founded after the sixteenth century. For the Serbian geographer Cvijić[39] however, they
represented settlements dating back to the Middle Ages. In
Thessaly it seems probable that in some cases these villages were
new foundations, true colonization villages established in order to
open up new lands in the plain for cultivation. Others may have
represented a regrouping of the Greek population or the replan-
ning of existing villages by landlords anxious to exercise greater
control over their tenants and to ensure the cultivation of their
estates. Many villages on çiftlik estates, however, did not have
this distinctive, regular form, though some were dominated by

konaks, and these towers were clearly one of the most characteristic features of the rural landscapes of the Thessalian plains
during this period. It is interesting to note that when the free
village of Boliana to the north of Elasson became a çiftlik of Ali
Pasha in the late eighteenth century, the only change in the form
of the village was the addition of a konak to house a detachment
of Albanian guards.[40] This practice may have been repeated elsewhere in the province.

The oppressiveness of the new landholding system and the
disorder and brigandage which characterized the later period of
Ottoman rule led to a new phase of rural depopulation in the plains
and the disappearance of some villages. The scale of this movement
has sometimes been exaggerated, but it appears to have reached
its peak during the second half of the eighteenth century and the
early nineteenth century.[41] Some peasants were attracted to the
towns and to centres of craft industries—Larissa, Volos, Tirnavos,
and Ambelakia. Many moved to other parts of the province or to
neighbouring provinces in search of more favourable tenancy
terms. Other migrants abandoned their plots to join the growing
number of outlaws in the mountains and forests. The persistence
of the plague and other endemic diseases such as malaria long after
they had disappeared from most of Western Europe, and the
devastation which accompanied the Russo-Turkish War (1768–
1774) and the War of Greek Independence (1821–32) also contributed to the depopulation of the plains. The Turkish population,
in particular, declined dramatically during this period. Many
Turkish villages disappeared completely and only the ruins of the
mosque and cemeteries remained to mark the site.[42] A number of
Greek villages were also abandoned, and while some were later reoccupied, others remained deserted. In the vilayeti of Velestinon,
for example, which had once contained seventy-two villages, only
twelve were still occupied by the beginning of the nineteenth
century.[43] Other villages declined in size and European travellers
provide many descriptions of once prosperous villages which had
declined to poor hamlets. Selos, for example, some 8 km north of
Elasson, had been a thriving village containing eighty houses, five
churches and two well-built stone bridges, but when Heuzey[44]
passed through it in the middle of the nineteenth century only
fifteen poor cottages were inhabited.

Unfortunately, although the rural settlement pattern of the plains was clearly restructured during this period it is difficult at present to establish a complete picture of the final pattern which emerged or to isolate and evaluate all the processes involved in the changes. Nevertheless, the evidence available illustrates that variations in the size and form of settlements—though reflecting differences in the size and extent of holdings and the nature of the terrain—were also closely related to spatial variations in the degree of security, the regulatory powers of the landlord and the nature of the tenancy terms.

One of the factors which explains the collapse of the land-holding system based on timars and the expansion of çiftlik estates was the impact of economic changes in Western and Central Europe. The expansion of towns, population and industry in the West during the eighteenth century resulted in a growing demand for the agricultural products of the Balkans and a rapid rise in the price of these goods. These demands provided a powerful incentive for landlords to seek complete control over their estates in order to exploit their tenants to the full and take maximum advantage of the new and lucrative markets in the West. Thus, although the peasants became increasingly impoverished, the eighteenth century was a period of unprecedented prosperity for the land-owning and commercial classes. Equally important, the growth of the urban population in the West and the rise of cotton manu-facturing stimulated the spread of two new 'colonial' crops—maize and cotton.[45] Both crops, together with another new crop, tobacco, were introduced on çiftlik estates in the second half of the eighteenth century, and their cultivation soon spread to all parts of the plains. Cotton in particular became the most important product of Thessaly. In the late eighteenth century, half of the province's cotton production was exported to Austria, Hungary and the German states and cotton accounted for two-thirds of the value of Austrian and German imports from Thessaly during this period. Forty per cent of grain production, half the tobacco production and considerable quantities of silk and wool were also exported to Western and Central Europe.[46]

The introduction of new crops was accompanied by changes in the system of farming in the plains. Before this period, extensive grain cultivation, wheat together with barley, formed the basis of the rural economy in the plains where half the cultivated area was under fallow each year. Areas of more intensive farming were limited to small irrigated gardens around the towns producing vegetables and fruits for the urban market, and to the edges of the plains and the foothills of the mountains where vines and tree crops (especially the olive and mulberry) created their own distinctive pattern of landuse. The new crops led to an intensification of agriculture with the extension of the irrigated area and also encouraged the reclamation of new land in low lying parts of the plains.[47] The traditional grain crops, however, remained important, and the fallow continued to be used by the villagers for their herds of cattle, sheep and goats, and in winter by pastoral folk from the Pindus mountains who often rented the stubbles from landowners and also grazed their animals on the extensive areas of permanent pasture in the plains. Close ties existed between the peoples of the mountains and the plains. During the winter months the villages and hamlets of the eastern Pindus, especially those of the Vlachs, were almost deserted as their inhabitants migrated with their herds to the lowlands, where each mountain village possessed long established rights of pasture in particular parts of the plain and where they could also purchase grain.[48]

It was men from these mountain communities, and others from neighbouring Epirus and Macedonia, who came to control much of the overland carrying trade with Western and Central Europe, as well as the commerce of the Balkan interior during the period of relative peace inaugurated by the Treaty of Karlowitz (1699). At this time, foreign traders knew little of the geography, economy and peoples of the Balkans or the local languages, so that, when trade with the West began to expand, much of it came under the control of a native Balkan merchant class. The lack of employment opportunities in the villages of the Pindus, the migratory habits of the men, their knowledge of difficult routes and their freedom from seignorial control persuaded many Vlachs and Greeks to become first carriers and muleteers, later commission agents and forwarders and finally independent merchants. By the second half of the eighteenth century Balkan wool and cotton was exported overland to Austria and the German states almost exclusively by these commercial groups who also transported goods imported from the West—processed colonial products, principally sugar

and coffee, and manufactures, glass, hardware and later textiles—
from the ports to chains of fairs in the Balkan interior. They became the chief and only suppliers of Russian furs to the Ottoman
provinces. Until the overland trade began to decline in the early
nineteenth century, the carriers, forwarding agents and merchants
from the Pindus prospered, and some became extremely wealthy.
In their mountain villages many built new and substantial houses
of stone and timber to replace the poor huts and tents of earlier
periods. They constructed richly decorated churches, founded
schools and contributed much to the intellectual advancement of
their fellow countrymen and to the development of Greek national
consciousness. The most wretched villages in the province were no
longer those in the mountains but the servile villages of the plains.[49]

The expansion of trade and the growing commercial contacts
with Western and Central Europe stimulated the demand for
handicraft products. Industrial output rose sharply during the
course of the eighteenth century, and Thessaly became the 'most
industrialized area in all Greece'.[50] As in the empire as a whole,
cotton and silk represented the major branches of industry and by
the end of the eighteenth century large quantities of red cotton
yarn, silk thread, cotton and silk cloth, towels, shawls, handkerchiefs and silk and woollen hoods (capotes) were being produced. Some finished textile goods were exported to the West,
but the major export was red cotton yarn[51] illustrating once again
the essentially colonial relationship between the province and the
economically more advanced nations of Europe.

The new textile factories in Austria and the German states
created a growing demand for red cotton yarn from Thessaly where
the main producing centres included Baba, Rapsani, Tzaritzena,
Tirnavos, Larissa, Farsala and the villages of Mount Ossa and
Pelion of which the most famous was that of Ambelakia. Situated
on the western slopes of Mount Ossa overlooking the Vale of
Tempe, Ambelakia, once a poor and insignificant hamlet acquired
by its activity the prosperous appearance of 'a borough of Holland'
during the second half of the eighteenth century.[52] In 1783 the
population numbered less than 1,500 but rose to 4,000 in 1798
and 6,000 in 1803. Cotton yarn was obtained from all the neighbouring parts of Thessaly and a part of the spinning was also
carried out by hand by the women and children of the village. The

rizari or madder, which formed the chief ingredient of the red dye, was imported from Anatolia where it grew wild, and was crushed in mills turned by horses. There were 24 factories where yarn was dyed, the value of the thread being more than doubled by this process. Some thread was also dyed blue for the local weaving industry. Each year, 2,500 bales of red cotton yarn were exported to Austria and the German states where the textile factories of Buda, Vienna, Leipzig, Dresden, Anspach and Bayreuth used growing quantities of yarn made in Ambelakia. Each manufacturing association possessed agents, who were all Ambelakiots, or branch establishments in all these towns. In 1778 the manufacturers of Ambelakia formed a single joint stock company in which every labourer had a share in order to reduce competition and to increase profits.[53]

Production of red cotton yarn was also important at Tirnavos during the eighteenth century, and much of the output from the dyeing factories was sold to Ambelakia. In addition there were 40 dyers producing several different colours of cotton yarn. Some cotton spinning was carried out in the town but all the yarn that was dyed for export and a third of that used by local weavers came from the surrounding villages. But the town was particularly famous for its weaving industry. There were 2,500 cotton weavers and 100 silk weavers, all working in their own homes and producing cotton cloth, cloth made of a mixture of silk and cotton called bukhasia and aladja, towels in the Turkish and Greek fashion interwoven with gold threads, and shawls for the head and waist.[54] At the height of its prosperity in the second half of the eighteenth century, the population may have reached some 20,000 inhabitants.[55] Cotton and silk cloth was also produced in the towns of Rapsani and Tzaritzena, and weaving was more important there than the manufacture of cotton yarn.

The major silk producing centres in Thessaly were the villages of Mount Pelion. In the late eighteenth century, the twenty-four villages of this region produced 25,000 okes of silk each year, about half of which was sent to the weavers of Tirnavos, and to the prosperous textile industry of Chios. Some silk thread was exported overland to the German states and by sea to Venice. The remainder was used locally for the manufacture of handkerchiefs, and silk hoods. Woollen hoods were also made by the villagers and exported through Salonica and Volos to all parts of the eastern Mediterranean.[56]

The reasons for the expansion of manufacturing activity in the villages of Mount Ossa and Pelion and in secondary urban centres such as Tirnavos and Tzaritzena rather than in the major towns, appear to be twofold. Both Tirnavos and Tzaritzena enjoyed judicial and administrative autonomy granted to them at the time of the Turkish conquest, while the villages of Mount Ossa and Pelion were free from seignorial control and enjoyed a degree of security as a result of their geographical isolation and the difficulties of access and communications. Their inhabitants also appear to have possessed initiative and entrepreneurial drive which enabled them to take full advantage of their liberties— though it is possible that the initial stimulus to development came from entrepreneurs from the major urban centres. During the course of the eighteenth century, all these communities were left alone by both bandits and government, and their industries flourished because they were left alone.[57]

Unfortunately, during the nineteenth century their industries also declined because they were left alone, because the Ottoman government failed to encourage them and to protect them against foreign manufacturers. In Britain, and later in other European countries, the industrial revolution created factories where, by the application of machinery and the division of labour, cheaper more uniform and regular goods could be produced. Already in the early nineteenth century, manufacturers in Thessaly had begun to feel the effects of the preference given to English cotton yarn in German markets, and as an ever larger number of European nations became producers and exporters of textiles, imported yarn and finished textile products gradually supplanted home manufactures in the Ottoman provinces. With the emergence of capitalism in the West, the decline of the handicraft industries in Thessaly, as in other Ottoman provinces, became inevitable.[58] The extension of capitulatory rights—special political and economic privileges which established import duties of 3 per cent until 1838 and 5 per cent between 1836 and 1862—did not permit the Ottoman government to protect domestic textile manufacturers from their European competitors or to introduce new industrial methods and techniques, and therefore only served to accelerate the decline.

There are many examples of the effects of this decline. When Urquhart visited Ambelakia in 1833, the export of cotton yarn had stopped, its industries had disappeared and for ten years the village had been deserted. Only the attractive mansions of the wealthier inhabitants, built in the Turkish manner but decorated in the style of Vienna, remained as evidence of its past prosperity (Fig. 4). In Tirnavos, there were only three dye factories in operation by the middle of the nineteenth century and the number of weavers working in the town had fallen dramatically. A cholera epidemic in 1813 greatly reduced the urban population and with the decline of manufacturing industry, many inhabitants were forced to seek employment in agriculture.[59]

Fig. 4. Mansion at Ambelakia.

The expansion of handicraft industries brought into being a number of settlements that were neither villages in the sense of being nucleated settlements of agricultural populations nor towns serving the surrounding countryside and which cut across the traditional, if somewhat ill-defined, division between urban and

rural settlements. The main urban centres in the province, however, remained unaffected by the economic impact of the West,
though the second half of the Ottoman occupation saw significant
changes in their internal characteristics and in the composition of
the urban population. The towns became less Jewish, less Armenian and less Turkish. Of particular importance was the sharp
decline in the Turkish population of several towns in Thessaly
between 1600 and 1800. Stoianovich (1960) has suggested that
the long and destructive wars between Turkey and her neighbours
during the seventeenth and early eighteenth centuries resulted in
heavy losses of manpower from the Turkish communities in many
Balkan towns, which became the major source of recruits for the
Ottoman armies after the end of the sixteenth century. The plague,
he points out, spread easily through the lowland towns and the
Turks, who formed a high proportion of the total urban population, became the chief victims. The practice of polygamy, he maintains, of abortion and other forms of birth control, and the spread
of venereal disease also contributed to the decline. However, it is
important to remember that the towns required a constant supply
of migrants from the countryside to maintain their population, but
most of them could not draw on an adequate reserve of Turkish
migrants from the surrounding rural areas which were inhabited
largely by Christian Greeks and Vlachs. The decline of the Turkish
population was therefore in some ways inevitable. In addition,
when much of Thessaly came under the control of Ali Pasha of
Janina there is evidence that a number of Turkish families, fearing
injustice and oppression at the hands of their new ruler, migrated
to towns outside his control (Leake, 1835).

But whatever the cause or causes of the decline, the effects are
clear. The Ottoman practice of restricting each religious community to particular quarters (mahallas) had to be modified, and Greeks
and Vlachs from the surrounding countryside, and in the late
eighteenth and early nineteenth centuries a growing number of
Albanians, settled in the Turkish quarters where the population
had diminished. When Leake (1835) visited the province at the
beginning of the nineteenth century he found that in Trikkala, for
example, many of the Turkish houses were in ruins or empty, and
some were let to Greeks. In others, only the rooms forming the
harem were occupied by Turks and the rest were let to Vlachs

from the Pindus mountains who came down to the plain with their flocks in order to escape the harsh winter climate or to obtain employment as artisans and labourers.

The architecture of the Muslim and non-Muslim quarters, however, was very similar so that the towns retained their distinctively Ottoman character in spite of changes in the communal structure of the urban population. Nevertheless, some changes did take place in the townscape of Thessaly during the second half of the Turkish occupation. The early houses in the towns had been little better than those in the neighbouring villages, consisting of single storey cottages built of mud-brick, and as late as the beginning of the nineteenth century many houses in Trikkala were still of this type, but beginning in the seventeenth century, large houses of two and sometimes three storeys made their appearance and spread rapidly in the eighteenth and nineteenth centuries—an expression no doubt, of the increased wealth of the urban land-owning classes as a result of the growing demand from the West for the agricultural products of the region. These houses were timber framed, the interstices filled with either wattle and daub or sundried bricks and then plastered over and painted with colour washes; the tiled roofs were only slightly inclined with wide eaves to give added shade. They had projecting upper storeys (Fig. 5) to ensure that the upper rooms were a reasonably rectangular shape and to increase the floor area where land was valuable or the site irregular. The projecting rooms with their tall windows set in rows, also caught the sunlight and breezes and enabled the women-folk to look out unobserved over the activities in the street below, 'they were the open eyes of the house and its link with the world around'.[60] Until the nineteenth century, because of the high cost of imported glass, the windows were simply open grilled casements with wooden shutters to protect them from the wind and rain. Of course, urban house types varied considerably in detail, but because of standardization of many architectural elements, e.g. timber lengths, they all exhibited a certain uniformity of style. These frail timber-framed houses had a relatively short life, and were often destroyed by fire. Yet only official buildings e.g. mosques (Fig. 6) and public baths, were constructed of stone or brick. In part, this reflected the Muslim's respect only for the permanence of God, which created a tradition of building anew

FIG. 5. Turkish house at Trikkala.

rather than of maintenance; it also resulted from the high cost of stone and brick, and the shortage of skilled stonemasons and bricklayers.[61]

Most houses overlooked narrow winding streets, some paved with cobble-stones, the rest unpaved, becoming muddy in winter and dusty in summer. There was little wheeled traffic and goods were generally brought into the town by mule. Other houses, often those belonging to the wealthiest families, were set in gardens which sometimes extended into the surrounding plain. In fact, most Ottoman towns were open and defenceless, unlike those of Western Europe where the citizens sheltered behind the walls for protection. Though they often appeared formless and unplanned,

FIG. 6. Mosque at Trikkala.

'there was a clear concept underlying the organization of an Ottoman town. . . the concept of the administrative, commercial, and
religious centre and the residential neighbourhoods spread
round'[62]

These functions remained unchanged during the second half of
the Turkish occupation. During the first centuries of their rule,
the Turks had created a series of military and administrative
centres, and administration continued to be the prime urban function. The towns were also important religious centres, and the role
of Islam—an essentially city-based religion—in the urbanization
process in Ottoman provinces should not be underestimated. In

contrast, the economic and commercial functions of the towns were limited. They offered a relatively small range of commercial services to the inhabitants of the surrounding countryside and only in a limited sense can they be regarded as 'central places'. The villagers sometimes brought their corn to mills in the nearby town; they sold vegetables to the weekly market there; and they visited the bazaar to buy goods produced by urban craftsmen. However, the importance of the numerous fairs in the province during this period illustrates that the manufacturing and exchange functions of the towns were poorly developed and inadequate. Far from serving the rural areas around, the towns were economically parasitic, and, as the home of the landowning class, much of the wealth from agriculture was concentrated there. Each town, furthermore, served only the surrounding area and because of the poor communications there was little or no differentiation in the services which each town offered, and little or no economic competition and interaction between different centres. A true urban system did not emerge until long after the end of Ottoman rule.

Conclusion

The state of Ottoman studies remains somewhat fragmented, with little interaction between the efforts of a limited number of research workers. A much clearer picture, however, of the economic and social changes which occurred during the Turkish occupation of the Balkan provinces and of the processes which brought about these changes is beginning to emerge. During the early Ottoman period in Thessaly, when the state exerted a high degree of control over the provinces, we know more about the processes operating than about their economic and social consequences. In the future, the publication of a full scale study of the Ottoman fiscal surveys by O. L. Barkan will greatly facilitate the use of this valuable source, and should provide much more detailed information about and spatial aspects of the economic and social changes which followed the Turkish conquest. In particular, further research is needed into the scale and duration of migrations from the plains; the impact of Ottoman urbanization policies on the internal characteristics of the towns; the effect of the numerous economic regulations on patterns of land-use, and the causes of rapid population growth during the sixteenth century and the economic and social consequences of this growth. For the later period when the political and economic initiative moves from the Ottoman state to the countries of North and North-west Europe, rich and varied documentary sources, principally from the West, provide a wealth of detailed information though sometimes difficult to interpret— about the profound changes which transformed the economic and social life of the province. But an analysis of the complex processes which brought about these changes has only just begun. Stoianovich's admirable researches, however, have created a valuable framework for further work necessitating the patient and careful collation of often fragmentary evidence. It is hoped that future work will provide a deeper understanding of the processes behind changes in the settlement pattern after the end of the sixteenth century; some indication of the spatial pattern of landuse on çiftlik estates; and finally more information about the level of urbanization in the province and about the factors influencing the size of urban centres. Paradoxically, at a time when the visual imprint of the Ottoman occupation is fast disappearing from the Balkan landscapes, especially in Greece, research into the Ottoman impact on the economic and social life of the region is becoming more organized, more interesting and more rewarding.

Acknowledgements

I am indebted to Michael P. Drury (Lecturer in Geography) and David J. Bennison (Research Student in Geography) of the University of Durham, for their helpful suggestions and corrections.

14. Notes

1. P. Coles, *The Ottoman Impact on Europe*, Thames and Hudson, London (1967).
2. S. J. Shaw, 'The Ottoman view of the Balkans' in *The Balkans in Transition*, ed. by C. and B. Jelavich, University of California Press, Berkeley and Los Angeles (1963), pp. 56–80.
3. One notable exception was the existence of a Serbian orthodox hierarchy with its centre at Peč.

4. C. A. Frazee, *The Orthodox Church and Independent Greece 1821–1852*, Cambridge University Press, Cambridge (1969).

5. L. S. Stavrianos, *The Balkans Since 1453*, Holt, Rinehart and Winston, New York (1961).

6. The English military adviser, Leake (1835), commented on the occasional severity of the winters in the Thessalian plains. He records that during 1779 and 1799 many Vlach shepherds from the Pindus mountains lost all their sheep as a result of a particularly harsh winter in the upper plain.

7. Michel Sivignon, *La Thessalie: analyse d'une province grecque*, Lyon, Institut des Etudes Rhodaniennes des Universités de Lyon, Mémoires et Documents 17 (1975).

8. A. Bon, *Le Péloponnèse Byzantin jusqu' en 1204*, Paris (1951).

9. D. Nicol, *Meteora—the Rock Monasteries of Thessaly*, London (1963).

10. O. L. Barkan, 'Les déportations comme méthode de peuplement et de colonisation dans l'Empire ottoman', *Revue de la faculté des sciences économiques de l'Université d'Istanbul*, 11 (1949/50), 67–131.

11. H. Antoniadis-Bibicou, 'Villages désertés en Grèce, Un bilan provisoire', in *Villages désertés et histoire économique XIe–XVIIIe siècle*, ed. by F. Braudel, Sevpen, Paris (1965), p. 343–417;
J. Cvijić, *La peninsule balkanique: géographie humaine*, Paris (1918);
A. E. Vacalopoulos, 'La retraite des populations grecques vers les régions éloignees et montagneuses pendant la domination turque', *Balkan Studies*, 4 (1963), 265–76.

12. H. Inalçik, 'Ottoman methods of conquest', *Studia Islamica*, 2 (1954), 103–30.

13. M. Franco, *Essai sur l'histoire des Israelites de l'empire Ottoman depuis les origines jusqu' à nos jours*, Librairie A. Durlacher, Paris (1897).

14. O. L. Barkan, 'Essai sur les données statistiques des registres de recensement dans l'Empire ottoman aux XVe et XVIe siècles', *Journal of the Economic and Social History of the Orient*, 1 (1958), 9–36.

15. S. J. Shaw, 'The aims and achievements of Ottoman rule in the Balkans', *Slavic Review*, 21 (1962), 617–22.

16. G. Finlay, *A History of Greece*, Vol. 5, Clarendon Press, Oxford (1877).

17. H. Inalçik, op. cit. (1954);
B. Cook, *Population Pressure in Rural Anatolia 1450–1600*, Oxford University Press, London (1972).

18. O. L. Barkan, 'Research on the Ottoman fiscal surveys' in *Studies in the Economic History of the Middle East from the Rise of Islam to the Present Day*, ed. by M. A. Cook, Oxford University Press, London (1970), pp. 163–171.

19. F. Braudel, *La Méditerranée et le monde Mediterranéen à l'époque de Philippe 11*, 2 vols. Librairie Armand Colin, Paris (1966);
O. L. Barkan, op. cit. (1970).

20. T. Stoianovich, 'The conquering Balkan Orthodox merchant', *Journal of Economic History*, 20 (1960), 234–313;
    O. L. Barkan, op. cit. (1970).
21. O. L. Barkan, op. cit. (1970).
22. Ibid.
23. F. Braudel, op. cit.
24. T. Stoianovich, op. cit. (1960).
25. O. L. Barkan, op. cit. (1970).
26. L. Güçer, 'Le commerce intérieur des céréales dans l'Empire ottoman pendant la seconde moitie du XVIème siècle', *Revue de la faculté des sciences économiques de l'université d'Istanbul*, I (1950), 163–88;
    Authorizations were given for certain provincial cities to purchase grain in other provinces, but only if they were suffering from an acute shortage or famine. In the sixteenth century, for example, the state authorized the transport of grain from Thessaly to the city of Tripoli (Syria) and to the province of Tripoli (North Africa) (L. Güçer op. cit.). Permission was sometimes given for exports outside the Empire, particularly to Venice and the North Italian cities, and there is evidence that with or without official permission, grain was exported to Western Europe from Thessaly through the port of Volos during the sixteenth century (F. Braudel op. cit.).
27. O. L. Barkan, 'Quelques observations sur l'organisation économique et sociale des villes ottomanes des XVIe et XVIIe siècles', *Recueils de la Société Jean Bodin*, VII (1955), 289–311.
28. G. Baer, 'Guilds in Middle Eastern history' in *Studies in the Economic History of the Middle East from the Rise of Islam to the Present Day*, ed. by M. A. Cook, Oxford University Press, London (1970), pp. 11–30.
29. S. J. Shaw, *Between Old and New. The Ottoman Empire under Sultan Selim III, 1789–1807*. Harvard University Press, Cambridge, Mass. (1971).
30. L. S. Stavrianos, op. cit.
31. T. Stoianovich, 'Land tenure and related sectors of the Balkan economy', *Journal of Economic History*, 13 (1953), 398–411.
32. L. Heuzey, *Excursion dans la Thessalie Turque en 1858*. Societe d'Edition 'Les Belles-Lettres', Paris (1927).
33. H. Inalçik, 'Land problems in Turkish history', *Muslim World*, 45 (1955), 221–28.
34. T. Stoianovich, 'Factors in the decline of Ottoman society in the Balkans', *Slavic Review*, 21 (1962), 623–632;
    Idem (1953), op. cit.
35. W. M. Leake, *Travels in Northern Greece*, London (1835).
36. A law of 1856, one of several reforms enacted during the period known as the Tanzimat, prohibited the transformation of free villages into ciftliks and also protected the cultivator by regulating relations between landowner and

sharecroppers. In practice, however, the new reforms were not enforced. Heuzey (1927) writes of a landowner at Palama, for example, who had imprisoned a sharecropper for attempting to leave the village.

37. M. Wagstaff, 'The study of Greek rural settlement: a review of the literature', *Erdkunde 23* (1969), 306–317;
    J. Cvijić, op. cit.
38. F. Brandel, op. cit.
39. J. Cvijić, op. cit.
40. L. Heuzey, *Le Mont Olympe et l'Acarnanie.* Librairie de Firmin Didot Frères, Fils et Cie, Paris (1860).
41. H. Antoniadis-Bibicou, op. cit.
42. D. Urquhart, *Turkey and its Resources.* London (1833).
43. W. M. Leake, op. cit.
44. L. Heuzey, op. cit. (1860).
45. T. Stoianovich, and G. C. Haupt, 'Le maïs arrive dans les Balkans'. *Annales, économies, sociétés et civilisations* 17 (1962), 84–93;
    T. Stoianovich, op. cit. (1953).
46. L. A. Felix-Beaujour (1800). *Tableau du commerce de la Grèce formé d'après une année moyenne depuis 1787 jusqu' en 1797.* Paris (1800);
    T. Stoianovich, op. cit. (1960).
47. T. Stoianovich, op. cit. (1962).
48. W. M. Leake, op. cit.
49. T. Stoianovich, op. cit. (1960).
50. L. A. Felix-Beaujour, op. cit.
51. Ibid.
52. D. Urquhart, op. cit.
53. L. A. Felix-Beaujour, op. cit.;
    W. M. Leake, op. cit.;
    F. Boulanger, *Ambelakia*, Paris (1875). Reprinted 1970.
54. L. Heuzey, op. cit. (1927).
55. W. M. Leake, op. cit.
56. D. Urquhart, op. cit.
57. T. Stoianovich, op. cit. (1960).
58. C. Issawi (1966). *The Economic History of the Middle East 1800–1914.* University of Chicago Press, Chicago, London (1966).
59. L. Heuzey, op. cit. (1927).
60. G. Goodwin. *A History of Ottoman architecture*, Thames and Hudson, London (1971).
61. Ibid.
62. Ibid.

15

Aspects of the Development of Capitalism in Yugoslavia The Role of the State in the Formation of a 'Satellite' Economy

JOHN B. ALLCOCK

Introduction

The programme of scholarship of which this paper forms a part is largely concerned with the attempt to understand the historical development of a particular society—Yugoslavia. An enterprise of this sort, however, is not carried on without reference to theory of a more general nature: the investigator brings to the task of research analytical tools of a variety of kinds—ranging from specific hypotheses to broad frames of reference—with the aim of ordering the data of experience. This discussion may be regarded as an account of an encounter with one such set of general assumptions.

The approach which will be examined here is that of Andre Gunder Frank. The discussion which follows does not in any way set out to be a general critique or evaluation of his work, but an assessment of its applicability in a specific historical case. In broad terms I regard his major thesis—that 'underdevelopment' is intimately and necessarily related to 'development' as correct.[1] In

particular it is a considerable advance on that variety of the sociology of development which encapsulates the problem within the
confines of individual, organically conceived 'societies'. His work
is doubly welcome for its attack on varieties of sociology which see
the major solution to the problem of 'underdevelopment' in the
engineering of the correct motivations—especially the correct
'entrepreneurial' motivations—in the countries concerned.[2] In
looking at the economic history of Yugoslavia, however, I have
been impressed by the value of Frank's analysis of the emergence
of satellitic economies around developed 'metropolitan' centres. At
the same time, however, it has become clear that certain key features of economic development/underdevelopment in the Balkans
do not fit easily within Frank's model.

Frank's ideas about the relationship between the developed,
capitalist, 'metropolis' and the underdeveloped 'satellite' were
built upon the basis of four years' research and teaching in Brazil,
Chile and Mexico, from 1962–6: and in that fact lies the clue to
the major difficulty arising in any attempt to generalize his scheme.[3]
The relationship which he documents may provide us with an
adequate interpretation of the economic histories of Brazil and
Chile; but I wish to argue in this paper that he has partly over-
generalized his case. A consideration of the development/under-
development problem in another historical context might well
serve to refine what is at present a rather crude approach to the
problem.

The Latin American societies with respect to which Frank has
formulated his argument have been characterized by a very distinctive historical development, the peculiarities of which can be
briefly highlighted through a brief comparison with the situation
in the Balkans. Both Latin America and the Balkan Peninsula, at
the beginning of the nineteenth century, were divided between
great colonial empires: in the former case the area was partitioned
between Spain and Portugal, and in the latter between the Ottoman
and Habsburg Empires. In spite of this initial similarity, however,
the structure of the Eastern European empires was quite different
from that of the Atlantic ones. The establishment of empire by the
Iberian powers entailed the enserfment and annihilation of largely
aboriginal populations—a feature entirely absent in the Balkans.
The colonies of European settlers which they established in the

New World were supported upon a basis of *latifundia* agriculture, which, although common on the Pannonian Plain, were relatively uncommon in the Balkan Peninsula.[4] The dominant feature of the demography and economy of Southern and Eastern Europe was the smallholding peasant.

In addition to these factors, the institutional structure of both the Ottoman and Habsburg states (and their successors after 1918) differed considerably from those established across the Atlantic— especially with regard to their economic organization. The state came to play an active and direct role in the economic affairs of the Balkans, especially in the inter-war period. In Latin America, on the other hand, the reverse was true, with laissez faire attitudes and policies predominating.[5] Although Frank himself implicitly recognizes these differences[6] he does not pursue their implications for the relationship between capitalist development and under-development. My argument is this : that social structural differences of the kind adumbrated here—*what* precisely it is that is developing/underdeveloping—have crucial significance for our general understanding of these processes.

There is not sufficient space in a paper such as this to elaborate in full a comparative analysis of the development of capitalism in Latin America and in the Balkans. The argument will be confined to one aspect of this problem : attention will be focussed upon the nature and importance of the economic involvement of the state in Yugoslav economic history.

State and Economy in Yugoslavia

Nicholas Spulber remarks that, 'the state has been a prime mover in economic change in eastern Europe'.[7] In many respects this has been substantially true of Yugoslav economic history : but the areas which later came to compose Yugoslavia were only united after the First World War, having been divided since the Middle Ages between the Ottoman and Habsburg spheres of influence. They brought with them into the new union quite different economic and political traditions, which were often very much at variance with one another. It will be useful to first review very briefly the diverse economic and socio-political developments which form the background to South Slav union in 1918.

The South Slavs before the War of 1914–18

The Ottoman Empire was founded on the basis of the amassing of booty: and until the time of its final demise in 1918 it never fully adjusted itself to any other order.[8] Within our present purposes, two main aspects of the Ottoman economy deserve note: the part played by the state in drawing off and consuming surplus produce, and its endeavours to control the economy.

Although all land in the non-Arab part of the Empire was declared, during the sixteenth century, to appertain to the state, in fact the state at this time received relatively little of the direct revenue of the land. Under the Ottoman feudal system the fief-holders were tax-collectors, either in person or by proxy, and they received taxes from their fief in lieu of cash payment. The state's revenues from agriculture were therefore largely limited to the taxes extracted from state-managed lands (miri). In this respect the Ottoman feudal system was never strong enough to sustain the huge apparatus of the slave Household of the Sultan, which was a permanent and substantial drain on the resources of the Empire. This situation was aggravated after the sixteenth century by the exhaustion of opportunities for further military expansion. Under these circumstances land-holding in the Empire underwent a series of radical changes. Firstly the fief-holding spahis attempted to consolidate their own economic security, and that of their descendants, by converting their lands into hereditable property. Secondly, on the death of the fief-holders, the state attempted to make good its revenue deficiency by insisting on its rights to the reversion of the estate, thus increasing its role in the direct extraction of surplus from agriculture.

Whereas the activities of the state in agriculture were thus mainly 'extractive', in industry and commerce this was reinforced by a 'regulative' interest. Although the guilds played a central role in the urban life of the Empire, their functions were strictly subordinated to state control. (For example, they were prevented from taking full advantage of their monopoly position by laws fixing the maximum prices for goods.) The roots of this desire for control, at least in part, seem to have lain in the fact that urban craftsmen and traders were always regarded as at least potentially subversive by the authorities. In many parts of the Empire commerce was very largely in the hands of non-Muslim minorities, especially Jews, Syrian Christians and Armenians. Although Islam has been noted for its religious tolerance, the state saw fit to guard itself continually against possible challenges from this source by such regulations as the prohibition against the free movement of craftsmen.

One aspect of the Ottoman economy which has attracted frequent comment was the Islamic prohibition on usury. It is clear that this was never absolutely enforced, and that, although the majority of usurious activity was carried on by Infidels, not all Muslims considered themselves bound strictly by religious orthodoxy in this matter. However, the embargo was sufficiently strong to operate as an effective barrier to the development of commercial banking and credit in the Empire until the second half of the nineteenth century. The Banque Impériale Ottomane was established in Istanbul in 1863 (an Anglo-French bank, in spite of its name) serving mainly the requirements of the state. Banks serving more general requirements only began to develop after 1890.

Although the involvement of the Ottoman state in the economy of the Empire was persistent and pervasive, it was usually negative and even reactionary in tone. The main concerns of the Porte were always the extraction of revenue and the establishment of control. Much of this pattern was carried over into the Serbian state, in the nineteenth century; and since Serbia was to be one of the dominant components of the new Yugoslav state after 1918, the Ottoman influence was prolonged into the modern period.

After more than two and half centuries of obscurity as an outpost of the Ottoman Empire, the Serbian state emerged again in the first decades of the nineteenth century as an independent social and political entity.[9] In twelve years of guerilla war-fare, following the first uprising in 1804, peasant armies led firstly by Karadjordje Petrović and latterly by Miloš Obrenović succeeded in wresting a considerable degree of autonomy from their Turkish overlords. By 1830 the liberated territory had been recognized by the Sultan as an independent principality, covering 38,000 sq. km with a population of just over 700,000.

The new ruling elite, for all its imitation of Ottoman dress and manners, was not composed of great landed magnates: they were peasants, though rather more wealthy than their fellows. The fire in their bellies was not the romantic Byronesque nationalism which lit neighbouring Greece, but a concern for the establishment of a peaceful political order conducive to the development of their livelihood—the trade in livestock—freed from the depredations of bandits and lawless Turkish janissaries. Initially their campaign had been directed, not at the overthrow of the Ottoman order, but the effective restitution of their rights under that order, including an end to the conversion of holdings by Turkish landlords and owners.

Throughout the nineteenth century the new Serbia expanded its territory southwards from its base on the Danube-Sava, by a combination of military preparedness and diplomatic opportunism. By the outbreak of the Great War in 1914 it extended from Belgrade to the Greek border, giving flesh to the ideal of Serbia as a 'Balkan Piedmont', proclaimed by its more extravagant ideologues. Political growth, however, ran ahead of economic growth. Railway building only began in Serbia in 1884, financed largely by the state with French assistance. Some non-ferrous ores were being mined in eastern Serbia in the last decade of the century.

A tariff war, initiated by the Austrians in 1906 with the intention of reducing the Serbs to economic servitude, failed completely. Indeed, through driving the Serbs to find other markets for their exports (still largely livestock products) their dependence on the Dual Monarchy was eased, and the rudiments of a domestic manufacturing industry began to appear.

A number of important elements of the Ottoman involvement in the economy were perpetuated under the Serbian state. Full constitutional autonomy was not secured in the first uprisings, the final link with the Porte only being severed in 1878. Until that time the Serbian government had to pay a variety of levies and taxes to the Sultan, amounting to 2,300,000 groša annually. Whereas the collection of these dues had been decentralized under the Turkish feudal system, under the new order the state became directly involved in the extraction of surpluses from the peasantry. In this connection, the government continued the Turkish practice of retaining a state monopoly on a number of important goods.

In addition to this, the new masters of the Serbian principality took over the predisposition of their predecessors to try and control commerce and industry. To a large extent, in the early years of independence, the same reasons for seeking control held good. The bulk of commercial activity, especially of an international nature, continued to be in the hands of non-Serbs—in this case a group of wealthy merchants, Orthodox in religion but ethnically distinct, known variously as 'Cincars', 'Greeks' or 'Macedonians'. Such was their strength that the suggestion was repeatedly canvassed throughout the nineteenth century that they should be confined by law to the wholesale trade. A number of decrees were issued attempting to control their activities by, for example, limiting their operations to a certain specified number of 'varoši', or market towns, and by licencing the opening of taverns and coffee houses. (Tavern keepers were usually also usurers; and this side of business also tended to be in non-Serb hands.)

In the field of credit provision a number of state-backed institutions were established in the second half of the century (especially the Uprava fondova, 1862, and the Okružna štedionica, 1871, whose purpose was to counter this growth of private usury. An indication of the importance of the state in the market for credit is given by figures relating to the incidence of public sales for debt in Serbia, in the period 1891–5; just over 75 per cent of such sales were to the account of the state.[9a]

A series of measures dating back to 1860 were instituted providing for a protected minimum homestead for the peasant, which was secure against foreclosure for debt. The stated purpose of these measures was to resist the process of pauperization of the peasant, and the formation of a landless rural proletariat. Similarly, in the case of craft industry, legislation from 1847 onwards was directed at the support of this section of the population, and their protection in the face of competition from imported manufactured goods. In fact, the guilds were only abolished in Serbia in 1910. In both of these cases the interest of the state in inflating the number of its tax-paying citizens was clearly a prominent motivation.

In many respects the economic activity of the state can be seen in this period as directly responsible for the stimulation of some classes of capitalistic enterprise. Government military contracts were a noted source of enrichment; and the disposal of the estates of former Turkish landlords and owners took on the character of a racket.[10] One of the most important methods of accumulation in the later part of the century was the trade in government bonds, which changed hands almost like paper money. From 1867–1906, the state issued twenty-three lots of loan stock; and there rapidly emerged a class of people who were able to make a living entirely from the exchange of government securities.

Manufacturing industry, however, was slow to develop. The census of 1866 provided for no category of industrial workers: by 1890 there were only 800 such workers (excluding miners) in the whole of Serbia. As we have already noted, though, this situation began to change after 1906, and over 400 manufacturing enterprises were established between 1906 and 1914.

By the turn of the century Serbia was developing a small, but coherent domestic bourgeoisie. The non-Serb elements had all but lost their distinctive character. There was little development of a middle class of free professionals, such as lawyers, and doctors, especially outside the larger towns; an industrial proletariat worth the name did not exist; and the small artisan class was too closely allied to the peasantry to constitute an independent force. The ruling economic elite was therefore effectively unchallenged. Particularly important, in our consideration of the emergence of capitalism in Serbia, was the beginnings of a ring of 'satellite' areas on its periphery, in Macedonia, Southern Hungary and parts of Croatia, and most notably Bosnia. By the outbreak of hostilities in 1914 a capitalist economy was becoming clearly formed in the area; but the precise nature of this process is incomprehensible without reference to the role of the state.

In the lands under Habsburg sovereignty, however, we find a strongly contrasted picture. Here, with the noteworthy exception of Bosnia-Hercegovina (to be discussed below) the state played a fairly minimal role in the direction of economic affairs.[11] As Jászi and others have observed, one of the few things which held the Austro-Hungarian Empire together for so long was the penetration of its economic organization by capitalism. The relatively developed industry of Bohemia and Silesia was heavily dependent upon their other areas of the Empire for food, raw materials and markets for their goods. These parts of the Dual Monarchy which were later to be included in Yugoslavia were among those regions which stood in an economically satellitic relationship to the more developed centres. The major role of the state, in these circumstances, was the facilitation of free trade between the various component parts of the Empire, allowing the free flow of raw materials and manufactured goods to develop. This became the mainstay of Habsburg economic policy in the period from 1850 to the outbreak of war in 1914.

The one important area of activity in which the state was positively involved was railway construction and management: though even here the field was shared with private enterprise. In Croatia-Slavonia the state owned and directed 850 km of the 1,914 km of track in operation in 1914, and directed a further 761 km which were under private ownership. A roughly comparable situation prevailed in Slovenia, where 875 km of the total of 1,701 km of track were owned by the state. This involvement was, of course, generally in accord with an emphasis on free trade as an instrument of the economic integration of the Empire; for free trade in principle without the means of commercial exchange in a viable transport system would have been meaningless.

The reluctance of the Habsburg monarchy to play an active role in economic life is vividly indicated by its policy with respect to forestry. Very large areas of the South Slav parts of the Monarchy were wooded (34 per cent of the total area of Croatia-Slavonia in 1895) and huge tracts of this were owned by the state, especially in the parts which had previously composed the Military Frontier, and on the Crown Lands in Slovenia. Commercial exploitation of these resources gradually got under way during the nineteenth century; but the most vigorous development was left to private enterprise—and mainly foreign capital at that. In the early years of the twentieth century, moreover, the state sold-off a number of its enterprises in this sector to private owners, rather than invest the necessary capital in the modernization necessary if they were to succeed in an increasingly competitive industry.

Under these conditions, therefore, the Slav areas of the Empire, became steadily more completely oriented towards the centres of capitalism in Vienna and Budapest. There was very little development of a native bourgeoisie; and that which did develop was dominated by small shopkeepers and (especially in Slovenia), such intellectuals as clerics and teachers. The same development of a colonial economy can be observed in agriculture. Unlike Serbia, the Slav areas of the Habsburg Empire contained many large estates. These were typically owned by Austrian and Magyar nobles, rather than by indigenous Slav aristocrats. Following the reforms of 1848 these large landowners tended to increase their hold upon the peasantry, so that by 1905, about a quarter of the agricultural land in Croatia-Slavonia, was held by a mere 209 owners. In Slovenia centralization was probably even more pronounced. The state held about 27 per cent of all forest lands, and fifty seven large private estates accounted for 92,504 ha of forest. In Carniola forty estate holders alone controlled a quarter of the land.

This process of reducing the Slav lands within the Monarchy to a colonial status encountered an interesting minor counter-current in Slovenia, in the guise of Slovene nationalism. Instead of working directly towards the goal of a Slovene state, which has been the characteristic first priority of European nationalist movements, the main thrust of the movement was directed against economic and cultural 'germanization', in a very 'low level' and every-day sense. In this respect the municipal councils and the 'Landtag' became the battleground of Slovene national identity, rather than the 'Reichstrat' in Vienna. Macartney tells us that:[12]

> The Slovenes now (i.e. 1890) controlled all the rural districts in Carniola, except the German ethnic islet of Gottschee and one other, and even most of the towns, including Laibach itself, where they gained the majority on the Municipal Council in 1882. In 1883, they acquired the majority in the Landtag itself, and in 1887 the German members of that body were reduced to ten representatives of the Great Landlords' Curia. Outside Carniola, the Slovenes were fully holding their own in South Styria, and gaining ground in Gorizia, Istria and even Trieste. Only in Carinthia was the trend still towards Germanization.'

Slovene domination at these lower levels of government was fully used to resist economic colonization. The first public electricity plant was constructed by the city of Ljubljana in 1897; and the provincial assembly of Carniola, at the turn of the century, fully backed plans for rural electrification. In banking, also, the initiative for the foundation of Slovene credit institutions came from within the political parties. For example, the Ljubljanska kreditna banka was founded in 1900 as a result of initiative from within the Liberal Party, led by Ivan Hribar, then mayor of Ljubljana. A major impetus in the development of a cooperative credit system came from the clerical Slovene Peoples Party. The Krajnska deželna banka began operations in 1910 on the basis of a measure enacted by the Carniola Provincial Diet the previous year. So successful were these efforts, that by the outbreak of war in 1914, mortgage and public bond financing in Carniola was entirely in the hands of national financial institutions.

An important exception to the general Habsburg pattern of laissez faire and the minimum direct involvement of the state in the economy is to be found in Bosnia-Hercegovina, which the Austrians occupied in 1878. The pretext for this move was a peasant rebellion in Hercegovina, in 1874, which rapidly spread throughout the province. Fearing that the Serbs, already active in supplying aid to the rebels, and rapidly expanding their economic interests in the area, might use the disturbances as an excuse to occupy it, Vienna took pre-emptive action and moved troops in herself. Although this move was presented as the institution of a 'protectorate' with the aim of restoring order, in 1908 the region was fully and formally annexed.

Here the general economic policy of the Empire was apparently reversed, in that the economic development of the area was totally under the guidance of the state.[13] This course of events does not represent a real change of policy, but is a reflection of the political realities behind occupation. The move was initially vigorously resisted by the Hungarian half of the Monarchy (and by a substantial portion of the German-speaking population too, who doubted the wisdom of adding still larger numbers of Slavs to the population of the Empire). Money for the administration of the occupation was perpetually hard to come by, and the project had to be as nearly self-supporting as possible. State involvement in the economy—especially the extraction of mineral wealth—became a vital source of income to underwrite these costs, since in such a poor area increased taxation had relatively limited prospects.[14]

The occupation had been conducted with Austrian troops, and was effectively an Austrian economic and political preserve; but because of the controversial nature of the enterprise, the administration of Bosnia-Hercegovina remained with the Common Minister of Finance, who became virtually the dictator of the province. All commercial and industrial projects in the province had to be either licenced or initiated through his department. By means of a rather slanted interpretation of the Moslem law on forests of 1868, all forests became state lands. A great deal of work was completed under the occupation in laying down a substructure of transport facilities. The extraction of the immense mineral resources of the area was begun—especially iron ore—and a number of elementary processing plants were constructed.

In order to counter growing Serbian economic penetration, the state also took a direct hand in the setting-up of credit and financial institutions. A chain of savings banks (the Sreska pomočna zaklada) were founded during the early years of occupation. In 1895 Austrian and Hungarian capital participated in the founding of the Privilegovana zemaljska banka za Bosnu i Hercegovinu, which because of its extended branch system soon became one of the leading financial institutions in the region. The state even gave sympathetic support to the growing cooperative credit system. The major exception to this practice seems to have been trade. The new addition to the Empire provided eagerly grasped opportunities for expanding the markets for the products of metropolitan industries. Even so, members of the Austrian civil service appear to have played a role similar to that of the servants of the East India Company, in supplementing their salaries with the proceeds of private commercial enterprise.

At this juncture of the argument it would be useful to review the account of the history of the South Slav lands in the period before the Great War, in the light of the general concepts and relationships developed by Frank.

On the fringes of the declining Ottoman Empire (itself suffering under the impact of the expanding capitalism of the Western European metropolitan areas) there emerged during the nineteenth century a strong Serbian state. Although this area remained one of the most under-developed regions of Europe, it developed a small but coherently organized, politically hegemonic and indigenous bourgeoisie. A key feature of Serbian society in this period was the active involvement of the state in the economy, both in a manner reminiscent of the old Ottoman pattern, and in newer and more 'positive' ways. The Serbian economic 'metropolis' began at this time to gather to itself an economically 'satellitic' periphery, particularly in Macedonia, and in the centres of Serb settlement in Southern Hungary, Croatia-Slavonia and Bosnia.

Those parts of the Habsburg Empire, however, which were destined to become elements of the new Yugoslav state after the war, were emphatically placed in a satellitic and subservient position vis-a-vis the major economic centres of the Empire, although their economies were significantly more developed than that of the Serbian kingdom. Their *per capita* income was higher; their economies were less dependent upon agriculture; they had developed financial institutions of a reasonably sophisticated nature.

The First World War and the Birth of the Yugoslav State

The unification of the South Slavs in a common state at the end of the First World War may be regarded as a major historical surprise.[15] This is particularly the case since the formation of such a state was not part of the aims of Slavs on either side at the outset of hostilities. Within the Austro-Hungarian Empire the 'Yugoslav Idea' mainly implied support for a 'trialist' solution to the problem of the position of Slavs within the Monarchy. (In other words, the Slav population of the Empire should be combined into a third self-governing unit under the Habsburg dynasty, to balance the German-speaking and the Magyar components.) On the other hand, Serbian war aims were quite unmistakable: the Serbs sought the continued expansion of the Serbian state to include all ethnic Serbs within the Balkans. Up until the early part of 1917 these two forces, represented by the Yugoslav Committee and by the Serbian Government in Exile, pursued their policies with almost complete disregard for each other. It does not seem to be an exaggeration to say that they were forced into the common policy initiated by the Declaration of Corfu, in July 1917, by the weight of external circumstances, and the logic of events.

Among the most significant results of the war, however, were the complete dismemberment of both the Habsburg and the Ottoman Empires. From the point of view of the present discussion two very noteworthy considerations follow from these events. Firstly, Austrian chances of becoming a major European capitalist power were finally shattered, and the area began to assume a satellitic character vis-a-vis the more developed centres. Secondly, the Balkan Peninsula as a whole was opened up to the penetration of western European capital—which was a particularly dramatic shift for the ex-Ottoman parts of the region.

In the newly-constituted 'Kingdom of the Serbs, Croats and Slovenes', Serbia rapidly assumed the dominant position. The reasons for this are not difficult to find. Serbia was, in the first place, the only component of the new kingdom to bring with it its own army. Thus Slav units from the forces of the Dual Monarchy, which became integrated into the defence forces of the new state, were placed under the control of the Serbian officer corps. Furthermore, at the conclusion of hostilities, large numbers of administrative personnel who were either Austrians, Magyars or Turks, left their posts with the retreat of their armies from the Balkans. Once again, in many cases Serbs were found to fill the breach, placing them in a highly advantaged position in the civil administration. Serbs were not an absolute majority of the population of the new state, by any means; but they did constitute its largest ethnic group. But the most important factor in establishing Serb hegemony was undoubtedly their strong conscious unity under the Karadjordjević dynasty, and the solidarity of the Serbian bourgeoisie, both of which contrasted with the manifest disunity of the opposition.[16] It was, therefore, not altogether surprising that the constitution which was framed as a basis for the conduct of the affairs of the new state should have been little more than a modified version of the pre-war Serbian constitution.

The process of integration into a unified, centralistic state was fought doggedly by the ex-Habsburg Slavs—most of all by the Croats. Croatian union with the Dual Monarchy had always been a personal union of Crowns—never the full absorption of the Croats into a Magyar state. Persistent attempts by Hungary to whittle away the safeguards of Croatian independence had been constantly resisted in a struggle lasting for three hundred years. We have already discussed the process by which Slovene independence had been gradually enlarged throughout the nineteenth century. It now seemed that all these efforts were to be nullified at a blow, and that the Serbs were to try and undo by decree the work of generations.

The Yugoslav Economy in the Inter-war Years

Just as Serbs succeeded in imposing their own political institutions on the new South Slav state, through the Vidovdan constitution, so the economic policies and practices of Serbia, rather than Austria–Hungary, became the framework within which economic affairs came to be regulated. This process was facilitated by the fact that the northern areas, previously integrated within the Austro–Hungarian economic system, were now cut off from their established markets by state boundaries. In 1919 the natural focus of the transport network of which Slovenia was a part lay in Vienna, and the main communication links of Zagreb were with Budapest: a single railway track linked the ex-Habsburg lands to Belgrade. These regions, therefore, in the immediate post-war period, underwent an ordeal of acute economic dislocation, as they gradually became adjusted to the new political realities.[17]

Under these circumstances we encounter a set of developments which are of central interest to our argument; for in the inter-war years two processes are clearly discernible with respect to the Yugoslav economy. Firstly, the entire Yugoslav economy is drawn into an increasingly satellitic relationship vis-a-vis the metropolitan areas of Europe. Secondly, within Yugoslavia, the development of capitalism becomes heavily centred upon a strong, centralizing state, which comes to play a leading role in all sectors of economic life.

The Character and Importance of Foreign Investment

With the collapse of the old Empires during the Great War, Yugoslavia was opened up to the incursion of European capital to a much greater extent. The first substantial amounts of foreign capital coming into the country after 1918 mainly took the form of government loans. These were raised mainly in the United States and France, and were used largely for currency stabilization, military reconstruction, and the repair and extension of the railway system. By 1931 the Yugoslav Government had accumulated a total foreign long-term debt of 572·9 million U.S. dollars—the equivalent of over forty dollars *per capita*, and a ratio only exceeded among the southern and eastern European countries by Rumania.[18]

Table I

Percentage of Foreign Participation in Share Capital of Corporations in All and in Selected Industries, 1937

Country	Partici-pation in total share capital	Mining	Cement bauxite glass	Electric power	Timber	Metallurgy	Chemicals and oils	Textiles
France	25·00	36·14	48·77	66·91	10·74	22·40	2·28	6·72
Great Britain	17·38	52·42	·16	—	41·20	1·36	23·17	3·46
United States	14·95	0·02	—	17·64	—	0·38	43·82	—
Germany*	11·13	1·13	22·46	0·05	20·04	16·80	5·33	48·43
Italy	9·45	2·30	0·64	—	14·00	—	—	—
Belgium	7·41	6·00	2·64	—	—	—	19·07	—
Switzerland	5·91	1·34	23·56	12·66	11·70	3·14	0·47	13·52
Monaco†	3·25	—	—	—	—	55·84	—	—
Netherlands	2·21	0·57	—	—	1·02	—	3·03	16·74
Sweden	1·30	—	—	2·31	—	—	2·77	—
Hungary	1·30	0·02	1·77	0·43	—	0·04	0·06	—

	Col 1	Col 2	Col 3	Col 4	Col 5	Col 6	Col 7	Col 8
Luxembourg	0·59	0·06	—	—	—	—	—	11·13
Rumania	0·11	—	—	—	—	0·04	—	—
Other	0·01	—	—	1·30	—	—	—	—
	100·00	100·00	100·00	100·00	100·00	100·00	100·00	100·00
Total share capital	D. 7,441·0	D. 877·5	D. 247·7	D. 669·6	D. 327·5	D. 417·4	D. 571·6	D. 296·9
Foreign owned‡	D. 3,282·3	D. 607·5	D. 91·6	D. 555·9	D. 94·5	D. 136·6	D. 399·3	D. 67·4
Percentage	44·1%	69·2%	37·0%	83·0%	28·8%	32·7%	69·9%	22·7%
Total indebtedness	D.11,150·0	D. 736·6	D. 510·3	D. 485·2	D. 1,207·2	D. 918·1	D. 588·0	D. 731·1
Foreign indebtedness	D. 2,832·8	D. 364·0	D. 213·9	D. 408·5	D. 582·5	D. 256·0	D. 308·2	D. 257·0
Percentage	25·4%	49·4%	41·9%	84·2%	43·8%	27·9%	52·4%	35·2%

Source: J. Tomasevich in R. Kerner, (1949), pp. 190–1.

*Germany's share includes the Austrian and the Czechoslovak shares.

†Monaco's share represents the bulk of holdings of the Vienna Kreditanstalt in Yugoslavia before 1931. Chief owners of Monaco's share were actually some British and Belgian banks.

‡Total foreign participation is estimated; participation in various industries as represented in shareholders' meetings.

The authors of a PEP study, *Economic Development in S. E. Europe*, estimated that in 1931–2 the servicing of this external public debt consumed nearly 30 per cent of all Yugoslav exports.[19]

The influx of private capital was stimulated by, and followed on, this securing of state loans, and by the stabilization of the currency. By 1927 it was flooding into the country from such large creditors as France, the U.S.A., Great Britain and Czechoslovakia, but also from Italy, Switzerland, Holland, Belgium—much of it still funnelled in through the big commercial banks of Vienna and Budapest. Statistics of private funds on which great reliance can be placed, are difficult to come by and estimates of the growth of Yugoslav foreign indebtedness vary. A contemporary Yugoslav source suggests that more than 51 per cent of the value of shares declared at shareholders' meetings in Yugoslavia, in 1938, was in foreign ownership.[20] In 1937, France alone owned a quarter of the total foreign share capital in the country, followed by Great Britain, the United States, and then Germany (which by this time effectively included Austrian and Czech holdings also). Statistical information on the nature and extent of foreign participation in the share capital of various industries is given in Table I.

Although domestic savings did follow the lead set by foreign investors, there is no doubt that following the war of 1914–18, the pace and direction of economic development in Yugoslavia were established by outside interests. In fact, so thorough was European economic penetration of the Balkans in general, that Stavrianos has written of the 'new imperialism' which, belying their political independence as nation-stakes, replaced the hegemony of the Turkish and Austro–Hungarian empires in the Balkans.[21]

Foreign investment in Yugoslavia had three main characteristics, which we will now investigate in detail:

the expansion of transport;
the development of extractive industries;
the financing of the state itself.

The Expansion of Transport

The new Yugoslav state, at the end of the war, found itself with a poorly-integrated rail network, consisting of some 5,600 miles of track constructed on three different gauges. Huge areas of the country were without rail transport at all.[22] A plan was prepared in 1920 for the reconstruction of 870 miles of old track, and the opening of nearly 1,900 miles of new line. This impressive plan, which at the time seemed almost impossible in such an impecunious state and over such terrain, was, with the exception of the planned link between Belgrade and Kotor, completed in less than twenty years, largely with the financial backing of foreign capital, and with technical assistance from abroad. In 1925 the line connecting Zagreb with Split was opened, providing a long sought rail link between the Adriatic coast and its hinterland.[23]

By 1937, foreign investors owned 40 per cent of the stock in Yugoslav transport.[24] The development of a modern transport system was the *sine qua non* of further economic development in the area. On the basis of the new railway system, the industrial concerns of Western Europe drew out of Yugoslavia increasing amounts of raw materials to serve the constantly growing needs of their own industry, and to meet the relatively diminishing domestic supplies of these goods. The extraction and rudimentary processing of industrial raw materials, particularly metals, illustrates well this aspect of the development of Yugoslav industry between the wars.

The Development of Extractive Industries

Yugoslavia is relatively poorly endowed with the major materials of industrial activity—coal and iron ore—and in spite of the considerable expansion of the mining of both commodities, the country remained a net importer of them right up to the Second World War. However, Yugoslavia is relatively well-supplied with various non-ferrous ores, particularly with copper, lead and bauxite. The production of these ores was one of the most noteworthy features of Yugoslav industry in the period between the wars. With the exception of the production of hydro-electric power, this was also the sector of the Yugoslav economy in which foreign capital was most heavily engaged. By 1937, very nearly 50 per cent of the share capital of all mining corporations was in foreign hands.

Copper was extracted in Croatia and Bosnia before the war by Austrian interests. However, production on a large scale did not

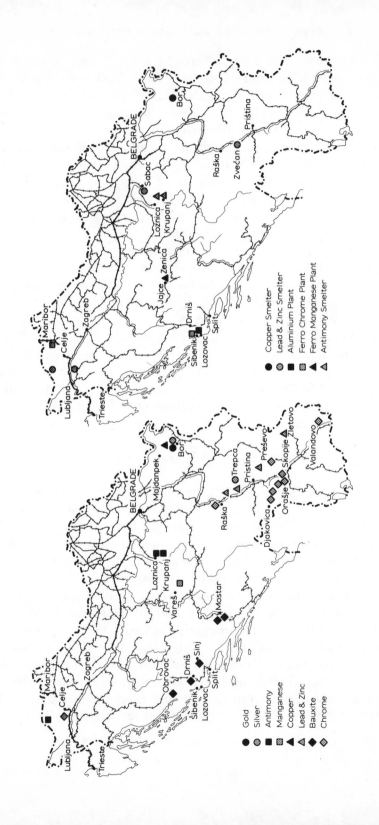

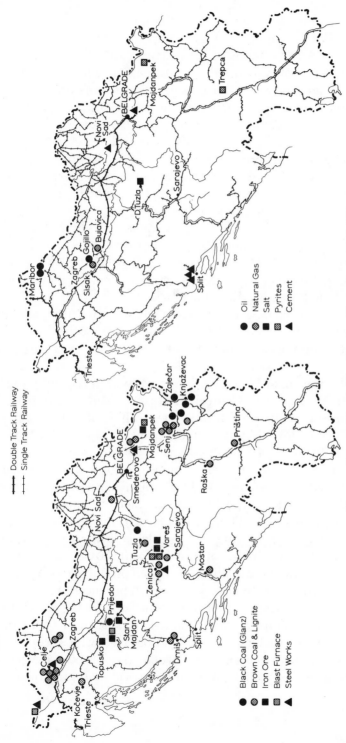

Fig. 1. *Source*: Naval Handbook—Yugoslavia Vol. III.

really begin until 1919, when the French Compagnie Francaise des Mines de Bor began operations at Bor, in eastern Serbia. Production rose from 16,000 tons of ore in 1919 to 493,000 tons in 1930; by the outbreak of war in 1939, output had reached 987,000 tons, and took Yugoslavia into third position in the rank order of copper production in Europe. Virtually the whole of this output was exported, until a refinery was started in 1938, but the manufacture of copper in a refined state remained at a low level.[25]

Not only was the Bor mine the largest in Europe, but also for years it was one of the most profitable mining enterprises in the world. In 1936, its share capital was expanded from F.Fr. 15 millions to F.Fr. 60 millions; and in 1940, this was doubled by the absorption of a part of the huge surplus of F.Fr. 149 millions accumulated by the company. Although dividends fluctuated between 2 per cent (1931) and 7.3 per cent (1936), very few shares ever changed hands, the largest single shareholder remaining the Paris banking house of Mirabaud et Cie.[26]

Lead and zinc have been mined in Yugoslavia for many centuries, particularly in Slovenia and there are large deposits in southern Serbia. The mining and smelting of these metals on a large scale was begun by the Austrians at Mežica, just inside the Yugoslav frontier in Slovenia. These workings were acquired after the war by a British concern, Central European Mines Limited. The smelter had a capacity of 15,000 tons. This enterprise was very quickly overshadowed by the rapid expansion of the Trepča mines, also in the hands of a British company. Production from a single mine at Trepča—the Stari Trg mine—reached 700,000 tons in 1939 (of lead and zinc ores). This single mine produced 80 per cent of Yugoslavia's output of lead and zinc ore, and quantities of silver and pyrites also. The greater part of this output was given only rudimentary processing in Yugoslavia, being exported in the form of concentrates. By the outbreak of war, however, Yugoslavia rivalled Germany as the leading European producer of lead ore, and ranked as third or fourth largest European producer of zinc.

Because exploitation rights were secured from the state at very low cost, and exemption was granted from several types of tax (import duty on machinery, etc.) and because wages were so low in comparison with the rest of Europe, the Trepča concern was able to compete very effectively on the world market. Tomasevich reports that, in 1933, the cost of working lead/zinc ore at Trepča was only 14s.4d. per ton, compared with a cost of 30s. per ton at the Broken Hill Mine—Australia's largest lead producer. 'Trepča was actually the cheapest lead producer in the world. . . . Its output was always sold four or five years in advance'.[27]

These two illustrations, from the production of copper and lead/ zinc, embody the general position of the mining industry in Yugoslavia in the period under consideration. The country rapidly became an important producer of a wide range of non-ferrous ores.[28] The greater part of this output was exported to the more advanced industrial countries, for whom it often provided a key resource. Over 90 per cent of Yugoslavia's lead, and 60 per cent of its zinc went to Belgium. After the war of 1914–18, when Germany sought to replace her former French sources of bauxite, exports of that commodity rose rapidly; and by 1938 Yugoslav production went almost exclusively to Germany, which derived about 40 per cent of her needs from this source.

But, in each case the development of Yugoslav mineral resources was very heavily dependent upon foreign capital, as well as foreign markets. Apart from the examples already cited, British capital (Trepča again) was active in the mining of silver and chrome in Macedonia (Allantini Mines Ltd). German funds became more and more heavily involved as German rearmament got under way. Aside from the bauxite interests already mentioned, the Germans invested huge sums in the extraction of chrome (Jugo-Chrome A.G.) and antimony (Montania A.D.—A German–Swiss venture), becoming the largest purchaser of both these ores by 1938.[29]

The satellite nature of Yugoslav industrial development in relation to the needs of Western European industry is illustrated very well by the fact that, in spite of the development of the extraction and initial processing of many mineral, and particularly metal, ores there never emerged a sizeable manufacturing industry to utilize these products. The output of Yugoslav mines was exported to the more advanced countries, where it was worked up into finished products. In spite of vigorous industrial protection, the Yugoslav manufacturing industries in general remained under-developed, and certainly dependent upon Europe (particularly Germany) for the machinery they needed.

Foreign Capital and the Financing of the State

The third area in which the already developed capitalist countries can be seen to have had a direct influence on the development of the Yugoslav economy is in the financing of the state itself. We have already noted the substantial sums borrowed abroad by the state in the period before 1926, for the purposes of currency stabilization. A further loan of F.Fr. 1,015,000 was negotiated in 1931 for the same purpose.[30] But this very direct form of support is only one of a number of ways in which the state came to depend upon external finance.

Partly because taxation in such an underdeveloped economy was a very inadequate source of funds for the state,[31] the government was often compelled to turn to the foreign money lender. But very little of this money was used to increase the productive capacity of the country, most of it being consumed by the administrative apparatus. Later loans were then used to service the interest on earlier ones, since these had not been productive enough to service themselves. This was a particularly pressing problem in Yugoslavia, since most foreign loans carried very heavy interest and other charges. Usually the nominal rate of interest was between 6 per cent and 9 per cent; but this was rapidly inflated to a burden of between 8 per cent and 12 per cent by low issue price, high commission charges, and so on.[32]

As international credit came to be less and less readily available, during and following the great depression, the governments of the Balkan states were forced to find more and more security for their international borrowing. Yugoslavia, in common with many others, was obliged to mortgage the revenues of the state monopolies to this purpose.

Modifying and accentuating this picture of the importance of foreign participation in the development of capitalism in Yugoslavia between the wars, are two important processes which took on increasing significance with the approach of war. These are, the increasing cartelization of both production and commerce, and the extension of German influence, particularly on trade. These two developments are, of course, closely interconnected, since the development of cartels was in many cases a part of German policy for the control of industry in Yugoslavia. But cartelization was also in large measure a consequence of the high level of industrial protection instituted by the state.

In 1939, there were 80 cartels and similar bodies operating in the country, and registered with the Ministry of Trade and Industry under the decree of 1934. (Numerous 'wild'—i.e. unregistered bodies were also in existence). Although, according to Kukoleča, cartels controlled only 5·76 per cent of existing factories, they accounted for 22·36 per cent of all industrial investments in the country, because cartelized enterprises owned the biggest and most modern plants. Many Yugoslav cartels were merely branches of international ones (especially German) and thereby completely dominated by outside interests.[33]

Table II

Cartels and Their Role in the Yugoslav Economy: 1938

Branch of Industry	Cartelized factories as per cent of total no.	Capital in cartelized industry as per cent of total	Per cent of labour force in cartelized industry	Per cent of motive power in cartelized industry	Per cent of cartelized enterprises predominantly or exclusively foreign owned
Industrial stone and cement	15·00	69·70	40·80	79·70	97·05
Metal production	50·00	47·50	43·86	59·85	17·96
Metal manufacturing	17·57	38·16	21·06	38·16	20·13
Ceramics, bricks and glass	8·67	9·42	8·89	16·67	—
Timber	2·46	0.96	2·51	2·31	15·97
Paper and Printing	10·26	30·02	15·53	42·34	7·95
Chemicals	21·43	52·06	33·58	62·95	67·67
Food	3·56	24·57	25·57	16·93	51·64
Textiles	4·19	8·47	6·89	6·11	81·11

Source: Adapted from S. M. Kukoleča (1939), pp. 221, 222, 226.

A good example of the growth of one such cartel is found in the lead/zinc ore extraction industry. The central place of the British-owned Trepča Mines Ltd. in Yugoslav production has already been noted. This company was acquired in the mid-thirties by the Anglo–American Selection Trust Ltd. In 1939, when the company already controlled 80 per cent of Yugoslav lead production, properties belonging to three other companies were also brought into the organisation—those of Kopaonik Mines Ltd., Novo Brdo Mines Ltd., and Zletovo Mines Ltd.[34] Tomasevich has estimated that between a quarter and a third of the cartels operating in Yugoslavia in 1939 were of an international character:

> Foreign ownership, influence, and control gave the economy of pre-war Yugoslavia a semi-colonial character.[35]

Discussion of the inter-war economic history of Yugoslavia would be incomplete without a consideration of the expansionist policies of Germany, particularly after the depression.[36] While it is possibly an exaggeration to say, with Tomasevich, that 'most of the industrialisation measures in south eastern Europe after 1935 were actually part of the German rearmament plans', the expansion of German economic ties with Yugoslavia during the thirties was clearly a conscious political device to ensure the continuing dependence of her economy on German markets, and, consequently, the continued diplomatic compliance of Belgrade with Nazi territorial ambitions.[37] The French loans of 1931 and 1935, although they had all the earmarks of direct diplomatic subsidisation, were too little and too isolated to reverse this trend. As war drew nearer the Yugoslav government found itself in the increasingly embarrassing position of having its closest economic ties with its fiercest diplomatic rivals.

The chief instrument of German economic penetration was the exploitation of trade agreements. In an era of atrophied world trade, the Balkan countries (which had been particularly hard-hit by the depression, because of their dependence upon agriculture) were eager to grasp the opportunities for favourable trade agreements held out to them by the Germans. The new trade treaty between Germany and Yugoslavia in 1934, exchanged 'most favoured nation' treatment of German exports to Yugoslavia for large import quotas of meat, wheat, corn, livestock, prunes and timber. This was accompanied by special price agreements between PRIZAD (Yugoslavia's Chartered Corporation for the export of agricultural products) and numerous German control boards, which granted prices for Yugoslav products at rates sometimes considerably above the general world level. The resulting large commodity credits to Germany were then used as a lever to secure further favours, and to direct production in Yugoslavia to suit Germany's needs.

Economic sanctions against Italy, in 1935 and 1936, served only to force Yugoslavia further into the German economic orbit— particularly since Italy had been one of the largest importers of Yugoslav soft timber. Attempts by Britain and Czechoslovakia to provide alternative outlets did not succeed in offsetting German trading initiatives.

The reorientation of Yugoslav trade during the thirties is summarized in the following table.

Table III

The Reorientation of Yugoslav Trade, 1933–37 (in 000's of dinars)

Country	Average, 1933–5		1936		1937	
	Exports to	Imports from	Exports to	Imports from	Exports to	Imports from
Italy	731·8	461·5	137·2	101·7	587·1	429·8
France	62·8	153·1	86·2	101·3	393·3	90·8
Great Britain	161·1	328·4	431·7	346·9	464·6	409·1
Germany	606·6	491·5	1039·1	1087·6	1361·3	1694·4

Source: Tomasevich, 1949, p. 209.

Following the Anschluss of Austria in March, and the dismemberment of Czechoslovakia in September of 1938, the position became even more serious. For not only did these moves show to all the small neighbours of Germany that their days were numbered, but both Czech and Austrian financial interests in Yugoslavia fell directly under German control. The fall of Czechoslovakia was particularly damaging, since it also cut off Yugoslavia from the principal source of its armaments, in the Skoda and Brno works, and it excluded the country from its fourth most important market for exports, as well as the supply of some of its raw materials.[38]

Against this background, neither the German ultimatum of March 1941, nor its acceptance by the Cvetković government, can come as a surprise to the historians.

The Role of the State in the Development of Capitalism

From the foregoing discussion it will be evident that, in general terms, Frank's analysis of the incorporation of under-developed areas into satellitic dependence upon developed 'metropolitan' areas in Latin America is substantially reflected in the economic history of Yugoslavia in the inter-war period. However, within the framework of these overarching processes, the most important internal force shaping the development of a capitalistic economy in Yugoslavia was the state. It was the action of public authority in the economy which gave to economic changes in the country during this period their distinctive direction and impetus. The ways in which the state became implicated in the development of capitalism in Yugoslavia are complex; but they may be conveniently summarised under four main headings:

> through its involvement in banking and credit;
> through its fiscal policies;
> through the central importance to industrial development of the military build-up in the Balkans;
> through its direct participation in productive enterprises.[39]

The Involvement of the State in Banking

The end of the war in 1918 saw Yugoslavia with a particularly imperative need for credit in view of the massive destruction caused by hostilities.[40] Not only did the rural population need to restock and rebuild, but industrial and social overhead capital were terribly depleted. The widespread and continued dearth of funds is suggested by the fact that, in the period from 1925–7, loans from domestic banks to industrial users carried interest charges of between 20 per cent and 30 per cent. In this situation the state became vitally important both as a source of credit and as a guarantor of other credit institutions.

Although the banking system of Yugoslavia was, by western

European standards, primitive, as in the majority of the Balkan countries the banks were the primary domestic financial institutions. The PEP survey estimated that even in the advanced areas (Czechoslovakia, Austria and Hungary) only 15–20 per cent of investment took place through the stock exchanges, and in the Balkans this proportion was probably less than 10 per cent.[42] The surface picture of banking in Yugoslavia was of a variety of independent institutions; but in fact the banks were either heavily centralized around the state, or closely linked with foreign enterprises.

The centre-piece of the system was the National Bank (Narodna banka Kraljevine Jugoslavije)—the direct descendant of the Privileged National Bank of Serbia, and established by statute. Officially government holdings of the share capital of the bank (and those of government agencies) were limited to 20 per cent of the total. However, the fifteen largest shareholders (including other banks) were all under some form of government influence, which, together with the fact that some 3 per cent of the shares were held by the bank's own pension fund, gave the state control over an absolute majority of the shares.[43]

Government nominees also provided a majority in the administrative hierarchy of the Chartered Agrarian Bank (Privilegovna agrarna banka). This bank was founded by decree in 1929; and up to 1939 its funds were limited almost entirely to its share capital of 700 million dinars. This was made up from subscriptions from the following sources:

the government	120 million D.
Government controlled agencies	120 million D.
the general public and co-operative societies	460 million D.

The chairman and seven of the fourteen other members of its council were appointed by royal decree, on the recommendation of the government; the remaining seven were elected by the shareholders. State control over the bank's policy was thereby assured.

The main purpose of the bank was to provide both short-term loans and long-term mortgage loans to private agriculture and co-operative societies, for the improvement of their equipment, buildings or live-stock. (Credits were also advanced through PRIZAD, after its foundation in 1930.) The initial aim of the bank was to remedy the acute shortage of rural credit which had afflicted Yugoslavia since even before the war, by making credit available at rather more favourable rates than were current on the open market.

At first sight, the bank's record is impressive. In the first seven years of its operation (1930–36) it lent mortgages to more than 20,000 borrowers, amounting to 572 million dinars, and other credits totalling 370 millions.[43] However, closer inspection reveals a less favourable picture. Firstly, the sums involved were but a drop in the ocean of needs—especially after 1932. Mirković informs us that in 1936 the total indebtedness of agriculture amounted to 6,000 million dinars.[44] Secondly, the regional distribution of loans was nothing if not significant. The following table gives figures showing the distribution by banovine (prefectures) of the 337 million dinars disbursed in 1930.

Table IV

Regional Distribution of Loans (1930) from the Chartered Agrarian Bank

Banovina	per cent	Banovina	Per cent
Dunavska	58·00	Zetska	4·00
Drinska	17·00	Moravska	3·60
Savska	6·40	Vardarska	0·88
Vrbaska	5·10	Dravska	0·02
Primorska	5·00		

Source: Mirković (1952), p. 89.

In other words, more than three-quarters of the loans granted by the bank went to areas with a predominantly Serb population. Finally, as a response to need, the distribution of loans appears to have been far from adequate, in that a heavy proportion of the bank's funds went to the wealthier peasants. In 1930, loans of more than 50,000 dinars were granted to some 1,200 borrowers. The deepening agrarian crisis of the depression years compelled it to restrict its activity considerably, so that in the immediate pre-war period it did little more than maintain the volume of credit outstanding.

The State Mortgage Bank (Državna hipotekarna banka) was

the successor to the old Serbian Uprava fondova, which expanded with the establishment of the Yugoslav state to take in a number of smaller banks and the business of several Austro–Hungarian mortgage banks. It was, apart from the National Bank, probably the most important financial institution in the country—especially in Montenegro and Macedonia, where commercial banking was particularly under-developed. Like the other major banks, it too was closely controlled by the government. In the early years of the existence of the South Slav state it adhered to its main purpose, of granting mortgage loans to individuals, enterprises and public bodies. As public confidence in Yugoslav banking became severely tested during the depression years, however, funds increasingly flowed into the State Mortgage Bank and the Postal Savings Bank (Poštanska Štedionica). The basic reason for this was that these two institutions enjoyed government guarantee and were presumed not to be exposed to freezing.[45] While greatly strengthening these banks, this movement naturally weakened commercial banking in general.

Unfortunately, the funds which they attracted were used during the thirties more and more for the financing of government deficits, and for the needs of the state-owned industrial enterprises. Towards the end of the decade, defence needs became the most important beneficiaries of this policy. After 1939 the State Mortgage Bank became mainly an agency for discounting Treasury Bills, and rediscounting them at the National Bank, thereby helping the government to evade the provisions of the latter's charter.

The Yugoslav government's position of control in the banking system was therefore used principally for political and administrative ends, rather than for progressive economic policies. As a direct consequence of this situation, the majority of both long and short term financing of industry came through the commercial banks. The most developed part of the private banking system was undoubtedly to be found in Ljubljana and Zagreb, where many Croatian and Slovenian banks still carried into the Yugoslav state ties dating back to the old links with Vienna and Budapest. In Zagreb, for example, the General Yugoslav Banking Corporation (Opšte jugoslovensko bankarsko društvo) and the Croat General Credit Bank (Hrvatska seveopća kreditna banka) both had extensive ties with foreign capital—the latter for example was an affiliate of the Hungarian General Credit Bank. Although Slovene banks were generally freer of foreign involvement than others in Yugoslavia, the Ljubljana Credit Institute for Commerce and Industry (Kreditni zavod za trgovino in industrijo) was originally the main Yugoslav branch of the Austrian Kredit-Anstalt Bankverein. When this went bankrupt in 1931, its Yugoslav operations were taken over by Slovene and German interests.[46]

This pattern of banking organisation in Yugoslavia had much more far-reaching consequences than one might expect, since the participation of the banks in industrial development extended much further than merely the lending of money to entrepreneurs. It was widespread practice for banks to either buy up, or secure controlling interests in industrial enterprises, and to participate very directly in their control. Thus an understanding of the structure of banking is necessary to an appreciation of the important mechanisms of state and foreign influence on industry.

Fiscal Problems

The over-riding feature of the fiscal policies of the Yugoslav government between the wars was the establishment of industrial protectionism. Tomasevich has interpreted the growth of protective tariffs as a direct consequence of political independence,[47] but it is by no means certain that this policy can be understood solely in these terms. Certainly the rationale is obscure if one approaches the matter entirely from an economic point of view. The greatest chances for economic development in Yugoslavia—as in the Balkans generally in this period—lay in the expansion of agriculture; and this area of production did grow more rapidly than any other section of the Yugoslav economy in the period under review. In this light the economic motives behind the protection of manufacturing industry, and the implied attempt to compete with the already developed manufacturing industries of the West, are puzzling.

In the event, Yugoslavia developed tariffs which were amongst the highest in Europe. An investigation by the Austrian Chamber of International Commerce, in 1927, reported that Yugoslavia imposed an average tariff of more than 33 per cent over 402 items.[48] These rates were on the increase after 1925, although hand in hand with the general raising of tariff walls went a policy of granting 'most favoured nation' status to those countries with whom Yugoslavia had trade treaties. Even under these conditions, protection was considerable right up to the outbreak of war.

In fact, the purely economic motives behind protectionism were almost certainly secondary to purely political ones: and, in particular, military considerations predominated. The drive towards independence in Yugoslav steel production was certainly motivated by military demands, and was responsible for the high levels of protection of the Bosnian steel industry, and the chemical industry, but, if the initiating impulses of the policy of protectionism were mainly political, there were clearly some important economic consequences following it. The drive to achieve independence was particularly successful in a number of commodities, notably textiles. Ironically, one of the major consequences of the states policy of ensuring its military independence was the deepening of the penetration by foreign interest. High industrial tariffs served to increase the profitability of domestic industry; and, under conditions of extreme scarcity of capital at home, the promise of good profits drew in more foreign investment.

At the same time, protectionism made it more difficult for the agrarian producer; it increased the cost of consumer goods, diverted investment further from farming, and raised the cost of capital investment in the countryside, by making such improvements as farm machinery and fertilizers prohibitively expensive.[49] The majority of small enterprises, both industrial and agrarian, were therefore heavily dependent upon their own resources for financing.

The Military Build-up in the Balkans

All the Balkan countries shared in some measure in the developments which are the subject of this paper; and the military build-up during the inter-war years is no exception to this, although it is arguable that the military situation of Yugoslavia was more difficult than that of most of her neighbours in this period. The Peace of Versailles by no means marked a final settlement of Yugoslavia's matters with its neighbours. At the Paris conference there was hardly a stretch of her international frontiers which was not contested with one or another of the seven bordering states. The problems of reaching a settlement were particularly difficult with respect to Italy, which had set great store by the promises of the Treaty of London of 1915. Negotiations with the Italians dragged on until The Treaty of Rome, in 1924, and even then honour was not felt to be satisfied on all sides. The wider strategic issues also bore heavily upon Yugoslavia. Throughout the twenties and thirties, her fate was dominated by the concern of the Great Powers to erect a 'cordon sanitaire' against bolshevism. Equally as time passed, it became evident that Yugoslavia could not avoid entanglement in German plans for expansion.[50] In the strategic situation of the Balkans at this time, then, a high level of expenditure on preparation for war is not altogether surprising; and Yugoslavia follows a pattern matched by neighbouring governments in this respect.

During the fiscal year 1920–21, the budget for the Ministry of the Army and Navy amounted to nearly 1,121 million dinars.[51] By 1937, this figure had risen to 2,273 millions, or 22 per cent of all government disbursements.[52] For the three years from 1935 to 1937, the Yugoslav government spent approximately 26 per cent of its total budgetary expenditure on defence. Naturally, the full extent of military expenditure was not disclosed in the budget; and the authors of the PEP survey, speaking of the Balkans in general, estimated that 40 per cent might be a more accurate assessment of the size of this item.

Leaving aside for a moment the question of the growth of the military burden on the exchequer, and the issue of whether or not this was justified by the international situation in the Balkans, it is worth placing these figures in the context of other disbursements by the Yugoslav government in this period. During the fiscal year 1930–31, in which the expenditure of the Ministry of the Army and Navy stood at 2,189 million dinars; the Ministry of Health spent only 178 millions, and the Ministry of Agriculture 56 millions.[53] In view of the rapid collapse of Yugoslav resistance in 1941, one can only ask whether this money was well spent?

State Participation in Productive Enterprises

The final aspect of the influence of the state upon economic change in Yugoslavia is its direct participation in production and marketing. This participation took three forms: the operation of state-owned enterprises; the control of monopolies; the provision of government marketing agencies.

The Yugoslav state was either the sole or joint proprietor of a tremendously wide range of industrial enterprises, ranging from the production of opium in Macedonia to the manufacture of aircraft parts. The most important of these activities were the ownership and exploitation of forests, mining and metallurgical concerns, and the railways.

In 1940, the state owned over 37 per cent of the forest area of Yugoslavia.[54] The real weight of the government's involvement in the industry is only realized when one takes into consideration the fact that the proportion of economically usable forest owned by the state (as opposed to merely wooded land) was much higher than this. One single state-owned enterprise in Bosnia—the huge *Šipad* estates—contributed no less than 25 per cent of the country's total softwood exports in the immediate pre-war period.[55]

The mining enterprises at Ljubljana and Vareš, both state-owned, between them produced about 90 per cent of the country's iron ore, until further mines were opened in 1936. The Bosnian steel mills at Zenica were also government property, and several armaments factories were either wholly or partly owned by the state.[56]

Whereas the government's conduct of its forestry interests may be considered as exemplifying the ideal of state control, in setting standards in the technical and organizational development of the industry, which could be followed with benefit by other concerns, its control of the railways appears in nothing like as favourable a light. Clearly, the possession of such a resource gave to the state a very useful instrument for the stimulation and development of the Yugoslav economy. Yet the potential of this kind of participation in the economy, if it was realized, was never utilized. In fact, the reverse was the case, in that concessionary rates were used as incentives to attract foreign industry. The basic freight rate was 1,020 para per 100 kg/100 km for loads of between five and ten thousand kilos. At this rate were transported bauxite, iron, bricks, tiles, coal, copper, petrol. A rate 70 per cent higher was paid for manure and fertilizer, and a rate 250 per cent higher for hay and straw.[57] While large foreign owned industrial firms gained the lowest rates for their goods, the small agricultural producer was heavily penalized. Government ownership of the railways was almost as important as a tool of political patronage, as it was a means of stimulating and facilitating economic development.[58]

Ownership of these various productive enterprises was very important to the state as a source of income.

'The income from the state economy, not including enterprises directed by the state monopolies, amounted in the budgetary period 1926/7–1929/30 to between 28 and 39 per cent of all anticipated budgetary income.'[59]

This point is reinforced by reference to figures for the year 1937–8, in Table V.

Table V

Analysis of the Revenues of the Yugoslav Government: 1937–8

Nature of source of revenue	Thousands of dinars	Per cent of total revenue
Direct taxes	2,962,919	22·5
Indirect taxes	3,165,459	26·6
Monopolies	2,068,245	17·3
State enterprises	3,777,884	31·4
Various	100,311	2·2

Source: *NIDH*, p. 258 (adapted).

The government also participated as a producer in those fields where it had a trading monopoly, owning several sugar mills and all processing facilities for salt and tobacco.

The Yugoslav government's monopolies were very important to its revenues, as the figures quoted in Table V indicate; in that fiscal year more than 17 per cent of its income was secured by this means. A major point to be noted, in connection with these figures, is the regressive nature of government monopolies, which was further exaggerated by the nature of the commodities subject to monopoly control—salt, tobacco, kerosene and matches. These items would form the bulk of the cash purchases of many poorer rural families. This regressive effect is strengthened when we take into consideration the nature of other forms of indirect taxation. In particular, government levies were imposed on sugar and electric light, Seton-Watson's comment, that the effect of government policy was to place a 'tax on production' may not be true as far as tobacco and sugar are concerned, but the taxes on electric power (90 per cent of which was consumed by industry) and on oil products certainly can be regarded in this light.[60]

Finally we turn our attention to the question of the state's direct involvement in the marketing of agricultural produce. The most significant form of involvement here was government intervention in the wheat market. With the onset of the depression a chartered company—PRIZAD—was established, with the principal aims of circumventing the foreign companies who were exporting Yugoslav grain, and reducing the role of the middlemen, thus supporting the incomes of grain producers.[61] The deepening of depression, with the consequent 'reagrarization' of the economies of a number of the major importers of Yugoslav grain, coincided with the bumper harvest of 1931–2. The bottom dropped out of the market for Yugoslav wheat abroad.

The government attempted to meet the crises by changing the status of PRIZAD, establishing it as a monopoly trader in wheat, rye, and wheat and rye flour, in June 1931. Its intentions were to maintain their domestic price at a level above export parity, and then to sell as much grain as possible on the home market, at artificially high prices, using the differential between this price and the purchase price to fund exports. Although established with substantial state credits, the size of the bumper crop completely exhausted both funds and storage facilities; and the result was generally agreed to be an unmitigated disaster. The government can not be held responsible for the unusually large crop that year; but it can be called on to account for the machinery by which its policy was operated. Its biggest defect seems to have been its insistence that grain would only be collected in lots of 50 metric tons or more. Since the great majority of the peasants had nothing like this amount to sell, PRIZAD's policy can be seen to have strengthened the grip of the middlemen on the peasantry, undermining its own first intentions. In following years the export monopoly of wheat was abolished, and PRIZAD concentrated its efforts on meeting export quotas of grain. There is no doubt that for those peasants who did have marketable surpluses of wheat in the 'thirties, this continued intervention was of some benefit.

The importance of the state's participation in the economy in the inter-war period is suggested by the fact that, in 1938, it controlled directly nearly 10 per cent of the value of shares declared at shareholders' meetings. (See Table VI.)

Table VI

The Pattern of Ownership in Yugoslav Enterprises, 1938

Category of ownership	Value of shares declared at shareholders' meetings in 1938. (In dinars)	Per cent of total
Foreign ownership	2,387,029,369	51·52
State ownership	488,315,350	9·67
Financial institutions	452,502,752	9·76
Holding companies	116,761,682	2·51
Other shareholders	1,229,027,744	26·54

Source: Mirković (1952), p. 59.

The classification which Mirković gives us here does not provide a set of mutually exclusive categories. Because of the heavy involvement of the state in banking, to which we have already referred in detail the influence of the state was probably greater than these figures indicate. In fact, it is no exaggeration to say that in the inter-war period the state was the biggest capitalist in Yugoslavia.

Conclusion

We have not examined in this paper the details of the 'development of underdevelopment' in Yugoslav society between the wars, with respect to agriculture and small-scale domestic industry, since we have principally been concerned to lay out in broad strokes the general shape of the relationship between state and economy. On the basis of the foregoing sketch, we are now able to summarize the main elements of this relationship.

The dominant feature of the Yugoslav economy in the inter-war period is the increasing penetration of foreign capital and, after the depression years in particular, the rapid reduction of the country to a position of economic satellite to other developed western European centres—especially Germany. However, the pace and direction of this movement can not be understood without some detailed knowledge of the institutional structure of Yugoslavia, and in particular knowledge of the nature of the state and its role in the economy. The key position of the state in the economy, as we have briefly shown, was a legacy of structures and policies which have deep historical roots in the Ottoman and Habsburg Empires. This became an especially important feature of Yugoslav society because of the success of Serbia in securing a dominant political position within the new South Slav union. From this position of pre-eminence within the economy, the policy of successive Yugoslav governments led a progressive deepening of the penetration of foreign capital, and facilitated the satellization of the Yugoslav economy. Large foreign-nominated enterprises entered the country under the direct sponsorship of the state, supported by tax concessions, favourable freight charges and similar incentives.

One of the most noteworthy consequences of the action of the state is seen in what it prevented, rather than in what it facilitated. We have repeatedly emphasized throughout the foregoing discussion, the enormous capacity of the Yugoslav state to absorb within itself the accumulated surplus of the country's economy. We have not, in the space available here, examined in detail the size and character of the administrative apparatus of the country, but we have noted the repeated tendency to divert funds both into the operation of that edifice, and into the financing of the state's own vast network of economic enterprises. (Corruption too, of course, accounted for a large amount of 'wastage' here.) Under these circumstances, both the accumulation of private and social capital in the country was seriously inhibited. Industry and agriculture remained small in scale, primitive in technology and starved of investment funds. It is no exaggeration to say that, in the case of Yugoslavia, the hinge between development and underdevelopment was the state.

15. Notes

1. It is questionable, however, that development and underdevelopment are related in this way only in capitalist economies. That there may be common

features relating capitalistic forms of development, and the development of satelitic economies in socialist Eastern Europe, is never acknowledged by Frank.

2. A. G. Frank, *The Sociology of Development and the Underdevelopment of Sociology*, Pluto Press (Reprinted from *Catalyst*) (1971).

3. A. G. Frank, *Capitalism and Underdevelopment in Latin America: historical Studies of Chile and Brazil*, Monthly Review Press (1967).

4. Also, in the latter instance, the large estate frequently represented a particular pattern of consumption, rather than a distinctive mode of production.

5. Frank himself intimates this point with respect to Chile: 'The audacity and vision of Montt in the use of the resources and administrative capacity of the state in railroad development can be justly appreciated only by taking into account the deep prejudice which existed against state intervention and which in almost all the rest of the Latin American countries resulted, as an inevitable alternative, in foreign investors taking charge of the task'. (Frank, op. cit. 1967).

6. In his essay on Brazil (Frank, op. cit. 1967) Frank stresses that the analysis of Brazilian economic history in terms of European notions of 'feudalism' is quite inappropriate. He never follows up the implications of this point: namely, that it limits his ability to generalize his argument to those countries which were characterized by this type of socio-economic structure.

7. N. Spulber, *The State and Economic Development in Eastern Europe*, Random House (1966), p. 12. In spite of my general agreement with Spulber on this point, his formulation of the issue is problematic. '(The state) . . . has spurred the process of modernization—it has developed complex administrative services, created developmental banks, encouraged the growth of certain industries (mostly connected with defence). It has further attempted to both deepen and channel processes started by other 'prime movers' of change—e.g. foreign investors and 'non-indigenous' entrepreneurs. Finally, it has sought with widely varying degrees of success, before the advent of the Communist regimes, to accelerate the growth of the private industrial sector by providing protection, subsidies, or tax exemption to private investors, by relying heavily on foreign lending, and by directly expanding its own investment and ownership holdings in the economy.'

In looking at the role of the state in the economy we frequently adopt a very westernized view of the state—in 'executive' terms. Spulber is here presenting as analogues of contemporary 'development policies' the actions of governments which were often by-products of quite different aims. This is a somewhat anachronistic view.

8. This brief discussion of the Ottoman economy has been compiled on the basis of the following sources:

N. Vučo, *Privredna istorija naroda FNRJ*, Belgrade (1948);

H. A. R. Gibb, and H. Bowen, *Islamic Society and the West*, Vol. 1, Parts I and II, Oxford University Press (1950 and 1957);

P. F. Sugar, *The Industrialisation of Bosnia-Hercegovina*; 1878–1918, University of Washington Press (1963);

J. Tomasevich, *Peasant Politics and Economic Change in Yugoslavia*, Stamford University Press (1955);

L. S. Stavrianos, *The Balkans Since 1453*, Holt Rinehart and Winston (1958);

P. Coles, *The Ottoman Impact on Europe*, Thames and Hudson (1968).

9. This brief review of the Serbian economy is based mainly on the following sources:

D. J. Popović, *O Cincarima; Prilozi pitanju postanka našeg gradjanskog društva*, 2nd ed., Belgrade (1937);

C. Kostić, 'Postanak i razvitak "Čaršije", (primer "čaršije" Bajine Bašte)', *Glasnik etnografskog instituta SAN-a* IV–VI (1955–57);

T. Stoianovich, 'The social foundations of Balkan politics 1750–1941', in *The Balkans in Transition*, ed. by C. and B. Jelavich, University of California Press (1963);

T. Stoianovich, 'The conquering Orthodox merchant', *Journal of Economic History*, XX (1960);

N. Vučo, op. cit. (1948);

J. Tomasevich, op. cit. (1955);

T. Stavrianos, op. cit. (1958).

9a. N. Vučo, op. cit., p. 222.

10. N. Vučo, op. cit., p. 213.

11. The major sources consulted in preparing this discussion of the economy of the Habsburg areas are:

O. Jaszi, *The Dissolution of the Hapsburg Monarchy*, University of Chicago Press (1929);

C. A. Macartney, *The Hapsburg Empire*, Weidenfeld and Nicholson (1969);

T. Hočevar, *The Structure of the Slovenian Economy, 1848–1963*, Studia Slovenica (1965);

N. Vučo, op. cit. (1948);

J. Tomasevich, op. cit. (1955);

T. Stavrianos, op. cit. (1958);

T. Stoianovich, op. cit. (1963).

V. Dedijer, 'Nova država u medjunarodnim odnosima', in, *Istorija Jugoslavije* (2nd ed.), ed. by I. Božić, *et al.*, Prosveta, Belgrade (1973).

12. C. A. Macartney, op. cit., p. 645.

13. P. F. Sugar, op. cit.

14. Nevertheless, Vučo informs us (N. Vučo, op. cit. (1948), p. 274) that the total tax receipts for the province grew from 7,747,081 kr. in 1887 to

17,095,000 kr. in 1904. Undoubtedly this was due in part to the greater efficiency of the Austrian fiscal system.

15. This extremely complex set of historical factors has been discussed in: Ivo Lederer, *Yugoslavia at the Paris Peace Conference: A Study in Frontier Making*, Yale University Press (1963).

16. For more detailed information relating to the political circumstances surrounding the founding of the Yugoslav state, see:
'Ustav kraljevine Srba, Hrvata i Slovenaca, od 28 juna 1921', *Službene novine Kr. SHS.*, 142–A, 28 juna 1921, pp. 1–6;
S. K. Pavlovitch, *Yugoslavia*, Benn. (1971);
S. Clissold (ed.), *A Short History of Yugoslavia*, Cambridge University Press (1966);
E. N. Mittleman, *The Nationality Problem in Yugoslavia: A Survey of Developments, 1921–1953* (2nd ed.), Ph. D., New York University (1954).
For a rather hysterical, but nevertheless informative discussion of this topic, written from a Croatian point of view, see, F. Tudjman, 'Hrvatska politika u prvim godinama borbe protiv Vidovdanskog centralističko-hegemonističkog poretka', *Kritika*, no. 14 (1970).

17. See, with reference to this point, T. Hočevar, op. cit. (1965), pp. 121 ff. and 128;
S. Dimitrijević, *Privredni razvitak Jugoslavije od 1918–1941, g.* Belgrade (1962);
L. S. Stavrianos, op. cit. (1958), Chs 21, 31, 32.

18. Figures from, *Political and Economic Planning* (PEP) (1945), p. 108.
Full details of the foreign loans negotiated by the Yugoslav state in the period 1918–36 are given in, Naval Intelligence Division, Geographical Handbook, *Jugoslavia*, Vol. III, p. 259 (Hereafter cited as NIDH).

19. PEP p. 110. See also, A. Basch, *The Danube Basin and the German Economic Sphere*, Kegan Paul, Trench, Trubner & Co. (1944), p. 24–25.

20. V. Rozenberg, and J. Kostić, *Tko Finansira jugoslovensku privredu?* Belgrade (1939);
M. Mirković, *Ekonomska struktura Jugoslavije, 1918–41*, Zagreb (1952), p. 29. Mirković believes that this is an underestimation of the role of foreign capital, since less than two thirds of the nominal value of companies was declared at such meetings. Tomasevich has argued a similar point; but estimates that in 1938 total foreign participation in share capital stood at roughly 44 per cent of the total, and that foreign investment at this time equalled a third of all corporate financial resources. (See J. Tomasevich, 'Foreign economic relations, 1918–1941' in Kerner (1949), pp. 186–7.) The PEP study (op. cit., p. 109) also cite a figure of roughly 50 per cent; but the authors add that this may be an overestimate.

21. L. S. Stavrianos, op. cit. (1958), p. 141–9.

22. At the end of the war there were no railways in operational condition in Montenegro at all; in Bosnia-Herzegovina only 10 per cent of the track was built on standard gauge. See S. Dimitrijević, op. cit., pp. 6–7.

23. See *NIDH*, p. 420;
W. S. Vucinich, *Serbia Between East and West*, Part 8, 'The Danube–Adriatic Railway', Stamford University Press (1954).

24. J. Tomasevich, 'Foreign Economic relations, 1918–41' in, *Yugoslavia*, ed. by R. Kerner, University of California (1949), p. 188.
From the point of view of the Yugoslav economy in this period 'transport' and 'railways' are almost synonymous. Until 1935, the country had no roads at all that could be described as first class by the standards of western Europe. Even in 1940 the authors of the NIDH estimated that only 4 per cent of Yugoslav roads were 'adequate for modern heavy traffic', and only about twice that percentage were 'practicable for tourist cars or lorries with a high clearance'. (Loc. cit., p. 392).

25. This discussion of the Yugoslav extractive industries is based, except where noted, on the *NIDH*, pp. 190 ff.

26. J. Tomasevich, op. cit. (1949), p. 189–90.

27. J. Tomasevich, op. cit. (1949).
See also M. Mirković, op. cit. (1952), pp. 60–62.
The sales of Trepča output were almost all under foreign control, all being handled by the Anglo-American Metals Co., Trepča and the Compagnie Française des Mines de Bor, together produced two-thirds of Yugoslavia's output of pyrites. I have been unable to find detailed information relating to the royalty situation in Yugoslavia. It would, of course, be valuable to have a detailed picture here.

28. In 1938, Yugoslavia was also fourth among European producers of bauxite, the leading European producer of chrome and antimony, and an important producer of gold, silver and manganese.

29. J. Tomasevich, op. cit. (1949), p. 179 claims that most of the measures of industrialization in Yugoslavia after 1935 were actually part of German rearmament plans.

30. J. Tomasevich, op. cit. (1949), pp. 186–7. For this loan French banks put up F.F. 675 millions.

31. Nevertheless, Tomasevich has calculated that, in 1931, the state extracted the staggering burden of between 3,200 and 4,000 millions dinars in taxes on agriculture, both direct and indirect. (J. Tomasevich, op. cit. (1955), p. 702). This represented between 40 per cent and 50 per cent of the total cash income from agriculture. That this was taxation to the limit is partly illustrated by the level of rural indebtedness in Yugoslavia in this period, and in particular by the necessity for a moratorium on peasant debts, which the government was compelled to announce in 1932.

32. *PEP* (1945), p. 110;
   Royal Institute for International Affairs (RIIA), *The Balkan States*, I, 'Economic', Oxford University Press (1936), pp. 99–100.
33. S. M. Kukoleča, 'Karteli i njihov značaj za jugoslovensku privredu', in, Yugoslavia, Ministry of Social Welfare, *Socijalni arhiv*, Vol. V (1939), pp. 203–37.
34. *NIDH*, op. cit., pp. 192–3.
35. J. Tomasevich, op. cit. (1949), p. 193.
36. This account of the reorientation of Yugoslav trade is based on: A. Basch, op. cit. (1944);
   RIIA, op. cit. (1936);
   J. Tomasevich, op. cit. (1949).
37. Ibid.
38. J. Tomasevich, op. cit. (1949), pp. 212–3 reports that after the annexation of Austria and Czechoslovakia, Germany took more than 50 per cent of Yugoslav exports, and supplied about 50 per cent of her imports. By acquiring control over the investments of these countries in Yugoslavia, German influence on the corporate structure of the Yugoslav economy was vastly strengthened. German pressure on the Yugoslav currency in this period further weakened her powers of resistance: the dinar was forced down from 14·80 against the mark in July 1940, to 17·82 in September.
39. I have deliberately excluded a discussion of agriculture from this paper, as it is intended to form the basis of a second essay.
40. The immense damage caused by the war cannot be under-estimated as a source of Yugoslavia's economic difficulties in this period. See in this respect, D. Mitrany, *The Effect of the War in South-east Europe*, Yale University Press, and Carnegie Endowment for International Peace (1936);
   S. Dimitrijević, op. cit. (1962), p. 5;
   M. Mirković, op. cit. (1952), p. 11;
   J. Tomasevich, op. cit. (1955), Ch. 12.
41. J. Tomasevich, op. cit. (1955), p. 639;
   J. Tomasevich, op. cit. (1949), p. 185 informs us that 'after 1932, the nominal interest rates were limited by law to about 10 per cent, depending on the discount rate of the National Bank, but effective rates . . . were never below 12–15%'.
42. 'Political and economic planning'. *Economic Planning in South-east Europe*, PEP/OUP (1945).
   This account of the Yugoslav banking system between the wars is based, except where otherwise acknowledged, on *NIDH*, op. cit., pp. 261–75, and J. Tomasevich, op. cit. (1955), Ch. 27, *passim*.
43. M. Mirković, op. cit., p. 89.

44. Ibid.
45. The Poštanška stedionica was possibly the most successful of the Yugoslav banking enterprises. It had a very sound reputation, and never had to impose a moratorium. It showed a profit of 114 million dinars in 1940.
46. Additional information relating to the Slovene banks can be found in T. Hočevar, op. cit. (1965), pp. 163 ff.
   For discussion of the role of banking in industry, see M. Mirković, op. cit. (1952), pp. 55 ff.
   On the banking collapse of 1931, see M. Mirković, op. cit., pp. 53–4.
47. J. Tomasevich, op. cit. (1949), p. 197;
   F. Hertz, *The Economic Problems of the Danubian States*, Gollancz (1947), especially pp. 69 ff.
48. Cited in F. Hertz, op. cit. (1947), pp. 70–1. This discussion of Yugoslav policies of protectionism is based mainly on the following:
   J. Tomasevich, op. cit. (1949), pp. 197 ff.;
   S. M. Kukoleča, op. cit. Part IV, 'Privredna i fiskalna politika kao faktor industrijalizacije' (1941);
   M. Mirković, op. cit. (1952), pp. 94–5; *NIDH*, op. cit., p. 163;
   T. Hočevar, op. cit. (1965), pp. 121 ff.
49. J. Tomasevich, op. cit. (1949), p. 199;
   ibid. op. cit. (1955), p. 448.
50. The grounds for this assumption are several. The authors of the PEP survey (PEP, op. cit. (1945), pp. 118–9) refer to the large 'unclassified' item which regularly appeared in Yugoslav and other Balkan government budgets. For the years in question this was 15·8 per cent of total budgetary expenditure. J. Vasiljević, 'Stvaranje ratne mornarice Kraljevine Jugoslavije (octobar, 1918–septembar 1923)', in, Institut za Savremenu Istoriju, *Istorija XX Veka: Zbornik Radova*, Vol. XI, ISI, Belgrade (n.d.) p. 228, refers to a category of 'extraordinary expenditure' (*Vanredni rashodi*), which in the figures he gives for 1920–1 amount to nearly 52, out of a total of 1,121 millions. Tomasevich (1955, p. 694) estimates that military expenditure came to between 28 and 35 per cent *per annum* of all government expenditure for administration, throughout the inter-war period. He also remarks that 'certain military expenditures were also probably financed through the Ministry of the Interior and Ministry of Transportation'.
51. Ibid. p. 228.
52. *NIDH* op. cit., p. 256.
53. J. Tomasevich, op. cit. (1955), p. 693; L. S. Stavrianos, op. cit., p. 640.
54. *NIDH* op. cit., p. 138.
55. Ibid., pp. 218–9.
56. *NIDH* op. cit, pp. 185–90;
   J. Tomasevich, op. cit. (1949), p. 176. It is an ominous economic and

political sign that in 1937 these key mills were enlarged and modernized with the aid of Krupp's of Essen.

57. M. Mirković, op. cit., p. 95.

58. The number of befezzed Muslims in service on the state railways became a national joke after the Yugoslav Muslim Organization entered the ruling coalition. The leader of the party was given ministerial responsibility for the railways.

59. S. Dimitrijević, op. cit., p. 14.

60. H. Seton-Watson, *Eastern Europe Between the Wars. 1918–1941*, 3rd ed. (1962) (originally published 1945), p. 131.

61. A fairly full account of the operations of PRIZAD is contained in J. Tomasevich, op. cit. (1955), pp. 629–35.
    See also, M. Mirkovic, op. cit. (1952), pp. 45–6.

Selected Further Reading

The following list contains those books of more specialist interest on the history and geography of the Balkans. This allows readers to follow up any particular themes which may have been found of interest in the various chapters of this book.

Adams, John Clinton, *Flight in Winter* (An account of the Serbian retreat in 1915) Princeton University Press, Princeton, New Jersey (1942).

Alexander, John, *Yugoslavia Before the Roman Conquest*, Thames and Hudson, Southampton (1972), 175 pp.

Amery, Julian, *Sons of the Eagle: A Study of Guerilla War*, London (1948), 354pp.

Ancel, J., *Peuples et nations des Balkans*, Colin, Paris (1930), 220pp.

Auty, D., *Yugoslavia*, London (1965), 252pp.

Auty, D., *Tito: A Biography*, London (1970), 344pp.

Avakumović, I., *History of the Communist Party of Yugoslavia*, Aberdeen (1964), 207pp.

Bailey, Frank E., *British Policy and the Turkish Reform Movement: a Study in Anglo-Turkish Relations, 1826–1853*, Harvard Historical Studies, Vol 51, Cambridge, Mass. (1942).

Barker, E., *Macedonia: its place in Balkan Power Politics*, Royal Institute of International Affairs (1950), 129pp.

Barker, T. M., *Double Eagle and Crescent: Vienna's Second Turkish Siege and its Historical Setting*. State University of New York Press (1968).

Dumitru Berciu, *Romania before Burebista*, London (1967), 215pp.

Betts, R. R., (eds) *Central and South East Europe 1945–1948*, Oxford University Press, London (1950).

Black, Cyril E., *The Establishment of Constitutional Government in Bulgaria*, Princeton—London (1943 reprinted 1970), 344pp.

Blaisdell, Donald C., *European Financial Control in the Ottoman Empire*, Columbia University Press, New York (1929).

Blanc, A., *Géographie des Balkans* (Que sais-je? series) No. 1154, 124pp.

Blumenfeld, Yorick, *Seesaw: Cultural Life in Eastern Europe*, New York, Harcourt Brace and World Inc., New York (1968).

Bohmann, Alfred, *Menschen and Grenzen*, Vol. 2, *Bevölkerung ünd Nationalitäten in Südosteuropa*, Verlag Wissenschaft and Politik, Köln (1969).

Brown, J. F., *The New Eastern Europe: the Khruschev Era and After*, Pall Mall Press, London (1966), 306pp.

Brown, J. F., *Bulgaria Under Communist Rule*, London (1970), 339pp.

Burks, R. V., *The Dynamics of Communism in Eastern Europe*, Princeton University Press, Princeton, New Jersey (1961).

Byrnes, Robert F., (ed.), *Yugoslavia* (Mid-European Studies Centre), F. A. Praeger, New York (1957), 241pp.

The Cambridge Medieval History, 2nd ed., Vol. 4, Pt. 1, *Byzantium and its Neighbours* (ed. J. M. Hussey), Cambridge University Press.

Campbell, John and Philip Sherrard, *Modern Greece*, Nations of the Modern World, London (1968), 426pp.

Carey, J. P. C., and A. G., *The Web of Modern Greek Politics*, Columbia University Press, New York (1968), 240pp.

Châttaigneau, Y and Sion, J., *Pays Balkaniques*, Tome 7 2e Partie (Géographie Universelle Series), Colin, Paris (1934), pp. 395–575.

Clissold, Stephen (ed.) *A Short History of Yugoslavia: From Early Times to 1966*, Cambridge University Press (1966), 280pp.

Coles, Paul, *The Ottoman Impact on Europe*, Harcourt, Brace and World, New York (1968).

Cvijić, J., *La Péninsule Balkanique: Géographie Humaine*, Colin, Paris (1918), 528pp.

Davison, Roderic H., *Reform in the Ottoman Empire (1856–1876)*, Gordian Press, New York (1963), 483 pp.

Dedijer, Vladimir, *The Road to Sarajevo*, London (1967), 552pp.

Dedijer, Vladimir, *Tito: His Self Portrait and Struggle with Stalin*, London (1953), 456pp.

Dellin, L. A. D. (ed.), *Bulgaria* (East Central Europe under the Communists), Thames and Hudson, London (1957), 457pp.

Devereux, R. E., *The First Ottoman Constitution Period: a Study of the Midhat Constitution and Parliament*, Johns Hopkins Press, Baltimore (1963).

Djilas, Milovan, *The New Class: An Analysis of the Communist System*, New York (1957), 214pp.

Djordjević, Dimitrije, *Révolutions nationales des peuples balkaniques, 1804–1914*, (French trans.), Institute of History, Belgrade (1965), 252pp.

Edouard, J., Driault and Michel Lheritier, *Histoire diplomatique de la Grèce de 1821 à nos jours*, 5 vols, Paris (1925–26).

Dvornik, Francis, *The Slavs: Their Early History and Civilization*, American Academy of Arts and Sciences, Boston, Mass. (1956), 394pp.

Dvornik, Francis, *The Slavs in European History and Civilization*, Rutgers University Press, New Brunswick, New Jersey (1962), 688pp.

Earle, Ward M., (ed.), *Turkey, the Great Powers, and the Bagdad Railway*, London, Macmillan (1923, reprinted 1966), 364pp.

Evans, S. G., *A Short History of Bulgaria*, Lawrence and Wishart, London (1960), 254pp.

Finlay, George, *A History of Greece, from its Conquest by the Romans to the Present Time*, B.C. *146 to* A.D. *1864*, new ed. Vol. 7, Zeno, London (1877 Oxford reprinted 1970).

Fischer-Galaţi, Stephen A., (ed.) *Eastern Europe in the Sixties*, Praeger, New York (1964).

Fischer-Galaţi, Stephen A., *The Socialist Republic of Rumania*, Baltimore (1969), 114pp.

Fischer-Galaţi, Stephen A., *Twentieth Century Rumania*, Columbia University Press, New York (1970), 248pp.

Forster, Edward S., *A Short History of Modern Greece, 1821–1956*, 3rd ed., Methuen and Co., London (1958).

Gimbutas, M., *The Slavs*, Thames and Hudson (1971), 240pp.

Gimbutas, M., *The Bronze Age Cultures in Central and Eastern Europe*, Mouton, The Hague (1965), 681pp.

Geographical Essays on Eastern Europe, ed. N. J. G. Pounds. Mouton, The Hague (1961), 159pp.

Geographical Handbook Series, Naval Intelligence Division: *Jugoslavia*, 3 vols., *Greece* 3 vols. *Albania* 1 vol., London (1943–45).

Halpern, J. and B., *A Serbian Village in Historical Perspective*, Holt, Rinhart and Wilson, New York (1972), 152pp.

Halperin, E., *Der siegreiche Ketzer: Titos Kampf gegen Stalin* (1957) Eng. trans., *The Triumphant Heretic: Tito's Struggle Against Stalin*, London (1958), 324pp.

Hamm, H., *Rebellen gegen Moskau: Albanien-Pekins Brückenkopf in Europa* (1962). Eng. trans., *Albania: China's Beachhead in Europe*, London, Weidenfeld and Nicolson (1963), 180pp.

Haumant, E., *La Formation de la Yougoslavie* (*XVe XXe siècles*) Institute of Slavic Studies, Paris, 753pp.

Heppell, Muriel and Singleton, Frank B., *Yugoslavia*, Nations of the Modern World Series, London (1961), 236pp.

Heurtley, W. A. *et al.*, *A Short History of Greece From Early Times to 1964*, Cambridge University Press, (1965).

Higgins, J., *Travels in the Balkans*, Barrie and Jenkins, London (1972), 144pp.

Hillgruber, A., Hitler, König Carol and Marshall Antonescu, *Die deutsch-rumäniscen Beziehungen 1938–1944*, Wiesbaden (1965), 382pp.

Hoptner, J. B., *Yugoslavia in Crisis, 1934–1941*, Columbia University Press, New York (1963), 328pp.

Hory, L. and Martin Broszat, Der Kroatische Ustacha-Staat, 1941–1945 (Schriftenreihe der Vierteljahrshefte für Zeitgeschichte Nr 8). Stuttgart (1965), 184pp.

Ionescu, Ghica, *Communism in Rumania, 1944–1962*, London (1964), 378pp.

Ionescu, Ghica, *The Politics of the European Communist States*, (The Nature of Human Society Series). Weidenfeld and Nicolson, London (1967). 304pp.

Iorga, Nicolae, *Geschichte des Osmanischen Reiches*, 5 vols Gotha (1908–13), 486pp.

Iorga, Nicolae, *Histoire des Roumains et de la romanité orientale*, 5 vols, Bucurest (1937).

Ippen, Theodor, "Beitrage zur inneren Geschichte Albaniens im XIX. Jahrhundert," in *Illyrisch-albanische Forschungen* . . ., ed. Ludwig von Thalloczy, Vol. 1. München-Leipzig, (1916), pp. 342–385.

Hoffman, G. W., *The Balkans in Transition*, Von Nostrand Searchlight Series, New York (1963), 124pp.

Jelavich, Charles and Barbara, *The Balkans* (The Modern Nations in Historical Perspective Series), Prentice-Hall Inc., New Jersey (1965), 148pp.

Kanapa, Jean, *Bulgarie d'hier et d'aujourd'hui: le pays de Dimitrov*, Editions Sociales, Paris (1953), 236pp.

Kerner, Robert J., (ed.) *Yugoslavia*, Berkeley (1949), 558pp.

Khristov, H., D., Kossev and D., Angelov, *A Short History of Bulgaria*, (Eng. trans. 1963), Sofia (1969), 366pp.

Kostelski, Ž., *The Yugoslavs* (the history of the Yugoslavs and their states to the creation of Yugoslavia), New York (1952), 498pp.

Lederer, I. J., *Yugoslavia at the Paris Peace Conference: a Study in Frontiermaking*, New Haven and London (1963), 351pp.

Macartney, C. A., and Palmer, A. W., *Independent Eastern Europe: A History*, St Martin's Press, New York (1962).

Macdermott, Mercia, *A History of Bulgaria, 1393–1885*, London (1962), 356pp.

Maconochie, Alexander, Cpt., *A Summary View of the Statistics and Existing Commerce of the Principal Shores*, London (1818).

McNeill, W. H., *Greek Dilemma: War and Aftermath*, Gollancz, London (1947), 240pp.

McNeill, W. H., *Greece: American Aid in Action, 1947–1956*, Twentieth Century Fund, New York (1957), 240pp.

Markert, Werner (ed.), *Jugoslawien* (In Zusammenarbeit mit zahlreichen Fachgelehrten herausgegeben von Werner Markert) Östereuropa-Handbuch, Köln-Graz (1954), 400pp.

Mateley, I. M., *Romania: A Profile*, Pall Mall Press, London (1971), 292pp.

Mavrocordato, John, N., *Modern Greece: A Chronicle and A Survey, 1800–1931*, London (1931).

Mellor, R. E. H., *Eastern Europe: A Geography of the Comecon Countries*, Macmillan Press, London (1975), 358pp.

Miller, William, *A History of the Greek People 1821–1921*, London (1922).

Miller, William, *The Ottoman Empire and its Successors 1801–1927*, 4th ed. Cambridge University Press (1936). (With appendix for 1927–36.)

Mitrany, David, *The Land and the Peasant in Rumania: The War and Agrarian Reform 1917–1921*, Oxford University Press (1930), 628pp (reprinted 1968).

Montias, John M., *Economic Development in Communist Rumania*, Cambridge, Mass.–London (1967), 328pp.

Moodie, A. E., *The Italo–Yugoslav Boundary—a Study in Political Geography*, Philip, London (1945), 421pp.

Moore, W. E., *Economic Demography of Eastern and Southern Europe*, League of Nations, Econ. Financial and Transit Dept., Geneva (1945).

Myres, J. L., *Geographical History in Greek Lands*, Clarendon Press, Oxford (1953), 381pp.

Newbigin, M. L., *Geographical Aspects of Balkan Problems*, Constable, London (1915).

O'Ballance, Edgar, *The Greek Civil War, 1944–1949*, Faber and Faber, London (1966), 237pp.

Obolensky, Dimitry, *The Byzantine Commonwealth: Eastern Europe, 500–1453*, Weidenfeld and Nicolson, London (1971), 445pp.

Osborne, R. H., *East-Central Europe: A Geographical Introduction to Seven Socialist States*, Chatto and Windus, London (1966), 379pp.

Ostrogorsky, George, *Geschichte des byzantinischen Staates* (Eng. Trans. *History of the Byzantine State*, 2nd ed., 1968), Oxford (1965), 616pp.

Palmer, A. W., *Yugoslavia*, Oxford University Press, London (1964).

Palmer, A. W., *The Gardeners of Salonika: the Macedonian Campaign, 1915–18*, André Deutsch, London (1965).

Palmer, A. W., *The Lands Between: A History of East-Central Europe Since the Congress of Vienna*, Weidenfeld and Nicolson, London (1970).

Pano, Nicholas, C., *The People's Republic of Albania*, Johns Hopkins Press, Baltimore (1968), 185pp.

Pounds, Norman J. G., *Eastern Europe*, Longmans, Green and Co. Ltd., London (1969), 910pp.

Remak, Joachim, *Sarajevo* (the story of a political murder), Weidenfeld and Nicolson, London (1959), 301pp.

Ramsaur, Ernest, E., *The Young Turks: Prelude to the Revolution of 1908*, Princeton University Press, Princeton, New Jersey (1957).

Riker, Thad, W., *The Making of Roumania* (*a study of an international problem*) *1856–1866*. London (1931), 592pp.

Ristelhueber, Rene, *Histoire des peuples balkaniques* (Eng. trans., *A History of the Balkan Peoples*, 1971). Twayne Publishers, New York (1950), 470pp.

Roberts, H. L., *Rumania: Political Problems of an Agrarian State*, New Haven, Conn. (1951), 414pp.

Rothschild, Joseph, *The Communist Party of Bulgaria: Origins and Development, 1883–1936*, Columbia University Press, New York (1959), 354pp.

Royal Institute of International Affairs, *South-Eastern Europe*, London (1939), 203pp.

Runciman, Steven, *The Fall of Constantinople, 1453*, Cambridge University Press (1965), 256pp.

Runciman, Steven, *The Great Church in Captivity*, (a study of the Patriarchate of Constantinople from the eve of the Turkish conquest to the Greek War of Independence), Cambridge University Press (1968), 455pp.

Sanders, Irwin, T., *Balkan Village*, University of Kentucky Press, Lexington (1949), 291pp.

Sanders, Irwin, T., (ed.) *Collectivization of Agriculture in Eastern Europe*, University of Kentucky Press, Lexington (1958), 214pp.

Seton-Watson, Hugh, *Eastern Europe Between the Wars, 1918–1941*, 3rd rev. ed. Cambridge University Press (1967), 445pp.

Seton-Watson, Hugh, *The East European Revolution*, 3rd ed., Methuen, London (1956), 406pp.

Seton-Watson, Hugh, *A History of the Roumanians from Roman Times to the Completion of Unity*, Cambridge (1934), 596pp, (reprinted 1963).

Shoup, Paul, *Communism and the Yugoslav National Question*, Columbia University Press, New York (1968).

Singleton, F. B., *Background to Eastern Europe*, Pergamon, London (1965).

Singleton, F. B., *Twentieth Century Yugoslavia*, Macmillan, London (1976).

Skendi, Stavro, (ed.) *Albania* (Mid-European Studies Series), London (1957), 389pp.

Skendi, Stavro, *The Albanian National Awakening, 1878–1912*, Princeton (1967), 498pp.

Spector, S. D., *Rumania at the Paris Peace Conference*, (A study of the diplomacy of Ioan I.C. Bratianu, New York (1962), 368pp.

Stadtmuller, G., *Geschichte Südosteuropas, Geschichte der Völker und Staaten*, Munchen (1950), 527pp.

Stavrianos, L. S., *Balkan Federation* (A history of the movement toward Balkan unity in modern times), Hamden, Conn. (1964), 338pp.

Stavrianos, L. S., *The Balkans Since 1553*, Chs 3–12, New York (1958), 970pp.

Stoianovich, Traian, *A Study in Balkan Civilization*, New York (1967), 215pp.

Svoronos, Nicholas, G., *Histoire de la Grèce moderne*, "Que sais-je?" No. 578 (PUF) Paris (1972), 128pp.

Swire, Joseph, *Albania: The Rise of a Kingdom* (1929) Williams and Norgate, London, 560pp. (reprinted 1971).

Swire, Joseph, *King Zog's Albania*, R. Hale, London (1937), 207pp.

Swire, Joseph, *Bulgarian Conspiracy*, London (1939).

Todorov, Kosta, *Balkan Firebrand: The Autobiography of a Rebel, Soldier and Statesman*, Chicago (1943).

Todorov, N. *et al.*, *Bulgarie-Aperçu Historique et Géographique*, Akademia na Naukite, Sofia (1965), 269pp.

Tomasevich, Jozo, *Peasants, Politics, and Economic Change in Yugoslavia*, Stanford, California, London (1955), 743pp.

Toynbee, Arnold, J., *The Western Question in Greece and Turkey*, 2nd ed. Constable and Co., London (1923), (reprinted 1970).

Trouton, R., *Peasant Renaissance in Yugoslavia 1900–1950: A Study of the Development of Yugoslav Peasant Society as Affected by Education*, Routledge and Kegan Paul, London (1951), 344pp.

Turrill, W. B., *The Plant Life of the Balkan Peninsula: A Phyto-geographical Study*. Clarendon Press, Oxford (1929), 490pp.

Warriner, D. (ed.), *Contrasts in Emerging Societies: Readings in the Social and Economic History of South-eastern Europe in the Nineteenth century*, Athlone Press, University of London (1965) 402pp.

West, Rebecca, *Black Lamb and Grey Falcon: A Journey Through Yugoslavia*, London (1941), 653pp. (reprinted 1967).

Wiesner, Joseph, *Die Thraker: Studien zu einem versunkenen volk des Balkanraumes*, W. Kohlhammer, Stuttgart (1963), 256pp.

Wilkinson, H. R., *Maps and Politics: A Review of the Ethnographic Cartography of Macedonia*. Liverpool University Press (1951), 366pp.

Winner, I., *A Slovenian Village: Žerovnica*, Brown University Press, Providence, Rhode Island (1971), 267pp.

Wolff, Robert, L., *The Balkans in Our Time*, Harvard University Press (1974), 647pp.

Woodhouse, C. M., *The Story of Modern Greece*, London (1968), 318pp.

Subject Index